Strategic Marketing Planning

Second edition

Colin Gilligan

Emeritus Professor of Marketing
Sheffield Hallam University and Visiting Professor,
Newcastle Business School

and

Richard M. S. Wilson

Emeritus Professor of Business Administration & Financial
Management at Loughborough University Business School and
Visiting Professor in the Department of Information Science at
Loughborough University

AMSTERDAM • BOSTON • HEIDELBERG • LONDON • NEW YORK • OXFORD
PARIS • SAN DIEGO • SAN FRANCISCO • SINGAPORE • SYDNEY • TOKYO
Butterworth-Heinemann is an imprint of Elsevier

Butterworth-Heinemann is an imprint of Elsevier
Linacre House, Jordan Hill, Oxford OX2 8DP, UK
30 Corporate Drive, Suite 400, Burlington, MA 01803, UK

First edition 2003
Second edition 2009

British Library Cataloguing in Publication Data
A catalogue record for this book is available from the British Library.

Library of Congress Cataloguing in Publication Data
A catalogue record for this book is available from the Library of Congress

ISBN: 978-1-85617-617-0

Composition by Macmillan Publishing Solutions
www.macmillansolutions.com

Printed and bound in Great Britain
09 10 11 12 13   10 9 8 7 6 5 4 3 2 1

Contents

Preface to the Second Edition

Over the past decade the marketing environment has changed in a series of dramatic and far-reaching ways. Amongst some of the most significant of these changes has been the emergence of what we refer to within this book as 'the new consumer' and 'the new competition.' This new consumer is typically far more demanding, far more discriminating, much less brand loyal, and far more willing to complain than in the past, whilst the new competition is frequently far less predictable and often more desperate than previously. At the same time, we have seen the ever-faster pace of technological change and the emergence of new delivery systems. Within the environment as a whole, we have seen and been affected by a series of unpredictable events, including the bombing of the twin towers in New York, the unprecedented rise – and then fall – in oil prices in 2008–2009, tensions in the Middle East, and a global economic crisis that began to emerge in 2007–2008. Together, these changes have led to a very different type of marketing reality which has had major implications for the marketing planning and strategy processes. The question of how marketing planners might respond to the new marketing reality is therefore an underlying theme of this book.

In practice, many marketing planners have responded by focusing to an ever greater degree upon short-term and tactical issues, arguing that during periods of intense environmental change, traditional approaches to planning are of little value. Instead, they suggest, there is the need to develop highly sensitive environmental monitoring systems that are capable of identifying trends, opportunities and threats at a very early stage, and then an organizational structure and managerial mindset that leads to the organization responding quickly and cleverly.

Within this book we question these sorts of assumptions and focus instead upon the ways in which the marketing planning process can be developed and managed effectively and ***strategically***. We therefore attempt to inject a degree of rigour into the process arguing that rapid change within the environment demands a ***more*** strategic approach rather than less.

The origins of this book can be seen to lie in our earlier book, *Strategic Marketing Management: Planning, Implementation and Control*. This was first published in 1992, with the second edition appearing five years later and the third edition in 2005. The very positive response that we received to the book appears to have been due, at least in part, to the way in which we assumed a certain level of knowledge on the part of the reader and then attempted to develop this further. This led us, in turn, to write the first edition of *Strategic Marketing Planning* which was published in 2003. The approach that we took within the book was essentially similar to that of *Strategic Marketing Management*, in that we did not return to first principles but relied instead upon the reader coming to this material with a solid grounding in the subject. The same approach is reflected in this second edition. As in the past, we have tried to give emphasis not just to the changes that are taking place within the marketing environment, but also to their implications for marketing planning and marketing strategy. In doing this, we have refocused parts of the book and included new material covering areas that have developed significantly over the past few years, including experience marketing, e-marketing, and the management of competitive *dis*advantage.

The primary markets for the book can therefore be seen to include:

- Students reading for degrees involving marketing, but especially MBA candidates and those studying for a specialist Master's degree in marketing

- Senior undergraduates following business studies and business related programmes

- Students of the Chartered Institute of Marketing who are preparing for the Diploma examinations

- Marketing practitioners who will benefit from a comprehensive review of current thinking in the field of strategic marketing planning.

Colin Gilligan, Sheffield
Richard M.S. Wilson, Loughborough

Acknowledgement

Our thanks go to Janice Nunn for all the effort that she put in to the preparation of the manuscript.

Overview of the Book's Structure

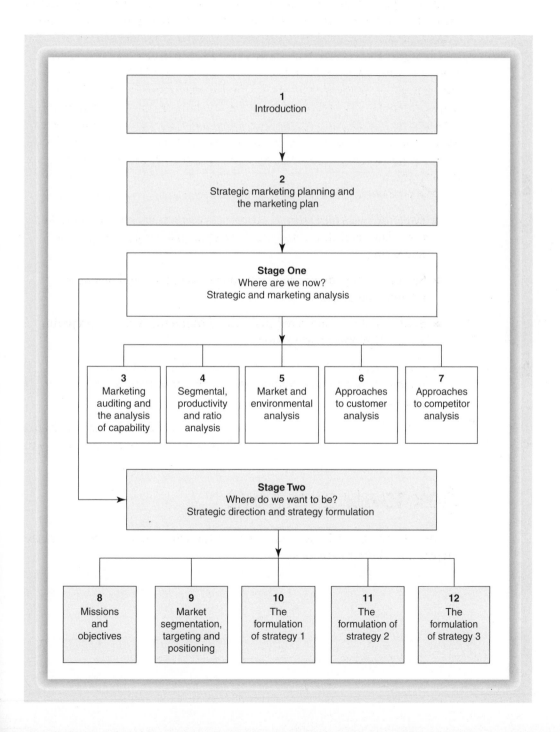

1
Introduction

2
Strategic marketing planning and
the marketing plan

Stage One
Where are we now?
Strategic and marketing analysis

3
Marketing
auditing and
the analysis
of capability

4
Segmental,
productivity
and ratio
analysis

5
Market and
environmental
analysis

6
Approaches
to customer
analysis

7
Approaches
to competitor
analysis

Stage Two
Where do we want to be?
Strategic direction and strategy formulation

8
Missions
and
objectives

9
Market
segmentation,
targeting and
positioning

10
The
formulation
of strategy 1

11
The
formulation of
strategy 2

12
The
formulation
of strategy 3

CHAPTER 1

Introduction

1.1 LEARNING OBJECTIVES

When you have read this chapter you should be able to:

(a) define marketing in strategic terms;

(b) understand the basic structure of the book and how this chapter establishes the context for what follows;

(c) specify the characteristics of strategy and strategic decisions;

(d) understand the nature of the debate about the future role of marketing and its contribution to management, enhancing organizational effectiveness;

(e) appreciate the changing emphases within marketing and the implications for the ways in which marketing strategies are developed.

1.2 THE NATURE OF MARKETING (OR, 'DELIVERING VALUE AND WINNING CUSTOMER PREFERENCE')

The question of what marketing is and what it entails has been the focus of a considerable amount of work over the past 60 years. From this, numerous definitions have emerged, with differing emphases on the process of marketing, the functional activities that constitute marketing, and the orientation (or philosophy) of marketing. The Chartered Institute of Marketing, for example, for a long time defined it as:

> *the management process for identifying, anticipating and satisfying customer requirements profitably.*

A slightly longer but conceptually similar definition of marketing was proposed by the American Marketing Association (AMA) in 1985:

Marketing is the process of planning and executing the conception, pricing, promotion distribution of ideas, goods and services to create exchanges that satisfy individual and organizational objectives.

Although this definition, or variations of it, was used by a variety of writers for a number of years (see, for example, McCarthy and Perreault, 1990; Kotler, 1991), Dibb *et al.*, 2005; Littler and Wilson (1995, p. 1) pointed to the way in which its adequacy was increasingly being questioned in European textbooks (e.g. Foxall, 1984; Baker, 1987).

They went on to suggest that too many definitions of marketing have presented marketing as a *functional* process conducted by the organization's marketing department, whereas the role of marketing today is increasingly being conceptualized as an organizational philosophy or 'an approach to doing business'. This strategic as opposed to a functional approach to marketing was initially captured both by Drucker (1973) who, almost forty years ago, put forward a definition of marketing orientation: McDonald (1989, p. 8):

Marketing is a management process whereby the resources of the whole organization are utilized to satisfy the needs of selected customer groups in order to achieve the objectives of both parties. Marketing, then, is first and foremost an attitude of mind rather than a series of functional activities.

and subsequently by

Marketing is so basic that it cannot be considered a separate function on a par with others such as manufacturing or personnel. It is first a central dimension of the entire business. It is the whole business seen from the point of view of its final result, that is, from the customers' point of view.

Although Drucker's definition had a significant effect upon patterns of marketing thinking, it has increasingly been recognized that it too has a number of limitations. Perhaps the most significant shift in emphasis since Drucker wrote this is to be found in the importance that is now attached to *competitive position* in a changing world and that the marketing concept is the managerial orientation which recognizes that success primarily depends upon identifying changing customer wants and developing products and services that match these better than those of competitors (Doyle, 1987; Wilson and Fook, 1990).

More recently, writers such as Vargo and Lusch (2004), Jobber (2006) and Kotler and Keller (2008) have all pointed to the way in which a new perspective on marketing, characterized by a focus on intangible resources, the co-creation of value, and the management of relationships, has emerged that demands a very different type of definition of marketing. Recognition of this highlights some of the inadequacies of the AMA definition within what is now a very different business environment. It could therefore be said that the AMA definition is more of a list than a definition and is therefore clumsy and inconvenient to use; that it cannot ever be comprehensive; and that it fails to provide a demarcation as to what necessarily is or is not *marketing*.

It was in an attempt to reflect the very different role that marketing now plays that the Chartered Institute of Marketing (CIM) revised its definition in 2008, seeing it as:

> *The strategic business function that creates value by stimulating, facilitating and fulfilling customer demand.*

Underpinning the definition is the CIM's belief that marketing creates value

> *by building brands, nurturing innovation, developing relationships, creating good customer service and communicating benefits.*

The contrasting emphases on customers and competitors that are highlighted by these more recent definitions of marketing can be highlighted, as in Figure 1.1. If an enterprise is managed a little better than customers expect, and if this is done in a slightly better way than competitors can manage, then the enterprise should be successful.

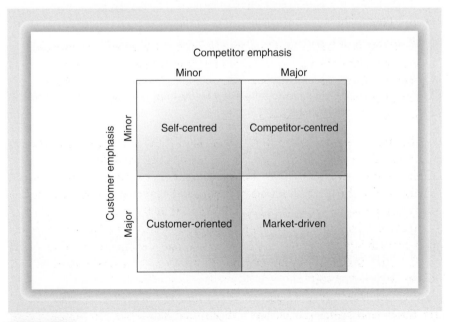

FIGURE 1.1 *Customer and competitor orientations (adapted from Day, 1990)*

Within Figure 1.1, the customer-oriented and competitor-centred categories speak for themselves. The self-centred category is characterized by an introspective orientation that focuses on year-on-year improvements in key operating ratios, or on improvements in sales volume without making direct comparisons with competitors. Such an orientation is potentially disastrous when viewed in strategic terms. At the opposite extreme is a market-driven approach to marketing, which seeks to balance responsiveness to customers' requirements on the one hand with direct competitor comparisons on the other (see Illustration 1.1).

Illustration 1.1   But is your organization *really* market-driven?
When Peter Drucker first outlined the marketing concept over 50 years ago, he equated marketing with customer orientation, arguing that for a firm to be market-driven meant always putting the customer first and innovating continuously to improve the delivered value. Subsequently, it has been recognized that Drucker's perspective lacked strategic content in that it gives emphasis to the organizational culture, but fails to provide guidance on *which* customers to serve and how to serve them. Equally, Drucker's initial views failed to take explicit account of competitors and the discipline of profit in the analysis of product and market opportunity. It is because of this that *customer* orientation has been replaced with the broader concept of *market* orientation.

Given this, we can see marketing operating at three levels:

1. Marketing as a *culture* characterized by a set of values and beliefs that highlights the importance of the customer's interests

2. Marketing as a *strategy* concerned with the choice of products, markets and competitive stance

3. Marketing as the set of *tactics* (essentially the seven Ps of the expanded marketing mix) that provides the basis for the implementation of the business and competitive strategy.

Recognition of this has led Webster (1999, pp. 239–40) to argue that the extent to which an organization is market-driven can be measured against eleven dimensions:

1. The extent to which a customer focus pervades the entire organization

2. The commitment to delivering value

3. The identification and development of distinctive competencies

4. The formation of strategic partnerships

5. The development of strong relationships with strategically important customers

6. The emphasis upon market segmentation, targeting and positioning

7. The use of customer information as a strategic asset

   8. The focus on customer benefits and service

   9. Continuous improvement and innovation

   10. The definition of quality based on meeting customers' expectations

   11. A commitment to having the best information technology available.

   For Day (1990), the characteristics of a market-driven organization can be stated more succinctly:

   ■ An externally oriented culture that emphasizes superior customer value

   ■ Distinctive capabilities in market sensing as a means of anticipating the future

   ■ Structures that are responsive to changing customer and market requirements.

   The significance of being market-driven has, in turn, been highlighted by a series of studies, including one amongst 600 managers in France, the USA, Germany, Japan and the UK, which found that 'the single strongest influence on company performance is innovativeness. Further, a market-oriented company culture was found to have a positive impact in all five countries, while customer orientation, by itself, has virtually no influence on bottom line performance' (Webster, 1999, p. 241). It is the recognition of this that, as Webster suggests, highlights the need for firms to innovate continuously in order to exceed the customer's evolving definition of value.

Given the nature of these three comments, the essential requirements of marketing can be seen to be (Wilson, 1988, p. 259):

   1. The identification of consumers' needs (covering *what* goods and services are bought; *how* they are bought; by *whom* they are bought; and *why* they are bought);

   2. The definition of target market segments (by which customers are grouped according to common characteristics – whether demographic, psychological, geographic, etc.); and

   3. The creation of a *differential advantage* within target segments by which a distinct competitive position relative to other companies can be established, and from which profit flows.

The way in which a differential advantage might be achieved – and sustained – is through the manipulation of the elements of the *marketing mix*. This mix has traditionally been seen to consist of the 'four Ps' of marketing: Product, Price, Promotion and Place. Increasingly, however, but particularly in the services sector, it has been recognized that these four Ps are far too limited in terms of providing a framework both for thinking about marketing and for planning marketing strategy. It is because of this that a

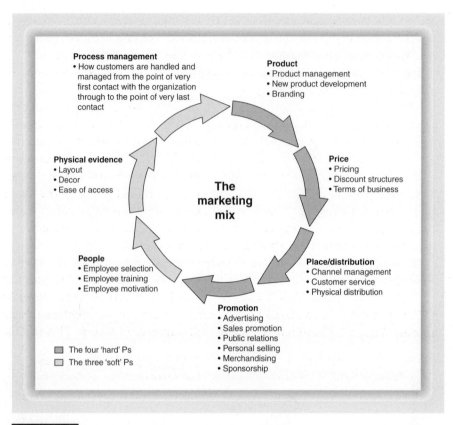

Process management
• How customers are handled and managed from the point of very first contact with the organization through to the point of very last contact

Product
• Product management
• New product development
• Branding

Physical evidence
• Layout
• Decor
• Ease of access

The marketing mix

Price
• Pricing
• Discount structures
• Terms of business

People
• Employee selection
• Employee training
• Employee motivation

Place/distribution
• Channel management
• Customer service
• Physical distribution

Promotion
• Advertising
• Sales promotion
• Public relations
• Personal selling
• Merchandising
• Sponsorship

☐ The four 'hard' Ps
☐ The three 'soft' Ps

FIGURE 1.2   *The elements of the marketing mix*

far greater emphasis is now given to the idea of an expanded mix that has three additional elements:

■ People

■ Physical evidence

■ Process management.

The detail of both the traditional 'hard' elements of the mix and the 'softer' elements appears in Figure 1.2.

1.3   THE MANAGEMENT PROCESS

Management can be looked at from a variety of viewpoints. It may be seen from one perspective as being largely an *attitude* that reflects a willingness to debate issues and resolve them through the use of appropriate techniques and procedures. Alternatively, management may be viewed in terms of its *responsibility for achieving desired* objectives, which requires the selection of means to accomplish prescribed ends as well as the articulation of those ends. This view of management can be analysed further by focusing on its *task orientation* (e.g. in the functional context of marketing) or on its *process orientation* (i.e. the way in which the responsibility is exercised). In either case it has been suggested that decision-making and management are the same thing (Simon, 1960, p. 1).

The process of decision-making is rendered problematic on account of the existence of risk and uncertainty. In the face of risk or uncertainty, some managers postpone making a choice between alternative courses of action for fear of that choice being wrong. What they typically fail to recognize in this situation is that they are actually making another choice – they are deciding *not to decide* (Barnard, 1956, p. 193), which favours the *status quo* rather than change. This is not a means of eliminating risk or uncertainty, since it seeks to ignore them rather than to accommodate them: the imperative to adapt is one that cannot be ignored.

If the central question in the management process concerns the need to make decisions, we need to know what decisions should be made and how they should be made. This book intends to deal with both these issues by following the first two stages in a sequence that reflects a problem-solving routine. Figure 1.3 summarizes the overall sequence of stages. This is done

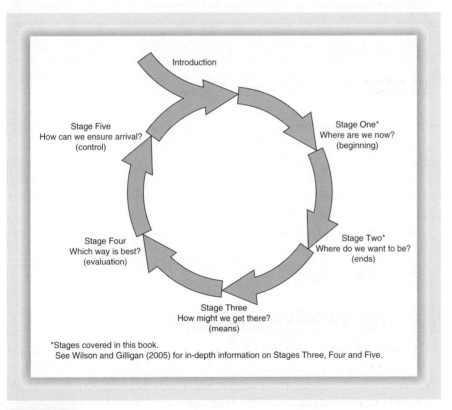

FIGURE 1.3   *The framework*

against the background of a discussion in Chapter 2 of the nature and role of strategic marketing planning and the structure of the marketing plan.

Stage One of this process (strategic and marketing analysis) raises the question of where the organization is now in terms of its competitive position, product range, market share, financial position and overall levels of capability and effectiveness. In addressing this question we are seeking to establish a base line from which we can move forward. Chapters 3 to 7 address Stage 1.

Stage Two (strategic direction and strategy formulation) is concerned with where the organization should go in the future, which requires the specification of ends (or objectives) to be achieved. While top management in the organization will have some discretion over the choice of ends, this is often constrained by various vested interests, as we shall see later in this chapter. Chapters 8 to 12 address Stage Two.

Stage Three of the management process deals with the question of how desired ends might be achieved, something which begs the question of how alternative means to ends might be identified. This strategy formulation stage requires creative inputs, which cannot be reduced to mechanical procedures. Stage Three is not directly addressed in this book, but is examined in detail in Wilson and Gilligan (2005).

Stage Four focuses on the evaluation of alternative means by which the most preferred (or 'best') alternative might be selected. The need to choose may be due to alternatives being mutually exclusive (i.e. all attempting to achieve the same end) or it may be a consequence of limited resources (which means that a rationing mechanism must be invoked). Again, Stage Four is not directly addressed in this book, but see Wilson and Gilligan (2005).

Stage Five covers the implementation of the chosen means, and the monitoring of its performance in order that any corrective actions might be taken to ensure that the desired results are achieved. Since circumstances both within the organization and in its environment are unlikely to stay constant while a strategy is being pursued, it is necessary to adapt to accommodate such changes. Stage Five is not addressed in this book but, again, see Wilson and Gilligan (2005).

We therefore begin by focusing upon the nature of strategy and strategic decisions, before turning to an examination of some of the issues facing strategic marketing planners currently and then, in Chapter 2, the detail of the strategic marketing planning process.

1.4 STRATEGIC DECISIONS AND THE NATURE OF STRATEGY

Strategic decisions are concerned with seven principal areas:

1. They are concerned with the scope of an organization's activities, and hence with the definition of an organization's boundaries.

2. They relate to the matching of the organization's activities with the opportunities of its substantive environment. Since the environment is continually changing, it is necessary for this to be accommodated via adaptive decision-making that anticipates outcomes – as in playing a game of chess.

3. They require the matching of an organization's activities with its resources. In order to take advantage of strategic opportunities it will be necessary to have funds, capacity, personnel, etc., available when required.

4. They have major resource implications for organizations – such as acquiring additional capacity, disposing of capacity, or reallocating resources in a fundamental way.

5. They are influenced by the values and expectations of those who determine the organization's strategy. Any repositioning of organizational boundaries will be influenced by managerial preferences and conceptions as much as by environmental possibilities.

6. They will affect the organization's long-term direction.

7. They are complex in nature, since they tend to be non-routine and involve a large number of variables. As a result, their implications will typically extend throughout the organization.

Decision-making (whether strategic or tactical) is but a part of a broader problem-solving process. In essence Johnson *et al.* (2008) suggest that this consists of three key aspects: analysis, choice and implementation.

Strategic analysis focuses on understanding the strategic position of the organization, which requires that answers be found to such questions as:

■ What changes are taking place in the environment?

■ How will these changes affect the organization and its activities?

■ What resources does the organization have to deal with these changes?

■ What do those groups associated with the organization wish to achieve?

Strategic choice has three aspects:

■ The generation of strategic options, which should go beyond the most obvious courses of action

■ The evaluation of strategic options, which may be based on exploiting an organization's relative strengths or on overcoming its weaknesses

■ The selection of a preferred strategy that will enable the organization to seize opportunities within its environment or to counter threats from competitors.

Strategic implementation is concerned with translating a decision into action, which presupposes that the decision itself (i.e. the strategic choice) was made with some thought being given to feasibility and acceptability. The allocation of resources to new courses of action will need to be undertaken, and there may be a need for adapting the organization's structure to handle new activities as well as training personnel and devising appropriate systems.

We have given some thought to strategic decisions, but what is meant by strategy? Hofer and Schendel (1978, p. 27) have identified three distinct levels of strategy in a commercial context. These are:

1. Corporate strategy, which deals with the allocation of resources among the various businesses or divisions of an enterprise;

2. Business strategy, which exists at the level of the individual business or division, dealing primarily with the question of competitive position;

3. Functional level strategy, which is limited to the actions of specific functions within specific businesses.

Our main concern within this book is in relation to business strategy (i.e. level (2) above) and the way in which this links to marketing as a set of functional activities (i.e. level (3) above), notwithstanding definitions on pp. 1–3 above.

Different authorities have defined strategy in lots of different ways; there is no standard definition. However, a range of elements that most writers seem to subscribe to in discussing strategy have been put forward by Simmonds (1980, pp. 7–9) as follows:

1. Strategy is applicable to business within defined boundaries. While the boundaries may change, the strategy applies at any one time to actions affecting a delimited area of demand and competition.

2. There are specified direct competitors. These are competitors selling essentially the same products or services within the defined demand area. Indirect competitors are those operating outside the defined business and whose products are not direct substitutes. Indirect competition is usually ignored or covered by the concept of price elasticity of demand.

3. There is zero-sum competition between the direct competitors for the market demand, subject to competitive action affecting the quantity demanded. Demand within the defined market varies over time. This variation in demand is largely independent of supplier

strategies, and is often referred to as the *product life cycle*. At its simplest it is depicted as a normal curve over time with regularly growing then declining demand.

4. Strategy unfolds over a sequence of time periods. Competition evolves through a series of skirmishes and battles across the units of time covered by the product life cycle.

5. Single period profit is a function of:
   - the price level ruling for the period
   - the accumulated volume experience of the enterprise
   - the enterprise's achieved volume as a proportion of capacity.

6. Market share has intrinsic value. Past sales levels influence subsequent customer buying, and costs reduce with single-period volume and accumulated experience.

7. Competitors differ in market share, accumulated experience, production capacity and resources. Competitors are unequal, identified and positioned. Objectives differ. Enterprises composed of ownership, management and employee factions and operating a range of different businesses have different objectives. Strategic business thinking, however, will usually express these as different time and risk preferences for performance within an individual business, measured in financial terms.

8. Within a given situation there will be a core of strategic actions that will be the essential cause of change in competitive position. Non-strategic (or contingent) actions will support strategic actions and should be consistent with them, but will not change competitive position significantly.

9. Identification of an optimal core of strategic actions requires reasoning (or diagnosis), is not attained through application of a fixed set of procedures, and is situational. In short, thinking is required.

Taken together, these elements present a view of business strategy that sees it as a chosen set of actions by means of which a market position relative to other competing enterprises is sought and maintained. This gives us the notion of competitive position.

It needs to be emphasized that 'strategy' is not synonymous with 'long-term plan', but rather consists of an enterprise's attempts to reach some preferred future state by adapting its competitive position as circumstances change. While a series of strategic moves may be planned, competitors' actions will mean that the actual moves will have to be modified to take account of those actions.

We can contrast this view of strategy with an approach to management that has been common in the UK. In organizations that lack strategic direction there has been a tendency to look inwards in times of stress, and for management to devote their attention to cost-cutting and to shedding unprofitable divisions. In other words, the focus has been on *efficiency* (i.e. the relationship between inputs and outputs, usually with a short time horizon) rather than on *effectiveness* (which is concerned with the organization's attainment of goals – including that of desired competitive position). While efficiency is essentially introspective, effectiveness highlights the links between the organization and its environment. The responsibility for efficiency lies with operational managers, with top management having the primary responsibility for the strategic orientation of the organization.

Figure 1.4 summarizes the principal combinations of efficiency and effectiveness.

An organization that finds itself in cell 1 is well placed to thrive, since it is achieving what it aspires to achieve with an efficient output/input ratio. In contrast, an organization in cell 4 is doomed, as is an organization in cell 2 unless it can establish some strategic direction. The particular point to note is that cell 2 is a worse place to be than is cell 3, since in the latter the strategic direction is present to ensure effectiveness even if rather too much input is currently being used to generate outputs. To be effective is to survive, whereas to be efficient is not in itself either necessary or sufficient for survival.

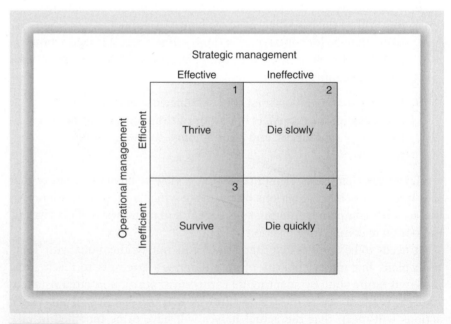

FIGURE 1.4 *Efficiency versus effectiveness (adapted from Christopher et al., 1987)*

Effectiveness in marketing terms can therefore be seen to be the ability on the part of management to search out and embrace changing markets and structures and then reflect this in the marketing strategy.

In crude terms, to be effective is to do the right thing, while to be efficient is to do the (given) thing right. An emphasis on efficiency rather than on effectiveness is clearly wrong. But who determines effectiveness? Any organization can be portrayed as a coalition of diverse interest groups each of which participates in the coalition in order to secure some advantage. This advantage (or inducement) may be in the form of dividends to shareholders, wages to employees, continued business to suppliers of goods and services, satisfaction on the part of consumers, legal compliance from the viewpoint of government, responsible behaviour towards society and the environment from the perspective of pressure groups, and so on. Figure 1.5 illustrates the way in which a range of interest groups come together to sustain (and, indeed, constitute) an organization. In so far as the inducements needed to maintain this coalition are not forthcoming, the organization ceases to be effective. Thus, for example, employees may go on strike in furtherance of a pay dispute; shareholders may be unwilling to subscribe

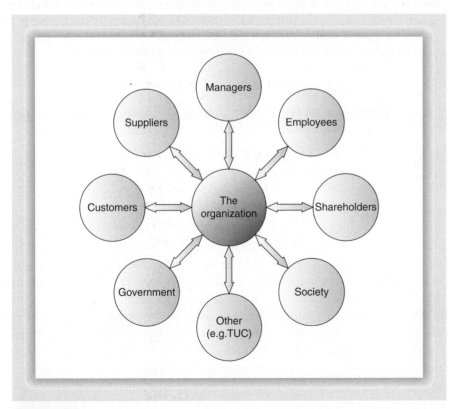

FIGURE 1.5   *Interest groups*

further capital if the value of their shares has fallen due to bad management; consumers may have defected in the light of superior market offerings from competitors; and each of these will remove one vital element from the coalition.

It should be apparent from this view of an organization that management's freedom of movement is constrained by virtue of the expectations of the various interest groups within the coalition. We are unable to assume that a clean slate exists on which any strategy might be drawn, since this may be against the interests of members of the coalition. What we can say, therefore, is that any strategy is potentially available in so far as it ensures that the interests of coalition members are protected. If this is not so the organization cannot be effective, and if it is not effective it will not survive.

The failure to achieve an appropriate balance between operational and strategic management has been illustrated at various times by numerous organizations, including Marks & Spencer, Vodafone, the Post Office (subsequently – and unsuccessfully – renamed Consignia and then, more recently, Royal Mail Group) and virtually all of the major flag carrier airlines. In the case of the Post Office, the British government set out its vision for the future of the organization in its report *Counter Revolution: Modernizing the Post Office Network*. The report highlighted a variety of issues, including:

- The organization's failure to come to terms with the service requirements of increasingly sophisticated and demanding customers

- The lack of any real competitive stance, that led to other service providers (such as TNT, Federal Express, DHL and UPS) being able to capture a substantial share of the organization's most profitable business

- The slow adoption of new technologies

- A belief that the brand equals the branch network.

With approximately 18 500 branches or outlets in 1999/2000, compared with less than one-fifth of this number amongst its most obvious competitors, the organization had proved to be slow and monolithic in its response to the far more focused and agile behaviour of others. In order to overcome this – and indeed to survive – a number of significant changes were needed to the loss-making branch network, the most obvious of which was to identify with a far greater clarity exactly where and how the Post Office brand could best add value to the communications chain for business customers and consumers alike. The organization's response to this challenge was seen by the public to be perverse in that it announced in 2005 a fundamental review of its branch network and then a series of significant cuts to this, something that reduced levels of customer access and customer service.

The difficulties of balancing both the operational and the strategic dimensions of management has also been illustrated by Hoover's problems in coming to terms with the challenges posed by Dyson's entry to the vacuum cleaner market, and by the ways in which the major airlines such as BA, KLM and Lufthansa all experienced difficulties in meeting the challenge of the low-cost, no-frills entrants to the airlines market, such as Ryanair and easyJet. In the case of BA, for example, having been hit by the low-cost carriers and then by a series of other factors – including the 2001 foot and mouth outbreak, the slowdown in the USA and in the global economy, and the turmoil in the aviation industry after the terrorist attacks in the USA in September 2001 – the company responded by developing and then selling bring text bach its own low(ish) cost airline, Go!, in a management buyout for a little over £100 million. Eleven months later, Go! was taken over by easyJet for £374 million in a deal that strengthened BA's competitor yet further.

Given the nature of these comments, it should be apparent that achieving a consistent balance between operational and strategic issues is inherently problematic, although it is the ability to do this that ultimately determines the organization's overall level of marketing effectiveness.

The question of what determines marketing effectiveness has been the subject of a considerable amount of research, and is an issue to which we return at various points in the book. At this stage, therefore, we will limit ourselves to an overview of the sorts of factors that contribute to the effectiveness of marketing activity (see Illustration 1.2).

Illustration 1.2 The dimensions of marketing effectiveness

Although it is tempting to identify the characteristics of marketing effectiveness and to believe that the straightforward adoption of these will lead to business success, it is also potentially simplistic and dangerous, since it can lead to the view that this is the formula for success.

Nevertheless, there are certain elements that appear to contribute to effectiveness, and it is in this way that the list below should be seen:

- A strong sense of vision amongst the member of the senior management team
- A strong customer orientation across all aspects of the business and a fundamental recognition of the importance of the customer
- A detailed recognition of the relative value of different segments and customer groups and a clear policy of targeting and positioning
- A clarity and ambition of marketing objectives
- A detailed understanding of the organization's assets and competencies
- A detailed understanding of the market
- A willingness to redefine the market and create and exploit windows of opportunity

- The creation of one or more market breakpoints
- An emphasis upon differentiation and the leveraging of strong selling propositions
- A fundamental understanding of the strategic importance of competitive advantage
- The innovative management of each of the elements of the marketing mix
- A balanced product portfolio
- A commitment to product and process innovation
- An emphasis upon the coordination of activities across the organization
- A recognition of the fundamental importance of implementation.

1.5 THE MARKETING/STRATEGY INTERFACE

On the basis of a literature review, Greenley (1986, p. 56) has drawn some distinctions between strategic planning (seen as being of a long-term nature) and marketing planning (seen as being an annual exercise), including those listed in Table 1.1.

These differences indicate that strategic planning logically precedes marketing planning, by providing a framework within which marketing plans might be formulated. As Cravens (1986, p. 77) has stated:

Understanding the strategic situation confronting an organization is an essential starting point in developing a marketing strategy.

This understanding can be derived from an assessment of:

- Organizational capabilities
- Threats from environmental forces
- Competitors' strengths and weaknesses
- Customers' needs

and fits into an iterative setting, as shown in Figure 1.6.

The strong interdependence of strategic and marketing planning is clearly seen in this diagram. We can use this interdependence to develop the marketing mix (of Figure 1.2 above) into a set of elements from which a competitive strategy might be developed (as in Figure 1.7). The aim should be to build strength in those elements that are critical to achieving superiority in areas deemed important by customers. In this way the organization should be able to challenge its competitors from a position in which it can use its relative strengths.

Table 1.1 Differences between strategic planning and marketing planning

Strategic planning	Marketing planning
Concerned with overall, long-term organizational direction	Concerned with day-to-day performance and results
Provides the long-term framework for the organization	Represents only one stage in the organization's development
Overall orientation needed to match the organization to its environment	Functional and professional orientation tends to predominate
Goals and strategies are evaluated from an overall perspective	Goals are subdivided into specific targets
Relevance of goals and strategies is only evident in the long term	Relevance of goals and strategies is immediately evident

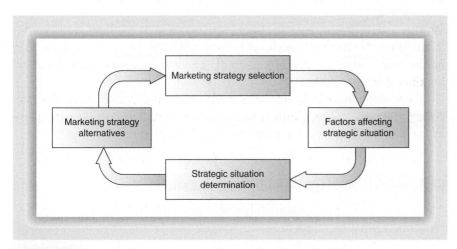

FIGURE 1.6   *The marketing strategy process*

The potential benefits of a strategic underpinning to marketing planning are probably apparent, but what about the problem of implementation? If implementation is ineffective, the carefully devised strategy will be unable to help in improving the organization's performance.

The question becomes, therefore: 'Given a specific type of strategy, what marketing structures, policies, procedures, and programs are likely to distinguish high performing business units from those that are relatively less effective, efficient, or adaptable?' (Walker and Ruekert, 1987, p. 15). Part of the answer is undoubtedly the extent to which the organization reflects a customer orientation.

Product
- Functional
- Technical developments planned
- Packaging
- Service levels
- Range extensions/deletions

Customer
- Customer targets
- Researching customer needs by segment
- Segmenting the market by customer needs
- Distribution channels
- Export

Distribution
- Identifying appropriate channels
- Accessing successful distributors
- Stock and service levels
- Operating costs

Price
- List prices
- Discount structure

Advertising and promotion
- Target audience
- Communication objective
- Media
- Advertising weight
- Promotion plans and timing
- Point of sale

Sales force
- Customer priorities
- Product priorities
- Incentives and rewards

Manufacturing
- Sustainable quality and volume levels
- Cost reduction programme:
  - raw material usage
  - yields
  - manpower
- Quality enhancement

FIGURE 1.7 *Elements of a competitive strategy (source: Milton and Reiss, 1985)*

Left-handed and right-handed organizations

The issue of customer orientation has been discussed by Doyle (1994, pp. 7–9) in terms of what he refers to as *left-handed* and *right-handed* organizations. For many senior managers, he argues, the principal business objectives are profitability, growth and shareholder value. There is, however, a danger in these, he suggests, in that they ignore the customer even though:

> *satisfied customers are the source of all profits and shareholder value. Customers can choose from whom they buy, and unless the firm satisfies them at least as well as competitors, sales and profits will quickly erode. Customer satisfaction should therefore be a prime objective and measure of the performance of managers.*

This led Doyle to highlight the differences between the two types of organization. In the case of left-handed or financially driven organizations, he suggests that the key planning mechanism is the financial plan or budget, with costs, expenses, debt and assets – and the elements of the marketing mix – all being controlled in order to achieve financial goals; this is illustrated in Figure 1.8. The consequence of this is that, when sales begin to

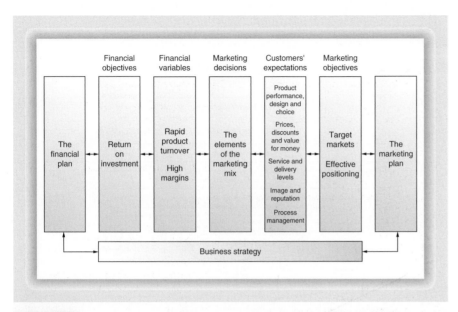

FIGURE 1.8 *The left-handed and right-handed organization (adapted from Doyle, 1994)*

slip, there is a tendency to cut back on areas such as advertising and R&D in order to maintain or boost profits.

By contrast, right-handed or market-driven organizations have as their primary focus the objective of satisfying customers. This involves defining and understanding market segments, and then managing the marketing mix in such a way that customers' expectations are fully met or exceeded. The difference between the two approaches, Doyle argues, is that 'Business decisions flow back from an understanding of customers rather than from a financial requirement.'

He went on to suggest that the market-led approach, which is based on the idea of achieving market leadership through superiority in meeting customers' needs, has typically been associated with Japanese organizations. By contrast, the financially driven approach has all too often been a reflection of British and US organizations. The idea of a left- versus right-handed orientation leads in turn to the notion of *wrong-side-up* and *right-side-up* organizations (see Figure 1.9). Given the importance to any organization of its customers, it follows that staff must be customer-led. Doyle argues that the truly fundamental importance of this has been recognized by relatively few organizations; those that have are the ones that achieve true customer delight.

Among those that have come to recognize the real significance of a customer orientation are Amazon, Tesco, Singapore Airlines, Caterpillar and, for a short time, in the 1980s, Scandinavian Airlines. Jan Carlzon, the

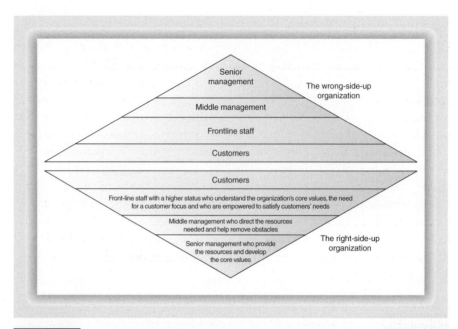

Senior management

The wrong-side-up organization

Middle management

Frontline staff

Customers

Customers

Front-line staff with a higher status who understand the organization's core values, the need for a customer focus and who are empowered to satisfy customers' needs

Middle management who direct the resources needed and help remove obstacles

Senior management who provide the resources and develop the core values

The right-side-up organization

FIGURE 1.9   *The two types of organization (adapted from Doyle, 1994)*

airline's Chief Executive at the time, recognized at an early stage the importance of what he referred to as 'moments of truth'; these are the occasions when the customer deals with the organization's staff and is exposed to the quality of service and type of personal contact. Carlzon's thinking in turning round and revitalizing what was at the time a poorly performing airline was therefore straightforward. Because the airline's frontline staff, many of whom are in relatively junior positions, are the customer's only really visible point of contact with the airline, he argued that managers need to ensure that all staff understand and act out the values that senior management claims are important. This means they need to be the most customer-oriented, best-trained and most strongly motivated employees in the business. However, the reality in many cases is that these are the people who least understand the core values and are often only poorly trained. The net effect of this is that the organization fails to deliver to the customer what it promises.

In an attempt to overcome this, organizations have responded in a variety of ways, including downsizing, developing flatter structures and by supporting and empowering staff. In this way, a more firmly customer-led business in which frontline employees are more highly trained and motivated to satisfy customers' needs should emerge: this is illustrated in Figure 1.9.

Marketing's mid-life crisis

We started this chapter by talking about the nature of marketing and its contribution to the overall management process. However, whilst the arguments in favour of marketing, with its emphasis upon the identification of customers' needs and the delivery of customer satisfaction, are (or appear to be) strong, there was an increasing recognition throughout the 1990s that marketing was (or might be) facing what is loosely referred to as a 'mid-life crisis'. The basis for this comment was that, although a whole generation of management writers agreed upon the importance of consumer sovereignty, and hence the apparent and pivotal importance of marketing, there was a widespread and growing concern that 'something is amiss, that the (marketing) concept is deeply, perhaps irredeemably, flawed, that its seemingly solid theoretical foundations are by no means secure and that the specialism is teetering on the brink of serious intellectual crisis' (Brown, 1995, p. 42).

In developing this argument, Brown – who has been one of the wittiest and most vocal critics of marketing as it has traditionally been perceived and practised – made reference to a variety of commentators:

- Piercy (1991, p. 15), for example, maintains that the traditional marketing concept 'assumes and relies on the existence of a world which is alien and unrecognizable to many of the executives who actually have to manage marketing for real'.

- Gummeson (1987, p. 10) states that 'the present marketing concept … is unrealistic and needs to be replaced'.

- Rapp and Collins (1990, p. 3) suggest that 'the traditional methods … simply aren't working as well any more'.

- Brownlie and Saren (1992, p. 38) argue that 'it is questionable whether the marketing concept as it has been propagated can provide the basis for successful business at the end of the twentieth century'.

- Michael Thomas (1993) who, after 30 years of disseminating the marketing message, made the frank (and frankly astonishing) confession that he is having serious doubts about its continuing efficacy.

Hooley and Saunders (1993, p. 3), however, pursued a rather different line of argument, suggesting instead that the marketing concept had come of age in that, whereas even ten years earlier many senior managers had not *really* understood marketing, there appeared now to be a far deeper and wider appreciation of the concept and of the benefits that it was capable of delivering. To a very large extent this was due to the succession

> ### Illustration 1.3   But does marketing work?
>
> The question of whether marketing 'works', in the sense that it contributes to or is the principal influence upon higher and more sustained levels of business performance, has been the subject of a number of studies. Some of the best known of these were conducted by:
>
> - Hooley and Lynch (1985), who examined 1504 British companies and concluded that the high performing organizations were characterized by a significantly greater market orientation, strategic direction and concern with product quality and design than the 'also rans'
> - Narver and Slater (1990), who focused upon the marketing orientation of the senior managers in 140 North American strategic business units (SBUs) and identified not only a very strong relationship between marketing orientation and profitability but also that the highest degree of marketing orientation was manifested by managers of the most profitable companies
> - Kohli and Jaworski (1990), who conducted a series of semi-structured interviews with marketing practitioners in the USA and discovered a high degree of managerial understanding of the three key component parts of the marketing concept (*customer orientation, coordination* and *profitability*), and that the perceived benefits of the marketing philosophy included better overall performance, benefits for employees and more positive customer attitudes
> - Wong and Saunders (1993), who, as the result of a study of matched Japanese, American and British companies, demonstrated that organizations classified as 'innovators', 'quality marketeers' and 'mature marketeers' were significantly more successful in terms of profits, sales and market share than those classified as 'price promoters', 'product makers' and 'aggressive pushers'.

of studies that highlighted the contribution that effective marketing programmes are capable of making to organizational performance and success: a number of these are summarized in Illustration 1.3. However, despite this sort of evidence there was still a question mark over the direction that marketing should take in the future. Without doubt, one of the triumphs of marketing as a discipline over the past three decades had been the way in which it has been accepted in a host of areas by managers who previously had denied its value and scope for contributing to the sector's performance. Included within these are healthcare, not-for-profit organizations, leisure, religious movements, cultural organizations, and the political arena.

Nevertheless, there is still a significant degree of scepticism about the value and future role of marketing. In discussing this, Brown (1995, p. 43) focuses upon four stages of marketing acceptance. The first of these, *realization*, is characterized by a general acceptance that the marketing concept is sound, but that there is often a problem with its implementation; the most common manifestation of this would be that of getting senior management to accept and embrace the concept. The net effect of this in many organizations has been 'a preoccupation with making marketing work through a heightened understanding of organizational politics and interfunctional rivalry ... [and] a programme of internal marketing' designed to ensure that organizational transformation takes place.

The second position is *retrenchment* in which, again, the concept is seen to be sound, but there are certain circumstances in which it is either inappropriate or of little immediate relevance; many managers in the very fastest moving high-tech industries have, for example, argued that this is the case. Other sectors and markets in which its role and contribution is, it is argued, of little real value include commodity markets, public administration and poorly developed markets in which either there is a significant imbalance between demand and supply and/or an almost complete absence of infrastructure.

The third position, *rearrangement*, demands a far more fundamental reappraisal of marketing so that it can more easily and readily come to terms with the very different realities of today's markets. Webster (1988), for example, has argued for a move away from the position in which marketing and strategic management have, for many commentators, become synonymous. Instead of a myopic preoccupation with market share, competitor activity and so on, marketing should, he claims, return to its roots of a true customer focus. A broadly similar line of argument has been pursued by Christopher *et al.* (1991), who highlight the fundamental importance of marketing relationships rather than one-off transactions.

The fourth, final and most radical position is that of *reappraisal* which, according to Brown (1995, p. 45), gives acknowledgement to:

> the simple fact that the marketing concept has not succeeded and is unlikely to prove successful in its present form. Despite the latter-day 'triumph' of marketing, the failure rate of new products is as high as it ever was – possibly higher. Consumerism, the so-called 'shame of marketing', is still rampant, especially in its virulent 'green' mutation. Selling has not, contra to the marketing concept, been rendered redundant, because few products actually sell themselves. Companies in countries where the marketing message has not been received loud and clear, such as Japan and Germany, continue to outperform their Anglo-American counterparts and, even in the latter milieux, businesses can still succeed without the aid of modern marketing.

Redefining marketing: coming to terms with the challenges of the next decade and the move towards the era of consent

Against the background of our comments so far it is apparent that there is a strong case both for redefining marketing (see our earlier comments) and for thinking about the very different role that it should play in the first quarter of the twenty-first century. For many managers the need for this has been highlighted by the way in which a series of fundamental changes have taken place within many markets, which demand a new and possibly radical rethinking of strategies underpinned by a very different marketing paradigm. Prominent among these changes are:

- A series of significant demographic shifts, accompanied by a number of far-reaching social changes. In the case of the UK, for example, the proportion of the population aged over 50 is now greater than that under 16. At the same time, one in four children now lives with a lone parent, whilst 31 per cent of the population now lives alone. (Source: ONS, 2008). In *The Times* (17 January 2009, p. 12) it states that singles make up 31 per cent of UK households and this is expected to increase to 40 per cent – by far the main category of household.

- A significant shift in the balance of power between retailers and manufacturers

- The relative decline of a number of the megabrands as the result of attacks from low-branded, low-priced competitors

- The redefinition of their business and redrawing of boundaries within many organizations. In the case of the supermarkets, for example, 28 million UK shoppers now regularly buy clothes, electrical goods and furniture from the big grocery chains (George, Asda's clothing range, now has a bigger turnover than Gap or H&M in the UK, whilst Sainsbury's Turange is now seen to be a serious competitor for Top Shop)

- The disappearance within many industrial organizations of staff marketing departments, and their replacement by more focused functions with specific line responsibilities

- The decline in the demand for certain specialist marketing skills, including the collection and analysis of data

- The emergence of a 'new' type of consumer who demands a far higher value-added offer (refer to Chapter 6)

- The growth of social networking

- The development of a 24-hour society

- Markets that are characterized by infinitely more aggressive – and desperate – levels of competition

- The rapid growth of the Internet and on-line marketing. In 2006, for example, the Internet advertising market overtook that of national press advertising and the time that European consumers spend online overtook the time spent reading newspapers and magazines. (Source: Jupiter Research, 2006). Amongst the consequences of this was that in 2008 Google became the dominant force in British advertising

- The fragmentation of the media which has led to the emergence of several hundred television channels (this compares with just three main channels 25 years ago) and very different media habits

- A far greater understanding of the implications of behaviour upon the environment and a consequently greater emphasis within organizations upon the triple bottom line (this theme is developed later in the chapter).

It was against the background of the emergence of these sorts of changes that Kashani (1996, pp. 8–10) conducted an international study of 220 managers with a view to identifying the challenges that marketing managers were facing, how these might best be met, and what the implications for marketing might be. The findings suggested that, in order of importance, the principal challenges were seen to be:

1. High and rising levels of competition across virtually all markets

2. Far higher levels of price competition

3. An increasing emphasis upon and need for customer service

4. A demand for higher levels of product quality

5. Higher rates of product innovation

6. Changing and less predictable customer need

7. The emergence of new market segments

8. The growing power of distribution channels

9. Growing environmental ('green') concerns

10. Increases in government regulations

11. European integration

12. Increasing advertising and promotional costs

At the same time, there is now a far greater concern with the environment and a much greater awareness of the finite nature of many resources, something that has led to the idea of the triple bottom line in which attention is paid not just to economic outcomes of marketing activity, but also to the social and environmental dimensions. It is this that, in turn, suggests that marketing has now reached the 'age of consequences'.

The increasing volatility of markets has also been referred to in a number of recent books, such as *The State We're In* (Hutton, 1995), *The End of Affluence* (Madrick, 1995), *The End of Work* (Rivkin, 1995) and *The Age of Turbulence* (Greenspan, 2007), all of which argue that the developed Western economies are facing a major step-change in their fortunes as unemployment levels rise, deficits persist and purchasing power declines. There appear to be two major forces that are contributing to these changes. The first is globalization, which leads to an opening up of domestic markets and to the threat of low priced foreign entrants. The second contributory factor is that of the seemingly ever faster pace of technological change. Together these demand that managers have a far more detailed understanding not only of their current and potential markets and of their organization's ability to capitalize upon the undoubted opportunities that exist, but also of the ways in which these threats might best be minimized; in essence, this is a case for marketers to recognize the fundamental need for their behaviour patterns to be what Ries and Trout (1986) discuss in terms of being faster, more focused and smarter. In the absence of this, an organization's ability to compete is reduced dramatically.

A broadly similar theme has been pursued by Ridderstråle and Nordström (2004) who, in their book *Karaoke Capitalism*, argue the case for the radically different approach of what they term 'the hollow corporation'. They suggest that:

A single corporate model has dominated business life for some 100 years – that of the vertically integrated company. This was a corporation where most activities were carried out internally. The firm made what it sold. This traditional model is crumbling. IT in general, and the Internet in particular, have ushered in a new age of information that has made markets more efficient and so shifted the advantage to those who play the markets most shrewdly. In essence, we have moved from a world of building to one of buying and the more non-core activities you place outside the firm, the higher the value you can generate. Amongst the techniques for doing this are the use of 'white-labelling' – the practice whereby a company supplying a product or service sells it to more than one distributor, with each one adding its own label before selling it to the end-user, and outsourcing.

The net effect of this is the move on the part of an ever greater number of companies to being little more than a brand. However, it is the 'brand carrier' which takes responsibility for developing and then delivering on the brand promise.

Amongst the examples of the organizations to have done this with enormous success that Ridderståle and Nordström cite are Dell, Ikea, Nike and Sony Ericsson: 'If, for example, you buy a pair of trainers from Nike or a phone from Sony Ericsson, they are not actually made by Nike or Sony Ericsson, but the company that is selling to the final consumer has to accept responsibility for the entire chain.'

They go on to suggest that a modern company, is 'like a Lego model. Once, activities and units were welded together. Today you can take them apart and move the pieces around.'

In making out the case for 'Karaoke Capitalism', the two authors have highlighted the way that although the boundaries of firms were always moved backwards and forwards, the boundaries today are moving more quickly, with more and more activities being shifted outside the corporation. These changes, Freedman (2004) has argued, are being driven by politics and technology, including the liberalization of international trade (the average level of tariffs in industrial countries is now less than a tenth of the level before the Second World War) and the growth of IT, with personal computers, the Internet and fibre-optic cables all being capable of transferring huge amounts of data at high speed and low cost. These factors, he suggests, have exposed companies to ever more global competition, putting ever more pressure on them to cut costs by outsourcing and offshoring, both of which have become ever easier, but which have significant implications for business behaviour.

But, although the new market environment demands more innovative thinking and more creative ways of tackling the market, there are, in many organizations, significant barriers to this. These are illustrated in Figure 1.10.

Given the nature of these opposing forces and of the likelihood of those on the right-hand side leading to a failure on the part of the organization to change, the marketing planner needs to focus upon a number of issues,

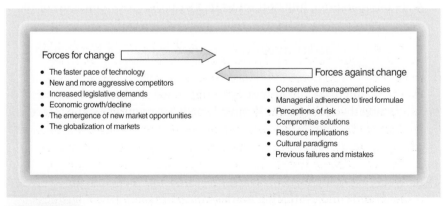

FIGURE 1.10   *The conflicting environmental and organizational forces*

including what Hamel and Prahalad (1994, pp. 49–71) refer to in terms of 'learning to forget'. (This is an issue that is developed in detail in Chapter 11.) In arguing for this, they suggest that far too many managers, while acknowledging at an intellectual level the need for change, fail to accept it at an emotional level. In other words, while they are aware of the environmental changes taking place and accept the need to behave more proactively, they are often far too constrained by day-to-day pressures and resist the need for change.

In order to overcome this myopia, Fisk (2006) makes a case for what he terms 'smart marketing' that is characterized by far clearer differentiation and more accurate targeting, whilst Wind (1996, p. 7) has argued that there needs to be a far greater emphasis upon being close to the customer, together with a far more fundamental recognition of the importance of customer satisfaction, the need for customer relationship building, an emphasis upon understanding customer value and the enhanced product offering, and that brand equity stems from a loyal customer base.

The implications of what both Fisk and Wind suggest can be seen to be far-reaching, including the way in which marketing needs to be looked at from a pan-organizational perspective rather than from the far narrower departmental perspective that predominates in many organizations. In turn, this different approach demands a rethinking of an organization's vision, objectives, strategies and structures, as well as of the sorts of skills that its staff need.

In discussing this, Wind (1996, p. 7) argues that managers need to ask – and answer – 12 questions:

1. Is marketing and its focus on meeting and anticipating customers' needs widely accepted as a business philosophy?

2. Are the business and corporate strategies focused on creating value for all the stakeholders?

3. Do the objectives include customer satisfaction and the creation of value?

4. Is the marketing function integrated with the other functions of the company as part of the key value-creating process?

5. Are the key marketing positions market segment (or key account) managers?

6. Are products viewed as part of an integrated product and service offering that delivers the desired benefit positioning for the target segment?

7. Is the marketing strategy global in its scope?

8. Is full use being made of market research and modelling in generating and evaluating marketing and market-driven business strategies?

9. Is there an emphasis upon information technology as an integral part of the organization's marketing strategies?

10. Does a significant part of the marketing effort constitute innovative practices not previously used by the organization and its competitors?

11. Are strategic alliances for co-marketing activities being formed, and are marketing strategies based on the development of long-term relationships with clients?

12. Is there a sufficient focus of attention and resources upon message effectiveness (instead of media power) and value-based pricing (instead of discounting)?

He goes on to argue that it is not enough just to answer 'yes' to these 12 questions, but that there is also a need to recognize the interrelationships between many of the questions and that the corporate vision and objectives *must* reflect a marketing orientation. This, in turn, highlights the critical importance of ensuring that the organizational architecture (this embraces the culture, structure, processes, technology, resources, people, performance measures and incentives) is focused upon the implementation of the new marketing paradigm. This paradigm, Wind suggests, can best be summed up in terms of building upon the historical role of marketing as the linkage between the organization and the environment, but that also focuses upon the 12 questions above, and which, in turn, has implications for marketing as:

- The leading business philosophy

- The knowledge and wisdom centre of the company that provides all organizational members with concepts and findings about customers and tools for measuring and forecasting customer behaviour and models and decision-support systems for improving the quality of marketing and business decisions

- The growth engine that, through creative marketing strategies that utilize technology and mobilize the other business functions of the company, stimulates the top-line growth of the company.

Fisk's view (2006) is that marketers need to start thinking and executing plans differently. Recognizing that what has worked in the past no longer necessarily works today demands different patterns of thinking and a much higher degree of innovation. In the case of communications, for example, he suggests that it involves moving from the communications free-for-all to an era of consent in which consumers and prospectors are asked how and when they want to talk to you.

> ### Illustration 1.4   The Opposable Mind
>
> Within the hotels business, traditional thinking over many years had led to the emergence of two main business models: large hotels whose economies of scale allowed them to provide business travellers with extra services, and small hotels that offered a greater degree of customer intimacy, but little else. The conventional wisdom was that in order to offer secretarial services, a variety of dining rooms and entertainment and meeting rooms, the hotel needed revenue from at least 1000 rooms. Isadore Sharpe, the founder of Four Seasons, recognized that many business travellers wanted intimacy and service. It was by bringing together the two seemingly contradictory business models that the Four Seasons strategy emerged.
>
> Equally, in 2000, when Procter & Gamble was losing market share to lower cost generic and own-store brands, views within the organization were polarized between those who wanted to cut costs and compete on price, and those who wanted to invest heavily in new products in order to compete on the basis of innovation and added value. The newly appointed Chief Executive, A.G. Lafley, pursued a strategy of outsourcing half of all new product development to small companies and laboratories, thereby cutting costs, but also getting the innovation needed.
>
> In the case of Red Hat, the largest supplier of Linux open-source software, the founder, Bob Young, questioned the industry views and succeeded by focusing upon the product, service levels and the quality of consulting to such a degree that large organizations decided that they could safely switch to Linux freeware from the more traditional and far more expensive suppliers such as Microsoft and Oracle.
>
> *Source*: How to Rise Above the Either/or Dilemma, R. Evans, *Financial Times*, 20 December 2007, p. 14.

The need for different patterns of thinking has also been highlighted by Martin (2007), who argues that too many strategists in the past have taken an either/or approach that has oversimplified the complexities of the world. What is required instead, he suggests, is a more integrative and advanced thought process that allows for contradictions to be embraced. In his book *The Opposable Mind* he pursues this idea and highlights the way in which success is increasingly based on an ability to reconcile contradictions and integrate possibly very different views, something that has been at the heart of the success in recent years of Four Seasons hotels, P&G, and Red Hat (refer to Illustration 1.4).

Given the nature of these comments, it should be apparent that marketing is facing a series of fundamental challenges and that many planners are reappraising how marketing might best contribute to the overall management of an organization. As part of this debate, Figure 1.11 attempts to pull together the kinds of relationships that should or might realistically exist between marketing and other areas of a marketing organization. Within this there are several areas to which attention needs to be paid, but most obviously the characteristics of corporate management (the long-term

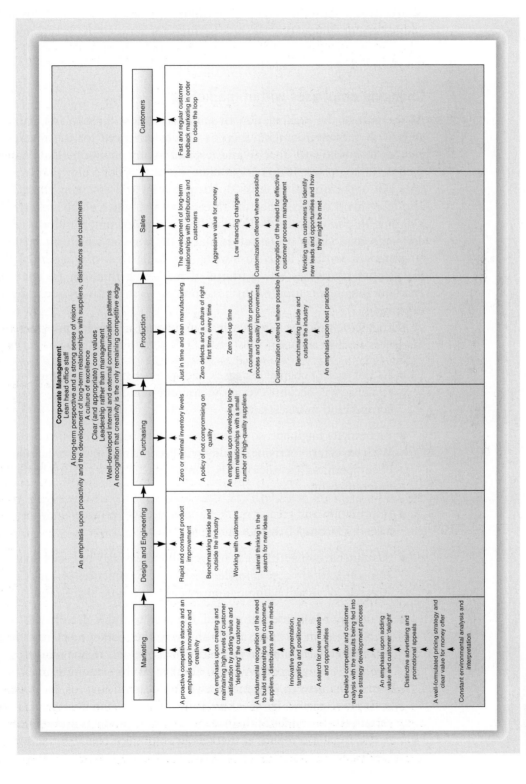

FIGURE 1.11 *Marketing and its contribution to effective management*

perspective, a sense of vision, clear values, proactive patterns of thought and behaviour, and so on), the process linkages between marketing and the other functions, and to the sorts of factors that characterize the effective management of each of the five functions identified.

Changing emphases within marketing

As the part of the organization that interacts most directly and immediately with the environment, there is an obvious need for the marketing planner to investigate, analyse and respond to any environmental changes that are taking place. If this is not done – or if it is done only poorly – not only will opportunities be missed, but potential and emerging threats are also more likely to become actual threats, both of which will be reflected in a decline in performance. Because of this, the marketing planner needs to develop a clear vision of the future and of the ways in which the business environment is most likely to develop. In doing this, it is essential that the planner recognizes how patterns of marketing thinking are changing and how the organization might best come to terms with areas of growing importance.

Recognizing this, we can identify a number of marketing priorities that marketers need to address:

- As the pace of change increases, the speed of anticipation and response will become ever more important and time-based competition more essential

- As markets fragment, so customization will become ever necessary. With expectations rising, quality will become one of the *basic* rules of competition (in other words, a 'must have') rather than a basis for differentiation

- Information and greater market knowledge will provide a powerful basis for a competitive advantage

- Sustainable competitive advantage will increasingly be based upon an organization's core competences. The consequences of a lack of strategic focus will become more evident and more significant

- As market boundaries are eroded, the need to think globally will become ever more necessary. In this way, the marketing planner will be able to offset temporary or permanent declines in one market against growing opportunities in another. At the same time, of course, the need to recognize the strategic significance of size and scale is increasing. However, in going for size, the marketing planner should not lose sight of the need for tailoring products and services to the specific demands of markets by thinking globally but acting locally

- Differentiation will increasingly be based upon service

- Partnerships with suppliers and distributors will become far more strategically significant

- Strategic alliances will become more necessary as a means of entering and operating within markets, partly because they offer the advantages of access to greater or shared knowledge, but also because of the sharing of costs and risks

- There will be a far greater emphasis upon product, service and process innovation

- There will be a need to recognize the greater number and complexity of stakeholders' expectations.

In turn, these marketing priorities have substantial implications for organizational structures and cultures. Doyle (1994, pp. 384–6), for example identified the 10 most obvious of these as being the need to:

1. Break hierarchies and reorganize around flatter structures

2. Organize around small(er) business units

3. Develop self-managing teams

4. Re-engineer

5. Focus upon developing networks and alliances

6. Move towards transactional forms of organization

7. Become a true learning organization

8. Emphasize account management in order to integrate specialist expertise across the organization for the benefit of the customer

9. Recognize the importance of 'expeditionary marketing' so that, instead of focusing upon what Hamel and Prahalad (1994) refer to as *blockbuster innovation* designed to get it right first time, the organization concentrates upon developing a stream of low cost fast-paced innovative products

10. Rethink the way in which the board of directors operates so that it focuses to a far greater extent upon strategic direction rather than control and day-to-day management.

Marketing and a shift of focus

Many of the sorts of changes to which we have referred are reflected in the way in which we have seen a move from the sort of mass marketing that prevailed up until the mid-1970s, through just-in-time thinking and time-based competition, to the far greater emphasis today upon one-to-one

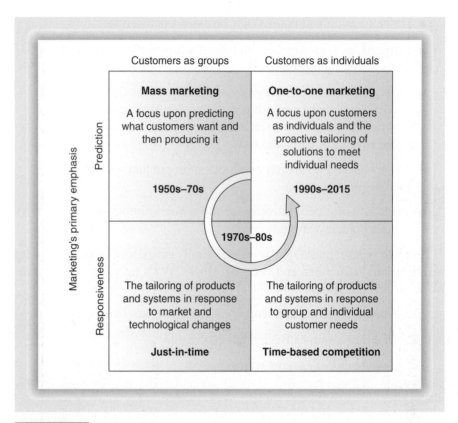

FIGURE 1.12   *The shift from mass marketing to one-to-one marketing (adapted from Datamonitor Analysis, 1996)*

marketing. This is illustrated in Figure 1.12. These changes are also reflected in Table 1.2 (see p. 36), which shows the emergence of different marketing paradigms, culminating in today's paradigm of electronic marketing (the role of the Internet in marketing is discussed in greater detail in Chapter 11 of the book).

Although the most obvious driver for this move towards the emerging paradigm of electronic marketing is the development of the technology itself, there are several underlying factors that have led analysts to question marketing practices and the need for a degree of rethinking. In 1993, for example, Coopers & Lybrand (as it then was) surveyed 100 companies and concluded that marketing departments were 'ill focused and over-indulged'. In the same year, McKinsey released a report suggesting that 'marketing departments have shown themselves to be "unimaginative", generating "few new ideas", and have simply stopped "picking up the right signals" … many consumer goods CEOs are beginning to think that marketing is no longer delivering'. A year later, Booz Allen Hamilton issued a report warning that 'brand managers were failing to get to grips with commercial realities'.

Table 1.2 Marketing's four paradigms: the shift from mass marketing to electronic marketing

	Mass marketing (traditional paradigm)	Target marketing (transitional paradigm)	Customer marketing (the new paradigm)	Electronic marketing (the emerging paradigm)
Key characteristics	Mass selling	Marketing segmentation	A focus upon key customers and database management	The Internet
Underlying assumptions and approaches	■ Consumers are satisfied with a standard product ■ Resellers are used to reach the consumer ■ Heavy advertisers will be successful	■ Markets consist of distinct and definable groups ■ Success is gained from clear customer targeting and the development of a strong position within particular segments ■ Targeting can be achieved through market analysis	■ Databases enable organizations to store and interrogate customer information to provide insight ■ Performance is improved by focusing on individual's needs ■ The costs of customization are reducing all the time ■ Technology now allows for direct marketing	■ Customer are more demanding, more discriminating and less loyal; they demand more information and are capable of processing this effectively ■ Buyers want 24-hour access to develop a dialogue ■ Markets are increasingly global in their nature
Weaknesses and failings	■ A lack of focus and the subsequent waste of resources ■ It ignores the demand for individual responses	■ Large and profitable segments attract numerous players ■ Customers shift from one segment to another and may belong to contradictory segments ■ Segments may be illusory ■ Some financial services organizations	■ 'Databases' are often just lists of names and addresses rather than detailed customer profiles ■ Database management and database mining skills are often more limited than is needed	■ Customers may be concerned about security

Given the nature of these (and other) comments, a number of marketing strategists have come to recognize the need for a far stronger and tighter focus upon customers, far better and more effective feedback systems, and a generally more strategic approach to customer management – something that has helped in this movement away from the traditional mass marketing paradigm.

So why do great companies fail?

Long-term success is typically based on a combination of investment, innovation, the creation of value and – very importantly – a strong emphasis upon strategic management, something to which Ormerod (2006) refers in his book *Why Most Things Fail*. In his analysis of US firms, he points to the way in which only 33 of the top 100 firms in 1919 were still in the list 60 years later. Taking the US firms as a whole, the rate of extinction averages 10 per cent a year over a long period. Although 'extinction' includes both liquidations and mergers and it is often difficult to disentangle the two, Ormerod's key point is that as independent entities, firms regularly disappear and that those that succeed in the long-term do so because of the quality of their strategies.

However, the quality and consistency of strategic thinking in many organizations has been severely criticized over the past few years. De Kare-Silver (1997), for example, highlights two studies: one from the consulting firm Kalchas CSC Index, which suggested that 'only one in ten companies had the information or insight needed to make truly worthwhile strategic decisions'; and one from *Business Week* (1996), which claimed that 'only 6% of executives rated their company highly for long-term planning skills'.

This led Hamel and Prahalad (1994) to suggest that in many organizations there is an inherent tension between their past and their future, which, unless it is addressed in a radical way, ultimately leads to the organization's decline and failure. This is illustrated in Figure 1.13.

In discussing this, de Kare-Silver (1997) suggests that those organizations that do manage to overcome this tension have several common features:

- A clear sense of purpose and direction
- Clearly articulated strategies
- Continuous investment
- A focus of resources and effort
- A commitment to the long-term
- A determination to overcome roadblocks

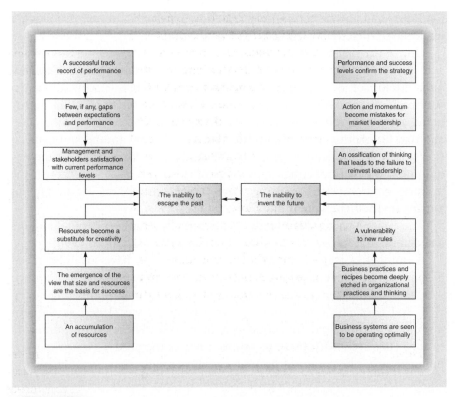

FIGURE 1.13   *Escaping the past and inventing the future (adapted from Hamel and Prahalad, 1994)*

- A relentless focus on *making* their future

- An emphasis on implementation.

In essence, he suggests they understand competitive advantage and what it takes to win. It is this sort of issue that effective strategic marketing planning is designed to address.

The four horsemen of the corporate apocalypse and the emergence of the neo-marketing organization

Given what has been discussed so far within this chapter, it can be argued that there are two types of organization: those with a marketing department, and those with a marketing soul. Those with a marketing department tend to believe still that the business models and formulae that have worked well in the past will continue to work well in the future, despite the sorts of often radical changes that have affected and still are affecting the vast majority of markets. Those with a marketing soul can be seen to be those organizations in which the senior management team has recognized that the way in which marketing had for a long time been interpreted was far too functional and far too limited. It is this that has led to the rise of what might be termed the neo-marketing organization.

One of the first highly credible criticisms of marketing came from Brady and Davies (1993), two consultants working for the management consultancy McKinsey & Co. They argued that 'doubts are surfacing about the very basis of contemporary marketing'. They went on to say that 'costly brand advertising often dwells on seemingly irrelevant points of difference' and that 'marketing departments are often a millstone around an organization's neck'. As evidence of this, they suggested that there were far too few examples of new marketing frameworks or fresh approaches: 'Although the business environment has changed dramatically, marketers are simply not picking up the right signals any more.'

These views have subsequently been echoed by a number of other authors and commentators (see, for example, Brannan, 1993; Thomas, 1994).

A number of factors appear to have conspired to have invalidated traditional patterns of marketing thought, the four most significant of which were the saturation of numerous markets, globalization, market fragmentation, and corporate downsizing. Referred to by Brown (1995) as the four horsemen of the corporate apocalypse, he argues that, if organizations are to cope effectively with these pressures, there is the need for a neo-marketing approach, characterized by four key dimensions that together help to create a far more customer-centric and competitive organization:

1. *A far stronger corporate philosophy* in which emphasis is given to 'treat(ing) each customer as if they are the only one'.

2. *The much greater and more effective use of teams* from across the organization, with these teams having to meet specific targets such as the development of a new brand for an emerging segment or the re-launch of a product line. Having achieved the objectives, the team then disbands. Clusters therefore form, break and reform on a regular basis in order to move in time with the rhythm of the market.

3. *The better use of alliances* in areas such as R&D, so that knowledge can be shared more effectively and mutual advantage can be gained through corporate symbiosis.

4. *IT-driven thinking* that provides a far greater insight into customers' patterns of thinking and behaviour, and helps to overcome the confusion caused by market fragmentation and saturation. By using information technology strategically, the marketing planner gains a far greater understanding of buying habits, cross-brand elasticities, marketing sensitivities and market structures, and in this way can raise barriers to entry and move further towards 'owning the customer'.

1.6 SUMMARY

This chapter has sought to offer some ideas constituting a framework for the rest of the book. We began by considering the nature of management and of the management process. The process is often characterized in the following stages:

- Planning
- Decision-making
- Control.

These are related to a series of questions:

- Where are we now?
- Where do we want to be?
- How might we get there?
- Which way is best?
- How can we ensure arrival?

In this book we focus very largely on the first two of these questions.

Strategy can be seen as a normative matter concerning what an organization would like to achieve. As such, it:

- Guides the organization in its relationship with its environment
- Affects the internal structure and processes of the organization
- Centrally affects the organization's performance.

Marketing, via its policies and programmes relating to product, price, service, distribution and communications, can provide the means to facilitate the attainment of a strategy.

The extent to which the strategy is achieved provides a measure of the organization's effectiveness. Any organization's effectiveness depends upon the balance between what is desired and what is achieved on the one hand, and paying due regard to the requirements of all stakeholders, whether internal or external, on the other. It is through the process of organizational control that managers seek to achieve organizational effectiveness, and this gives a reference point for all that follows. However, it should be apparent from what has been discussed within this chapter that marketing is undergoing a series of significant changes and that this is being reflected in the ways in which the subject is defined. If, though, marketing is to succeed, it must offer the customer a clear and meaningful value proposition. In the absence of this, marketing is of little value. Recognizing this, we can contrast what might loosely be called the traditional physical product sequence of 'make the product and sell the product', with the value delivery sequence that is based on a clear understanding of what value means to the customer and which then reflects the idea of 'choose the value, provide the value and communicate the value'. It is this theme that provides the basis for much of what is said in the subsequent chapters.

CHAPTER 2

Strategic Marketing Planning and the Marketing Plan

2.1 LEARNING OBJECTIVES

When you have read this chapter you should understand:

- **(a)** the nature and purpose of strategic planning;
- **(b)** the ten schools of strategic thinking;
- **(c)** the dimensions of effective planning;
- **(d)** the pros and cons of marketing planning;
- **(e)** the structure of the marketing plan.

2.2 INTRODUCTION

Within this chapter we focus upon the nature of strategic marketing planning and the development of the marketing plan. In doing this we concentrate initially upon patterns of thinking in strategic management and then, against this background, on the nature and structure of the marketing plan. However, before doing this it is worth remembering a comment that is made in *Alice in Wonderland*:

> *If you don't know where you are going, any road will get you there.*

It is for this reason that we argue throughout this chapter for a clarity of thinking about the organization's environment, managerial objectives, organizational capabilities, the nature of any constraints that exist, and indeed anything else that impinges upon the process of effective planning and implementation.

2.3   THE ROLE OF STRATEGIC MARKETING PLANNING

Strategic marketing planning is typically seen to be concerned with the definition of marketing objectives and how over, say, a three- to five-year period, these objectives might best be achieved. There is, however, a substantial body of admittedly largely anecdotal evidence to suggest that, although a majority of businesses have plans, these are often used primarily to control spending. Largely because of the rate of environmental change over the past 10 years, there has also been a growing cynicism about formal planning, with many of its detractors arguing that, in a volatile environment, there is little to be gained from planning since both the underlying assumptions and the plan itself are quickly invalidated. It is also often argued that plans frequently suffer from a lack of realism, stifle creativity, lead to a degree of inflexibility in terms of dealing with the unexpected, and frequently give the illusion of control. (These points are discussed in greater detail at a later stage in this chapter.) However, this misses the point, since the *process* of planning is often as important as the plan itself. The essential value of the planning process is that it forces the planning team to question assumptions, tests the rigour of the team's thinking, and provides an opportunity to rehearse the future. In order to plan more effectively, the team therefore needs to use the corporate, divisional or brand vision as a guiding star, and to view planning as a learning process rather than as an exercise in control.

Strategy and planning

The strategic marketing planning process is concerned with the development of strategies that are based on the planning team's assessment of the market and perceptions of managerial expectations and organizational capability. However, before we examine the detail of the marketing planning process, it is worth recognizing that strategy and planning are probably two of the most overworked and misunderstood words in the management lexicon. Given this, we need to clarify what is meant by strategy (a number of definitions of strategy appear in Illustration 2.1).

Mintzberg and Strategy

For Mintzberg (1987), strategy is concerned with five Ps:

1. Planning, which deals with the direction of the organization

2. Ploys, which are designed to deal with and outwit the competition

3. Patterns, which represent a logical stream of actions

4. Position, which relates to how the organization is located in the market place

5. Perspectives, which reflect the management team's view of the world.

Illustration 2.1 Defining strategy

Over the past 50 years a considerable amount has been written about strategy, and from this a variety of definitions and strategic perspectives have emerged. However, one of the first to discuss strategy in a structured way was the Chinese General Sun Tzu (1963), who, in his book *The Art of War*, suggested that it was better to overcome one's enemies by wisdom rather than by force alone:

> One should appraise a war first of all in terms of five fundamental factors and make comparisons of various conditions of the antagonistic sides in order to assess the outcome. The first of the fundamental factors is politics; the second, weather; the third, terrain; the fourth, the commander; and the fifth, doctrine.

One of the first of the more recent writers to define strategy was Drucker (1955), who described it as the answer to two fundamental questions: What is our business, and What should it be?

Following on from this, Chandler (1962) described strategy as:

> the determination of the basic long-term goals and objectives of an enterprise and the adoption of courses of action and the allocation of resources necessary for carrying out these goals.

Although Johnson, Scholes & Whittington (2008) argue against giving a definition of strategy on the grounds that all too often such definitions lead to overly long discussions about the semantics, they suggest that strategy is:

> the direction and scope of an organization over the long term: ideally, which matches its resources to its changing environment and in particular its markets, customers or clients so as to meet stakeholder expectations.

An alternative approach has been proposed by Stacey (2007), who argues that only rarely is strategy the deliberate set of actions that most writers suggest, and that it is instead a far more organic approach:

> there is a strong tendency to slip into talking about it as a response that 'the organization' makes to 'an environment'. When we do that, we depersonalize the game and unwittingly slip into understanding it in mechanical terms, where one 'thing' moves in predetermined ways in relation to another 'thing'. The inevitable result is lack of insight into the real complexities of strategic management because in reality organizations and their environments are not things, one adapting to other, but groupings of people interacting one with another.

He goes on to suggest that there are, in essence, eight different types of strategy:

1. Planned strategies, which represent a series of deliberate and precise intentions

2. Entrepreneurial strategies, which emerge as the result of a personal vision

3. Ideological strategies, which reflect the collective vision of the management team

4. Process strategies, which result from the leadership controlling the process

5. Umbrella strategies, which emerge from a set of broad objectives set by the leadership

6. Disconnected strategies, as the result of sub-units being only loosely connected

7. Consensus strategies, where members converge on patterns

8. Imposed strategies, where the external environment or a parent company dictates patterns of action.

The extent to which a strategy (be it planned, entrepreneurial or any of the others identified by Mintzberg) is achieved is determined to a large extent by the ways in which organizational resources are managed; something that is achieved through the business and marketing planning process. The arguments in favour of planning are straightforward, and include:

■ Organizations must plan to coordinate their activities

■ Organizations must plan to ensure the future is taken into account

■ Organizations must plan to be rational

■ Organizations must plan to control.

In practice, however, planning frequently encounters a series of problems, the eight most critical of which were highlighted by Richardson and Richardson (1989):

1. How best to identify and manage organizational stakeholders

2. How to anticipate long(er)-term futures and develop the most appropriate product or market portfolio in order to leverage competitiveness

3. How to plan for things that might foreseeably go wrong with mainstream plans

4. How to manage product and market 'dreams' into reality

5. How to seek out major cost-cutting and contribution-creating opportunities and make the required changes to enhance productivity

6. How to create a responsive team culture whereby resources come together to meet changing market conditions and heighten customer satisfaction

7. How to create a base for innovation and then to harness the ability of the enterprise to change effectively its products, services and processes

8. How to make the most of unexpected opportunities and respond positively to shock events.

Perspectives on strategic thinking

In discussing current thinking on strategy and how strategic perspectives have developed, Mintzberg *et al.* (1998) suggest that:

> we are all like the blind man and the strategy process is our elephant. Everyone has seized some part or other of the animal and ignored the rest. Consultants have generally gone for the tusks, while academics have preferred to take photo safaris, reducing the animal to two dimensions. As a consequence, managers have been encouraged to embrace one narrow perspective or another – like the glories of planning or the wonders of core competencies. Unfortunately, the process will only work for them when they deal with the entire beast as a living organism.

To illustrate this, Mintzberg has identified ten views of the strategy process and how they have developed; these are summarized in Table 2.1.

Table 2.1 A summary of the ten schools of strategic thinking (adapted from Mintzberg *et al.*, 1998)

School	Advocates	Key themes and characteristics
The Design School	Selznick	Strategy development focuses very largely upon matching internal strengths and weaknesses with external opportunities and threats. Clear and simple strategies are developed by senior managers as the result of detailed and conscious thought and are then communicated to others further down the organizational hierarchy
The Planning School	Ansoff	In many ways similar to the Design School, the Planning School is based on a series of formal and distinct steps characterized by checklists and frameworks. Highly cerebral and formal in its nature, it is typically driven by staff planners rather than senior managers as the key players
The Positioning School	Porter	Based firmly upon the work of writers such as Michael Porter, the Planning School emerged from earlier work on strategic positioning by organizations such as the Boston Consulting Group and the PIMS researchers, and reflects thinking on military strategy and the ideas of Sun Tzu (1963). Strategy is 'reduced' to a series of generic positions that are chosen as the result of formal analyses of industry situations. Planning is seen to be a highly analytical process, with emphasis being placed upon hard data. Amongst the frameworks to have emerged from the planning school are strategic groups, value chains, and game theories
The Entrepreneurial School	Schumpeter	The Entrepreneurial School gives emphasis to the role of the chief executive, with strategies being based not so much upon detailed designs, plans, positions and framework, but upon visions of the future and the organization's place within this. A key element of the school is the argument that all organizations need a visionary leader

(Continued)

Table 2.1	Continued	
School	**Advocates**	**Key themes and characteristics**
The Cognitive School	March and Simon	The Cognitive School is concerned not so much with the type or nature of strategy as with the mental processes that underpin any strategy that emerges. Areas of particular emphasis have proved to be cognitive biases and aspects of information processing
The Learning School	Cyert and March; Hamel and Prahalad	With its origins in the ideas of incrementalism (a series of small steps rather than any large one), venturing and emergent strategy (strategy grows from a series of individual decisions rather than as the result of a tightly defined process), strategy development is seen to take place at all levels within the organization. There is an emphasis upon retrospective sense-making ('we act in order to think as much as we think in order to act') and a belief that strategy formulation and implementation are interlinked
The Power School	Allinson (micro) and Pfeiffer *et al.* (macro)	Seen by many to be a relatively minor school, the Power School gives emphasis to the idea that strategy making stems from power. This power can be seen both at a micro-level in that strategy emerges as a result of politicking between organizational actors, and at a macro-level in terms of external alliances, joint ventures and network relations
The Cultural School	Rhenman; Normann	Whereas the power school concentrates on self-interest and fragmentation, the cultural school is based on a common interest, with strategy development being seen as a social process rooted in the organizational culture. One of the most influential forces in the thinking in this area proved to be the impact of Japanese management in the 1970s and 1980s, as it became evident that difficult-to-copy cultural factors could contribute to competitive advantage
The Environmental School	Hannan and Freeman; Pugh	Whereas much thinking on strategy rests upon how the organization uses its degrees of freedom to develop strategy, the Environmental School focuses upon the significance and implications of demands placed upon the organization by the environment. Included within this is 'contingency thinking', in which consideration is given to the responses expected of the organization as the result of specific environmental conditions, and 'population ecology', which argues that there are significant constraints upon strategic choice
The Configuration School	Chandler; Mintzberg *et al.*; Miles and Snow	Seen by many to be a more extensive and integrative school of thought than those referred to above, this is characterized both by the view that the organization is a configuration of coherent clusters of characteristics and behaviours, and by the belief that change must be seen as a dramatic transformation

In practice, of course, managers are unlikely to adhere to the views and perspectives of any single school because, as Mintzberg *et al.* (1998) suggest:

> these people have to deal with the entire beast of strategy formation, not only to keep it as a vital force but also to impart real energy to the strategic process. The greatest failings of strategic management have occurred when managers took one point of view too seriously. This field had its obsession with planning. Then came generic positions based on careful calculations, now it is learning, and

doubtless other perspectives, waiting in the wings, will be greeted with similar enthusiasm before making their exit.

A categorization of approaches to strategy formulation has also been proposed by Whittington (1993), who has suggested that there are four principal or generic approaches to strategy formulation:

1. The classical approach

2. The evolutionary approach

3. The processual approach

4. The systemic approach.

A summary of these four approaches appears in Table 2.2.

The significance of these four approaches – and indeed the differences between them – needs to be understood in some detail by the reader, since the way in which the organization views strategy and the strategy-making process has significant implications for the way in which the marketing strategist goes about the development of marketing strategy. Perhaps the most obvious of these implications can be seen in terms of whether emphasis is placed largely upon a *deliberate* or an *emergent* strategy. In commenting upon this, Mintzberg (1994, pp. 24–5) suggests that:

> *intentions that are fully realized can be called* deliberate *strategies. The literature of planning recognizes both cases, with an obvious preference for the former. What it does not recognize is the third case, which we call* emergent *strategy, where a realized pattern was not expressly intended. Actions were taken, one by one, which converged in time in some sort of consistency or pattern. For example, rather than pursuing a strategy (read plan) of diversification, a company simply makes diversification decisions one by one, in effect testing the market. First it buys an urban hotel with restaurant, and then another of these, etc., until the strategy (pattern) of diversifying into urban hotels with restaurants finally emerges.*
>
> *As implied earlier, few, if any, strategies can be purely deliberate, and few can be purely emergent. One suggests no learning, the other, no control. All real world strategies need to mix these in some way – to attempt to control without stopping the learning process. Organizations, for example, often pursue what may be called* umbrella *strategies: the broad outlines are deliberate while the details are allowed to emerge within them. Thus emergent strategies are not necessarily bad and deliberate ones good; effective strategies mix these characteristics in ways that reflect the conditions at hand, the ability to predict as well as the need to react to unexpected events.*

Table 2.2	The four generic approaches to strategy formulation	
Approach	**Advocates**	**Key themes and characteristics**
The classical approach	Ansoff; Sloan and Porter	The essential underpinning is economic theory, with its advocates arguing that profit maximization is an important objective and that the strategist's task is to position the organization or business unit in such a way that this can be achieved. Rigorous intellectual analysis represents an essential input to the process, and is designed to contribute to the organization achieving a degree of control over the internal and external environment
The evolutionary approach	Henderson (of the Boston Consulting Group); Friedman; Peters	Similar in a number of ways to the Classical School of thought, strategy evolutionists differ in that they believe that because the strategist cannot control the environment, the idea of a single strategy route is inappropriate. Instead, they argue, the planner needs to recognize the options open to the organization and keep these options open for as long as possible. Its advocates also argue that because large organizations are inherently slow and inflexible, the notion of an all-embracing strategy is unrealistic. In turn, this leads to a belief that long-term strategies can often be counterproductive and that higher levels of long-term performance can often be achieved by a sense of fast-moving, short-term cost-reduction processes. In discussing this, Fifield (1998, p. 9) summarizes a key theme in terms of 'In a competitive market place the organization should launch as many small initiatives as possible and see what works. The competitive processes inherent in the market place should then allow the best initiatives to flourish and an overall strategy should begin to emerge as a pattern from the market place. In this way, we can see that the idea is that the market dictates the strategy, not the manager'
The processual approach	Mintzberg; Hamel	This pattern of thought can be seen to have emerged from the Evolutionary School, and is based on the idea that a worthwhile strategy can only emerge as the result of the strategist's detailed involvement in the day-to-day activities of the business. They recognize that the environment is too powerful and unpredictable for the strategist to overcome or manage it purely on the basis of intellectual analysis and that – unlike the evolutionists – markets are not sufficiently or inherently efficient to allow for performance maximization. Given that organizations represent a collection or coalition of individuals and interests, goals – and strategy – emerge as the result of a bargaining process. They believe strongly that planning and implementation need to be firmly interlinked, and that the classical school's ideas of strong central corporate planning departments are of little value. Mintzberg in particular believes that (effective) strategy involves a series of small steps that then coalesce into a pattern, and that the key to high(er) performance is an emergent rather than a deliberate strategy. This view is also based firmly upon the idea that in the absence of the right competencies, strategy and plans are to all intents meaningless
The systemic approach	Whittington; Morgan	This reflects a belief that there is no one strategy model that is applicable to all types of organization, but that both the objectives and the strategy process are the result of the strategist's social and cultural backgrounds and of the social context in which they are operating. This view gives emphasis to the way in which strategy and the strategy process are not necessarily objective and rational but, particularly in multinational corporations (MNCs), are a reflection of an amalgam of possibly very different forces that have their origins in social systems. The most obvious ways in which these differences are manifested within an MNC include attitudes to profit, risk, group versus individual decision-making, levels of accountability, timescales and indeed the notion of the free market. Advocates of the systemic school argue that a focus upon implementation is essential and that this is significantly influenced by organizational sociology

2.4   SO WHAT IS MARKETING STRATEGY?

At its simplest, strategy means knowing where you want to go and then deciding upon how best to get there. Strategic marketing can therefore be distilled down to the planner deciding – with complete clarity – in which markets the organization wants (or is able) to compete, and then how exactly it will do this (see Figure 2.1).

Given this, an effective marketing strategy can be seen to be based upon four key dimensions:

1. Being close to the market

2. Developing valid assumptions about environmental trends and market behaviour

3. Exploiting the competencies of the organization

4. Developing a realistic basis for gaining and sustaining competitive advantage.

A slight variation on this, which reflects the 'three Cs' of marketing strategy, is illustrated in Figure 2.2.

An organization's marketing strategy is not developed in isolation; instead it needs to be developed against the background of and within the constraints imposed by the organization's overall corporate plan. There is therefore a cascade process, with the marketing strategy emerging from the corporate strategy, and the marketing plan and tactics then emerging from the marketing strategy. An integral part of any marketing strategy is the competitive strategy. In other words, *how* – in detail – will the organization compete within the market place?

Although there are numerous dimensions to any competitive strategy (many of which are discussed in detail in later chapters), competitive strategy at its most extreme can be seen to be about being better than the competition in every function and at every level. The reality for many organizations is often very different, since the organizational culture and overall level of

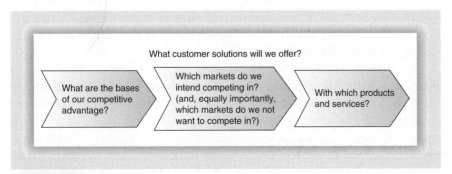

What customer solutions will we offer?

What are the bases of our competitive advantage?

Which markets do we intend competing in? (and, equally importantly, which markets do we not want to compete in?)

With which products and services?

FIGURE 2.1   *The key dimensions of marketing strategy*

In developing the strategic marketing plan, the strategist needs to take as one of the starting points the analysis of the three Cs of strategy: Customers, Competitors and Capabilities.

Customers: Who are they? When, where and how do they buy? What motivates them? How is the market currently segmented? How might it be segmented?

Competitors: Who are they? What strategies are they pursuing? What are their strengths and weaknesses? What are their areas of vulnerability? How are they most likely to develop over the next few years?

Capabilities: What are the organization's relative strengths and weaknesses in each of the market segments in which it is operating? What levels of investment are available? How might the capabilities best be leveraged?

FIGURE 2.2   *The three Cs of marketing strategy*

capability prevent this. (See Illustration 2.2 in which we discuss the idea of organizational DNA.) However, regardless of capability, the strategic marketing planning process needs to begin with the identification of key issues, both externally and internally. Externally, these include the general environment, the markets, customers and competitors. Internally, the key issues are both real (e.g. budgetary or production constraints) and imaginary or artificial (e.g. an attitude of 'we can't do it that way' or 'it just wouldn't work').

Having identified these key issues, the next step is their analysis, followed by the strategy and action plans, and then implementation, monitoring, control and feedback (see Figure 2.3).

The approach that is reflected in Figure 2.3 can be termed a logical, sequential and rational approach to planning, in that it is based on a highly structured view of how an organization operates. In practice, the planning process is often far less structured. Stacey, for example, whose work is based on chaos theories of management that reflect his view that strategy is a far more dynamic and unpredictable process than is typically acknowledged, has argued for a far more organic approach to strategy and planning. Here, however, we focus largely upon a structured approach to thinking about the process of marketing planning and implementation.

An alternative framework for thinking about strategy is illustrated in Figure 2.4. Here, the core organizational values and defining competencies drive the core purpose of the business and, in turn, the vision or what we have labelled 'the Olympic goal'. Strategies and action plans then emerge from this, with areas such as operational efficiency, the organizational structure, people, and customer service all being aspects of the implementation process. This is then developed in greater detail in Figure 2.5, which explores how the organization might achieve its objective.

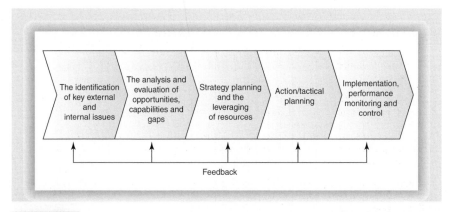

FIGURE 2.3   *The strategic marketing planning process*

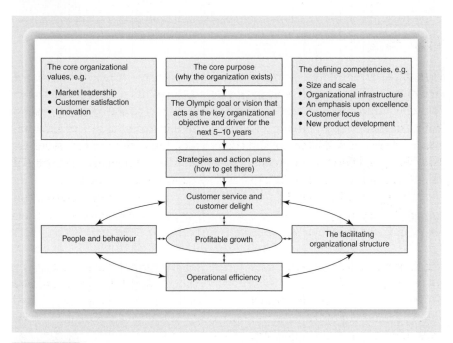

FIGURE 2.4   *The Olympic goal as the driver for strategic marketing planning*

However, despite all the attention that has been paid to strategy and to the factors that influence it, the reader needs to recognize that an organization cannot really claim to have a strategy if it simply carries out many of the same activities as its competitors, but only a little better. If it does this, it is merely operationally more efficient. An organization can only really claim to have a robust strategy when major points of difference exist between what it is doing and what its competitors are doing. In the absence of this, the organization runs the risk of a self-inflicted vulnerability and of falling into the trap of action **without** strategy.

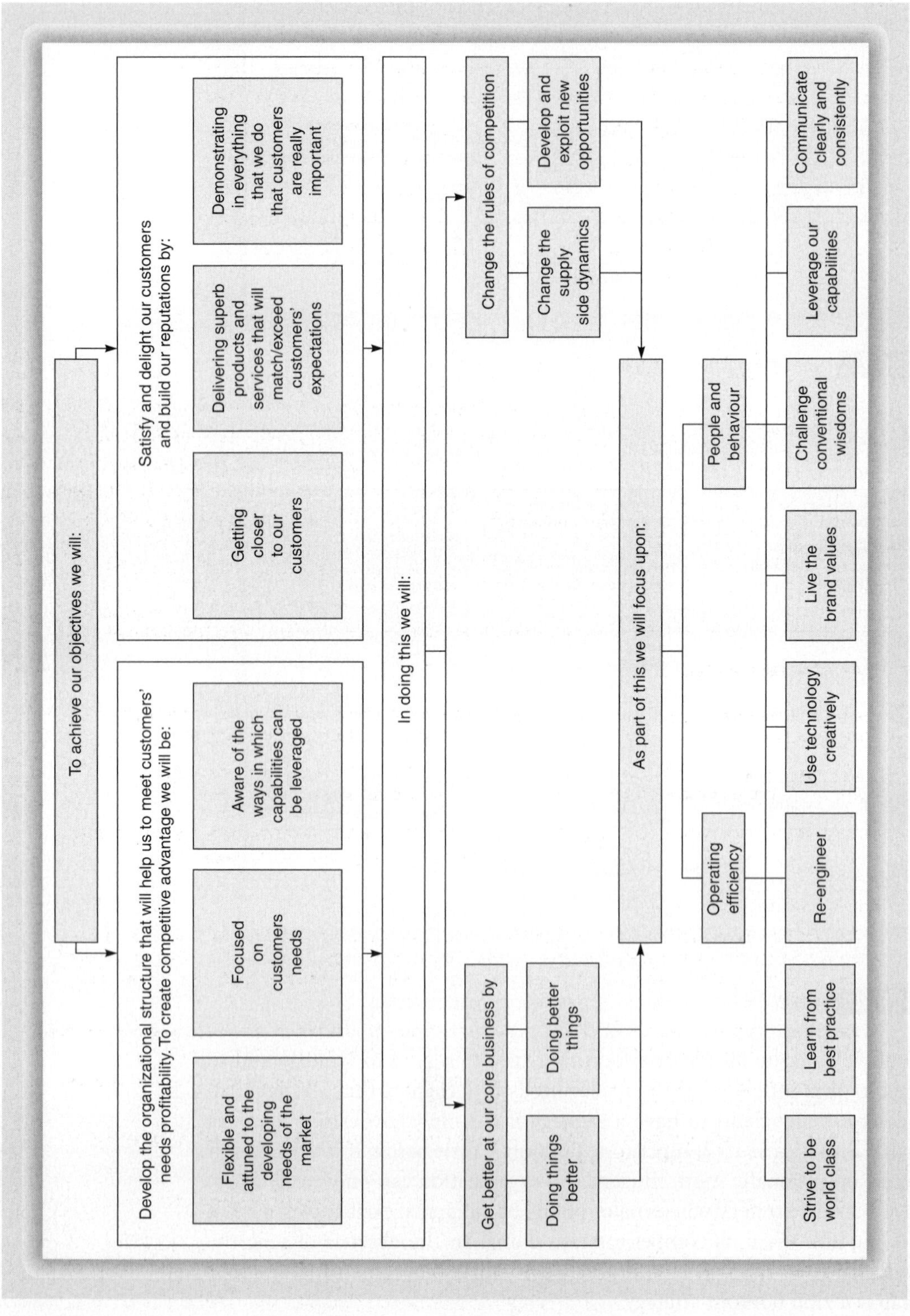

To achieve our objectives we will:

Develop the organizational structure that will help us to meet customers' needs profitably. To create competitive advantage we will be:

Flexible and attuned to the developing needs of the market

Focused on customers needs

Aware of the ways in which capabilities can be leveraged

Satisfy and delight our customers and build our reputations by:

Getting closer to our customers

Delivering superb products and services that will match/exceed customers' expectations

Demonstrating in everything that we do that customers are really important

In doing this we will:

Get better at our core business by

Doing things better

Doing better things

Strive to be world class

Learn from best practice

Re-engineer

Use technology creatively

Live the brand values

Challenge conventional wisdoms

Leverage our capabilities

Communicate clearly and consistently

As part of this we will focus upon:

Operating efficiency

People and behaviour

Change the supply side dynamics

Change the rules of competition

Develop and exploit new opportunities

FIGURE 2.5 Developing and implementing strategies

In discussing this, Neilson and Pasternack (2005) of the consultants Booz Allen Hamilton develop the concept of organizational DNA which, they suggest, is one of the primary determinants of performance. In essence, they argue, there are seven organizational types, only three of which are healthy (refer to Illustration 2.2). The implications of these profiles for planning and, more importantly, for implementation are significant and highlight the ways in which, despite the attention that might be paid to a planning process, if the underlying DNA of the business is unhealthy, little that is different or meaningful is likely to be achieved. Instead, the organization simply zig-zags towards the land of the lost.

Illustration 2.2 Planning and the significance of organizational DNA

In their book *Results: Keep What's Good, Fix What's Wrong and Unlock Great Performance*, Neilson and Pasternack (2005) use the Booz Allen Hamilton DNA profiling tool (see www.orgdna.com) to identify seven types of organization, three of which are healthy and in which planning – and implementation – work effectively. In the other four, a host of factors, including political infighting, a lack of focus and multiple layers of management, conspire to create an environment in which little is likely to be achieved (refer to Figure 2.6). Depressingly, their research suggests that 60% of businesses fall into this category.

The healthy DNA profiles ...

The military organization: Typically driven (hard) by a small and focused senior leadership team, it succeeds as a result of a well-thought-out and superior business model and superior execution.

The resilient organization: Sensitive to the market and sufficiently flexible to cope with these changes, the management team has a clear focus upon the strategy and its implementation.

The just-in-time organization: Although it suffers from a degree of inconsistency, there is typically a clear understanding of what is needed to succeed and a high degree of flexibility that allows it to meet market demands.

And the unhealthy DNA profiles ...

The out-grown organization: With strategies, structures, systems and processes more suited to an earlier phase in its life, the outgrown organization often has its decision-making concentrated in the hands of a small number of managers who are increasingly out of touch both with the market and what this demands of the organization.

The over-managed organization: Characterized by high levels of bureaucracy, a highly political environment and too many layers of management, the organization typically suffers from paralysis by analysis.

The passive-aggressive organization: Although strategies and plans are developed without argument, the organization then struggles with their implementation.

The fits-and-starts organization: Typically staffed with large numbers of talented and motivated managers, they rarely agree on the direction of the business.

FIGURE 2.6 *The seven types of organizational DNA*

2.5   THE THREE DIMENSIONS OF PLANNING

According to Piercy (2002, p. 586) the strategic marketing planning process consists of three principal and interrelated dimensions:

1. An *analytical* dimension, which is concerned with a series of techniques, procedures, systems and planning models

2. A *behavioural* dimension, which relates to the nature and extent of the participation, motivation and commitment from members of the management team

3. An *organizational* dimension, which is concerned with information flows, structures, processes, management style and culture.

The effectiveness of the planning process – and hence the ultimate value of the plan – is therefore determined by the way in which these three dimensions are managed. Where, for example, there is a culture in which there is little openness, creativity or involvement from staff across marketing and other parts of the business, the value of any analysis and planning is likely to be reduced dramatically. Equally, if the organizational dimension inhibits information flows and/or an emphasis upon implementation, again the value of the planning process and the plan is reduced.

However, although planning has an inherent and logical attraction (a summary of the most commonly claimed benefits of marketing planning appear in Figure 2.7), the reality in many organizations is that the planning process is often managed relatively badly. In attempting to explain why this is so, a variety of issues have been highlighted. Piercy (2002, pp. 583–5), for example, argues that there are ten principal planning pitfalls. These include:

1. *An emphasis upon analysis rather than planning*, which leads to managers becoming preoccupied with tools and techniques rather than thinking creatively about objectives, positioning and strategy

2. *Information instead of decisions*, where there is a constant demand for ever more information before decisions are taken

3. *Incrementalism*, which leads to this year's plan being an often minor development of what has gone before rather than something that raises fundamental questions about issues of capability, objectives and markets

4. *Vested interests*, which lead to an emphasis upon maintaining the *status quo* and the safeguarding of empires and budgets

5. *An organizational mindset*, which refuses to accept plans that move away from the well-accepted and the well-rehearsed approaches of the past

Amongst the most frequently claimed benefits of marketing plans and marketing planning are that:

1. The process of planning encourages or forces managers to think ahead and to examine in detail how the environment may develop and where opportunities and threat exist or might come from

2. Following on from this, the planning process leads managers to think in detail about organizational capabilities, priorities, objectives and policies

3. If clearly and realistically developed, the objectives that emerge from the planning process provide the basis for the development of performance standards and the more effective control of the organization

4. Plans should lead to a better co-ordination of company efforts and the more effective utilization of assets

5. By thinking about the future, managers should be better prepared for any unexpected environmental developments

6. By being involved in the development of the plan, managers should feel a (greater) sense of ownership and have a better understanding of their responsibilities and what is expected of them.

FIGURE 2.7   *The benefits of marketing planning*

6. A general *resistance to change* amongst members of the management team

7. *Little ownership of the plans* and a corresponding absence of commitment

8. *Inadequate resourcing* of the plan

9. *A focus upon planning per se* rather than planning and implementation

10. *A diminishing interest* in the plan as a result of its not having been taken seriously in the past and a general shift towards planning simply becoming an annual, time-consuming, irksome and essentially pointless ritual.

The pitfalls and difficulties of marketing planning have also been highlighted by McDonald (2007), who has suggested that the ten most common barriers to (effective) marketing planning are:

1. *A confusion between marketing tactics and marketing strategy,* and an emphasis upon the easier and more predictable short-term issues and performance at the expense of those that are more complex and uncertain long term

2. *A separation of the marketing function from day-to-day operations*, with the result that plans are developed without the immediacy of contact with the market

3. *A confusion between marketing as a function and marketing as a far broader business concept*; the implications of this are seen most obviously in terms of marketing being seen to be synonymous with sales, or advertising, or customer service, rather than as the driving organizational philosophy

4. *Organizational barriers* that lead to company activities being structured around functional activities rather than customer groups

5. *A lack of detailed analysis*, and an emphasis instead upon preconceptions and conventional wisdoms

6. *A confusion between process and output*; something that is manifested most obviously in terms of models such as SWOT being seen as an end in themselves rather than as the basis for providing real insight to issues of capability

7. *A lack of knowledge and skills*

8. *The lack of a systematic approach to planning* and a reliance instead upon something that is rather more *ad hoc*

9. *The failure to prioritize objectives* on the basis of their impact upon the organization, their urgency and their implications for resources

10. *Hostile corporate cultures* that lead to marketing and, by extension, marketing planning being viewed as less important than other parts of the business.

Given the nature of these comments, it would seem that planning rarely works as well as it should. However, at an intellectual level, few managers would argue against the notion of planning. Instead, it is the way in which planning is often practised that appears to create problems.

Recognizing this, the marketing planner needs to think in detail about how the planning process – and therefore the plans – might be improved. However, before doing this, it is worth thinking about four observations made by Giles (1995):

1. Better planning does not invariably lead to better implementation

2. Over-sophistication hinders ownership of the plan

3. Ownership tends to make implementation work, irrespective of the strategy

4. Sophistication follows ownership and implementation.

Managing the marketing planning process (effectively)

If you buy into a strategy, you have to buy into the consequences *of that strategy. (Anon)*

In the light of what has been said so far, it should be apparent that, if the planning process is to be effective, it is not simply a case of imposing a planning structure upon members of the marketing team. Instead, there is the need to demonstrate, first, that planning is a living and meaningful process, and secondly, that the plan is designed to be a working document – in other words, it is designed to be something that is used on a day-to-day basis to guide and inform decisions. Recognizing this, we can identify a number of initial guidelines:

- The planning format needs to be standardized so that managers across the business are familiar with the process and structure

- There needs to be an inbuilt flexibility so that, as the external environment changes, the plan can be modified to reflect these changes

- The plan needs to be based upon opportunity-oriented and strategic thinking rather than simply being a reiteration of what has gone before

- The priorities and strategy should not be hidden in the detail of the plan, but should instead be immediately apparent.

In addition, the planner needs to think about how to improve levels of commitment and support to the planning process. Some of the ways in which this might be done are examined at a later stage, although at this point it is worth referring to Figure 2.8, in which we show the five levels of commitment and support that typically exist.

The lost art of planning and strategy

The implications of a poorly-developed and poorly-implemented approach to planning have been spelled out by a variety of writers, including de Kare-Silver (1997) who, in his book *Strategy in Crisis*, suggested that many companies have lost the art of planning and strategy-making. They spend too much time, he argues, looking inward at process change, organization and systems, and do not allocate enough time or effort to planning their future, determining where they want to be in their markets, and how they are going to beat competitors. In these circumstances, he suggests, planning processes are typically reduced to annual form-filling and extrapolating numbers without any serious debate about the future. In making this comment, he points to a variety of studies and statements from senior managers:

Only 20 per cent of CEOs surveyed put strategy as their starting point in building their company ... As few as 6 per cent of business people in the United States would rate their company excellent at planning for the long-term future ... We don't have a strategy, what's the point when the world is so uncertain?

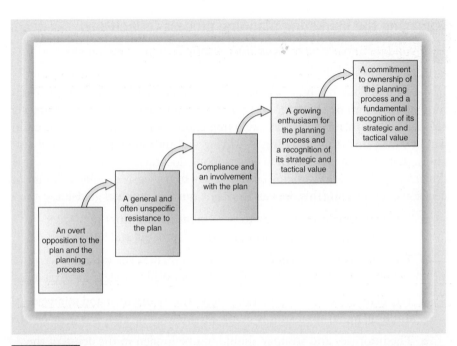

FIGURE 2.8 *The ladder of planning commitment and support (adapted from Jobber, D. (2004, p. 757)*

To support his argument, de Kare-Silver cites the results of a survey of 100 chief executives of the top 100 companies based in the UK and the United States that was carried out by the consultancy firm Kalchas Group. The results suggested that only 14 put 'strategy' at the top of their list of priorities; this is illustrated in Table 2.3.

He goes on to say that:

This low ranking for strategy is confirmed by other surveys. For example, another piece of research reviewed in the book Maximum Leadership *(1995) concluded that only 20 per cent of CEOs described strategy formulation as their defining role. While most acknowledged its importance, at the same time they put other items such as people, change management and core competencies ahead on their list of priorities: In reality, many of the CEOs we interviewed felt entirely comfortable saying they believed the days of top-down strategy formulation are past.*

Insofar as it is possible to identify the characteristics of those organizations in which managers have *not* lost sight of the significance of planning and strategy, they are that:

- There is a clear sense of purpose and direction
- Strategies are clearly articulated

Table 2.3	Where would strategy typically rank on your agenda? (adapted from de Kare-Silver, 1997)	
Suggested priority agenda items		**Average rankings**
People management		1
Financial performance		2
Stockholders		3
Customers		4
Re-engineering		5
Future strategy		6
New products		7
Technology		8
Information management		9
Regulatory environment		10

- There is continuous investment in people, products, processes and markets

- Resources and effort are clearly focused upon those elements that are seen to be important and that give or contribute to competitive advantage

- There is a commitment to the long term

- The management team is determined to overcome obstacles and roadblocks

- There is an emphasis upon implementation

- Managers are concerned with creating their own future, rather than having it created for them by others.

In essence, de Kare-Silver suggests, they not only understand competitive advantage and what it takes to win, but they also recognize that marketing excellence is achieved not through ignorance and guesswork, but through a detailed understanding of the organization's markets and organizational capabilities, and a clear focus upon segmentation and differentiation.

However, a problem for many managers who do attempt to develop and implement a more strategic approach to their markets is that the majority of the best-known and most widely used strategy tools are increasingly being seen as out of date. The Boston Consulting Group's (1970) growth-share matrix and Porter's five forces and three generic strategies, for example, were all developed against the background of a very different business environment from the one within which many managers operate today and, as a consequence, have a number of limitations (these are touched upon in later parts of this book). In order to overcome this, de Kare-Silver argues for what he terms the Market Commitment model, suggesting that it is this that helps managers to come to terms with the way in which competitive advantage might possibly be built and sustained.

The model is based upon two building blocks: commitment and competitive advantage. The first of these stems from de Kare-Silver's belief that in focusing upon the future, high-performing management teams demonstrate a commitment to win and an almost messianic focus that is so strongly articulated that competitors back away, recognizing that the market will be dominated by the key player.

The second building block of the model is competitive advantage. Research by de Kare-Silver and the Kalchas Group led him to suggest that there are four prime areas that differentiate organizations and most frequently influence purchases decisions. These are:

1. Performance

2. Price

3. Emotion

4. 'Service hustle'.

The absolute ideal, he suggests, is the superior performance of the product or service, sold at the most leveraged price, with extraordinary levels of service and compelling emotional values. In practice, of course, there tends to be a focus upon just one or two of these areas rather than all four, and the task of the strategist is therefore to identify which of these is (or are) the most appropriate. Toyota, BMW and Mercedes, for example, focus upon product quality, performance and the development of advances in the product. Marriott Hotels and First Direct base their advantage on delivering very high service levels. Aldi and Wal-Mart use price as the lever, whilst Coca-Cola, Marlboro and Disney base their thinking on the establishment of powerful emotional values with their brands, and the building of customer relationships.

The structure of the marketing plan

Against the background of what we have said so far, we can now turn to the structure of the marketing plan: this appears in Table 2.4, together with an indication of the tools and techniques that might be used at each stage. Deliberately, we have opted for something that is highly-structured and through which the planner moves in a step-by-step way.

Table 2.4	The marketing plan
Key headings of the plan	**Tools, techniques and outcomes**
1. Executive summary	
2. The background to the plan and the context for what follows (a summary of the position reached and the strategic progress made)	
3. The vision for the organization, the mission and aspirations (e.g. to create superb products and services, to develop and expand the markets in which the company is active, and to create stakeholder value by achieving an exceptional financial performance that will be reflected in the company's share price), and strategic intent (e.g. to gain leadership within defined strategic groups and markets, as well as achieving an excellent financial performance)	
4. Market overview and situational analysis (the statement of where we are currently, the factors that have contributed to this, and a review of what has been going well and what has been going badly and is in need of attention)	
5. Internal analysis: strengths, weaknesses and measures of capability	■ Strengths and weaknesses and their implications ■ Resource analysis ■ Assets and competences ■ Measures of capability ■ Portfolio analysis ■ Product and brand life cycle positions ■ The reality check (why should anyone buy from us?) ■ Strategic intent and strategic reality (what do we want to do, and what are we *really* capable of achieving?) ■ Benchmarking (how do we perform relative to others?)
5(a). *The preliminary assessment of strengths and weaknesses and initial thinking on how to leverage capability*	
6. External analysis and the market audit	■ SLEPT analysis ■ Opportunities and threats: basic beliefs, implications and must do's ■ Market trends and implications ■ Performance/importance analysis ■ Customer analysis, including customers' perceptions of the organization, measures of satisfaction, and measures of loyalty ■ Areas of company–customer mismatch ■ Competitor analysis ■ Market product, brand and technology life cycle analysis

(Continued)

| Table 2.4 | Continued |

Key headings of the plan	Tools, techniques and outcomes
6(a). *Preliminary assessment of the opportunities and threats: the issues that emerge from the analysis, including the critical success factors*	
7. Critical issues analysis and thinking on positioning in order to reduce competitive threats and how to exploit opportunities	■ Strategic imperatives and priorities ■ Marketing priorities
8. The principal assumptions underpinning the plan	■ Critical success factors (the areas in which the organization must excel if it is to outperform its competitors and achieve success) and how these are changing ■ Life cycle projections ■ Probable customer and competitor moves and developments ■ The scope for leveraging capability (what can we do to reinvent the marketing proposition and/or the industry?)
9. The target market and its characteristics	■ Customer and consumer issues ■ Strategic groups ■ Segmentation, targeting and positioning ■ Market space analysis
10. The marketing objectives by market, product group, segment and brand	■ The Ansoff matrix ■ Competitive stance and competitive advantage ■ Profits forecast and sensitivity analysis
11. The positioning statement	
12. The marketing and competitive strategy and the competitive stance	The *type* of strategy ■ The big idea – the killer or winning proposition ■ Competitive targets and priorities ■ Issues of differentiation and the competitive stance ■ Approaches to leveraging capability: the three actions/things that would make a difference ■ Breakpoint thinking ■ Segmentation, targeting and positioning
13. The management of the seven Ps of the marketing matrix	■ The seven Ps (Product, Price, Place, Promotion, People, Physical evidence and Process management) ■ Aspects of customer service/establishing the service levels
14. The development of the brand	■ Market mapping ■ Competitive advantage, selling proposition(s) and brand values ■ The 'big idea' and breakpoint thinking ■ The bases for differentiation and competitive advantage ■ Leveraging assets and strategy ■ The delivery of greater value
15. Budgets	
16. Review and the possible reformulation of the objectives	

(*Continued*)

Table 2.4	Continued
Key headings of the plan	**Tools, techniques and outcomes**
17. The action plan	
18. Implementation and control	▪ Issues of responsibility and accountability ▪ Deadlines, intermediate targets and measures of performance ▪ Internal marketing ▪ The McKinsey 7S
19. Contingency thinking (what are we going to do if some of the planning assumptions prove not to be valid and/or our objectives and/or environmental conditions change?)	▪ Scenario and 'what if'? thinking

Note: Within this structure, the setting of the budget appears at a relatively late stage. In many organizations, of course, the budget (or at least the initial budget) is allocated at the beginning of the planning cycle, and the planner is therefore faced with the task of developing the plan within this constraint.

Marketing planning and the significance of mindset

In his book *The Mind of the Strategist*, Kenichi Ohmae (1983) claimed that successful strategy was more to do with a particular mindset than with detailed and highly objective analysis. Written in 1975, at the time of a tremendous upsurge in Japanese global economic power, the book was translated into English in 1983 and proved to be particularly successful and influential, since it was at this stage that American business was being hit particularly hard by Japanese firms. Perceived by many to hold the secret to Japanese management thinking, the book was in fact a warning against a belief in a 'Made in Japan' miracle of business strategy.

Ohmae, a consultant with McKinsey, argued in the book that a considerable amount of Japanese strategy was often based on creativity and intuition – a view that was at odds with the common perception of remorseless Japanese logic and detailed planning, something that was, in turn, reflected in the often small and frequently poorly resourced strategic planning units of Japanese companies. Despite this, Japanese firms at the time were often outstanding performers in the market place.

Ohmae contrasted this with the way in which he saw many large American firms being run rather like the Soviet economy in its heyday, with managers feeling that they needed to plan ahead comprehensively and control in detail each stage of the process. In these circumstances, he suggested, creativity and intuition get lost. He also suggested that in these types of organization those who step outside the well-established and clearly-defined planning parameters are often penalized, whilst those who understand and work the system are rewarded.

In commenting on this, Merriden (1998) suggests that:

If creativity and intuition are the key, then the central thrust of Ohmae's argument is that successful strategies result not from rigorous

1. What issues are you facing in your business today, what are the market dynamics, and how are they changing?

2. What actions have your competitors taken in the last three and five years that have had a significant effect upon your organization?

3. What actions have you taken over the last three and five years that have had a significant effect upon the competition?

4. What are the most dangerous and far-reaching actions that your competitors might take, both in the short term and the long term?

5. What are the most effective steps that you could take in the next three years?

FIGURE 2.9 *Five questions for the marketing planner and strategist*

analysis but from a particular state of mind. 'In strategic thinking', he argues, 'one first seeks a clear understanding of the particular character of each element of a situation and then makes the fullest use of human brainpower to restructure the elements in the most advantageous way.' Brainpower on its own is not enough. Hence, at the heart of a Japanese business, there is often a single, talented, forceful strategist, who has 'an idiosyncratic mode of thinking in which company, customers and competition merge'. These three Cs, as Ohmae called them, are all-important, but for the Japanese it is the customer who has always been at the heart of the Japanese approach to strategy.

Ohmae goes on to suggest that an effective strategy is one through which a company can gain significant ground on its competitors at an acceptable cost to itself, and outlines four ways of achieving this. The first is a clear focus on the key factors for success, and a concentration of major resources at an early stage on a single strategically significant function. The second is to build on superiority by employing technology not currently being exploited by your rivals. The third is to pursue aggressive initiatives that upset 'the rules of the game'. The final route is to make full use of what Ohmae calls 'strategic degrees of freedom', focusing on areas in which competitors are not involved.

Given the nature of these comments, we can identify a number of questions that marketing planners and strategists need to ask themselves on a regular basis (see Figure 2.9). It is the answer to these questions that (should) help to focus attention upon some of the more significant issues that underpin the development of the strategic marketing plan.

Testing and evaluating the plan

In testing and evaluating the strategy and plan, a number of criteria need to be considered – the three most obvious of which relate to the plan's *appropriateness* (does it, for example, strengthen and exploit the current position?); its *feasibility* (can it be successfully implemented?); and its *desirability* (does it close any planning gaps, and are the risk levels acceptable?). A slightly different approach to evaluation is encapsulated in Table 2.5, where the plan is tested against a number of criteria.

Having developed the plan and applied the initial test that appears in Table 2.5, there is then the need to take the evaluation a stage further with a straightforward five-stage test.

1. The objectives

To what extent are the objectives measurable, stretching, and motivating, with clear interim steps?

2. A long-term view

Does the plan reflect a long-term perspective, and is there a clear picture of how the future will be or might be different?

Table 2.5 Testing the strategy and plan					
To what extent does the strategy and plan:	To a very high degree				Not at all
1. Build upon and exploit our strengths	•	•	•	•	•
2. Address our weaknesses	•	•	•	•	•
3. Leverage and strengthen our competitive position	•	•	•	•	•
4. Exploit emerging opportunities	•	•	•	•	•
5. Provide a basis for meaningful differentiation	•	•	•	•	•
6. Hurt the competition	•	•	•	•	•
7. Leverage marketing assets	•	•	•	•	•
8. Strengthen our image and reputation	•	•	•	•	•
9. Develop our routes to market	•	•	•	•	•
10. Build customer loyalty	•	•	•	•	•
11. Reflect product and/or process innovation	•	•	•	•	•
12. Coordinate resources – including staff – across the organization	•	•	•	•	•
13. Make best use of resources	•	•	•	•	•
14. Satisfy the criteria of simplicity	•	•	•	•	•
15. Satisfy the criteria of flexibility	•	•	•	•	•

3. The allocation of resources	Are the resources needed for the plan understood in detail, and has this level of resource been committed?
4. Competitive advantage	What are the bases of competitive advantage for the company? How significant are they? To what extent are they capable of being leveraged and how are they to be used?
5. Simple	By ensuring that the strategy is clear, concise and simple, the chances of successful implementation increase dramatically.

Assuming that the plan satisfies these criteria, the focus needs then to switch to that of implementation.

The difficulties of implementation

It has long been recognized that it is one thing to develop the strategy and the strategic plan. It is another to implement the plan effectively and translate strategy into action. One of the first to explore this in detail was the Prussian staff officer Karl von Clausewitz (1984) who, in his book *On War*, suggested that 'everything in strategy is very simple, but that does not mean that everything in strategy is very easy'. He went on to say that 'countless minor incidents – the kind you can never really foresee – combine to lower the general level of performance, so that one always falls short of the intended goal'. He referred to this phenomenon as 'friction' and believed it to be the principal reason why strategies fail.

Although von Clausewitz was discussing strategy in terms of war, a similar theme has been pursued by numerous business writers, including Ansoff (1984), Dromgoole *et al.* (2000) and Mintzberg *et al.* (2005). In some instances, the factors that cause the strategy to fail are built into the strategy itself, in that the underlying assumptions are flawed and/or the underlying environmental conditions change. As an example of this, the car makers General Motors and Ford both assumed for many years that the sports utility vehicle market in the USA, where both companies had considerable strengths, would continue to grow. Faced, however, in 2008 with rapidly rising fuel prices, customers began looking for smaller and more economical vehicles. Equally, the unexpected rejection by customers of 'New Coke' in 1985 forced the Coca-Cola company into a very different marketing strategy, whilst in 2004 the US pharmaceutical group Merck was unexpectedly forced into withdrawing one of its key products, the arthritis treatment drug Vioxx.

Given examples such as these, there are five possible guidelines for the planner:

- Ensure that the underlying marketing strategy is as realistic as possible

- Check the external and internal environmental assumptions and conditions on a regular basis

- Recognize the pivotal importance of ongoing communication so that staff understand what the plan entails and what it demands of them

- Be prepared for the unexpected and have contingencies in place. Faced with the rapid rise in the price of oil in mid-2008, for example, when oil reached almost $150 a barrel, many organizations were forced into having to think very differently and put in place contingency actions. Airlines, for example, began rethinking routes, mothballing aircraft and imposing additional levies on passengers

- If market conditions change significantly, be willing to dramatically revise or even drop the plan and begin again.

In an attempt to summarize the primary contributors to poor or ineffective implementation, Piercy and Morgan (1990) have pointed to:

1. The separation of planning activities from the day-to-day management of market, products and brands

2. The hopeless optimism that leads to plans being developed that are divorced, almost totally in some cases, from reality

3. Issues associated with the implementation of the plan being recognized at too late a stage, with the result that the plan that emerges simply cannot be taken further without the injection of new resources, capabilities, systems and people

4. A denial of any potential implementation problems (this is sometimes manifested in terms of senior management taking the approach that 'if this is the way that we say it is going to be, this is the way it is going to be'). In the absence of buy-in, ownership and commitment, even the most logical of plans is unlikely to be implemented fully

5. Implementation being seen almost as an after-thought and a tidying up of loose ends rather than as something that needs to be an integral part of the planning process from the outset

6. Any barriers or potential implementation problems that are identified are not analysed in sufficient detail, and managers then either over-react or react inappropriately.

McDonald (1989) offers a broadly similar perspective when discussing the problems of implementation, pointing to:

1. Too little support from senior management, with the result that too few resources are available and levels of buy-in are low

2. The lack of a plan for planning so that few of the team really understand what is required and how the plan will be used

3. The absence of line management support

4. Confusion over the planning terminology

5. A focus upon numbers rather than clearly stated objectives and strategies

6. Too great an emphasis upon detail

7. The emergence of planning as a once-a-year ritual rather than as an ongoing process that involves analysing markets, capabilities and strategic options

8. The failure to distinguish properly between the short- and the long-term and between the operational and the strategic dimensions

9. The failure to integrate marketing planning with corporate planning

10. The temptation to leave planning to a (separate) planning team rather than seeing it to be the responsibility of those who manage the business.

Piercy (2008) has highlighted a series of broadly similar issues, suggesting that, if the planning – *and implementation* – processes are to work effectively, there is the need for the formulization of marketing planning across the organization, supported by high levels of management involvement; a thoroughness which includes resources and rewards; a recognition of the behavioural issues associated with planning; and a culture which ensures that the plan is used.

In addition to these points, Freedman (2003) has pointed to the problems of:

- Strategic inertia which leads to managers being unwilling to change, despite what the plan demands

- A lack of stakeholder commitment

- Strategic drift

- Strategic dilution which is characterized by a lack of clarity about the plan's ownership and drivers

- Strategic isolation in communication is poorly developed and the plans increasingly become disconnected from the focus of activity

- The failure to monitor and understand the progress being made

- Initiative fatigue in which (too much) action becomes mistaken for strategy

- A level of impatience in which the timetable for results is unrealistically short

- The failure to celebrate success.

In order to overcome these sorts of problems, Piercy and Morgan (1990) advocate taking four steps:

- Turn planning upside-down. Start with those things that line executives see as most critical. Work back from this to begin putting together a strategic plan.

- Make participation a controlled variable to get the right blend of line executives and planning analysts, departmental and political interest, 'change champions' and 'culture carriers', to weld strategy and implementation together.

- In all strategic plans, demand explicit, costed, researched implementation strategies for every key item. Reject out-of-hand any plan that does not explicitly address implementation issues.

- Challenge all strategic plans that do not show how the plan gains the commitment of the people who run the business, and that ignore the importance of consistency between what has to be done and what the organization is going to try to do.

Having started this section with a quotation from von Clausewitz, it is perhaps appropriate to finish with a quotation from another military strategist. The Prussian Field Marshal Helmuth von Moltke once said that 'no plan survives contact with the enemy'. In business terms, this would be that 'no plan survives contact with reality' and that what looks to be robust as a planning document may not work out in practice.

2.6 SUMMARY

Within this chapter we have examined the nature and role of strategic marketing planning and illustrated some of the different perspectives that have emerged over the past few years. We have also examined the dimensions of marketing strategy and planning and how the planning process might be made to work effectively. Against this background we have introduced the structure of the marketing plan, and it is this that provides the framework for the remainder of the book.

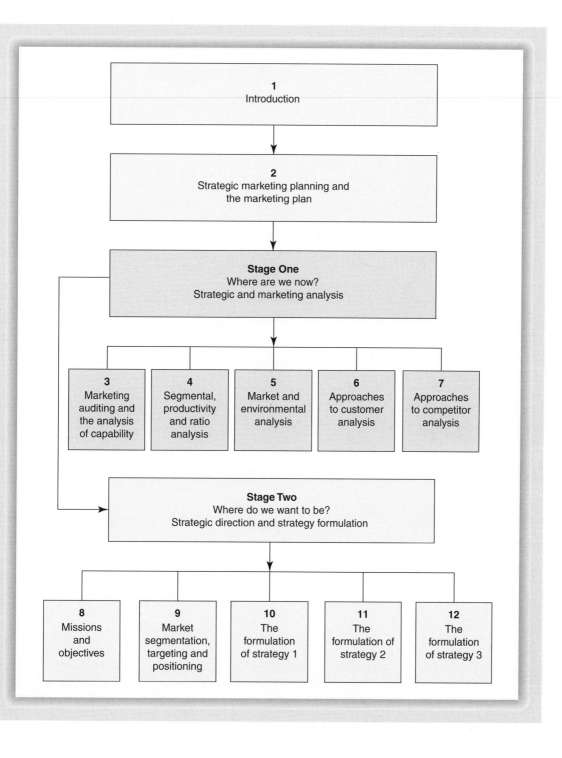

Where Are We Now? Strategic and Marketing Analysis

Our primary concern in Stage One is with the ways in which organizations can most clearly identify their current position and the extent of their marketing capability. With the background of the picture that emerges from this analysis, the marketing planner should be in a far better position to begin the process of deciding upon the detail of the organization's future direction and the ways in which strategy is to be formulated. The starting point in this process of strategic and marketing analysis involves a detailed marketing audit and review of marketing effectiveness. Together, the two techniques are designed to provide the strategist with a clear understanding of:

- The organization's current market position
- The nature of environmental opportunities and threats
- The organization's ability to cope with the demands of this environment.

The results of this analysis are then incorporated in a statement of Strengths, Weaknesses, Opportunities and Threats (SWOT), and subsequently a measure of capability.

Although the marketing auditing process is, as we discuss in Chapter 3, a relatively underutilized activity, a growing number of planners, strategists and writers have over the past few years highlighted the nature of its potential contribution to effective strategy formulation. Although there is no single format for the audit, it is generally acknowledged that, if the process is to be worthwhile, account needs to be taken of six dimensions:

1. The marketing environment
2. The current marketing strategy

3. Organizational issues

4. The marketing systems in use

5. Levels of marketing productivity

6. Marketing functions.

Used properly, marketing auditing and a review of marketing effectiveness are recognized as potentially powerful analytical tools that are capable of providing the planner with a detailed understanding of the organization's marketing capability and the nature of the environment that it is likely to face.

This process of analysis is taken a step further in Chapter 4, in which we discuss the ways in which the planner can establish patterns of resource allocation and its productivity by relating inputs (resources or costs) to outputs (revenues and profits). By doing this, the process of cost-effective planning is capable of being improved significantly.

Against this background we turn, in Chapters 5, 6 and 7, to the environment as a whole and then to the various ways in which competitors and customers can be analysed.

It has long been recognized that marketing strategy is to a very large extent driven by the strategist's perception of competitors and customers, and because of this the failure to analyse competitors' and customers' potential response profiles in depth is likely to be reflected in strategies that lack an adequate underpinning.

In the case of competitors, our understanding of how competitive relationships develop and operate has increased greatly over the past few years, largely as the result of the work of Michael Porter. Porter's work is based on the idea that the nature and intensity of competition within an industry is determined by the interaction of five key forces:

1. The threat of new entrants

2. The power of buyers

3. The threat of substitutes

4. The extent of competitive rivalry

5. The power of suppliers.

Analysis of these allows, in turn, for the identification of strategic groups, and for a far clearer identification of the relative position, strengths and objectives of each competitor. In the light of this, the arguments in favour of a competitive intelligence system are compelling. However, as we point out in Chapter 7, the value (and indeed the existence) of such a system is determined to a very large extent by the belief in competitive monitoring on the part of top management. Without this, the evidence that emerges from the work of numerous writers suggests that the organization will be largely introspective, with competitive analysis playing only a minor role in the planning process.

Broadly similar comments can be made about the role and value of customer analysis (refer to Chapter 6). As with competitive behaviour, our understanding of how buyers behave has advanced significantly in recent years. All too often, however, evidence suggests that firms devote relatively little attention to detailed customer analysis, assuming instead that because they interact with customers on a day-to-day basis they have a sufficient understanding of how and why markets behave as they do. Only rarely is this likely to be the case and, recognizing that customer knowledge is a potentially powerful source of competitive advantage, the rationale for regular and detailed analyses of customers is therefore strong.

CHAPTER 3

Marketing Auditing and the Analysis of Capability

3.1 LEARNING OBJECTIVES

When you have read this chapter you should understand:

- **(a)** the nature, structure and purpose of the marketing audit;

- **(b)** the nature of the contribution made by the marketing audit to the overall management audit;

- **(c)** the need for a regular review of marketing effectiveness and how such a review might be conducted;

- **(d)** why a regular review of strengths, weaknesses, opportunities and threats is necessary;

- **(e)** how the marketing effectiveness review, SWOT and TOWS analysis and the marketing audit contribute to the marketing planning process.

3.2 INTRODUCTION

Although the process of marketing auditing is a fundamental underpinning for the marketing planning process, it is for many organizations still a relatively under-utilized activity. This is despite a substantial body of evidence that suggests that an organization's performance in the marketplace is directly influenced by the marketing planner's perception of three factors:

1. The organization's current market position

2. The nature of environmental opportunities and threats

3. The organization's ability to cope with environmental demands.

Given this, the marketing audit is designed to provide the strategist with a clear understanding of these three dimensions and, in this way, provide a firm foundation for the development of strategy, something that is reflected in a comment by McDonald (1995, p. 28):

> *Expressed in its simplest form, if the purpose of a corporate plan is to answer three central questions:*
>
> > *Where is the company now?*
> > *Where does the company want to go?*
> > *How should the company organize its resources to get there?*
>
> *then the audit is the means by which the first of these questions is answered. An audit is a systematic, critical and unbiased review and appraisal of the environment and of the company's operations. A marketing audit is part of the larger management audit and is concerned (specifically) with the **marketing environment and marketing operations**.*

(emphasis in original)

What is a marketing audit?

The marketing audit is, in a number of ways, the true starting point for the strategic marketing planning process, since it is through the audit that the strategist arrives at a measure both of environmental opportunities and threats and of the organization's marketing capability. The thinking that underpins the concept of the audit is therefore straightforward: it is that corporate objectives and strategy can only be developed effectively against the background of a detailed and objective understanding of both corporate capability and environmental opportunity. The audit is, therefore, the process through which the marketing planner identifies and evaluates the organization's strengths and weaknesses against the background of the market and the opportunities and threats that exist. Having done this, the planner is then in a far stronger position to develop the strategy and decide upon a meaningful market position.

Definitions of the audit have also been proposed by a variety of authors, all of whom highlight the need for the audit to be a systematic, critical, and impartial review of the total marketing operation. In essence, therefore, the audit must embrace the marketing environment in which the organization – or the business unit – is operating, together with the objectives, strategies and activities being pursued. In doing this, the planner needs to take an objective view of the organization and its market and must not be affected by preconceived beliefs.

Given this, the three major elements and potential benefits of the marketing audit can be seen to be:

1. The detailed analysis and understanding of the external environment and internal situation

2. The objective review and evaluation of past performance and present activities

3. The clearer identification of future opportunities and threats.

These three elements can then usefully be viewed against the background of comments made by Ansoff (1968), who has suggested that, 'irrespective of the size of the organization, corporate decisions have to be made within the constraint of a limited total resource'. Recognizing this, the strategist is then faced with the task of producing 'a resource allocation pattern which will offer the best potential for meeting the firm's objectives'. The marketing audit can therefore be seen in terms of providing a sound basis for this process of resource allocation. In this way, any strategy that is then developed should be far more consistent both with the demands of the environment and with the organization's capabilities and strengths.

The rationale for the audit is therefore straightforward and, in a number of ways, can be seen to derive from the more commonly known and widely accepted idea of the financial audit which, together with audits of other functional areas, is part of the overall management audit. The nature of this relationship is illustrated in Figure 3.1.

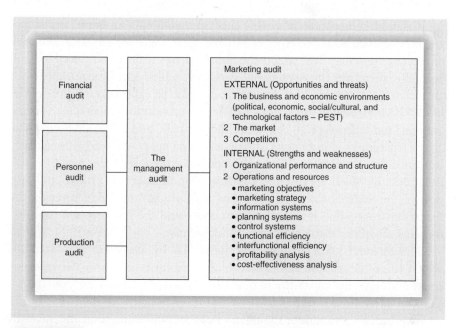

FIGURE 3.1   *The place of the marketing audit in the overall management audit*

The structure and focus of the audit

In terms of its structure, the marketing audit consists of three major and detailed diagnostic steps. These involve a review of:

1. The organization's environment, the ways in which it is likely to change and the probable impact of these changes upon the organization. It is this analysis that then provides the basis for a detailed understanding of the opportunities and threats that exist or are likely to emerge

2. Its marketing strategy, structures, systems, processes and culture, and the extent to which they are capable of dealing with the demands of the environment (in essence, this is the identification and analysis of the organization's strengths, weaknesses and capabilities)

3. Its marketing activities and, in particular, the components of the marketing mix and how well – or badly – they have been managed.

It should be apparent from this that the first of these is designed to establish the various dimensions of the marketing environment, the ways in which it is likely to change, and the probable impact of these changes upon the organization. The second stage is concerned with an assessment of the extent to which the organization's marketing systems are capable of dealing with the demands of the environment whilst the final stage involves a review of the individual components of the marketing mix.

It should be apparent from this that, in conducting an audit, the strategist is concerned with two types of variable. First, there are the *environmental* or *market variables*, over which the strategist has little or no direct control. Secondly, there are the *operational variables*, which can be controlled to a greater or lesser extent. This distinction can also be expressed in terms of the *macro-environmental forces* (political/legal, economic/demographic, social/cultural, and technological) that affect the business, and *micro-environmental actors* (customers, competitors, distributors and suppliers) who subsequently influence the organization's ability to operate profitably in the market place. Regardless of which approach to categorization is used, the process and purpose of the audit is the same. It begins with an *external audit* covering the macro-environmental forces referred to above and the markets and competitors that are of particular interest to the company.

The *internal audit* then builds upon this by assessing the extent to which the organization, its structure and resources relate to the environment and have the capability of operating effectively within the constraints that the environment imposes.

In doing this, the auditor should not view the marketing audit and its result in isolation but should instead, as we observed earlier, give full recognition to the way in which it sits within the general framework of the overall management audit and alongside the audits of the other management functions (refer back to Figure 3.1). In this way the strategist should arrive at an accurate measure not just of environmental opportunity but also of the ability of the organization as a whole to respond effectively.

With regard to the question of how frequently the audit should be conducted, this is typically influenced by several factors, the most important of which are the nature of the business, the rate of environmental change, and the planning cycle (annual, bi-annual). In so far as it is possible to provide a reasonably definitive guideline, it is that the organization should undertake a full audit at the beginning of each major planning cycle, supplemented by less intensive but more frequent reviews of specific or key areas as conditions change.

The stages of the audit

In conducting a marketing audit, a majority of commentators advocate a step-wise procedure. In this way, they argue, the approach ensures a degree of consistency that allows for a comparison from one period to another. For Grashof (1975), these steps are:

1. Pre-audit activities in which the auditor decides upon the precise breadth and focus of the audit

2. The assembly of information on the areas that affect the organization's marketing performance – these would typically include the industry, the market, the firm and each of the elements of the marketing mix

3. Information analysis

4. The formulation of recommendations

5. The development of an implementation programme.

Cannon's approach (1968, p. 102) is broadly similar, and again consists of five distinct stages: these are illustrated in Table 3.1.

Although for many organizations it is the assembly of information that proves to be the most time-consuming, it is (in terms of Grashof's suggested framework) Stages 3 and 5 that often prove to be the most problematic. In analysing information, the auditor therefore needs to consider three questions:

1. What is the *absolute* value of the information?

2. What is its *comparative* value?

3. What *interpretation* is to be placed upon it?

Table 3.1	Cannon's five stages of audit (Cannon, 1968)
Stage	**Key elements**
Step 1 Define the market	*Develop:* ■ Statement of purpose in terms of benefits ■ Product scope ■ Size, growth rate, maturity state, need for primary versus selective strategies ■ Requirements for success ■ Divergent definitions of the above by competitors ■ Definition to be used by the company
Step 2 Determine performance differentials	■ Evaluate industry performance and company differences ■ Determine differences in products, applications, geography and distribution channels ■ Determine differences by customer set
Step 3 Determine differences in competitive programmes	*Identify and evaluate individual companies for their:* ■ Market development strategies ■ Product development strategies ■ Financing and administrative strategies and support
Step 4 Profile the strategies of competitors	■ Profile each significant competitor and/or distinct type of competitive strategy ■ Compare own and competitive strategies
Step 5 Determine the strategic planning structure	*When size and complexity are adequate:* ■ Establish planning units or cells and designate prime and subordinate dimensions ■ Make organizational assignments to product managers, industry managers and others

It is generally acknowledged that, if these questions are answered satisfactorily, the recommendations will follow reasonably easily and logically. The only remaining problem is then the development of an effective implementation programme.

It should be apparent from the discussion so far that a marketing audit, if carried out properly, is a highly specific, detailed and potentially time-consuming activity. Because of this many organizations often do not bother with a full audit, and opt instead for a less detailed, more general and more frequent *review of marketing effectiveness*, coupled with an analysis of strengths, weaknesses, opportunities and threats.

In doing this, the typical starting point is a straightforward analysis or review of strengths and weaknesses that is designed simply to highlight the key issues internally and externally. An example of this appears in Figure 3.2.

Having done this initial analysis, the next step is to plot each of these elements into the sort of grid that appears in Figure 3.3, with each feature being linked to the customer's perception of their significance.

At the same time that this is being done, the initial external analysis designed to identify opportunities and threats can be conducted, with the

Strengths	Weaknesses
• Product quality and reliability • Product performance • High levels of after-sales service • Brand reputation • Low maintenance costs	• Limited product range • Higher prices than the direct competitors • High after-sales prices

FIGURE 3.2 *The initial analysis of strengths and weaknesses*

		Significance to the customer	
	Low		High
Strengths +10	• Low maintenance costs	• After-sales service levels	• Product quality and reliability
0		• Brand reputation	• Product performance
Weaknesses −10	• Limited product range	• Prices • After-sales costs	

FIGURE 3.3 *Customer perceptions of the significance of the strengths and weaknesses Significance to the customer*

results then being brought together in the form of a provisional situational analysis. However, in conducting the external audit, the planner needs to make sure that the analysis does not simply lead to a list of opportunities and threats, but that the issues are plotted on to the sort of matrix shown in Figure 3.4.

		Low		High
	High	Develop a scenario plan	Think about possible contingency plans	Analyse and plan in detail
Significance to the organization		Review periodically	Monitor on an ongoing but general basis	Monitor closely and plan
	Low	Monitor in very general terms	Review periodically	Monitor and review

FIGURE 3.4 *Probability of occurrence*

Having done this, the results can be used as the basis for the next stage, that of the identification of the product/market opportunities (refer to pages 327–30 and to the Ansoff matrix) and to the identification and evaluation of the strategic alternatives open to the organization. Having identified these, they can then be given an initial attractiveness rating by identifying the contribution that each is capable of making to the filling of the planning gap (refer to pages 330–1).

3.3 REVIEWING MARKETING EFFECTIVENESS

Marketing effectiveness is to a very large extent determined by the extent to which the organization reflects the five major attributes of a marketing orientation, namely:

1. A customer-oriented philosophy

2. An integrated marketing organization

3. Adequate marketing information

4. A strategic orientation

5. Operational efficiency.

Each of these dimensions can be measured easily by means of a checklist, and an overall rating then arrived at for the organization. It needs to be recognized, however, that an organization's marketing effectiveness is not always reflected in current levels of performance. It is quite possible, for example, for an organization to be performing well simply by force of circumstances rather than because of good management – in other words, good performance may be due to being in the right place at the right time as opposed to anything more fundamental. A change in strategy as the result of an effectiveness review might well have the result of improving performance from good to excellent. Equally, an organization may be performing badly despite seemingly excellent marketing planning. Again, the explanation may well be environmental rather than poor management. Recognizing this, the purpose of going through the process of a marketing effectiveness rating review is to identify those areas in which scope exists for marketing improvement. Action, in the form of revised plans, can then be taken to achieve this.

With regard to the process of arriving at a measure of marketing effectiveness, the procedure is straightforward and involves managers from a number of departments (not just marketing) scoring the organization's performance on each of the five dimensions referred to above. Scores are then summarized in order to arrive at an overall perception of marketing effectiveness. In practice, and as might be expected, few companies achieve a score in the highest range; among the few to have done this are organizations such as IKEA, W.L. Gore, Amazon.com and a small number of the airlines, such as Emirates, Cathay Pacific and Singapore Airlines. The majority of companies, however, cluster around the fair-to-good range, suggesting that scope exists for improvement in one or more of the five areas.

Having conducted a review of marketing effectiveness, the marketing planner may decide that the results provide sufficient insight into the organization's capabilities. There is, however, a strong argument for viewing the marketing effectiveness rating review simply as the jumping-off point for a more detailed analysis of strengths, weaknesses, opportunities and threats.

3.4   THE ROLE OF SWOT ANALYSIS

Although SWOT analysis is one of the best-known and most frequently used tools within the marketing planning process, the quality of the outputs often suffer because of the relatively superficial manner in which it is conducted. There are several ways in which SWOT analyses can be made more rigorous – and therefore more strategically useful – and this is something to which we will return at a later stage in this chapter. However, before we turn to the detail of the SWOT, it is perhaps worth summarizing the key elements of the four dimensions. These are illustrated in Figure 3.5.

Identifying opportunities and threats

Opportunities multiply as they are seized (Sun Tzu, circa 500 BC)

Faced with a constantly changing environment, managers need to develop a marketing information system (MkIS) that is capable of tracking trends and developments within the market place. Each trend or development can then be categorized as an opportunity or a threat, and an assessment made of the feasibility and action needed if the organization is either to capitalize upon the opportunity or minimize the impact of the threat.

However, in examining opportunities and threats the reader needs to recognize that these can never be viewed as 'absolutes'. What might appear at first sight to be an opportunity may not be so when examined against the organization's resources, its culture, the expectations of its stakeholders, the strategies available, or the feasibility of implementing the strategy. Instead, it might simply be a change within the market that is of little real or immediate consequence. At the risk of oversimplification, however, the purpose of strategy formulation is to develop a strategy that will take advantage of the opportunities and overcome or circumvent the threats.

For our purposes, an opportunity can be seen as any sector of the market in which the company would enjoy a competitive advantage. These opportunities can then be assessed according to their attractiveness and the organization's probability of success in this area, as illustrated in Figure 3.6.

STRENGTHS: Areas of (distinctive) competence that:

- Must always be looked at relative to the competition
- If managed properly, are the basis for competitive advantage
- Derive from the marketing asset base

WEAKNESSES: Areas of relative disadvantage that:

- Indicate priorities for marketing improvement
- Highlight the areas and strategies that the planner should avoid

OPPORTUNITIES: Environmental trends with positive outcomes that offer scope for higher levels of performance if pursued effectively:

- Highlight new areas for competitive advantage

THREATS: Trends within the environment with potentially negative impacts that:

- Increase the risks of a strategy
- Hinder the implementation of strategy
- Increase the resources required
- Reduce performance expectations

FIGURE 3.5 *SWOT: A summary*

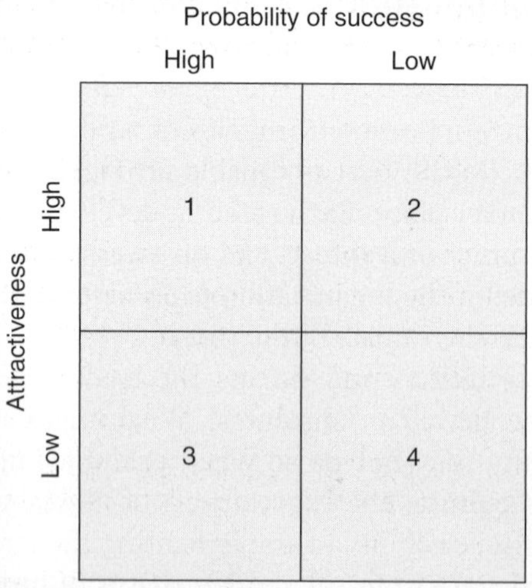

Probability of success

	High	Low
Attractiveness **High**	1	2
Attractiveness **Low**	3	4

Cell 1 consists of opportunities offering the greatest scope, and management should focus upon these. Cell 4, by contrast, represents those opportunities that are either too small or the organization is unlikely to be able to exploit effectively. Cells 2 and 3 offer certain attractions, and management should examine these closely to see whether scope exists either for improving their attractiveness or increasing the probability of success.

FIGURE 3.6 *The opportunity matrix*

The probability of success is influenced by several factors, but most obviously by the extent to which the organization's strengths, and in particular its distinctive competences, match the key success requirements for operating effectively in the target market *and* exceed those of its competitors.

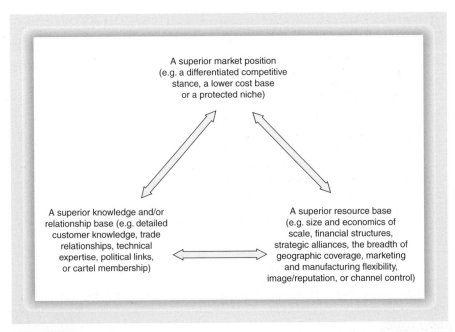

FIGURE 3.7 *Sources of competitive advantage (adapted from McDonald, 1990)*

However, competence by itself is rarely sufficient in anything more than the short term since, given time, competitive forces will erode this competence. Because of this the strategist needs to concentrate upon developing competitive advantages that are sustainable over time. The bases of a sustainable competitive advantage are illustrated in Figure 3.7 and are discussed in greater detail in Chapter 11.

However, at the same time as generating opportunities, the external environment also presents a series of threats (a threat being a challenge posed by an unfavourable trend or development in the environment which, in the absence of a distinct organizational response, will lead to the erosion of the company's market position).

Threats can be classified on the basis of their seriousness and the probability of their occurrence. An example of how this can be done is illustrated in Figure 3.8.

Given the nature of these comments, it can be seen that, by putting together a picture of the major opportunities and threats facing the business, the marketing planner is attempting to arrive at a measure of the market's overall attractiveness. In essence, four possibilities exist:

1. An *ideal* business, which is characterized by numerous opportunities but few (if any) threats

2. A *speculative* business, which is high both in opportunities and in threats

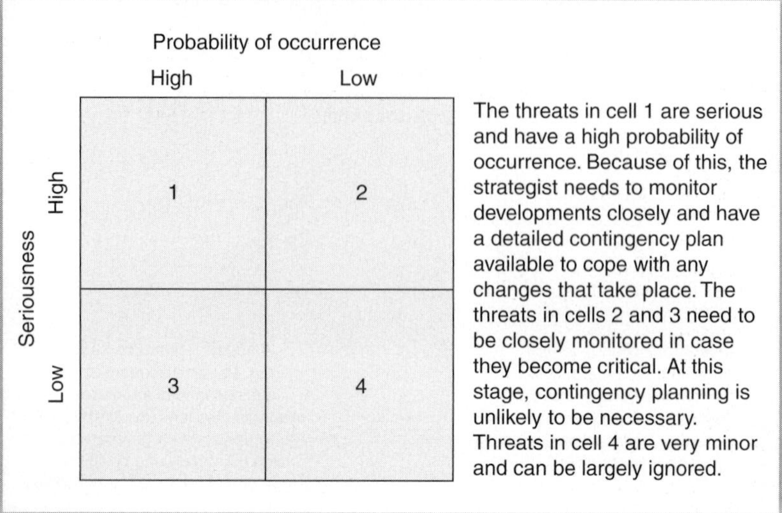

Probability of occurrence

The threats in cell 1 are serious and have a high probability of occurrence. Because of this, the strategist needs to monitor developments closely and have a detailed contingency plan available to cope with any changes that take place. The threats in cells 2 and 3 need to be closely monitored in case they become critical. At this stage, contingency planning is unlikely to be necessary. Threats in cell 4 are very minor and can be largely ignored.

FIGURE 3.8 *The threats matrix*

3. A *mature* business, which is low both in opportunities and threats

4. A *troubled* business, which is low in opportunities but high in threats.

Identifying and evaluating strengths and weaknesses

Although in many markets it is often a relatively simple process to identify a whole series of environmental opportunities, few organizations have the ability or the competences needed to capitalize upon more than a small number of these. Each business therefore needs to evaluate its strengths and weaknesses on a regular basis. This can be done by means of the sort of checklist illustrated in Figure 3.9.

Each factor is rated by management or an outside consultant according to whether it is a fundamental strength, a marginal strength, a neutral factor, a marginal weakness, or a fundamental weakness. By linking these ratings, a general picture of the organization's principal strengths and weaknesses emerges. Of course, not all of these factors are of equal importance either in an absolute sense or when it comes to succeeding with a specific business opportunity. Because of this, each factor should also be given a rating (high, medium or low) either for the business as a whole or for a particular marketing opportunity. Combining performance and importance levels in this way injects a greater sense of perspective to the analysis, and

Strengths	Performance					Importance		
	Fundamental strength	Marginal strength	Neutral	Marginal weakness	Fundamental weakness	High	Medium	Low
Marketing factors								
1 Relative market share	___	___	___	___	___	___	___	___
2 Reputation	___	___	___	___	___	___	___	___
3 Previous performance	___	___	___	___	___	___	___	___
4 Competitive stance	___	___	___	___	___	___	___	___
5 Customer base	___	___	___	___	___	___	___	___
6 Customer loyalty	___	___	___	___	___	___	___	___
7 Breadth of product range	___	___	___	___	___	___	___	___
8 Depth of product range	___	___	___	___	___	___	___	___
9 Product quality	___	___	___	___	___	___	___	___
10 Programme of product modification	___	___	___	___	___	___	___	___
11 New product programme	___	___	___	___	___	___	___	___
12 Distribution costs	___	___	___	___	___	___	___	___
13 Dealer network	___	___	___	___	___	___	___	___
14 Dealer loyalty	___	___	___	___	___	___	___	___
15 Geographical coverage	___	___	___	___	___	___	___	___
16 Sales force	___	___	___	___	___	___	___	___
17 After sales service	___	___	___	___	___	___	___	___
18 Manufacturing costs	___	___	___	___	___	___	___	___
19 Manufacturing flexibility	___	___	___	___	___	___	___	___
20 Raw material advantage	___	___	___	___	___	___	___	___
21 Pricing	___	___	___	___	___	___	___	___
22 Advertising	___	___	___	___	___	___	___	___
23 Unique selling propositions	___	___	___	___	___	___	___	___
24 Structure of competition	___	___	___	___	___	___	___	___
Financial factors								
25 Cost of capital	___	___	___	___	___	___	___	___
26 Availability of capital	___	___	___	___	___	___	___	___
27 Profitability	___	___	___	___	___	___	___	___
28 Financial stability	___	___	___	___	___	___	___	___
29 Margins	___	___	___	___	___	___	___	___
Manufacturing factors								
30 Production facilities	___	___	___	___	___	___	___	___
31 Economies of scale	___	___	___	___	___	___	___	___
32 Flexibility	___	___	___	___	___	___	___	___
33 Workforce	___	___	___	___	___	___	___	___
34 Technical skill	___	___	___	___	___	___	___	___
35 Delivery capabilities	___	___	___	___	___	___	___	___
36 Supplier sourcing flexibility	___	___	___	___	___	___	___	___
Organizational factors								
37 Culture	___	___	___	___	___	___	___	___
38 Leadership	___	___	___	___	___	___	___	___
39 Managerial capabilities	___	___	___	___	___	___	___	___
40 Workforce	___	___	___	___	___	___	___	___
41 Flexibility	___	___	___	___	___	___	___	___
42 Adaptability	___	___	___	___	___	___	___	___

FIGURE 3.9 *Strengths and weaknesses analysis (adapted from Kotler, 1988)*

leads to four possibilities emerging. These are illustrated in Figure 3.10 in the form of a performance–importance matrix.

In Figure 3.10 Cell 1 consists of those factors that are important but in which the organization is currently performing badly. Because of this the organization needs to concentrate on strengthening these factors. Cell 3

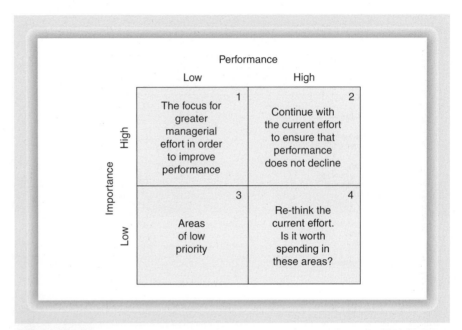

FIGURE 3.10 *The perfomance–importance matrix*

consists of unimportant factors. Cell 2 is made up of factors in which the business is already strong but in which it needs to maintain its strengths. Improvements here, while often desirable, have low priority. Cell 4 is made up of unimportant factors in which (possibly as the result of over-investment in the past) the business is unnecessarily strong.

Another way of looking at issues of performance and importance involves focusing specifically upon the organization's performance relative to the competition. The framework for this is illustrated in Figure 3.11.

On the basis of this sort of analysis it should be apparent that, even when a business has a major strength in a particular area, this strength does not invariably translate into a competitive advantage. There are several possible explanations for this, the two most prominent of which are that it may not be a competence that is of any real importance to customers, or that it is an area in which competitors are at least equally strong. It follows from this that, in order to benefit from the strength, it *must* be relatively greater than that of the competitor.

Having identified the organization's weaknesses, the strategist needs to return to the analysis of these (see Figure 3.9) and consider again their relative importance. There is often little to be gained from overcoming all of the organization's weaknesses, since some will be unimportant and the amount of effort needed to convert them to a strength would quite simply not be repaid. Equally, some strengths are of little real strategic value, and to use them in anything other than a peripheral way is likely to prove of

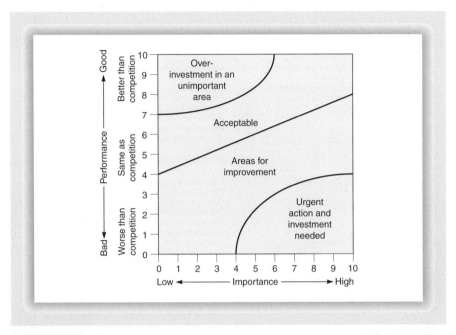

FIGURE 3.11 *Performance–importance and the competition (adapted from Slack et al., 1998)*

little real value. Recognizing this, the marketing planner should focus upon those areas of opportunity in which the firm currently has major strengths or where, because of the size of the opportunity and the potential returns, it is likely to prove cost-effective in acquiring or developing new areas of strength.

On occasions, organizations suffer not because of a lack of individual, departmental or divisional strengths, but quite simply because the various departments or divisions do not work together sufficiently well. As part of the SWOT process the strategist therefore should also pay attention to the quality of interdepartmental and divisional relationships with a view to identifying any dysfunctional areas. One of the ways in which this can be done is by conducting a periodic survey in which each department is asked to identify the strengths and weaknesses both of itself and of each other department with which it interacts. Action can then be taken to overcome areas of conflict, misunderstanding and inefficiency. An example of the results of an attempt to identify interdepartmental strengths and weaknesses appears in Figure 3.12. These are based on a consultancy project conducted by one of the authors several years ago. The client company operated in the engineering field, and was a subsidiary of a far larger multinational organization. The company had a strong financial orientation and was rapidly being overtaken by its competitors: for obvious reasons, the client's name has been omitted.

	Strengths	Weaknesses
Marketing	Market development Advertising Dealer development Competitor analysis	Long-term planning Liaising with sales Liaising with production Profitable new product development Identifying small but potentially profitable gaps in the market Expectations regarding quality and manufacturing capability Pricing Relations with corporate management
Sales	None identified	Expectations regarding delivery times Providing market feedback Often sell what can only be made with difficulty Little apparent awareness of costs Ignores small orders Patchy productivity Levels of training Sales staff turnover
Production	Quality	Slow to change Unwilling to cooperate with marketing and sales Often late in delivering Tend to want to make what they are good at A lack of flexibility caused by a strong trade-union presence Rising costs Lack of strong management Ageing plant Inadequate training in CAD/CAM
Personnel	Junior management and shop-floor training	Representation at board level Long-term senior management development Poor negotiating skills Willingness to give in to trade-union pressure Lack of real personnel management skills
Finance	Tight cost control Credit control Relationship with corporate management Access to significant financial resources	Over-emphasis on short-term returns Lack of vision Unwilling to cooperate with marketing and sales Unwilling to provide finance for major programmes of new product development Unrealistic reporting demands

FIGURE 3.12   *Identifying interdepartmental strengths and weaknesses*

Issues of capability

Although the analysis of strengths and weaknesses is a valuable step in the auditing process, the reader needs to recognize that strengths and weaknesses by themselves are of little real planning value. Instead, they should be seen as a step towards the planner coming to terms with the broader issue of capability. In doing this, the planner is giving recognition to the way in which the value of any strategy or plan is ultimately determined not by strengths and weaknesses, but by the organization's capability and the extent to which it is able to outperform its competitors.

Although capability has been defined in several ways, it is, in essence, the ability of the management team to get things done. In arriving at a measure of capability, the marketing strategist needs to come to terms with seven principal areas:

1. *Managerial capability*. This includes not just the abilities of individuals, but also – and perhaps more importantly – that of the team.

2. The *managerial culture* and the organizational DNA (for a discussion of organizational DNA, refer back to Illustration 2.2).

3. *Financial capability*. This is determined in part by the availability of funds, but also by the expectations of how they are used, the extent to which the management team is willing to take risks when investing, and the returns that are expected.

4. *Operational capability*. This involves the levels of day-to-day efficiency and effectiveness.

5. *Distribution capability*. This is determined by a combination of geographic reach or coverage, penetration (the proportion of possible outlets), and the quality of these distributors.

6. *Human resource capability*. This is a reflection of the nature and experience of staff throughout the business.

7. *Intangible factors* (such as the brand). In the case of a powerful brand, capability is extended enormously because it provides the opportunity not just for brand stretching, but also for pricing at a premium, gaining access to the strongest forms of distribution and increasing levels of customer loyalty.

At the same time, however, the planner also needs to understand the factors that inhibit capability. Typical examples of this include attitudes to risk and an adherence to a well-developed business model.

Making SWOT analyses more effective

Although SWOT analysis is a potentially useful input to the strategic marketing planning process, in practice it often suffers from a number of weaknesses. Amongst the most common of these are that:

- The planner fails to relate strengths and weaknesses to critical success factors

- Strengths and weaknesses are seen in absolute terms rather than in relation to the competition

- The elements of the analysis are insufficiently specific

- Competitors' capabilities are underestimated and/or misunderstood

- The focus is upon marketing specific issues rather than reflecting a broader company perspective

- Emphasis is placed largely upon the 'hard' or quantifiable elements, and fails to take account of managerial attitudes, cultures, capabilities and competencies.

The implications of this have been highlighted by numerous writers (e.g. Weihrich, 1982; Piercy, 1991; Doyle, 2002; Johnson *et al.*, 2008; McDonald, 2007) all of whom have also argued that, as a result, its full potential is rarely realized.

In suggesting this, Piercy claims that 'the use of this tool has generally become sloppy and unfocused – a classic example perhaps of familiarity breeding contempt'. There are, he believes, several factors that have contributed to this, the most obvious of which are that:

(a) *because the technique is so simple it is readily accessible to all types of manager;*

(b) *the model can be used without a need for extensive information systems;*

(c) *it provides planners with a structure that allows for a mixture of the qualitative and quantitative information, of familiar and unfamiliar facts, of known and half-known understandings that characterize strategic marketing planning.*

In order to make better use of the SWOT framework, Piercy proposes five guidelines:

1. *Focus the SWOT* upon a particular issue or element, such as a specific product market, a customer segment, a competitor, or the individual elements of the marketing mix.

2. Use the SWOT analysis as a mechanism for developing a *shared vision* for planning. This can be done by pooling ideas from a number of sources and achieving a team consensus about the future and the important issues.

3. *Develop a customer orientation* by recognizing that strengths and weaknesses are largely irrelevant unless they are recognized and valued by the customer. One of the ways in which this can be done is by applying the McDonald's 'so what?' test, in which the planner looks at each of the claimed benefits from the viewpoint of the consumer and, by asking 'well, so what?', tries to assess its *true* significance (see pages 429–30). By doing this, the planner is also likely to move away from the trap of making a series of so-called *motherhood statements* (a motherhood statement is warm,

reassuring and difficult to argue against). As an example of the most common of motherhood statements to emerge in analyses of strengths is the suggestion that 'we are committed to the customer'. The reality, Piercy argues, is often far removed from this.

4. In the same way that strengths and weaknesses must always be viewed from the viewpoint of the customer, so the analysis of opportunities and threats must relate to *the environment that is relevant to the organization's point of focus*. Anything else simply leads to a generalized – and largely pointless – set of comments.

5. The final guideline is concerned with what Piercy refers to as *structured strategy generation*. This involves:

   - *Matching strategies* – strengths *must* be matched to opportunities, since a strength without a corresponding opportunity is of little strategic value.

   - *Conversion strategies* – while often difficult, these are designed to change weaknesses into strengths and threats into opportunities. As an example of this, competitors may well be growing and proving to be an increasing threat. However, by recognizing that a head-on battle is likely to prove expensive and counterproductive, the emphasis might shift to developing strategic alliances that then provide both organizations with a greater combined strength – which in turn allows them to capitalize upon growing opportunities.

   - *Creative strategies* for developing the business – these emerge as the result of a detailed analytical process rather than the vague and unfocused lines of thought to which we referred earlier.

   - *Iteration* – as the planner goes through the process of identifying hidden strengths, matching strengths to opportunities, converting weaknesses to strengths, and so on, there is a periodic need to go back to the beginning of the process in order to identify how the situation that is emerging changes the SWOT model and any initial assumptions.

SWOT analysis can also be made more effective by thinking:

- To what extent has the relative importance of the various elements been identified?

- To what extent have the implications of each of the elements been examined?

- To what extent does the management team *really* recognize the significance of the elements?

- To what extent have attempts been made in the past to manage the SWOT analysis outcomes proactively?

SWOT to TOWS

The limitations that Piercy suggests typically characterize SWOT analyses have also been highlighted by Weihrich (1982). His principal criticism of SWOT is that, having conducted the analysis, managers frequently then fail to come to terms with the strategic choices that the outcomes demand. In order to overcome this he argues for the TOWS matrix which, while making use of the same inputs (threats, opportunities, weaknesses and strengths), reorganizes them and integrates them more fully into the strategic planning process. To do this involves the seven steps illustrated in Figure 3.13. The TOWS matrix is then illustrated in Figure 3.14.

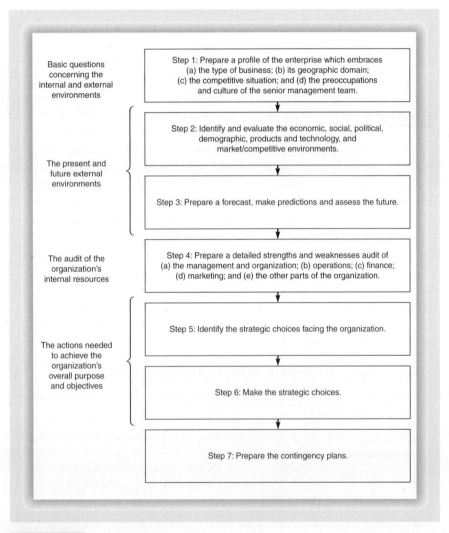

FIGURE 3.13   *The TOWS framework*

Internal elements / External elements	Organizational strengths	Organizational weaknesses
Strategic options		
Environmental opportunities (and risks)	S-O: Strengths can be used to capitalize or build upon existing or emerging opportunities	W-O: The strategies developed need to overcome organizational weaknesses if existing or emerging opportunities are to be exploited
Environmental threats	S-T: Strengths in the organization can be used to minimize existing or emerging threats	W-T: The strategies pursued must minimize or overcome weaknesses and, as far as possible, cope with threats

FIGURE 3.14   *The TOWS matrix (adapted from Weihrich, 1982)*

Very obviously, the matrix outlined in Figure 3.14 relates to a particular point in time and there is therefore a need to review the various inputs on a regular ongoing basis in order to identify how they are changing and the nature of the implications of these changes. It is also often useful if, when planning and having made particular assumptions, the planner then produces TOWS matrices for, say, three and five years ahead, with a view to identifying how the strategic options and priorities may change. In this way there is a greater likelihood that the planning team will come to terms with what the future really demands.

Figure 3.15 illustrates how Mercedes–Benz used the TOWS matrix in its cars division.

But are SWOT and TOWS analyses of any real value?

Although TOWS analysis can be seen to add another dimension to the traditional thinking about strengths, weaknesses, opportunities and threats, a fundamental question can be raised about just how useful this sort of analysis is within today's markets. In commenting on this, Walton (1999) argues that its value is limited, suggesting that 'compared with the steady state of the 1960s and 1970s, today's markets are characterized by an exponential increase in the rate of change, brought about by a combination of social, technological, legislative and other forces'. The implications of this are then reflected by the way in which 'as more organizations change from portrait

Strategies
Tactics
Actions
	Internal strengths
	
	1 Cash position
	2 Luxury car image
	3 New car models
	4 Location dose to suppliers
	5 Engineering and technology
		Internal weaknesses
		
		1 High costs
		2 Venturing into unrelated
		  businesses
		3 Organizational diversity
		4 Reliance on past successes
		  and bureaucracy
		5 Long cycle for new model
		  development
		6 Relatively weak position in
		  Japan

External opportunities
 	
1 Demand for luxury cars
2 Eastern Europe, especially
  East Germany
3 Prosperity through EC
  1992
4 Electronics technology
	S-O strategy
	
	1 Develop new models (using
	  high-tech) and charge
	  premium prices
	2 Use financial resources to
	  acquire other companies or
	  increased production capacity
		W-O strategy
		
		1 Reduce costs through
		  automation and flexible
		  manufacturing
		2 Manufacture parts in Eastern
		  Europe
		3 Reorganizations
		4 Daimler-Benz management
		  holding companies

External threats
 	
1 Decrease in defence needs
  because of easing of
  East–West tensions
2 BMW, Volvo, Jaguar,
  Lexus, Infinity in Europe
3 BMW in Japan
4 Diesel emissions
5 Renault/Volvo cooperation
6 Political instability in
  South Africa
	S-T strategy
	
	1 Transform defence sector to
	  consumer sector
	2 Develop new models to
	  compete especially in Europe
		W-T strategy
		
		1 Retrench in South Africa
		2 Form strategic alliance with
		  Mitsubishi to penetrate the
		  Japanese market

FIGURE 3.15   *TOWS analysis for Mercedes–Benz car division 1990 (source: Weihrich, 1993)*

to landscape structures, the mayhem of the operational day-to-day activity often gets in the way – not only of a true understanding of the nature and pattern of competition, but also of the more added-value appreciation of the implications for business strategy'.

Amongst the sorts of factors that have contributed to this planning mayhem are mega-brands, mega-retailers (including category busters such as Toys 'R' Us and Wal-Mart) and the sort of technological convergence that we have seen in the software, consumer electronics and telecommunications markets. For Walton (1999, p. 35), convergence has the effect of making competitive appraisal more difficult, and can be the consequence of:

industry boundaries blurring and turf disputes opening up between new competitors.

  Consider how the last decade has seen supermarkets move successfully into petrol, and petrol stations increasingly move

into food. And how new markets attract players from all quarters.
For example, the direct marketing industry has attracted creative
agencies, computer software houses, fulfilment businesses and door-
to-door distribution companies, each bringing different competencies
and skill sets to the market opportunity.

Technological convergence can produce even more thrills and spills
for marketers. The last two years have shown how digital technology
has brought what we have traditionally known as the photographic,
video and audio markets all closer together, with significant
implications. For instance, for the consumer, who has the brand
authority in digital cameras? A film brand like Kodak, a camera brand
like Olympus, a video brand like JVC or an imaging brand like Canon?

Given this, and what might be seen to be the Pavlovian tendency in
mature and highly competitive markets for firms to converge (discussed in
Chapter 11 (pages 441–2) in terms of the phenomenon of strategic herding),
the implications for competition – and therefore for market and competitive
analysis – are significant. As organizations merge, the industry *status quo*
changes dramatically and the idea of the traditional enemy being outside the
gates begins to disappear and is replaced by higher levels of internal competition. This internal competition is often geographic in its nature and, for organizations operating across the EU, is typically made more difficult by the degree
of cultural diversity that exists – something that Walton suggests has 'created a
kind of tragi-comic *Jeux Sans Frontières* assault course which can lead to "euro-
mush" marketing resulting from conflicting harmonization demands'.

At the same time, with brand strategies now performing a far more pivotal role within marketing and a greater number of management teams
beginning to copy what might loosely be termed the Virgin model of brand
architecture that is characterized by a far greater degree of mobility across
category boundaries, marketing planners need to adopt a far broader perspective of competition. The 'Maginot-line' approach to SWOT analysis that many planners have pursued in the past tends to be based on a
functional rather than a brand view of competition, and is likely to miss
potential new market entrants. The likelihood of this has in turn been
compounded by the way in which, because consumers today are far more
familiar with brands and open to new patterns of brand thinking, the scope
for moving into and out of markets has increased dramatically.

Given the nature of these changes, the implications for SWOT analysis
are potentially significant and provide the basis for a number of modifications to the traditional approach (see Figure 3.16).

The rise of asset- and competency-based thinking

Although TOWS analysis undoubtedly represents an improvement upon the
rather more mechanistic examination of strengths, weaknesses, opportunities

1 Consider the degree and implications of change to be anticipated in a market – high/medium/low. Is there one major factor you can identify as a window of opportunity or that could be used against you by a competitor as a killer threat? What is on the radar? And who is looking?

2 Within a market or category, what slots are already owned, being actively pursued and/or contested, and by whom?

3 What is the current phase of industry concentration? As we shift from 'middle game' to 'end game', what are the end game options? Does the industry leader have a future direction? What is our best long-term winning strategy or exit?

4 What industries and technologies are converging with our market? Can we zoom out and see proximate industries? For whom is our market an 'appetizing lunch'? Can the consumer-value equation be met in a new and radical way?

5 What brand franchises are relevant to a category and can travel quickly and easily from, to and into it? What consumer-relevant brand properties are available to existing and potential market entrants? How robust is our brand architecture against the market and against the competition? Have we got some big guns?

6 How strong is the enemy within? What do we do about the 5th Column?

7 What is the 'diplomatic status' of the market place? What is the network of alliances? What extra problems and opportunities does this present? Who is tied up?

8 Who currently sets the industry agenda? How strongly is it controlled? How easy will it be to change the industry agenda?

9 Do the industry bandwagons have a role for us? Benchmark with caution!

10 Above all, can you identify a major disruption or a transformational initiative?

FIGURE 3.16 *A checklist for the 'post-modern SWOT' (adapted from Walton, 1999)*

and threats that underpins many marketing plans, Davidson (2007, pp. 34–5) has argued for an alternative way of diagnosing an organization's current position and a way forward. His method of asset- and competency-based marketing (ACM) reflects the idea that any business consists only of *assets* (these are the 'things' that the organization owns and typically include brands, property, databases, supply chains and cash) and *competences* (these are the skills created by staff both individually and in groups, and might include brand development, database management, cost management and trade marketing). The challenge for the marketing planner is therefore one of how best to recognize the organization's real assets and then, through the competences, how best to exploit them.

He argues that for each asset it is essential that there is a corresponding competency. Without this, it is unlikely that the asset will be exploited. For an asset such as a brand, the competency needed is brand management; for databases it is database management and customer service. The issue for the planner is therefore initially that of the recognition of the organization's asset and then, against the background of a detailed understanding of market needs and opportunities, how these can best be leveraged and exploited.

For Davidson, the advantage of ACM is that it 'divides the "strengths" into two key and separate elements – assets and competences – and stresses the process of matching these both with each other, and with future opportunities'. He goes on to say that:

> *Many successful marketers do this instinctively, but due to lack of a systematic processes even they can miss big opportunities. Using ACM those opportunities which are best for a particular company can be revealed systematically. The company can exploit them better than others by capitalizing on its assets, and matching them to its distinctive competences. The result is long-term competitive advantages that are exploitable and sustainable.*

The application of ACM revolves around a six-step process that involves:

1. *Identifying the organization's exploitable assets and competences.* To do this, the planner begins by listing all of the company's brand assets and competences and then focuses upon those that offer scope for competitive advantage and superior customer value. For Disney, the competency is customer service; for Nike it is brand positioning; for P&G global brand development; and for Marks & Spencer it is the management of their suppliers.

2. *Reviewing the extent to which these assets and competences are being exploited currently.* In doing this, Davidson highlights a series of action points that include:
   - Reprioritizing markets, channels, customers or brands, to generate the better utilization of assets
   - Redeploying assets by buying, selling, developing and milking brands or physical assets
   - Identifying the new competences that are needed to exploit assets.

3. *Identifying the future shape of the industry and market.* By doing this, the planner can see more clearly how a market is likely to change and the sorts of assets and competences that will be needed for the organization to compete effectively in the future.

4. *Deciding how the organization's assets need to change over the next five years.* As part of this, the planner needs to focus upon the prospects of current markets, brands and other assets with a view to identifying whether they will deliver the sorts of returns that the organization demands.

5. *Building and exploiting assets and competences.*

6. *Matching assets and competences with future opportunities.*

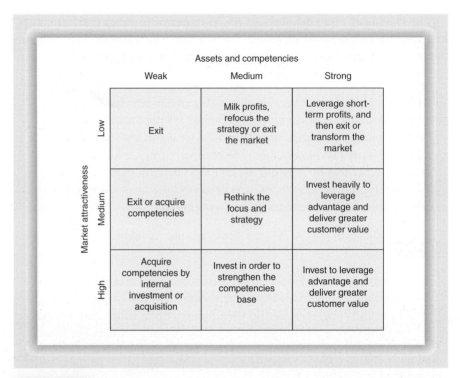

FIGURE 3.17 *The asset- and competency-based marketing framework for market prioritization (adapted from Davidson, 2007)*

The outputs from ACM thinking should, Davidson argues, more easily enable the marketing planner to:

■ Move assets into areas of higher return

■ Fully exploit all assets and competences

■ Ensure assets and competences are well matched with opportunities

■ Identify new competences that must be developed in the future

■ Spread the marketing mindset by embracing efficient delivery of superior customer value throughout the company.

These ideas are summarized in Figure 3.17.

3.5 COMPETITIVE ADVANTAGE AND THE VALUE CHAIN

Having analysed the strengths and resources of the organization, the marketing planner then needs to think about the ways in which these resources can best be used to contribute to the organization's performance. In other words, how might these resources best be used as a means of gaining and

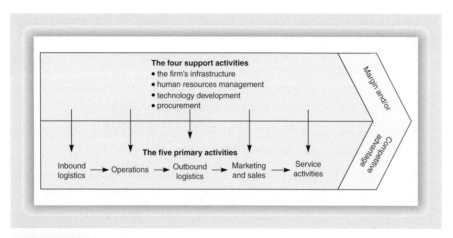

FIGURE 3.18   *The value chain (adapted from Porter, 1985a)*

maintaining a competitive advantage? One of the ways in which this can be done is by means of the *value chain* and a detailed understanding of competitive advantage (in this chapter we highlight some of the issues associated with competitive advantage, but a far fuller and more detailed analysis is provided in Chapter 11).

Although value analysis has its origins in accounting and was designed to identify the profit of each stage in a manufacturing process, a considerable amount of work has been done in recent years in developing the concept and applying it to measures of competitive advantage. Much of this work has been conducted by Michael Porter, who suggests that an organization's activities can be categorized in terms of whether they are *primary activities* or *support activities* (see Figure 3.18).

The five primary activities identified by Porter are:

1. *Inbound logistics*, which are the activities that are concerned with the reception, storing and internal distribution of the raw materials or components for assembly

2. *Operations*, which turn these into the final product

3. *Outbound logistics*, which distribute the product or service to customers. In the case of a manufacturing operation, this would include warehousing, materials handling and transportation. For a service, this would involve the way in which customers are brought to the location in which the service is to be delivered

4. *Marketing and sales*, which make sure the customers are aware of the product or service and are able to buy it

5. *Service activities*, which include installation, repair and training.

Each of these primary activities is, in turn, linked to the support activities, which are grouped under four headings:

1. The *procurement* of the various inputs

2. *Technology development*, including research and development, process improvements and raw material improvements

3. *Human resources management*, including the recruitment, training, development and rewarding of staff

4. The *firm's infrastructure* and the approach to organization, including the systems, structures, managerial cultures and ways of doing business.

Porter suggests that competitive advantage is determined to a very large extent by how each of these elements is managed and the nature of the interactions between them. In the case of inbound logistics, for example, many organizations have developed just-in-time systems in order to avoid or minimize their stockholding costs. In this way, the value of the activity is increased and the firm's competitive advantage improved. Equally, in the case of operations, manufacturers are paying increasing attention to lean manufacturing processes as a means of improving levels of efficiency. Porter's message is therefore straightforward. Managers, he suggests, need to examine the nature and dimensions of each of the nine activities with a view to identifying how the value added component can best be increased. He then goes on to argue that value chain analysis should not simply stop with the manager's own organization, but in the case of a manufacturer should also include the suppliers and distribution networks, since the value of much of what an organization does will be magnified or constrained by what they do.

3.6 CONDUCTING EFFECTIVE AUDITS

At an earlier stage in this chapter we made reference to the characteristics of effective audits, suggesting that if they are to be worthwhile they should be *comprehensive, systematic, independent* and *conducted on a regular basis*. These points are discussed below.

Comprehensive auditing

For the auditing process to be worthwhile it is essential that it covers *all* of the major elements of the organization's marketing activity, including those that seemingly are doing well, rather than just a few apparent trouble spots. In this way a distinction can be drawn between the *marketing audit* and a *functional audit*, which would focus far more specifically upon a particular element of marketing activity, such as sales or pricing. As an example of this, a functional audit might well suggest that a high salesforce turnover and low morale is due to a combination of inadequate sales training and a poor compensation package. A more fundamental reason, however, might be that the company has a poor or inadequate product range and an inappropriate pricing and advertising strategy. It is the comprehensiveness of the marketing audit that is designed to reveal these sorts of factors and to highlight the fundamental causes of the organization's problems.

Systematic auditing

In carrying out the audit it is essential that a sequential diagnostic process is adopted, covering the three areas to which reference was made earlier: the external environment, internal marketing systems, and specific marketing activities. This process of diagnosis is then followed by the development *and implementation* of both short-term and long-term plans designed to correct the weaknesses identified and, in this way, improve upon levels of marketing effectiveness.

Independent auditing

There are several ways in which the marketing audit can be conducted. These include:

- A self-audit in which managers use a checklist to assess their own results and methods of operation

- An audit by a manager of the same status but drawn from a different department or division within the organization

- An audit by a more senior manager within the same department or division

- The use of a company auditing office

- A company task force audit group

- An audit conducted by an outside specialist.

Of these, it is generally recognized that an audit conducted by an outside specialist is likely to prove the most objective and to exhibit the independence that any internal process will almost inevitably lack. Adopting this approach should also ensure that the audit receives the undivided time and attention that is needed. In practice, however, many large companies make use of their own audit teams (something that 3M, for example, has pioneered).

This question of who should conduct the audit has been the subject of a considerable amount of research and discussion in recent years with, as indicated above, the argument revolving around the issue of objectivity (in other words, how objective can a line manager be in conducting an evaluation of activities for which he has direct responsibility?). It is largely because of this that it has been suggested that outside consultants should be used to ensure impartiality. This is likely to prove expensive if done annually, and the answer is increasingly being seen to lie in a compromise whereby an outside consultant is used every third or fourth year, with line managers from different departments or divisions being used in the intervening periods. Alternatively, an organization might opt for what is in essence a composite approach, with an external auditor being used initially to validate line managers' self-audits, and subsequently to integrate them to produce an audit result for the marketing function as a whole.

To a large extent, however, it can be argued that the supposed difficulties of achieving impartiality are overstated since a sufficiently well-structured and institutionalized auditing process can overcome many of these difficulties. There is a need, therefore, for managers to be trained in how best to use auditing procedures and, very importantly, for the audit process to be endorsed by senior management. Without top management commitment to the audit process and, in turn, to the need to act on the results that emerge, the entire exercise is likely to prove valueless.

Regular auditing

If the company is to benefit fully from the auditing process, it is essential that it be carried out on a regular basis. All too often in the past companies have been spurred into conducting an audit largely as the result of poor performance. Ironically, this poor performance can often be traced to a myopia on the part of management, stemming from a failure to review activities on a sufficiently regular basis – something that has been pointed to by Shuchman (1950), who commented that: 'No marketing operation is ever so good that it cannot be improved. Even the best *must* be better, for few if any marketing operations can remain successful over the years by maintaining the *status quo*.'

But why bother with a marketing audit?

Although we have so far argued the case for marketing auditing to be carried out on a regular basis, many organizations quite simply do not bother to do this until things go wrong. Most typically, this would be manifested in terms of declining sales, a loss of market share, under-utilized production capacity, a demoralized salesforce, reduced margins, and so on. Faced with these sorts of problems the temptation for management is to firefight and hence fall into the trap of crisis management. In many cases this is characterized by the rapid launching and dropping of products, price-cutting, and attempts at drastic cost reduction. While this sort of response will often have an immediate and apparent pay-off, it is unlikely that it will solve any underlying and fundamental problems. The audit is designed to avoid the need for crisis management by both identifying and defining these fundamental problems before they have any opportunity to affect the organization. Carrying out a regular and thorough marketing audit in a structured manner will therefore go a long way towards giving a company a knowledge of the business, the trends in the market, and where value is added by competitors, as a basis for setting objectives and strategies. These points have been highlighted in a summary of the ten most common findings of marketing audits:

1. A lack of knowledge of customers' behaviour and attitudes

2. A failure to segment markets effectively

3. The absence of marketing planning procedures

4. Reductions in price rather than increases in volume

5. The absence of market-based procedures for evaluating products

6. Misunderstanding company marketing strengths

7. Short-term views of the role of promotion

8. A perception that marketing is limited just to advertising and sales activity

9. Inappropriate organizational structures

10. Insufficient investment in the future, particularly in the area of human resources.

The auditing process

The auditing process should begin with agreement being reached between the organization's marketing director and the marketing auditor – whether someone from inside or outside the organization – regarding the specific objectives, the breadth and depth of coverage, the sources of data, the report format and the time period for the audit. Included within this should be a plan of who is to be interviewed and the questions that are to be asked.

With regard to the question of *who* is to be questioned, it needs to be emphasized that the audit should never be restricted to the company's executives; it should also include customers, the dealer network, and other outside groups. In this way, a better and more complete picture of the company's position and its effectiveness can be developed. In the case of customers and dealers, for example, the auditor should aim to develop satisfaction ratings that are capable of highlighting areas in need of attention.

Once the information has been collected the findings and recommendations need to be presented, with emphasis being given to the type of action needed to overcome any problems, the timescale over which remedial action is to be taken, and the names of those who are to be responsible for this.

Components of the audit

Within the general framework of the external and internal audits, there is the need to focus upon six specific dimensions: These are:

1. *The marketing environment audit*. This involves an analysis of the major macroeconomic forces and trends within the organization's task environment. This includes markets, customers, competitors, distributors, dealers, and suppliers.

2. *The marketing strategy audit*. This focuses upon a review of the organization's marketing objectives and strategy, with a view to determining how well suited they are to the current and forecasted market environment.

3. *The marketing organization audit*. This aspect of the audit follows on from point (2), and is concerned specifically with an evaluation of the structural capability of the organization and its suitability for implementing the strategy needed for the developing environment.

4. *The marketing systems audit*. This covers the quality of the organization's systems for analysis, planning and control.

5. *The marketing productivity audit*. This examines the profitability of different aspects of the marketing programme and the cost-effectiveness of various levels of marketing expenditure.

6. *The marketing functions audit*. This involves a detailed evaluation of each of the elements of the marketing mix.

How are the audit results used?

Having conducted the audit, the question that then arises is how best to use the results. In some companies a considerable amount of time, effort and expense is given over to the auditing process, but the corrective action that is then needed simply falls by the wayside. To ensure that the results are incorporated most effectively within the strategic planning process, the major findings of the audit need to be incorporated within an appropriate framework. This can be done in one of several ways, although undoubtedly the most useful are the SWOT and TOWS frameworks discussed earlier. This should focus on the key internal strengths and weaknesses in relation to the principal external opportunities and threats, and include a summary of the reasons for good or bad performance. It is against the background of this document that the strategist should begin planning at both the functional and the corporate levels.

3.7 SUMMARY

Within this chapter we have focused upon the role and structure of marketing auditing and SWOT and TOWS analysis. In doing this we have highlighted the way in which the marketing audit represents an important first step in the marketing planning process and how, as a result, the value of much of what follows within this process is determined by the thoroughness of the audit procedure. It is therefore essential that the audit exhibits a number of characteristics, the four most significant of which are that it is:

1. Comprehensive in its coverage of the elements of the organization's marketing activity

2. Systematic

3. Independent

4. Conducted on a regular basis.

The purpose of the audit is to provide the strategist with a clear understanding both of environmental opportunities and threats, and of the organization's marketing capability. In doing this the strategist begins by focusing upon the principal macro-environmental forces (political/legal, economic/demographic, social/cultural and technological) that affect the business. He then moves on to consider the micro-environmental actors (customers, competitors, distributors and suppliers) who influence the organization's ability to operate effectively in the marketplace. The internal audit builds upon this by providing an understanding of the extent to which the organization, its structure and resources relate to the environment and have the capability of operating effectively within the constraints that the environment imposes.

In addition to conducting the marketing audit, the strategist needs to carry out regular reviews of the organization's marketing effectiveness. This can be done most readily by means of a checklist that embraces five principal areas:

1. The nature of the customer philosophy

2. The marketing organization

3. Marketing information

4. The strategic perspective

5. Operational efficiency.

Against the background of the picture that emerges from the audit and the review of marketing effectiveness, the strategist should have a clear understanding of both the environment (opportunities and threats) and the organization's marketing capability (strengths and weaknesses). It is this that provides the basis for subsequent marketing planning.

CHAPTER 4

Segmental, Productivity and Ratio Analysis

4.1 LEARNING OBJECTIVES

When you have read this chapter you should be able to:

(a) understand how cost and profit analysis can be applied to marketing segments;

(b) appreciate the role of marketing experimentation in improving the allocation of marketing effort;

(c) recognize the value of segmental productivity analysis;

(d) perceive critically how ratio analysis can be used in order to appreciate the current position;

(e) appreciate the relevance of strategic benchmarking.

4.2 INTRODUCTION

In relation to the question 'Where are we now?', it is useful to know how resources have been utilized and with what returns. To this end, it helps to think of the organization as a bundle of projects or activities. This is relevant whether the organization is large or small, commercial or non-commercial, engaged in manufacturing or service rendering. Typical projects might be defined as:

- Reformulation and relaunch of product X
- Continued market success with service Y
- The successful development and launch of project Z.

We might go further and define projects or activities in terms of *missions*: a mission in this context represents the provision of a product or range of products at a particular level of service to a particular customer or customer group, in a particular area. Figure 4.1 illustrates this (see also Chapter 8).

An organization's mix of projects – or missions – will be constantly changing, and each has resource implications and profit consequences. For example, the scarcity of resources inevitably means that choices must be made in rationing available resources (whether in the form of funds, management time, etc.) among competing activities. It may be that new activities can only be adopted if old ones are deleted, thereby freeing resources. But how might a manager know which activities are worth retaining, which should be added to the portfolio, and which should be deleted? One starting point is to establish the cost and profit performance of each of the organization's existing activities.

We can think of cost as being equivalent in broad terms to *effort*, so what we are initially seeking to establish is how the available effort has been applied to the various activities in which the organization is engaged, and how productive this has been. Before we can really get to grips with this, however, we need to clarify our understanding of some important categories of cost (see Wilson, 1999, 2001).

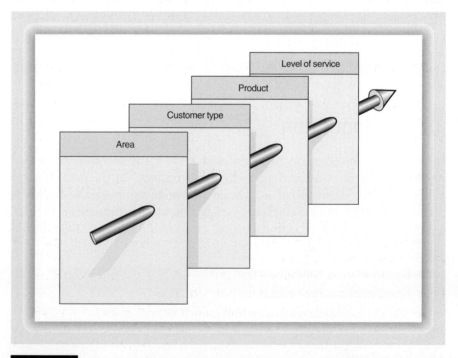

FIGURE 4.1 *Multi-dimensional mission characteristics (from Barrett, 1980)*

4.3   THE CLARIFICATION OF COST CATEGORIES

Many of the costs of marketing are not satisfactorily identified, since marketing functions are not always carried out by the marketing department. (It could be argued – as was suggested in Chapter 1 – that any members of an organization who deal with customers are carrying out a marketing function even though they may not be recognized in any formal sense as members of the marketing staff.) This is one definitional problem, but not the only one. Another definitional problem concerns the traditional focus adopted by accountants, which puts product costing at the centre of their costing systems. This traditional preoccupation with the manufacturing costs of products and factory processes emphasizes the attributes of whatever is currently being made. Such an orientation fails to deal with patterns of consumer preferences and competitive positioning by market segment. The attributes of market segments – from which profit is derived – are fundamentally different from those attributes that characterize production processes. Any analysis based on product costing will generate insights that are limited by their origins, thereby failing to support marketing orientation.

Whatever cost object (or activity) is selected as the focus of attention, some costs will be direct (in the sense of being traceable to the activity – such as direct labour, and direct material inputs into a unit of manufactured output, or a salesperson's salary and expenses in relation to the sales territory in which that individual operates) while others will be indirect. By definition, indirect costs cannot be traced directly to cost objects, so any procedure whereby these costs are assigned to cost objects will mean that the resulting full (or 'absorbed') cost is inaccurate to an unknown extent. The assigning of a 'fair share' of indirect costs, along with direct costs, to cost objects is at the heart of *absorption costing* (of which activity-based costing, or ABC, is a variant).

A particular cost item can only be termed direct or indirect once the cost object has been specified. This could be, for example, a particular market offering, a product range, a brand, a customer or customer group, a channel, a sales territory, an order, and so on. Thus a salesperson's salary will be indirect in relation to the individual product lines sold (assuming the salesperson carries a range of products), but it will be a direct cost of the territory in which that individual is operating. In the same way, the costs of distributing various products to wholesalers may be indirect with regard to the goods themselves but direct if costing the channel of distribution of which the wholesalers are part.

The same basic problems arise in attempting to determine the full cost of a cost object in every type of organization, whether a service company, a retailing enterprise, a factory or a non-commercial entity. For example, a garage (as one type of service organization) will treat the servicing of each customer's car as a separate job (or cost object), to which will be assigned the direct cost of the mechanic's time, materials, and parts, plus an allowance (usually applied as an hourly rate and associated with the utilization of mechanics' time) for the use of indirect factors (including power, equipment, rent, rates, insurance, salaries of reception, supervisory and stores staff, etc.). A similar approach is applied by firms of solicitors or accountants, by consulting engineers, architects and management consultants. Non-commercial organizations typically provide services (such as healthcare, defence, education and spiritual guidance) and use resources in carrying out their various activities in much the same way as do commercial undertakings. The logic of absorption costing is equally applicable to non-commercial as to commercial enterprises.

4.4 MARKETING COST ANALYSIS: AIMS AND METHODS

Establishing a base line for marketing planning can be seen to be concerned with the allocation of total marketing effort to cost objects (also known as segments), along with the profit consequences of these allocations. It is generally found, however, that companies do not know the profit performance of segments in marketing terms. Useful computations of marketing costs and profit contributions in the multi-product company require the adoption of analytical techniques that are not difficult in principle, but are not widely adopted in practice on account of, *inter alia*, the preoccupation with factory cost accounting that exists.

The fact that most companies do not know what proportion of their total marketing outlay is spent on each product, sales territory or customer group may be due to the absence of a sufficiently refined system of cost analysis, or it may be due to vagueness over the nature of certain costs. For instance, is the cost of packaging a promotional, a production or a distribution expense? Some important marketing costs are hidden in manufacturing costs or in general and administrative costs, including finished goods inventory costs in the former and order-processing costs in the latter.

Since few companies are aware of costs and profits by segment in relation to sales levels, and since even fewer are able to predict changes in sales volume and profit contribution as a result of changes in marketing effort, the following errors arise:

1. Marketing budgets for individual products are too large, with the result that diminishing returns become evident and benefits would accrue from a reduction in expenditure

2. Marketing budgets for individual products are too small and increasing returns would result from an increase in expenditure

3. The marketing mix is inefficient, with an incorrect balance and incorrect amounts being spent on the constituent elements – such as too much on advertising and insufficient on direct selling activities

4. Marketing efforts are misallocated among missions and changes
in these cost allocations (even with a constant level of overall
expenditure) could bring improvements.

Similar arguments apply in relation to sales territories or customer
groups as well as to products. The need exists, therefore, for planning
and control techniques to indicate the level of performance required and
achieved as well as the outcome of shifting marketing efforts from one segment to another. As is to be expected, there exists great diversity in the
methods by which managers attempt to obtain costs (and profits) for segments of their business, but in large part the cost data are inaccurate for
such reasons as those listed below:

- Marketing costs may be allocated to individual products, sales
  territories, customer groups, etc., on the basis of sales value or
  sales volume, but this involves circular reasoning. Costs should be
  allocated in relation to causal factors, and *it is order-getting marketing
  expenditures that cause sales to be made* rather than the other way
  round: managerial decisions determine order-getting marketing costs.
  A different pattern typically applies to order-filling (e.g. logistics) costs,
  since sales volume will cause (or drive) order-filling costs: order-getting →
  sales volume → order-filling. Furthermore, despite the fact that success is
  so often measured in terms of sales value achievements by product line,
  this basis fails to evaluate the efficiency of the effort needed to produce
  the realized sales value (or turnover). Even a seemingly high level of
  turnover for a specific product may really be a case of misallocated sales
  effort. (An example should make this clear: if a sales representative
  concentrates on selling Product A, which contributes £50 per hour of
  effort, instead of selling Product B, which would contribute £120 per
  hour of effort, then it 'costs' the company £70 for each hour spent on
  selling Product A. This is the *opportunity cost* of doing one thing rather
  than another, and is a measure of the sacrifice involved in selecting
  only one of several alternative courses of action.)

- General indirect and administrative costs are arbitrarily (and
  erroneously) allocated to segments on the basis of sales volume.

- Many marketing costs are not allocated at all as marketing
  costs since they are not identified as such but are classified as
  manufacturing, general or administrative costs instead.

Marketing cost analysis has been developed to help overcome these
problems, and aims to:

1. Analyse the costs incurred in marketing goods/services (embracing
order-getting and order-filling aspects) so that, when they are
combined with product cost data, overall profit can be determined

2. Analyse the costs of marketing individual product lines to determine profit by product line

3. Analyse the costs involved in serving different classes of customers, different territories and other segments to determine their relative profit performance

4. Compute such figures as cost per sales call, cost per order, cost to put a new customer on the books, cost to hold £1's worth of inventory for a year, etc.

5. Evaluate managers according to their actual controllable cost responsibilities

6. Evaluate alternative strategies or plans with full costs.

These analyses and evaluations provide senior management with the necessary information to enable them to raise questions regarding which classes of customer to cultivate, which market offerings to delete or encourage, which channels may be preferable and so forth. Such analyses also provide a basis from which estimates may be developed of the likely increases in sales volume, value or profit (i.e. outputs) that a specified increase in marketing effort (i.e. input) might create. In the normal course of events, it is far more difficult to predict the outcome of decisions that involve changes in marketing outlays in comparison with changes in production expenditure. It is easier, for instance, to estimate the effect of a new machine in the factory than it is to predict the impact of higher advertising outlays. Similarly, the effect on productive output of dropping a production worker is easier to estimate than is the effect on the level of sales caused by a reduction in the sales force.

The basic approach of marketing cost analysis is similar to that of product costing. Two stages are involved (see Figure 4.2):

1. Marketing costs are initially reclassified from their *natural* expense headings (e.g. salaries) into *functional* cost groups (e.g. sales expenses) in such a way that each cost group brings together all the costs associated with a particular marketing activity

2. These functional cost groups are then apportioned to the cost object/ segment of interest (e.g. product lines, customer groups, channels of distribution, etc.) on the basis of measurable criteria that bear as close an approximation as possible to a causal relationship with the total amounts of the functional cost groups.

Once the natural indirect expenses have been reclassified on a functional basis, they are then charged to the segment in line with the usual benefit criterion (i.e. the segment is only allocated with that portion of each functional cost group that can be related to it on some approximation of a

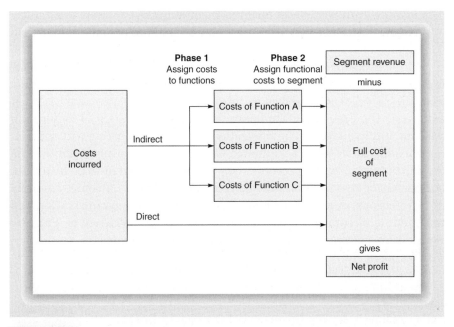

FIGURE 4.2   *Determining segmental costs (from Wilson and Chua, 1993)*

cause and effect basis). The logical basis of allocation may be apparent from an analysis of the underlying data, but it is important to observe that some costs vary with the characteristics of one type of segment only. Thus inventory costs depend on the characteristics of products rather than on those of customers, whereas the cost of credit depends on the financial integrity and number of customers rather than on regional factors. Accordingly, not all functional costs should be allocated to products, customers and territorial segments. Allocation should only be made when an actual or imputed cause and effect relationship between an underlying activity and some resultant cost that is relevant to the segment(s) can be identified.

It must be remembered when using marketing cost analysis that any cost allocation involves a certain degree of arbitrariness, which means that an element of approximation is inevitably contained within the allocation. Furthermore, it remains necessary to supplement the analysis of marketing costs with other relevant information and with managerial judgement.

Marketing cost analysis is the joint responsibility of the financial controller and the marketing manager, with the financial controller supplying most of the information and the marketing manager supplying most of the judgement. Nevertheless, the marketing manager must be fully aware of the method and limitations of marketing cost analysis. The high cost of establishing and maintaining a marketing costing system is justified by the benefits derived from increasing the efficiency of marketing effort. The risks involved in adopting marketing cost analysis before the benefits have been demonstrated can be reduced by initially confining the analysis to a sample of products, customers or territories, and by making periodic rather than continuous analyses.

Since a fundamental objective of marketing cost analysis lies in increasing the productivity of expenditures and not necessarily in their reduction, the manager who wishes to introduce marketing cost analysis must emphasize the desire to make better use of existing resources rather than reducing future budgets. The integration of marketing costing with marketing research can assist in this matter. Confining any costing system to data provided from accounting records risks forcing that system to be historical, but marketing research can provide estimates of future outcomes resulting from variations in marketing effort (with or without experimentation and the building of complex models), which enable the efficiency of alternate expenditure patterns to be pre-determined and evaluated in accordance with corporate aims.

See Illustration 4.1.

Illustration 4.1   My biggest mistake (David Bruce)

(David Bruce, 42, failed his maths 'O' level five times before leaving school to work for a brewery. In 1979, he came off the dole queue to open the Goose and Firkin pub in London after raising a loan against his home. By 1988 he had built a chain of 18 pubs, which he sold for £6.6 m, intending to retire with his £2 m share. However, he could not resist going back into business and is now trading as Inn Securities and building up a chain of Hedgehog and Hogsheads pubs outside London.)

My biggest mistake was not paying proper attention to my accounts in the early days of the Firkin pubs. We had opened the Goose and Firkin in London in 1979, and I was working 18 lousy hours a day, seven days a week, brewing the beer in the cellar and surviving on adrenalin. I had eight staff and a part-time book-keeper.

Everybody said the pub would not work, but people were queuing to get in. It was tremendously exciting and I was on a complete high. The tills were ringing, my break-even point was £2500 a week, but the pub never did less than £4500.

So why, I thought, if one has created this extraordinary thing, should one scuttle back home to Battersea and spend hours doing boring old paperwork? The turnover was so good I did not even bother with profit and loss accounts. (And you have to bear in mind that I did not have a natural aptitude for figures.)

In May 1980, I opened the Fox and Firkin in Lewisham. I trained a brewer to look after the Goose, but he promptly broke his leg, leaving me to deal with both pubs. There was even less time to do paperwork.

Then I opened another pub in London and, because the experts doomed us to failure I thought it would be easier if the pubs traded under separate companies. Each one had a different accounting year – it was a good lesson in how not to run a business.

By the time we had opened our fourth pub in 1981, our solicitors, Bishop and Sewell, had watched our progress with great interest and assumed we were incurring a hideous tax bill, so they suggested we met with accountants Touche

Ross. My wife, Louise, and I went along with what little financial information we had, plus a couple of audits that showed we had traded at a loss from day one.

In fact, while the turnover for the first year was £1 m, we had made losses of £86 000. One of their corporate finance partners said that if I did not appoint a chartered accountant to the board as financial director immediately we would go bust within a couple of months. So I took on someone from a major brewery, who introduced systems such as stock control and weekly profit and loss accounts.

But that did not solve the immediate problems. Touche Ross also said I would have to sell one of the pubs, the Fleece and Firkin in Bristol, because it was costing too much in time and money. Reluctantly I put it on the market.

By now it was obvious that I should have appointed a finance director at the beginning. The bank was getting nervous, my borrowings were rising, and I was not producing a profit.

If the bank had pulled the rug we would have gone down personally for £500 000. Touche Ross advised me to sell a small percentage of the equity, which of course I did not want to do. Eventually I struck a satisfactory deal with 3i (Investors in Industry), which bought 10 per cent of the business and gave us a loan. Better cash control enabled us to turn a loss into a profit, and the following year, on a turnover of £1.6 m, we showed a profit of £47 000.

Touche Ross, who charged us under £5000 to sort the problem out, have done my audits ever since. Paul Adams, our managing director, is the resident chartered accountant. He has kept costs down and introduced budgets that the staff can stick to.

In hindsight the solutions were obvious, but I was the victim of my own success. If the turnover had not been so good, I would have realized a lot sooner how close I was to bankruptcy.

Source: As told to journalist Corinne Simcock, *The Independent on* Sunday: Business, 16 December 1990, p. 20.

4.5 AN ILLUSTRATION OF SEGMENTAL ANALYSIS

As discussed above, a segment is any cost object that is of interest, and is synonymous with the notion of activity, project or mission as appropriate. Thus, for example, marketing segments may be one – or a combination – of the following:

- Product line or range

- Channel of distribution

- Sales representative or territory

- Customer or customer/industry group

- Size of order.

It is possible to vary the degree of aggregation of segments, as shown in Figure 4.3. Initially the segment of interest must be selected (e.g. territory,

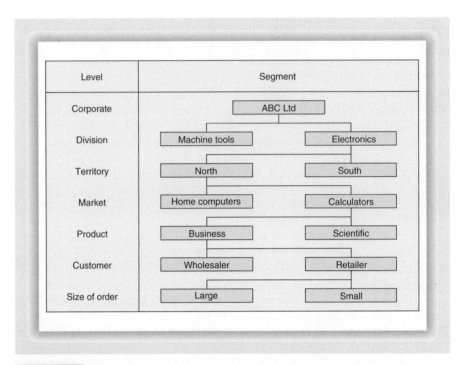

Level	Segment
Corporate	ABC Ltd
Division	Machine tools / Electronics
Territory	North / South
Market	Home computers / Calculators
Product	Business / Scientific
Customer	Wholesaler / Retailer
Size of order	Large / Small

FIGURE 4.3 *Segmental levels (adapted from Ratnatunga, 1983)*

customer, etc.), and then the preferred approach to costing. Essentially there are two major alternatives:

1. Absorption (or full) costing

2. Variable (or direct or marginal) costing.

Our earlier discussion dealt with the first of these, and we saw that this approach involves charging both direct and a portion of indirect costs to the segment in question. When set against the segment's revenue, the result is a net profit figure.

Figure 4.4 provides an example of the net profit picture in an organization operating through three different channels of distribution.

The net profit figure reflects the result of the allocation of effort as shown by the total of:

■ Costs of goods sold

■ Direct marketing costs

■ Indirect marketing costs.

Once this allocation has been set against the revenue figure, channel by channel, it is evident that the validity of the net profit figures that emerge

£'000s		Channel			Total
	A	B		C	
Revenue	875	950		1,225	3,050
Cost of goods sold	325	285		490	1,100
Gross profit	550	665		735	1,950
Direct marketing costs	265	245	450	960	
Indirect marketing costs	330	275	250	855	
Total marketing costs	595	520		700	1,815
Net profit	(45)	145		35	135

FIGURE 4.4 *Profit analysis by channel*

depend critically upon the adequacy of the means by which indirect costs are apportioned.

4.6 AN ALTERNATIVE APPROACH TO SEGMENTAL ANALYSIS

The alternative approach to segmental analysis is the variable costing approach, in which only direct costs are allocated to arrive at a measure of profit known as *marketing contribution*. The data from Figure 4.4 have been reworked in Figure 4.5 to illustrate the variable costing approach.

It has been assumed that the cost of goods sold figures in Figure 4.4 included £700 000 of variable manufacturing costs; that the direct costs are all of a marketing nature and can be split into fixed and variable components as shown in Figure 4.5, and that the indirect costs are all non-allocable to channels. The result is a clear statement that sufficient revenue is being generated via each channel to cover the variable costs and the directly allocable fixed costs. Moreover, there is sufficient total contribution to cover the indirect costs and the fixed manufacturing costs while still making a net profit of £135 000.

4.7 CUSTOMER PROFITABILITY ANALYSIS

An approach to segmental analysis that is of increasing interest is customer profitability analysis (CPA). If marketing effort is to be directed at customers or market segments with the greatest profit potential, it is essential that marketing

£'000s	Channel			Total
	A	B	C	
Revenue	875	950	1,225	3,050
Variable COGS	225	175	300	700
Manufacturing contribution	650	775	925	2,350
Variable direct marketing costs	115	105	190	410
Variable contribution	535	670	735	1,940
Fixed direct marketing costs	150	140	260	550
Marketing contribution	385	530	475	1,390
Indirect costs				855
Fixed manufacturing costs				400
Net profit				135

FIGURE 4.5 *A direct costing profit statement*

managers have information showing both the existing picture with regard to customer profitability and prospects for the future. Customer profitability analysis has been defined (Anandarajan and Christopher, 1987, p. 86) as:

> *the evaluation, analysis and isolation of:*
>
> - *all the significant costs associated with servicing a specific customer/group of customers from the point an order is received through manufacture to ultimate delivery;*
>
> - *the revenues associated with doing business with those specific customers/customer groups.*

The implementation of CPA can be achieved by a series of steps that parallel the steps suggested earlier for other types of segmental analysis. In outline, these steps are:

- *Step 1* – clearly define customer groups and market segments in a way that distinguishes the needs of customers in one group from those of customers in another group.

- *Step 2* – for the customer groups or market segments of interest, identify those factors that cause variations in the costs of servicing those customers. This can be done by identifying the key elements of the marketing mix used for each customer group or segment, from which some indication of the costs of servicing each group should be drawn.

- *Step 3* – analyse the ways in which service offerings are differentiated between customer groups. For example, terms of trade may vary between home-based and overseas customers, or between large and small customers, as might the level of service (i.e. speed of delivery) to key accounts.

- *Step 4* – clearly identify the resources that have been used to support each customer group or segment (including personnel, warehouse facilities, administrative back-up, etc.).

- *Step 5* – determine ways in which the costs of resources (Step 4) can be attributed to customer groups.

- *Step 6* – relate revenues and costs to each customer group, with profit emerging as the difference.

The total of the costs for a given customer group is a measure of the effort that has been allocated to that group, and the profit is a measure of the return from that effort. Until the existing pattern of allocation is known, along with its profitability, it is not possible to devise ways of improving that allocation.

See Illustration 4.2.

Illustration 4.2   Evolution

New technologies are beginning to make mass customization feasible, and information systems are allowing us to identify the profitability of each customer.

Tower Records recently started offering its customers the top 40 lines of groceries. It was a publicity stunt, of course – a protest at the way supermarkets have started cherry picking their business by selling records from the Top 40 chart.

Tower's initiative amounts to little more than a puff of hot air, but behind it lies an issue of growing importance. Cherry picking is hardly new, but its extent and nature are changing. Increasingly the most aggressive and successful cherry pickers are coming from 'outside' the industry concerned – and as such these are invaders with a difference. They're changing the nature of the market itself.

To see what's happening, we need to take a step back. Consider, for example, how people acquired their clothes 50 years ago. Basically, they had three ways to do it. First, if they were rich, they could go to their tailor, who provided a high quality, high convenience, high service offer, with bespoke fitting at a high price. Secondly, you could buy mass manufactured garments, which offered standard quality and standard sizes at low prices but with low service and low convenience. Thirdly, you could make them yourself, buying cloth and thread and slaving over a hot sewing machine. This way you got bespoke fitting at a very low price, but the service and convenience elements were reduced.

Buying bespoke

Since then, mass manufacturing has swept nearly all before it. Its ongoing technological revolution has forced down prices and improved quality at such a rate that 'Royal' service and DIY have (in most sectors) become tiny niches for the very rich and the very poor respectively. Economies of scale were worth it, but came at a price. Everything was standardized and averaged, and there was, to varying degrees, cross-subsidization between customers.

Today, that's changing. As new technologies are increasing the feasibility of mass customization and information systems are allowing identification of individual customer profitability, marketers are rightly questioning the validity of the mass production trade-off. Inspired by the total quality movement ('you can have better quality and lower prices'), they're racing to offer Royal, bespoke products and services at standard prices – an inspiring agenda that will keep them busy for decades.

At the same time, they're realizing that their customer base usually falls into three groups. The first group (let's call them the Superprofits) actually generates 150 per cent of their profits even though it only accounts for, say, 60 per cent of customers, and makes a crucial contribution to overheads even if its profitability is marginal. The third group actually costs money to serve.

De-averaging is now the order of the day. The big drive now is to 'fire' or otherwise lose the loss makers while going all out to deepen the relationship with the Superprofits.

So far, so good. This is classic segmentation taken to its next logical level. But de-averaging has a sting in the tail. In many a company it threatens to set off a chain reaction that unravels the ties that bound it together into a single entity in the first place. Instead of having one mass production business that dominates the market with its brands, de-averaging implies the return of a three-tiered business structure of Royals, standards and DIY, each with their own distinct brands and marketing strategies.

Cherry picking costs

Without the mass markets and their economies of scale, the advantages that gave mass production its tremendous edge begin to go into reverse. Many of these businesses are, in effect, cross-subsidization businesses, and if cross-subsidization falls apart, so do they.

Tower Records' beef is that sales of Top 40 records basically subsidize other titles, allowing it to offer a wider range and therefore a better service. If the Top 40 goes, the whole proposition goes.

Ditto credit cards. Heavy borrowers who pay extortionate interest rates on high levels of rollover debt are subsidizing wily users who pay off their debts each month and get an excellent service for free. But a traditional credit card operator cannot cherry pick its own Superprofits, because ending the cross-subsidization would destroy the rest of its business.

Likewise banks. Current account holders whose balances are so low and transactions so frequent that they cost a fortune to serve are being subsidized by affluent customers with higher balances. Banking is ripe for a redivision into Royal, standard and DIY, but it's almost impossible for existing mass players to do this.

Or take insurance. It's all about averaging and cross-subsidization. Clever marketers have made good money by de-averaging – distinguishing high-risk customers from those who are low-risk. But the better the match gets between premium and risk, the less incentive there is to bet: high-risk people won't be able to afford the premium, and very low-risk types will realize they're better off investing their own premiums.

The real challenge comes when an outsider who hasn't got the same sort of cross-subsidizing structure targets another industry's Superprofits. Almost by definition, they can make a better offer – like the supermarkets and Tower Records, or, perhaps, category killers poaching high profit business from mass merchandisers, or car companies and charities marketing credit cards. In each case, the victim company is no longer doing the segmenting. It is being segmented.

We can expect more of this as technological development reduces the volume of business needed to cover infrastructure costs (thereby lowering barriers to entry), or as specialist operators see big opportunities in creating cherry-picking platforms for 'outsider' brands.

It's tempting to label the first type a niche player and the second type a brand extender and to think that's the end of it. But beware: jargon suffocates thought. It may be just the beginning. Behind such brands and marketing strategies there might be much more than meets the eye. A completely new industrial – and brand – landscape may be emerging.

Source: Mitchell, 1997.

An example follows, ABC Ltd, which illustrates in detail how the above approach might be implemented. This approach has been in existence for at least 80 years, but renewed interest in it has been generated over the last 25 years or so under the banner of activity-based costing (ABC).

ABC Ltd: an exercise on segmental analysis

The profit and loss account for last month's operations of ABC Ltd is given in Figure 4.6, showing a net profit of £14 070. (The numbers in this example are only intended to show how the calculations can be done.)

Derek Needham, ABC's chief executive, is interested in knowing the profit from each of the company's three customers. Since this cannot be known from Figure 4.6 as it stands, he asks his management accountant, Alan Lovell, to carry out the necessary analysis.

In addition to the five *natural* accounts shown in the profit and loss account, Mr Lovell has identified four *functional* accounts:

1. Personal selling

2. Packaging and dispatch

3. Advertising

4. Invoicing and collection.

His investigations have revealed that:

1. Salaries are attributable as follows:

   ■ Sales personnel £15 000

   ■ Packaging labour £13 500

	£	£
Sales revenue		255 000
Cost of goods sold		178 500
Gross profit		76 500
Expenses		
Salaries	37 500	
Rent	7500	
Packaging materials	15 180	
Postage and stationery	750	
Hire of office equipment	1500	
		62 430
Net profit		£14 070

FIGURE 4.6 *ABC Ltd: profit and loss account*

- Office staff £9000.

  Sales representatives seldom visit the office. Office staff time is divided equally between promotional activities on the one hand and invoicing/collecting on the other.

2. The rent charge relates to the whole building, of which 20 per cent is occupied by offices and the remainder by packaging/despatch.

3. All the advertising expenditure is related to Product C.

4. ABC Ltd markets three products, as shown in Figure 4.7. These products vary in their manufactured cost (worked out on absorption lines), selling price, and volume sold during the month. Moreover,

Product	Manufactured cost per unit	Selling price per unit	Number of units sold last month	Sales revenue	Relative bulk per unit
A	£105	£150	1000	£150 000	1
B	£525	£750	100	£75 000	3
C	£2100	£3000	10	£30 000	6
			1110	£255 000	

FIGURE 4.7 *ABC Ltd: basic product data*

Customer	Number of sales calls in period	Number of orders placed in period	Number of units of each product ordered in period		
			A	B	C
Charles	30	30	900	30	0
James	40	3	90	30	3
Hugh	30	1	10	40	7
Totals	100	34	1000	100	10

FIGURE 4.8 *ABC Ltd: basic customer data*

their relative bulk varies: Product A is much smaller than Product B, which in turn is only half the size of Product C (see Figure 4.7).

5. Each of ABC's three customers requires different product combinations, places a different number of orders, and requires a different amount of sales effort. As Figure 4.8 shows, James received more sales calls, Charles placed more orders, and Hugh made up most of the demand for Product C.

Using the data that have been presented, and making various assumptions that we feel to be appropriate, we can apply absorption costing principles in order to determine the net profit or loss attributable to each of ABC's customers. On the basis of our analysis we may be able to suggest what course of action be considered next, but the main aim is to address the question 'Where are we now?'

Among the given data we are told that office staff divide their time equally between two functional activities:

1. Advertising (i.e. order-getting)

2. Invoicing and collections.

It seems reasonable to assume (in the absence of other guidance) that space, postage and stationery, and office equipment are used equally by these two functions. The calculations that follow are based on this assumption, but any other reasonable (and explicit) basis could be acceptable.

Rent is payable on the basis of:

■ 20 per cent office space (i.e. £1500)

■ 80 per cent packaging and despatch space (i.e. £6000).

All packaging materials are chargeable to packaging and despatch (which is a clear-cut example of a direct functional cost). Since packaging costs will vary with the bulk of the products sold rather than with, say, the number of

Product	Number of units sold		Relative bulk per unit		Packaging units
A	1000	×	1	=	1000
B	100	×	3	=	300
C	10	×	6	=	60
	1110				1360

FIGURE 4.9   *ABC Ltd: packaging units*

units sold or sales revenue, we need to take note of the causal relationship between the bulk of sales and packaging costs (see Figure 4.9).

This can be done by computing (as in Figure 4.9) a measure termed 'packaging units', which incorporates both the number of units and their relative bulk. Even though only 10 units of Product C are sold during the month, the relative bulk of that product (with a factor of 6) ensures that it is charged with a correspondingly high amount of packaging effort (hence cost) per unit relative to products A and B.

The bases for determining the rates by which to apply functional costs to segments can be built up in the following way:

1. *Assign natural expenses to functional activities* (see Figure 4.10).

2. *Select bases for assigning functional costs to segments.*

   - Sales calls can be used for personal selling expenses (although this assumes all calls took an equal amount of time)
   - The packaging costs vary in accordance with the number of packaging units handled, so a rate per product can be established by taking bulk and the number of units handled into account

Natural expense	Personal selling	Packaging and despatch	Advertising	Invoicing and collection
Salaries	£15 000	£13 500	£4500	£4500
Rent	–	£6000	£750	£750
Packaging materials	–	£15 180	–	–
Postage and stationery	–	–	£375	£375
Hire of equipment	–	–	£750	£750
Total	£15 000	£34 680	£6375	£6375

FIGURE 4.10   *ABC Ltd: assigning natural expenses*

- Advertising can be related to the number of units of Product C sold during the period (which assumes that advertising was equally effective for all sales, and that all its benefits were obtained during the period in question)
- The costs of invoicing can be assumed to vary in accordance with the number of orders (hence invoices) processed during the period.

  Relevant calculations are given below:

$$\text{Cost per sales call} = \frac{\text{functional costs}}{\text{no. of sales calls}} = \frac{£15\,000}{100} = £150.00$$

$$\text{Packaging costs} = \frac{\text{functional costs}}{\text{no. of packaging units}} = \frac{£34\,680}{1,360} = £\,25.50$$

$$
\begin{aligned}
\text{Product A} &= £25.50 \times 1 & &= £\,25.50 \\
\text{Product B} &= £25.50 \times 3 & &= £\,76.50 \\
\text{Product C} &= £25.50 \times 6 & &= £153.00
\end{aligned}
$$

$$\text{Advertising cost} = \frac{\text{functional costs}}{\text{units of C sold}} = \frac{£6375}{10} = £637.50$$

$$\text{Invoicing cost per order} = \frac{\text{functional costs}}{\text{no. of orders}} = \frac{£6375}{34} = £187.50$$

3. *Assign functional costs to segments.* Before this step can be executed fully it is necessary to calculate the cost of goods sold on a customer-by-customer basis. The given data in Figure 4.7 include the manufactured cost per unit of each product, and from the given data in Figure 4.8 we can see how many units of each product are bought by each customer. From this we can calculate the data given in Figure 4.11.

   We can now turn to the assigning of functional costs to segments. If we take the case of Charles, we know that he can be attributed with a total of £35370 (see Figure 4.12). A similar computation needs to be carried out for James and Hugh, which gives us the data in Figure 4.13.

   Finally, the revenue generated from each customer must be calculated as in Figure 4.14.

4. *Compile a net profit statement.* All the pieces can now be put together to show the profit or loss of each customer account with ABC Ltd. The resulting figures (Figure 4.15) show that Charles and Hugh are profitable accounts, while James is marginally unprofitable.

		Customer					
		Charles		James		Hugh	
Product	Unit COGS	Units	COGS	Units	COGS	Units	COGS
A	£105	900	94 500	90	9450	10	1050
B	£525	30	15 750	30	15 750	40	21 000
C	£2100	0	0	3	6300	7	14 700
			£110 250		£31 500		£36 750

FIGURE 4.11 ABC Ltd: determining cost of goods sold by customer

30 sales calls	@ £150.00		£4500
30 orders	@ £187.50		£5625
Packaging costs for:			
Product A 900 × £25.50		£22 950.00	
Product B 30 × £76.50		£2 295.00	
Product C		0	
			£25 245
Advertising			0
Segmental marketing cost			£35 370

FIGURE 4.12 ABC Ltd: Charles' costs

James				Hugh			
40 sales calls	@ £150.00	£6000.00		30 sales calls	@ £150.00	£4500.00	
3 orders	@ £187.50	£562.50		1 orders	@ £187.50	£187.50	
Packaging				Packaging			
A 90 × £25.50	£2295			A 10 × £25.50	£255		
B 30 × £76.50	£2295			B 40 × £76.50	£3060		
C 3 × £153.00	£459			C 7 × £153.00	£1071		
		£5049.00				£4386.00	
Advertising 3 × £637.50		£1912.50		Advertising 7 × £637.50		£4462.50	
Segmental marketing cost		£13 524.00		Segmental marketing cost		£13 536.00	

FIGURE 4.13 ABC Ltd: costs of James and Hugh

	Unit selling price	Charles		James		Hugh	
Product		*Units*	*Revenue*	*Units*	*Revenue*	*Units*	*Revenue*
A	£150	900	135 000	90	13 400	10	1500
B	£740	30	22 500	30	22 500	40	30 000
C	£3000	0	0	3	9000	7	21 000
			£157 500		£45 000		£52 500

(Customer)

FIGURE 4.14 *ABC Ltd: revenue by customer*

	Charles	James	Hugh	ABC Ltd
Sales revenue	£157 500	£45 000	£52 500	£255 000
COGS	110 250	31 500	36 750	178 500
Gross profit	47 250	13 500	15 750	76 500
Marketing expenses	35 370	13 524	13 536	62 430
Net profit	£11 880	£(24)	£2214	£14 070

(Customer)

FIGURE 4.15 *ABC Ltd: net profit by customer*

In productivity terms (see pages 136–8 below), it is evident that there are significant variations from one customer to another. Taking Charles first, we have:

Inputs	£	Outputs	£
COGS	110 250	Sales revenue	157 500
Marketing	35 370		
	£145 620		£157 500

$$\text{Productivity} = \frac{\text{Outputs}}{\text{Inputs}} = \frac{£157\,500}{£145\,620} = 1.08$$

This productivity index of 1.08 is better than the figure of 1.06 for ABC Ltd as a whole (as shown in Figure 4.16), and considerably in excess of the figures for James and Hugh. It is in excess of unity, which is, *prima facie*, a good thing.

Taking James next, we have:

Inputs	£	Outputs	£
COGS	31 500	Sales revenue	45 000
Marketing	13 524		
	£45 024		£45 000

$$\text{Productivity} = \frac{\text{Outputs}}{\text{Inputs}} = \frac{£45\,000}{£45\,024} = 0.99$$

Since this index is below unity (i.e. outputs are less than inputs) it follows that a loss is being made, and the loss (£24) is the amount by which the value of the inputs consumed in servicing James exceeds the output generated from his account.

Turning now to Hugh, we have the following picture:

Inputs	£	Outputs	£
COGS	36 750	Sales revenue	52 500
Marketing	13 536		
	£50 286		£52 500

$$\text{Productivity} = \frac{\text{Outputs}}{\text{Inputs}} = \frac{£52\,500}{£50\,286} = 1.04$$

The index is greater than unity, but not as large as that for Charles, or for that relating to ABC Ltd as a whole. This overall position is given below:

Inputs	£	Outputs	£
COGS	178 500	Sales revenue	255 000
Marketing	62 430		
	£240 930		£255 000

$$\text{Productivity} = \frac{\text{Outputs}}{\text{Inputs}} = \frac{£255\,000}{£240\,930} = 1.06$$

A summary is provided in Figure 4.16.

Interpretation of data

A danger in using an absorption-based approach in segmental analysis is that the 'bottom line' might be taken as a criterion for action. It should not be: the aim is to determine the net profit as a criterion for investigation. (In a sense, of course, this is one type of action, but the type of action that

	Charles	James	Hugh	ABC Ltd as a whole
Outputs (£)	157 500	45 000	52 500	255 000
Inputs (£)	145 620	45 024	50 286	240 930
Productivity index	1.08	0.99	1.04	1.06

FIGURE 4.16 *ABC Ltd: productivity by segment*

should be avoided is the eliminating of James's account due to the marginal loss revealed in Figure 4.15.)

Charles's account contributed almost 85 per cent of the total net profit, and he bought three times as much from ABC Ltd as did Hugh, and more than three times the purchases of James. However, the number of sales calls to Charles was fewer than to James, although Charles placed a much larger number of orders than both James and Hugh together.

The mix of products purchased clearly affects the profit performance of different customer accounts. While the COGS does not vary from one product to another (being 70 per cent of sales revenue for each product line), the variation in relative bulk of the product lines caused differences in packaging costs. Thus Charles (whose orders were for 900 units of A, 30 of B, and none of C) was charged with relatively less packaging cost than either James or Hugh due to the smaller packaging bulk of Product A. On a similar basis, since Charles bought no units of C his account was not charged with any advertising costs, so the profit performance of Charles's account would clearly be better than either of the others.

One possible way forward could be to consider calling less often on James; to encourage Charles to place fewer (but larger) orders; and to rethink the wisdom of the advertising campaign for Product C.

It is vital to recognize that this net profit approach to segmental analysis can only raise questions: it cannot provide answers. (The reason for this, of course, is that the apportionment of indirect costs clouds the distinction between avoidable and unavoidable costs, and even direct costs may not all be avoidable in the short run.)

The application of the above steps to a company's product range may produce the picture portrayed in Figure 4.17.

The segment could equally be sales territory, customer group, etc., and after the basic profit computation has been carried out it can be supplemented (as in Figure 4.18) by linking it to an analysis of the effort required to produce the profit result. (Clearly this is a multivariate situation in which profit depends upon a variety of input factors – as suggested by

Product	% contribution to total profits
Total for all products	100.0
Profitable products:	
A	43.7
B	35.5
C	16.4
D	9.6
E	6.8
F	4.2
Sub-total	116.2
G	−7.5
H	−8.7
Sub-total	−16.2

FIGURE 4.17   *Segmental profit statement*

Product	% contribution to total profits	% total selling time
Total for all products	100	100
Profitable products:		
A	43.7	16.9
B	35.5	18.3
C	16.4	17.4
D	9.6	5.3
E	6.8	10.2
F	4.2	7.1
Sub-total	116.2	75.2
Unprofitable products:		
G	−7.5	9.5
H	−8.7	15.3
Sub-total	−16.2	24.8

FIGURE 4.18   *Segmental productivity statement*

Figure 4.1 – but developing valid and reliable multivariate models is both complex and expensive.) As a step in the direction of more rigorous analysis, benefits can be derived from linking profit outcomes to individual inputs – such as selling time, in the case of Figure 4.18.

From Figure 4.18 it can be seen that Product A generates 43.7 per cent of total profits, requiring only 16.9 per cent of available selling time. This is highly productive. By contrast, Product E produces only 6.8 per cent of total profits but required 10.2 per cent of selling effort. Even worse, however, is the 24.8 per cent of selling effort devoted to Products G and H, which are unprofitable.

A number of obvious questions arise from this type of analysis. Can the productivity of marketing activities be increased by:

- increasing net profits proportionately more than the corresponding increase in marketing outlays?

- increasing net profits with no change in marketing outlays?

- increasing net profits with a decrease in marketing costs?

- maintaining net profits at a given level but decreasing marketing costs?

- decreasing net profits but with a proportionately greater decrease in marketing costs?

If these analyses are based purely on historical information they will provide less help than if they relate to plans for the future. One way of overcoming the limitations of historical information is to plan and control the conditions under which information is gathered. This can be achieved through *marketing experimentation.*

A themed double issue of *Journal of Marketing Management* edited by Roslender and Wilson (2008) focuses on customer analysis.

4.8   MARKETING EXPERIMENTATION

In conducting marketing experiments, the marketing planner sets out to identify all the controllable independent factors that affect a particular dependent variable, and some of these factors are then manipulated systematically in order to isolate and measure their effects on the performance of the dependent variable.

It is not possible, of course, to plan or control all the conditions in which an experiment is conducted; for example, the timing, location and duration of an experiment can be predetermined, but it is impossible to measure such uncontrollable conditions as those caused by the weather or competitors' activities and eliminate their effects from the results. Irrespective of these uncontrollable influences, the fact that experiments are concerned with the deliberate manipulation of controllable variables (i.e. such variables as price and advertising effort) means that a good deal more confidence can be placed in conclusions about the effects of such manipulation than if the effects of these changes had been based purely on historical associations or guesswork.

Studies of marketing costs can provide the ideas for experiments. Questions such as the following can be answered as a result of marketing experimentation.

1. By how much (if any) would the net profit contribution of the most profitable market offerings be increased if there were an increase in specific marketing outlays, and how would such a change affect the strategy of competitors in terms of the stability of, say, market shares?

2. By how much (if any) would the net losses of unprofitable market offerings be reduced if there were some decrease in specific marketing outlays?

3. By how much (if any) would the profit contribution of profitable market offerings be affected by a change in the marketing effort applied to the unprofitable market offerings, and *vice versa*, and what would be the effect on the total marketing system?

4. By how much (if any) would the total profit contribution be improved if some marketing effort were diverted to profitable territories or customer groups from unprofitable territorial and customer segments?

5. By how much (if any) would the net profit contribution be increased if there were a change in the method of distribution to small unprofitable accounts, or if these accounts were eliminated?

Only by actually carrying out properly designed marketing experiments can management realistically predict with an acceptable degree of certainty the effects of changes in marketing expenditure on the level of sales and profit of each differentiated product, territory or customer segment in the multi-product company.

4.9   THE NATURE OF PRODUCTIVITY

Productivity can be considered either at a macro-level (i.e. in relation to entire industries or whole economies) or at a micro-level (i.e. in relation to particular organizations, or in relation to particular activities within organizations). Our interest is in the latter – productivity at a micro-level – although we must avoid being too introspective by focusing exclusively on one organization or function as if it were independent of its context.

At its simplest, productivity can be conceived of as the relationship between outputs and inputs. Thus marketing productivity can be expressed as:

$$\frac{\text{marketing outputs}}{\text{marketing inputs}}$$

Sevin (1965, p. 9) has defined marketing productivity in more specific terms as:

> *the ratio of sales or net profits (effect produced) to marketing costs (energy expended) for a specific segment of the business.*

This equates productivity and profitability, which seems acceptable to some writers (such as Thomas, 1984, 1986) but not to others (e.g. Bucklin, 1978). The major objection to Sevin's definition is due to the effects of inflation, since sales, net profit and costs are all financial flows subject to changes in relative prices. For example, any increase in the value of sales from one period to another during inflationary times will be made up of two elements:

1. An increase due to a higher physical volume of sales

2. An increase due to higher prices.

If the value of the pound sterling (in terms of its purchasing power) were constant this would remove the problem, but since this is not the case it means that any financial data are necessarily suspect. The answer is to make some adjustments to ensure that measurement is made in *real* terms rather than simply in *monetary* terms – and to make these adjustments to both numerator and denominator in a way that allows for differential rates of inflation. Once measurement is made in real terms, it is possible to use the ratio that emerges as an index of efficiency. This can be used in relation to two types of question:

1. How much output was achieved for a given input?

2. How much input was required to achieve a given output?

These questions can be asked retrospectively (as above) or prospectively (for example, how much output should be achieved from a given mix and quantity of inputs?). The first relates to the notion of *technical efficiency* (whereby the output from a given input can be maximized), whereas the second relates to the notion of *economic efficiency* (whereby the input costs for a given output can be minimized).

Having specified in operational terms the numerator (output) and the denominator (input), and having eliminated the impacts of inflation, the result represents a measure of resource allocation (i.e. the pattern of inputs) and resource utilization (i.e. the generation of outputs), and these can be depicted via *ratio pyramids*, which we will look at later in this chapter. What we need to recognize at this point is that the array of ratios within a ratio pyramid can give us a vivid picture of the manner in which the organization has allocated its resources, and the efficiency with which those resources have been utilized. The next step, of course, is to consider how the allocation and its efficiency might be improved, which will mean changes in inputs (*cf.* causes) and outputs (*cf.* effects). In turn, this requires an understanding of the causal relationships between inputs and outputs.

Let us be a little more specific and consider a particular productivity index from the distribution domain. The relevant output may be expressed in terms of the number of orders shipped during a given period, and the associated input may be the number of labour hours worked in the period. Thus:

$$\text{productivity index} = \frac{\text{number of orders shipped}}{\text{number of labour hours worked}}$$

It will be apparent that this index relates one physical measure to another, and hence there is no need to worry about inflationary distortions. However, had the numerator been expressed in terms of the *sales value* of orders shipped, and/or the denominator in terms of the *cost* of labour hours worked, it would have been necessary to adjust the figures to eliminate the effects of inflation – even though the index that results is a true ratio (i.e. it is not stated in terms of specific units).

It should also be apparent that any productivity index that is calculated is meaningless in isolation from some comparative figure. With what should an index be compared? There are a number of alternatives that will be examined later in more detail, but for the present we should be aware that:

- *Internal comparisons* can be made with figures from previous periods (which give a basis for trend analysis) or figures representing efficient or desired performance (which give a basis for budgetary control)

- *External comparisons* can be made with other organizations operating within the same markets (e.g. via competitive benchmarking).

The importance of external reference points cannot be overemphasized. As Christopher (1977) has stated:

> *Business success is achieved where the client is, more than in our plants. External returns from the market are more appropriate measures than internal returns on investment. Success is more in manufacturing satisfied, repeat customers than in manufacturing products.*

4.10   THE USE OF RATIOS

Whether the primary interest is in the productivity of an organization as a whole, or in the productivity of a highly specific activity within an organization, ratios can be computed at a suitable level of aggregation. Their value lies in the relative measures (as opposed to absolute measures) on which they are based.

It is possible to calculate a great range of ratios, but a word of warning is needed to ensure that only useful ratios are calculated. Thus, for example, the ratio of:

$$\frac{\text{advertising expenditure}}{\text{miles travelled by sales representatives}}$$

within a given period is not likely to be very useful for at least two reasons:

1. It seeks to relate two input factors (rather than one input and one output)

2. The resulting ratio (of advertising expenditure per mile travelled by sales representatives) is not meaningful.

On the other hand, the ratio of:

$$\frac{\text{incremental sales}}{\text{incremental promotion expenditure}}$$

relates one input to a relevant output, and is potentially useful as a measure of promotional effectiveness. Discretion, therefore, is most important in choosing which ratios to calculate as a means towards assessing productivity within marketing.

Another warning needs to be given over the way in which ratios tend to average out any patterns in the underlying data. Consider the case of a seasonal business making 90 per cent of its sales in the first six months of every year and the remaining 10 per cent during the other six months. Average monthly sales over the whole year will differ significantly from the average monthly sales in each half year, so care must be taken when choosing the period over which data are gathered and the frequency with which ratios are calculated.

At an organizational level the ultimate financial measure of short-term efficiency is the relationship between net profit and capital employed, typically expressed in percentage terms as the rate of return on capital employed or the rate of return on investment (ROI):

$$\text{ROI} = \frac{\text{net profit}}{\text{capital employed}} \times 100$$

This ratio shows the return (i.e. net output) that has been generated by the capital employed (i.e. input) during a given period of time. Problems exist in connection with the definitions (and hence measurement) of both numerator and denominator, which highlights another note of caution in using ratios: always be sure to establish the definition of numerators and denominators. For example, is the net profit pre-tax or post-tax? Is the capital employed based on historic cost or replacement cost figures?

Given that profit is the residual once costs have been deducted from sales revenues, it is clear that ROI can be improved by increasing sales revenues, by decreasing costs, or by reducing capital employed – or by any combination of these.

This gives us the basic idea underlying the ratio pyramid. At the apex is ROI, but this can be broken down into two secondary ratios:

$$\text{Primary ratio:} \quad \frac{\text{net profit}}{\text{capital employed}}$$

$$\text{Secondary ratios:} \quad \frac{\text{net profit}}{\text{sales revenue}} \times \frac{\text{sales revenue}}{\text{capital employed}}$$

Each of the secondary ratios can help explain the ROI. The first is the profit rate on sales and the second is the capital turnover. Their interrelationship is such that:

$$\text{profit rate} \times \text{capital turnover} = \text{ROI}$$

Even the secondary ratios are highly aggregated, so it is necessary to proceed to measure tertiary ratios on moving down the ratio pyramid, using its structure as a diagnostic guide.

The general cause of any deviation in ROI from a target rate may be found by computing the profit ratio and the capital turnover ratio, but this is only a starting point. Before corrective action can be taken a study of specific causes must be made, and hence *tertiary ratios* need to be worked out.

Tertiary ratios are those that constitute the secondary ratios. The profit ratio reflects the relationship between the gross profit rate, the level of sales revenue, and operating costs (i.e. net profit + operating costs = gross profit), while the rate of capital turnover is affected by the level of sales revenue and the capital structure mix (of fixed and working capital, etc.). From these details it is a simple step to compute four tertiary ratios as follows (see Figure 4.19):

1. $\dfrac{\text{Gross profit}}{\text{Sales revenue}}$

2. $\dfrac{\text{Sales revenue}}{\text{Operating costs}}$

3. $\dfrac{\text{Sales revenue}}{\text{Fixed assets}}$

4. $\dfrac{\text{Sales revenue}}{\text{Working capital}}$

Figure 4.19 also shows many other levels of the ratio pyramid that can be identified, and the process of decomposing broad ratios into their component

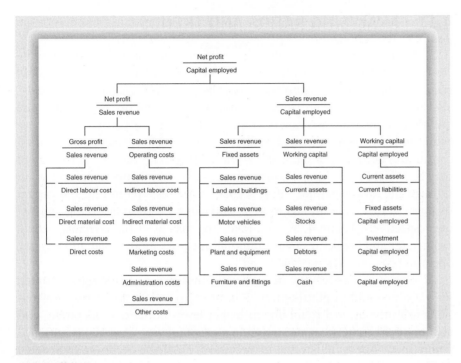

FIGURE 4.19 *Ratio pyramid*

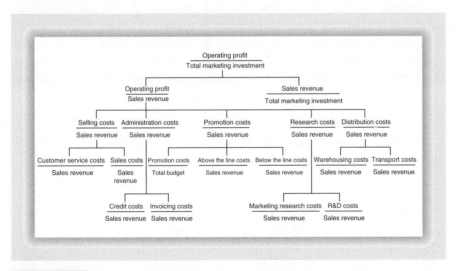

FIGURE 4.20 *Marketing ratio pyramid*

parts can be continued further and further until the reasons for overall outcomes are known.

A variation on Figure 4.19, relating specifically to marketing, is provided by Figure 4.20.

4.11   ANALYSING RATIOS AND TRENDS

It is possible to indicate trends in a company's performance over time by plotting successive ratios on a graph. Some important trends may only become apparent over a number of months (or even years), and ratio analysis can ensure that such trends do not develop unnoticed. In asking the question 'Where are we now?', it is often helpful to consider where we came from by means of trend analysis. Figure 4.21, for example, shows a continuing decline in a company's profitability. The causes for this trend may be found by breaking it down into its secondary components and so on through the ratio pyramid. These secondary trends – profit rate and capital turnover – are shown in Figure 4.22, and can be seen to be falling and rising respectively. Figure 4.23 then takes the former of these trends (falling profit rate) and breaks it down into a falling gross profit trend and a rising operating cost to sales revenue trend.

It may prove necessary in a specific instance to work right through the ratio pyramid in plotting trends in order to isolate the causes of variations from the desired trend line in higher levels of the ratio hierarchy, and also to apply some imagination and common sense. This last mentioned requirement can be illustrated in two ways. First, the declining ROI noted in Figure 4.21 may be thought, *prima facie*, to be due to the falling net profit to sales revenue trend shown in Figure 4.22, and so the rising capital turnover trend as in Figure 4.22 may be ignored. But ROI is clearly the combined outcome of a particular level of profit and a particular quantity of capital investment, so any variation in either will inevitably affect the ROI. Furthermore, a rising aggregate trend of capital turnover will almost certainly conceal many more compensating highs and lows in tertiary and

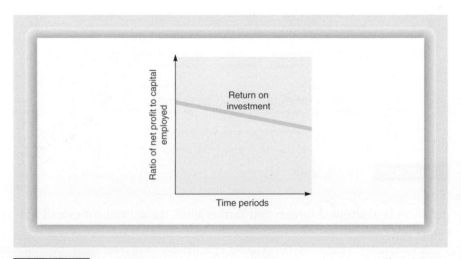

FIGURE 4.21 *Primary trend*

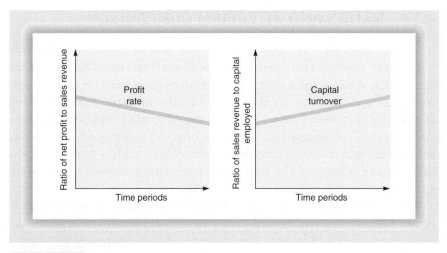

FIGURE 4.22 *Secondary trends*

subsequent levels of the ratio hierarchy. It follows that attention in the light of a falling ROI should not necessarily be focused exclusively on the net profit trend, but some consideration should be given to the rate and trend of capital turnover.

The second common-sense point to note is that a rising operating cost to sales revenue trend, as in Figure 4.23, cannot be controlled until the specific items that cause the trend have been identified and appropriate steps taken to bring them under control. Of course, the extent to which the decline of the profit rate (a secondary trend) is caused by either of its constituent tertiary trends should be carefully established.

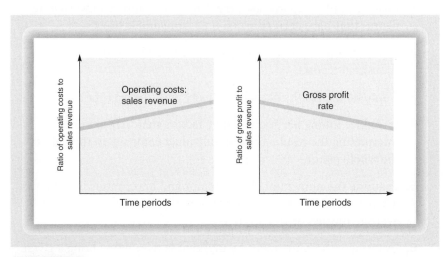

FIGURE 4.23   *Tertiary trends*

4.12   RATIOS AND INTERFIRM COMPARISON

In many industries – and especially in those in which operating methods, technology, product characteristics and general operating conditions are very similar – it is helpful to have comparative figures both for the company concerned and for other companies within the industry. From published accounts it is possible to see the primary, secondary and tertiary ratios (hence trends) of competing companies, but no reasons for divergences between companies' results can be discerned from such accounts due to a lack of detail relating to the lower part of the ratio pyramid (i.e. below the tertiary level) and so there is no guidance for future actions.

One major cause of divergence between the results of any two companies can be found in their use of differing accounting techniques and definitions. This will be seen, for example, if two companies purchase a similar asset each at the same point and one company chooses to depreciate the asset over four years while the other company chooses to take a 100 per cent depreciation allowance in the first year. It follows, therefore, that a meaningful comparison must be based on common definitions and usage. This can best be achieved (for comparative purposes) by a central organization, and for this reason the Centre for Interfirm Comparison was set up.

While interfirm comparison figures are expressed in relation to quartiles and the median (i.e. if all results are ranked in descending order of size, the median is represented by the figure that comes half-way down, and the third quartile is three-quarters of the way down), the following example (OPQ Ltd) simplifies this by just giving the general approach to interfirm comparisons. The necessary steps in such an exercise are:

1. Ensure that the reports, etc., that are to be compared incorporate figures that have been prepared on a comparable basis

2. Compute the required ratios, percentages and key totals from submitted reports

3. Compare the results of each company with the aggregate results

4. Introduce intangible or qualitative factors that may aid in interpreting the results of each individual company in the light of the whole picture

5. Examine the numerator, denominator and lower ratios in instances where a ratio differs significantly from the external standard (or average, median or whatever)

6. Determine the adjustment (if any) that is required to bring a given company's divergent ratio into line with the aggregate norm.

OPQ Ltd – ratio analysis

The following is a simple example of interfirm comparison. Figure 4.24 shows the ratios of OPQ Ltd, a firm in a light engineering industry, for the two years 2007 and 2008.

This looks like a success story. Profit on assets employed has gone up from 8.25 per cent to 10 per cent due to an increase in the firm's profit on

	Ratio	Unit	2007	2008
1	Operating profit / Assets employed	%	8.25	10.0
2	Operating profit / Sales revenue	%	5.5	6.1
3	Sales revenue / Assets employed	times	1.5	1.65
3(a)	Assets employed / Average daily sales revenue	days*	249	222
4	Production cost of sales / Sales revenue	%	71.0	70.4
5	Distribution and marketing costs / Sales revenue	%	17.7	17.7
6	General and administrative costs / Sales revenue	%	5.8	5.8
7	Current assets / Average daily sales revenue	days*	215	188
8	Fixed assets / Average daily sales revenue	days*	34	34
9	Material stocks / Average daily sales revenue	days*	49	45
10	Work-in-progress / Average daily sales revenue	days*	53	46
11	Finished stocks / Average daily sales revenue	days*	52	39
12	Debtors / Average daily sales revenue	days*	61	54

*Days required to turn the asset item over once.

FIGURE 4.24 *OPQ's own figures*

sales (Ratio 2) and the better use it seems to have made of its assets (Ratios 3 and (3(a)). The higher profit on sales seems to have been achieved through operational improvements, which results in a lower ratio of cost of production (Ratio 4). The firm's faster turnover of assets (Ratio 3) is due mainly to a faster turnover of current assets (Ratio 7), and this in turn is due to

Ratio			Firm				
			A	B	C	D	E
1	Operating profit / Assets employed	%		18.0	14.3	10.0	7.9	4.0
2	Operating profit / Sales revenue	%		15.0	13.1	6.1	8.1	2.0
3	Sales revenue / Assets employed	times		1.20	1.09	1.65	0.98	2.0
3(a)	Assets employed / Average daily sales revenue	days*		304	335	222	372	182
4	Production cost of sales / Sales revenue	%		73.0	69.4	70.4	72.5	79
5	Distribution and marketing costs / Sales revenue	%		8.0	13.1	17.7	13.7	15.0
6	General and administrative costs / Sales revenue	%		4.0	4.4	5.8	5.7	4.0
7	Current assets / Average daily sales revenue	days*		213	219	188	288	129
8	Fixed assets / Average daily sales revenue	days*		91	116	34	84	53
9	Material stocks / Average daily sales revenue	days*		45	43	45	47	29
10	Work-in-progress / Average daily sales revenue	days*		51	47	46	60	52
11	Finished stocks / Average daily sales revenue	days*		71	63	39	94	22
12	Debtors / Average daily sales revenue	days*		36	84	54	18	26

*Days required to turn the asset item over once.

FIGURE 4.25 *The interfirm comparison*

accelerated turnovers of material stocks (Ratio 9), work-in-progress (Ratio 10), finished stocks (Ratio 11) and debtors (Ratio 12).

The firm's illusion of success was shattered when it compared its ratios with those of other light engineering firms of its type. Figure 4.25 is an extract from the results – it gives the figures of only five of the 22 participating firms. OPQ Ltd's figures are shown under letter C. In this year, the firm's operating profit on assets employed is well below that of two other firms, and this appears to be due to its profit on sales (Ratio 2) being relatively low. This in turn is mainly due to the firm's high distribution and marketing expenses (Ratio 5). In the actual comparison further ratios were given, helping Firm C to establish to what extent its higher Ratio 5 was due to higher costs of distribution and warehousing; higher costs of advertising and sales promotion; or higher costs of other selling activities (e.g. cost of sales personnel).

4.13 A STRATEGIC APPROACH

A strategic-oriented approach to answering the question 'Where are we now?' can be provided from the PIMS database. PIMS stands for Profit Impact of Market Strategy, and refers to an objective approach to analysing corporate performance using a unique database. Some 3000 strategic business units (SBUs) have contributed over 25 000 years' experience to this database (see Buzzell and Gale, 1987).

PIMS research on what drives business profits has become more widely known over the last 30 years as more evidence has become available. We know that there is, in general, a range of factors that we can quantify and that relate to margins or to return on capital employed (ROCE). But does the evidence show that these factors work in specific industries – do they actually explain the spread that dwarfs differences between industries?

PIMS results from examining real profits of real businesses suggest that the determinants of business performance can be grouped into four categories (see Figure 4.26):

1. Market attractiveness

2. Competitive strength

3. Value-added structure

4. People and organization.

The first category contains factors in the business situation that affect its performance. Customer bargaining power, market complexity, market growth and innovation are obvious examples.

The second group describes how a business differs from its competitors in its market situation. Share position, customer preference relative to competitors' offerings, market coverage and product range all have an effect.

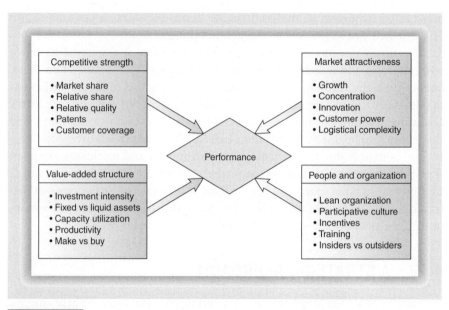

FIGURE 4.26   *PIMS can quantify how strategic factors drive performance*

The third category quantifies the way a business converts inputs into outputs: it includes investment intensity, fixed/working capital split, employee productivity, capacity use and vertical integration.

People and organization, an area in which PIMS has only recently built up comparable data, includes managers' attitudes, skill and training mix, personnel policies, and incentives. Figure 4.27 shows the impact of these factors on business profits tracked across PIMS' 3000 businesses. Some factors are more important than others, but each has an influence that is both measurable and explainable. The positioning of a business on the chart can be described as its 'profile'.

To test whether the profile of a business can explain its profits, irrespective of the industry in which it operates, PIMS looked at the performance of businesses with 'weak' and 'strong' profiles in each of five sectors. Weak and strong profiles were picked in terms of position on each of the 15 variables in Figure 4.28. Factors related to people and organization were omitted from the exercise because the available sample at the time was not large enough to examine them by sector.

The results are startling! In every industry sector where there were enough observations to test, a business with a weak profit makes a 6 per cent return on sales (ROS) or 10 per cent return on capital employed (ROCE) over a four-year period. In contrast, a strong-profile business makes 11 per cent ROS or 30 per cent ROCE. The gap in profit performance between strong and weak businesses in each sector is bigger than the standard deviation in each group. So the profile does a better job of explaining

Factor	−	Effect on ROCE	+
Market attractiveness			
Market growth	Low		High
Innovation	Zero, very high		moderate
R&D spend	Zero, very high		Moderate
Marketing spend	High		Low
Contract size	Large		Small
Customer complexity	Complex		Simple
Competitive strength			
Relative share	Low		High
Relative quality	Worse		Better
Differentiation	Commodity		Differentiated
Customer spread	Narrow		Broader
Product range	Narrow		Broader
Value-added structure			
Investment/sales	High		Low
Capacity use	Low		High
Vertical integration	Low		High
Employee productivity	Low		High
People and organization			
Attitudes	Restrictive		Open
Training	Little		Substantial
Incentives	Weak		Strong

FIGURE 4.27 *Impact of strategic factors on performance (source: PIMS database)*

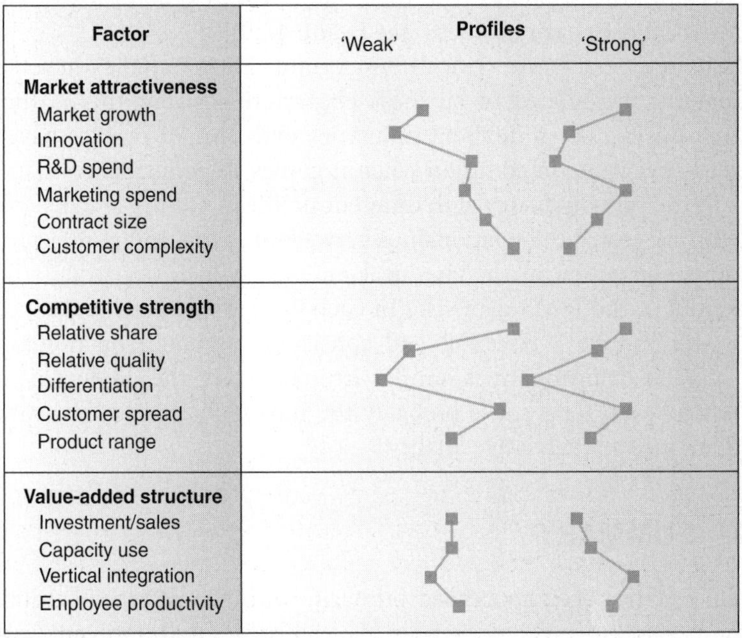

FIGURE 4.28 *PIMS profiles*

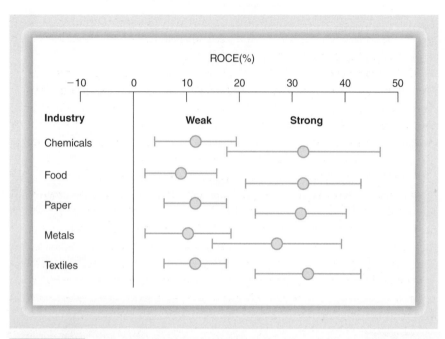

FIGURE 4.29   *PIMS profiles 2 (source: PIMS database)*

differences in performance than the industry each business is in. The profile represents the strategic logic that shapes the real competitive choices facing managers in each business (see Figure 4.29).

These new results are critically important. Earlier studies have shown how margins are related to business characteristics, but this is the first time that businesses in different industries with similar profiles have been shown to have more in common when it comes to performance than businesses in the same industry with different profiles.

PIMS also tested the relationships between margins and profile variables in various subsectors in the chemical industry, which is particularly well represented in the PIMS database. In each case the determinants included in the profile have a powerful and consistent influence on profits. The effect of each determinant is similar irrespective of the product category. This is true even for what is probably the most subjective of the variables that PIMS measures: relative quality.

4.14   SUMMARY

This chapter has been concerned primarily with the pattern of utilization of resources and its efficiency within the enterprise. Both ratio analysis and productivity analysis can help in establishing the pattern of resource utilization and its productivity by relating inputs (resources consumed or costs) to outputs (revenue). From this base, marketing managers are able to derive greater insights into relationships between inputs and outputs to help them in planning (and controlling) future activities.

If the utilization of 'effort' (i.e. resources) across an organization's various activities can be measured and related to the revenues generated by those activities, it is possible to determine their productivity. In essence, this is the ratio of outputs/inputs. While the outputs are fairly easy to establish with precision, the same is not true of the inputs, so most of the discussion has focused on the measurement of inputs.

The starting point is the specification of the cost objects of interest, for example, the productivity of operating via different channels, or serving different customer groups. Costs will be *direct* or *indirect*, depending upon the cost objects of interest. Full cost needs to be determined for each cost object (i.e. segment), and the ways in which this can be done have been discussed. Once this has been done the productivity of each segment can be measured, and from these measurements questions can be raised about the adequacy of each segment's productivity. For example, can effort be reallocated from Segment A to Segment B to improve these segments' productivity?

The key role of ratio analysis and productivity analysis lies in the basis they give for raising questions in the light of the existing state of play. Such techniques cannot generate answers as to what to do next.

A pyramid of marketing ratios was constructed to show the pattern of ratios (reflecting resource utilization and productivity) across relevant activities in a way that highlights interdependencies in an overall context.

Finally, the strategic approach provided by PIMS was outlined, which adds extra dimensions to the analysis of 'Where are we now?'.

Market and Environmental Analysis

5.2 INTRODUCTION

The changing business environment (or the emergence of a newmarketing reality)

If there is a single issue or theme which now links all types and sizes of organization, it is that of the far faster pace of environmental change and the consequential greater degree of environmental uncertainty than was typically the case even a few years ago. This change and uncertainty has been manifested in a wide variety of ways, and has led to a series of environmental pressures and challenges with which managers need to come to terms: a number of these are illustrated in Figure 5.1. Although the 12 points identified in Figure 5.1 are not intended either as a complete or a definitive list of the sorts of challenges that managers now face, they go some way towards illustrating the nature of the ways in which organizational environments are changing and how the pressures upon managers

1. Higher levels of over-capacity in many markets, and the increasingly global nature of many markets' tendency for strategic herding.

2. Product proliferation and ever-tighter levels of product parity.

3. Shorter product life cycles.

4. The emergence of a customer who is more demanding and discriminating (refer to Chapter 6).

5. A decline in levels of loyalty.

6. An increasing complex, aggressive and inter-connected competitive environment (refer to Chapter 7).

7. The erosion of many of the traditional bases of competitive advantage and the loss of differentiation.

8. Downward price pressures.

9. Media fragmentation, rising promotional costs and declining promotional returns.

10. Changing patterns of distribution and a significant shift in the balance of power between manufacturers and intermediaries.

11. Rapid changes in technology.

12. An increased emphasis upon environmental and 'green' issues.

FIGURE 5.1 *Changing environmental pressures*

are increasing. They also illustrate the point made in Chapters 1 and 2 that strategic marketing planning is an essentially iterative process. It is iterative for a number of reasons, the most significant of which being that, as the company's external environment changes, so opportunities and threats emerge and disappear only to re-emerge perhaps in a modified form at a later stage. Because of this, the marketing planner needs to recognize the fundamental necessity both for an environmental monitoring process that is capable of identifying in advance any possible opportunities and threats, and for a planning system and organizational structure that is capable of quite possibly radical change to reflect the environment so that the effects of threats are minimized and that opportunities are seized.

In essence, therefore, in formulating the marketing plan, the planner is concerned with matching the *capabilities of the organization* with the *demands of the environment*. In doing this, the planner is faced with a difficult problem, since what we typically refer to as *the environment* encapsulates a wide variety of influences. The difficulty lies, therefore, in coming to terms with this diversity in such a way that it contributes to effective decision-making, since it is this that has a direct influence upon performance.

This difficulty in coping with the environment can be viewed under two headings:

1. Understanding the *extent* to which the environment affects strategy

2. Understanding the ways in which environmental pressures can be *related* to the capabilities of the organization.

A possible danger that has been highlighted by several commentators is that of adopting a 'balance sheet' approach to environmental analysis – simply listing all possible environmental influences and then categorizing each as either an opportunity or a threat. If environmental analysis is limited to this alone, the strategist is left with far too broad and unsophisticated a picture of what really affects the organization. In addition, such an approach is likely to lead to the organization responding in a fragmented way rather than in a more integrated and strategic fashion.

This chapter therefore focuses on the various elements of the marketing environment with a view to illustrating the nature of their interaction and, subsequently, their effect on the organization. Against this background, we then move on to consider the ways in which an effective environmental monitoring process can best be developed and then, subsequently, how environmental forces are capable of determining the nature of the strategy pursued. We begin, however, by examining an approach to analysing the environment.

5.3   ANALYSING THE ENVIRONMENT

When the rate of change inside the company is exceeded by the rate of change outside the company, the end is near.
        (Jack Welch, former Chief Executive Officer, General Electric)

No organization exists in a vacuum. Marketing strategy must therefore develop out of a detailed understanding of the environment. Given this, the planner must:

■ Know *what* to look for

■ Know *how* to look

■ Understand *what* he or she sees

■ Develop the strategy and plan that takes account of this knowledge and understanding.

In analysing the environment, the majority of commentators argue for a stepwise approach. This involves an initial audit of general environmental influences, followed by a series of increasingly tightly-focused stages that are designed to provide the planner with an understanding of the *key oppor-tunities and threats* as a prelude to identifying the organization's *strategic position*. This process includes four principal stages:

1. The initial audit of the environment with a view to identifying the type of environment and how it is likely to change over the next few years.

2. An assessment of the organization's position within the environment and its ability to cope with environmental pressures. A detailed discussion of how this can be done appears in Chapter 7. In essence, however, this involves a combination of *strategic group analysis* in which competitors are mapped in terms of their similarities, dissimilarities, their capabilities and the strategies they follow, and *market share analysis* to highlight their relative degrees of market power.

3. The identification of emerging opportunities and threats and an assessment of the organization's strength to manage these effectively.

4. The preliminary identification of the marketing strategy.

At this point we will examine the first three stages of this stepwise approach; the fourth stage is discussed in Chapters 11 and 12. The first step in the process involves the *initial audit* of the environment with a view to identifying its current structure and how this is likely to change. The starting point for this involves the strategist in developing a list of those factors which are likely to have an impact on the organization and which will therefore need further analysis. In doing this, the purpose is to develop a detailed under-standing of what environmental factors have influenced the organization in the past, and the degree to which any changes that are taking place are likely to increase or reduce in impact. Although quite obviously such a list has to be company-specific, it is possible to identify a broad framework to help with this audit. This framework, which is typically referred to as PEST (Political, Economic, Social and Technological) analysis, is illustrated in Figure 5.2.

Against this background, the strategist can then move to an assess-ment of the *nature of the environment*. In essence, this is concerned with answering three questions:

1. How uncertain is the environment?

2. What are the sources of this uncertainty?

3. How should this uncertainty be dealt with?

Levels of uncertainty are directly attributable to the extent to which envi-ronmental conditions are dynamic or complex. *Dynamism* is due largely to the rates and frequency of change, while *complexity* is the result either of the diversity of environmental influences, the amount of knowledge required to

POLITICAL/LEGAL FACTORS
Political and legal structures
Political alliances
Legislative structures
Monopoly restrictions
Political and government stability
Political orientations
Taxation policies
Employment legislation
Foreign trade regulations
Environmental protection legislation
Pressure groups
Trades union power

SOCIO-CULTURAL FACTORS
Demographics
Lifestyles
Social mobility
Educational levels
Attitudes
Consumerism
Behaviour and behaviour patterns
Zeitgeists

ECONOMIC FACTORS
Business cycles
Money supply
Inflation rates
Investment levels
Unemployment
Energy costs
GNP trends
Patterns of ownership
The nature and bases of competition
domestically and internationally
Trading blocks

TECHNOLOGICAL FACTORS
Levels and focuses of government and
industrial R&D expenditure
Speed of technology transfer
Product life cycles
Joint ventures
Technological shifts
The direction of technological transfer
The (changing) costs of technology

FIGURE 5.2   *The PEST framework for environmental auditing*

cope with them, or the extent to which environmental factors are interconnected. The implications for environmental analysis of these different types of environmental condition are illustrated in Figure 5.3.

Environment types

The question of *how* to categorize environments has been discussed in some detail amongst others by Miles (1980, Chapter 9), who developed a framework for a comprehensive and systematic analysis of environment types. The model calls for a 'measurement' response by those performing the analysis and is based upon the answers to six questions:

1. How complex is the environment? (Complexity is a measurement of the number of different environmental forces which have an impact, or potential impact, upon the organization.)

2. How routine and standardized are organizational interactions with elements of the environment?

3. How interconnected and how remote, initially, are the significant environmental variables?

	Simple/static	Dynamic	Complex
		Conditions	
Aims	To achieve thorough (historical) understanding of the environment	To understand the future rather than simply relying on past experiences	The reduction of complexity Greater structural understanding
Methods	Analysis of past influences and their effect on organizational performance Identification of key forces Analysis of existing relationships	Managers' sensitivity to change Scenario planning Contingency planning Sensitivity planning	Specialist attention to elements of complexity Model-building
Dangers	The sudden emergence of unpredicted change Mechanistic organizational structures Lack of skills Focus on existing relationships Lack of willingness to accept that conditions are changing Stereo-typed responses	Management myopia Mechanistic organizational structures Lack of skills Inappropriate forecasting Failure to recognize significant new players	Unsuitable organizational structure or control systems Inappropriate reactions Inappropriate focuses Over-reaction

FIGURE 5.3 *Handling different environmental conditions (adapted from Johnson, Scholes and Whittington, 2008)*

4. How dynamic and how unpredictable are the changes taking place around the organization?

5. How receptive is management to the ways in which environmental pressures adversely affect the input and output processes of the organization?

6. How high is flexibility of choice and to what extent is the organization constrained from moving into new areas?

Using this checklist of questions, the strategist should then be able to establish the organization's environmental position on a number of continua:

Simple	↔	Complex
Routine	↔	Non-routine
Unconnected	↔	Interconnected
Proximate	↔	Remote
Static	↔	Dynamic
Predictable	↔	Unpredictable
High input receptivity	↔	Low input receptivity
High output receptivity	↔	Low output receptivity
High domain choice flexibility	↔	Low domain choice flexibility

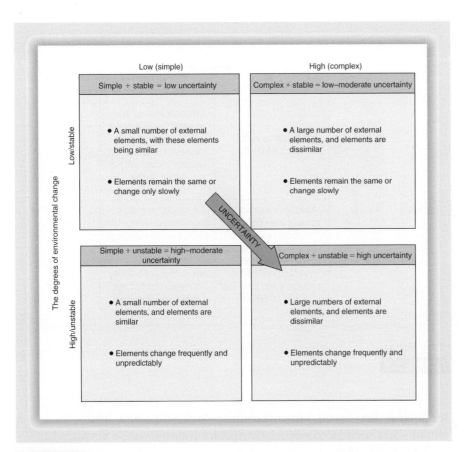

Low (simple)   High (complex)

| Simple + stable = low uncertainty | Complex + stable = low–moderate uncertainty |

• A small number of external elements, with these elements being similar

• A large number of external elements, and elements are dissimilar

• Elements remain the same or change only slowly

• Elements remain the same or change slowly

UNCERTAINTY

| Simple + unstable = high–moderate uncertainty | Complex + unstable = high uncertainty |

• A small number of external elements, and elements are similar

• Large numbers of external elements, and elements are dissimilar

• Elements change frequently and unpredictably

• Elements change frequently and unpredictably

(Left vertical axis: The degrees of environmental change — Low/stable, High/unstable)

FIGURE 5.4   *Degrees of environmental complexity (adapted from Daft, 1998)*

Taken together, these elements can then be incorporated into the matrix shown in Figure 5.4.

In turn, changes taking place within the environment can be plotted as in Figure 5.5. Here, the two key dimensions are the immediacy of an event taking place and then its likely impact upon the organization.

The implications of environmental change

Undoubtedly one of the major problems faced by managers comes when the organization, having operated for some time in a largely predictable environment, is faced with having to come to terms with a far more complex, uncertain and possibly malevolent environment. Among those who have had to do this in recent years are the major clearing banks, which have been faced with a very different type of competition, initially from telephone banking and then, subsequently, from Internet banking. Equally, Hoover has had to come to terms with a very clever, fast-moving and unpredictable competitor in the form of Dyson. Elsewhere, BA was challenged initially by

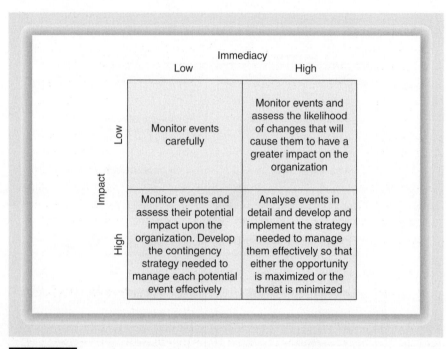

FIGURE 5.5 *Issues of immediacy and impact*

Virgin and then by the low-cost airlines such as Ryanair, whilst the music industry has been faced with challenges for Internet music downloads.

The significance of changes such as these needs to be seen in terms of *how* the organization monitors the environment and, subsequently, *how* it *responds*. Quite obviously, what is appropriate to a static environment is not likely to be suited to either a dynamic or a complex environment.

Static, dynamic and complex environments

With regard to the question of how the organization monitors the environment, evidence suggests that, in *broadly static conditions*, straightforward environmental scanning is likely to be a useful and generally adequate process. In a *dynamic environment*, however, the organization is typically faced with major change in the areas of technology and markets, with the result that decisions can no longer be based upon the assumption that what broadly has happened in the past will continue in the future. As a consequence of this, the focus needs to be upon the future with a far greater degree of inspirational interpretation. Among the techniques that have been used to do this is Delphic forecasting (see Wills *et al.*, 1972). The results are then used as the basis for building alternative scenarios.

This idea of alternative futures can then be used to identify the likely impact upon consumers, suppliers, competitors, government, the financial institutions, their probable responses, and subsequently their impact upon the organization.

For organizations faced with a *complex* environment, many of the issues and problems to which reference has been made are exacerbated.

Regardless, however, of the degree of complexity in the environment, there appear to be certain common strands in the ways in which managers cope with their environments. The most significant of these is that managers develop over time what can loosely be referred to as the accepted wisdom of the industry and the workable solutions to the various situations that are likely to emerge. One consequence of this is that the major competitive threats to organizations often come from companies *outside* the industry which, on entering the market, adopt a strategy that falls outside this area of standardized expectation, allowing for the conventional wisdom of response to change to be challenged.

5.4 THE NATURE OF THE MARKETING ENVIRONMENT

The marketing environment has been defined in a variety of ways. One view, for example, has referred to it in terms of factors that are outside the system's control but which determine, in part at least, how the system performs. For our purposes, however, the definition that we will work with is that an organization's marketing environment is made up of those forces that lie outside the organization and which exert some degree of influence upon the ways in which marketing management develops relationship with the firm's target markets.

Within the environment there are two distinct components: the *micro-environment* and the *macro-environment*. These are illustrated in Figure 5.6.

The *micro-environment* is made up of those elements that are closest to the company and that exert the greatest and most direct influence over its ability to deal with its markets. This includes the organization itself, its suppliers, its distribution network, customers, competitors and the public at large. The *macro-environment* consists of the rather broader set of forces that have a bearing upon the company, including economic, demographic, technological, political, legal, social and cultural factors. Together, these elements of the environment combine to form what we can loosely refer to as the *non-controllable* elements of marketing, which in many ways act as a series of constraints on the parameters within which the marketing planner is required to operate.

In labelling these elements as non-controllable, the reader should recognize that, in some cases at least, the marketing planner may well adopt a highly proactive stance in an attempt to alter the nature and impact of the environment upon the organization – for example, by attempting a merger or takeover in order to minimize a competitive threat. Equally, a large organization may well lobby the government in order to have legislation

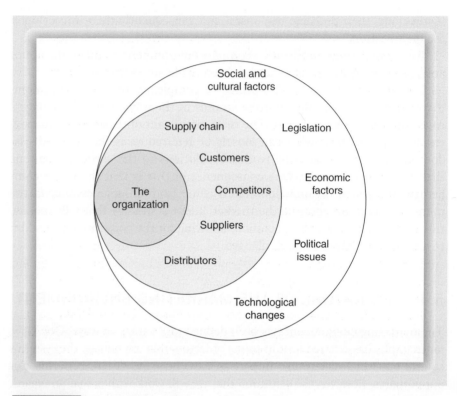

FIGURE 5.6   *The organization's marketing environment*

developed or changed so that the company benefits in some way. The car, foodstuffs, defence cigarette and brewing industries, for example, all have powerful lobby groups that attempt to exert a degree of influence over government to ensure that any legislation is beneficial (or at least not harmful) to their interests. In other cases, however, the organization may adopt a rather more reactive stance and simply view the environment as something that has to be lived with and responded to.

Regardless of which approach an organization adopts, it needs to be recognized that the environment is a significant determinant both of strategy and organizational performance, something which has been reflected in the work of a considerable number of writers, including Baker (1985, p. 85), who has described it as 'the ultimate constraint upon the firm's strategy'; Drucker (1969), who referred to the environment of the 1960s and 1970s as the 'age of discontinuity'; and Toffler (1970, p. 28) who, in looking ahead, referred to it as a time of 'future shock'. In making these comments, each author was giving recognition to the volatility and, indeed, the potential malevolence of environmental factors. As an example of this, the early 1970s witnessed an oil price crisis which, in turn, precipitated an economic upheaval throughout the world. This was reflected for some considerable time in higher levels of unemployment, high interest rates, the development of new economic thinking and, perhaps most importantly, reduced levels of business confidence. More recently, of course, the bombing of the World Trade Center in September 2001 had major economic, political and social implications. More recently still we have again seen significant and very rapid changes in the price of oil, and a major credit crisis as well as more regionalized upsets such as Sars and Avian flu.

In the case of the oil crisis, although this was without doubt a significant environmental upset, its impact was obviously felt far more directly by some organizations than others. It should therefore be remembered that what is a key environmental issue for one organization is not necessarily a key environmental issue for another. For a multinational corporation, for example, the major areas of concern are likely to be government relations, spheres of influence and the various political complexions throughout the world. For a retailer, the more *directly* important environmental influences are likely to be customer tastes and behaviour, and interest rates, while for a manufacturer in the high-technology fields it is issues of technological development and speeds of obsolescence that are most important.

The question of the extent to which environmental change, particularly of something as significant as the oil crisis, can be anticipated by business organizations has been the subject of considerable discussion and, in the case of the oil crisis, has led to both a 'yes' and a 'no' answer. 'Yes' in the sense that the techniques of environmental analysis undoubtedly existed at the time, but 'no' in that few people were willing, or indeed able, to recognize that one economic era was in the process of coming to an end, that another was about to start, and that balances of power throughout the world were beginning to change in a number of significant ways.

Although a number of commentators have suggested that environmental change of this magnitude is so rare as to be seen almost as a one-off, other writers' views differ and suggest that it is simply the *scale* of the oil crisis that separates it from the more commonly experienced and less dramatic forms of environmental change. The lesson to be learned in either case is straightforward, in that it points to the need for companies to engage in careful, continuous and fundamental monitoring of the environment with a view to identifying *potential* threats before they become *actual* threats, and opportunities before they are missed. In the absence of this, the organization runs the risk of falling victim to what Handy (1994, pp. 7–8) refers to as the 'boiled frog syndrome', which is discussed in Illustration 5.1. This has in turn led to the idea of 'strategic windows', a concept that has been discussed by Abell and Hammond (1979, p. 63).

Strategic windows

The term *strategic window* is used to describe the fact that there are often only limited periods when the 'fit' between the 'key requirements' of a market

Illustration 5.1   The parable of the boiled frog
All organizations are faced with a series of environmental changes and challenges. The principal difference between the effective and the ineffective organization is how well it responds, something that was encapsulated several years ago in one of the most popular of management fables, the parable of the boiled frog. What is now referred to as 'the boiled frog syndrome' is based on the idea that, if you drop a frog into a pan of hot water, it leaps out. If, however, you put a frog into a pan of lukewarm water and turn the heat up very slowly, it sits there quite happily not noticing the change in the water's temperature. The frog, of course, eventually dies. The parallels with the management and development of any organization are – or should be – obvious. Faced with sudden and dramatic environmental change, the need for a response is obvious. Faced with a much slower pace of change, the pressures to respond are far less (this is the 'we are doing reasonably well and can think about doing something else at some time in the future' phenomenon), with the result that the organization becomes increasingly distant from the *real* demands of its customers and other stakeholders. Given this, think seriously about whether you are one of the frogs that is sitting quite happily in a pan of increasingly hot water. If so, why, what are the possible consequences and what, if anything, are you going to do about it?

and the particular competences of a firm competing in that market is at an optimum. Investment in a product line or market area has to be timed to coincide with periods in which a strategic window is open, i.e. where a close fit exists. Disinvestment should be considered if, during the course of the market's evolution, changes in market requirements outstrip the firm's capability to adapt itself to the new circumstances.

The strategic window concept can be useful to incumbent competitors as well as to would-be entrants into a market. For the former, it provides a way of relating future strategic moves to market evolution and of assessing how resources should be allocated to existing activities. For the latter, it provides a framework for diversification and new entry.

The consequences of failing to identify strategic windows can, of course, be significant and are typically manifested in terms of a loss of opportunity, market share or competitive advantage. This was illustrated by the Swiss watch industry in the 1970s and 1980s, when it failed to recognize the significance of new, low-price market segments, new quartz technology, and a new, low-cost and aggressive form of competition from Japan and, subsequently, Hong Kong. The net effect of this was that the Swiss saw their share of the world watch industry drop from 80 per cent in 1948 to just 13 per cent in 1985.

That they have subsequently fought back with the Swatch watch is, in one sense at least, incidental. Perhaps the more important lesson to be learned from their experience is that a different approach to environmental monitoring might well have led to the industry avoiding the traumas that it undoubtedly faced.

The new marketing environment

Among the legacies of the economic and social turbulence of the last 25 years has been the emergence of a new type of consumer and the development of a new type of competitive environment (refer to Chapters 6 and 7). Taken together, these changes have led to what is for many organizations a radically different and far more demanding marketing environment than has been the case in the past. The consequences of these changes have been felt in a variety of ways, but most obviously in terms of the need for a different approach to management. This is typically discussed in terms of the need for managers to be more creative, innovative, flexible, dynamic, forward-looking and willing to take risks. However, in making this comment and identifying the characteristics of a new approach, we run the risk of making a series of largely self-evident points, but then failing to develop the sort of culture in which these elements prosper.

Environmental uncertainty and its implications have been discussed by numerous commentators over the past few years, including Charles Handy (1994) in *The Empty Raincoat*, and Tom Peters (1992) who, in *Liberation Management*, referred to the extreme changes that some organizations now face as 'crazy days'. Crazy days, he argued, are increasingly being faced by managers, and call for responses which often fall outside the traditional, well-understood and well-rehearsed patterns of managerial behaviour. Often, he suggests, it is the case that, if an organization is to survive let alone prosper, managers need to pursue much more radical and truly innovative strategies than ever before. He refers to these new patterns of behaviour as 'crazy ways', going on to argue that crazy days demand crazy ways.

Although others have suggested that Peters perhaps goes too far in his ideas of how to respond, it can be argued that they provide a useful starting point or underpinning of thinking about how best to manage the marketing process. In essence, what Peters is arguing for is a move away from the traditional to the more radical. This post-modern approach has, in turn, been developed by a wide variety of other commentators (see, for example, Brown, 1995; Nilson, 1995; and Ridderstråle and Nordström, 2000, 2004), all of whom have argued in one way or another for more innovative responses and patterns of managerial thinking and behaviour.

This theme has also been developed by Hamel and Prahalad (1994) who, in *Competing for the Future*, encapsulate many of these ideas in terms of what they label 'the quest for competitiveness'. This quest, they suggest, typically involves one or more of three possible approaches: *restructuring*, *re-engineering* and *reinventing the industry and/or strategies*; these are discussed in Chapter 11. In many cases, however, they claim that, whilst many managers over the past few years have placed emphasis upon the first two of these, they have failed to recognize the real significance – and, indeed, the strategic necessity in environments that are changing rapidly and unpredictably – of the third.

The implications of this are significant, and highlight one of the two key themes of this book: first, that in common with many other parts of a business, the marketing process needs to be managed in a truly strategic fashion and, secondly, that there is an ever greater need for innovation. These changes also highlight the need for organizations to be far closer to their markets than has typically been the case in the past and to have a far more detailed understanding of market dynamics. Without this, it is almost inevitable that any marketing programme will lack focus.

Responding to the changing market by coming to terms with the future

One of the principal themes that we pursue throughout this book is that the marketing environment is changing ever more dramatically and, for many organizations, ever more unpredictably. Faced with this, the marketing planner can take one of three approaches:

1. To ignore what is happening and accept the consequences of strategic drift and wear-out

2. To respond quickly or slowly, but largely reactively

3. To try to predict the nature of the changes and then manage them proactively.

The implications of the first of these in fast-moving markets are in most cases far too significant for this to be a realistic option for the majority of organizations, and so it is really only the second and third with which we need to be concerned here. In deciding whether to respond quickly or slowly, the planner needs to think about the opportunities or threats posed by the changes taking place, the time for which any window of opportunity is likely to be open, and the organization's ability to respond. Thus, the third option is in many ways the most desirable, but is typically dependent upon the quality of the environmental monitoring system that exists and the planner's ability to identify *how* to respond.

Although this third option is potentially the most difficult, it highlights a key issue for the marketing strategist: recognizing that an important part of planning and strategy is about the future; how can the organization get to the future first? It is the failure to do this and for external change to move ahead faster than management learning that typically creates significant problems for the marketing planner.

Recognizing this allows us to identify five types of manager:

1. Those who make it happen

2. Those who think they make it happen

3. Those who watch it happen

4. Those who wonder what happened

5. Those who fail to realize that anything has happened.

The likelihood of the last two of these occurring increases dramatically when the organization has a poorly-developed or non-existent marketing information system, and can lead to managers suffering from psychological recoil when they finally do recognize the nature and significance of changes taking place. In these circumstances, the marketing planner can then either continue to deny the nature and significance of market changes or respond to these changes.

5.5   THE EVOLUTION OF ENVIRONMENTAL ANALYSIS

Recognition of the potential significance of environmental change highlights the need for a certain type of organizational structure and culture, which is then reflected both in a balanced portfolio of products and in an adaptive management style supported by a well-developed intelligence and information monitoring system. Without this, the likelihood of the firm being taken unawares by environmental changes of one sort or another increases dramatically. Against the background of these comments, the need for environmental analysis would appear self-evident. All too often, however, firms appear to pay only lip service to such need. In commenting on this, Diffenbach (1983) has identified three distinct stages in the evolution of corporate environmental analysis:

1. An *appreciation stage*, typically resulting from the emergence of books and articles that argue the case for looking beyond the short-term and for considering the wider implications of the economic, technological, social and political factors that make up the business environment.

2. An *analysis stage*, which involves finding reliable sources of environmental data, compiling and examining the data to discuss trends, developments and key relationships. It also includes monitoring developments and anticipating the future. It was the emergence of this thinking which led to the appearance in the 1960s and 1970s of numerous books on environmental scanning, Delphic analysis and environmental forecasting (see, for example, Wills *et al.*, 1972).

3. The *application stage*, in which very real attempts are made to monitor the environment, assess the implications for change and incorporate staff evaluations into strategy and plans.

Assuming therefore that a firm intends to develop an effective system for environmental analysis, there is a need first to identify those dimensions that are likely to have the greatest impact upon the organization and, secondly to establish a mechanism whereby each of these elements is monitored on a regular basis. For most companies these elements are contained within the PEST analytical framework referred to earlier. Although in practice other factors can be added to this list, we will for convenience use this framework as a prelude to illustrating how environmental factors influence, and occasionally dictate, strategy. However, before examining these various dimensions, it is worth making brief reference to the ways in which organizations scan their environments.

In essence, there are three approaches to scanning, with these being characterized by an increasing degree of structure, systemization, sophistication and resource intensity.

1. *Irregular systems*, which predominate in companies with a poorly-developed planning culture and in which the focus is upon *responding* to environmentall-generated crises. The net effect of this is that emphasis is simply placed upon finding solutions to short-term problems, with little real attention being paid to identifying and assessing the likely impact of future environmental changes.

2. *Periodic models*, which represent a general development of the irregular system and which are more systematic, resource intensive and sophisticated. The environment is reviewed regularly and a longer-term perspective is developed.

3. *Continuous models*, which represent yet a further development and involve focusing upon the business environment generally and upon the long-term as opposed to short-term and specific issues.

The argument for continuous environmental monitoring in order to identify strategic issues and market signals in advance of their impact upon the company is a strong one, and has led Brownlie (1987, pp. 100–5) to identify the three basic premises upon which continuous environmental analysis is based:

1. The determinants of success are dictated by the business environment

2. The firm's response to environmental change therefore represents a fundamental strategic choice

3. A knowledge of the business environment must precede the acquisition of any degree of control over it.

Acknowledging the validity of these three assumptions leads to a recognition that effective management cannot take place in an information vacuum, or indeed in circumstances in which information is at best partial and poorly-structured. There is therefore an obvious need for the organization to develop an effective information system that *collects*, *analyses* and then *disseminates* information both from within and outside the company.

There are, however, problems that are commonly associated with the first of these – information collection and the development of a worthwhile database. Brownlie identifies these as being that all too often the information is:

- Poorly structured

- Available only on an irregular basis

- Often provided by unofficial sources

- Qualitative in nature

- Ambiguous in its definitions

- Opinion based

- Poorly quantified

- Based on an insecure methodology

- Likely to change.

Because of problems such as these, the need to collect and analyse environmental information in a well-structured and usable fashion is essential, and it is this that frameworks such as PEST are designed to achieve. It must be emphasized, however, that the organization should avoid focusing just upon the immediate *task environment*, since all too frequently history has demonstrated that the most significant threats faced by companies often come from firms outside the task environment. We have already pointed to the example of the Swiss watch industry, which was significantly damaged by the introduction of microchips and digital technology on the part of firms that the Swiss did not see as competitors. Equally, companies in markets as prosaic as carbon paper were decimated by photocopying technology, while in the same period the British motorcycle manufacturers of the 1960s, seeing their competitors as being one another, were taken by surprise by the Japanese. In making these comments we are therefore arguing for a *breadth* of perspective within the general structure of PEST analysis.

However, although the environment exerts a significant and obvious influence upon the organization, it should not necessarily be seen as the most direct determinant of strategy. Porter (1980, Chapter 1), for example, has argued that industry structure is a more important factor than environmental conditions, since it typically exerts a strong influence in determining the competitive rules of the game, as well as the strategies potentially available to the firm. Recognizing this, the key issue for the planner lies in developing the ability of the firm to deal with them.

However, before going on to consider some of the ways in which industry structure influences strategy, we need to examine the various dimensions of the political, economic, social and technological environments. It is this that provides the basis of the next section.

5.6 THE POLITICAL, ECONOMIC, SOCIAL AND TECHNOLOGICAL ENVIRONMENTS

At the beginning of this chapter we suggested that effective marketing planning is based on two important analytical ingredients. First, market opportunity must be analysed and, secondly, the company's ability to take advantage of these opportunities and cope with threats must be assessed.

Under the first heading, there are four basic building blocks:

1. Customers must be analysed to determine how the market can be segmented and what the requirements of each segment are

2. Competitors must be identified and their individual strategies understood

3. Environmental trends (social, economic, political, technological) affecting the market must be isolated and forecasted

4. Market characteristics in terms of the evolution of supply and demand and their interaction must be understood.

It is point 3 to which we now turn our attention. We do this by examining each of the elements of the PEST framework in turn, and then try to bring them together in Illustration 5.3 (see p. 178), where we make reference to what we term world-changing megatrends.

The political (and legal) environment

Marketing decisions are typically affected in a variety of ways by developments in the political and legal environments. This part of the environment is composed of laws, pressure groups and government agencies, all of which exert some sort of influence and constraint on organizations and individuals in society.

With regard to the legislative framework, the starting point involves recognizing that the amount of legislation affecting business has increased steadily over the past two decades. This legislation has been designed to achieve a number of purposes, including:

- Protecting companies from each other so that the size and power of one organization to damage another is limited

- Protecting consumers from unfair business practice by ensuring that certain safety standards are met, that advertising is honest, and that generally companies are not able to take advantage of the possible ignorance, naivety and gullibility of consumers

- Protecting society at large from irresponsible business behaviour.

It is important therefore that the marketing planner is aware not only of the current legislative framework, but also of the ways in which it is likely to develop and how, by means of industry pressure groups and lobbying of parliament, the direction of legislation might possibly be influenced so that it benefits the company. At a broader level, the strategist should also be familiar with the way in which legislation in other countries differs, and how this too might provide opportunities and constraints. The Scandinavian countries, for example, have developed a legislative framework to protect consumers that is far more restrictive than is generally the case elsewhere in Europe. Norway, for example, has banned many forms of sales promotion, such as trading stamps, contests and premiums, as being inappropriate and unfair methods for sellers to use in the promotion of their products. Elsewhere, food companies in India require government approval to launch a new brand if it will simply duplicate what is already on offer in the market, while in the Philippines food manufacturers are obliged to offer low-price variations of their brands so that low-income groups are not disadvantaged.

Although legislation such as this tends to be country-specific, examples such as these are potentially useful in that they highlight the need for marketing managers to be aware not just of the situation in their immediate markets, but also of how legislation might develop in order to restrict marketing practice. In a broader sense, marketing planners also need to monitor how public interest groups are likely to develop and, subsequently, influence marketing practice. In commenting on this in the context of American pressure groups, Salancik and Upah (1978) have suggested:

There is some evidence that the consumer may not be King, nor even Queen. The consumer is but a voice, one among many. Consider how General Motors makes its cars today. Vital features of the motor are designed by the United States government; the exhaust system is redesigned by certain state governments; the production materials used are dictated by suppliers who control scarce material resources. For other products, other groups and organizations may get involved. Thus, insurance companies directly or indirectly affect the design of smoke detectors; scientific groups affect the design of spray products by condemning aerosols; minority activist groups affect the design of dolls by requesting representative figures. Legal departments also can be expected to increase their importance in firms, affecting not only product design and promotion but also marketing strategies. At a minimum, marketing managers will spend less time with their research departments asking 'What does the consumer want?' and more and more time with their production and legal people asking 'What can the consumer have?'

In the light of comments such as these, the need for careful and continual monitoring of the political and legal environment should be obvious, since at the heart of all such analysis is the simple recognition of the idea of political risk.

The economic and physical environments

Within the majority of small- and medium-sized enterprises (SMEs), the economic environment is typically seen as a constraint, since the ability of a company to exert any sort of influence on this element of the environment is, to all intents and purposes, negligible. As a consequence, it is argued, firms are typically put into the position of responding to the state of the economy. Having said this, larger companies, and particularly the multinationals (MNCs), are perhaps able to view the economic environment in a rather different way since they are often able to shift investment and marketing patterns from one market to another and from one part of the world to another in order to capitalize most fully on the global opportunities that exist. For a purely domestic operator, however, the ability to do this is generally non-existent. For both types of company there is still a need to understand *how* the economic environment is likely to affect performance, a need which received a significant boost in 2008–2009 in the wake of the financial crisis, when parallels were being drawn between that period and the Great Depression of the 1930s. More specifically, however, the sorts of changes that are currently taking place in the economic environment can be identified as:

1. A significant shift in the balance of power between the major economies, with countries such as China and India both exerting an ever greater influence

2. A higher degree of economic inter-connection

3. Very high and rising levels of debt within many countries within the developed world

4. High levels of Third World debt

5. Rapidly fluctuating commodity prices

6. Very different patterns of consumer expenditure.

The significance of changes such as these should not be looked at in isolation, but should be viewed instead against the background of changes in the *political/economic balances of power* (e.g. the rise and then the relative decline of Japan over the past 40 years, the opportunities today in Central and Eastern Europe, and the economic development of China and India), and major changes in the *physical environment*.

Concern with the physical environment has increased dramatically over the past few years, with the origins being traceable to the publication in the 1960s of Rachael Carson's book *Silent Spring* (1963). In this, Carson drew attention to the possibly irrevocable damage being done to the planet and the possibility that we would exhaust the world's resources. This concern was echoed in the coining of the phrase 'eco-catastrophe' and reflected subsequently in the formation of powerful lobby groups such as Friends of the Earth and Greenpeace, which have had an impact upon business practice. The five major areas of concern expressed by pressure groups such as these are:

1. An impending shortage of raw materials

2. The increasing costs of energy

3. Increasing levels and consequences of pollution

4. An increasing need for governments to become involved in the *management* of natural resources

5. The need for management teams to take a very much more informed view of sustainable development, to which we must add the causes and consequences of global warming.

The social, cultural and demographic environments

It should be apparent from what has been said so far that a broad perspective needs to be adopted in looking at the economic environment. From the viewpoint of the marketing planner, analysis of short-term and long-term economic patterns is of vital importance. In doing this, arguably the most useful and indeed logical starting point is that of demography, since not only is demographic change readily identifiable, but it is the size, structure and trends of a population that ultimately exert the greatest influence on demand. There are several reasons for this, the two most significant of which are, first, that there is a strong relationship between population and economic growth and, secondly, that it is the absolute size of the population that acts as the boundary condition determining potential or primary demand. A detailed understanding of the size, structure, composition and trends of the population is therefore of fundamental importance to the marketing planner. It is consequently fortunate that, in the majority of developed countries, information of this sort is generally readily available and provides a firm foundation for forecasting.

At the same time, a variety of other equally important and far-reaching changes are currently taking place, including:

1. *The growth in the number of one-person households.* The size of this SSWD group (single, separated, widowed, divorced) has grown dramatically over the past few years, with 64 per cent of the UK's 24.4 million households consisting of just one or two people.

Amongst the factors that have contributed to this are young adults leaving home earlier, later marriage, a rise in the divorce rate, a generally greater degree of social and geographic mobility, and higher income levels that give people the freedom to live alone if they wish to do so. The implications for marketing of changes such as these have already proved significant in a variety of ways and have been reflected in an increase in demand for more starter homes, smaller appliances, food that can be purchased in smaller portions, and a greater emphasis upon convenience products generally. (At this stage, the reader might usefully turn to the Appendix of Chapter 6, where some of the drivers of consumer change are discussed.)

2. *A rise in the number of two-person cohabitant households.* It has been suggested by several sociologists that cohabitation is becoming increasingly like the first stage of marriage, with more people of the opposite sex sharing a house. At the same time, the number of households with two or more people of the same sex sharing has also increased.

3. *An increase in the number of group households.* These are households with three or more people of the same or opposite sex sharing expenses by living together, particularly in the larger cities. These look set to increase yet further. The needs of these non-family households differ in a variety of ways from those of the more conventional family household, which in the past has typically provided the focus for marketing attention. By virtue of their increasing importance, non-family households are likely to require ever more different strategies over the next few years if full advantage of the opportunities they offer is to be realized.

4. *A much greater degree of social mobility.*

At the same time a variety of other significant demographic shifts are taking place throughout the world, all of which need to be reflected in the planning process. These include:

1. *An explosion in the world's population,* with much of this growth being concentrated in those nations which, by virtue of low standards of living and economic development, can least afford it.

2. *A slowdown in birth rates* in many of the developed nations. Many families today, for example, are opting for just one child and this has had significant implications for a variety of companies. Johnson & Johnson, for example, responded to the declining birth rate by very successfully repositioning its baby oil, baby powder and baby shampoo in such a way that the products also appealed to young female adults. Similarly, cosmetics companies have placed a far

greater emphasis on products for the over-50s. The implications of this slowdown in the birth rate are illustrated perhaps most dramatically in countries such as Japan in which the ratio of over-50s to the under-16s is greater than in any other nation.

3. *An ageing population*, as advances in medical care allow people to live longer. One result of this trend, which has in turn been exacerbated by the slowdown in the birth rate, has been an increase in the number of empty nesters (see the section on the family life cycle on pages 352–4) who have substantial sums of discretionary income and high expectations (see Illustration 5.2).

4. *Changing family structures* as a result of:
   - Later marriage
   - Fewer children
   - Increased divorce rates
   - More working wives
   - An increase in the number of career women.

5. *Higher levels of education* and an increasing number of families in what has traditionally been seen as the middle class.

6. *Geographical shifts* in population and, in Britain at least, the emergence of a North–South divide characterized by radically different levels of economic activity and employment. In parallel with

---

Illustration 5.2   Disney and the Silver Yen

The implications of the increasingly skewed demographic profiles of North America, much of Western Europe and Japan have had significant implications for large numbers of organizations. Kellogg's Optovita brand, for example, was specifically targeted at the growing over 50s segment whilst companies such as Saga have focused almost entirely on this market.

A similar recognition of the value of the 'grey' market was at the heart of Disney's revised thinking in Japan in 2008. Faced with a significant decline in the country's birth rate, Disney began focusing upon a previously largely ignored demographic group, the over-60s. The company recognized that the largest group of customers having both the money and the time is now mostly retired. To attract this part of society, which it labelled 'the Silver Yen', the company began offering a cut-price season ticket and made older people Tokyo Disneyland's core target.

This move, which was unprecedented throughout the Disney empire, was in many ways a simple recognition of a market reality that many others had previously talked about, but failed to respond to effectively.

A slightly more unusual example of a revised market focus is that of Pascha, Germany's largest brothel, which offers a 50 per cent afternoon discount scheme for those over 66 and reduced entry prices to the establishment's night club at 9.00 pm.

this, there has been the urbanization of society, with 33 per cent of the population now living in just 3 per cent of the UK land area.

7. *A growth in the number of people willing to commute long distances to work*, and an upsurge in the opportunities for telecommuting whereby people can work from home and interact with colleagues via the Internet.

The net effect of changes such as these has been significant, and is continuing to prove so, with the marketing strategies of nearly all companies being affected in one way or another. At their most fundamental, these changes have led to a shift from a small number of mass markets to an infinitely larger number of micromarkets differentiated by age, sex, lifestyle, education and so on. Each of these groups differs in terms of its preferences and characteristics and, as a consequence, requires different, more flexible and more precise approaches to marketing that no longer take for granted the long-established assumptions and conventions of marketing practice. The implications of these trends are therefore of considerable significance and, from the viewpoint of the strategist, have the advantage of being both reliable and largely predictable, at least in the short- and medium-term. There is thus no excuse either for being taken unawares by them or for ignoring them.

Social and cultural change: an overview

Taken together, the changes that we have pointed to in this section can be seen as fundamental, and have been described in various ways. The media theorist Marshall MacLuhan (1964), for example, labelled it the Age of the Global Village. Drucker (1969) referred to it as the Age of Discontinuity; Toffler (1970) as the Age of Future Shock; Galbraith (1977) as the Age of Uncertainty; and Albrecht (1979) as the Age of Anxiety.

Although each of these was commenting some years ago, their thinking is still in many ways valid. However, for us the implications of much of what has been said is that we are now living in the Age of Consequences.

The technological environment

The fourth and final strand of the environment considered here is that of technology. Seen by many people as the single most dramatic force shaping our lives, technological advance needs to be seen as a force for 'creative destruction' in that the development of new products or concepts has an often-fatal knockout effect on an existing product. The creation of the xerography photocopying process, for example, destroyed the market for carbon paper, while the development of cars damaged the demand for railways. The implications for the existing industry are often straightforward: change or die. The significance of technological change does, however, need to be seen not just at the corporate or industry level, but also at the national level, since an economy's growth rate is directly influenced by the level of technological advance.

Technology does, therefore, provide both opportunities and threats, some of which are direct while others are far less direct in their impact. As an example of this, the development of the contraceptive pill led to smaller families, an increase in the number of working wives, higher levels of discretionary income, and subsequently to a greater emphasis on holidays, consumer durables, and so on. Recognizing then that the impact of technology is to all intents inevitable, the areas to which Kotler (1988, pp. 154–6) suggests the marketing planner should pay attention include:

1. *The accelerating pace of technological change*. In his book *Future Shock*, Toffler (1970) makes reference to the accelerative thrust in the invention, exploitation, diffusion and acceptance of new technologies. An ever greater number of ideas are being developed, and the time period between their development and implementation is shortening. This theme was developed further by Toffler (1980) in *The Third Wave*, in which he forecast the rapid emergence and acceptance of telecommuting (the electronic cottage) with direct implications for such things as family relationships, home entertainment and, less directly, levels of car exhaust pollution.

2. *Unlimited innovational opportunities*, with major advances being made in the areas of solid-state electronics, robotics, material sciences and biotechnology.

3. *Higher research and development budgets*, particularly in the USA, northern Europe and Japan. One implication of this is that organizations are likely to be forced into the position of spending ever greater amounts on R&D simply to stay still.

4. *A concentration of effort in some industries on minor product improvements* that are essentially defensive, rather than on the riskier and more offensive major product advances.

5. *A greater emphasis upon the regulation of technological change* in order to minimize the undesirable effects of some new products upon society. Safety and health regulations are most evident in their application in the pharmaceutical, foodstuffs and car industries, although across the entire spectrum of industry far more emphasis today is being given to the idea of technological assessment as a prelude to products being launched commercially.

A broadly similar view of the major changes taking place within the environment appears in Illustration 5.3, which highlights what have been termed 'world-changing megatrends'. From the viewpoint of marketing, the implications of each of these areas are potentially significant, and argues

Illustration 5.3 World-changing megatrends

It should be apparent from what has been said so far that the marketing planner is faced with an increasingly volatile – and malevolent – environment. However, underpinning this is a number of what might be termed 'megatrends' that have a long-term and, in many cases, fundamental effect upon the pattern, structure and practices of business. These include:

1. The explosive and accelerating power of information and communication technologies

2. The globalization of markets, patterns of competition and innovation

3. The fundamental shifts from a world economy based on manufacturing and the exploitation of natural resources to one based on knowledge, information, innovation and adding value

4. The accelerated decoupling of the 'real' global economy from the 'virtual' economy of financial transactions

5. Geographic rebalancing and the emergence of a new world economic order

6. The twilight of government

7. Sector convergence

8. The emergence of unprecedented new forms of business organization, both within and between firms

9. A shift in the economic 'centre of gravity' of the business world from large multinationals to smaller, nimbler and more entrepreneurial companies

10. The increase in the social, political and commercial significance of environmental considerations

11. An exponential increase in the velocity, complexity and unpredictability of change.

Source: Lewis (2005).

the case for careful technological monitoring in order to ensure that emerging opportunities are not ignored or missed. This, in turn, should lead to more market-oriented, rather than product-oriented, research and to a generally greater awareness of the negative aspects of any innovation.

5.7 COMING TO TERMS WITH INDUSTRY AND MARKET BREAKPOINTS

A fundamental element of any competitive marketing strategy should be the anticipation – or precipitation – of major environmental or structural change. Sometimes referred to as *industry breakpoints*, the consequences of major change are seen in a variety of ways, but most obviously in terms of how a previously successful strategy is made obsolete. An understanding of how breakpoints work and how they might best be managed is therefore an essential part of strategic marketing.

In discussing industry breakpoints, Strebel (1996, p. 13) defines them as:

> *a new offering to the market that is so superior in terms of customer value and delivered cost that it disrupts the rules of the competitive game: a new business system is required to deliver it. The new offering typically causes a sharp shift in the industry's growth rate while the competitive response to the new business system results in a dramatic realignment of market shares.*

The other way in which to think about breakpoints is in terms of the way in which once a breakpoint has been created, the existing players need either to respond, and possibly to respond dramatically, or recognize the often significantly negative implications upon their position and performance in the marketplace.

There are numerous examples of industries in which the phenomenon has been experienced (think, for example, about the implications of the Internet for both the holiday industry and the book market; the effects of the low-cost airlines upon the traditional players; the impact upon Nestlé, Mars and Unilever of the launch of Häagen–Dazs; and Eastman Kodak's need to come to terms with a disruptive breakpoint in the form of digital photography) although in many instances it appears that managers have learned little from the lessons of other markets in which traumatic change has already taken place. However, given the seemingly ever greater pace of competition, shorter product, market and brand life cycles, and the consequently more intensive search for competitive advantage, it is almost inevitable that at some stage a majority of managers will be faced with the problems that breakpoints create.

A breakpoint on a slightly smaller scale was illustrated in 2002/2003 by the popularity of the Atkins Diet. The high-protein regime that the diet demands was reflected in significant shifts in demand for food products, with sales of meat increasing substantially and sales of carbohydrates such as bread and pasta falling.

According to Strebel (1996, p. 13), there are two basic types of breakpoint:

1. *Divergent breakpoints*, which are associated with sharply increasing variety in the competitive offerings and consequently higher value for the customer

2. *Convergent breakpoints*, which are the result of improvements in the systems and processes used to deliver the offerings, with these then being reflected in lower delivered costs.

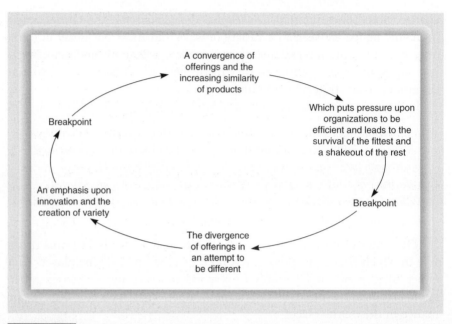

FIGURE 5.7 *The evolutionary cycle of competitive behaviour (adapted from Strebel, 1996)*

These are illustrated in Figure 5.7. With regard to the specific causes of breakpoints, it appears that they can be created by a variety of factors, including:

- Technological breakthroughs that provide the innovative organization with a major competitive advantage but, in turn, put competitors at a disadvantage

- The economic cycle, which, in a downturn, forces a radical rethink of the product and how it is to be marketed

- A new source of supply that offers scope for major reductions in cost

- Changes in government policy

- Shifts in customer values and/or expectations

- The identification by one company of new business opportunities, with the result that there is a divergence in competitors' responses and behaviour as they try to work out how best to exploit these opportunities

- Shifts within the distribution network that lead to changes in the balance of power between manufacturers and retailers, and very different sets of expectations

- New entrants to the market who bring with them different sets of skills and expectations, as well as a different perspective

- Declining returns, which force a radical rethink of how the company is operating and how it should develop in the future.

Given the significance of breakpoints, it is obviously essential that, wherever possible, the marketing planner identifies when breakpoints are most likely to occur and the form they will take. In the absence of this the organization will be forced into a reactively responsive mode. However, it can be argued that a majority of managers are particularly badly-equipped to identify breakpoints, especially in organizations with a closed culture, since their experience is largely irrelevant in new markets and new business systems. As an example of this, the established players in the computer industry focused much of their effort upon their existing products, markets and technologies, and had little cause or incentive to look at a redefinition of the product and market in the way that Apple did.

Nevertheless, planners need to come to terms with the dynamics of their industry and, in particular, with the sorts of pressures that we referred to earlier and which, sooner or later, lead to breakpoints occurring. In so far as a framework for this can be identified, it stems from the way in which there is a tendency for the competitive cycle to fluctuate between *divergence* (variety creation) and *convergence* (the survival of the fittest).

Faced with what, on the face of it, appears to be ever more rapid environmental change, marketing planners need to address a series of issues. Amongst the most prominent of these are:

- How to best balance short-run and long-run goals and actions

- How to become more firmly market focused and customer-driven

- How to manage customers more effectively and, in particular, ever higher expectations and lower levels of loyalty

- How to segment markets more creatively and strategically

- How best to achieve leadership in selected market segments

- How best to add value and differentiate the company's offer

- How to price in order to gain competitive advantage

- How to develop an effective distribution strategy

- How to deal most effectively with new technologies

- How to cope with shifting market boundaries and the globalization of markets

- How to improve the marketing information, planning and control systems.

5.8 COMING TO TERMS WITH THE VERY DIFFERENT FUTURE: THE IMPLICATIONS FOR MARKETING PLANNING

Predicting the future is the easy part. It's knowing what to do with it that counts.

(Faith Popcorn, 2001)

Given the nature of our comments so far, it should be apparent that the marketing planner must be concerned with the future. A fundamental consideration for many firms is therefore the question of how the organization can get to the future before its competitors. In discussing this, and how, by getting to the future first, organizations can create a possibly significant competitive advantage, Hamel and Prahalad (1994) suggest that: 'Companies that create the future are rebels. They break the rules. They are filled with people who take the other side of an issue just to spark a debate.'

They go on to suggest that, because so many markets are now dramatically more competitive than in the past, the traditional idea of being better, faster and smarter (which has led to the three words running together in the form of the management mantra 'betterfastersmarter') is no longer enough. Instead, there is the need for managers to recognize the fundamental importance of innovation and creativity being in many markets the only truly sustainable forms of competitive advantage. However, if this is to be achieved, run-of-the-mill large companies need to take on many of the mindsets of smaller organizations that are characterized by a far greater degree of flexibility and speed of response. It was this pattern of thinking and the difficulties of achieving it that led Kanter (1989) to refer to the idea of getting elephants to dance. In the absence of this, managers face the danger of simply drifting into the future. In order to avoid this, Hamel and Prahalad (1994) argue that managers need to recognize the importance of three rules:

1. *Step off the corporate treadmill.* To do this, managers need to avoid an over-preoccupation with day-to-day issues and to focus instead upon the smaller number of issues that are *really* important and will contribute to competitive advantage.

2. *Compete for industry foresight and learn to forget.* This involves spending time identifying how the market will or can be encouraged to move and then quite deliberately forgetting some of the traditional rules of competition and patterns of behaviour.

3. *Develop the (new) strategic architecture*, and concentrate upon leveraging and stretching the strategy in such a way that far greater use is made of the organization's marketing assets.

In coming to terms with these areas, the marketing planner needs to understand which of the factors that are typically taken for granted (the conventional wisdoms), both within the organization and the market as a whole, can either be questioned or eliminated. The planner also needs to identify the two or three strategic actions which, if taken, would make a real difference to the organization's performance in the marketplace.

Looking to the future

In many organizations there is a temptation to focus upon the short-term. There are several obvious explanations for this, the most obvious of which stems from the (greater) feeling of security that managers derive from concentrating upon the comfort zone of the areas and developments that are essentially predictable. A more fundamental explanation, however, emerged from a survey in the *Asian Wall Street Journal*. The study, which covered large firms and multinational corporations, illustrated the extent to which many senior managers are forced to demonstrate higher and more immediate short-term results than in the past. The implications for strategic marketing planning are significant, since strategic planners have little incentive to think and act long-term if they know that they will be evaluated largely on the basis of short-term gains and results. The sorts of trade-offs that emerge from this have, in turn, been heightened as the pace of change within the environment, and the need to manage ambiguity, complexity and paradox, has increased.

Nevertheless, the strategic marketing planner must, of necessity, have some view of the longer-term and of the ways in which markets are likely to move. In discussing this, Doyle (2002) identified ten major trends within the environment:

1. The move towards what he termed the *fashionization of markets,* in which an ever greater number of products and markets are subject to rapid obsolescence and unpredictable and fickle demand

2. The *fragmentation* of previously homogeneous markets and the emergence of micro-markets

3. The *ever higher expectations* of customers

4. The greater pace of *technological change*

5. *Higher levels of competition*

6. The *globalization* of markets and business

7. Expectations of *higher service*

8. The *commoditization* of markets

9. The *erosion of previously strong and dominant brands*

10. A series of new and/or greater governmental, political, economic and social *constraints*.

Although the list is by no means exhaustive (it fails, for example, to come to terms with the detail of a series of major social and attitudinal changes) and, in a number of ways, focuses upon the broadly obvious in that much of what he suggested is simply a continuation of what exists currently, it does provide an initial framework for thinking about the future.

A somewhat different approach has been taken by Fifield (1998), who has focused upon tomorrow's customer. He suggests that this customer will not simply be a replication of the customer of the past, but will instead be characterized by a series of traits that include being:

- Inner-driven and less susceptible to fashion and fads

- Multi-individualistic and multi-faceted

- Interconnected, with a far stronger awareness of different facets of their lives

- Pleasure seeking

- Deconstructed, in that they will view work, family and society in a very different way than in the past

- Unforgiving, in that customers will not expect more, but they will demand more and retaliate if and when this is not provided.

A slightly different and more focused view of the future has been spelled out by Hill and Lederer (2002) who, in their book *The Infinite Asset* map out a future of world brand domination. In a few years, they suggest, we will see brand-based business models become the dominant corporate life form. The implication of this is that the successful twenty-first century corporation will not be a collection of buildings, equipment and products, but a collection of brands and the activities that support them. In short, brands will exceed marketing. However, in making out this case, they argue that there is a need to forget about conventional notions of a brand simply being a name or a term that identifies a company or product. Instead, they suggest that there is the need to think about 'intersections' – points where two (or more) brands might meet. As an example of this, they talk about branding dream teams (e.g. Apple and Microsoft) and highlight the marketing potential of liaisons such as this.

The emergence of hypercompetition and the erosion of traditional competitive advantage

Since the early 1990s, a wide variety of markets has witnessed an increase in the nature and intensity of competition. Referring to this as the 'era of hypercompetition', D'Aveni (1999, p. 57) suggests that 'domestic upstarts and foreign entrants have entered markets with a ferocity that has toppled national oligopolies and well-established industry leaders'. As just one example of this, he points to the way in which Microsoft, Intel, Compaq, Dell and a host of clone manufacturers from Asia have battered the once invincible IBM. (Authors' Note: Subsequently, IBM has sold its laptop business to the Chinese manufacturer Lenovo.)

D'Aveni (1999) suggests that:

> *hypercompetition is characterized by constantly escalating rivalry in the form of rapid product innovation, shorter design and product life cycles, aggressive price and competence-based competition, and experimentation with new approaches to serving customer needs. Hypercompetitors engage in an unrelenting battle to re-position themselves and to outmanoeuvre their competitors. By being customer-oriented, by turning suppliers into alliance partners and by attacking competitors head on, global hypercompetitors destroy the existing norms and rules of national oligopolies.*

Given this, the implications for how firms operate are significant. If an organization is to win an advantage, it must seize the initiative. It 'must serve customers better than its competitors and must do things that competitors cannot or will not react to or even understand' (D'Aveni, 1999, pp. 57–8). To rely upon traditional thinking and defensive strategies as opposed to attempting to disrupt and unsettle the competition will almost inevitably lead to the firm's position being eroded. It is because of this that a number of commentators now believe that the idea that competitive advantages based upon the traditional ideas of quality, competencies, entry barriers and economies of scale is rapidly losing validity. Instead, success is far more likely to come from a reinvention of the rules of competition within the marketplace.

This move towards hypercompetitive markets appears to have been driven by four factors:

1. *The demand by customers throughout the world for higher quality at lower prices*. In the USA, for example, numerous low-cost foreign competitors have entered price-sensitive market sectors with a higher value for money offer than the well-entrenched players. Having established a foothold in the market, they have gone on to expand the market and capture significant share.

2. *The speed of technological change and the information revolution* that has led to the traditional 'owners' of markets being outsmarted by new players who move faster and in very different ways. As an example of this, First Direct rewrote some of the rules of banking by being the first in the UK to offer 24-hour telephone and then Internet banking.

3. *The emergence of aggressive and well-funded competitors* who take a long-term view and are willing to lose possibly substantial sums of

money in the early years in order to dominate a market with long-term strategic potential and significance.

4. *Changes in government policies that have led to the collapse of traditional entry barriers*. Examples of this include legislation on competition within the EU, the reduction of tariffs, and the trend worldwide towards privatization and deregulation that has allowed non-traditional competitors to break up long-standing oligopolies.

Competing (effectively) in hypercompetitive markets

Faced with an increasingly hypercompetitive market, the marketing strategist is faced with a number of options. However, underpinning all of these has to be the recognition that the traditional competencies are likely to become increasingly less relevant as the rules of the competitive game change. The astute competitor therefore plays upon this by disrupting the product market and/or the factor (input) market.

In order to disrupt the product market, there are several possibilities, the most obvious of which involve:

1. *Changing the bases of competition* by redefining the meaning of quality on the product and then offering it at a lower price, a strategy that was pursued by easyJet when it entered the airlines market.

2. *Modifying the boundaries of the market* by bundling and splitting industries. In the mobile phone market, for example, the astute competitors recognized that it is the air time that offers the greatest opportunities to make money, not the hardware. Because of this, the major players, particularly in the early years, focused upon building the customer base by offering cellular phones at very low prices. Equally, Microsoft and Intel split the personal computer business by capturing the value that at one stage was held by the PC manufacturers.

To disrupt the factor or input market, the strategist needs to focus upon one or more of three possibilities:

1. *Redefining the knowledge that is critical to success*. Dell, for example, by opting for direct selling through the Internet and telephone ordering, assembly to order and outsourced delivery, undercut many of the traditional players.

2. *Applying competencies developed outside the industry*. This approach is illustrated by First Direct's use of IT and telephone selling expertise developed in other sectors.

3. *Altering the sums of money needed to survive within a particular sector*. The so-called 'category killers', such as Toys 'R' Us, Wal-Mart and Car Supermarket, are all examples of this sort of approach.

Given the nature of these comments, it is apparent that, within hyper-competitive markets, the rules of competition change dramatically. In order to survive and prosper, firms need to behave in a very different way, characterized by far more rapid innovation, aggressive price- and competence-based competition, new approaches to meeting customers' needs, and very different mindsets.

Market domination and third-wave companies

For many organizations faced with or facing massively changed environments and ever greater customer expectations, the nature of the strategic marketing planning challenges with which they need to come to terms are radically different from those of the past. The implications of this, according to Vollman (1996, p. 5), are that organizations generally, but manufacturing firms in particular, need to recognize the need to dominate their markets. It is the failure to do this, he argues, which will almost inevitably lead to the decline and probable death of the organization. In making this comment, he believes that the nature and scope of change over the past few years has led to such a change in the competitive environment that what contributed towards the profile of a winning organization in the past does not necessarily apply today.

These 'third-wave' companies differ from their predecessors in a variety of ways although, in nearly every instance, he suggests they reached their current position not by a series of evolutionary moves, but by a transformative leap which gave them a profile of dominance. However, it needs to be recognized that domination is not necessarily about *size* (General Motors, for example, despite being the biggest automotive company, for many years failed to dominate the industry. Instead, it was the initially smaller organizations such as Toyota that set the pace of competition), *monopolistic competition* or *profitability*. Rather it is the degree of influence they exert within their market sector(s).

The alternative to market domination, Vollman argues, is organizational death, with this happening quickly or, more frequently, very slowly (see 1996: ch. 1, Figure 1.5 and the supporting discussion). The signs of organizational decay are often identifiable long before crises become apparent. Included within these are a loss of market share, possession of the wrong set of competencies, slow(er) or slowing growth patterns, a loss of employee morale, poor product and process development, and the failure to recognize competitors' true capabilities (see Figure 5.8).

Faced with problems such as these, organizations typically respond in one of a number of ways, including:

- Improvement programmes such as time-based competition, quality and flexibility. However, in many markets these sorts of initiatives no longer provide the basis for competitive advantage, but are instead 'commodities of process'. In other words, without them you will not survive, but with them you are simply a player in the market.

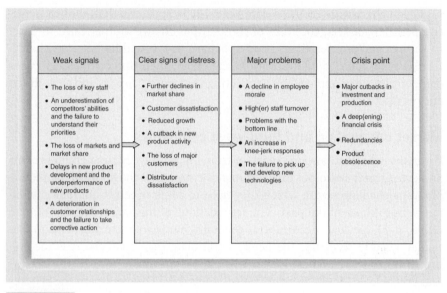

Weak signals	Clear signs of distress	Major problems	Crisis point
• The loss of key staff • An underestimation of competitors' abilities and the failure to understand their priorities • The loss of markets and market share • Delays in new product development and the underperformance of new products • A deterioration in customer relationships and the failure to take corrective action	• Further declines in market share • Customer dissatisfaction • Reduced growth • A cutback in new product activity • The loss of major customers • Distributor dissatisfaction	• A decline in employee morale • High(er) staff turnover • Problems with the bottom line • An increase in knee-jerk responses • The failure to pick up and develop new technologies	• Major cutbacks in investment and production • A deep(ening) financial crisis • Redundancies • Product obsolescence

FIGURE 5.8 *The signs of impending doom*

- Financial restructuring and downsizing which, whilst apparently helpful in the short-term, often do little to change the organizational culture.

- Management changes, which are characterized by a reshuffling of job titles, responsibilities and structures, rather than any real change in focus and direction.

By contrast, dominant organizations typically exhibit a very different set of characteristics and responses, including:

- Paradigm shifts that reflect a recognition that the old set of operating assumptions is no longer valid.

- Proactive rather than reactive changes, with these being made possible because of:
  High levels of responsiveness and flexibility
  A high degree of anticipation and forecasting of how the market is likely to develop
  The creation of change in the marketplace as the result of a series of marketing initiatives.
- Enterprise transformation that, because of a fundamental recognition on the part of management of the significance of environmental change and the consequent inadequacy of current structures and systems, leads to radically different ways of doing business.

The combined effect of these sorts of initiatives is that, in the successful organizations (Vollman, 1996, p. 7):

> the very shape and structure of the enterprise have had to change, their competencies and capabilities have changed, their resources have changed, their outputs have changed, their attitude to customer service has changed and their fundamental raison d'être has changed.
>
> In the unsuccessful, their missions have reverted back to 'doing core business', crisis management has replaced strategy and 'passengers' (such as cost) replace 'drivers' (such as customer satisfaction). They certainly are not the companies they once were – they have indeed been transformed. But no one was steering the change towards dominance.

5.9 APPROACHES TO ENVIRONMENTAL ANALYSIS AND SCANNING

Against the background of our discussion so far, it should be clear that environmental analysis and forecasting are capable of making a major contribution to the formulation of strategy. Indeed, it has been argued by a number of strategists that environmental analysis and forecasting is the true starting point of any effective planning system, since strategy is based not only on a detailed understanding of the firm's capacity, but also on a full knowledge and appreciation of environmental forces and changes that are likely to have an impact on the firm. At its most extreme, the failure to do this is highlighted by Theodore Levitt's ideas of 'Marketing Myopia', which he discussed in his now classic *Harvard Business Review* article (1960, pp. 45–56).

In this article Levitt argued that declining or defunct industries generally reached this position because of a product rather than a marketing orientation. In other words, they focused too firmly on products rather than the environment in which they operated. As a consequence, these companies were often taken by surprise by environmental change, found it difficult to respond and, in many cases, either lost significant market shares or were forced into liquidation.

A system of environmental analysis and forecasting consists of two elements: the first of these is concerned with the *generation* of an up-to-date database of information, while the second involves the *dissemination* of this information to decision-makers and influencers. The effectiveness of such a system, and in particular of this second part, is in practice likely to be influenced by a variety of factors, including:

- The technical skills of those involved in the process of analysis and forecasting

- The nature of the managerial environment that exists within the company.

The significance of this second point is, in many companies, all too often ignored, but highlights the importance of a planning culture that is both endorsed and promoted by top management. In addition, the managerial environment affects the process in the sense that, in large companies at least, those who are involved in the mechanics of analysis and forecasting are rarely the decision-makers themselves. Instead, they are generally in an advisory role. This role can lead to the emergence of an important political process within the system, whereby the analyst presents information in such a way that the decision-maker's perception of the environment and, in turn, the options open to the company, are distorted in a particular way. By the same token, the decision-maker will often place a particular interpretation on the information presented by the analyst, depending on his or her perception of the analyst's track record. In commenting on this political process, Brownlie (1987, p. 99) suggests that:

> students of history will recognize that many a bloody political intrigue was spawned by the jealously guarded, and often misused, privilege of proximity to the seat of power which was conferred on privy counsellors and advisors. Thus in addition to the technical skills demanded of environmental analysts and forecasters, astute political skills could be said to be the hallmark of an effective operator.

It should therefore be recognized that the effectiveness of a planning system is not determined solely by its methodology, but that it is also affected by several other factors, including the willingness and ability of a management to recognize and subsequently respond to the indicators of coming environmental change.

Taken together, these comments argue the case for what we can refer to as *formal environmental scanning*, a process that covers the full spectrum of activities firms use in order to understand environmental changes and their implications. The essential element of formal environmental scanning is that it should be seen as an activity that becomes an *integral* part of the ongoing process by which companies develop, implement, control and review strategies and plans at both the corporate and the business unit levels.

In practice, the precise role of an environmental scanning process is influenced by a variety of factors, the most significant of which is typically that of management expectations. This, in turn, is often a function of the size of the organization and managerial perceptions of the complexity of its environment. Thus, in the case of many small firms, the focus is likely to be on the general trends that are likely to influence short- and medium-term levels of performance. In large firms, however, and in particular the multinationals, the focus tends to be far broader, with a greater emphasis being placed upon longer-term and more fundamental issues, including possible changes in the political, economic, social and technological variables that provided the focus for the first part of this chapter.

Having said this, the complexity of the scanning process varies greatly from one company to another and is typically determined by two factors:

1. Perceptions within the company of the degree of environmental uncertainty (most typically this is a function of the rate of environmental change)

2. Perceptions of the degree of environmental complexity (this is generally influenced by the range of activities and markets in which the firm is currently and prospectively involved).

The significance of this second factor needs to be seen in terms of the implications for the structure of the scanning process that the firm then develops. Recognizing the dangers of overload within a system, there is a need for those involved in scanning to organize the process in such a way that the environment can be reduced to something manageable, while at the same time ensuring that extraneous factors are not ignored. What this means in practice is that a process of filtration generally operates in which the full breadth of environmental stimuli is reduced to something more manageable.

The question of who should decide on these elements has been referred to by Ansoff (1984), who has argued that it is the *user* of the information who should exert the major influence. In practice, however, it is often the scanner who determines the choice of approach.

Returning for a moment to the filtration process through which a structure is imposed upon the full breadth and complexity of the environment, Brownlie (1987, pp. 110–12) identifies three levels:

1. *The surveillance filter*, which provides a broad and generally unstructured picture of the business environment. However, although this picture is broad it will, by virtue of the perceptions of those involved, 'be selective and partial'.

2. *The mentality filter*, which emerges as the result of past successes and failures, and in turn leads to the idea of *bounded rationality* (by which a manager's ability to make optimal decisions is constrained by factors such as complexity and uncertainty), allowing those involved to cope with the volume and complexity of the information being generated. However, while this mentality filter is undoubtedly useful in helping to provide a structure, bounded rationality can create problems in that environmental signals that are extreme in nature and outside the manager's historical experience are likely to be perceived as being of little significance and subsequently screened out. There is a need, therefore, to balance the benefits of the mentality filter with a willingness to assess and possibly incorporate novel and perhaps extreme signals.

3. *The power filter*, which is essentially an attitude of mind on the part of top management and reflects a willingness to incorporate material in the strategic decision-making process that falls outside the bounds of previous practice and preconceived notions. Recognition by the scanner of the existence of an attitude such as this is then likely to be reflected in the scanner's own willingness to build into the process a breadth of perspective rather than a straightforward identification and assessment of largely predictable environmental changes.

Against the background of comments such as these it is possible to identify the features that are most likely to lead to an effective environmental scanning system. These include:

- Top management involvement and commitment

- A detailed understanding of the dimensions and parameters of the scanning model that it is intended should operate

- An established strategic planning culture.

In addition, attention needs to be paid to the *boundaries of the firm's environment* and hence to those areas that are deemed to be either relevant or irrelevant, and to the *time horizon* that is felt to be meaningful. In the case of the chemicals and pharmaceuticals industries, for example, the planning time horizon – and hence the scanning period – may easily be in excess of 30 years, while in the fashion clothing industry it may be a year or less.

Recognition of these sorts of issues has led Diffenbach (1983) to identify the specific difficulties of environmental analysis that act as deterrents to the development and implementation of an effective scanning system:

1. The interpretation of results and the assessment of their specific impact upon the organization is rarely clear-cut

2. The output of environmental analysis may be too inaccurate, general or uncertain to be taken seriously

3. A preoccupation with the short-term pre-empts attention being paid to longer-term environmental issues

4. Long-term environmental analyses are often treated sceptically

5. In diversified businesses the amount of analysis needed is likely to be both considerable and complex, particularly when interrelationships are considered

6. Perceptions and interpretations of scenarios identified may differ significantly between one manager and another.

However, for many marketing managers, one of the biggest and most enduring problems is that of understanding their markets. Without this understanding, they lose touch with the market, are taken by surprise by shifts in customers' expectations, are slow to react to competitors, and fail to make full use of their distribution channels. The net effect of this is that they then fail to anticipate the nature and direction of changes within the market, constantly miss opportunities and, when they do respond, typically behave slowly and counter-productively. By contrast, managers within the truly market-driven organization are notable for the way in which they sense how their markets are likely to change, the nature of the opportunities that this is likely to create and how these opportunities can then best be exploited.

In discussing the difference between the two types of organization and what determines whether an organization is market driven, Day (1996a, p. 12) highlights the importance of market learning:

> *Market learning involves much more than simply taking in information. The learning process must give managers the ability to ask the right questions at the right time, absorb the answers into their mental model of how the market behaves, share the new understanding with others in the management team and act decisively. Effective learning about markets is a continuous process that pervades all decisions. It cannot be spasmodic.*

This effective learning process, which is illustrated in Figure 5.9, consists of several distinct stages:

- *Open-minded enquiry* based on the belief that decisions need to be based on a detailed and broad understanding of the market, and that conventional wisdoms and preconceived notions and beliefs are dangerous

- *Widespread information distribution* to ensure that managers across the organization develop a greater market understanding

- *Mutually informed mental models*, which are used in the interpretation of information and ensure that issues that are deemed to be strategically important are examined

- *An accessible organizational memory* to ensure that the organization keeps track of what has been learned so the information and knowledge can continue to be used.

The process is then reinforced by a deliberate reflection on the outcomes of the strategies and tactics that have been developed and, by means of integrated databases, the augmentation of the organizational memory.

The dangers of misjudging the market

The potentially significant implications of misjudging a market have been highlighted by Vodafone's experiences in Japan. Part of the rationale for

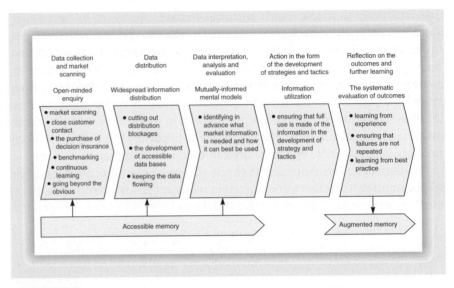

Data collection and market scanning	Data distribution	Data interpretation, analysis and evaluation	Action in the form of the development of strategies and tactics	Reflection on the outcomes and further learning
Open-minded enquiry	Widespread information distribution	Mutually-informed mental models	Information utilization	The systematic evaluation of outcomes
• market scanning • close customer contact • the purchase of decision insurance • benchmarking • continuous learning • going beyond the obvious	• cutting out distribution blockages • the development of accessible data bases • keeping the data flowing	• identifying in advance what market information is needed and how it can best be used	• ensuring that full use is made of the information in the development of strategy and tactics	• learning from experience • ensuring that failures are not repeated • learning from best practice

Accessible memory	Augmented memory

FIGURE 5.9   *The organizational learning process (adapted from Day, 1996a)*

entering the market in 2001 was that the lessons that the company learnt in the Japanese market would give it a technological and marketing advantage over its domestic and European competitors. In the event, the company had problems rolling out to the rest of the organization some of the technologies perfected in Japan, whilst in Japan itself the company failed to produce the 'must-have' handset for Japanese consumers. Instead, it made what is now seen to be one of its biggest errors of judgement – the introduction of a range of inappropriate 3G Nokia handsets from the European market. The customers' rejection of these had the effect of delaying further the company's roll-out of 3G technology.

Marketing techniques developed in Europe proved also to be flawed when exposed to the nature of the Japanese market and, in particular, customers' expectations of service level. The company found itself lagging behind its principal competitors, NTT DoCoMo and KDDI, and was then forced to invest £1.3 billion in an attempt to match the levels of service they were delivering.

Faced with this, the company announced in 2006 its withdrawal from the market.

5.10   SUMMARY

Marketing strategy is concerned with matching the capabilities of the organization with the demands of the environment. There is therefore a need for the strategist to monitor the environment on an ongoing basis so that opportunities and threats facing the organization are identified and subsequently reflected in strategy.

In analysing the environment a stepwise approach is needed. This begins with an initial audit of general environmental influences, followed by a series of increasingly tightly-focused stages designed to provide the strategist with a clear understanding of the organization's strategic position.

Although a variety of approaches can be used for analysing the environment, arguably the most useful is the PEST framework. This involves the strategist focusing in turn upon the Political/legal, Economic, Social/cultural and Technological elements of the environment. Each of these elements has been discussed in detail.

The environmental conditions faced by an organization are capable of varying greatly in their complexity, and need to be reflected both in the ways in which environmental analysis is conducted and in the ways in which strategy is subsequently developed. The consequences of failing to take account of a changing environment have, as discussed, been illustrated by a wide variety of organizational experiences, including those of the Swiss watch industry in the 1970s.

It is widely recognized that the pace of environmental change is increasing and that the need for organizations to develop a structured approach to environmental analysis, with the results then being fed into the strategic marketing planning process, is greater than ever. Despite this, the evidence suggests that in many organizations environmental scanning systems are only poorly developed. If this is to change, top management commitment both to the development of a scanning system and to the incorporation of the results into the planning process is essential.

CHAPTER 6

Approaches to Customer Analysis

6.1 LEARNING OBJECTIVES

When you have read this chapter you should be able to understand:

(a) the factors that influence consumer behaviour;

(b) the structure of the consumer buying decision process;

(c) the nature of organizational buying;

(d) how an understanding of buying processes can be used in the development of marketing strategy;

(e) why relationship marketing is becoming an increasingly important strategic marketing tool and how a relationship marketing programme can be developed.

6.2 INTRODUCTION

The great illusion of the marketplace is a simple one: that it is supply-based; that those who produce and those who create sustain the market; that if you build it, they come. The great reality of the marketplace is simpler still: nobody who produces is in control. Nobody who sells is in control. If you build it, they will come only if they want to, and if they decide to leave, there is nothing – not cutting your prices, not increasing your supply, not getting on your knees and begging for sales (or offering loyalty cards) – that can stop them. When the world gets tired of cappuccino machines, they are

> *gone. The great reality of the marketplace is that it is demand-based.*
> *Customers own it lock, stock and barrel.*
>
> (Taylor and Watts, 1998)

It has long been recognized that marketing planning is ultimately driven by the marketing planner's perception of how and why customers behave as they do, and how they are likely to respond to the various elements of the marketing mix.

In the majority of markets, however, buyers differ enormously in terms of their buying dynamics. The task faced by the marketing planner in coming to terms with these differences is consequently complex. In consumer markets, for example, not only do buyers typically differ in terms of their age, income, educational levels and geographical location, but more fundamentally in terms of their personality, their lifestyles and their expectations. In the case of organizational and industrial markets, differences are often exhibited in the goals being pursued, the criteria employed by those involved in the buying process, the formality of purchasing policies, and the constraints that exist in the form of delivery dates and expected performance levels.

Despite these complexities, it is essential that the marketing planner understands in detail the dynamics of the buying process, since the costs and competitive implications of failing to do so are likely to be significant. In the case of new product development, for example, it is generally recognized that some 80 per cent of all new products launched fail, a statistic that owes much to a lack of understanding of customers' expectations. It is for these sorts of reasons that a considerable amount of research has been conducted in the post-war period in order to provide us with a greater understanding of buying patterns, and to enable us to predict more readily *how* buyers will behave in any given situation. Within this chapter we therefore focus upon some of the factors that influence buying behaviour and how subsequently they influence marketing strategy. It does need to be emphasized, however, that a series of interrelationships exist between this material and the areas covered in Chapter 9, in which we examine approaches to segmentation, targeting and positioning. The reader might therefore find it useful at this stage to turn briefly to Chapter 9 to identify the nature of these interrelationships before continuing.

6.3 COMING TO TERMS WITH BUYER BEHAVIOUR

Irrespective of whether the marketing planner is operating in a consumer, industrial or organizational market, there are eight questions which underpin any understanding of buyer behaviour:

1. Who is in the market and what is the extent of their power with regard to the organization?

2. What do they buy?

3. Why do they buy?

4. Who is involved in the buying?

5. How do they buy?

6. When do they buy?

7. Where do they buy?

8. What are the customers' 'hot' and 'cold' spots? ('Hot' spots are those elements of the marketing offer that the customer sees as being particularly important and reassuring – and on which the organization delivers. 'Cold' spots are those elements that alienate the customer. An example of this might be poor or inconsistent service.)

It is the answers to these questions which should provide the marketing planner with an understanding of the ways in which buyers are most likely to respond to marketing stimuli. It then follows from this that the organization that makes the best use of the information should be in a position to gain a competitive advantage. For this reason, a considerable amount of time, effort and money has been spent over the past few decades in attempting to provide the marketing planner with a series of answers.

The starting point for much of this work has been a straightforward stimulus–response model of the sort illustrated in Figure 6.1. Here, stimuli

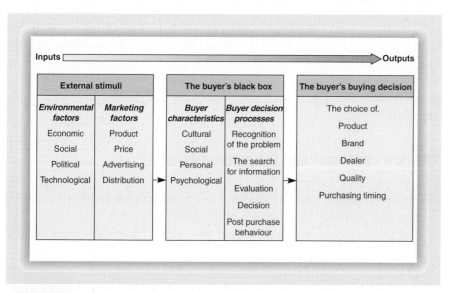

FIGURE 6.1 *A stimulus–response model of buyer behaviour*

in the form both of the external environment and the elements of the marketing mix enter the buyer's 'black box' and interact with the buyer's characteristics and decision processes to produce a series of outputs in the form of purchase decisions. Included within these is the question of whether to buy and, if so, which product and brand, which dealer, when, and in what quantities. The task faced by the marketing planner therefore involves understanding how this black box operates. To do this, we need to consider the two principal components of the box: first, the factors that the individual brings to the buying situation; secondly, the decision processes that are used. We will therefore begin by focusing upon these background factors – cultural, social, personal and psychological – as a prelude to examining the detail of the decision process itself.

However, before doing this, we need to highlight just one of the major changes of the past few years, that of the emergence of what might loosely be termed 'the new consumer'. The new consumer is typically far more demanding and far more discriminating than consumers of the past, as well as being far less brand loyal and much more willing to complain. In many ways, the emergence of this new type of consumer represents one of the biggest challenges for marketers, since their expectations of organizations and their relationships that they demand are very different from anything previously experienced. The characteristics and marketing implications of the new consumer are examined in some detail at a later stage in the chapter (see pages 217–21), although Illustration 6.1 provides the reader with an overview of some of their key features.

Taking just one of the characteristics listed in Illustration 6.1 – the changed and changing roles of men and women – its significance can perhaps be appreciated by the fact that more than 40 per cent of new cars that are bought privately are now bought by women; this compares with less than 6 per cent in 1970. From the viewpoint of the car manufacturers, the implications have been enormous and have had to be reflected not just in terms of the design of cars, but also the nature of the market research that is conducted, the advertising and promotion that is carried out, and the approach to selling.

The new consumer and the youth market

The differences that exist between the new consumer and the old are even more apparent – and more extreme – in the case of young(er) consumers (for our purposes here, we see these as being aged between 4 and 19), in that this segment, when compared with other customer groups, is also typically:

- Far more media literate

- Infinitely more advertising literate

Illustration 6.1   The emergence of the new consumer

In many ways, the most significant and far-reaching legacies for marketing of the economic and social changes and turbulence of the late 1980s and early 1990s are reflected in what we might loosely refer to as the emergence of the 'new' consumer and the 'new' competitor (the dimensions of the new competitor are discussed in Chapter 7). Although neither is necessarily new in any absolute sense, they differ in a series of ways from traditional consumers and competitors in that their expectations, values and patterns of behaviour are all very different from that with which marketing planners traditionally had to come to terms. The consequences of this are manifested in several ways but, in the case of the new consumer, by the way in which the degree of understanding of customers' motivations must be far greater and the marketing effort tailored more firmly and clearly to the patterns of specific need. We can therefore see the new consumer as being characterized by:

- The development of new value systems
- A greater emphasis upon value for money
- Higher levels of price awareness and price sensitivity
- An increased demand for and a willingness to accept more and exciting new products
- Less technophobia
- Lower levels of brand and supplier loyalty, and the development of what might be referred to as customer and brand promiscuity
- A greater willingness to experiment with new products, ideas and delivery systems
- A generally far more questioning and sceptical attitude towards government, big business and brands
- Higher levels of environmental awareness
- Fundamental changes in family structures and relationships
- The changed and changing roles of men and women.

In essence, therefore, one can see the new consumer to be very different from consumers of the past in that they are typically:

1. Far more demanding
2. Far more discriminating
3. Much less brand loyal
4. Much more willing to complain than customers in the past.

These themes are explored in greater detail in the Appendix to this chapter.

- Much more brand literate, brand aware, brand sensitive and brand discriminating
- Far more technologically literate.

To a large extent, these higher levels of media, advertising, brand and technological literacy can be seen to be the direct result of having been exposed to a far greater number and a much larger variety of media than any previous generation. Included within this are 24-hour television, satellite broadcasting, and a huge upsurge in the numbers of newspapers and far more finely-targeted magazines. The advertising literacy then follows directly from this in that the sheer number of advertisements to which they have been exposed is higher than ever before. Brand literacy emerges from brands having been an integral part of lifestyles for as long as this generation has been alive, something that was not always the case with older consumers. Equally, the technological literacy follows from their exposure to technologies such as the Internet and information technology from a very early age. The combined effect of this is the emergence of a very different type of young buyer who has very different and often much more unpredictable patterns of buying, and who is typically very aware of the subtleties of brand differences.

In many ways, the emergence of this new type of consumer, be it in the teen market or Generation Y, represents one of the biggest challenges for marketers, since their expectations of organizations and the nature of the relationships that they demand are very different from anything previously experienced. Recognizing this, if marketers fail to come to terms with this development, the implications for organizational performance and marketing planning are significant, something that is discussed at a later stage in the chapter (refer to pages 217–21).

6.4   FACTORS INFLUENCING CONSUMER BEHAVIOUR

From the viewpoint of the marketing planner, the mix of cultural, social, personal and psychological factors that influence behaviour (illustrated in Figure 6.2) is largely non-controllable. Because of the influence they exert upon patterns of buying, it is essential that as much effort as possible is put into understanding *how they interact* and, ultimately, *how they influence* purchase behaviour. In doing this, it is important not to lose sight of the differences that exist between customers and consumers, and the implications of these differences for strategy. The term 'consumer' is typically taken to mean the final user, who is not necessarily the customer (the buyer). In the case of foodstuffs such as breakfast cereals, for example, the buyer (generally still the housewife) acts on behalf of her family. For the marketing mix to be effective, it is quite obviously essential that the strategist therefore understands not just what the *customer* wants (e.g. value for money), but also what the *consumer* wants (e.g. taste, free gifts, image).

The significance of culture

The most fundamental of the four influencing forces, and hence the logical starting point for any analysis of behaviour, is the buyer's set of *cultural*

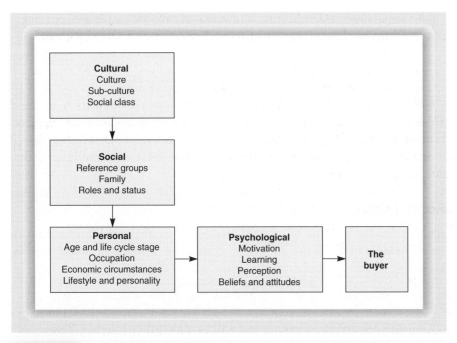

FIGURE 6.2 *Factors influencing consumer behaviour*

factors. These include culture, sub-culture and social class. Of these, it is the culture of the society itself that typically proves to be the most fundamental and enduring influence on behaviour, since human behaviour is very largely the result of our socialization, initially within the family and then, increasingly, within a series of other institutions such as schools, friendship groups, clubs, and so on. It is from this that we learn our set(s) of values, perceptions, preferences and behaviour patterns. Schiffman and Kanuk (1983, pp. 404–20), for example, suggest that, in the Western world at least, these include achievement, success, efficiency, progress, material comfort, practicality, individualism, freedom, humanitarianism, youthfulness and practicality. It is these which, to a very large extent, determine and drive our patterns of behaviour.

This broad set of values is then influenced in turn by the sub-cultures in which we develop. These include nationality groups, religious groups, racial groups and geographical areas, all of which exhibit degrees of difference in ethnic taste, cultural preferences, taboos, attitudes and lifestyle.

The influence of sub-cultures is subsequently affected by a third set of variables: that of *social stratification* and, in particular, *social class* and reflects the view that:

1. People within a particular social class are more similar than those from different social classes

2. Social class is determined by a series of variables, such as occupation, income, education and values, rather than by a single variable

3. Individuals can move from one social class to another.

Although research in recent years has led to a modification of these ideas as the degree of overall social mobility has increased, the most important single implication of social class is the still valid assumption that it exerts a significant degree of influence in areas such as clothing, cars, leisure pursuits and media preferences.

Social factors

Against this background of cultural forces, the strategist needs then to turn to an examination of the influence exerted by a series of social factors, including reference groups, family, social role and status.

Reference groups can be divided into four types:

1. *Primary membership groups*, which are generally informal and to which individuals belong and within which they interact. These include family, neighbours, colleagues and friends.

2. *Secondary membership groups*, which tend to be more formal than primary groups and within which less interaction typically takes place. Included within these are trade unions, religious groups and professional societies.

3. *Aspirational groups*, to which an individual would like to belong.

4. *Dissociative groups*, whose values and behaviour the individual rejects.

The influence exerted by reference groups tends to vary considerably from one product and brand to another, as well as at different stages of the individual's life stage. Among the products and brands that typically have been found to be influenced most directly by reference group behaviour are cars, drinks, clothing and cigarettes. The influence of reference groups does, however, change over the course of the product life cycle. In the introductory stage, for example, the question of *whether* to buy is heavily influenced by others, although the influence upon the choice of brand may not necessarily be particularly significant. In the growth stage, the group influences both product and brand choice, while in maturity it is the brand but not the product that is subject to this influence. The influence of reference groups in the decline stage is almost invariably weak in terms of both the product and brand choice.

The implications of these findings are significant and provide the marketing planner with a series of guidelines, the most important of which centres around the need to identify the *opinion leaders* for each reference group. Our understanding of opinion leadership has developed considerably over the past few years, and whereas at one time it was believed that opinion leadership was limited primarily to prominent figures within society, this is no longer seen to be the case. Rather, it is recognized that an individual may well be an opinion leader in certain circumstances, but an opinion follower in others. Quite obviously, this makes the task of identifying opinion leaders more difficult and gives emphasis to the need to understand not just the demographic but particularly the psychographic characteristics of the group that the strategist is attempting to influence.

For many products, however, it is the family that exerts the greatest single influence on behaviour, even though, as we suggest elsewhere in this chapter, the size and structure of the family unit has changed considerably over the past 20 years. This includes both the *family of orientation* (parents, brothers and sisters) and the *family of procreation* (spouse and children). The significance of the family as a determinant of buying behaviour has long been recognized, and for this reason it has been the subject of a considerable amount of research in order to identify the roles and relative influence exerted by different family members. Although it is not our intention to examine this area in detail, there are several general conclusions that have emerged from this research:

- The involvement of both partners within a relationship upon purchase decisions varies greatly from one product category to another, with women still playing the principal role in the purchasing of food and clothing. Although this has changed somewhat over the past few years as the proportion of working women has increased and divorce rates have escalated, the Institute of Grocery Distribution has estimated that, in the UK, women still account for some 80 per cent of food purchases.

- Joint husband and wife (or partner) decision-making tends to be a characteristic of more expensive product choices, where the opportunity cost of a 'wrong' decision is greater.

At a more general level, however, research in the USA has identified three patterns of decision-making within the family and the sorts of product category with which each is typically associated. These are:

1. Husband-dominant – life insurance, cars and consumer electronics

2. Wife-dominant – washing machines, carpets, kitchenware and non-living-room furniture

3. Equal – living-room furniture, holidays, housing, furnishings and entertainment.

Although this research is useful in that it distinguishes between the different decision-making patterns, the results need to be treated with a degree of caution, if only because of the ways in which roles within the family have changed (and indeed still are changing) significantly.

The final social factor that typically influences purchase behaviour consists of the individual's actual and perceived *roles* and *statuses*, both within society in general and within groups in particular. The significance of status symbols and the messages they communicate has long been recognized. The obvious implication, however, for the marketing strategist is to position products and brands in such a way that they reinforce the messages suited to particular individuals and groups.

Personal influences on behaviour

The third major category of influences upon behaviour is made up of the buyer's set of *personal characteristics*, including age and life-cycle stage, occupation, economic circumstances, lifestyle and personality. The majority of these factors have been used extensively by marketing strategists in segmenting markets; this is discussed further on pages 350–2 and 357–65.

Psychological influences

The fourth and final set of influences upon behaviour consists of the four principal *psychological factors* – motivation, perception, learning, and beliefs and attitudes. The first of these, motivation, is in many ways both the most important to understand and the most complex to analyse. The starting point involves recognizing the differences between *biogenic* needs, which are physiological (hunger, thirst and discomfort), and psychogenic needs, which are essentially psychological states of tension (these include the need for esteem and the desire for recognition or belonging). It is these needs which, when they become sufficiently intense, create a motivation to act in such a way that the tension of the need is reduced. The search to understand the detail of this process has led to a considerable amount of research over the past 100 years and, in turn, to a variety of theories of human motivation. The best known of these are the theories of Marshall, Freud, Veblen, Herzberg, Vroom and Maslow.

The first of these, the Marshallian model, is in many ways the most straightforward and is based on the idea that a person's behaviour is inherently rational and motivated by economic factors. The economic individual therefore attempts to maximize total satisfaction by buying goods and services from which the marginal utility is, in theory at least, equivalent to the marginal utility of the alternatives. Although such an overtly rational view of behaviour has long been criticized as being too partial and inadequate an explanation, it has been argued that the Marshallian model contributes the following to our understanding of buyer behaviour:

1. It is axiomatic that every buyer acts in the light of his own best interest. The question is whether an economist would describe these actions as 'rational'.

2. The model is normative in the sense that it provides a logical basis for purchase decisions, (i.e. how one *should* decide rather than how one *actually* decides).

3. The model suggests a number of useful behavioural hypotheses, e.g. the lower the price, the greater the sales; the lower the price of substitute products, the lower the sales of this product; the lower the price of complementary products, the higher the sales of this product; the higher the real income, the higher the sales of this product, provided that it is not an 'inferior' good; the higher the promotional expenditure, the higher the sales.

Freud's work, by contrast, suggests that the psychological factors that influence behaviour are for the most part unconscious and that, as a consequence, we can only rarely understand our true motivations. Equally, in the process of growing up and conforming to the rules of society, we repress a series of urges. The obvious implication of this for marketing is that a consumer's *stated* motive for buying a particular brand or product may well be very different from the more fundamental *underlying* motive. Thus, in the case of a fast car, the stated motive might be the ability to get from A to B quickly. The underlying motive, however, might well be the desire for status and to be noticed. Similarly, with an expensive watch, the stated motive might be the product's reliability while the real – and unconscious – motive might again be status and the desire to impress others.

The best-known exponent of Freudian theory in marketing was Ernest Dichter who, in the 1950s, developed a series of techniques, under the general heading of *motivational research*, designed to uncover consumers' deepest motives. Motivational research was subjected to a considerable amount of criticism on the grounds that buyers were subsequently being manipulated and persuaded to act against their own interests. Two of the most vociferous opponents of motivational research proved to be Galbraith and Packard. Galbraith (1958), for example, levelled a series of criticisms against the development of the consumer society, arguing that consumers were being persuaded to act against their true interests. Packard's criticisms, in his book *The Hidden Persuaders* (1957), were aimed even more specifically at techniques of motivational research and raised the spectre of the wholesale manipulation of society by marketing people for their own ends. Largely because of the subsequent publicity, motivational research became a less acceptable research technique and this, coupled with a whole series of problems experienced in its use, led to its gradual decline.

The Freudian view that a consumer's stated motives may well be very different from the true motives is echoed in Veblen's (1899) socio-psychological interpretations of behaviour. Many purchases, he argued, are motivated not by need but by a desire for prestige and social standing. Although Veblen's views, and in particular his emphasis upon conspicuous consumption, have subsequently been modified by research findings, his contribution to our understanding of buyer behaviour is significant, not least because it stresses the importance of social relationships as an influence upon choice.

The fourth major theory of motivation, one which has received considerable attention from marketing analysts over the past 30 years, was developed by Herzberg. Labelled the 'two-factor theory' of motivation, it distinguishes between *satisfiers* (factors that create satisfaction) and *dissatisfiers* (factors that create dissatisfaction). In the case of a car, for example, the absence of a warranty would be a dissatisfier. The existence of a warranty, however, is not a satisfier since it is not one of the principal reasons for buying the product. These are more likely to be the car's looks, its performance and the status that the buyer feels the product confers upon the driver.

There are several implications of this theory for marketing, of which two are particularly significant. First, the seller needs to be fully aware of the dissatisfiers which, while they will not by themselves sell the product, can easily 'unsell' it. The second implication, which follows logically from this, is that the strategist needs to understand in detail the various satisfiers and then concentrate not just upon supplying them, but also giving them full emphasis in the marketing programme.

The fifth and final principal theory of motivation was put forward by Maslow, who suggested that behaviour can be explained in terms of a hierarchy of needs starting with an individual's *physiological needs* (hunger and thirst) and then moving successively through *safety needs* (protection and security), *social needs* (a sense of love and belonging), *esteem needs* (self-esteem, status and recognition by others), and culminating in *self-actualization needs* (the individual's self-development and self-realization).

The model suggests that a person begins by concentrating upon satisfying the most important and most basic physiological needs before moving on to the higher levels of need. Thus, as each level is satisfied, the next level is likely to become the focus of attention.

Although, from the viewpoint of the marketing strategist, Maslow's theory is arguably of less direct value than that of, say, Herzberg, it is of value in that it provides yet another insight into the ways in which products fit into the goals and lives of consumers.

Issues of perception

Against the background of an understanding of the factors influencing motivation, the marketing strategist needs then to consider the influence of *perception*, since it is the way in which motivated individuals perceive a given situation that determines precisely how they will behave. It has long been understood that, because of the three elements of the perceptual process: selective attention, selective distortion and selective retention, individuals can perceive the same object in very different ways. It is the failure to recognize and take account of this that often leads to a confusion of, for example, advertising messages. Research in this area has provided a series of insights into the perceptual process, and subsequently to a series of guidelines for marketers. In the case of *selective attention*, for example, simply because of the enormous number of stimuli that we are exposed to each day (more than 2200 advertisements alone), a substantial number are either ignored or given only cursory attention. If a marketing message is to succeed it therefore has to fight against this screening process. This can be done in one of several ways, including:

1. The use of black and white advertisements when others are in colour, or vice versa.

2. The use of shock messages – in 1990, for example, the RSPCA drew attention to the number of stray dogs being destroyed each year by showing a mountain of bodies. Equally, Benetton has over the years run a series of highly controversial advertisements, while French Connection UK coveted controversy with the ambiguity of the FCUK logo.

3. The sheer size of the advertisement.

4. Substantial money-off offers.

5. The unexpected – a glue manufacturer used his product to stick a car to a hoarding in London some 15 feet above the pavement.

However, even when a message does reach the consumer, there is no guarantee that it will be interpreted in the way that was intended. Each person modifies information in such a way that it fits neatly into that person's existing mindset. This process of *selective distortion* means that messages that confirm preconceived notions are far more likely to be accepted than those that challenge these notions. Although a mindset can be changed, this is typically both costly and time-consuming. However, one example of where this has been done with considerable success is with Japanese products. The image and reputation of the majority of Japanese products in the 1960s was generally poor, a factor that had implications for, among other things, distribution and pricing. Throughout the 1970s, 1980s and 1990s, however, the Japanese concentrated on quality and product innovation to the point at which even the most die-hard and conservative European or American was forced to admit that, in many markets, it is now the Japanese who set the pace.

A similar example is that of the car manufacturer, Skoda. Long seen as rugged, cheap and utilitarian, Skoda's takeover by Volkswagen in the 1990s and a heavy investment in new product development, manufacturing and marketing has led to a radical repositioning of the brand; this is discussed in Illustration 6.2.

Illustration 6.2   The repositioning of Skoda

Throughout the 1980s and into the early 1990s, Skoda was a byword for everything that was wrong with east European products in general and their cars in particular. With a reputation for being ugly, unreliable and for rusting away, the brand had little credibility in western markets. Following the collapse of communism and the Socialist Republic of Czechoslovakia in 1989, the new government immediately embarked on a programme of industrial privatization. Among the companies put up for sale was Skoda. In 1990, Volkswagen Group, intent on expanding into eastern Europe, took a 30 per cent share of the company and gained managerial control (it subsequently increased its shareholding to 70 per cent and then total ownership). Specialists from Germany were sent to the main Skoda factory to re-engineer the production line, retrain the workers, update the designs, and encourage suppliers to adopt just-in-time practices. Within the first 10 years of VW's control and with an investment of £1 billion and a further £1 billion planned, Skoda launched three new models and invested heavily in an advertising campaign designed to reposition the brand in consumers' minds. In doing this, the company decided to confront the problem head-on.

Typical of the poster campaign was a sleek image of a shadowy, powerful car with a Skoda badge and the line 'No, really …'. In a television campaign, three stooges – a politician, a self-important car show official and a car park attendant – all mistake the gleamingly up-to-date new Skoda for something else. The pay-off line is, 'It's a Skoda. Honest.'

Underpinning the campaign was the fundamental recognition that any attempt at repositioning had to be based upon a series of radical changes and improvements to the product itself. In the absence of this, any attempt at repositioning would undoubtedly fail. The new Skoda models therefore emphasized quality, the driving experience, the Volkswagen link/heritage and value for money.

Previously, the traditional Skoda driver was a 56-year-old man with little interest in design or performance, and who wanted basic low-cost and no-frills transport. Although the company was intent on repositioning the brand by appealing to a younger market and more women (young, middle-class women make up the largest single group of customers for small cars), it also recognized it could not afford to alienate its traditional markets, which had a 76 per cent loyalty/repurchase rate.

Source: *Weekend FT Magazine, Financial Times*, 29 April 2000, pp. 22–3, 40.

The third element of perception is that of *selective retention*. Quite simply, individuals forget much of what they learn. Therefore, to ensure that a message is retained, it needs to be relevant, generally straightforward, one which reinforces existing positive attitudes and which, in the case of certain products, is catchy. Many people, for example, still remember simple advertising slogans such as 'You've been Tangoed', 'Beanz Meanz Heinz', 'Drinka Pinta Milk a Day', 'Go to work on an egg' and 'Guinness is good for you', even though, in some cases, the message has not been used for well over 30 years.

Once individuals have responded to an advertisement, they go through a process of learning. If the experience with the product is generally positive, the likelihood of repeat purchase is obviously increased. If, however, the experience is largely negative, not only is the likelihood of repeat purchase reduced, but the negative attitude that develops is likely to be extended to other products from the same manufacturer and possibly the country of origin. It is the set of *beliefs* and *attitudes* that emerge both from our own experiences and from those of individuals in our reference groups that build up a set of product and brand images. These, in turn, lead us to behave in relatively consistent ways. An obvious problem that can therefore be faced by a manufacturer stems from the difficulties of changing attitudes and images once they have been established.

6.5 THE BUYING DECISION PROCESS

Having identified the various factors that influence behaviour, the marketing strategist is then in a position to examine the buying process itself. This involves focusing on three distinct elements:

1. The buying roles within the decision-making unit

2. The type of buying behaviour

3. The decision process.

The five buying roles

In the majority of cases, and for the majority of products, identifying the buyer is a relatively straightforward exercise. In some instances, however, the decision of what to buy involves several people, and here we can identify five distinct roles:

1. The *initiator*, who first suggests buying the product or service

2. The *influencer*, whose comments affect the decision made

3. The *decider*, who ultimately makes all or part of the buying decision

4. The *buyer*, who physically makes the purchase

5. The *user(s)*, who consume(s) the product or service.

Identifying who plays each of these roles, and indeed *how* they play them, is important since it is this information which should be used to determine a wide variety of marketing decisions. In the case of advertising, for example, the question of who plays each of the buying roles should be used to decide on who the advertising is to be aimed at, the sort of appeal, the timing of the message, and the placing of the message.

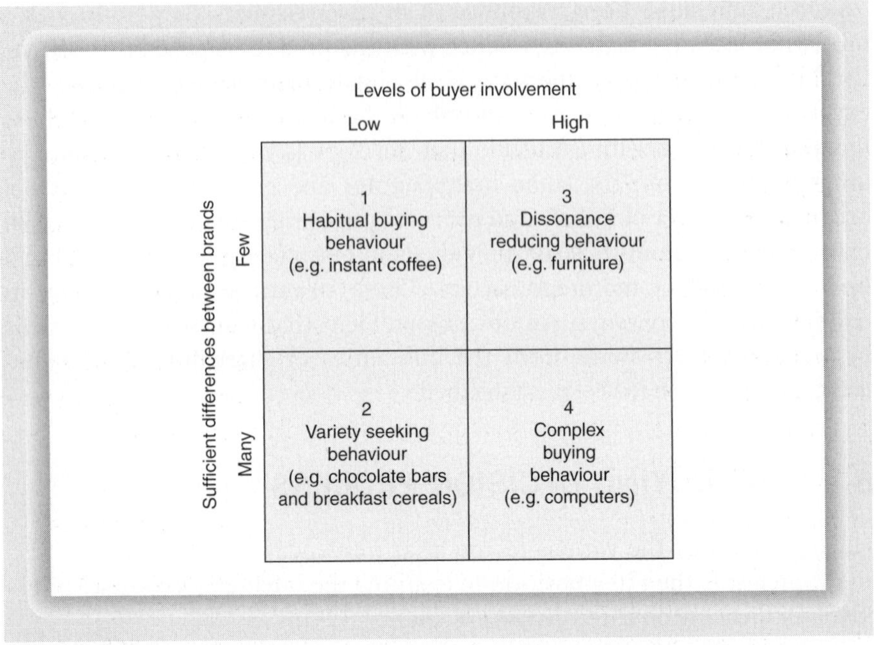

FIGURE 6.3   *The four types of buying behaviour (adapted from Assael, 1987)*

Different types of buying behaviour

So far in this discussion we have referred simply to 'buying behaviour'. In practice, of course, it is possible to identify several types of buying decision and hence several types of buying behaviour. The most obvious distinction to make is based on the expense, complexity, risk and opportunity cost of the purchase decision – the process a consumer goes through in deciding on a new car or major holiday, for example, will be radically different from the process in deciding whether to buy a chocolate bar. Recognition of this has led to the identification of four types of buying behaviour, depending on the degree of buyer involvement in the purchase and the extent to which brands differ. This is illustrated in Figure 6.3.

Understanding the buying decision process

The third and final stage that we are concerned with here is the structure of the buying decision process that consumers go through. In other words, precisely *how* do consumers buy particular products? Do they, for example, search for information and make detailed comparisons, or do they rely largely upon the advice of a store assistant? Are they influenced significantly by price or by advertising? Questions such as these have led to a considerable amount of research into the buying process and subsequently to consumers being categorized either as deliberate buyers or compulsive buyers.

To help in coming to terms with this, a series of models have been proposed that focus not simply upon the purchase *decision*, but upon the *process* leading up to this decision, the decision itself and then, subsequently, post-purchase behaviour.

Here, the process begins with the consumer's *recognition of a problem*, or perhaps more commonly, a want. This may emerge as the result of an internal stimulus (hunger or thirst) or an external stimulus in the form of an advertisement or a colleague's comment. This leads to the *search for information*, which might be at the level simply of a heightened awareness or attention to advertising, or at the deeper level of extensive information searching. In either case, the search process is likely to involve one or more of four distinct sources:

1. *Personal sources*, such as family, friends, colleagues and neighbours

2. *Public sources*, such as the mass media and consumer organizations – typical examples would be the Consumers' Association's *Which?* magazine for consumer durables, *Vogue* for fashion and *What Car?* for cars

3. *Commercial sources*, such as advertising, sales staff and brochures

4. *Experimental sources*, such as handling or trying the product.

The relative importance of each of these varies greatly from person to person and product to product. Typically, therefore, the consumer might gain the greatest amount of information from commercial sources such as newspapers and advertisements. However, the information that is most likely to influence behaviour comes from personal sources such as friends (word of mouth). Each type of source plays a different role in influencing the buying decision. Commercial information, for example, plays an informing function, while personal sources perform a legitimizing and/or evaluation function.

By gathering information in this way, consumers develop an awareness, knowledge and understanding of the various brands in the market. An obvious task then faced by marketing strategists is how best to ensure that their brand stands out from the others available and is subsequently purchased. In essence, this involves moving the product or brand from the *total set* available, through to the consumer's *awareness set* and *consideration set* to the *choice set*, from which the consumer ultimately makes the buying decision.

However, for this to be done effectively, the strategist needs to have a clear understanding of the criteria used by consumers in comparing products. Much of the research in this area has focused primarily upon the cognitive element, suggesting that consumers make product judgements on a rational basis (see Illustration 6.3). Whether this is the case in practice is, of course, highly debatable and contradicts much of what we have already said.

Illustration 6.3 Customers buy benefits, not products

Recognition of the idea that customers do not buy products but are instead interested in the benefits gained from using the product has long been at the heart of successful marketing. This has been commented on by, among others, McDonald (1995, pp. 102–3):

> The difference between benefits and products is not just a question of semantics. It is crucial to the company seeking success. Every product has its features: size, shape, performance, weight, the material from which it is made, and so on. Many companies fall into the trap of talking to customers about these features rather than what those features mean to the customer. This is not surprising. For example, if, when asked a question about the product, the salesman could not provide an accurate answer, the customer might lose confidence and, doubting the salesman, will soon doubt his product. Most salesmen are therefore very knowledgeable about the technical features of the products they sell. They have to have these details at their fingertips when they talk to buyers, designers and technical experts.

However, being expert in technical detail is not enough. The customer may not be able to work out the benefits that particular features bring and it is therefore up to the salesman to explain the benefits that accrue from every feature he mentions.

A simple formula to ensure that this customer-oriented approach is adopted is always to use the phrase 'which means that' to link a feature to the benefit it brings:

> 'Maintenance time has been reduced from 4 to 3 hours, **which means that** most costs are reduced by … '
>
> 'The engine casing is made of aluminium, **which means that** six more units can be carried on a standard truck load, which means that transport costs are reduced by … '

McDonald goes on to argue that companies should undertake detailed analyses to identify the full range of benefits *they are able to offer* the customer as a prelude to identifying the range of benefits that *customers actually want* or will respond to. Benefits typically fall into four categories:

1. *Standard benefits*, which arise from the company and its products

2. *Double benefits*, which bring a benefit to the customer and subsequently, through an improvement in the customer's product, to the end-user

3. *Company benefits*, which emerge as the result of a relationship that develops by virtue of having bought a particular product – a typical example would be worldwide service backup

4. *Differential benefits*, which distinguish the product from those offered by competitors.

Nevertheless, there are several interesting factors that have emerged from this research that merit consideration. These include the need to think about:

1. The *product's attributes*, such as its price, performance, quality and styling

2. Their *relative importance* to the consumer

3. The consumer's perception of each *brand's image*

4. The consumer's *utility function* for each of the attributes.

By understanding consumers' perceptions in this way, the strategist can then begin modifying the product offer. This can be done in one of six ways:

1. Changing the physical product by, for example, adding features (real repositioning)

2. Changing beliefs about the product by giving greater emphasis to particular attributes (psychological repositioning)

3. Changing beliefs about competitors' products by comparative advertising and 'knocking copy' (competitive depositioning)

4. Changing the relative importance of particular attributes – as a product moves through the product life cycle, for example, and consumers become more familiar with the concept and the technology, the emphasis in the advertising can be shifted from, say, reassuring consumers about reliability and service backup, to a range of additional uses

5. Emphasizing particular product features that previously have been largely ignored

6. Changing buyers' expectations.

Against the background of these comments, the strategist should then be in a position to consider the act of purchase itself and, in particular, *where* the purchase will be made, the *quantities* in which it will be made, the *timing*, and the *method* of payment.

An overview of models of consumer behaviour

Throughout the 1960s attempts were made to integrate a variety of theories, research findings and concepts from the behavioural sciences into a general framework that could be used to explain and predict consumer behaviour. In doing this, the principal writers (such as Nicosia, 1966; Engel *et al.*, 1968; Sheth, 1969) moved away from the general perspective that had previously been adopted by economists and which in a number of ways is typified by

Marshall's work and the Marshallian model of 'economic man'. Instead of viewing consumer behaviour simply as a single act made up of the purchase itself and the post-purchase reaction, a far greater recognition was given to the consumer's psychological state before, during and after the purchase.

But although these so-called 'comprehensive models' of consumer behaviour have been of value in extending our understanding of the decision process, their value has been questioned in recent years. One of the first to do this was Foxall (1987, p. 128), who suggested:

- The models assume an unrealistic degree of consumer rationality

- Observed behaviour often differs significantly from what is described

- The implied decision process is too simplistic and sequential

- Insufficient recognition is given to the relative importance of different types of decisions – each decision is treated by comprehensive models as being significant and of high involvement, but the reality is very different and by far the vast majority of decisions made by consumers are relatively insignificant and of low involvement

- The models assume consumers have a seemingly infinite capacity for receiving and ordering information – in practice, consumers ignore, forget, distort, misunderstand or make far less use than this of the information with which they are presented

- Attitudes towards low-involvement products are often very weak and only emerge after the purchase, not before as comprehensive models suggest

- Many purchases seem not to be preceded by a decision process

- Strong brand attitudes often fail to emerge even when products have been bought on a number of occasions

- Consumers often drastically limit their search for information, even for consumer durables

- When brands are similar in terms of their basic attributes, consumers seemingly do not discriminate between them, but instead select from a repertoire of brands.

In the light of these criticisms, it is perhaps not surprising that the results that have emerged from attempts to test the models have proved disappointing.

Behavioural economics and the significance of irrationality

As markets have become more crowded and competitive, and customers more demanding and discriminating, behavioural economists have focused in ever greater detail upon the ways in which decision-making differs from the perfectly rational ideal that underpins classical economic thinking. The – not surprising – conclusion is that consumers are systematically irrational. In discussing this, Whyte (2008) goes on to suggest that:

> *we are apathetic, favouring options that require no action or that*
> *preserve the status quo. We are herd followers, doing things that*
> *are bad for us simply because others do them. We are hopeless at*
> *statistics, buying insurance and lottery tickets even when the odds*
> *make them a bad deal … And these are only a few of many irrational*
> *biases.*

For the behavioural economists who have focused upon these irrational patterns of behaviour, this highlights not just the need that many consumers have for strong external guidance, but also – and more importantly – how we can be guided, with consumers irrationally being used to nudge the market in a particular direction.

The ways in which this can be done have been examined in detail by Thaler and Sunstein (2008) in their book *Nudge*. Amongst the examples that they explore of how nudge marketing can be used effectively is that of the financial services sector. Faced with increasingly skewed demographic profiles across much of the developed world, governments and pensions companies have spent substantial sums trying to persuade consumers to invest in pension schemes. The results in many cases have been mixed, largely because investments like this require the consumer to opt **in**. For Thaler and Sunstein, the solution is to change what they term the *decision architecture*. This would mean that joining a pension scheme would be the default option when someone takes up a new job. In other words, the employer structures the choices so that the individual has to actively opt **out** as opposed to actively opting in.

6.6   THE RISE OF THE NEW CONSUMER AND THE IMPLICATIONS FOR MARKETING PLANNING

We suggested in Illustration 6.1 that the 1990s saw the emergence of a very different type of consumer. This theme has been developed by Lewis and Bridger (2000) who, in their book *The Soul of the New Consumer*, suggest that consumers have evolved from being conformist and deferential children, reared on the propaganda of the post-Second World War era and prepared to trust mass advertising, into free-thinking, individualistic adults, who are sceptical of figures of authority and believe in what Sigmund Freud called 'the narcissism of small differences' (see Figure 6.4).

Reflecting the change from an era of austerity to one of affluence, these consumers have largely exhausted the things they *need* to purchase and are

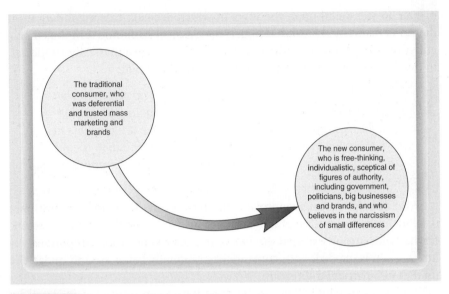

FIGURE 6.4 *The shift from the old to the new consumer*

now concentrating on what they *want* to buy. In this sense, shopping is not merely the acquisition of things but the buying of identity.

While 'old consumers' were typically constrained by cash, choice and the availability of goods whereas 'new consumers', Lewis and Bridger (2000) suggest, are generally short of time, attention and trust (this is the cash-rich/time-poor generation that we discuss in greater detail on pages 247–9). Mass society has shattered and been reduced to a mosaic of minorities:

> *In a hypercompetitive world of fragmented markets and independently-minded, well-informed individuals, companies that fail to understand and attend to the needs of New Consumers are doomed to extinction. Currently, the average life of a major company only rarely exceeds 40 years. In the coming decade, any business that is less than highly successful will find that lifespan reduced by a factor of at least 10.*

Even though such a drastic picture and such short timescales can be questioned, the overall picture that emerges is significant and has major implications for the marketing planner. Perhaps the first of these is the need for organizations to reconnect with their customers. Even giant consumer products companies with powerful brands and long trading histories – such as Levi Strauss, Kellogg's, Marks & Spencer and Coca-Cola – can lose touch with the new consumers, whose behaviour often transcends the traditional categories such as age, ethnic identity and even income.

The second main implication of the new consumer is that consumer products companies must become much better at directing their messages to increasingly critical audiences who have access to technology. The proliferation of Internet sites, for example, has enabled groups of consumers to publicize instantaneous and often highly critical reviews of new products, services or films that can be far more influential than the formal advertising campaigns. However, from the company's point of view, improving technology and growing consumer sophistication also enable them to become smarter. New advertising channels, such as Internet sites, video screens at supermarket checkouts and interactive television all enable suppliers to find more willing buyers. Companies are also becoming better at stimulating a street 'buzz' about their products by influencing select opinion formers, rather than by focusing largely upon mass advertising hype. Amongst those to have done this are companies such as Disney, Apple, Virgin and Starbucks, all of which have caught the *zeitgeist* and created innovative means such as viral marketing to deliver their message to new consumers.

This theme of a very different and far more assertive type of consumer has also been developed by the advertising agency Publicis, which, in its report *The New Assertiveness* (2002), suggest:

> *infuriated by the pressures of 21st-century living and a feeling of having little control over many aspects of their lives, consumers are attempting to regain control and vent their frustration through their buying habits … Seventy per cent of those surveyed believe the future is more uncertain than it was in their parents' day – an anxiety that has been increased since September 11. Many now feel vulnerable to the possibility that anything could happen, at any time.*

The study argues that:

> *This insecurity and frustration is breeding a new generation of consumer. Increasingly, we are buying products or services to cheer ourselves up – 31 per cent of adults surveyed said their consumption was motivated by this, a figure that rose to 50 per cent among 15- to 24-year-old respondents.*

The report also highlighted the way in which consumers' expectations of product quality and levels of service are outstripping satisfaction. Ninety-six per cent of respondents had made a complaint about a product or service during the previous 12 months.

The findings of the study were seen by the agency to present both a warning and an opportunity to brand owners.

Competitive intensity, the new consumer and the rise of complicated simplicity (or the law of increasing individuality)

With markets becoming ever more competitive and consumers more demanding, organizations can respond in any one of a number of ways.

However, underpinning many of these is the need to individualize and tailor services to the consumers' needs to a far greater extent than has typically been the case in the past. This sort of response, which can be labelled 'complicated simplicity', highlights the end of a mass audience-oriented approach and the need for the far greater acceptance of an audience-of-one approach. This shift is being driven, in part at least, by the consumer empowerment movement which (amongst other things) demands a far greater degree of price transparency. The implications of this are potentially significant, since organizations face the pressure of cutting costs and maintaining profitability, while having little opportunity to raise prices.

Complicated simplicity also highlights the need for organizations to take greater account of developments such as the 'ninety-nine lives' trend first identified by Faith Popcorn, the American trend forecaster. This involves recognizing that a consumer can play a variety of roles (e.g. mother, wife, manager, outdoor enthusiast) and that typecasting under a single broad heading is likely to be of little real value. This expectation of individual attention is, of course, at odds with the general trend of the past 30 years of mega-mergers and conglomeration. Amongst those to have used technology to come to terms with this individualization is Amazon.com, which outmanoeuvred the established market leader, Barnes & Noble, partly by developing a new business model but also by tailoring its message and response to consumers as individuals.

Another contributor to complicated simplicity is the move across society to Me, Myself and I Inc. With government as well as organizations across Europe, the USA and Japan slowly dismantling the cradle-to-grave welfare state, levels of corporate loyalty are declining rapidly. At the same time, long-term permanent employment is disappearing and greater numbers of people are beginning to work for themselves. Faced with this, the implications for marketing are potentially significant, and are likely to be seen most obviously in terms of consumers' far higher expectations and their demands for individual treatment.

The genie of the super-powered consumer

Arguably, one of the most significant and far-reaching legacies for marketing of the social and economic turbulence of the 1980s and 1990s was the emergence of what we have termed 'the new consumer'. This new consumer exhibits a number of characteristics that (as we suggested earlier), can perhaps best be summarized in terms of buyers who are now far more demanding, far more discriminating, much less loyal and far more willing to complain. This type of consumer has, over the past few years, developed even further, with the emergence of what might loosely be termed the 'super-powered consumer'. The super-powered consumer is typically media-literate, has access to his/her own mass-media channel of communication (the Web), has a number of tools for a fast response to problems (the mobile phone), and often has a public relations strategy and an ability to hurt companies. They are also often well-informed and frequently politicized in their behaviour patterns. Examples of the super-powered consumer in action include the anti-global brand demonstrations in Seattle in 1999, French farmers attacking the 'imperialism' of McDonald's, European and North American customers asking questions of Nike about their manufacturing policies in South-East Asia, and the green lobby forcing the British government to change its policy on genetically-modified foods.

In a number of ways the emergence of the super-powered consumer represents something of a paradox. Marketers have worked hard to create this type of consumer by giving them greater access, more information and more influence over how business is done, and how brands communicate. Having been encouraged to ask questions, consumers have responded by becoming far more discriminating and cynical, with the result that marketing planners are now under far greater pressure and need to respond with communication that is far more open.

The new consumer and the new radicalism

In her book *The Customer Revolution* (2001), Patricia Seybold argues that, because of the Internet, customers are more easily able to influence a company's behaviour. Websites such as TheCorporateLibrary.com, for example, have an extensive list of articles and reports on the behaviour of companies, and this, she argues, provides the basis for small shareholders to begin exerting a greater power and influence than in the past. The implication of this is that a company can be measured not just through the traditional measures of profit and loss, return on assets and the price/earnings ratio, but also on the quality of customer relationships. To help with this, Seybold has developed a 'customer value index' that gives investors a way to measure company performance by looking at the present and future value of its customer base. The net effect of this is that measures such as customer satisfaction, customer retention and share of wallet become easier and more meaningful.

In many markets, she suggests, there are now three types of customer: those who are *price sensitive* and concerned about costs; those who are *service sensitive* and who focus upon areas such as quality and delivery; and those who are *commitment sensitive* and look for long-term relationships.

6.7   ORGANIZATIONAL BUYING BEHAVIOUR

Although there are certain factors common to both consumer and organizational buying behaviour, there are also numerous points of difference. Perhaps the most obvious feature of commonality in approaching the two areas is the fundamental need to understand how and why buyers behave as they do. There are, however, certain features of organizational buying which are not found in consumer markets. These typically include the following:

- Organizations generally buy goods and services to satisfy a variety of goals such as making profits, reducing costs, meeting employees' needs, and meeting social and legal obligations.

- A greater number of people are generally involved in organizational buying decisions than in consumer buying decisions, especially when the value of the purchase is particularly high. Those involved in the decision usually have different and specific organizational responsibilities and apply different criteria to the purchase decision.

- The buyers must adhere to formal purchasing policies, constraints and requirements.

- The buying instruments, such as requests for quotations, proposals and purchase contracts, add another dimension not typically found in consumer buying.

Although quite obviously, as with consumers in consumer markets, no two companies behave in the same way, both research and experience have demonstrated that patterns of similarity do exist in the ways in which organizational buyers approach the task of buying, and that they are sufficiently uniform to simplify the task of strategic marketing planning.

In analysing patterns of organizational buying, the starting point is in many ways similar to that for consumer markets, with the strategist posing a series of questions:

- *Who* makes up the market?

- What *buying decisions* do they make?

- Who are the *key participants* in the buying process?

- What are the *principal influences* upon the buyer, and what organizational rules and policies are important?

- What *procedures* are followed in selecting and evaluating competitive offerings, and how do buyers arrive at their decisions?

The three types of organizational buying decision

Much of the research conducted over the past 40 years into the nature of the industrial buying process has made either explicit or implicit use of a categorization first proposed in 1967 by Robinson, Faris and Wind. There are, they suggested, three distinct buying situations or buy classes, each of which requires a different pattern of behaviour from the supplier. They are the straight rebuy, the modified rebuy and the new task.

Of these, the *straight rebuy* is the most straightforward and describes a buying situation where products are reordered on a largely routine basis, often by someone at a fairly junior level in the organization. Among the products ordered in this way is office stationery. Here, the person responsible for the ordering simply reorders when stocks fall below a predetermined level and will typically use the same supplier from one year to another until either something goes wrong or a potential new supplier offers a sufficiently attractive incentive for the initial decision to be reconsidered. The implications of this sort of buying situation are for the most part straightforward, and require the supplier to maintain both product and service quality. Perhaps the biggest single problem in these circumstances stems from the need on the part of the supplier to avoid complacency setting in and allowing others to make an approach that causes the customer to reassess the supplier base.

The second type of buying situation – the *modified rebuy* – often represents an extension of the straight rebuy and occurs when the buyer wants to modify the specification, price or delivery terms. Although the current supplier is often in a relatively strong position to protect the account, the buyer will frequently give at least cursory consideration to other possible sources of supply.

The third type of buying situation – the *new task* – is the most radical of the three, and provides the marketing strategist with a series of opportunities and challenges. The buyer typically approaches the new task with a set of criteria that have to be satisfied and, in order to do this, will frequently consider a number of possible suppliers, each of whom is then faced with the task of convincing the buyer that his product or service will outperform or be more cost-effective than the others. The buyer's search for information is often considerable and designed to reduce risk. Where the costs are high there will typically be several people involved in the decision, and the strategist's task is therefore complicated by the need not just to identify the buying participants, but also their particular concerns and spheres of influence. In doing this, the strategist should never lose sight of the significance of attitudes to risk and the ways in which individuals may work to reduce their exposure to it. Amongst those to have focused upon this is McClelland (1961), who almost 50 years ago was suggesting that 'A great part of the efforts of business executives is directed towards minimizing uncertainties.'

Who is involved in the buying process?

A major characteristic of organizational buying is that it is often a group activity, and only rarely does a single individual within the organization have sole responsibility for making all the decisions involved in the purchasing process. Instead, a number of people from different areas and often with different statuses are involved either directly or indirectly. Webster and Wind (1972, p. 6) were the first to refer to this group as the decision-making unit (DMU) of an organization and as the buying centre, and defined it as 'all those individuals and groups who participate in the purchasing decision-making process, who share some common goals and the risks arising from the decisions'. There are, they suggest, six roles involved in this process (although, on occasions, all six may be performed by the same person):

1. *Users* of the product or service, who in many cases initiate the buying process and help in defining the purchase specifications

2. *Influencers*, who again help to define the specification, but who also provide an input to the process of evaluating the alternatives available

3. *Deciders*, who have the responsibility for deciding on product requirements and suppliers

4. *Approvers*, who give the authorization for the proposals of deciders and buyers

5. *Buyers*, who have the formal authority for selecting suppliers and negotiating purchase terms

6. *Gatekeepers*, who are able to stop sellers from reaching individuals in the buying centre – these can range from purchasing agents through to receptionists and telephone switchboard operators.

Although Webster and Wind's categorization of buying centre roles is the best known and the most widely used, a variety of other analytical approaches have been developed. Hill (1972), for example, has argued the case for analysing the buying centre not on the basis of the participants' roles, but on the basis of functional units. There are, he suggests, five such units:

1. *Control units*, which are responsible for the policy-making which influences buying and which imposes certain constraints – these might include buying where possible only from British suppliers or from local small firms

2. *Information units*, which provide information relating to the purchase

3. *The buying unit*, which consists of those with formal responsibility for negotiating the terms of the contract

4. *User units*, consisting of anyone in the organization who will be involved in using the product or service

5. *The decision-making unit*, which consists of those in the DMU who will make the decision.

Of these, it is only the control, information and decision-making units that he believes are of any real importance in influencing buying decisions.

Although the size, structure and formality of the buying centre will quite obviously vary depending both upon the size of the organization and the product decision involved, the strategist needs always to consider five questions:

1. Who are the principal participants in the buying process?

2. In what areas do they exercise the greatest influence?

3. What is their level of influence?

4. What evaluative criteria do each of the participants make use of and how professional is the buying process?

5. To what extent in large organizations is buying centralized?

The principal influences on industrial buyers

Much of the early research into industrial buying processes was based on the assumption that industrial buyers, unlike consumers, are wholly rational. More recently it has been recognized that, while economic factors play a significant role, a variety of other elements also needs to be taken into account. Included within these are the culture of the organizations, the expectations of senior managers, attitudes to risk, the direct and indirect costs of the 'wrong' decision being made, the degree of choice within the market, patterns of past behaviour and their outcomes, and so on.

The question of what influences buyers and how various sources of information are perceived has also been examined by a variety of writers, one of the earliest and still most influential of whom was Webster (1970). He was particularly interested in the relative importance of formal and informal information sources, and how they differ from consumer markets. His findings suggest that informal sources tend to be used far less frequently in industrial markets than in consumer markets, and that salespeople are often regarded as highly reliable and useful sources of information. By contrast, opinion leadership, which often plays a significant role in consumer markets, was found to be largely ineffective; a possible explanation of this is the perception that no two companies experience the same problem and that there is therefore little to be gained. Perhaps the most significant single finding to emerge from Webster's research was the significance of the role that the industrial salesperson is capable of playing *throughout* the buying process.

The relative importance of sources of information has also been examined by Martilla (1971) and Abratt (1986). Martilla's work led to a series of conclusions that are broadly similar to those of Webster although, in addition, he highlighted the importance of word-of-mouth communication within firms, particularly in the later stages of the adoption process. Abratt's research, which focused on high-technology laboratory instrumentation, adds a further dimension to our understanding of the buying process by suggesting that, in markets such as these, buying personnel often have 'only a token administrative function'. Instead, the question of what to buy is the responsibility of groups of two to three people, with the most significant purchasing criteria proving to be product reliability and technical and sales service backup, while price was relatively unimportant.

However, perhaps the most underestimated and, in research terms, ignored elements of the buying process is that of the *gatekeeper*. Although the identity of the gatekeeper is often difficult to determine, it is the gatekeeper who in many organizations either blocks or facilitates access and who can therefore play a pivotal role in determining which products are even considered by the DMU.

How do industrial buyers arrive at their decisions?

One of the major differences between consumer and industrial buying decisions is the buying motive. Whereas the majority of consumer purchases are made for the individual's personal consumption or utility, industrial purchases are typically designed to reduce operating costs, satisfy legal obligations, provide an input to the manufacturing process, and ultimately to make money. But although the buying motive may well be different, the decision sequence is in many ways similar to that of the consumer process.

This buying process, which is based on Robinson *et al.*'s (1967) concept of a buy-grid model, begins with the recognition of a problem, can be sparked off by either internal or external stimuli. Internal stimuli typically include: the decision to develop a new product, and the recognition that this will require new equipment or materials; machine breakdowns; the belief on the part of the purchasing manager that better prices or quality can be obtained from an alternative supplier; curiosity; and organizational policy decisions. External stimuli include: the launch of a new product by a competitor; advertisements; sales representatives; and ideas that emerge as the result of trade shows.

This recognition of a problem is then followed by a *general need description*, in which the buyer identifies the characteristics and quantity of the products required to overcome the problem. This leads to the development of *product specifications* and, subsequently, to a *search for suppliers*.

The question of precisely *how* buyers select suppliers has been the subject of a considerable amount of research. However, in so far as it is possible to identify a common theme in this process of deciding between suppliers, it is the reduction, containment and management of risk.

It appears that buyers typically cope with risk in several ways, including:

- Exchanging technical and other information with their customers and prospects

- Dealing only with those suppliers with whom the company has previously had favourable experiences

- Applying strict (risk-reducing) decision rules

- Dealing only with suppliers who have a long-established and favourable reputation

- The introduction of penalty clauses relating to, for example, late delivery

- Multiple sourcing to reduce the degree of dependence upon a single supplier.

Although for many buyers the pursuit of a risk-reducing strategy has a series of attractions, it needs to be recognized that such a strategy can also possess drawbacks. The most obvious of these stems from the way in which it is likely to lead to the company becoming and remaining a follower rather than becoming a leader. Developments both in product and process technology on the part of a supplier often provide significant opportunities for the development of a competitive edge and, unless this is recognized by the company, it runs the risk of adopting new ideas only when they have been well tried by others.

Perhaps the final aspect of risk that needs to be considered here stems from the significance of post-purchase dissonance. Undoubtedly the best-known writer on dissonance is Festinger (1957), who has referred to it as a state of psychological discomfort. This discomfort is, in essence, the result of the individual questioning whether the decision made is correct. According to Festinger, a buyer will try to reduce this discomfort by seeking reassurance for the decision. This can be done by, for example, seeking the support of others, avoiding conflicting messages such as competitive advertising, and searching for editorials and advertisements that state how good the product just purchased is. The more expensive and significant the purchase, the greater the dissonance is likely to be. The implications for a supplier in these circumstances should be obvious: buyers need reassurance and this can best be provided by continuing to 'sell' the product and providing supporting evidence of the wisdom of the decision even after the sale itself has been made. Other ways in which dissonance can be reduced include giving emphasis to the quality of the after-sales service, maintaining regular contact with customers, and giving prominence in advertising to the market leaders who have also bought the product.

Having decided upon the choice of supplier, the buyer moves on to the *order-routine specification* by identifying such features as the technical specification, the order quantities, delivery schedules, maintenance requirements and payment terms.

The final stage involves a *review of suppliers' performance* and is designed, in one sense at least, to close the loop by feeding back information that will be used when purchasing in the future.

Although this sequential approach to organizational decision-making is undoubtedly useful and provides a series of insights into the various phases of buying, it should be realized that it fails to give full recognition to the complexity of the behavioural factors that are likely to influence those involved in making specific purchase decisions. Because of this, other models of organizational buying have been proposed, including *the interaction approach*, which places emphasis upon the nature of the process and relationships that develop both within and between buying and selling organizations.

Thus:

- Buyers and sellers are both seen to be active participants, and buyers often attempt to influence what they are offered

- Relationships are often long-term and based on mutual trust rather than any formal commitment

- Patterns of interaction are frequently complex and extend within the organizations as well as between organizations

- Emphasis is given to supporting these relationships as well as to the process of buying and selling

- Links between buyers and sellers often become institutionalized.

This approach to modelling industrial buying has, in turn, provided one of the foundations for the work of Hakansson (1981) and the IMP (International Marketing and Purchasing of Industrial Goods) group. Their research focused upon industrial buying and selling behaviour in five European countries – West Germany (as it was at the time), the UK, France, Italy and Sweden – and led to the development of a model that views this behaviour as a process in which both sides play active roles within a given environment. They suggest that four elements influence the patterns of buyer–seller interaction:

1. The interaction process

2. The participants in this process

3. The interaction environment

4. The atmosphere created by this interaction.

The real value of this model, which makes use both of interorganizational theory and new institutional economics thinking, is that it gives far greater emphasis than earlier work to the idea that industrial buying and selling is concerned with the management of relationships (refer to the discussion that begins in section 6.8 of this chapter).

The significance of relationships was also illustrated in 2005 when Ashridge Management College conducted a study designed to identify why industrial (B2B) organizations lost customers. The biggest single cause was found to lie not amongst what for many commentators are the obvious 'hard' elements of price, quality and delivery, but quite simply company indifference and the failure to manage effectively the customer relationship. This was illustrated by the way in which they summarized the reason for the percentage of lost customers in terms of:

1. Death (1%)

2. Business relocation (3%)

3. The development of new relationships (5%)

4. A lower price offered by a competitor (9%)

5. Dissatisfaction with the product, including issues of quality and delivery (14%)

6. Company indifference and the failure to manage the relationship effectively (68%).

The industrial buying process and issues of corruption

A somewhat different approach to thinking about the nature of the industrial buying process has been highlighted by the work of the research group Transparency International (1997) (www.transparency.org). The organization produces each year a corruption perceptions index based on the political and business practices of 180 countries across the world. Amongst those at the bottom of the list and seen to be the most corrupt in 2008 were Somalia, Myanmar (previously Burma), Iraq, Haiti and Afghanistan. Those that were seen to be the least corrupt were Denmark, New Zealand, Sweden, Singapore and Finland (the UK was rated 16th, whilst the USA was 18th).

6.8   THE GROWTH OF RELATIONSHIP MARKETING

Against the background of everything that we have said about the consumer and organizational buying processes, we can now turn to an issue that affects virtually all marketers, regardless of the nature of their customer base or indeed their product or service: the question of how to build, develop and nurture relationships.

A major focal point for a considerable amount of marketing thinking over the past 20 years has been the notion of loyalty and how long-term, cost-effective relationships might be developed with customers. In many ways, the idea of relationship marketing can be seen to be a logical development of the way in which the focus of marketing has changed from the

Transaction marketing	Relationship marketing
A focus on single sales	A focus on customer retention and building customer loyalty
An emphasis upon product features	An emphasis upon product benefits that are meaningful to the customer
Short timescales	Long timescales recognizing that short-term costs may be higher, but so will long-term profits
Little emphasis on customer retention	An emphasis upon high levels of service that are possibly tailored to the individual customer
Limited customer commitment	High customer commitment
Moderate customer contact	High customer contact, with each contact being used to gain information and build the relationship
Quality is essentially the concern of production and no-one else	Quality is the concern of all, and it is the failure to recognize this that creates minor mistakes which lead to major problems

FIGURE 6.5 *Transaction versus relationship marketing (adapted from Christopher et al., 1991)*

early 1980s view that marketing is essentially a business function to the idea that, more realistically, it is – or should be – an organizational attitude, ethos and culture (see Chapter 1). Given this, it follows that the nature of any relationship between an organization and its markets should be based on a recognition of their fundamental interdependence, something which, in turn, has major implications for the ways in which the organization interacts with its customer base.

One of the most powerful drivers for relationship marketing has been what is in many ways the straightforward recognition of the fact that the costs of gaining a new customer, particularly in mature and slowly declining markets, are often high. Given this, the marketing planner needs to ensure that the existing customer base is managed as effectively as possible. One way of doing this is to move away from the traditional and now largely outmoded idea of marketing and selling as a series of activities concerned with transactions, and to think instead of their being concerned with the management of long(er)-term relationships. This is illustrated in Figure 6.5.

The potential benefits of this sort of approach are considerable and can be seen not just in terms of the higher returns from repeat sales, but also in terms of the opportunities for cross-selling, strategic partnerships and alliances. Clutterbuck and Dearlove (1993), for example, cite a study by Bain & Co., who suggest that, depending upon the type of business, a 5 per cent increase in customer retention can result in a profitability boost of anywhere from 25 to 125 per cent. The advantages are, of course, then increased further when the potential lifetime value of the customer is taken into account. In essence, therefore, the attractions of a loyal customer base can be seen in terms of the greater scope for profit from four main areas:

1. The price premium that loyal customers are or may be willing to pay

2. Customer referrals

3. A reduction in marketing costs

4. The value of a greater number of purchases.

Developing the relationship strategy

In developing the relationship strategy, the marketing planner needs to focus upon four steps:

1. Analysing the gap between target and existing behaviour

2. Identifying what needs to be done to close the gap

3. Formulating a programme of benefits that satisfy customers' needs in order of importance of each within the segment

4. Formulating a communications plan to modify the behaviour of target groups.

However, before doing this, there is the need to:

- Identify the *key* customers, since it is with these, particularly in the early stages, that the most profitable long-term relationships can be developed.

- Determine which customers *want* a relationship. Although it is easy to assume that customers will benefit from – and will therefore want – a relationship, the reality is that not all customers want to move beyond anything more than a straightforward transaction. The normal reason for this is that, for a relationship to work, there is the need for an investment of time and effort from both sides. Although the organization may be willing to do this, it does not necessarily follow that the customer has the same commitment.

- Following on from this, categorize customers in terms of their current or future potential with a view to the nature of any relationship then being tailored to their potential.

- Examine in detail the expectations of each segment for both sides.

- Identify how, if at all, the two can work together more closely in a cost-effective and profitable way.

- In the case of relationships in the commercial sector, appoint a relationship manager in each of the two organizations so that there is a natural focal point and think about how operating processes on both sides might need to be changed so that cooperation might be made easier.

- Go for a series of small wins in the first instance and then gradually strengthen the relationship.

- Recognize from the outset that different customers have very different expectations and that these need to be reflected in the way in which the relationship is developed.

As part of this, there is also the need to think about how customers can be managed and how the customer database might be used. As the prelude to this, six questions need to be posed:

1. How much do you know about the current customer base?

2. How good is the database?

3. How good is the management of the database?

4. What needs to be done to exploit it further?

5. What else does the organization need to know about customers?

6. How can this be achieved?

The position of relationship marketing within the customer loyalty chain is illustrated in Figure 6.6. The ways in which it was used strategically by SAS is then discussed in Illustration 6.4.

Although it might be argued that the movements of a buyer through the various stages from prospects to partners in Figure 6.6 should be straightforward and seamless, the reality in many instances is that organizations unwittingly erect a series of barriers that slow down or stop this movement. The first can be seen to be that of the way in which, in many cases, organizations make it difficult to do business with them. While this might seem to be something of a paradox, these barriers often exist in terms of inappropriate opening hours, unhelpful sales staff, uncompetitive prices, poor product configurations, slow delivery, and so on. The second barrier occurs at a later stage, when the customer deals with the organization on a regular basis, but no real effort is made to get close to the customer by building a relationship. Instead, each sale takes the form of a one-off transaction, an approach which goes at least part of the way towards explaining why long-standing customers 'suddenly' move to another supplier.

Given this, the arrow on the right-hand side of Figure 6.6 shows how customers can – and almost inevitably will – move back down the loyalty chain if the relationship is not managed proactively.

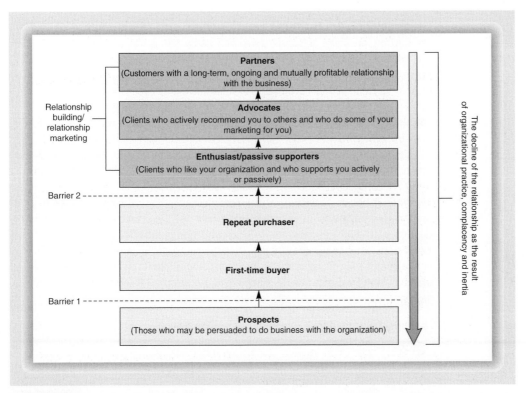

FIGURE 6.6   *Relationship marketing and the customer loyalty chain*

Relationship marketing and the marketing mix

There are numerous ways in which relationships can be managed proactively, including by redefining and extending the marketing mix. As markets have become more competitive, the extent to which the marketing planner can differentiate purely on the basis of the traditional four Ps has become increasingly more difficult and more questionable. To overcome this, as we mentioned in Chapter 1, the focus in many markets has moved to the 'softer' elements of markets and the additional three Ps of People, Physical evidence and Processes that include proactive customer service. In emphasizing the softer elements of marketing, the marketing planner is giving explicit recognition to the way in which the product or service is typically delivered through people and that it is the organization's staff who have the ability to make or break the relationship. This, in turn, is influenced either positively or negatively by organizational processes and the effectiveness of process management (which is concerned with the ways in which the customer is handled, from the point of very first contact with the organization through to the last). The third of the soft Ps (Process management) relates

Illustration 6.4   Building relationships and the moments of truth

Jan Carlzon, president of Scandinavian Airlines System (SAS), achieved fame as the result of the way in which he turned SAS from heavy losses to healthy profit in the mid-1980s. In his book, Carlzon (1987, p. 3) says that each of his 10 million customers came in contact with approximately five employees for an average of 15 seconds each time. He referred to these contacts as moments of truth, suggesting that, for SAS, these were 'created' 50 million times a year, 15 seconds at a time.

It is statistics such as these that indicate the scale of opportunity for managing and building relationships – or, as Clutterbuck and Dearlove (1993, p. 101) define these critical encounters, OTSU (Opportunities To Screw Up).

When things do go wrong – and almost inevitably they will sooner or later in any long-term relationship – the question is how well the organizations handle the complaint. In examining this, the TARP organization in the USA concluded that when a customer complains and feels that the complaint is handled properly, he or she comes away satisfied and is likely to be *more loyal* to that brand or supplier than a customer who has never experienced a problem. Related to customer segment brand loyalty, the findings were as follows:

Experienced no problem	87 per cent
Satisfied complainant	91 per cent
Dissatisfied complainant	41 per cent
Non-complainant	59 per cent

Two key issues emerge here: first, dissatisfied customers should be encouraged and assisted to complain, but secondly, the complaint must be resolved to the customer's complete satisfaction.

Where customers remain dissatisfied, the implications are significant because not only will they fail to buy again, they tend not to keep quiet about their experiences. Statistics surrounding this issue are quoted ubiquitously, but all tend to tell the same story. Gerson (1992), for example, states that a dissatisfied customer will tell ten people about his experiences; approximately 13 per cent of dissatisfied customers will tell up to 20 people. Customers who are satisfied or have had their complaints satisfactorily resolved will tell between three and five people about their positive experience.

The stark reality of these statistics is that three to four customers have to be satisfied for every one who remains dissatisfied – a 4:1 ratio against.

to the way in which the customer is handled throughout the customer journey from point of first contact through to the point of last contact. Included within this is the notion of proactive customer service and the ways in which levels of customer satisfaction can be leveraged by proactive rather than reactive service standards and initiatives.

The development of relationship marketing concepts and the emphasis placed upon the organization's staff has led, in turn, to a greater clarity of thinking about the differences that exist between what might loosely be termed the three dimensions of marketing: *external marketing*, which is concerned with the traditional four Ps of marketing and how they contribute to the development of the external profile of the organization or brand; *internal marketing*, which is concerned with the ways in which senior management communicate the organizational values and priorities to their staff; and *interactive marketing*, which is concerned with the ways in which staff then interact with the customer or client base.

Relationship building and the growth of loyalty marketing

For many customers in the consumer goods sector, the most obvious manifestation of relationship marketing over the past few years has been the growth of customer loyalty schemes. The rationale for many of these has been the straightforward recognition that, particularly in mature markets, the costs to an organization of recruiting a new customer are typically far greater than those associated with keeping an existing one. Because of this, marketing campaigns that are designed to build customer loyalty offer – or appear to offer – considerable strategic benefits. Recognizing this, the mid-1990s saw an upsurge in the number of organizations developing loyalty marketing programmes. Amongst the most proactive in this were the major food retailers.

However, calculating the *potential* value of a customer, as opposed to the value of each transaction, involves a very different approach to marketing and customer service, something that has forced many organizations to rethink how they use their internal accounting and data management systems. Having done this, they should then be in a far better position to communicate with customers in a more focused and strategic way, and apply the 80:20 rule (Pareto's Law) in order to target the 20 per cent of customers who generate the largest revenues and/or the greatest profits. The value of loyalty schemes can therefore be seen to lie in *how* the knowledge gained from customer databases is used.

There are, however, questions that can be raised about the long-term benefits of loyalty schemes. In the case of the food retailers, for example, it might be argued that the cards are a zero-sum game in that, ultimately, the total amount of food bought will remain the same and that the discounts that the cards give to customers will translate into lower gross margins for supermarkets. In commenting on this, Denison (1994) has suggested that, in the long term:

> *loyalty schemes are not particularly effective. As schemes proliferate, what began as a 'reward' turns into an 'incentive' – or bribe. As companies try to outbid each other's incentives they risk slipping*

into loyalty wars – price wars by another name. And as consumers learn to shop around for the best schemes, marketers risk fuelling the very promiscuity they set out to combat. Until companies invent a means of introducing switching costs for customers, the future benefits of many loyalty schemes will be very marginal. They could end up in a lose–lose situation.

If this happens, it could be the result of a certain amount of muddled thinking as marketers confuse retention with loyalty: a customer may return again and again, not out of any loyalty but out of sheer habit. Others assume that greater customer satisfaction must bring increased loyalty. But as British Airways' head of customer relations, Charles Weiser, has pointed out, this isn't necessarily the case. Defection rates among BA passengers who declare themselves satisfied are the same as among those who make complaints.

A similar line of argument has been pursued by Mazur (1999), who has pointed to the proliferation of loyalty schemes and to the dangers of loyalty cards simply being taken for granted by consumers. In making this comment, Mazur points to a Mintel report (1998) which found that:

- There is extensive cross-ownership of cards. In the case of online mileage schemes, for example, frequent travelers will typically have cards from 3–4 airlines and then choose an airline because of its flight times, prices and destinations, with the card's mileage points then being used as a reward.

- Less than one-third of those surveyed suggested that a loyalty card influenced where they shopped.

- The most significant short-term driver for a card to be introduced was because a major competitor has already launched one.

Mazur (1999) also points to research by the Marketing Forum which found that 'while active drivers of [retailer] loyalty included own brands, staff and customer service, product quality, price and product range, loyalty schemes come well down the list of what makes people go to certain shops'. It is this that, she suggests, highlights the way in which the concept of loyalty in retailing and airlines at least, has been brought into question and that a loyalty scheme will only work if it is just one part of a long-term strategy.

Perhaps surprisingly, despite the huge growth in the number of loyalty schemes (there are currently 27 million reward cards in circulation in the UK; in the airline business, travellers had accumulated more than 17 trillion frequent miles by the end of 2007 worth more than $850 billion), many of the benefits often go unclaimed by consumers. A study by the International Consumer Loyalty Programme (2005), for example, revealed that in each year in the UK 23 per cent of card holders with £460 million worth of points fail to redeem these points.

It is because of issues such as this and the sorts of paradox highlighted by our earlier comment about airline passengers that in recent years there has been a significant re-evaluation and rethinking of the concept of loyalty and the role of loyalty schemes. In doing this, we need initially to go back to the initial thinking about the nature and role of loyalty.

One of the first to explore in detail the attractions of customer loyalty was Reicheld (2006), who argued that organizations need to focus upon customer retention for five main reasons:

1. Acquiring customers is typically expensive and so the more you keep, the less you need to spend (it is this idea that has led others to suggest that 5 per cent uplift in customer retention could lead to companies doubling their profits)

2. The longer a customer stays, the more profitable he becomes

3. Established customers have lower servicing costs

4. Loyal customers provide more word-of-mouth recommendations

5. As loyal customers, they are less price-sensitive.

In many ways, it is Reicheld's work that has provided the foundation for much of what has been written about customer loyalty and loyalty marketing over the past decade, although increasingly his five basic tenets are being called into question. Reinartz and Kumar (2002), for example, have argued that, in many sectors (their primary focus was the retail, mail order, hi-tech, and financial services markets), long-term customers are often the least profitable. There are several reasons for this, but most obviously this is because they demand ever more from the organization. Research by Ehrenberg has also disputed the supposed link between loyalty and profitability.

The idea that loyal customers have lower servicing costs has also been questioned by Reinartz and Kumar (2002) who, in their research, simply found no evidence for this assertion. If anything, they suggest, the opposite may be true.

With regard to word-of-mouth recommendation, East found that across 15 categories (these included cars, credit cards, car insurance, home insurance, ISPs and mobile air time), the longer a customer stays, the less likely that customer is to recommend. He identifies several possible explanations for this, the most obvious of which is the loss of novelty as in that the customer starts to take the company for granted.

Reicheld's final point regarding the loyal customer's willingness to pay a price premium has also been questioned by Reinartz and Kumar who suggests that it is loyal customers who most typically demand more and who most resent an organization profiting from their loyalty.

Recognition of this sort of research has led Reicheld in recent years to accept that some of the ideas on which thinking about loyalty marketing has been based may indeed be questionable and has led him to suggesting instead that there is just one number that a company needs to know: the customer's willingness to recommend products or services to a friend. However, even this can be questioned in that, as a concept, it is essentially very loose, with recommendations potentially ranging from a positive statement if pushed, through to unprompted and unkindled enthusiasm. Secondly, a willingness to recommend does not automatically have a link to lifetime value or any of the other dimensions that are typically associated with loyalty marketing.

Given the cost of many long-running loyalty schemes and the questions that are increasingly being asked about their value, it is worth viewing loyalty schemes from a different standpoint. Rather than the simplistic idea of (so-called) loyalty schemes being based on the idea that customers have the potential for being inherently loyal, organizations such as Tesco have developed schemes such as their Club Card which capture huge amounts of customer information. This information is then analysed in detail so that very focused customer profiling then becomes possible. This profiling then allows for far more per use customer targeting, a far clearer and more meaningful offer to different customer groups, and a series of benefits and incentives in the form of special offers and points that can be redeemed either with Tesco or at theme parks, cinemas, and so on.

From the company's point of view, the information generated can then be used in a variety of ways including:

- The more precise management of the product range

- New product development

- Pricing strategies that more precisely meet the needs and price sensitivities of different target groups

- Merchandising so that the product portfolio is based on *detailed* insights to customer profiles and purchasing patterns

- Inventory management

- Promotions, with greater rewards being offered to loyal customers

- Levels of customer service, with greater attention being paid to the stock levels and promotions on those products bought by loyal customers

- The measurement of promotional and media effectiveness

- Customer acquisition by matching new products such as the entry to financial services and the launch of Tesco.com to specific customer types

- Targeted communications (20 per cent of Tesco's coupons are redeemed against an industry average of 0.5 per cent).

Relationship marketing myopia

Although relationship marketing and relationship management has an obvious attraction, Piercy (1999) has identified what he terms 'relationship marketing myopia', or the naive belief that every customer wants to have a relationship with their suppliers. He goes on to suggest that 'customers differ in many important ways in the types of relationship they want to have with different suppliers, and that to ignore this reality is an expensive indulgence'.

This, in turn, leads him to categorize customers in terms of those who are:

- *Relationship seekers* – customers who want a close and long-term relationship with suppliers

- *Relationship exploiters* – customers who will take every free service and offer, but will still move their business elsewhere when they feel like it

- *Loyal buyers* – those who will give long-term loyalty, but who do not want a close relationship

- *Arm's-length, transaction buyers* – those who avoid close relationships and move business based on price, technical specification or innovation.

This is illustrated in Figure 6.7.

In categorizing customers in this way, Piercy gives recognition to the need for relationship strategies to be based upon the principles of market segmentation and customers' relationship-seeking characteristics:

Relationship investment with profitable relationship seekers is good. Relationship investments with exploiters and transactional customers are a waste. The trick is going to be developing different marketing strategies to match different customer relationship needs.

Piercy's comments are interesting for a variety of reasons, and raise the question of whether there is a direct link between customer satisfaction and customer loyalty. Although intuitively a link between the two might appear obvious, the reality is that there is little hard evidence to suggest that anything more than an indirect relationship exists. Instead, it is probably the case that it is customer *dissatisfaction* that leads to customer disloyalty, although even here the link may be surprisingly tenuous. Whilst this might at first sight seem to be a strange comment to make, the reality in many markets is that there is often a surprisingly high degree of inertia within the customer base. (Gary Hamel, in a TV interview, has referred to this in terms of customer friction being a potentially major source of profits for

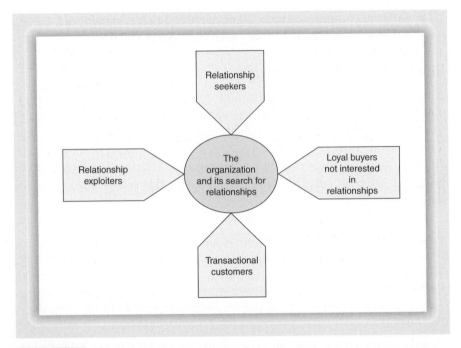

Customers and the nature of their relationship needs

many companies.) Given this, customers or consumers may be in a position where they simply cannot be bothered to change their source of supply until levels of dissatisfaction reach a very high level.

Piercy's ideas about the need to rethink approaches to relationship marketing have, in turn, been taken a step further by Frederick Newell (2003), who in his book *Why CRM Doesn't Work* highlighted many of the failures of the numerous customer relationship management (CRM) initiatives. With Frost & Sullivan having estimated that spending on CRM now exceeds $12 billion worldwide and is expected to double again in the next few years, the costs of a radical rethink are high. For Newell, there is now the need to move away from CRM to what he refers to as CMR, the customer management of relationships. Arguing that this is more than just a matter of semantics, Newell suggests the need for a new balance of power that allows 'the customer to tell us what she's interested in, what kind of information she wants, what level of service she wants to receive, and how she wants us to communicate with her – where, when and how often'.

However, an argument can be developed to suggest that both CRM and CMR fail to come to terms with the real complexities of consumer choice, something that can only become more problematic as the range of products and services available becomes ever wider. In these circumstances, any benefit to the customer that then justifies the idea of a relationship diminishes a proposition. As an example of this, loyalty cards – one of the original drivers of CRM – were seen at one stage as a way of engaging the customer's attention but, as Newell acknowledges, the advantage is marginal now that practically every airline and retail chain offers one or more. In the USA, 60 million people now belong to frequent-flyer programmes, something that led Newell to acknowledge that 'half of all members of loyalty programmes are free riders, enjoying benefits without spending more at the business that provides them'. Recognizing this, the real value of cards to the issuer is to provide data on customers' purchasing patterns, but if an organization is to pursue the CMR rather than the CRM philosophy, the company must use the information not just to sell more, but to 'make their lives easier and create emotional loyalty to the business relationship'.

Developing the customer community

Given some of the problems faced with the now traditional approach to relationship marketing campaigns (e.g. a survey undertaken in 2006 by Bain & Co. concluded that one in five executives believe that CRM initiatives had damaged customer relationships), Hunter (1997) has argued that, although marketing success needs to be based on the development of a loyal customer base, ensuring that product or service offerings meet customers' needs, having an ongoing competitive intelligence system, effective and efficient sales channels and – most importantly from our standpoint at this stage – building new business around current customers, the ways in which this is done need to be rethought. Amongst the ways in which he believes this can be done is by building an interdependent relationship with the customer in which each relies on the other for business solutions and successes. Hunter refers to this in terms of building a customer community which – given the average company loses 20–40 per cent of its customer base each year – is strategically important.

For Hunter, the customer community, based on integrated one-to-one marketing contact databases and value-based marketing, is an approach that allows for the building of truly strategic relationships with customers. Amongst the models that illustrate the central ideas and processes of the customer community and provide the framework for implementing it is the service–profit chain.

Developed by Heskett et al. (1994), the service–profit chain attempts to show the interrelationship of a company's internal and external communities, and highlights how customer loyalty that translates into revenue growth and profits might be achieved. It does this by establishing relationships between profitability, customer loyalty and employee satisfaction. The links in the chain are as follows:

- Profit and growth are stimulated primarily by customer loyalty
- Loyalty is a direct result of customer satisfaction

- Satisfaction is largely influenced by the value of services provided to customers

- Value is created by satisfied, loyal and productive employees

- Employee satisfaction, in turn, results primarily from high-quality support services and policies that enable employees to deliver results to customers.

The significance of customer promiscuity

One of the principal themes pursued throughout this book is that many of the traditional assumptions that have been made about customers and that have driven thinking on marketing strategy are quite simply no longer appropriate. Rather than being able to take customer loyalty for granted, the reality for many planners is that, as customers have become more demanding, more discriminating, less loyal and more willing to complain, levels of customer promiscuity have increased dramatically. In a number of ways, this can be seen to be the logical end point of the sorts of ideas discussed in 1970 by Alvin Toffler in his book *Future Shock*: he predicted that we would be living in a world of accelerating discontinuities where 'the points of a compass no longer navigated us in the direction of the future'.

Amongst Toffler's predictions was that, as the pace of change accelerates, so the nature of relationships becomes much more temporary. For marketers, the most obvious manifestation of this is a fracturing of the relationship between the organization and its markets and the decline of brand loyalty. This disconnection between consumers and brands is then exacerbated by vicarious living, a phenomenon that has been explored by Crawford Hollingworth (2001) of Headlight Vision. Hollingworth has argued that 'We live in a world where there is so much choice and information and so many different experiences that we believe that we have had, but in fact we haven't actually had.'

With customers now faced with so many stimuli in the form of advertising, promotions, point-of-sale offers, poster sites and sponsorship, the danger is that of a considerable amount of marketing activity simply becoming white noise. Given this, there is a need to rethink the nature of the relationship between the consumer and the brand. Amongst the ways in which this can be done is by focusing upon added value and the extra value proposition (EVP), customer-driven strategies and permission marketing (refer to the discussion in Chapter 11). In the absence of this, there is the very real danger of competitive oblivion, particularly as Web-based strategies reduce market entry barriers and costs.

An additional problem stems from what Hamel (2001) has referred to as the end of friction as a reliable service of profits (friction is defined by Hamel as customer ignorance or inertia). For many banks, for example, a substantial part of their revenue is often derived from the problems that customers face in identifying and/or choosing alternatives. However, with a generally greater degree of customer scepticism or cynicism, far higher expectations, increasing

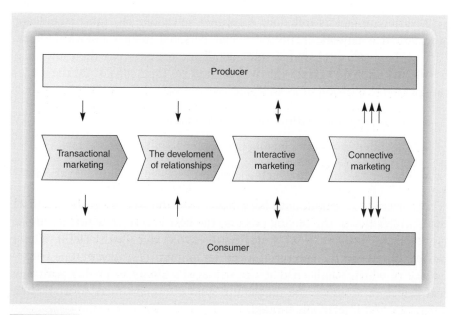

Producer

Transactional marketing

The develoment of relationships

Interactive marketing

Connective marketing

Consumer

FIGURE 6.8   *The move from transactional to connective marketing*

levels of customer promiscuity and the ease of access to alternatives via the web, friction is likely to become a far less common phenomenon.

Relationship marketing: the next stage of thinking

Although relationship marketing has undoubtedly had a major impact upon marketing thinking and upon the ways in which organizations interact with their customers, relationship marketing should not be seen as an end in itself. Instead, the marketing planner should think about how this sort of thinking might be moved ahead yet further, something that is made possible by the better management of databases, far more effective targeting, and the greater scope for one-to-one marketing. This is illustrated in Figure 6.8.

Here, the marketing planner focuses not just upon getting even closer to the customer, but also upon the development of a series of far more strategic and inherently cleverer interactions that are based upon true customer insight. However, in doing this, the planner needs to understand in detail the potential that each customer offers, since this then provides the basis for far better approaches to market segmentation.

6.9   SUMMARY

Within this chapter we have focused on the detail of consumer and industrial buying structures and processes, and on the ways in which an understanding of these contributes to effective marketing planning.

A variety of factors influence consumer behaviour, the most significant of which are a network of cultural, social, personal and psychological forces. Each of these was discussed in some detail and the nature of their interrelationships explored. Against this background we then considered the structure of buying decision processes, and in particular:

- The buying roles within the decision-making unit

- The different types of buying behaviour

- The process through which a consumer goes in making a decision.

A variety of attempts have been made over the past 40 years to model the complexities of the buying process, the best known of which are those proposed by Nicosia (1966), Engel *et al.* (1968) and Sheth (1973). These models have been the subject of a certain amount of criticism, one consequence of which has been that the strategist's ability to predict with any real degree of accuracy the probable response of consumers to marketing behaviour is still relatively limited.

Research into organizational buying behaviour has pursued broadly similar objectives to that in the consumer field, with attention being paid to the questions of:

- Who makes up the market?

- What buying decisions do they make?

- Who are the key participants in the buying process?

- What influences the buyer?

- How do buyers arrive at their decisions?

Each of these areas was examined in some detail and the best known of the models of organizational buying behaviour were reviewed. As with models of consumer behaviour, the majority of these have been heavily criticized, largely because of their poor analytical or predictive ability. There are, however, exceptions to this, as discussed, including Robinson *et al.*'s (1967) buy-grid model and Hakansson's (1981) interaction approach, in which use is made of interorganizational theory and new institutional economics thinking. It is in these areas that future developments in our understanding of organizational buying processes are most likely to be made.

APPENDIX: THE DRIVERS OF CONSUMER CHANGE

A variety of studies has been conducted over the past few years in an attempt to identify the principal drivers of change amongst twenty-first century consumers.

There are several features that are common to virtually all of these studies which suggest that Western societies are increasingly being characterized by:

1. Changing demographics

2. Changing family relationships

3. A significant cash-rich/time-poor segment

4. A search for (greater) value

5. The rise of ethical consumerism

6. An emphasis upon health and healthy lifestyles

7. A desire for indulgence and small treats as a reward for working hard and/or as a retreat from the pressures of the world.

Changing demographics

The youthful elderly

Although it has long been recognized that changing demographics in many countries are leading to increasingly elderly populations, less emphasis has been given to the characteristics of these people. The notion of the youthful elderly is based on the way in which, as the children of the 1960s move into middle age/late middle age, they are increasingly retaining their youthful lifestyles and attitudes (see, for example, Richardson, 2001). Benefiting from higher levels of health and fitness and having more money than previous generations, the youthful elderly expect – and are able – to live life to the full. In these circumstances, age largely becomes an attitude of mind.

Although this market has often been largely ignored by planners, its real size and value is shown by the way in which, in the UK, more than 48 per cent of the population is currently over 50. In 20 years, one in two adults will be over 50.

However, it needs to be recognized that, within the over-50s segment, major differences do exist. Although a growing number of retired people are healthier, more active, more affluent, want to have more fun, eat out more often, travel, and as a result are more experimental with food and are open to new technology (including the Internet), those dependent on state pensions are now having to pay more for their healthcare and becoming more entrenched in terms of attitude to new ideas and products. There is therefore a growing polarization within the group.

Ageing children (the under 14s)

At the same time that we are seeing the elderly becoming more youthful, we also have a series of changes that are affecting the children's market. In the case of the under 14s, numbers are currently declining. Between 2000 and 2007, for example, the 5–9 years age segment declined by 6 per cent, the

10–14s remained static and 15–19s increased by 5 per cent. By 2010, 5–9s will have declined by 11 per cent, 10–14s will have declined by 5 per cent and 15–19s will have increased by 5 per cent. By 2012, 5–9s will have declined by 13 per cent, 10–14s will have declined by 6 per cent and 15–19s will have increased by 6 per cent. The widening availability of technology and media means that children are exposed to the adult world much earlier and are now aware of advertising and its role by the age of 3. One result of this is that they are more demanding of brands and their environment, with this being due in part to more spoiling by time-pressured parents and the easy availability of luxuries. They are also more sophisticated and far more unforgiving with regard to brands. They expect entertainment and have low boredom thresholds.

Ageing children (the teens)

Although the teenage market has traditionally been seen to be amongst the fastest changing segments of consumer markets, a strong case can be made to suggest that this segment is now changing even faster than in the past. In part, this is because of the ways in which teenagers today have been exposed to a greater number of stimuli than those previously, and it is this that has led to a generation that is now far more advertising media, technologically and brand literate than any of those that have gone before. However, the 'teen' world is characterized by a series of paradoxes, with a continual seeking of new youth world/escapism (as adults invade their space) and for excitement, as well as increasing insecurity and the need to belong.

This manifests itself in a teen world that is characterized by:

- Living for today, with a heavy emphasis upon individual self-expression, mobility, freedom and hedonism

- A commercial and marketing overload that has led to those within this group being media literate, cynical and more demanding

- A group that has a strong appreciation of brands and their heritage; where there is a superficial idealism for the brand, the market has a tendency to reject it.

Changing family relationships

With the breakdown of the traditional family structure, a decline in the number of births to 1.64 per woman and a growth in the number of working women, family decision-making structures have undergone a series of fundamental changes. There is therefore a big question over who within the redefined family makes decisions and how these are arrived at. In essence:

- Democracy and individualism have replaced traditional family hierarchies and children play a far greater role. They are no longer protected from the adult world in the way they were previously.

- Because the number of working and career women has increased dramatically, male/female/family dynamics have changed. Independence is now an economic possibility for a greater number of women – with the economics of divorce having contributed to this. However, a number of commentators have identified a culture of guilt surrounding the question of how to be a good mother, whilst at the same time working full-time and pursuing a career.

There are now no set life-stages and less age-appropriate behaviour. Children are exposed to a greater number of stimuli (half of all 4-year-olds have a television in their bedroom) and are far more brand-conscious. Adults stay young longer. The age at which many have children is getting later as they concentrate on having 'fun' (this is the rise of 'middle youth' – people in their 30s and 40s who still haven't 'settled down', something that has been manifested in the rise of adventure holidays targeted at this group).

The rise of the cash-rich/time-poor segment

Because more and more people are working longer hours, the service sector has grown enormously to fill the time gap. The idea of getting someone to do something for you is no longer unacceptable (laziness/snobbery). Instead, it is a sign of valuing your life. Other factors that have led to the growth of the service sector to serve this market include:

- Seventy-six per cent of women of working age are now employed and, whilst statistics show that women still do the majority of housework, young women are less inclined to do it than their mothers were. The number of single-person households is also increasing and so these people have no one else to do it for them.

- The desire to fully exploit the little time people do have. They are therefore willing to pay for time, quality and simplicity – life is too short to do it yourself. This is not a return to Edwardian hierarchy (i.e. 'I am too good to clean'), but rather 'I don't have enough time to clean, so I will pay someone to do it for me'.

- The 24-hour society that has been driven by:
  - The Internet being 'open' 24 hours, helping to confirm this notion of the 24-hour society
  - Home delivery and combination of products when and where you want them
  - An increase in stress-related diseases.

However, at the same time that we have seen the rise of the cash-rich/time-poor segment, there has also been a growth in the time-rich/cash-poor segment, a factor that has implications for the value-for-money offer.

A search for (greater) value

Against the background of the factors discussed in the above section, there is increasingly the emergence of two (or three) nations within society (see Illustration 6.5), characterized by:

- Forty per cent of households are affluent, but one in three is poor and getting poorer

- The wealthiest 5 per cent of UK society own 42 per cent of the total national wealth, whilst the bottom 50 per cent own just 6 per cent of national wealth (the top 25 per cent own 74 per cent of the wealth)

- High levels of price consciousness continue to thrive, and retailers are set to capitalize on this with the growth of retailers such as Wal-Mart, Aldi and Netto

- Even the wealthier, older households will feel squeezed as more of their discretionary income goes on health, education and private insurance

Illustration 6.5   The rise of the three-nation society

In the mid-1990s, the Henley Centre highlighted the ways in which there is an interaction of time and money and how this has led to the emergence of a sizeable time-poor/cash-rich segment in society. The profile of this segment, which they referred to as 'the first nation', differs sharply from those segments labelled the second and third nations; the characteristics of the three segments are illustrated in Figure 6.9. The 20 per cent of the people in this first nation are characterized by being willing to spend money to save time, something that distinguishes them from the other 80 per cent. By virtue of their income levels, this segment of society also has open to it a greater spectrum of product choices and has responded by being more willing than other segments to pass on to others some aspects of life management.

The first nation	The second nation	The third nation
20% of the population	50% of the population	30% of the population
40% of consumer spending	50% of consumer spending	10% of consumer spending
Cash-rich	Cash-constrained	Cash-poor
Time-poor	Time-constrained	Time-rich

FIGURE 6.9   *The three-nation society*

- Consumers are becoming even more demanding of quality and see price/value solutions more than price *per se* to be important

- Home shopping, with much more prominent pricing cues, will help to fuel the price mentality.

The rise of ethical consumerism

Because of the large numbers of financial, food, health and environmental scares over the past decade, a greater cynicism about government, politicians, big business and brands has emerged.

Ethical consumerism has been a response to this and reflects the desire to gain control over one's life. Buying ethical products from a supermarket, for example, involves no major life changes, but is an easy way to make the consumer feel he or she is making a difference. In these circumstances, prices are often of less importance than how the product is positioned.

An emphasis upon health and healthy lifestyles

Because of the growing awareness of the ability and personal responsibility for individuals to influence their own health, the greater evidence regarding links between diet and disease, and the shift from the welfare state to the individual, there has been an upsurge in the emphasis given to lifestyle management. Underpinning this is the recognition that diet is an important contributor to healthiness ('I am more concerned about what I eat and drink than I used to be'), and that children today are increasingly exposed to smoking, pollution, drugs, stress and a lack of exercise. There is, though, a general confusion over how to eat healthily, 'the advice given on healthy eating is always changing' and a (growing?) body of consumers who just opt out or cannot afford to participate ('I would like to eat healthier foods but it costs a lot more to buy the right things').

The desire for indulgence and small treats

With society generally becoming wealthier, the rises in consumers' disposable income and the number of people considering themselves 'middle class', tastes and aspirations are changing. Stressful lifestyles and time famine means there is a greater need for pampering and enhanced leisure time. Even in times of economic hardship small indulgences remain intact; in fact, these are increasingly seen as being essentials.

CHAPTER 7

Approaches to Competitor Analysis

7.1 LEARNING OBJECTIVES

When you have read this chapter you should be able to understand:

(a) the importance of competitor analysis;

(b) how firms can best identify against whom they are competing;

(c) how to evaluate competitive relationships;

(d) how to identify competitors' likely response profiles;

(e) the components of the competitive information system and how the information generated feeds into the process of formulating strategy.

7.2 INTRODUCTION

Competition is defined by the perceptions of the customer and not by the (mis)perceptions of the members of a management team. (Anon)

We suggested in Chapter 6 that the past 10 years have seen the emergence of a very different type of consumer who is characterized by a very different type of value system and far higher expectations. At the same time, a new type of competitor appears to have emerged along with a different type of competitive environment. This new environment can be seen to be characterized by:

- Generally higher levels and an increasing intensity of competition

- New and more aggressive competitors who are emerging with ever greater frequency

- Changing bases of competition as organizations search ever harder for a competitive edge

- The emergence of new technologies, including the Internet, which have dramatically lowered barriers to entry and operating costs, thereby allowing companies to enter and leave a market far more quickly and far more easily

- Wider geographic sources of competition as trade barriers are reduced

- More frequent niche attacks

- More frequent strategic alliances

- A quickening of the pace of innovation

- The need for stronger relationships and alliances with customers and distributors

- An emphasis upon value-added strategies

- Ever more aggressive price competition

- Difficulties of achieving long-term differentiation, with the result that a greater number of enterprises are finding themselves stuck in the marketing wilderness with no obvious competitive advantage

- The emergence of a greater number of 'bad' competitors (i.e. those not adhering to the traditional and unspoken rules of competitive behaviour within their industries).

The implications of these changes, both individually and collectively, are significant and demand far more from an enterprise if it is to survive and grow. Most obviously, there is a need for a much more detailed understanding of who it is that the enterprise is competing against and the nature of their capabilities. However, in coming to terms with this, the marketing planner needs to focus not just upon the 'hard' factors (e.g. their size, financial resources, manufacturing capability), but also upon the 'softer' elements, such as their managerial cultures, their priorities, their commitment to particular markets and market offerings, the assumptions they hold about themselves and their markets, and their objectives. There is also a significant issue in terms of how organizations perceive their competitors, something that has become more difficult and complex as the result of the Internet making market entry and exit far easier. Without this understanding, it is almost inevitable that the marketing planner will fail to come to terms with the nature and significance of competitive threats. Given the nature of these comments, the need for, and advantages of, detailed competitive analysis should be apparent and can be summarized in terms of how it is capable of:

- Providing an understanding of your competitive advantage/ disadvantage relative to your competitors' positions

- Helping in generating insights into competitors' strategies – past, present and potential

■ Giving an informed basis for developing future strategies to sustain/
establish advantages over your competitors.

Although the vast majority of marketing planners and strategists acknowledge the importance of competitive analysis, it has long been recognized that
less effort is typically put into the detailed and formal analysis of competitors
than, for example, of customers and their buying patterns. In many cases this
is seemingly because marketing managers feel that they know enough about
their competitors simply as the result of competing against them on a day-by-
day basis. In other cases there is almost a sense of resignation, with managers
believing that it is rarely possible to understand competitors in detail and that,
as long as the company's performance is acceptable, there is little reason to
spend time collecting information (see Figure 7.1). In yet others, there is only
a general understanding of who it is that the company is competing against.
The reality, however, is that competitors represent a major determinant of
corporate success, and any failure to take detailed account of their strengths,
weaknesses, strategies and areas of vulnerability is likely to lead not just to
a sub-optimal performance, but also to an unnecessarily greater exposure to
aggressive and unexpected competitive moves. Other probable consequences of
failing to monitor competition include an increased likelihood of the enterprise
being taken by surprise, its relegation to being a follower rather than a leader,
and to a focus on short-term rather than more fundamental long-term issues.

There are numerous examples of organizations having been taken by
surprise by new competitors who introduce and then play by very different rules of the game. (Think, for example, of the way in which BA and the
other major European flag carriers have been hit by new entrants such as
easyJet and Ryanair; how Hoover and Electrolux were hit by Dyson; how
the major clearing banks were seemingly taken by surprise by the telephone
and Internet bankers; and how the American car industry was hit by the
Japanese.) It is apparent from these sorts of examples and the points made
above that competitor analysis is not a luxury but a necessity in order to:

■ Survive

■ Handle slow growth

- Complacency
- It can't happen here
- I don't want to hear it
- We have the information already
- Preconceived assumptions

FIGURE 7.1   *Attitudinal barriers to undertaking competitor analysis*

- Cope with change
- Exploit opportunities
- Uncover key factors
- Reinforce intuition
- Improve the quality of decisions
- Stay competitive
- Avoid surprises.

(See Kelly, 1987, pp. 10–14)

It follows from this that competitive analysis should be a central element of the marketing planning process, with detailed attention being paid to each competitor's apparent objectives, resources, capabilities, perceptions and competitive stance, as well as to their marketing plans and the individual elements of the marketing mix. In this way, areas of competitive strength and weakness can more readily be identified, and the results fed into the process of developing an effective marketing strategy. Better and more precise attacks can then be aimed at competitors and more effective defences erected to fight off competitors' moves. An additional benefit of competitor analysis, in certain circumstances at least, is that it can help in the process of understanding buying behaviour by identifying the particular groups or classes of customer to whom each competitor's strategy is designed to appeal. This can then be used as the basis for determining the most effective probable positioning strategy for the organization.

Recognition of these points leaves the strategist needing to answer five questions:

1. Against whom are we competing?
2. What strengths and weaknesses do they possess?
3. What are their objectives?
4. What strategies are they pursuing and how successful are they?
5. How are they likely to behave and, in particular, how are they likely to react to offensive moves?

Taken together, the answers to these five questions should provide the marketing strategist with a clear understanding of the competitive environment and, in particular, against *whom* the company is competing and *how* they compete. An example of this, which although it relates to Kodak in the 1970s, appears in Figure 7.2 and neatly illustrates the need to adopt a breadth of perspective in coming to terms with the complexity of the competitive environment.

It is against the background of the picture that emerges from this sort of analysis that the marketing strategist can then begin to formulate strategy. In the example cited in Figure 7.2, for example, the central issue for Kodak

Kodak's products	Principal competitor(s)	Kodak's market position	Intensity and bases of competition	Likelihood of new entrants	Kodak's core strategy
Instant cameras and instant film	Polaroid	Challenger to a well-established leader	High and increasing with greater emphasis being placed on innovation	High	Penetration pricing to sell cameras as fast as possible to build a base for the sales of film
Photographic paper	Fuji Photo Film Co	Leader but being threatened by Fuji and other Japanese companies	High – the attack is based on lower prices and statements of quality	Medium	Share maintenance by emphasizing the quality of Kodak paper and making consumers aware that some processors do not use Kodak paper
Office copiers	Xerox, IBM, 3M	Late entrant to a highly competitive market in which Xerox held a 75 per cent share	Very high with ever greater emphasis being given to innovation, cost and service	Very high (particularly from Japanese firms)	The establishment of a separate sales and service network utilizing the firm's image and marketing capabilities in the microfilm equipment area

FIGURE 7.2   The competitive environment for selected Eastman Kodak products in the late 1970s (Adapted from Business Week, 20 June 1977)

revolved around the costs, risks and possible long-term returns from penetrating new markets in instant cameras and office copiers, as opposed to sustaining and defending the company's position as the market leader in the photographic paper market. The principal environmental inputs to the company's strategic planning process at this time were therefore competitive forces and new technology. Subsequently, of course, the camera market has changed dramatically as the result of digital technology, the effects of which have been seen in terms of the decline of the film processing market and the demand for photographic paper, two markets in which Kodak held a dominant position. In the case of cameras, the principal players, such as Sony, Canon, Minolta and Samsung, have all proved to be very aggressive and fast-moving, with the result that Kodak is now a relatively small competitor.

Having developed a picture of the market in this way, the analysis can then be taken a step further by a compilation of each competitor's likely response profile; the various inputs needed for this are illustrated in Figures 7.3 and 7.4.

In using the model in Figure 7.4, the strategist begins by focusing upon the competitor's current strategy, and then moves successively through an examination of competitive strengths and weaknesses; the assumptions that the competitor appears to hold about the industry and itself; and then, finally and very importantly, the competitor's probable future goals and the factors that drive it. It is an understanding of these four dimensions which then allows the marketing strategist to begin compiling the detail of the response profile and to answer four principal questions:

1. Is the competitor satisfied with its current position?

2. What future moves is the competitor likely to make?

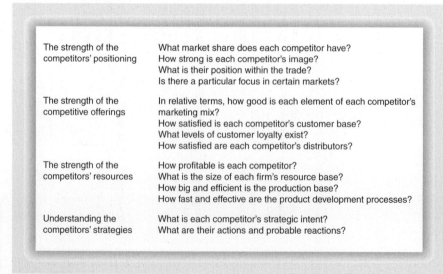

FIGURE 7.3　*Competitor analysis: step 1 – developing a general picture of the competition*

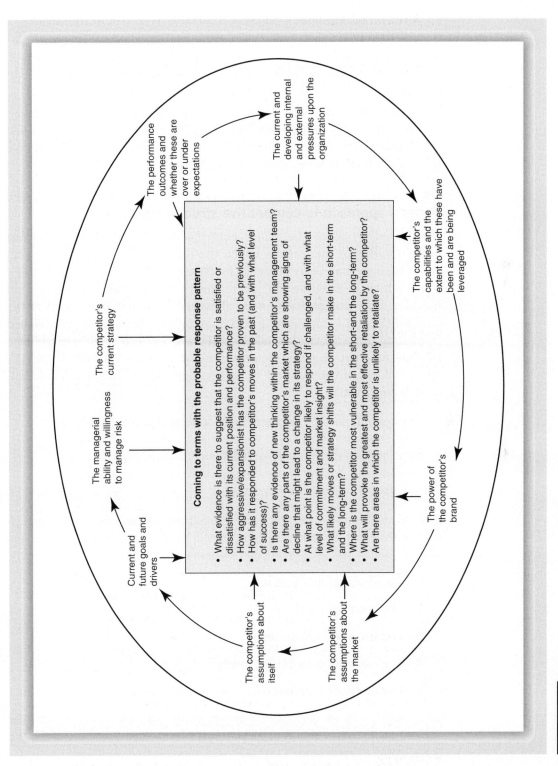

The performance outcomes and whether these are over or under expectations

The current and developing internal and external pressures upon the organization

The competitor's current strategy

The managerial ability and willingness to manage risk

Coming to terms with the probable response pattern

- What evidence is there to suggest that the competitor is satisfied or dissatisfied with its current position and performance?
- How aggressive/expansionist has the competitor proven to be previously?
- How has it responded to competitor's moves in the past (and with what level of success)?
- Is there any evidence of new thinking within the competitor's management team?
- Are there any parts of the competitor's market which are showing signs of decline that might lead to a change in its strategy?
- At what point is the competitor likely to respond if challenged, and with what level of commitment and market insight?
- What likely moves or strategy shifts will the competitor make in the short-term and the long-term?
- Where is the competitor most vulnerable in the short-and the long-term?
- What will provoke the greatest and most effective retaliation by the competitor?
- Are there areas in which the competitor is unlikely to retaliate?

The competitor's capabilities and the extent to which these have been and are being leveraged

Current and future goals and drivers

The competitor's assumptions about itself

The competitor's assumptions about the market

The power of the competitor's brand

FIGURE 7.4   *The development of a competitor's response profile*

3. In which segments or areas of technology is the competitor most vulnerable?

4. What move on our part is likely to provoke the strongest retaliation by the competitor?

Against the background of the answers to those questions, the marketing strategist needs then to consider two further issues: where are we most vulnerable to any move on the part of each competitor, and what can we realistically do in order to reduce this vulnerability?

Porter's approach to competitive structure analysis

Undoubtedly one of the major contributions in recent years to our understanding of the ways in which the competitive environment influences strategy has been provided by Porter (1980, Chapter 1). Porter's work, which is discussed in greater detail in Chapter 11, is based on the idea that 'competition in an industry is rooted in its underlying economics, and competitive forces that go well beyond the established combatants in a particular industry' (Porter, 1979, p. 138). He has also emphasized that the first determinant of a firm's profitability is the attractiveness of the industry in which it operates. The second determinant is competition:

> The central question in competitive strategy is a firm's relative position within its industry. Positioning determines whether a firm's profitability is above or below the industry average ... The fundamental basis of above average performance in the long run is sustainable competitive advantage.

This leads Porter to suggest that the nature and intensity of competition within any industry is determined by the interaction of five key forces:

1. The threat of new entrants

2. The power of buyers

3. The threat of substitutes

4. The extent of competitive rivalry

5. The power of suppliers.

This work is, as we commented above, examined in Chapter 11 and the reader may therefore find it of value to turn to the first part of that chapter before going any further.

7.3 AGAINST WHOM ARE WE COMPETING?

Identifying present competitors and new entrants

Although the answer to the question of who it is that a company is competing against might appear straightforward, the range of actual and potential competitors faced by a company is often far broader than appears to be the case at first sight. The strategist should therefore avoid competitive myopia both by adopting a broad perspective and recognizing that, in general, companies tend to overestimate the capabilities of large competitors and either underestimate or ignore those of smaller ones. In the 1970s, for example, the large manufacturers of computers were preoccupied with competing against one another and failed for some time to recognize the emergence and growing threat in the PC market posed by what were at the time small companies such as Apple. More recently, we have seen book retailers having to rethink their strategies, often in a radical way, as the result of Amazon.com having changed the competitive dynamics of book selling, whilst the travel sector has had to come to terms with customers' very different buying patterns through the Internet.

In a more general sense, business history is full of examples of companies that have seemingly been taken by surprise by organizations they had failed to identify as competitors, or whose competitive capability they drastically underestimated. In Chapter 5, for example, we referred to the experiences of the Swiss watch industry, which was brought to its knees in the late 1960s and early 1970s by new manufacturers of inexpensive watches that incorporated digital technology, a technology that, ironically, the Swiss themselves had developed. Equally, in the reprographic market, companies such as Gestetner suddenly and unexpectedly found themselves in the 1970s having to fight aggressive new entrants to the market such as Xerox. Xerox entered this market with a new, faster, cleaner and infinitely more convenient product to which Gestetner, together with a number of other companies in the market at the time, experienced difficulties in responding. Subsequently, Xerox itself has been faced with a new and aggressive wave of competition from a number of largely Asian competitors, including Canon. Similarly, the British and US television and motorcycle manufacturers either failed to recognize the Japanese threat or underestimated their expansionist objectives. The result today is that neither country has a domestic manufacturing industry of any size in either of these sectors. More recently, in the case of the music industry, the traditional players across the sector have been forced to come to terms with a very different type of competition in the form of Internet downloads, whilst in the soft drinks market both Coca-Cola and Pepsi have been faced with an aggressive and highly innovative competitor in Red Bull. Less drastic, but in many ways equally fundamental, problems have been experienced in the car industry with new players from countries such as Korea and Taiwan having emerged with high value-for-money offers.

It is because of examples such as these that astute strategists have long acknowledged the difficulties of defining the boundaries of an industry, and have recognized that companies are more likely to be taken by surprise and hit hard by *latent* competitors than by *current* competitors whose patterns of marketing behaviour are largely predictable. In other words, it is typically the new and often small firms that are not being monitored which frequently pose the biggest medium and long term threats. It is therefore possible to see competition operating at four levels:

1. Competition consists only of those companies offering a similar product or service to the target market, utilizing a similar technology, and exhibiting similar degrees of vertical integration. Thus, Nestlé (which makes Nescafé) sees Kraft Foods, with its Maxwell House brand, as a similar competitor in the instant coffee market, while Penguin sees its direct competitors in the chocolate snack bar market to be Kit-Kat's six pack, Twix and Club.

2. Competition consists of all companies operating in the same product or service category. Penguin's indirect competitors, for example, consist of crisps and ice-creams.

3. Competition consists of all companies manufacturing or supplying products that deliver the same service. Thus, long-distance coach operators compete not just against each other, but also against railways, cars, planes and motorcycles.

4. Competition consists of all companies competing for the same spending power. An example of this is the American motorcycle manufacturer Harley Davidson, which does not necessarily see itself as competing directly with other motorcycle manufacturers. Instead, for many buyers it is a choice between a Harley Davidson motorcycle and a major consumer durable such as a conservatory or a boat: this is discussed in greater detail in Illustration 7.1.

It should be apparent from this that the marketing strategist needs not only to identify those competitors who reflect the same general approach to the market, but also to consider those who 'intersect' the company in each market, who possibly approach it from a different perspective, and who ultimately might pose either a direct or an indirect threat. As part of this, the strategist needs also to identify potential new entrants to the market and, where it appears necessary, develop contingency plans to neutralize their competitive effect. Newcomers to a market can, as Abell and Hammond (1979, p. 52) have pointed out, enter from any one of several starting points:

■ They already sell to your customers, but expand their participation to include new customer functions which you currently satisfy (e.g.

Illustration 7.1   Harley Davidson and its perception of competition

Harley Davidson, the last remaining American motorcycle, is seen by many as one of the icons of the design world. As a symbol of freedom and adventure, the socio-economic profile of Harley Davidson owners differs significantly from that of virtually all other motorcycle riders. The late Malcolm Forbes, the owner of *Forbes* magazine, for example, rode Harleys with his 'gang' called the Capitalist Tools and did much to promote the bike among clean-cut executives known as Rich Urban Bikers (RUBs). This image has been reinforced by the bike's appearance in numerous commercials, including a Levi's advertisement in which a monstrous Harley is ridden on to a Wall Street dealing-room floor. Although it is acknowledged that the bikes are technically antiquated, few current or aspiring owners see this as a drawback. Most Harley owners do not actually ride the bikes a great deal. They are, as one commentator has observed, social statements rather than forms of transport. One consequence of this is that Harley Davidson, at least in the UK, competes only very indirectly with other motorcycle manufacturers. Instead, as Steve Dennis of Harley Street, a dealership specializing in used and customized bikes, puts it: 'We're competing against conservatories and swimming pools, not other bikes.'

Source: The Sunday Times, 23 September 1990.

they initially sell a component of a computer system and expand into other system components that you supply)

- They already satisfy customer functions that you satisfy but expand their participation into your customer market from activities in other customer markets (e.g. they initially sell pumps for oil exploration only and then expand into the marine pump business, where you are active)

- They already operate in an 'upstream' or 'downstream' business (e.g. Texas Instruments entered calculators from its position as a semiconductor manufacturer, while some calculator manufacturers have subsequently integrated backwards into the manufacture of semiconductors)

- They enter as a result of 'unrelated' diversification.

Taken together, these comments lead to two distinct viewpoints of competition: the *industry point of view* and the *market point of view*.

The industry perspective of competition

The industry perception of competition is implicit in the majority of discussions of marketing strategy. Here, an industry is seen to consist of firms offering a product or class of products or services that are close substitutes for one another; a close substitute in these circumstances is seen to be a product for which there is a high cross-elasticity of demand. An example of this would be a dairy product such as butter where, if the price rises, a

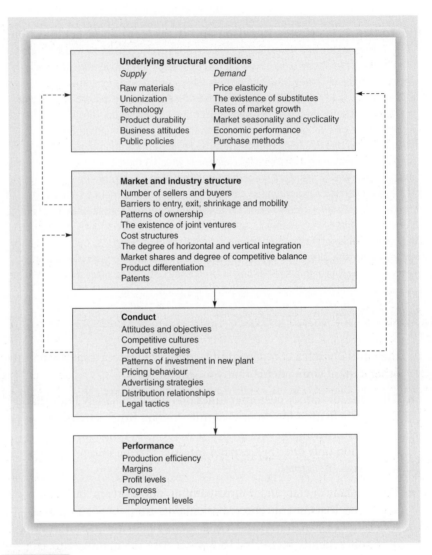

Underlying structural conditions

Supply

Raw materials
Unionization
Technology
Product durability
Business attitudes
Public policies

Demand

Price elasticity
The existence of substitutes
Rates of market growth
Market seasonality and cyclicality
Economic performance
Purchase methods

Market and industry structure

Number of sellers and buyers
Barriers to entry, exit, shrinkage and mobility
Patterns of ownership
The existence of joint ventures
Cost structures
The degree of horizontal and vertical integration
Market shares and degree of competitive balance
Product differentiation
Patents

Conduct

Attitudes and objectives
Competitive cultures
Product strategies
Patterns of investment in new plant
Pricing behaviour
Advertising strategies
Distribution relationships
Legal tactics

Performance

Production efficiency
Margins
Profit levels
Progress
Employment levels

FIGURE 7.5   *The competitive dynamics of an industry (adapted from Scherer, 1980)*

proportion of consumers will switch to margarine. A logical starting point for competitor analysis therefore involves understanding the industry's competitive pattern, since it is this that determines the underlying competitive dynamics. A model of this process appears in Figure 7.5.

From this it can be seen that competitive dynamics are influenced initially by conditions of supply and demand. These in turn determine the *industry structure*, which then influences *industry conduct* and, subsequently, *industry performance*.

Arguably the most significant single element in this model is the structure of the industry itself, and in particular the number of sellers, their relative market shares, and the degree of differentiation that exists between the competing companies and products.

The interrelated issue of the number of sellers and their relative market shares has long been the focus of analysis by economists, who have typically categorized an industry in terms of five types:

1. *An absolute monopoly*, in which, because of patents, licences, scale economics or some other factor, only one firm provides the product or service

2. *A differentiated oligopoly*, where a few firms produce products that are partially differentiated

3. *A pure oligopoly*, in which a few firms produce broadly the same commodity

4. *Monopolistic competition*, in which the industry has many firms offering a differentiated product or service

5. *Pure competition*, in which numerous firms offer broadly the same product or service.

Although industries can at any given time be categorized in these terms, competitive structures do of course change. The rail industry, for example, faced significant competition initially from bus companies such as National Express coaches, and then subsequently from Stagecoach and First Group after deregulation within the industry in 1980, and was forced into making a series of changes to its marketing strategy, which has continued following the privatized break-up of British Rail. Equally, patterns of competition in many other industries, such as cars, consumer electronics and white goods, have changed dramatically in a relatively short period as the result of the growth of import penetration. In the case of white goods such as refrigerators, washing machines, tumble driers and freezers, for example, the domestically-based manufacturers such as Hoover and Hotpoint found themselves in the 1980s facing new, aggressive and often price-based competition from, among others, Zanussi, Indesit, Electrolux and Candy, and then, in the 1990s, from Dyson. The issue that then needs to be faced is how best the challenged company can respond.

Although a substantial increase in levels of import penetration are in many ways the most conspicuous causes of a change in competitive structures, a series of other factors exist that can have equally dramatic implications for the nature and bases of competition. These include:

■ Changes within the distribution channels – the emergence of very powerful retail chains such as Tesco and Sainsbury's with groceries, B&Q in the DIY (do-it-yourself) sector, PC World with computers, and Toys 'R' Us with toys – has led to a significant shift in the balance of power between manufacturers and retailers, with the retailers adopting an ever-more proactive stance regarding product acceptance, new product development, price points, promotional activity and advertising support

■ Changes in the supplier base

- Legislation
- The emergence of new technology.

The market perspective of competition

As an alternative to the industry perspective of competition, which takes as its starting point companies making the same product or offering the same

---

Illustration 7.2   Substitutes for aluminium

The need to have a clear understanding of who exactly your competitors are and the nature of their strengths and weaknesses is illustrated below. In this we list some of the alternatives to aluminium. Although not all of the materials listed in the left-hand column are alternatives in each and every situation in which aluminium is used, the table goes some way towards illustrating how an overly-narrow competitive perspective could well lead to an organization being taken by surprise as customers switch to the alternatives.

Material	Advantages	Drawbacks
Mild steel	Very cheap	Weight
	Widely available	Rusts easily
Low-chrome ferritic stainless steel	Similar price	Weight
	Widely available	Rusts in sea water
Titanium	Strength (especially at temperature)	Cost
	Corrosion resistance	Processing (not easily extrudable)
Magnesium	Very lightweight	Vulnerable to fire
Polystyrene	Lightweight	Low strength
Unplasticated PVC	Reasonably cheap	No temperature/fire resistance
ABS, nylon engineering plastics	Lightweight	Cost
	Strong	
Wood	Cheap	Variable quality
	Widely available	Rots
Composites		
Aluminium MMCs	Stronger	Extra cost
	Stiffer	Processing difficulties
	Harder	
Fibre-reinforced plastics	Lighter for quality	Can lack toughness
	Stiffness/strength	Extra cost

service, we can focus on companies that try to satisfy the same customer needs or that serve the same customer groups. Theodore Levitt has long been a strong advocate of this perspective and it was this which was at the heart of his classic article 'Marketing Myopia'. In this article, Levitt (1960), pointed to a series of examples of organizations that had failed to recognize how actual and potential customers viewed the product or service being offered. Thus, in the case of railways, the railway companies concentrated on competing with one another and in doing this failed to recognize that, because customers were looking for transport, they compared the railways with planes, buses and cars. The essence of the market perspective of competition therefore involves giving full recognition to the broader range of products or services that are capable of satisfying customers' needs. This should, in turn, lead to the marketing strategist identifying a broader set of actual and potential competitors, and adopting a more effective approach to long-run market planning (see Illustration 7.2).

7.4 IDENTIFYING AND EVALUATING COMPETITORS' STRENGTHS AND WEAKNESSES

By this stage it should be apparent that the identification and evaluation of competitors' strengths, weaknesses and capabilities is at the very heart of a well-developed competitive strategy. The marketing planner should, as a first step, therefore concentrate upon collecting information under a number of headings as a prelude to a full comparative assessment. These include:

- Sales
- Market share
- Cost and profit levels, and how they appear to be changing over time
- Cash flows
- Return on investment
- Investment patterns
- Production processes
- Levels of capacity utilization
- Organizational culture
- Products and the product portfolio
- Product quality
- The size and pattern of the customer base
- The levels of brand loyalty
- Dealers and distribution channels
- Marketing and selling capabilities

- Operations and physical distribution

- Financial capabilities

- Management capabilities and attitudes to risk

- Human resources, their capability and flexibility

- Previous patterns of response

- Ownership patterns and, in the case of divisionalized organizations, the expectations of corporate management.

The signs of competitive strength in a company's position are likely to be:

- Important core competences

- Strong market share (or a leading market share)

- A pace-setting or distinctive strategy

- Growing customer base and customer loyalty

- Above-average market visibility

- Being in a favourably situated strategic group

- Concentrating on fastest-growing market segments

- Strongly differentiated products

- Cost advantages

- Above-average profit margins

- Above-average technological and innovational capability

- A creative, entrepreneurially alert management

- In a position to capitalize on opportunities.

Obtaining this sort of information typically proves to be more difficult in some instances than in others. Industrial markets, for example, rarely have the same wealth of published data that is commonly available in consumer markets. This, however, should not be used as an excuse for not collecting the information, but rather emphasizes the need for a clearly-developed competitive information system that channels information under a wide variety of headings to a central point. This information needs to be analysed and disseminated as a prelude to being fed into the strategy process.

The sources of this information will obviously vary from industry to industry, but will include most frequently the sales force, trade shows, industry experts, the trade press, distributors, suppliers and, perhaps most importantly, customers. Customer information can be gained in several ways, although periodically a firm may find it of value to conduct primary research among customers, suppliers and distributors to arrive at a profile

Significant buying factors	Our company	Competitors		
		1	2	3
Products				
Product design	Good	Exc	Fair	Good
Product quality	Good	Exc	Fair	Exc
Product performance	Good	Good	Fair	Good
Breadth of product line	Fair	Fair	Poor	Good
Depth of product line	Fair	Fair	Poor	Good
Reliability	Good	Exc	Fair	Exc
Running costs	Fair	Good	Equal	Good
Promotion and pricing				
Advertising/sales promotion	Fair	Exc	Fair	Good
Image and reputation	Fair	Exc	Fair/Poor	Exc
Product literature	Poor	Exc	Poor	Good
Price	Equal	Fair	Good	Equal
Selling and distribution				
Sales force calibre	Fair	Good	Poor	Good
Sales force experience/knowledge	Fair	Good	Fair	Exc
Geographical coverage	Good	Good	Poor	Good
Sales force/customer relations	Fair	Exc	Poor	Exc
Service				
Customer service levels	Fair	Exc	Poor	Exc
Performance against promise	Fair	Exc	Poor	Exc

The classification of factors from excellent (Exc) to poor should be determined by marketing intelligence, including studies of the perceptions of current and potential buyers, as well as those of suppliers and distributors.

FIGURE 7.6 *The comparative assessment of competitors*

of competitors within the market. An example of this appears in Figure 7.6, where current and potential buyers have been asked to rate the organization and its three major competitors on a series of attributes. A similar exercise can then be conducted among suppliers and distributors in order to build up a more detailed picture.

A variation on this approach is shown in Figures 7.7 and 7.8. In the first of these, a list of characteristics that can be associated with success in the sector in question has been identified and each main competitor (including ourselves – ABC Co.) has been evaluated on each of the characteristics. From the total scores it appears that Rival 2 is the strongest competitor, with Rival 1 being only marginally weaker than ABC Co. However, while the relative strengths of each competing enterprise are clearly visible in Figure 7.8, there is no indication of the relative importance of each of the key success factors. For example, it may be that relative cost position and ability to compete on price are the most important factors for competitive success within this sector, with technological skills, advertising effectiveness and distribution being relatively unimportant. These priorities can be indicated

Key success factor/strength measure	ABC Co	Rival 1	Rival 2	Rival 3	Rival 4
Quality/product performance	8	5	10	1	6
Reputation/image	8	7	10	1	6
Raw material access/cost	2	10	4	5	1
Technological skills	10	1	7	3	8
Advertising effectiveness	9	4	10	5	1
Distribution	9	4	10	5	1
Financial strength	5	10	7	3	1
Relative cost position	5	10	3	1	4
Ability to compete on price	5	7	10	1	4
Unweighted overall strength rating	61	58	71	25	32

Rating scale: 1 = Very weak; 10 = Very strong

FIGURE 7.7   *Unweighted competitive strength assessment*

Key success factor/strength measure	Weight	ABC Co	Rival 1	Rival 2	Rival 3	Rival 4
Quality/product performance	0.10	8/0.80	5/0.50	10/1.00	1/0.10	6/0.60
Reputation/image	0.10	8/0.80	7/0.70	10/1.00	1/0.10	6/0.60
Raw material access/cost	0.10	2/0.20	10/1.00	4/0.40	5/0.50	1/0.10
Technological skills	0.05	10/0.50	1/0.05	7/0.35	3/0.15	8/0.40
Advertising effectiveness	0.05	9/0.45	4/0.20	10/0.50	5/0.25	1/0.05
Distribution	0.05	9/0.45	4/0.20	10/0.50	5/0.25	1/0.05
Financial strength	0.10	5/0.50	10/1.00	7/0.70	3/0.30	1/0.10
Relative cost position	0.30	5/1.50	10/3.00	3/0.90	1/0.30	4/1.20
Ability to compete on price	0.15	5/0.75	7/1.05	10/1.50	1/0.15	4/0.60
Sum of weights	1.00					
Weighted overall strength rating		5.95	7.70	6.85	2.10	3.70

Rating scale: 1 = Very weak; 10 = Very strong

FIGURE 7.8   *Weighted competitive strength assessment*

by weights, as in Figure 7.8. From this it is now evident that Rival 1 is the market leader, followed by Rival 2, which is ahead of ABC Co. These profiles indicate quite clearly the relative importance of key success factors and the relative strength of each competitor on each of those factors.

Competitive product portfolios

In many cases, one of the most useful methods of gaining an insight into a competitor's strengths, weaknesses and general level of capability is by means of portfolio analysis. The techniques of portfolios analysis, which include the Boston Consulting Group matrix, are by now well-developed and are discussed in detail in Chapter 10. It might therefore be of value at this stage to turn to pages 384–91 in order to understand more fully the comments below.

Having plotted each major competitor's portfolio, the marketing strategist needs to consider a series of questions:

1. What degree of internal balance exists within each portfolio? Which competitors, for example, appear to have few, if any, 'cash cows' but a surfeit of 'question marks' or 'dogs'? Which of the competitors appears to have one or more promising 'stars' that might in the future pose a threat?

2. What are the likely cash flow implications for each competitor's portfolio? Does it appear likely, for example, that they will be vulnerable in the near future because of the cash demands of a disproportionate number of 'question marks' and 'stars'?

3. What trends are apparent in each portfolio? A tentative answer to this question can be arrived at by plotting the equivalent growth–share display for a period three to five years earlier, and superimposing on this the current chart. A third display that reflects the likely development of the portfolio over the next few years, assuming present policies are maintained, can in turn be superimposed on this to show the direction and rate of travel of each product or strategic business unit (SBU).

4. Which competitors' products look suited for growth and which for harvesting? What are the implications for us and in what ways might we possibly pre-empt any competitive actions?

5. Which competitor appears to be the most vulnerable to an attack? Which competitor looks likely to pose the greatest threat in the future?

In plotting a competitor's portfolio the marketing strategist is quite obviously searching for areas of weakness that subsequently can be exploited. A number of the factors that contribute to vulnerability are identified in Illustration 7.3.

At this point it is perhaps worth uttering a word of caution. The marketing strategist should not, of course, limit competitive analysis just to a series of marketing factors, but should also focus upon other areas, including financial and production measures. In this way it is possible to identify far more clearly which competitors within the industry are relatively weak and might therefore be vulnerable to a price attack or a takeover. Equally, it can identify which competitors within the industry should, by virtue of their financial strength or production flexibility, be avoided.

Illustration 7.3 What makes a competitor vulnerable?

A knowledge of a competitor's weaknesses can often be used to great effect by an astute marketing strategist. Amongst the factors that make a competitor vulnerable are:

Marketing factors

- Strength in declining market sectors
- Little presence in growing and high margin markets
- Low market share
- Distribution weaknesses
- Weak segmentation of the market
- Poor/confused and/or unsustainable positioning
- A weak reputation and/or poorly-defined image

Financial factors

- Cash flow problems
- Under-funding
- Low margins
- High-cost operations and/or distribution

Market- and performance-related factors

- Slow/poor growth
- An overdependence on one market
- An overdependence on one or a small number of customers

Product-related factors

- Outdated products and a failure to innovate
- Product weaknesses
- Weak or non-existent selling propositions

Managerial factors

- An over- and ill-justified confidence
- Managerial arrogance and a belief that the organization has an inalienable right to a place in the market
- A short-term orientation
- The poor management of staff
- The failure to focus upon what is important
- Competitive arrogance, competitive myopia and competitive sclerosis
- Managerial predictability and the adherence to well-tried formulae

Bureaucratic structures

- Product or service obsolescence/weaknesses
- A fiscal year short-term fixation

7.5 EVALUATING COMPETITIVE RELATIONSHIPS AND ANALYSING HOW ORGANIZATIONS COMPETE

In essence, five types of relationship can develop between an organization and its competitors:

1. *Conflict*, where the firm sets out to destroy, damage or force the competitor out of the market.

2. *Competition*, where two or more firms are trying to achieve the same goals and penetrate the same markets with broadly similar product offers.

3. *Coexistence*, where the various players act largely independently of others in the market. This may in turn be due to the marketing planner being unaware of the competition; recognizing them but choosing to ignore them; or behaving on the basis that each firm has certain territorial rights that, tacitly, each player agrees not to infringe.

4. *Cooperation*, where one or more firms work together to achieve interdependent goals. Typically, this is done on the basis of exchanging information, licensing arrangements, joint ventures and through trade associations.

5. *Collusion*, which, although typically illegal, has as its purpose that of damaging another organization or, more frequently, ensuring that profit margins and the status quo are maintained.

Given this, any analysis of *how* firms compete falls into four parts:

1. What is each competitor's current strategy?

2. How are competitors performing?

3. What are their strengths and weaknesses?

4. What can we expect from each competitor in the future?

However, before moving on to the detail of these four areas, the strategist should spend time identifying what is already known about each competitor. There are numerous examples of companies that have collected information on competitors only to find out at a later stage that this knowledge already existed within the organization but that, for one reason or another, it had not been analysed or disseminated. In commenting on this, Davidson (1987a, p. 133) has suggested that:

> Recorded data tends not to be analysed over time, and often fails to cross functional barriers. Observable data is typically recorded on a haphazard basis, with little evaluation. Opportunistic data is not always actively sought or disseminated.

This failure to collect, disseminate or make full use of competitive information is, for the majority of organizations, a perennial problem and often leads to the same information being collected more than once. It is, however, an issue that we discuss in greater detail at a later stage, and at this point we will therefore do no more than draw attention to it.

In attempting to arrive at a detailed understanding of competitive relationships, it is essential that each competitor is analysed separately, since any general analysis provides the strategist with only a partial understanding of competitors, and tells little either about potential threats that might emerge or opportunities that can be exploited. It is worth remembering, however, that what competitors have done in the past can often provide a strong indication of what they will do in the future. This is particularly the case when previous strategies have been conspicuously successful. Companies such as Mars, for example, have traditionally pursued an objective of market leadership, while the Japanese are often willing to accept long payback periods. Recognition of points such as these should then be used to guide the ways in which strategy is developed.

Other factors that need to be borne in mind include:

- Patterns of investment in plant

- Links with other competitors

- Patterns of advertising expenditure

- Relative cost positions

- Major changes in the senior management structure, but particularly the appointment of a new chief executive who might act as an agent for change.

Identifying strategic groups

In the majority of industries competitors can be categorized, at least initially, on the basis of the similarities and differences that exist in the strategies being pursued. The strategist can then begin to construct a picture of the market showing the strategic groups that exist. For our purposes here, a strategic group can be seen to consist of those firms within the market that are following a broadly similar strategy. An example of how strategic groupings can be identified is illustrated in Figure 7.9.

Having identified strategic groups in this way, the strategist then needs to identify the relative position and strength of each competitor. This can be done in one of several ways, including the categorizing of firms on the basis of whether their position within the market overall and within the strategic group is dominant, strong, favourable, tenable, weak or non-viable. Having done this, the strategist needs to consider the bases of any competitive advantages that exist. This is illustrated in Figure 7.10.

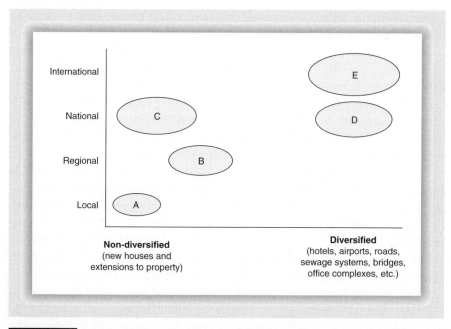

<figure>
International ... E

National ... C ... D

Regional ... B

Local ... A

Non-diversified
(new houses and
extensions to property)

Diversified
(hotels, airports, roads,
sewage systems, bridges,
office complexes, etc.)
</figure>

FIGURE 7.9 *Strategic groups in the construction industry*

Level	Competitive status	Examples
1	One or more sizeable advantages	Honda, Samsung, Lexus, and Coca-Cola
2	A series of small advantages that combine to form one large advantage	McDonald's
3	Advantages exist but these are either not recognized or not exploited fully	
4	No obvious or sustainable competitive advantages	Petrol retailers, estate agents and high street retail banks
5	Competitive disadvantages because of the organization's limited size, inflexibility, inefficient manufacturing practices, distribution networks, cost structures, cultures, lack of skills, or poor image	Eastern European car manufacturers before the expansion of the EU

FIGURE 7.10 *The five types of competitive status and the implications for competitive advantage (adapted from Davidson, 1987a)*

The experiences of many companies suggest that the easiest starting point from which to improve an organization's competitive position is Level 3, since this can often be achieved by good management. One example of a company that did this with considerable success was Beecham with its

Lucozade brand, which it respositioned over a number of years in order to take advantage of a growing market for energy drinks.

There are several points that emerge from identifying strategic groups in this way. The first is that the height of the barriers to entry and exit can vary significantly from one group to another. The second is that the choice of a strategic group determines which companies are to be the firm's principal competitors. Recognizing this, a new entrant would then have to develop a series of competitive advantages to overcome, or at least to neutralize, the competitive advantages of others in the group.

There is, of course, competition not just *within* strategic groups but also *between* them, since not only will target markets develop or contract over time and hence prove to be either more or less attractive to other firms, but customers might not fully recognize major differences in the offers of each group. One consequence of this is that there is likely to be a degree of comparison buying across groups, something which again argues the case for the marketing strategist to adopt a market, rather than an industry, perspective of competition.

Although in Figure 7.9 we have made use of just two dimensions in plotting strategic groupings, a variety of other factors can typically be expected to be used to differentiate between companies and to help in the process of identifying group membership. These typically include:

- Size and relative share

- The extent of *product* or *service diversity*

- The degree of *geographic coverage*

- The number and type of *market segments served*

- The type of *distribution* channels used

- The *branding* philosophy

- Product or service *quality*

- *Market position* (leader or follower)

- *Technological position* (leader or follower)

- *R&D capability*

- *Performance*

- *Cost structure* and behaviour

- Patterns of *ownership*

- Organizational *culture*

- The degree of *vertical integration*

- *Reputation*

The particular relevance to any given industry of these characteristics is in practice influenced by several factors, the most significant of which are the history and development of the industry, the types of environmental forces at work, the nature of the competitive activities of the various firms, and so on. It should be evident from this that each company does therefore have a different strategic make-up that needs to be profiled separately. Often, however, a strategy proves difficult to describe since it encompasses so many different dimensions, but Abell and Hammond (1979, p. 53) have outlined a useful framework for thinking about the strategic decision process:

- How does the competitor define the business in terms of customer groups, customer functions and technologies, and how vertically integrated is this competitor? And at a lower level of aggregation, how is the competitor segmenting the market and which segments are being pursued?

- What mission does this business have in its overall portfolio of businesses? Is it being managed for sales growth, market share, net profit, ROI or cash? What goals does it appear to have for each major segment of the business?

- What is the competitor's marketing mix, manufacturing policy, R&D policy, purchasing policy, physical distribution policy, etc.?

- What size are its budgets and how are they allocated?

In so far as it is possible to generalize, it is the third of these areas in which marketing managers find it most easy to collect information. This should not, however, be seen as a reason for ignoring the other three areas, since it is here that insights into what really drives the competition can best be gained.

This leads us to a position in which we are able to begin to construct a detailed list of the areas in which we need to collect competitive information. In the case of each competitor's current performance, this list includes sales, growth rates and patterns, market share, profit, profitability (return on investment), margins, net income, investment patterns and cash flow. Other areas to which attention needs to be paid include the identification of the importance of each market sector in which the competitor is operating, since this allows the marketing strategist to probe the areas of weakness or least concern at the minimum of risk.

The character of competition

The final area that we need to consider when examining how firms compete is what can loosely be termed 'the character of competition'. Because competition within a market is influenced to a very high degree by the nature of customer behaviour, the character of competition not only takes many forms, but is also likely to change over time. One fairly common way of examining the character of competition is therefore by means of an analysis of the changes taking place in the composition of *value added* by different firms. (The term 'value added' is used to describe the amount by which selling prices are greater than the cost of providing the bought out goods or services embodied in market offerings.) An analysis of changes in the value added component can therefore give the strategist an understanding of the relative importance of such factors as product and process development, selling, after-sales service, price, and so on, as the product moves through the life cycle.

The marketing planner can also arrive at a measure of the character of competition by considering the extent to which each competitor develops new total industry demand (primary demand) or quite simply competes with others for a share of existing demand (selective demand). When a competitor's objective is the stimulation of primary demand, it is likely that efforts will focus upon identifying and developing new market segments. Conversely, when a competitor concentrates upon stimulating selective demand, the focus shifts to an attempt to satisfy existing customers more effectively than other companies. The obvious consequence of this is that the intensity of competition on a day-to-day basis is likely to increase significantly.

7.6   IDENTIFYING COMPETITORS' OBJECTIVES

Having identified the organization's principal competitors and their strategies, we need then to focus upon each competitor's objectives. In other words, what drives each competitor's behaviour? A starting point in arriving at an answer to this is to assume that each competitor will aim for profit maximization either in the short-term or the long-term. In practice, of course, maximization is an unrealistic objective which, for a wide variety of reasons, many companies are willing to sacrifice. A further assumption can be made – that each competitor has a variety of objectives, each of which has a different weight. These objectives might typically include cash flow, technological leadership, market share growth, service leadership or overall market leadership. Gaining an insight into this mix of objectives allows the strategist to arrive at tentative conclusions regarding how a competitor will respond to a competitive thrust. A firm pursuing market share growth is likely to react far more quickly and aggressively to a price cut or to a substantial increase in advertising than a firm that is aiming for, say, technological leadership.

In a general sense, however, organizational and managerial objectives (as pointed out in Chapter 8) are influenced by a wide variety of factors, but particularly the organization's size, history, culture and the breadth of the operating base. Where, for example, a company is part of a larger organization, a competitive thrust always runs the risk of leading to retaliation by the parent company on what might appear to be a disproportionate scale. Conversely, the parent company may see an attack on one of its divisions as being a nuisance but little more, and not bother to respond in anything other than a cursory fashion. This has been discussed in some detail by Rothschild (1984), who argued that the potentially most dangerous competitive move involves attacking a global company for which this is the only business.

It follows that the marketing strategist should give explicit consideration to the relative importance of each market to a competitor in order to understand the probable level of commitment that exists. By doing this, it is possible to estimate the level of effort that each competitor would then logically make in order to defend its position. Several factors are likely to influence this level of commitment, the five most important of which are likely to be:

1. The proportion of company profits that this market sector generates

2. The managerial perceptions of the market's growth opportunities

3. The levels of profitability that exist currently and that are expected to exist in the future

4. Any interrelationships between this and any other product or market sector in which the organization operates

5. Managerial cultures – in some companies, for example, any threat will be responded to aggressively almost irrespective of whether it is cost-effective.

As a general rule of thumb, therefore, competitive retaliation will be strong whenever the company feels its core business is being attacked. Recognizing this, the marketing planner should concentrate on avoiding areas that are likely to lead to this sort of response, unless of course the target has a strong strategic rationale. This sort of issue is discussed in detail in Chapter 12.

7.7 IDENTIFYING COMPETITORS' LIKELY RESPONSE PROFILES

Although a knowledge of a competitor's size, objectives and capability (strengths and weaknesses) can provide the strategist with a reasonable understanding of possible responses to company moves such as price cuts, the launch of new products and so on, other factors need to be examined. One of the most important of these is the organization's culture, since it is this that ultimately determines how the firm will do business and hence how it will act in the future.

The issue of how a competitor is likely to behave in the future has two components. First, how is a competitor likely to respond to the general changes taking place in the external environment and, in particular, in the marketplace? Secondly, how is that competitor likely to respond to specific competitive moves that we, or indeed any other company, might make? For some companies at least, there is also a third question that needs to be considered: how likely is it that the competitor will initiate an aggressive move, and what form might this move be most likely to take? In posing questions such as these we are trying to determine where each competitive company is the most vulnerable, where it is the strongest, where the most appropriate battleground is likely to be and how, if at all, it will respond. In doing this, a potential starting point involves identifying each competitor's most probable reaction profile, the four most common of which are:

1. *The relaxed competitor*, who either fails to react or reacts only slowly to competitive moves. There are several possible reasons for this, the most common of which are that the management team believes that their customers are deeply loyal and are therefore unlikely to respond to a (better) competitive offer; they may fail to see the competitor's move or underestimate its significance; they may not have the resources to respond; the market might be of little real importance; or the focus may be upon harvesting the business. However, whatever the reason, the marketing strategies must try to understand why the competitor is taking such a relaxed approach.

2. *The tiger competitor*, who responds quickly and aggressively almost regardless of the nature and significance of any competitive move. Over time, firms such as this develop a reputation for their aggression and in this way create Fear, Uncertainty and Despair (FUD marketing) amongst other players in the market.

3. *The selective competitor*, who chooses carefully – and often very strategically – how, where and with what level of aggression they will respond to any competitive move. Such an approach is generally based not just on a clear understanding of the relative value of the organization's markets, but also on the costs of responding and the likelihood of the response proving to be cost-effective.

4. *The unpredictable competitor*, for whom it proves difficult or impossible to identify in advance how – or, indeed, if – they will respond to any particular move. The unpredictability of competitors such as this comes from the way in which in the past they may have responded aggressively on one occasion, but not at all on another when faced with what appears to be a broadly similar attack.

The significance of costs

In attempting to come to terms with the structure of competition, the marketing planner should also take account of *cost structures* and *cost behaviour*.

Cost structure is usually defined as the ratio of variable to fixed costs and is typically capable of exerting a significant influence upon competitive behaviour. In businesses where, for example, the fixed costs are high, profits are highly sensitive to volume. Companies are therefore forced to behave in such a way that plants operate as near to full capacity as possible. An example of this would be aluminium smelting. Where demand is price-sensitive, the industry is likely to be characterized by periodic bouts of aggressive price wars. Where, however, it is the case that variable costs are high, profits are influenced far more directly by changes in margins. Recognizing this, the marketing strategist needs to focus upon differentiating the product in such a way that prices and hence margins can be increased.

The second cost dimension is that of its behaviour over time and, in particular, how the organization can make use of learning and experience effects, as well as scale effects.

The influence of the product life cycle

Competitive behaviour is typically affected in several ways by the stage reached on the product life cycle (PLC). Although the PLC (see Chapter 12) is seen principally as a model of product and market evolution, it can also be used as a framework for examining probable competitive behaviour. Used in this way, it can help the strategist to anticipate changes in the character of competition. In the early stages of the life cycle, for example, advertising and promotion are generally high, and prices and margins are able to support this. The natural growth of the market allows firms to avoid competing in an overtly direct way. As maturity approaches and the rate of growth slows, firms are forced into more direct forms of competition, a situation that is in turn exacerbated by the often generally greater number of companies operating within the market. This greater intensity of competition manifests itself in several ways, but most commonly in a series of price reductions. The role of advertising changes as greater emphasis is placed upon the search for differentiation. In the final stages, some firms opt to leave the market, while others engage in perhaps even greater price competition as they fight for a share of a declining sales curve. It follows from this that the PLC is yet one more of the myriad of factors that the marketing strategist needs to consider in coming to terms with competitors.

7.8 COMPETITOR ANALYSIS AND THE DEVELOPMENT OF STRATEGY

Given the nature of our comments so far, how then does the analysis of competitors feed in to the development of a strategy? Only rarely can marketing strategy be based just on the idea of winning and holding customers. The marketing strategist also needs to understand how to win the competitive battle. As the first step in this, as we have argued throughout this chapter,

1. The market's key factors for success (KFS)	• Identify the KFSs for the industry • Inject resources where you can gain a competitive advantage
2. Relative superiority	• Exploit differences in competitive conditions between company and rivals using technology and the sales network
3. Developing aggressive initiatives	• Challenge assumptions about the way of doing business • Change the rules of the game • Challenge the status quo • Develop a fast-moving and unconventional strategy
4. Developing strategic degrees of freedom	• Be innovative • Open up new markets or develop new products • Exploit market areas untouched by competitors • Search for 'loose bricks' in their position

FIGURE 7.11 *Linking competitor analysis to strategy*

the planner must understand in detail the nature and bases of competition, and what this means for the organization. In the absence of this, any plan or strategy will be built upon very weak foundations. This involves:

- Knowing the strength of each competitor's position

- Knowing the strength of each competitor's offering

- Knowing the strength of each competitor's resources

- Understanding each competitor's strategy.

Against this background, the planner needs then to think about how this information can best be used. In discussing this, Ohmae (1983) argued for a focus upon four areas. These are illustrated in Figure 7.11.

It can be seen from this that it is through understanding the nature of the market's key success factors and issues of relative strength and weakness that the planner can start to move towards the development of the sorts of marketing initiatives and degrees of freedom that will underpin the strategy.

7.9 THE COMPETITIVE INTELLIGENCE SYSTEM

It should be apparent from everything that has been said in this chapter that the need for an effective competitive intelligence system (CIS) is paramount. In establishing such a system, there are five principal steps:

1. Setting up the system, deciding what information is needed and, very importantly, who will use the outputs from the system and how

2. Collecting the data

3. Analysing and evaluating the data

4. Disseminating the conclusions

5. Incorporating these conclusions into the subsequent strategy and plan, and feeding back the results so that the information system can be developed further.

A framework for developing a CIS is given in Figure 7.12. The mechanics of an effective CIS are in many ways straightforward and involve:

- Selecting the key competitors to evaluate. However, in deciding who these competitors should be, the planner should never lose sight of the point that we make about the way in which, in many markets, the *real* competitive threat comes not from the established players but from new and often very unexpected players who operate with different rules.

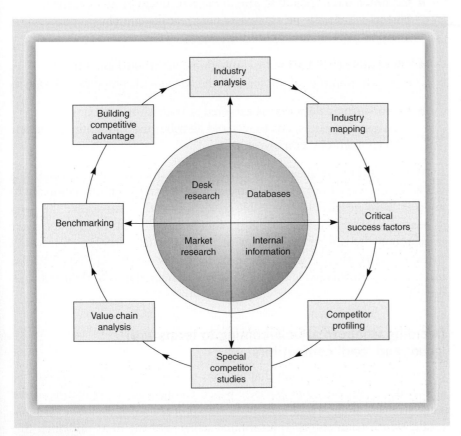

FIGURE 7.12   *Approaches to competitor analysis (source: Harbridge House)*

- Being absolutely clear about what information is needed, *how* it will be used and by whom.

- Selecting and briefing those responsible for collecting the information.

- Allocating the appropriate level of resource to the collection and evaluation processes.

- Publishing regular tactical and strategic reports on competition.

- Ensuring that the outputs from the process are an integral part of the planning and strategy development processes rather than a series of reports that are rarely used.

The sources of data are, as we observed at an earlier stage, likely to vary significantly from one industry to another. However, a useful framework for data collection involves categorizing information on the basis of whether it is recorded, observed or opportunistic. These include:

- **Recorded data**, including primary and secondary research, the business and trade press, government reports, company reports, analysts' reports, and public documents

- **Observable data**, including competitors' advertising and pricing, feedback from the sales force, and the analysis of competitors' products

- **Opportunistic data** that is gathered at trade shows; talking to packaging suppliers, customers and distributors; and random contact with competitors' employees.

With regard to the question of precisely what information is needed, this will of course vary from one industry to another and from one company to another. It is, nevertheless, possible to identify with relative ease the sorts of headings under which information should be gathered: include the *types* of customer the competitor deals with, their product portfolio, their advertising patterns, their prices, their distribution networks and type of sales force, their performance levels, and the key characteristics of their management team.

Deciding whom to attack: coming to terms with 'good' and 'bad' competitors

Given the sort of information that we refer to above, the strategist should be able to determine far more precisely which competitors are operating in the same strategic group. From here, he or she can then go on to decide far more readily which competitors to attack and when, and the basis on which this should be done. Equally, he or she is also able to decide which competitors are to be avoided. Although these issues are discussed in detail in Chapter 12, there are several points that can usefully be made at this stage.

Assuming that the company is to go on the offensive, the strategist needs to begin by deciding *which* competitors to attack. In essence, this represents a choice between strong and weak competitors, close and distant competitors, and good and bad competitors.

Although *weak competitors* are by their very nature the most vulnerable, the potential pay-off needs to be examined carefully. It may be the case, for example, that the share gained, while useful, is of little long-term strategic value, since it takes the company into segments of the market offering little scope for growth. Equally, these segments may require substantial long-term investment. By contrast, competing against *strong competitors* requires the firm to be far leaner, fitter and more aggressive, a point that has been argued in some considerable detail for more than two decades by Porter, and which was developed further in his book *The Competitive Advantage of Nations* (Porter, 1990). (See also the World Economic Forum's *The Global Competitiveness Report 2007–2008*, Porter *et al.*, 2007)

The second decision involves deciding between *close* and *distant* competitors. We have already commented that the majority of companies compete against those within the strategic group they most resemble. Thus, as we observed earlier, Nestlé's Nescafé is in direct competition with Krafts' Maxwell House. The strategist needs, in certain circumstances at least, to beware of destroying these close competitors, since the whole competitive base may then change. In commenting on this, Porter (1985a, pp. 226–7) cites some examples:

- Bausch & Lomb in the late 1970s moved aggressively against other soft lens manufacturers with great success. However, this led one competitor after another to sell out to larger firms such as Revlon, Johnson & Johnson and Schering–Plough, with the result that Bausch & Lomb now faced much larger competitors.

- A speciality rubber manufacturer attacked another speciality rubber manufacturer as its mortal enemy and took away market share. The damage to the other company allowed the speciality divisions of the large tyre companies to move quickly into speciality rubber markets, using them as a dumping ground for excess capacity.

Porter expands upon this line of argument by distinguishing between 'good' and 'bad' competitors. A good competitor, he suggests, is one that adheres to the rules, avoids aggressive price moves, favours a healthy industry, makes realistic assumptions about the industry's growth prospects, and accepts the general status quo. Bad competitors, by contrast, violate the unspoken and unwritten rules. They engage in unnecessarily aggressive and often foolhardy moves, expand capacity in large steps, slash margins and take significant risks.

The implication of this is that good competitors should work hard to develop an industry that consists only of good companies. Amongst the ways in which this can be done are coalitions, selective retaliation and careful licensing. The pay-off will then be that:

- Competitors will not seek to destroy each other by behaving irrationally
- They will follow the rules of the industry
- Each player will be differentiated in some way
- Companies will try to earn share increases rather than buying them.

It follows from this that a company can benefit in a variety of ways from competitors, since they often generate higher levels of total market demand, increase the degree of differentiation, help spread the costs of market development, and may well serve less attractive segments.

7.10   THE DEVELOPMENT OF A COMPETITIVE STANCE: THE POTENTIAL FOR ETHICAL CONFLICT

A key element of any marketing strategy involves the development of a clear, meaningful and sustainable competitive stance that is capable of providing the organization with an edge over its competitors. In doing this, organizations have responded in a variety of ways, ranging from, at one extreme, a series of actions that are both legally and ethically questionable through to, at the other extreme, an approach that discourages or prohibits doing business with particular customer groups. In the case of the Cooperative Bank, for example, its highly-publicized competitive stance has been based on an ethical platform that led the bank to stop dealing with customers deemed to be involved in 'unethical' activities. This policy, which was formulated in the 1990s, led in the first year to the bank severing its ties with twelve corporate customers, including two fox-hunting associations, a peat miner, a company that tested its products on animals, and others where it took the view that the customer was causing unreasonable environmental damage. The bank has also taken a stand against factory farming.

An ethical dimension – albeit one with an element of self-interest – was also at the heart of a strategy developed by British Alcan in 1989 to recycle used beverage cans. With the industry suffering in the late 1980s from problems of overcapacity, the price of aluminium on the world markets had dropped significantly and Alcan, in common with other aluminium producers, began searching for ways in which costs might be reduced. The aluminium recycling process offers a number of advantages, since not only are the capital costs of investing in a recycling operation as little as one-tenth of investing in primary capacity, but recycled aluminium also requires only one-twentieth of the energy costs. An additional benefit is that, unlike steel recycling, the recovery process does not lead to a deterioration in the metal. At the same time, however, the company was acutely aware of a series of environmental pressures and concerns and, in particular, the greater emphasis that was being given both by governments and society at large to the issue of finite world resources and to the question of recycling.

Faced with this, Alcan developed a highly proactive stance that involved the development of an infrastructure that was capable of collecting and recycling aluminium beverage cans. The success of the campaign was subsequently reflected by the way in which, between 1989 and 2005, the UK's recycling rate of aluminium cans, largely as the result of the Alcan initiative, increased from less than 2 per cent to more than 55 per cent.

However, for many other organizations the implications of an increasingly demanding and apparently competitively malevolent environment has led to the search for a competitive stance and a competitive edge almost irrespective of the cost. In doing this, the problem that can then be faced concerns the stage at which the need for managers to deliver seemingly ever higher levels of performance leads to actions that subsequently are deemed to be unacceptable, something which the senior management of British Airways was faced with in the early 1990s and which led to the infamous 'dirty tricks' campaign against Virgin (for a detailed discussion of this, the reader should refer to Gregory (1994) *Dirty Tricks*).

Ethics and market intelligence: the growth of corporate espionage

With many markets having grown enormously in their complexity in recent years, so the demand for increasingly detailed and effective market intelligence systems has escalated. Although many of the inputs to a market intelligence system can be obtained through relatively straightforward and conventional market research routines, the much more strategically useful – and indeed more necessary – information on competitors' intentions, capabilities and strategies can, as we saw in the British Airways example, often only be obtained by radically different approaches. Although the legality of many of these approaches has been called into question, the law, both in Europe and the USA, has in many instances failed to keep pace with the developments that have taken place in information technology and electronic data distribution.

The implication of this is that, whilst the techniques used to gain the more confidential forms of competitive information may not in the strictly legal sense be wrong, the ethics of the approach are arguably rather more questionable. The net effect of this is that, in many companies, the search for a competitive edge has led managers to enter what has been referred to as 'the twilight zone of corporate intelligence', in which the traditional boundaries of legal and ethical behaviour are blurred. This is illustrated in Figure 7.13,

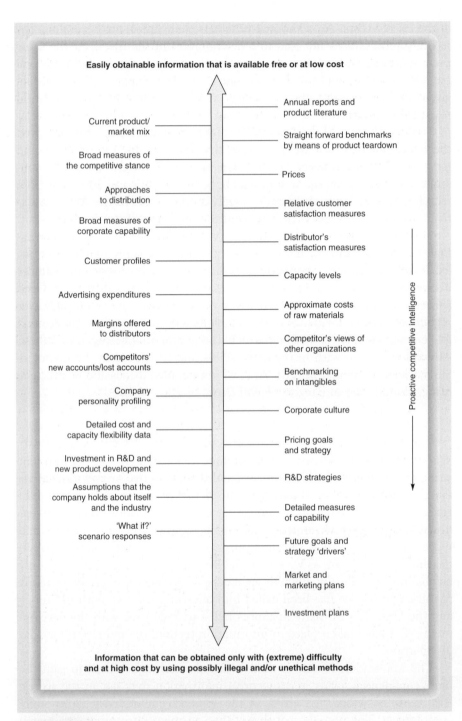

Easily obtainable information that is available free or at low cost

Current product/ market mix

Broad measures of the competitive stance

Approaches to distribution

Broad measures of corporate capability

Customer profiles

Advertising expenditures

Margins offered to distributors

Competitors' new accounts/lost accounts

Company personality profiling

Detailed cost and capacity flexibility data

Investment in R&D and new product development

Assumptions that the company holds about itself and the industry

'What if?' scenario responses

Annual reports and product literature

Straight forward benchmarks by means of product teardown

Prices

Relative customer satisfaction measures

Distributor's satisfaction measures

Capacity levels

Approximate costs of raw materials

Competitor's views of other organizations

Benchmarking on intangibles

Corporate culture

Pricing goals and strategy

R&D strategies

Detailed measures of capability

Future goals and strategy 'drivers'

Market and marketing plans

Investment plans

Proactive competitive intelligence

Information that can be obtained only with (extreme) difficulty and at high cost by using possibly illegal and/or unethical methods

FIGURE 7.13 *Managerial needs for competitive intelligence (adapted from Button, 1994)*

which represents a continuum of the types of competitive intelligence that are available, their sources and the difficulties of gaining access to them.

For many organizations, much of the market research effort over the past two decades, particularly in Europe, has been concentrated towards the upper part of the continuum. However, as competitive pressures grow, so the need for more and more confidential competitive intelligence increases. One consequence of this in the USA, and now increasingly in Europe, has been a growth in the number of agencies that specialize in obtaining the sorts of competitive information that, whilst increasingly being seen to be necessary, can only be obtained through what might loosely be termed as unconventional methods. Amongst the more extreme of these is what is referred to in the USA as 'doing trash', something which involves sifting through competitors' rubbish bins, using hidden cameras and listening devices, intercepting fax lines, bugging offices and planting misinformation. Although the leading competitive intelligence agencies have been quick to condemn this sort of approach – and indeed several agencies now publish codes of ethics – the ever greater pressures upon managers, particularly in international markets, demand ever more detailed competitive information, little of which may be obtained by adhering to traditional legal and ethical principles.

Because of this, managers are faced with what is possibly a dilemma since, whilst competitive pressures demand the information, traditional and ethical patterns of behaviour argue against the actions that will provide it. In these circumstances managers can respond in one of several ways, ranging from an adherence to truly ethical behaviour (and then living with the competitive consequences) through to a pragmatically straightforward belief that the ends justify the means and that, without the information, the organization will be at a competitive disadvantage.

Intelligence gathering and corporate culture

The work practices of competitive intelligence agencies have highlighted a series of differences between managerial cultures in Europe and the USA, with the general approach of European managers having proved to be far less aggressive and proactive than that of their American counterparts. A Conference Board report in 1988, for example, suggested that only 50 per cent of British managers view the monitoring of competitors' activities as 'very important'. This has, in turn, led to the suggestion by Button (1994, pp. 3–4) that:

there are two major differences between US and European companies. The culture is different, obviously. But also there is a greater degree of loyalty to the corporation in Europe than in the US. One consequence of this, together with the greater frequency of job-moving in the States, is that the incidence of security leaks is greater and US companies are more vulnerable to the corporate spy.

The differences and implications of the two cultures have also been highlighted by McGonagle and Vella (1993), who have suggested that the ethics of senior UK managers make them reluctant to engage in 'shady practices or covert operations'. By contrast, corporate intelligence agencies and their clients in the USA, whilst often stressing the ethical and legal standards to which they adhere, are rarely willing to discuss in detail the techniques they adopt (Button, 1994, p. 9):

> Although 'data detectives' don't necessarily lie, they tend not to tell the whole truth either. On the telephone, they regularly identify themselves as industry researchers, without disclosing their affiliation to a specific client. By focusing their introduction on the type of information they need rather than who they are and why they need it, plus an upfront statement that they are not interested in anything confidential or proprietary, interviewees are lulled into a false sense of security. Industry jargon is used with care so as not to appear overly knowledgeable and questions are carefully phrased to avoid suspicion. Ask an interviewee about their employer's weaknesses and they are liable to clam up. But when the victim is protected by their visual anonymity and physical distance from the caller, a question such as 'If you had a magic wand, which three things would you change about your manufacturing/distribution/pricing policy?' often produces the same information, without raising the alarm.

The significance of industrial espionage and the possible scale of the problem has been highlighted by a series of studies, one of the most useful being that of Johnson and Pound (1992), who found that 40 per cent of large US and Canadian firms had uncovered some form of espionage costing some $20 billion annually. The problems proved to be at their most acute in the high-technology industries, where the commercial returns between the leaders and the followers are potentially considerable. Hitachi, for example, pleaded guilty to obtaining confidential documents from IBM dealing with one of its computer systems. However, Berkowitz et al. (1994, p. 97) also cite the example of espionage occurring in other less esoteric industries, including the American cookie market, with Procter & Gamble claiming that 'competitors photographed its plants and production lines, stole a sample of its cookie dough, and infiltrated a confidential sales presentation to learn about its technology, recipe and marketing plan'. Procter & Gamble took action against the competitor and won $120 million in damages.

In an attempt to overcome the criticisms that have been made of industry practices, a number of competitive intelligence (CI) agencies have published ethics statements that emphasize that they will not lie, bribe or steal in the information gathering process. However, with levels of competition increasing at an ever greater rate, the pressures upon managers, and hence the CI agencies they employ, will invariably become greater.

These problems have in turn been highlighted by a series of newspaper revelations concerning the ways in which a number of governmental security services have been involved in commercial espionage for many years. In the case of the old Iron Curtain countries, for example, many of the security agencies, having lost much of their previous role, have now turned their attention to the commercial sector.

A high profile – and highly embarrassing – example of corporate espionage came to light in 2000 when Harry Ellison, the chief executive of Oracle, was found to have hired a private detective agency to spy on corporate supporters of Microsoft. Amongst the approaches used by the agency was the bribing of cleaning staff at one of the target organizations, something that some corporate detectives suggest is an unnecessary expense – in many cases employees further down the corporate ladder can be coerced into parting with secrets simply because they do not understand the value of the information.

Sifting through a rival's rubbish bins has been used by numerous firms and is helped by the way in which, in Britain at least, information is not regarding as property under UK theft law. Although the law may change, under the current system, if a person can prove they will return the discarded paper to the local municipal council – the legal owner of the rubbish – they cannot be charged.

For many firms, however, there is a more fundamental problem that has been highlighted by the Risk Advisory Group, a London-based specialist investigation agency. Their research suggests that some 80 per cent of all leaked company secrets can be traced to senior management, who are either aggrieved because they may have been overlooked for promotion, are preparing to set up on their own, or have found someone prepared to pay a large sum for the information. This is more likely in industries such as construction and oil and gas, where large contracts are at stake and where a relatively small piece of intelligence can boost a company's chances of winning a multi-million pound tender.

7.11 SUMMARY

Within this chapter we have emphasized the need for constant competitor analysis and for the information generated to be fed into the strategic marketing planning process.

Although the need for competitor analysis has long been acknowledged, a substantial number of organizations still seemingly fail to allocate to the process the resources that are needed, relying instead upon a far less detailed understanding of competitive capabilities and priorities. It does therefore need to be recognized that, if an effective system of competitive monitoring is to be developed, and the results used in the way intended, it is essential that there is top management commitment to the process.

In developing a structured approach to competitive analysis, the strategist needs to give explicit consideration to five questions:

1. Against whom are we competing?

2. What are their objectives?

3. What strategies are they pursuing and how successful are they?

4. What strengths and weaknesses do they possess?

5. How are they likely to behave and, in particular, how are they likely to react to offensive moves?

Taken together, the answers to these five questions can be used to develop a detailed response profile for each competitive organization, and the probable implications for competitive behaviour fed into the planning process.

Several methods of categorizing competitors have been discussed, including Porter's notion of strategic groups. We then examined the ways in which these ideas can be taken a step further by focusing upon the character of competition and how this is likely to change over the course of the product life cycle.

Particular emphasis was given to the need for the strategist to take account of each competitor's probable objectives, its competitive stance, and the relative importance of each market sector. Again, a variety of frameworks that can help in this process of understanding have been discussed, including portfolio analysis.

Against this background, we discussed the ways in which an effective competitive intelligence system (CIS) might be developed and the nature of the inputs that are required. Much of the information needed for such a system is often readily available, and emphasis therefore needs to be placed upon developing a framework which will ensure that this information is channelled, analysed and disseminated in the strategically most useful way.

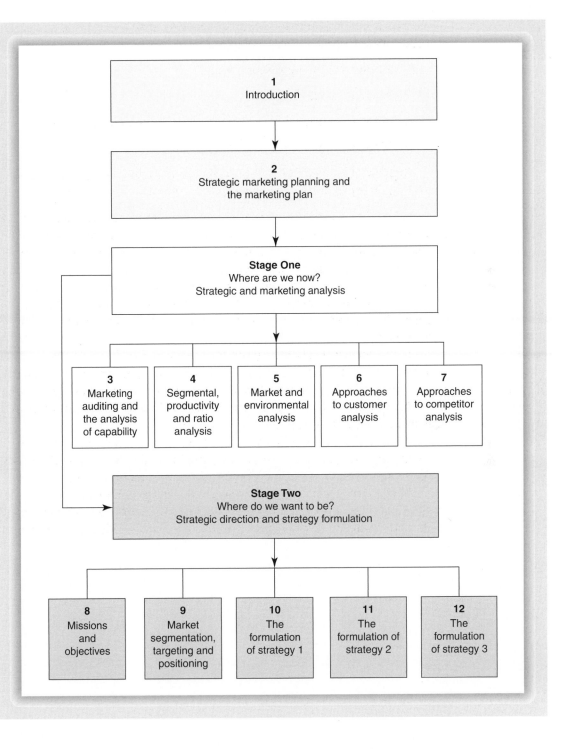

Where do We Want to Be? Strategic Direction and Strategy Formulation

Within this stage we focus on where the organization wants to go. In doing this we take as our foundation the material of Stage One, in which we examined where the organization is currently, the characteristics of its markets and the nature of its marketing capability.

We begin by considering the organizational mission and the nature of marketing objectives (Chapter 8). We then turn to an examination of the approaches that might be adopted when segmenting the market (Chapter 9). In Chapter 10 we examine a number of the models that have been developed to help in the process of strategy formulation, as a prelude – in Chapters 11 and 12 – to a discussion of the factors that influence the nature of the strategy to be pursued.

Mission statements have been the subject of considerable discussion in recent years, with the majority of commentators pointing to their potential for providing employees with a clear understanding of core corporate values. Although many organizations still lack a mission statement, while others have statements that reflect a degree of wishful thinking rather than reality, the guidelines for developing a meaningful corporate mission are now well developed. The significance of the mission statement can be further highlighted by recognizing that it is against the background of the mission statement that the strategist should set objectives at both the corporate and functional levels (in the case of marketing, these objectives revolve around two major dimensions: products and markets). It follows from this that a poorly developed mission statement is likely to have consequences for the nature and appropriateness of any subsequent objectives.

Following on from the discussion of mission statements, we turn our attention to the idea of vision and how the vision or picture of how the organization should look in three to five years' time helps to drive objectives and the marketing planning process.

As well as being influenced by the corporate mission, organizational objectives are typically influenced by a wide variety of other factors, including the nature and demands of the environment. The marketing strategist typically analyses the environment within the PEST (Political, Economic, Social and Technological) framework, the individual elements of which are – in the majority of markets – undergoing a series of significant and often unprecedented changes, each of which needs to be taken into account both when setting objectives and formulating strategies. It might therefore be of value to return to Chapter 5, to the discussion of some of the key changes that are taking place within the marketing environment, before proceeding.

The changing environment also has consequences for methods of segmentation. Effective segmentation is at the heart of a well-developed marketing strategy, and has implications for virtually everything else that follows in the strategy-making process. It is therefore a source of concern that work by a variety of writers (e.g. Saunders, 1987) has highlighted the fact that senior managers in many British organizations seemingly fail to recognize this, and pay little or no attention either to the need for segmentation or to the ways in which it can be carried out most effectively.

The strategic significance of segmentation is reinforced by the way in which decisions on how the organization's markets are to be segmented subsequently has implications for targeting and market positioning. The failure to segment effectively is therefore likely to weaken much of the marketing process.

In Chapters 10–12 we focus upon approaches to the formulation of marketing strategy. In the first of these chapters we consider some of the developments that have taken place over the past 30 years in techniques of portfolio analysis. The portfolio approach to management emerged largely as a result of the turbulence of the early 1970s and is based on the idea that an organization's businesses should be viewed and managed in a similar way to an investment portfolio, with a strategic perspective being adopted in the management of each major element.

Although a wide variety of portfolio techniques have been developed and have contributed to a greater understanding on the part of management of what is meant by strategy, research findings are beginning to emerge which suggest that usage levels of even the best-known methods are low. Several explanations for this have been proposed, including unrealistic expectations on the part of managers, difficulties with the data inputs, and an overzealous adherence to the strategic guidelines that typically accompany the models. Nevertheless, models of portfolio analysis need to be seen as one of the major developments in strategic thinking over the past 30 years and, if used wisely, are capable of contributing greatly to a structured approach to marketing management.

The type of marketing strategy pursued by an organization is often the result of the interaction of a series of factors, including past performance, managerial expectations and culture, competitive behaviour, the stage reached on the product life cycle, and the firm's relative market position. Porter (1980) has attempted to provide a structure for examining the strategic alternatives open to an organization and suggests that, in order to compete successfully, the strategist needs to select a generic strategy and pursue it consistently. The three generic strategies that he identifies are:

1. Cost leadership

2. Differentiation

3. Focus.

Dangers arise, Porter suggests, when the firm fails to pursue one of these and instead is forced or drifts into a 'middle-of-the-road' position, where the message to the market is confused and the likelihood of a successful competitive attack is increased.

A considerable amount of work has been done in recent years in drawing parallels between military warfare and marketing strategy, with a view to identifying any lessons that the marketing strategist might learn. A number of general lessons have emerged from this, and guidelines on how best either to defend a market position or attack other organizations are now well developed. Within Chapter 12 we have attempted to draw upon the experiences of successful organizations and to highlight particular dangers. Included within these is the danger of adhering to a particular strategy for too long a period, labelled 'strategic wear-out'. There is an obvious attraction in sticking to a well-proven strategy, although evidence exists to suggest that even the best formulated strategy has a limited life. The marketing strategist should therefore closely monitor the effectiveness of any given strategy, and be willing to change it in order to reflect the environment, different managerial expectations, and the progression through the product and market life cycles.

CHAPTER 8

Missions and Objectives

8.1 LEARNING OBJECTIVES

When you have read this chapter you should be able to understand:

(a) the purpose of planning;

(b) the nature of the corporate mission and how a mission statement can best be developed;

(c) the significance of vision;

(d) the factors influencing objectives and strategy;

(e) the nature of corporate objectives;

(f) the nature of marketing objectives.

8.2 INTRODUCTION

To be effective, a strategic planning system must be goal-driven. The setting of goals or objectives is therefore a key step in the marketing planning process since, unless it is carried out effectively, everything that follows will lack focus and cohesion. In terms of its position within the overall planning process, which forms the basis of this book, objectives setting can be seen to follow on from the initial stage of analysis and, in particular, the marketing audit, which provided the focus of Chapter 3 (see Figure 8.1).

By setting objectives, the planner is attempting to provide the organization with a sense of direction. In addition, however, objectives provide a basis for motivation, as well as a benchmark against which performance and effectiveness can subsequently be measured. The setting of objectives is thus at the very heart of the planning process, and is the prelude to the

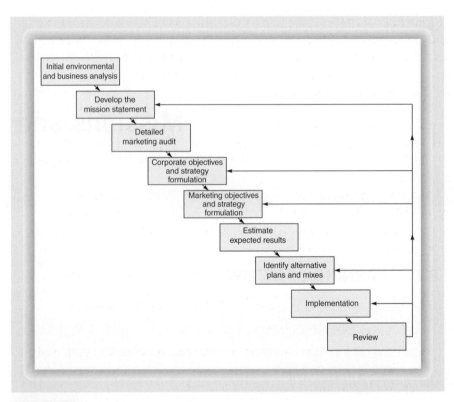

FIGURE 8.1 *The strategic planning process*

development of strategies and detailed plans. Perhaps surprisingly therefore, in view of its fundamental importance, the literature on *how* to set marketing objectives is surprisingly thin, something that is reflected in a comment made more than 20 years ago by McDonald (1984, p. 82):

> *The literature [on marketing planning] is not very explicit, which is surprising when it is considered how vital the setting of marketing objectives is. An objective will ensure that a company knows what its strategies are expected to accomplish and when a particular strategy has accomplished its purpose. In other words, without objectives, strategy decisions and all that follow will take place in a vacuum.*

Although the situation has undoubtedly improved since McDonald made this comment, the reality is that marketing planning appears in many ways to be one of those areas that is seen to be important, but which is subjected to relatively little fundamental scrutiny.

There are several possible explanations for this, the most obvious of which is that, in principle at least, the process of setting objectives is relatively straightforward and, as such, merits little discussion. The rest of the planning and strategy development process is then seen by some to follow easily and logically. In practice, however, the process is infinitely more difficult, particularly in divisionalized organizations, or where the company has an extensive product range being sold across a variety of markets. Regardless of whether we are talking about principles or practice, the sequence should be the same, beginning with an identification of the organization's current position and capabilities, a statement of assumptions about environmental factors affecting the business, and then agreement among stakeholders as to the objectives themselves.

In moving through this process, the majority of commentators recommend that the planner moves from the general to the specific and from the long term to the short term. This frequently translates into statements on three aspects of the business:

1. The nature of the current business (what business *are* we in?)

2. Where it should go (what business *should* we be in?)

3. How we should get there.

Identifying where the company is, however, is often far more difficult than it might appear, something which is reflected in a comment by the ex-Chairman of ICI, Sir John Harvey-Jones (1988):

> *There is no point in deciding where your business is going until you have actually decided with great clarity where you are now. Like practically everything in business this is easier said than done.*

Recognizing the validity of this point should encourage the marketing planner to focus not just upon the business's current position, but also *how* and *why* it has achieved its current levels of success or failure. Having done this, he or she is then in a far better position to begin specifying the *primary* or *most important* corporate objectives, as well as a series of statements regarding the key results areas, such as sales growth, market penetration and new product development, in which success is essential to the organization. Following on from this, the planner should then begin developing the *secondary* or *subobjectives*, such as geographical expansion and line extension, which will need to be achieved if the primary objectives are to be attained.

This process of moving from the general to the specific should lead to a set of objectives that are not just attainable within any budgetary or other constraints that exist, but that are also compatible with environmental conditions as well as organizational strengths and weaknesses. It follows from this that the process of setting objectives should form what is often referred to as an internally consistent and mutually reinforcing hierarchy. As an illustration of this, if we assume that corporate management is concerned first and foremost with, say, long-term profits and growth, it is these objectives that provide the framework within which the more detailed subset of operational objectives, including market expansion and product-specific increases in sales and share, are developed. Taken together, these then contribute to the achievement of the overall corporate objectives.

It is these operational objectives that are the principal concern of those in the level below corporate management. Below this, managers are concerned with objectives that are defined even more specifically, such as creating awareness of a new product, increasing levels of distribution, and so on. This hierarchy points in turn to the interrelationship, and in some cases the confusion, that exists between corporate objectives and marketing objectives. The distinction between the two is an important one and is discussed at a later stage in this chapter. However, as a prelude to this, and indeed to the process of objectives setting, there is a need for the strategist to decide upon the business mission. We therefore begin this chapter with a discussion of the role and purpose of planning as the background against which we can more realistically examine approaches to the development of the mission statement and, subsequently, corporate and marketing objectives.

8.3   THE PURPOSE OF PLANNING

In discussing the nature and role of the planning process, Jackson (1975) comments that:

> Planning attempts to control the factors which affect the outcome of decisions; actions are guided so that success is more likely to be achieved. To plan is to decide what to do before doing it. Like methods, plans can be specially made to fit circumstances or they can be ready made for regular use in recurrent and familiar situations. In other words, a methodical approach can be custom built or ready made according to the nature of the problems involved.

The purpose of planning can therefore be seen as an attempt to impose a degree of structure upon behaviour by allocating resources in order to achieve organizational objectives. This is reflected in a somewhat cumbersome but nevertheless useful comment by Drucker (1959), who suggests that:

> business planning is a continuous process of making present entrepreneurial decisions systematically and with best possible knowledge of their futurity, organizing systematically the effort needed to carry out these decisions against expectations through organized feedback.

While not particularly succinct, this definition has a certain value in that it highlights the three major elements of planning:

1. The need for systematic decision-making

2. The development of programmes for their implementation

3. The measurement of performance against objectives, as a prelude to modifications to the strategy itself.

It follows from this that if the planning process is to be effective, then the planner needs to give full recognition to the changing nature and demands of the environment, and to incorporate a degree of flexibility into both the objectives and the plan itself. Any failure to do this is likely to lead to a plan that quickly becomes out of date. Simmons (1972) pointed to the dangers of this both in the planning carried out by the Eastern bloc countries and by American business. In the case of the Eastern bloc countries in the 1940s, 1950s and 1960s, for example, he suggests that:

> They tried to impose a fixed five-year plan on changing conditions. Unfortunately, some American businesses are still making this mistake ... frequently a well constructed plan only six months old will be found to be very much out-of-date.

If, therefore, planning is to prove effective, there is an obvious need for a regular review process, something that is particularly important when the environment in which the organization is operating is changing rapidly. Amongst the examples that illustrate this are the high street coffee market, in which large numbers of new players have entered the market in recent years; the retail grocery market, in which Tesco has led with a series of innovations and put their competitors at a disadvantage; and the consumer electronics market, in which the pace of innovation is getting ever faster.

The principal purpose and indeed benefit of planning can therefore be seen in terms of the way in which it imposes a degree of order upon potential chaos and allocates the organization's resources in the most effective way. Among the other benefits are the ways in which the planning process brings people together and, potentially at least, leads to 'a shared sense of opportunity, direction, significance and achievement'. The planning process can therefore be seen to consist of four distinct stages:

1. Evaluation (where are we now, where do we want to go, and what level of resource capability do we have?)

2. Strategy formulation (how are we going to get there?)

3. Detailed planning

4. Implementation and review.

For many organizations, it is the implementation stage that proves to be the most difficult, but which paradoxically receives the least attention. There are several possible explanations for this. Peters and Waterman (1982, pp. 9–12), for example, suggest that all too often emphasis is placed upon what they refer to as the 'hard-ball' elements of strategy, structure and systems, with too little recognition being given to the significance of the 'soft-ball' elements of style, skills, staff and subordinate systems.

The problems of marketing planning

Although marketing planning has an inherent logic and appeal, McDonald (1995, p. 64) suggests that the vast majority of organizations experience significant problems in developing truly effective planning systems and cultures. There are, he believes, nine factors that contribute to this:

1. Too little support from the chief executive and top management. As a result, the resources that are needed are not made available and the results are not used in a meaningful way.

2. A lack of a plan for planning. As a consequence, too few managers understand how the plan will be built up, how the results will be used, the contribution that they are expected to make and the timescales that are involved.

3. A lack of support from line managers. A confusion over planning terms – remember that not everyone is familiar with Ansoff and the Directional Policy matrix.

4. Numbers are used instead of written objectives and strategies.

5. The emphasis is on too much detail, too far ahead.

6. Planning becomes a once-a-year ritual instead of an integral part of the day-to-day management process.

7. Too little thought or attention is given to the differences between operational or short-term planning and strategic planning.

8. There is a failure to integrate marketing planning into the overall corporate planning system.

9. The task of planning is left to a planner who fails to involve those who are actually managing the business.

McDonald goes on to suggest that far too many plans also fail to take sufficient account of the issues associated with the plan's implementation. The consequences of this, which have also been discussed by Bonoma (1985), are illustrated in Figure 8.2.

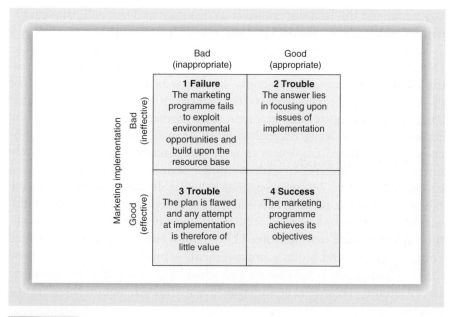

	Bad (inappropriate)	Good (appropriate)

1 Failure — The marketing programme fails to exploit environmental opportunities and build upon the resource base

2 Trouble — The answer lies in focusing upon issues of implementation

3 Trouble — The plan is flawed and any attempt at implementation is therefore of little value

4 Success — The marketing programme achieves its objectives

(Marketing implementation: Bad (ineffective) / Good (effective))

FIGURE 8.2   *The planning and implementation matrix (adapted from Bonoma, 1985)*

8.4   ESTABLISHING THE CORPORATE MISSION

Referring to Figure 8.1 it can be seen that, following an initial environmental and business analysis, the development of a mission statement is the starting point both for corporate and marketing planning, since it represents a vision of what the organization is or should attempt to become. This is typically expressed in terms of the two questions to which we have already referred: 'What business are we in?' and 'What business should we be in?'. It is the answer to this second question in particular that sets the parameters within which objectives are subsequently established, strategies developed and action programmes implemented. In the case of the UK drinks industry, a series of changes and market pressures have led to a radical reconfiguration of the market, with the focus today being not upon brewing, but upon licensing deals, hotels and restaurants. It is also the question that many organizations, when faced with a rapidly changing market environment, find difficult to answer. In the case of the high street retailer W.H. Smith, for example, the question of what business the organization should be in was thrown into sharp relief at the beginning of 2004, as it became increasingly evident that many of the company's core product lines, such as CDs, DVDs and even books, were being targeted by other Internet retailers such as Amazon, as well as seemingly very different types of retail organization such as Tesco. Equally, at the same time Boots found its core lines under attack both from the low-price retailers such as

Superdrug and the large supermarket chains such as Tesco and Sainsbury's, both of which offered convenience and relatively low prices.

Given these sorts of issues, the role of the mission statement should be seen in terms of the way in which it is – or should be – capable of performing a powerful integrating function, since it is in many ways a statement of core corporate values and is the framework within which individual business units prepare their business plans, something that has led to the corporate mission being referred to as an 'invisible hand' that guides geographically scattered employees to work independently and yet collectively towards the organization's goal. A similar sentiment has been expressed by Ouchi (1983, p. 74), who suggests that the deliberate generality of the mission statement performs an integrating function of various stakeholders over a long period of time. This is illustrated in the case of the earthmoving equipment manufacturer J.C. Bamford, which has a clearly stated policy of quality and product improvement, something of which everyone in the organization is fully aware and which acts as a consistent guideline in determining behaviour at all levels, but particularly within the planning process.

For a mission statement to be worthwhile, it should be capable of providing personnel throughout the company with a shared sense of opportunity, direction, significance and achievement, factors which are particularly important for large organizations with divisions that are geographically scattered.

The potential benefits of a strong binding statement of fundamental corporate values and good communication have been highlighted by a variety of writers, including Collins and Porras (1998), who have highlighted the importance of a powerful vision that is then driven throughout the organization. Equally, a study of European managers by Management Centre Europe found that what gave highly successful companies an edge over their competitors was the importance they attached to basic corporate values.

In many ways, therefore, the mission statement, the position of which within the overall planning process is illustrated by the acronym MOST (Mission, Objectives, Strategy, Tactics), represents a visionary view of the overall strategic posture of an organization and, as Johnson and Scholes (2002, p. 239) comment, 'is a generalized statement of the overriding purpose of an organization. It can be thought of as an expression of its *raison dêtre*.' Richards (1978) has referred to the mission in much the same way, calling it 'the master strategy' and suggesting that it is a visionary projection of the central and overriding concepts on which the organization is based. He goes on to suggest that 'it should not focus on what the firm is doing in terms of products and markets currently served, but rather upon the services and utility within the firm.'

It follows from this that any failure to agree the mission statement is likely to lead to fundamental problems in determining the strategic

direction of the firm. Recognizing this, the managment teams of The Body Shop and easyJet have both concentrated upon developing *and communicating to their staff* their mission statements. The rationale in each case is straightforward and is a reflection of the fact that a mission statement is of little value unless it is understood by everyone in the organization and *acted upon*.

In the case of easyJet, for example, the mission statement is:

to manage and extend Europe's leading value brand to more products and services, whilst creating real wealth for all stakeholders.

For The Body Shop, which is now owned by L'Oreal, the mission is based on the values of the company's founder, Anita Roddick, and reflects the view that business can be both profitable and responsible. This is encapsulated in the five principles that underpin the business:

- Opposition to animal testing
- The support of community trade
- The defence of human rights
- The protecting of the planet
- Activating individuals' self-esteem.

The characteristics of good mission statements

Good mission statements can be seen to exhibit certain characteristics, the most notable being that they are, as Wensley (1987, p. 31) has commented, 'short on numbers and long on rhetoric while (still) remaining succinct'. Having said this, Toyota's mission statement, expressed in 1985, did contain a useful and significant number. (Note: In 2009, Toyota overtook General Motors to become the world's largest car manufacturer.) Sometimes called the Global 10 mission, it expressed Toyota's intention to have 10 per cent of the world car market by the late 1990s. In many cases, however, the mission statement emerges as little more than a public relations exercise. In making this comment we have in mind the temptation that exists for over-ambition, which is typically reflected in the too frequent use of phrases such as 'first in the field', 'excellent', and so on. For a mission statement to be worthwhile, it is essential that it is realistic and specifies the business domain in which the company will operate. According to Abell (1980, Chapter 3), this domain is best defined in terms of three dimensions:

1. The *customer groups* that will be served
2. The *customer needs* that will be met
3. The *technology* that will satisfy these needs.

Given the nature of Abell's comments, the six tests for a successful mission statement are that it must:

1. Be sufficiently specific to have an impact on the behaviour of staff throughout the organization

2. Be founded more on customer needs and their satisfaction than on product characteristics

3. Reflect the organization's core skills

4. Reflect opportunities and threats

5. Be attainable

6. Be flexible.

Modifying the mission statement over time

Having developed a mission statement, it should not be seen as a once-and-for-all expression of the organization's purpose, but rather as something that changes over time in response to changing internal conditions, and external environmental opportunities and threats. A mission statement developed in the 1990s, for example, is unlikely to be appropriate today, when issues such as environmentalism and the green consumer are of considerably greater importance. Equally, the mission statement needs to reflect changing emphases as the organization grows, adds new products and moves into new markets. Over the past decade, for example, many of the drinks companies have, as we suggested earlier, moved away from the focus upon brewing that dominated for several decades to a far broader focus upon leisure, and in doing this have redefined their mission statements on several occasions.

Influences on the mission statement

In developing the mission statement for a company, there are likely to be five major factors that need to be taken into account:

1. The company's history and in particular its performance and patterns of ownership

2. The preferences, values and expectations of managers, owners and those who have power within the organization

3. Environmental factors, in particular the major opportunities and threats that exist and are likely to emerge in the future

4. The resources available, since these make certain missions possible and others not

5. Distinctive competences. While opportunities may exist in a particular market, it would not necessarily make sense for an organization to enter the market if it would not be making the fullest use of its areas of distinctive competence.

However, for the majority of organizations, the development of a mission statement often proves to be a difficult process, involving a series of decisions on strategic trade-offs between different groups of stakeholders both inside and outside the organization. These stakeholders can conveniently be grouped under three main headings:

1. *Internal stakeholders*, including owners, decision-makers, unions and employees

2. *External stakeholders*, such as the government, the financial community, trade associations, pressure groups and society

3. *Marketplace stakeholders*, including customers, competitors, suppliers and creditors.

Of these three groups it is the internal stakeholders who undoubtedly exert the greatest and most immediate effect upon the mission and subsequently the objectives pursued, since it is their expectations and patterns of behaviour that influence the organization most directly on a day-to-day basis.

The impact of external stakeholders is by contrast less direct, although still felt in a variety of ways. The implications of legislation, for example, in the form of, say, compulsory seat belts in the rear of cars, have an effect both upon the manufacturers of cars and seat belts. Equally, the financial community represents a significant influence in that the availability and cost of finance, as well as financial expectations in terms of returns, will all force the planner to behave in particular ways. In the case of pressure groups, the most obvious factor in recent years has been the emergence of environmental issues, with the 'greening' of business policies having subsequently been felt across a wide spectrum of products, including petrol, foodstuffs and white goods such as refrigerators.

The third category of stakeholders is made up of those in the marketplace. Of the four major types of marketplace stakeholder, it is customers and competitors who have the most obvious and direct impact upon planning since, in order to succeed, the company needs to understand in some detail their expectations and likely patterns of behaviour. It follows from this that both the organizational mission and the objectives pursued must of necessity be a direct reflection of both elements. By contrast, the influence of suppliers is generally seen to be less direct. There is, however, an obvious need for planning to take account of issues of supply availability, consistency and quality, since without this problems of shortfall or irregular supply are likely to be experienced.

Mission statements: the starting point

Before attempting to write a mission statement the strategist needs to spend time preparing a meaningful statement about the purpose of the firm. In doing this, it is important to recognize the organization's capabilities, the constraints upon it both internally and externally, and the opportunities that exist currently and those that might feasibly develop.

For a mission statement to be useful, it therefore needs to exhibit certain characteristics. It should, for example, focus upon *distinctive values* rather than upon every opportunity that is likely to exist. A statement that includes comments on producing the highest-quality product, offering the most service, achieving the widest distribution network and selling at the lowest price is both unrealistic and too ambitious. More importantly, it fails to provide the sorts of guidelines needed when trade-offs are necessary. Equally, the mission statement must define what we can refer to as the *competitive domain* within which the organization will operate. This competitive domain can be classified by a series of statements on scope:

1. *Industry scope*. This is the range of industries that are of interest to the organization. Some organizations, for example, will operate in just one industry sector, while others are willing to operate in a series. Equally, some organizations will only operate in an industrial or consumer goods market, while others are willing to operate in both.

2. *Geographical scope*. The geographical breadth of operations in terms of regions, countries or county groupings is again part of the mission statement, and varies from a single city right through to multinationals, which operate in virtually every country of the world.

3. *Market segment scope*. This covers the type of market or customer that the company is willing to serve. For a long time, for example, Johnson & Johnson sold its range of products only to the baby market. Largely because of demographic shifts, the company redefined its market segments and, with considerable success, moved into the young adult market.

4. *Vertical scope*. This refers to the degree of integration within the company. Thus, Ford, as part of its car manufacturing operations, has owned rubber plantations, glass manufacturing plants and several steel foundries. Others, by contrast, buy in everything and simply act as middlemen (refer back to our comments about the hollow corporation, page 27).

It should be apparent, therefore, that in developing the mission statement a variety of considerations need to be borne in mind. The end purpose, however, should be that of *motivation* by ensuring that stakeholders recognize the significance of their work in a far broader sense than simply that of making profits.

The third aspect of the mission statement is that it should only give emphasis to the *major policies* that the organization wishes to pursue. These policies are designed to narrow the range of individual discretion, with the result that the organization should operate in a more consistent manner.

The danger of bland mission statements: rethinking the approach by developing 'the awesome purpose'

Although mission statements have a potentially valuable role to play in clarifying what an organization stands for (its singular purpose), far too many mission statements have proved to be bland and meaningless. The extent to which this is the case was highlighted by Abrahams (1999), who in *The Mission Statement Book* analyses 301 corporate mission statements from America's top companies. The words used most frequently were: service (230 times); customers (211); quality (194); value (183); employees (157); growth (118); environment (117); profit (114); shareholders (114); leader (104); and best (102). Many of the 301 statements proved to be interchangeable and gave no real indication of the nature of the organization from which it emerged or any insight to what might make the organization distinctive. First-generation companies know instinctively what they stand for, but after several generations of management, the singular purpose to which we referred above becomes far harder to identify. One of the few vary large organizations not to have lost sight of this in its mission statement is Chrysler, which has as its mission 'To produce cars and trucks that people will want to buy, will enjoy driving, and will want to buy again.'

Mission statements have also been criticized by Piercy (1997, p. 181), who has suggested that numerous organizations are guilty of a 'holier than thou' posturing in which the mission statement is full of phrases such as 'we will be a market leader ... A total quality supplier ... A socially responsible producer ... A green/environmentally friendly firm, ... A global player ... A good corporate citizen ... a responsible partner with distributors ... [and] a caring employer'.

It was in an attempt to overcome this that the management consultant Nigel MacLennan (2000, p. 13) has argued that what companies need instead is an 'awesome purpose'. Awesome purpose, he suggests, is the framework into which every element of the organization's culture should be aligned. Examples of an awesome purpose include that of the Toyota 10 (page 305), to which reference was made earlier, and companies such as Ryanair and easyJet deciding to redefine the airlines market and, in this way, hitting hard and/or beating the established market players. Others who have taken a similar and seemingly impossible approach include the management team of Toyota, who pursued a vision of creating a car that would allow them to undercut the prices of German luxury cars while at the same time beating them on quality. The result was the Lexus.

The need for communication and the growth of visioning

Once a mission has been developed it is, of course, imperative that it is communicated to employees so that everyone in the organization is aware of it, since (as we suggested earlier) the statement is designed to provide a sense of vision and direction for the organization over the next 10–20 years. A mission statement is therefore of little value if employees are either not made aware of it or misunderstand it, or if it is revised every few years in response to minor environmental changes. There is, however, a need for it to be redefined either when it has lost its appropriateness or when it no longer defines the optimal course for the organization.

However, although mission statements have an undoubted value in that they are capable of highlighting an organization's core values, many mission statements have, as suggested above, been criticized in recent years on the grounds that they are far too general ('to be the best'), too ambitious ('to be the world leader') and too similar. Therefore, if a mission statement is to be meaningful, it is essential that it is firmly rooted in organizational realities, capabilities and competences. Without this, it is quite simply empty rhetoric.

It is partly in recognition of this that a greater emphasis is now being given to the idea of *visioning*. The thinking behind visioning is straightforward and designed to encourage management teams at the corporate level, the business unit or the brand level to think in detail about what they are trying to create. The vision can therefore be seen to be the picture that the planner has of what exactly the organization will look like in three or five years' time. In developing this picture of the future size and profile of the organization, there is an obvious need for a clear understanding both of the ways in which the environment might develop (or be encouraged to develop) and of the organization's competences. Against this background, an initially broad but then an increasingly detailed vision of the organization or brand in, say, three, five and ten years' time can be developed (an example of the Swatch vision appears in Illustration 8.1).

Illustration 8.1   The Swatch vision

One of the major successes of the last 25 years has been the Swiss Corporation for Microelectronics and Watchmaking (SMH). The company was formed in 1983 by the merger of two of Switzerland's biggest watchmakers, both of which were insolvent. The new company, under the leadership of Nicholas Hayek, developed the Swatch watch, which, Hayek openly admits, was the result not of detailed financial analysis but of a burning desire to rebuild the Swiss watch industry and a vision of how this might be done.

Hayek recognized that in order to beat his Asian competitors he would have to produce something distinctive. In the event, this was a watch with a European sense of style that, despite being built in a high-labour-cost environment, was able to compete against – and beat – watches from SMH's Japanese competitors such as Seiko.

Where visioning has been successful, it has therefore tended to reflect a clarity of managerial thinking about several areas, including:

- The size of the organization, business unit or brand in three, five or 10 years' time
- The image and reputation that will have been created
- The corporate and brand values that will be developed
- The nature of the customer base and the customer segments that will be served
- How these customers should perceive the organization or brand
- The geographic coverage that will have been achieved
- The overall position within the market and the competitive stance
- The links with other organizations.

The significance of vision has been highlighted by a variety of writers over the past few years, but most notably by Collins and Porras (1998), who argue the case not just for corporate (or brand) vision, but also for visionary product concepts and visionary market insights. However, vision cannot be developed in isolation, but needs to be based on the planner's clarity of thinking and understanding of organizational values. The ways in which the two dimensions come together and contribute to performance are illustrated in Figure 8.3.

In commenting on this, Hayek the CEO of Swatch to whom we referred on the previous page, said:

Everywhere children believe in dreams. And they ask the same question: Why? Why does something work a certain way? Why do we behave in certain ways? We ask ourselves those questions every day.

People may laugh – the CEO of a huge Swiss company talking about fantasy. But that's the real secret of what we've done.

Ten years ago, the people on the original Swatch team asked a crazy question: Why can't we design a striking, low-cost, high-quality watch and build it in Switzerland? The bankers were sceptical. A few suppliers refused to sell us parts. They said we would ruin the industry with this crazy product. But this was our vision and we won!

Having created the mission and the vision, the management team can then begin to focus upon the development of the specific objectives and the detail of the strategy. However, it is not enough for this strategy to be appropriate in that it builds upon organizational capabilities and environmental demands, it must also be implementable. The reader needs to recognize at this stage that there are numerous barriers to the effective implementation of any strategy, and that good leadership and well-developed patterns

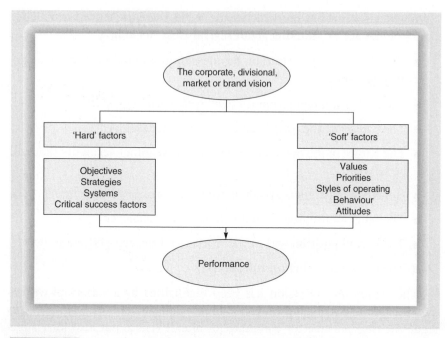

FIGURE 8.3 *Influences on the vision*

of communication are a fundamental part of overcoming these barriers. Without these, it is almost inevitable that the staff will have little real understanding of the core values or what is expected of them.

It is because of this that considerable emphasis in recent years has been given to the idea of *internal marketing*. This term, which is used to describe the work that is done within the organization in terms of training, motivating and communicating with the employees, was developed largely within the service sector. Increasingly, however, it is becoming recognized that it is a fundamental part of the marketing equation for any organization, since in its absence the ways in which employees interact with customers will lack true focus (see Figure 8.4).

Vision, inspiring commitments and leadership principles

Having developed the vision, be it at corporate, divisional, brand or market level, there is then the need to link this to a series of what might be referred to as inspiring commitments and then, in turn, to leadership principles; this is illustrated in Figure 8.5 and reflects how Shell Oils operated at the beginning of this decade.

Although it has often been argued that a fundamental underpinning for any marketing strategy, be it at the corporate, divisional or brand level, is a shared vision of what the management team is trying to achieve, research at Cranfield School of Management (see Kakabadse, 1999) has highlighted

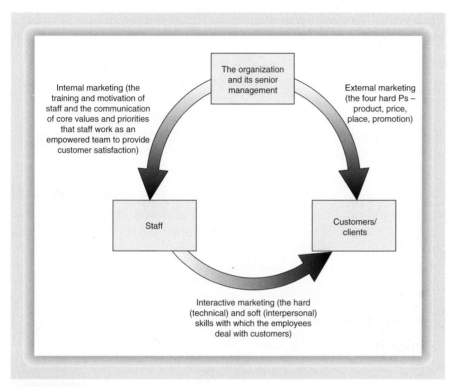

FIGURE 8.4   *The three dimensions of marketing*

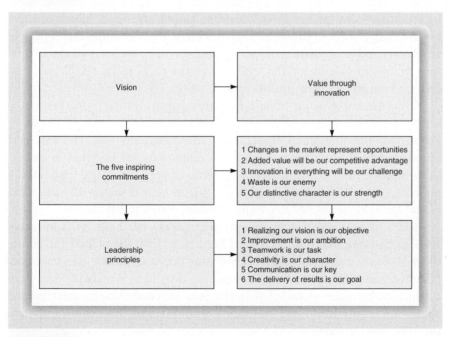

FIGURE 8.5   *The vision, inspiring commitments and leadership principles*

the degree of dissension that often exists within senior management teams. His findings suggested:

> the [senior] management of 20% of Swedish, 23% of Japanese, 30% of British, 31% of Austrian, 32% of German, 39% of French, 42% of Finnish, 46% of Spanish, 68% of Irish companies and 56% of top civil servants in the Australian Commonwealth government, report that the members of the top team hold deeply different views concerning the shape and direction of their organization – in effect differences of vision.

The common retort is that differences such as these are only to be expected and can be seen to be the sign of a healthy organization characterized by a degree of creative tension. However, the research suggests that this is not in fact the case and those differences in vision manifest themselves in a number of ways, including:

- Organizational turbulence

- An emphasis upon the short term

- Infighting

- Staff keeping their heads down.

In order to overcome this, Kakabadse argues for more open communication amongst senior management; the promotion of a stronger feedback culture from further down the organization; the development of more overtly shared values; attention to be paid to the detail of the differences in ambitions and goals that each person has for their own department, division or function; and for the (revised) vision then to be established and driven throughout the organization.

Although vision is an important early stage in the planning process, a series of studies suggest that staff are only rarely included in discussions about corporate brand and reputation. The consultants ORC, for example, found that only 6 per cent of European employees are involved in discussions at departmental level, compared with 12 per cent in the USA and 17 per cent in the Pacific Rim. In addition, 43 per cent of European employees do not know their employer's brand mission, vision or values.

Given that a considerable amount of emphasis has been given in recent years to the idea that there is a need for staff to 'live the brand', the failure to understand it has potentially significant implications for the process of planning and implementation. Recognizing this, BBC Worldwide has spent a considerable time ensuring that the organization's vision, strategy and values are family integrated and then communicated throughout the organization (see Illustration 8.2).

Illustration 8.2   Vision, strategy and values

BBC Worldwide is the BBC's international marketing arm, with a brief for marketing and selling BBC programmes overseas. The vision, strategy and values represent the framework from within which marketing planning takes place.

The vision

To be recognized as one of the UK's leading international consumer media companies, admired around the world for its outstanding products and exceptional commercial performance, thereby bringing substantial and growing benefit to the BBC – not just commercially but also creatively.

The strategy

BBC Worldwide aims to become a world-class marketing organization, able to understand, respond to and anticipate market needs better than its competitors. In particular, it will develop outstanding skills in driving value major brands across media and markets. It will continue to focus on developing the most creative, cost-effective and high-quality range of consumer media products on the market. It will build lasting partnerships with the BBC and independents that ensure unique access to the best of BBC brands and properties. And it will help make the BBC the natural first choice for talent.

Our UK strategy is to be the first choice provider of quality media products for many 'communities of interest' by exploiting the BBC's unique broadcast strengths across all media platforms, past and future, and in the majority of genres.

Our international strategy is to focus on fewer market segments, where the BBC has clear competitive advantage. It will understand these target segments better than its competitors, and will seek to build a robust cross-media business around major BBC brands.

The values

We have worked to identify the key behaviours which characterize successful performance at BBC Worldwide. We believe that these should define 'the way we do things around here'. Therefore, BBC Worldwide embraces these values and guiding behaviours:

- *Clarity* – we have a clarity of direction, purpose and goals
- *Responsibility* – we are responsible for creating our own success
- *Excellence* – we foster and encourage innovation and creativity as the life-blood of our business
- *Appreciation* – we fully appreciate and respect each other
- *Teamwork* – we are team players and believe in cooperation and collaboration at all levels
- *Effective* – we are committed to delivering high-quality products that delight our partners and customers.

8.5   INFLUENCES ON OBJECTIVES AND STRATEGY

Having developed the mission statement and the vision, the planner is then in a position to turn to the objectives and strategy. It has long been recognized that any organization represents a complex mix of cultural and political influences, all of which come to bear in some way on the objectives that are pursued. It follows from this that objectives and strategy are not simply set in a vacuum or just by reference to environmental factors, but rather that they emerge as the product of a complex interaction at various levels of the organization. This is reflected in Figure 8.6, which illustrates the various layers of cultural and political influences on objectives (and subsequently strategy), ranging from the values of society to the far more specific influences such as organizational objectives, individuals' expectations, and indeed the power structures that exist within and around the organization.

It logically follows that, if we are to understand fully the process of setting objectives, we need to recognize the complexities of these interrelationships.

These have been commented on by Johnson and Scholes (1988, pp. 113–15), and it is worth quoting them at some length:

- There are a number of cultural factors in an organization's *environment* which will influence the internal situation. In particular the values of society at large and the influence of organized groups need to be understood.

- The *nature of the business*, such as the market situation and the types of product and technology are important influences not only in a direct sense but in the way they affect the expectations of individuals and groups.

- Most pervasive of all these general influences is the organizational *culture* itself.

- At a more specific level, individuals will normally have shared expectations with one or more groups of people within the organization. These shared expectations may be concerned with undertaking the company's tasks and reflect the formal structure of the organization, e.g. departmental expectations. However, *coalitions* also arise as a result of specific events, and can transcend the formal structure.

- Internal groups and individuals are also influenced by their contacts with *external stakeholders* – groups which have an interest in the operation of the company such as customers, shareholders, suppliers or unions. For example, sales staff may be pressurized by customers to represent their interests within the company.

- Individuals or groups, whether internal or external, cannot influence an organization's strategies unless they have an influencing mechanism. This mechanism is called *power*, which can be derived in a variety of ways.

- Organizational *objectives* traditionally have been afforded a central/dominant role in influencing strategy, i.e. strategy is seen as the means of achieving preordained and unchangeable objectives. That is not our view. Whereas organizations do have objectives, which are often valuable in strategy formulation, they should not be regarded as an unchangeable set of expectations. They should be viewed as an important part of the strategic equation, and open to amendment and change as strategies develop.

- Objectives tend to emerge as the wishes of the most dominant coalition, usually the management of the organization, although there are notable exceptions. However, in pursuing these objectives the dominant group is very strongly influenced by their reading of the political situation, i.e. their perception of the power struggle. For example, they are likely to set aside some of their expectations in order to improve the chance of achieving others.

8.6   GUIDELINES FOR ESTABLISHING OBJECTIVES AND SETTING GOALS AND TARGETS

Few businesses pursue a single objective; instead they have a mixture, which typically includes profitability, sales growth, market share improvement, risk

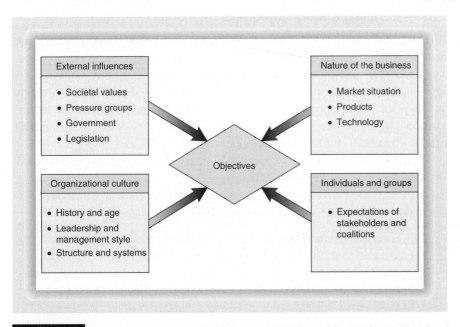

FIGURE 8.6   *Influences on organizational objectives and strategy (adapted from Johnson and Scholes, 1988)*

containment, innovativeness, usage, and so on. Each business unit should therefore set objectives under a variety of headings and then *manage by objectives*. In other words, it is the pursuit of these objectives that should provide the framework both for the planning and control processes. However, for this to work, several guidelines must be adhered to, with objectives being:

1. *Hierarchical*: going from the most important to the least important

2. *Quantitative*: in order to avoid ambiguity – the objective 'to increase market share' is not as satisfactory a guideline as 'to increase market share by 5 per cent' or indeed 'to increase market share by 5 percentage points within 18 months'

3. *Realistic*: it is only too easy for objectives to reflect a degree of wishful thinking; instead they should be developed as the result of a detailed analysis of opportunities, corporate capability, competitive strengths and competitive strategy

4. *Consistent*: it is quite obviously unrealistic to pursue incompatible objectives; as an example of this, to aim for substantial gains in both sales and profits simultaneously is rarely possible.

It is also essential that they satisfy the SMART criteria of being **S**pecific rather than general in their nature, **M**easurable, **A**ctionable, **R**ealistic and **T**ime-based. In the case of marketing objectives, there is also the need for them to be built upon to or fall out of the corporate objectives.

Primary and secondary objectives

Although for a long time economists argued that firms aimed to maximize profits, it is now generally recognized that the modern large corporation, managed by professionals, pursues a far broader and infinitely more diverse set of objectives. As a consequence, traditional views of profit maximization as the principal objective have been challenged by the reality of the behaviour of corporate management. With this in mind, two types of objective can be identified: *primary* and *secondary*.

Traditionally the primary objective was, as observed above, profit maximization. Other objectives are, however, often seen by managers to be of more immediate relevance and, as Chisnall (1989, p. 137) points out, may affect the organization's profit-earning ability:

> *These secondary objectives, which are not in any way inferior to the primary objective, are necessary if a company is to plan effectively for its future progress. In the short term, for instance, a profit maximization policy may be affected by changes in economic conditions which demand some restructuring of corporate resources to meet new levels of competition. Survival or market share defences may, in fact, become primary objectives.*

This issue of the multiplicity of objectives has also been discussed by Drucker (1955), who isolated eight areas in which organizational objectives might be developed and maintained:

1. Market standing
2. Innovation
3. Productivity
4. Financial and physical resources
5. Manager performance and development
6. Worker performance and attitude
7. Profitability
8. Public responsibility.

Rethinking business objectives: the significance of the triple bottom line and the alternative three Ps

The eighth of Drucker's objectives, public responsibility, has received far greater attention over the past few years than at any time since he first identified them almost 50 years ago. With a far greater emphasis having been given in recent years to the impact upon society of marketing behaviour, issues of sustainable development have led to the emergence of the triple bottom line and the alternative three Ps.

The triple bottom line is based on the idea that business should not simply pursue economic objectives, but that decisions should also reflect social and ecological considerations. This has, in turn, led to the three Ps of People, Planet and Profit, in which environmental quality and social equity are seen to be just as important as profit. Amongst the advocates of such an approach was Anita Roddick, the founder of The Body Shop. The Body Shop's corporate philosophy was – and still is – that social justice, human rights and spirituality are integral parts of modern business practice. With business and marketing decision-making having long been based on quantifiable measures such as efficiency, proponents of the triple bottom line argue that highlighting social issues and taking responsibility for business practice will increasingly prove to be the way in which firms will gain a competitive advantage.

Objectives and time horizons

It should be apparent by this stage that, in setting objectives, the marketing planner needs to take account of a wide variety of factors. Perhaps the final influence that we need to examine here before focusing upon the detail of corporate and marketing objectives is that of the time horizons involved. In the case of those industries that are highly capital-intensive, for example, the planning horizons tend to be considerably longer than is the case in faster-moving consumer goods markets. We can therefore usefully distinguish between the short, medium and long terms.

From the planner's point of view, the short term is concerned essentially with issues of tactics, while the long term is concerned with the major issues of strategy and the allocation and reallocation of resources. The medium term then sits neatly between these in that it provides the focus for determining how effectively resources are being used. Although there is perhaps an understandable temptation to tie each of these phases to specific periods of time (e.g. up to one year in the case of the short term, one to five years for the medium term and over five years for the long term), such an exercise is generally only useful when carried out in relation to a specific industry or company.

At a more general level, the significance of planning time horizons relates rather more to the degree of environmental change being experienced and the ability of the organization to respond by reallocating resources. A useful distinction (derived from economics) between long-term and short-term focuses on *capacity*. Within the short run capacity is given, hence the aim should be to make the best use of available capacity – whether this is defined in terms of sales personnel, productive facilities, distribution systems or any other resource constraint. One moves from the short run to the long run when capacity is increased (or reduced). Making extra capacity available involves capital expenditure/investment, and its existence – in whatever time frame – is usually associated with fixed (or establishment) costs. The significance of this from the point of view of establishing objectives can therefore be seen in terms of the need to identify objectives both for the short term and the long term. The long-term objectives will then be concerned with the direction in which the organization is heading, while the short-term objectives will be allied far more closely with the stages through which the organization will have to move in order to achieve this position.

The nature of corporate objectives

In the light of our discussion here and in Chapter 1, it should be apparent that corporate management, having established the corporate mission and vision, then has to take these a stage further by developing a series of specific objectives for each level of management. Most typically these objectives are expressed in terms of sales growth, profitability, market share growth and risk diversification. Because the majority of organizations generally pursue a number of objectives, it is, as we have seen, important that they are stated in a hierarchical manner, going from the most important to the least important, with this hierarchy being both internally consistent and mutually reinforcing. By doing this, the strategist is clarifying priorities so that if, at a later stage, a conflict of objectives emerges, a decision can then be made as to which particular objective is to dominate. At the same time it is essential that the objectives established are realistic both in terms of their magnitude and the timescale over which they are to be achieved. Almost invariably, however, organizations experience difficulties and conflicts in establishing objectives, problems that are in turn compounded by the need to establish multiple objectives. For example, it is seldom, if ever, possible for an organization to satisfy concurrently objectives of rapid growth *and* risk aversion, or to maximize both sales *and* profits. Recognizing this, Weinberg (1969) has identified eight basic strategic trade-offs facing firms:

1. Short-term profits versus long-term growth
2. Profit margins versus competitive position
3. Direct sales effort versus market development effort
4. Penetration of existing markets versus the development of new markets
5. Related versus non-related new opportunities as a source of long-term growth
6. Profit versus non-profit goals
7. Growth versus stability
8. A 'riskless' environment versus a high-risk environment.

It follows from this that the strategist has to decide upon the relative emphasis that is to be given to each of these dimensions. Any failure to do this is ultimately likely to lead to conflict and reduce the extent to which the objectives provide useful strategic guidelines.

However, while the need for clear objectives may well be self-evident, it is relatively unusual to find explicit references as to just *how* managers should go about developing these objectives in the first place. One of the few who has attempted to provide guidelines for formulating objectives is McKay (1972), who suggests that it is possible to identify two categories of issues that should be considered: the general issues that apply to all organizations, and the more specific, which force a more detailed examination. These general issues are:

- *Business scope* – what business should we be in?
- *Business orientation* – what approach is most appropriate for our business scope and to our purposes of survival, growth and profit?
- *Business organization* – to what extent is our organizational style, structure and staff policy suited to the orientation chosen?

- *Public responsibility* – is there a match between our selection of opportunities and the existing and future social and economic needs of the public?

- *Performance evaluation* – is there a match between our appraisal and planning systems?

The *specific* areas that then follow from this, he suggests, relate to each strategic business unit (SBU) and include:

- Customer classes

- Competitors

- Markets and distribution

- Technology and products

- Production capability

- Finance

- Environment.

Taking account of competitors' objectives

Objectives should never be set in a vacuum. Instead they should be set against the background of a detailed understanding of environmental demands and opportunities. In doing this, particular attention needs to be paid to the objectives that are likely to be pursued by competitors, since these will often have a direct impact upon subsequent levels of performance.

A competitor's objectives are likely to be influenced by many factors, but particularly by its size, history, managerial culture and performance. They are also affected by whether the company is part of a larger organization. If this is the case, the strategist needs to know whether it is being pressured to achieved growth or whether it is viewed by the parent as a 'cash cow' and is being milked. Equally, we need to know just how important it is to the parent: if it is central to the parent company's long-term plans, this will have a direct influence upon how much money will be spent in fighting off an attack. As mentioned earlier (Chapter 7), Rothschild (1984), for example, argues that the worst competitor to attack is the competitor for whom this is the sole or principal business, and who has a global operation.

There is therefore, as discussed in Chapter 7, a strong argument for the strategist to develop a detailed competitive map in which issues of competitive capability and priority figure prominently. In doing this, a useful assumption, at least initially, is that competitors will aim for profit targets and choose their strategies accordingly. Even here, however, organizations differ in the emphasis they put on short-term as opposed to long-term profits. In reality, of course, few organizations aim for profit maximization, be it in the short or long term, but instead opt for a degree of *satisficing* (a term coined by Simon (1960) to refer to an acceptable level of performance, typically across multiple objectives, rather than an optimal performance on just one). They have target profit figures and are satisfied to achieve them, even if greater profits could have been achieved by other strategies with perhaps a greater degree of risk.

An alternative approach is to assume that each competitor has a variety of objectives, each of which is of different importance and which has therefore a different weight in the minds of the members of the management team. Recognizing this, the marketing strategist needs to determine, at least in broad terms, the relative weighting that each competitor gives to areas such as current and long-term profitability, market share retention and growth, risk avoidance, technological leadership, distribution dominance, service, and so on. Knowing this provides an insight into whether each competitor is broadly satisfied with its current strategy and results, whether – and how – it will respond to different forms of competitive movement and attack, and so on. The competitor who, for example, is pursuing a service-based strategy is far more likely to respond aggressively to a similar competitive move than if the move is based on, say, an advertising-led attack by the same competitor.

The argument for looking in detail at your competitors as a prelude to developing your own objectives is, in many ways, self-evident, since what a competitor has done in the past will typically provide potentially strong insights to what the competitor is likely to do in the future. This is particularly the case when the organization has been performing strongly and the managerial priorities and mindsets have become well established. The management team will have developed a business model and, although it would be foolish to suggest that this is never reviewed or questioned, its success is likely to lead to its continued pursuit. Given this, a competitor's marketing strategists should, within certain parameters, be able to predict future patterns of behaviour. Firms such as GE, Mars, P&G and Kellogg's all have a focus upon brand leadership, whilst hotel chains such as Four Seasons have a focus on the premium end of the business market, an approach that is unlikely to change.

Having said this, competitive attitudes, objectives and strategies, but especially approaches to implementation, do of course change over time, even when a particular strategy is proving to be successful. History has shown though that the probability of change is far greater when a particular strategy is not working, or when there is a change in management at the top of the organization. There are therefore several specific factors that should be taken into account, as well as the rather more general issue of competitive posture referred to above. These include:

- *Each competitor's previous successes and failures*. It is quite normal to continue with a successful formula and to change one that is not working.

- *The volume and direction of investment in advertising and plant.* A rational competitor will concentrate advertising effort on the products and markets that appear to offer the greatest scope. Monitoring patterns of competitive advertising spend can therefore provide the strategist with a good indication of the directions in which to concentrate. Equally, a knowledge of competitors' investment in plant, which can often be picked up from equipment suppliers, planning applications and the trade press, provides an invaluable guide to profitable future plans.

- *Each competitor's relative cost position.* The starting point for this is to arrive at an assessment of each competitor's relative cost position in each major market sector. Working on the assumption that each competitor will have conducted a similar exercise, it is reasonable to suppose that they will give priority to cost-reduction strategies in those markets in which they are currently high-cost operators.

By focusing upon areas such as these, the strategist should be in a far better position to answer four fundamental questions:

1. What is each competitor seeking?

2. What is it that drives each competitor?

3. What is each competitor's potential competitive capability?

4. In what ways might this capability be translated into objectives and strategy?

It is against this background that the strategist can then define and perhaps redefine his or her own organization's objectives.

Developing offensive corporate objectives

Firms can be broadly classified as *proactive* or *reactive*. The former are characterized by an entrepreneurial and highly positive attitude to their markets, with a constant searching and pursuit of new business opportunities; in essence they try to shape the environment to fit the organization's resources and objectives. By contrast, reactive firms adopt a far more passive and less entrepreneurial posture, responding to rather than initiating environmental change. These contrasting styles have an obvious effect upon the sorts of objectives pursued and indeed, in most cases, upon subsequent levels of trading performance.

The implications of this for the way in which marketing objectives are set are reflected in the way in which there are few incentives for the marketing strategist to take an offensive approach within the marketplace unless ambitious marketing objectives have been set and a proactive and aggressive and high-performing marketing culture established.

With regard to the specific objectives that an offensive or proactive organization might pursue, these will depend to a large degree upon the organization's market position. If, for example, it is intent on increasing its market share, the starting point involves deciding upon which competitor(s) to attack. The options open to it are essentially:

1. *To attack the market leader.* This is typically a high-risk but potentially high-return strategy and one which makes sense if the leader is generally complacent or not serving the market as well as it might – Xerox, for example, chose to attack 3 M by developing a cleaner, faster and more convenient copying process (dry copying rather than wet). Equally, Dyson attacked Hoover with a technologically different product, whilst Airbus Industries attacked Boeing.

2. *To attack firms of its own size*, an approach in which is typically suited when they are either underfinanced or undermanaged.

3. *To attack local and regional firms.* This strategy was pursued with considerable success in the 1960s and 1970s by a small number of large brewers who gobbled up the small, regional brewers in the UK. It has been adopted subsequently by some of the major car producers such as Ford, who bought some of the smaller and specialist manufacturers such as Volvo and Aston Martin, and Volkswagen, who bought Skoda and Seat. (Note: Faced with a significant downturn in the economy, Ford sold Aston Martin in 2008.)

4. *To ignore the major players and to pursue instead* a flanking strategy that leads to the development and growth of a new market sector, something that has been done with considerable success by Ryanair and easyJet, both of whom sidestepped the major flag carriers.

Given the nature of these comments, it should be apparent that this question of *who* to attack is therefore at the very heart of an effective offensive strategy, since to make the wrong choice is likely to prove immensely costly.

Setting truly ambitious objectives: the significance of BHAGs

In discussing goals, Collins and Porras (1998) argue the case for what they term Big Hairy Audacious Goals (BHAGs). As examples of BHAGs, they point to a variety of organizations, including Boeing, which in the 1950s gained a significant advantage over its principal competitor Douglas aircraft (later to become McDonnell-Douglas) by establishing itself as the dominant player in the commercial aircraft industry with its 707, despite having little experience in that sector of the market. It then followed this in quick succession with the 727 (Douglas launched the DC-9 more than two years later), the 737 and then the 747 jumbo jet.

For Collins and Porras (1998, p. 94):

a BHAG engages people – it reaches out and grabs them in the gut. It is tangible, energizing, highly focused. People 'get it' right away; it takes little or no explanation.

Amongst the other organizations they cite as having or having had BHAGs are the cigarette manufacturer Philip Morris, which in 1961 was a sixth-place also-ran with less than 10 per cent of the tobacco market. The BHAG that the management team set themselves was that of replacing RJ Reynolds as the market leader, something that they achieved largely through their Marlboro brand. Other BHAGs include Sam Walton's objective of becoming the world's largest retailer (Wal-Mart), Walt Disney's ideas for the new type of amusement park that became Disneyland, IBM's reshaping of the computer industry in the 1960s, and Jack Welch's reshaping of General Electric.

In doing this, Welch stated that the first step – before all other steps – is for the company to 'define its destiny in broad but clear terms. You need an overarching message, something big, but simple and understandable'. In the case of GE, Welch developed the BHAG of 'To become number 1 or number 2 in every market we serve and revolutionize this company to have the speed and agility of a small enterprise.' Employees throughout GE fully understood – and remembered – the BHAG which was 'to become the number 1 or number 2 in every market we serve and to revolutionize this company to have the speed and agility of a small enterprise'. The compelling clarity of GE's BHAG can be contrasted with the difficult-to-understand, hard-to-remember 'vision statement' articulated by Westinghouse in 1989 which was based on a series of largely general and interchangeable comments about 'total quality, market leadership, technology, globalization, focused growth and diversification.'

The point that the reader needs to take from this is not that GE had the 'right' goal and Westinghouse had the 'wrong' goal. Rather, it is that GE's goal was clear, compelling and more likely to stimulate progress. Similar BHAG thinking was at the heart of the Amazon.com strategy, with Jeff Bezos becoming the biggest Internet bookseller by pursuing his GBF (Get Big Fast) philosophy.

Establishing the marketing objectives

Against the background of the comments made so far, we can identify a firm's competitive situation and hence its marketing decisions as being concerned with just two major elements: products and markets. This has been discussed by a variety of writers (see, for example, Ansoff, 1968; McKay, 1972; and Guiltinan and Paul (1988) and has led to the recognition that there are just four principal marketing objectives:

1. To establish and defend a clear position within the market
2. To defend and possibly increase market share

3. To grow the market, and

4. To sustain/grow levels of profitability.

To these, it is possible to add one other that reflects the growing importance of the social responsibility of business and the nature of the triple bottom line:

5. To deliver these in a socially responsible manner.

In many ways, the thinking that underpins these objectives can be seen to come together in Ansoff's ideas of a product/market matrix. This is illustrated in Figure 8.7.

The matrix in Figure 8.7 which focuses upon the product (what is sold) and to whom it is sold (the market), highlights four distinct strategic alternatives open to the marketing strategist:

1. Selling more existing products to existing markets

2. Extending existing products to new markets

3. Developing new products for existing markets

4. Developing new products for new markets.

Although in practice there are of course *relative* degrees of newness both in terms of products and markets – and hence the number of strategies

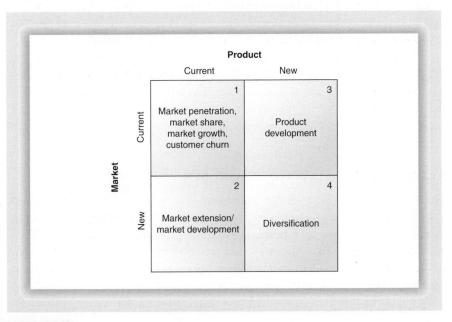

FIGURE 8.7 *Ansoff's growth vector matrix (source: Ansoff, 1957)*

open to the organization is substantial – Ansoff's matrix is useful in that it provides a convenient and easily understood framework within which marketing objectives and strategies can be readily developed, something that is reflected in Figure 8.8.

It follows from this that setting objectives and strategies *in relation to products and markets* is a fundamental element of the marketing planning process. These marketing objectives then represent performance commitments for the future, and are typically stated in terms of market share, sales volume, levels of sterling distribution, and profitability. For these to be worthwhile, however, they need to be stated both quantitatively and unambiguously. In this way they are capable of measurement, something which is not possible if they are stated only in broad directional terms.

The argument for explicit and quantitatively expressed objectives is therefore overpowering, since any failure to do this simply offers scope for confusion and ambiguity at a later stage, not just in terms of the sort of action required, but also in terms of the performance measurement standards that are to be used. In stating objectives they also need to be related to the fundamental philosophies and policies of a particular organization, something

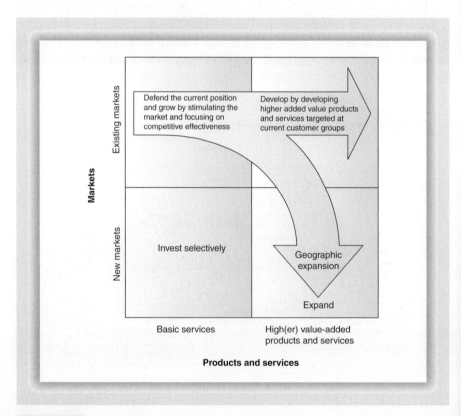

FIGURE 8.8 *Developing strategic direction*

which again argues the case for a clear and well-communicated mission statement. The *process* of setting objectives is therefore central to its effectiveness.

Ansoff's matrix revisited and expanded

Against the background of the comments so far, it should be apparent that marketing objectives relate to the four categories of Ansoff's product/market matrix, with decisions being needed on:

1. Existing products in existing markets

2. New products in existing markets

3. Existing products in new markets

4. New products in new markets.

But, although Ansoff's matrix is undoubtedly useful, the simplicity of a 2×2 matrix has a number of limitations. Recognizing this, Wills *et al.* (1972) have taken the matrix a step further by highlighting the degree of product and market newness and what this potentially means for planning and strategy; the expanded matrix is illustrated in Figure 8.9.

The general nature and direction of the choices between these strategic alternatives is influenced both by the product life cycle and the current shape of the company's product portfolio. This in turn leads to a series of choices for each product/market condition, choices that can be expressed in terms of five types of strategy:

1. *Maintenance* of the current competitive position

2. *Improvement* of the current competitive position

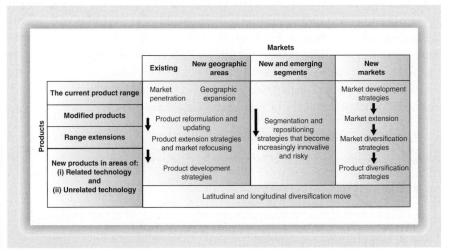

FIGURE 8.9   *Developing the Ansoff matrix*

3. *Harvesting*, which involves reducing or relinquishing the current competitive position in order to capitalize upon short-term profit and improve cash flow

4. *Exiting*, which typically occurs when the company is suffering from a weak competitive position or recognizes that the cost of staying in the market and/or improving upon the position is too high. As an example of this, ICI, now part of AkzoNobel, sold its loss-making European fertilizer business to Europe's second largest fertilizer producer, the Finnish company Kemira Oy. The decision to withdraw from this market sector was made after ICI had experienced losses for four years, despite having made major attempts to improve the business, including vigorous cost reductions and investment in new technology

5. *Entry* to a new sector.

However, while considering either the need or the feasibility of each of these strategies, the marketing planner needs to recognize the danger of adhering slavishly to any particular set of rules relating to the five categories and to be fully aware of the major constraints within which he or she is operating. Among the most commonly used and useful frameworks for identifying these is the concept of the limiting factor (a limiting factor might include costs of distribution that limit the market to a small geographic region, limitations on production capacity, and so on) and techniques of gap analysis, which are designed to highlight any gaps that exist between long-term forecasts of performance and the sales or financial objectives that have been set (see Figure 8.10).

In the case of Figure 8.10(a), the lowest curve represents a projection of expected sales from the organization's current portfolio of businesses. The highest curve traces the sales targets for the next five years, which, as can be seen, are more ambitious than the current portfolio will permit. The question that then quite obviously follows is how best to fill this strategic planning gap. The courses of action open to the strategist can then be examined in several ways. The first involves subdividing the gap into the *operations gap* and the *new strategies gap*. In the case of the *operations gap*, the approaches to reducing or eliminating it totally include:

- Greater productivity by means of reduced costs

- Improvements to the sales mix or higher prices

- Higher levels of market penetration.

In the case of the *new strategies gap*, the courses of action include:

- A reduction in objectives

- Market extension in the form of new market segments, new user groups or expansion geographically

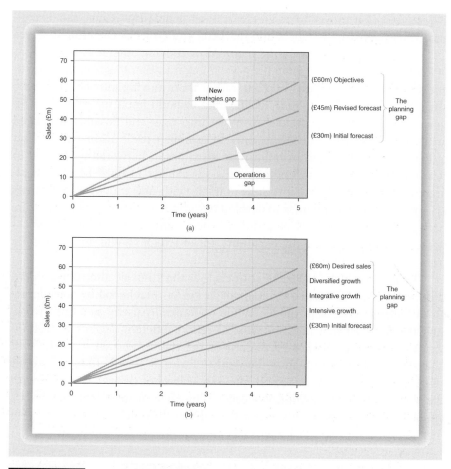

FIGURE 8.10   *The strategic planning gap*

- Product development

- Diversification by selling new products to new markets.

An alternative way of looking at the strategic planning gap is illustrated in Figure 8.10(b). Here, the solutions to the shortfall have been categorized as:

- Identifying further opportunities to achieve growth within the company's current business (intensive growth)

- Identifying opportunities to build or acquire businesses related to the current sphere of operations (integrative growth)

- Adding businesses that are unrelated to current operations (diversification).

In weighing up which of these alternatives to pursue, the planner needs to give consideration to a variety of issues. For many companies the most attractive option proves to be greater market penetration, since this is concerned with existing products and markets, and typically therefore involves less cost and risk than would be incurred by moving outside existing areas of knowledge. Equally, it generally pays an organization to search for growth within existing and related markets rather than moving into new markets, since by doing this it is more readily able to build upon its reputation. If, however, the company decides to move into new and possibly unrelated areas, there is then a need not only to establish itself against a new set of competitors, but also to build new distribution networks and come to terms with a different technology. This should not in itself be seen as an argument against moving into new markets with new products, but rather an argument for the planner to develop objectives and strategies against the background of a firm understanding of the organization's strengths, weaknesses and overall corporate capability, all of which should emerge clearly from the marketing audit.

The levels of risk associated with each of the strategic alternatives identified in the Ansoff matrix can perhaps be better understood by considering an extension to the basic model. While undoubtedly useful as a framework, Ansoff's four-cell matrix is not able to reflect different *degrees* of technological or market newness, or indeed of the risk associated with the four alternatives. By returning for a moment to Figure 8.7, it should be apparent that, all other things being equal, the lowest level of risk is associated with the market penetration strategy of cell 1. This then increases through cells 2 and 3, peaking in cell 4 with a strategy of diversification.

8.7 THE DEVELOPMENT OF STRATEGIES

In the light of what has been discussed so far, it should be apparent that a marketing objective is what the organization wants to achieve in terms of sales volume, market share, and so on (i.e. the ends). How the organization then sets out to achieve these objectives is the *strategy* (i.e. the means). An effective strategy statement should therefore make reference not just to the allocation of resources but also to timescales; inevitably it is broad in scope. Following on from this, the planner then moves to develop the *tactics* and *programme for implementation*. From the viewpoint of the marketing planner, the major aspects of strategy are the individual elements of the marketing mix. Before moving on, however, it is worth focusing on one of the other major influences upon strategic success. Although decisions are typically taken against a background of resource constraint, their effects can often be minimized by the strategist giving full recognition to the importance of the *leverage* that can be gained by the development of one or more *distinctive competences* to gain a comparative marketing advantage. Although the importance of distinctive competences has long been recognized, their strategic significance was highlighted by the results of a study carried out by the American management consultants, McKinsey & Co. Prominent among their findings was that:

> the distinguishing characteristic shared by (successful companies) was that they did one particular thing well. They had developed significant strength in one feature of their business which gave them a comparative advantage over their competitors.

It follows from this that, in developing strategies, the planner needs to identify these distinctive competences and build on them. As an example of how this can be done, the Dominos Pizza chain in the USA developed as its USP (unique selling proposition) rapid delivery times with a refund to the customer if delivery of the pizza took longer than it should.

The changing focus of strategic and marketing planning

Although portfolio analysis has been subjected to a number of criticisms, its contribution to strategic planning has undoubtedly been significant. However, at the beginning of the 1990s, a number of writers, including Mintzberg (1994) and Stacey (1991), began questioning the traditional and well-established lines of thinking about strategic planning. With its origins in the late 1960s and early 1970s, strategic planning had been held up by many as the most logical and effective way of devising and implementing the strategies that would improve the competitiveness of a business unit. However, Mintzberg argues that the creation in many large organizations of specialist departments staffed by strategic planners who were involved in the thinking but not the doing or the implementation has created a series of difficulties and tensions. The net effect of this, he suggests, is that 'strategic planning has long since fallen from its pedestal' (1994, p. 107). He goes on to say that:

> But even now, few people really understand the reason: strategic planning is not strategic thinking. Indeed, strategic planning often spoils strategic thinking, causing managers to confuse real vision with the manipulation of numbers. And this confusion lies at the heart of the issue: the most successful strategies are visions, not plans.

In making this comment, Mintzberg highlights the way in which the traditional approach to strategic planning is, in essence, *strategic programming*, an activity that involves articulating strategies or visions that already exist. What is needed, he believes, is that managers should understand the differences between planning and strategic thinking so that they can then focus upon what the strategy development process should really be. This process, he suggests, involves capturing what the manager learns from all sources (the soft insights from his or her personal experiences, the experiences of others throughout the organization, and the hard data from market research and the like) and then synthesizing that learning into a vision of the direction that the business should pursue.

Recognition of this means that the role of the planner changes significantly and, for Mintzberg, highlights the way in which the planner's contribution should be *around* rather than *inside* the strategy-making process. In other words, the planner should provide the analyses and data inputs that strategic thinkers need and not the one supposedly correct answer to the strategic challenge being faced.

This redefinition of roles illustrates, in turn, the distinction that needs to be made between the analytical dimension of planning and the synthesis, intuition and creativity that characterize effective strategic thinking. It also goes some way towards highlighting the way in which the formal and traditional approach to planning (Mintzberg, 1994, p. 109):

> *rests on the preservation and rearrangement of established categories, the existing levels or strategy [corporate, business, functional], the established types of products (defined as 'strategic business units'), and overlaid on the current units of structure [divisions, departments, etc.].*
>
> *But real strategic change requires not merely rearranging the established categories, but inventing new ones. Search all those strategic planning diagrams, all those interconnected boxes that supposedly give you strategies, and nowhere will you find a single one that explains the creative act of synthesizing experiences into a novel strategy. Strategy making needs to function beyond the boxes, to encourage the informal learning that produces new perspectives and new combinations. As the saying goes, life is larger than our categories. Planning's failure to transcend the categories explains why it has discouraged serious organizational change. This failure is why formal planning has promoted strategies that are extrapolated from the past or copied from others. Strategic planning has not only amounted to strategic thinking but has often impeded it. Once managers understand this they can avoid other costly misadventures caused by applying formal technique, without judgement and intuition, to problem-solving.*

These criticisms of the traditional logical and sequential approach to planning have, in turn, been developed by Stacey (1992), who in his book *Managing Chaos*, argues for a managerial emphasis upon adaptability, intuition, paradox and entrepreneurial creativity in order to cope with an unpredictable and, indeed, inherently unknowable future.

In many ways, Stacey's ideas are a reflection of chaos and complexity theories ('chaos' in these terms refers not to muddle and confusion, but to the behaviour of a system that is governed by simple physical laws but is so unpredictable as to appear random) in which the complexity of interaction between events is so great that the links between cause and effect either disappear or are so difficult to identify as to be meaningless. The implication of this for strategic planning is potentially far-reaching and, according to Stacey, highlights the importance of intuition and the need for managers to deal with problems in a truly holistic fashion. He goes on to suggest that managers 'must learn to reason through induction rather than deduction; and to argue by analogy, to think in metaphor and to accept paradox' (Stacey, 1994, p. 64).

Like Mintzberg, Stacey (1994, p. 65) argues for a greater creativity within organizations and refers to the scientific concept of the 'edge of chaos' as a metaphor for more independence of managerial thought:

> *Tucked away between stability and instability, at the frontier, non-linear feedback systems generate forms of behaviour that are neither stable nor unstable. They are continuously new and creative. This property applies to non-linear feedback systems no matter where they are found. All human organizations, including businesses, are precisely such non-linear feedback systems; and while it is not necessary or indeed desirable for all organizations to be chaotically creative all the time those that do should not think in terms of stability and adapting to their environment but in terms of using amplifying feedback loops or self-reinforcing mechanisms to shape customer needs.*

With regard to the detail of planning and strategy, Stacey's views rest upon the idea that, because of the nature and complexity of the business system, anything useful about the future is essentially unknowable, something which negates the value of the conventional planning wisdom that success depends upon developing a vision of where the company wants to be in five, ten or twenty years' time, the strategy that will achieve this, and a shared culture. Instead, he believes that:

> *managers should recognize that these strategic planning meetings every Monday morning serve a ritual rather than a functional purpose rather like the ceremonial laying of the foundation stone on a building. They should recognize too that those elaborate computer-modelled forecasts presented to the board to convince them of the wisdom of a proposed business venture are a fiction, and that their purpose is to allay anxiety rather than perform any genuinely predictive purpose. Real strategy is not derived from this sort of planning. No, real strategy emerges from group dynamics, from the politicking and informal lobbying in the corridors, from the complicated patterns of relationships and interplay of personalities, from the pressure groups that spring up after the formal meeting is*

over and real success lies not in total stability and 'sticking to your knitting', but in the tension between stability (in the day-to-day running of the business) and instability (in challenging the status quo). Instability is not just due to ignorance or incompetence, it is a fundamental property of successful business terms.

Given this, he suggests that creative organizations deliberately set out to encourage counter-cultures and subversion. Among the examples that he cites of organizations that have done this with a high degree of success is Honda, which, during the past decade, has hired large numbers of managers in mid-career from other organizations as a means of introducing a series of pressures, challenges and contention into the organization. The effect of this has been to encourage a culture of creative destruction, greater learning and an increase in flexibility (see also Stacey, 1991).

8.8 SUMMARY

In this chapter we have focused on four main areas:

1. The nature and purpose of planning

2. The significance of vision, and the corporate mission and vision

3. The nature and purpose of corporate and marketing objectives

4. How the thinking about the development of the marketing strategy might begin.

The starting point in the planning process involves the strategist in identifying where the organization is currently (where are we now?), and the short- and long-term direction for the organization (where do we want to be?). In addressing this second question, a variety of issues need to be considered, including:

■ Environmental opportunities and threats (see Chapter 3)

■ The organization's strategic capability (again, see Chapter 3)

■ Stakeholders' expectations.

Having done this, it then becomes possible to give far more explicit and realistic consideration to the question of how the organization should go about achieving its objectives.

As a background to the planning process there needs to be agreement on the corporate mission, the mission being an aspirational statement of what the organization is or should attempt to become. The significance of the mission statement has been highlighted by a wide variety of writers, most of whom have given emphasis to its integrating role and to the way in which it provides a strong binding statement of fundamental corporate values – so long as it avoids platitudinous statements.

In developing a mission statement, the strategist needs to take account of a variety of factors, including:

- The organization's history, performance and patterns of ownership
- Managerial values and expectations
- The environment
- Resource availability
- The existence of any distinctive competences.

Having developed a mission statement and then the vision, the planner is in a far stronger position to begin the process of establishing corporate and marketing objectives. Objectives are typically influenced by several issues, including:

- The nature of the business (products, markets and technology)
- External factors (societal values, pressure groups, government and legislation)
- Organizational culture
- Individuals and groups within the organization.

Having identified the organization's corporate and marketing objectives, the marketing planner needs to ensure that they satisfy certain criteria, the four most significant of which are that they are arranged hierarchically, that they are expressed quantitatively, that they are realistic and that there is internal consistency. It is at this stage also that the planner is in a position to identify the nature and size of any gaps that are likely to emerge between where the organization wants to go and where in practice it is capable of going. Once this has been done, it then becomes possible to begin the process of developing the strategies that are to be used to achieve the agreed objectives.

CHAPTER 9

Market Segmentation, Targeting and Positioning

9.1 LEARNING OBJECTIVES

When you have read this chapter you should be able to understand:

(a) the nature and purpose of market segmentation;

(b) the contribution of segmentation to effective marketing planning;

(c) how markets can be segmented, and the criteria that need to be applied if segmentation is to prove cost-effective;

(d) how product positioning follows from the segmentation process;

(e) the bases by which products and brands can be positioned effectively.

9.2 INTRODUCTION

In Chapters 5–7 we focused on approaches to environmental, customer and competitor analysis, and the frameworks within which strategic marketing planning can best take place. Against this background we now turn to the question of market segmentation, and to the ways in which companies need to position themselves in order to maximize their competitive advantage and serve their target markets in the most effective manner. It does need to be recognized, however, that for many organizations the strategic issues of market segmentation, market targeting and positioning often take on only a minimal role. A variety of authors (see, for example, Saunders, 1987; Solomon *et al.*, 2006) have all pointed to the way in which approaches to segmentation are often poorly thought out and then poorly implemented.

There are several possible reasons for views such as these, although, in the case of companies with a broadly reactive culture, it is often due largely to a degree of organizational inertia, which leads to the firm being content to stay in the same sector of the market for some considerable time. It is only when the effects of a changing environment become overwhelmingly evident that serious consideration is given to the need for repositioning in order to appeal to new sectors of the market. For other organizations, however, a well-thought-out policy of segmentation plays a pivotal role in the determination of success. It is the recognition of this that has led to the suggestion in recent years that the essence of strategic marketing can be summed up by the initials STP – segmentation, targeting and positioning. This is illustrated in Figure 9.1.

Not all writers are in favour of segmentation so before we examine the methods used to segment markets, it is worth looking briefly at their views. Bliss (1980), for example, has suggested that, while many marketing managers acknowledge the rationale of segmentation, many are dissatisfied with it as a concept, partly because it is inapplicable or difficult to apply in many markets, but also because emphasis is too often given to the techniques of segmentation at the expense of the market itself and the competitive situation that exists. Equally, Resnik *et al.* (1979) have suggested that changing values, new lifestyles, and the rising costs of products and services argue the case for what they call 'counter-segmentation'; in other words, an aggregation of various parts of the market rather than their subdivision. The majority of writers, however, acknowledge the very real strategic importance of segmentation and, in particular, the ways in which it enables the organization to use its resources more effectively and with less wastage.

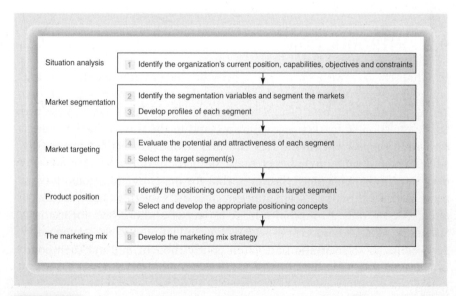

FIGURE 9.1   *The eight stages of the segmentation, targeting and position process*

9.3   THE NATURE AND PURPOSE OF SEGMENTATION

During the past 30 years, market segmentation has developed and been defined in a variety of ways. In essence, however, it is the process of dividing a varied and differing group of buyers or potential buyers into smaller groups, within which broadly similar patterns of buyers' needs exist. By doing this, the marketing planner is attempting to break the market into more strategically manageable parts, which can then be targeted and satisfied far more precisely by making a series of perhaps small changes to the marketing mix. The rationale is straightforward and can be expressed most readily in terms of the fact that only rarely does a single product or marketing approach appeal to the needs and wants of all buyers. Because of this, the marketing strategist needs to categorize buyers on the basis both of their characteristics and their specific product needs, with a view then to adapting either the product or the marketing programme, or both, to satisfy these different tastes and demands.

The potential benefits of a well-developed segmentation strategy can therefore be considerable, since an organization should be able to establish and strengthen its position in the market and, in this way, operate more effectively. Not only does it then become far more difficult for a competitor to attack, but it also allows the organization to build a greater degree of market sector knowledge and customer loyalty.

Although the arguments for segmentation appear strong, it is only one of three quite distinct approaches to marketing strategy which exist. These are:

1. Undifferentiated or mass marketing

2. Product-variety or differentiated marketing

3. Target or concentrated marketing.

These are illustrated in Figure 9.2.

Undifferentiated, differentiated and concentrated (or atomized) marketing

A policy of *undifferentiated* or *mass marketing* emerges when the firm deliberately ignores any differences that exist within its markets and decides instead to focus upon a feature that appears to be common or acceptable to a wide variety of buyers. Perhaps the earliest, best-known and most frequently quoted example of this is Henry Ford's strategy with the Model T, which buyers could have 'in any colour as long as it's black'. A more recent example of undifferentiated marketing is provided by Black & Decker, which in the late 1970s was faced with a drop in its worldwide market share of the power tool market from 20 to 15 per cent as Japanese firms began marketing their brands in a far more aggressive manner. In

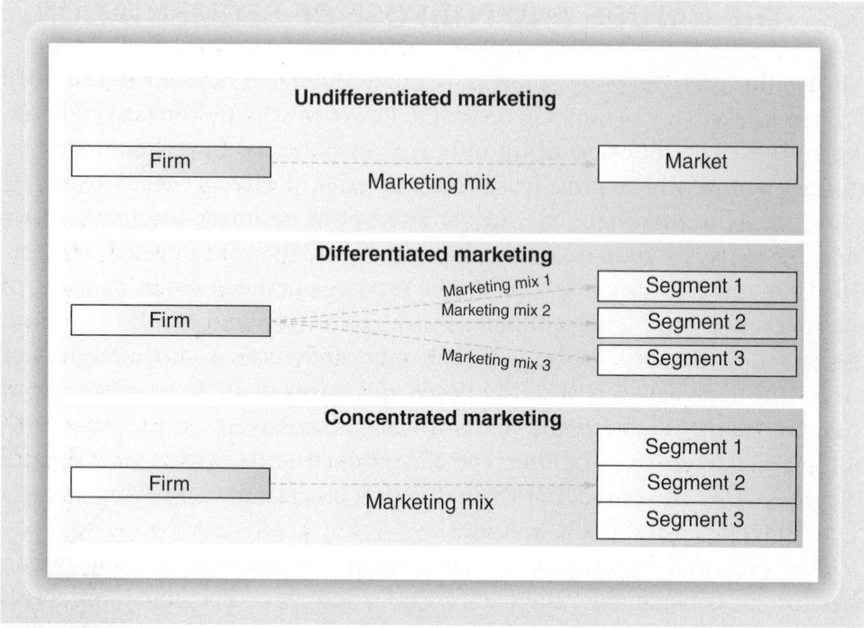

FIGURE 9.2 *Undifferentiated, differentiated and concentrated marketing*

an attempt to counter this, Black & Decker moved away from a policy of customizing products for each market and concentrated instead on making a smaller number of products that could be sold everywhere with the same basic marketing approach. The success of this undifferentiated global marketing strategy was subsequently reflected in the fact that, by the mid-1980s, Black & Decker had more than regained its 20 per cent share of the market. Subsequently, it has strengthened its position yet further.

The obvious advantage of an undifferentiated strategy such as this is that it offers scope for enormous cost economies in production, promotion and distribution, since the organization is dealing with a standardized product. At the same time it needs to be recognized that undifferentiated marketing is becoming increasingly rare, largely because of ever greater degrees of competition and the increasingly sophisticated and fragmented nature of the majority of developed markets. In these circumstances, the scope that exists for marketing a product aimed at a broad sector of the market is reduced significantly.

This de-massification of markets has led many organizations towards strategies of *product-variety marketing* and, ultimately, target marketing. As an example of this, Coca-Cola for many years produced only one type of drink for the entire market in the expectation that it would have a mass-market appeal. The success of the strategy is now part of marketing folklore. The company's strategy was changed, however, partly to cope with an increasingly aggressive competitive environment (think, for example, about the entry of Red Bull to the soft drinks market and its creation of the energy drinks sector, and the highly successful repositioning of Lucozade) and partly to develop and capitalize on different patterns of consumer demand. As a result, the company's marketing effort today now reflects buyers' needs for a far wider variety of tastes and demands, which are packaged in a number of different sizes and types of container. It should be emphasized that the move on the part of many organizations in recent years towards product-differentiated or product-variety marketing has often had as its primary purpose the need to offer existing buyers greater variety, rather than to appeal to new and different market segments. In many ways, therefore, product-variety marketing can be seen as an interim step in the move towards *target marketing*, in which the strategist identifies the major market segments, targets one or more of these segments, and then develops marketing programmes tailored to the specific demands of each segment.

For some organizations target marketing leads to a concentration of effort on a single target market with a single marketing mix. Referred to as *concentrated segmentation*, it is a strategy that has been pursued with great success by the piano makers Steinway. The company defines its market as the concert and professional pianist and, while others may buy the product, they are not part of the strategic target market. The obvious advantage of an approach such as this is that, having identified a particular market, the firm can then control costs by advertising and distributing *only* to the market segment it views as its primary target.

In so far as disadvantages exist with a strategy of concentration, they stem from the possibility of missed opportunities; it may be the case, for example, that significant opportunities exist elsewhere but that the firm's single-minded approach to just one part of the market fails to recognize this. Equally, the organization can prove vulnerable either to a direct and sustained attack by a competitor or to a downturn in demand within the target market. Because of this, many marketing strategists pursue a policy of *multiple segmentation*, in which the firm focuses upon a variety of different segments and then develops a different marketing mix for each. This is often described as a 'rifle' rather than a 'shotgun' approach, in that the company can focus on buyers they have the greatest chance of satisfying rather than scattering the marketing effort. An example of its use is that of Arcadia which pursues a highly segmented strategy with a series of retail concepts such as TOPSHOP, TOPMAN, Burton, Dorothy Perkins, Evans, Miss Selfridge, and Wallis. In doing this, specific attention is paid to a variety of distinct customer groups by means of different types of retail outlet, each with its own distinct target market, image and customer appeal.

The rationale for target marketing and multiple segmentation can be seen to be straightforward, and stems from an expectation on the part of the organization that it will be able to generate a higher total level of sales by making specific appeals to a variety of different target groups. At the same time, however, a strategy of multiple segmentation almost invariably leads to cost increases in several areas, including production, promotion, distribution, inventory and administration. The choice between undifferentiated marketing, product-variety marketing and target marketing therefore involves a series of trade-offs, the most obvious of which is an increase in cost against an expectation of higher total returns. As a prelude to deciding which of these three approaches to adopt, the strategist needs to identify clearly the organization's capability, the opportunities that exist and the level of market coverage that is possible or realistic.

Perhaps the most extreme example of a trade-off is to be seen in *customized* or *atomized marketing*, where the product or service is modified to match the specific demands of each buyer, an approach that is often used within the business-to-business sector by organizations with a relatively small number of large customers.

The development of segments over time

Having identified segments within a market, the strategist needs to recognize that this is not a once-and-for-all exercise, but rather one that needs monitoring and updating if it is to maintain its usefulness. This is illustrated by the ways in which attitudes to a given product's country of origin can change, possibly dramatically, over time. Thirty years ago, for example, attitudes in Britain to Japanese products were generally negative, largely because of perceptions of poor quality and inadequate levels of after-sales support. These attitudes changed throughout the 1970s and 1980s and today Japanese products are generally perceived very differently. The implications of this for preference patterns is significant and does, of course, need to be reflected in methods of segmentation. By the same token, Skoda for many years targeted a relatively poor segment of the market, but over the past decade has increasingly moved into a series of very different target markets (here, it might be useful to refer to Illustration 6.2, in which Skoda's changed approach is discussed).

9.4 APPROACHES TO SEGMENTING MARKETS

The majority of markets can be segmented in a variety of ways. For the marketing strategist, the process of identifying the potentially most effective way begins with an initial examination of the market, with a view to identifying whether 'natural segments' already exist.

In the USA in the 1960s, for example, both Volkswagen and Toyota identified the growth potential of a market sector that was concerned with car size and fuel economy, a segment that the three major domestic manufacturers had either failed to identify or had chosen to ignore. Following the

Arab–Israeli conflict of the early 1970s and the subsequent oil crisis, consumers became far more energy conscious and this part of the market grew dramatically. It was several years before domestic manufacturers were able to capitalize on these opportunities. Equally, Honda in the 1960s and 1970s identified and then targeted a young(er) and essentially middle-class market for small and medium-sized motorcycles in the USA that the other players within the market, such as Harley Davidson, had traditionally ignored. The advertising campaign featured college students riding the smaller Honda bikes and used the strapline 'You meet the nicest people on a Honda'. More recently, Mercedes, Porsche and BMW have all targeted the ageing baby boomer generation whose children have left home, have insurance policies maturing, are downsizing and rethinking their priorities, and who are not only searching for their lost youth, but more importantly have the money to indulge themselves.

There are several lessons to be learned from these sorts of examples, including the ways in which new segments can be identified by examining the sequence of variables that consumers consider when choosing a product. One way of doing this involves categorizing current consumer segments on the basis of a hierarchy of attributes. There are those, for example, whose major preoccupation is price (price-dominant), while others are more concerned with the brand (brand-dominant), quality (quality-dominant) or country of origin (nation-dominant).

In the case of hi-fi and audio equipment, for example, a buyer might only be willing to consider products from a Japanese manufacturer – this would be the first-level preference. The second-level preference may then be for, say, Sony followed by Panasonic. After this, issues of the price range and choice of outlet begin to emerge.

Recognition of hierarchies of attitudes such as these has led to the emergence of *market-partitioning theory*, with segments being determined on the basis of particular combinations such as quality/service/brand, price/type/brand, and so on. Underlying this is the belief that each combination will then reflect distinct demographic and psychographic differences.

The question of *how* to segment the market provides the basis for much of the remainder of this chapter. In essence, however, this involves deciding between *a priori* and *post hoc* methods. An a priori approach is based on the notion that the planner decides in advance of any research the basis for segmentation he or she intends to use. Thus, typically the planner will categorize buyers on the basis of their usage patterns (heavy, medium, light and non-users), demographic characteristics (age, sex and income) or psychographic profiles (lifestyle and personality). Having decided this, the planner then goes on to conduct a programme of research in order to identify the size, location and potential of each segment as a prelude to deciding on which of the segments the marketing effort is to be concentrated.

Post hoc segmentation, by contrast, involves segmenting the market on the basis of research findings. Thus, research might highlight particular attitudes, attributes or benefits with which particular groups of customers are concerned. This information can then be used as the basis for deciding how best to divide the market. One of the best-known – if oldest – examples of this is Haley's research into the toothpaste market in the early 1960s, which highlighted levels of concern among mothers about tooth decay in their children (Haley, 1963). Although a number of brands claiming decay prevention existed at the time, the size and potential for the growth of this segment had not previously been recognized. One result of Haley's work was to increase the number of companies that recognized the value of targeting this segment.

In making these comments, it must be emphasized that both a priori and post hoc approaches to segmentation have their place, and that their real value to the strategist depends largely on how much knowledge of the market the strategist has. If, for example, previous research or experience has enabled the planner to identify key segmentation dimensions within the market, then an a priori approach is likely to be adequate. When, however, the market is new, changing or unrelated to the planner's experience, a post hoc approach to determine the key segmentation variables is likely to prove more valuable.

9.5 FACTORS AFFECTING THE FEASIBILITY OF SEGMENTATION

Market segmentation works at two levels, the strategic and the tactical. At a strategic level it has a direct link to decisions on positioning. At a tactical level it relates to the question of which customer groups are to be targeted. However, for a market segment to justify attention, six conditions typically need to be satisfied. The segment must be:

1. *Measurable*. Although in many consumer markets measurement is generally a relatively straightforward exercise, it is often a more difficult process with industrial or technical goods. This is due largely to the relative lack of specific published data.

2. *Accessible*. In some cases it may be possible to identify a sizeable and potentially profitable segment but then, either because of a lack of finance or in-house expertise, this potential may be difficult to exploit.

3. *Substantial*. If the strategist is to justify the development of a segment, the exercise must be cost-effective. The size and value of the segment is therefore an important determinant of this decision. Size should, of course, be seen in relative rather than absolute terms, since what may be too small to be considered by one organization may be appropriate to another, smaller, company. Morgan, for

example, has concentrated on a very small and specialized part of the car market that is of no interest to the larger firms such as Ford, Toyota and Volkswagen.

4. *Unique* in its response, so that it can be distinguished from other market segments.

5. *Appropriate* to the organization's objectives and resources.

6. *Stable*, so that its behaviour in the future can be predicted with a sufficient degree of confidence.

Against the background of these six conditions, it should be possible to evaluate segments on the basis of two criteria: the attractiveness of the segment and the organization's ability to exploit the value of the segment.

9.6   APPROACHES TO SEGMENTATION

Although a wide variety of methods of segmentation have been developed over the past 40 years, their real value to the strategist in any given situation depends to a very large extent on the nature and characteristics of the product, and the market in which the company is operating. The task with which the strategist is faced involves deciding upon the most appropriate single method or combination of methods for dividing up the market. In the case of consumer goods, for example, the most commonly used methods have typically been geographic, demographic and benefit measures, while in the industrial sector they have typically been usage rate, source loyalty and location. Most of these measures, however, are at best partial, and the past few years have witnessed a growing willingness on the part of many companies, particularly in the consumer sector, to make greater use of more complex methods of segmentation in order to build up more detailed and useful pictures of their target markets. One result of this has been an upsurge of the interest expressed in behavioural and psychographic techniques as a means of gaining a greater insight into the question of *why* people behave in particular ways.

The thread that runs through all of these approaches is the need to understand in detail the structure of the market. This is most typically done by focusing on three areas:

1. Developing a spatial map of consumers' perceptions of brands within a given market sector

2. Identifying consumers' ideal points on this map so that demand for a particular product might then be estimated by examining its position in relation to the ideal

3. Developing a model that will then provide a basis for predicting consumers' responses to new and modified products.

This sort of picture of the market can then be taken a step further by superimposing a second map illustrating in greater detail consumer profiles. This might typically include sex (male versus female), age (young, middle-aged, old), income group (high earners versus low earners) and marital status.

9.7 THE BASES FOR SEGMENTATION

More than 30 years ago, Wind (1978, p. 317) commented that 'over the years almost all variables have been used as bases for market segmentation'. There are several possible explanations for this, the most significant of which is the difficulty that is typically encountered in putting into practice the normative theory of segmentation. In other words, while the marketing planner might well recognize that customer characteristics should determine strategy, all too often this is reversed, with managers focusing on the probable response of different segments to a previously determined strategy. Whilst, in the majority of circumstances, feedback will ensure that changes are subsequently made to the strategy to take account of the response received, it is often the case, that the approach taken is more similar to a strategy of product different than the normative approach which is typically advocated by writers in the area.

Although, as we observed earlier, a wide variety of variables have been used to segment markets, the majority of these can be grouped into four categories.

1. Geographic and geodemographic
2. Demographic
3. Behavioural
4. Psychographic.

Only rarely, however, can just one of these dimensions be used to segment a market effectively, something that is reflected both in Illustration 9.1 and in a comment by Wind (1978, p. 318):

In contrast to the theory of segmentation that implies that there is a single best way of segmenting a market, the range and variety of marketing decisions suggest that any attempt to use a single basis for segmentation (such as psychographic, brand reference, or product usage) for all marketing decisions may result in incorrect marketing decisions as well as a waste of resources.

Illustration 9.1   Recommendations for the bases of segmentation
Some of the most interesting work on market segmentation has been carried out in the USA by Yoram Wind (1978). One of the undoubted attractions of his work is its strong element of pragmatism and the recognition that he gives to the problems

typically experienced by marketing managers in trying to develop and implement an effective segmentation strategy. This has led him to a series of recommendations for the bases of segmentation, which Baker (1985, pp. 142–3) has neatly summarized:

For general understanding of a market

- Benefits sought (in industrial markets, the criterion used is purchase decision)
- Product purchase and usage patterns
- Needs
- Brand loyalty and switching pattern
- A hybrid of the variables above.

For positioning studies

- Product usage
- Product preference
- Benefits sought
- A hybrid of the variables above.

For new product concepts (and new product introduction)

- Reaction to new concepts (intention to buy and preference over current brand)
- Benefits sought.

For pricing decisions

- Price sensitivity
- Deal proneness
- Price sensitivity by purchase/usage patterns.

For advertising decisions

- Benefits sought
- Media usage
- Psychographic/lifestyle
- A hybrid of the variables above and/or purchase/usage patterns.

For distribution decisions

- Store loyalty and patronage
- Benefits sought in store selection.

9.8 GEOGRAPHIC AND GEODEMOGRAPHIC TECHNIQUES

Geographic approaches

Geographic segmentation – one of the earliest and still most commonly used methods of segmentation, within both the consumer and the industrial sectors – involves dividing markets into different geographical units such as countries, regions, counties and cities. The strategist then chooses to operate either in just a few or in all of these. Typically, however, if a company pursues this second approach, minor modifications are often made to the marketing mix used for different geographical areas in order to take account of different regional tastes and preferences. In the case of the car industry, for example, the majority of manufacturers, while selling a particular model throughout Europe, will typically make a series of minor changes to the design and to the way in which the product is promoted and sold in order to reflect local differences, preferences and legislative demands. Similarly, food manufacturers modify the taste of the product to cater for regional taste differences. Across Europe, for example, companies such as Nestlé vary the strength and flavour of coffee to reflect regional preferences for stronger or weaker coffees. With other products, such as consumer electronics, geographical differences also need to be reflected in strategy. Makers of stereo equipment, for example, offer products that vary by region. Europeans tend to want small, unobtrusive, high-performance equipment, while many Americans prefer large speakers that, as one anonymous commentator said, 'rise from the floor of living rooms like the columns of an ancient temple'.

Among the undoubted attractions of geographic segmentation to the strategist is its flexibility and its apparent simplicity. It is the combination of these, together with its broad applicability, that has led to its widespread use. At the same time, however, it is a relatively unsophisticated approach to categorization and one that at best gives only a partial view of buying motives.

Geodemographic and lifestyle approaches

Largely because of the limitations of geography, a considerable amount of work has been done in Britain over the past few years in an attempt to improve on the traditional methods of geographic segmentation. One outcome of this has been the development of a variety of geodemographic systems such as ACORN (A Classification Of Residential Neighbourhoods), which classify people by where they live. Based on the idea that 'birds of a feather flock together', it gives recognition to the fact that people with broadly similar economic, social and lifestyle characteristics tend to congregate in particular neighbourhoods and exhibit similar patterns of purchasing behaviour and outlook.

The essential purpose of geodemographics is therefore to provide the base for targeting customers in particular areas who exhibit similar behaviour patterns.

The first attempt to formalize this and demonstrate its potential to the strategist was carried out in Liverpool in 1973 by Richard Webber. Working subsequently with the Census Office at a national level, Webber applied techniques of cluster analysis to identify 38 separate neighbourhood types, each of which was different in terms of its population, housing and socio-economic characteristics. The potential value of this to the market research industry was subsequently recognized by Kenneth Baker (1982) of the British Market Research Bureau, who identified the scope that the system offered for controlling the fieldwork of the bureau's Target Group Index (TGI). The respondents in the TGI survey were categorized on the basis of Webber's neighbourhood groups, and illustrated graphically 'that respondents in different neighbourhood groups displayed significantly different propensities to buy specific products and services'.

Following this, Webber subsequently joined Consolidated Analysis Centres Inc. (CACI) and concentrated on developing the technique further in order to achieve higher levels of discrimination. The result was a classification of households that included agricultural areas, modern family housing owned by people with high incomes, older housing of intermediate status multiracial areas, high status non-family areas, and so on, that is used as a major method of market location. Specific applications of the technique include:

1. The identification of new retail sites

2. The selection of sales territories

3. The allocation of marketing resources

4. Media selection

5. Leaflet distribution

6. Decisions on which products and services to promote in particular retail outlets.

Using this profile, specific areas of high and low consumption can be identified from the ACORN 'buying power' indices, with consumers being classified under one of six headings: wealthy achievers, urban prosperity, comfortably off, moderate means, or hard pressed. The six categories are then further sub-divided. As an example of this, group Ø9 (part of the wealthy achievers) consists of older families living in the prosperous suburbs. By contrast, group 47 is made up of low income families living in terraced estates. Using information such as this, market targeting becomes both easier and far more accurate.

This work on the ACORN system of classification has led subsequently to a major reassessment of the ways in which geographic techniques might be used in the most effective way. One result of this has been the development of a variety of other geodemographic forms of classification, the common element of which is their use of census enumeration district (ED) data. ACORN, for example, uses regularly updated census variables that take account of the demographic, housing and social aspects of EDs. Their clustering techniques then enable customers to be matched to an ACORN type and, by the postcode, to the relevant ED.

Other geodemographic systems are broadly similar to this, although each uses a variety of other variables. MOSAIC, for example, includes financial data at postcode level and then relies on aggregated individual addresses within a postcode to reduce the errors encountered in matching postcodes to EDs. Other systems, base their clustering techniques on a larger sample and improvements to the grid referencing of EDs so that they more accurately match postcodes. Such developments represent a very real attempt to overcome some of the inevitable problems and inaccuracies of geodemographic analysis.

9.9   DEMOGRAPHIC SEGMENTATION

The second major method of segmentation, and probably the one most frequently used, rests on the assumption that markets can be subdivided into groups on the basis of one or more demographic variables such as age, sex, income, education, occupation, religion, race, nationality, family size and stage reached in the family life cycle. Here, we will concentrate on just three of these variables: age and the family life cycle; income and occupation; and sex.

An undoubted attraction of demographic segmentation is the wide availability and easy interpretation of the data, and it is this – together with the fact that not only can most consumer markets generally be divided relatively easily along these lines, but also that purchase behaviour often correlates highly with demographic segmentation – that have combined to make it such a convenient, easily understood and frequently used approach. In recent years, considerable attention has been paid to the ways in which specific demographic variables can be used more effectively, with the result that variables such as age and life cycle, income, and sex have all been greatly refined. As an example of this, firms such as Lego, Toys 'R' Us and the Early Learning Centre give full recognition to the differences that exist between children of various ages, with the result that toys are now designed to fall into highly specific age categories. In this way, not only is the development potential of the child maximized, but the task of choosing toys by parents, friends and relatives is made infinitely easier. A similar, if perhaps rather more esoteric, recognition of the importance of age and life cycle is reflected in the marketing strategies of various petfood manufacturers who, over the past few years, have developed different dog foods for puppies, adult dogs, older dogs, overweight dogs and dogs with 'sensitive stomachs'. More frequently, however, the significance of life cycle is reflected in the notion of a *family life cycle* (FLC).

The family life cycle

The idea of a FLC, which is illustrated in Figure 9.3, can be traced back to Rowntree's work in the early part of the twentieth century, and while

Stages in the family life cycle	Buying patterns
1 Bachelor stage: young, single people living at home	Few financial commitments. Recreation and fashion orientated Buy: cars, entertainment items, holidays
2 Newly married couples: young, no children	Better off financially than they are likely to be in the near future; high purchase rate of consumer desirables Buy: cars, white goods, furniture
3 Full nest 1: youngest child under six	House buying is at a peak; liquid assets are low Dissatisfied with level of savings and financial position generally Buy: medicines, toys, baby food, white goods
4 Full nest 2: youngest child six or over	Financial position is improving; a higher proportion of wives are working Buy: wider variety of foods, bicycles, pianos
5 Full nest 3: older married couples with dependent children	Financial position is improving yet further; a greater proportion of wives work and some children get jobs. Increasing purchase of desirables Buy: better furniture, unnecessary appliances and more luxury goods
6 Empty nest 1: older married couples, no children at home, head of household still in the workforce	Home ownership is at a peak; the financial situation has improved and savings have increased. Interested in travel, recreation and self-education. Not interested in new products Buy: holidays, luxuries and home improvements
7 Empty nest 2: older married, no children living at home, head of household retired	Substantial reduction in income Buy: medical products and appliances that aid health, sleep and digestion
8 Solitary survivor in the workforce	Income still high but may sell home
9 Solitary survivor, retired	Same medical and product needs as group 7 Substantial cut in income. Need for attention and security

FIGURE 9.3 *The family life cycle and its implications for buying behaviour (adapted from Wells and Gubar, 1966)*

changes have occurred since then to the pattern through which the family passes, the concept is still the same. Today, the nine-stage FLC that was developed by Wells and Gubar (1966) starting with a bachelor stage and culminating with the retired solitary survivor, is still the one to which reference is made most frequently. The potential strategic value of the FLC stems from the way in which it highlights the different and changing financial situation and priorities of the family as it moves through the nine stages. By recognizing and taking account of these differences, the strategist should be more easily able to develop a marketing programme that satisfies the *specific* rather than the general demands of target groups.

However, although the FLC has an apparent logic, the reality is often far more complex with personal relationships and family structures being far more fluid and very different from, say, 20 years ago. In part, this has been driven by rising divorce rates, the later age of marriage (and, indeed, a decline in the number of marriages), and the growth in the number of single-parent households, all of which have made the early ideas of a series of neat FLC stages far less meaningful.

Because of criticisms such as these, fundamental questions have been raised about the model's validity and usefulness. However, defenders of the model have argued that it is simply a summary demographic variable that combines the effects of age, marital status, career status (income), and the presence or absence of children. This can then be used *together* with other variables to reflect reality.

The psychological life cycle

As an extension both to the traditional thinking about the FLC and as a recognition of a number of fundamental – and increasingly evident – weaknesses of the FLC model, work recently has focused upon the idea of a *psychological life cycle*, in which chronological age by itself is not necessarily the factor of greatest significance in determining consumption patterns. Rather it is the transformation of attitudes and expectations that becomes a more important factor, something which is reflected in Neugarten's (1968) research in the USA:

> *Age has become a poor predictor of the timing of life events, as well as a poor predictor of a person's health, work status, family status, and therefore, also of a person's interests, preoccupations, and needs. We have multiple images of persons of the same age: there is the 70-year-old in a wheelchair and the 70-year-old on the tennis court. Likewise, there are 35-year-olds sending children off to college and 35-year-olds furnishing the nursery for newborns, producing in turn, first-time grandparenthood for persons who range in age from 35 to 75.*

The significance of the psychological life cycle is also illustrated by the emergence of the 'kidults' segment, to which we made brief reference earlier (see the Appendix to Chapter 6), and by the way in which important target markets for Microsoft's X Box and Sony's Playstation are young adults as well as teenagers. Equally, Reebok and Adidas brands are owned by as many 25- to 44-year-olds as 15- to 24-year-olds.

Income and occupation

The second major category of demographic variable focuses upon *income* and *occupation*, the combination of which is reflected in the JICNARS approach to social classification.

Developed in the immediate post-war period, the JICNARS classification of A, B, C1, C2, D and E social classes proved for many years to be a popular, enduring and easily understood method of classification. Increasingly, however, it was seen to be an imprecise method of segmenting a market, since social class today is a far less accurate predictor of income and spending patterns than was once the case. It has also been argued that social class gives little *real* insight into a household's level of disposable income, particularly where there are several wage earners. Largely because of this, a considerable amount of work has been done in recent years in an attempt to develop it further and to identify better alternative methods of discrimination. It was this that led in 1999 to the revised JICNARS approach to social classification that appears in Figure 9.4.

The problems of the early thinking on social class as a basis for segmentation have also been highlighted by O'Brien and Ford (1988, pp. 289–332), who commented:

> The trends today are towards a more disparate family group, less inclined to share their meals and leisure time as a household unit, but following their own interests and tastes with like-minded peers. Whether peer groups share the same 'social' background is less important than their shared pursuit. Equally, Social Class does not act as an accurate gauge of disposable income. A C2 or D may not intellectually be performing the same role in the job market as a B or C1, but may well have more cash with which to acquire the trappings of our society. The financial chains of private education are likely to constrain the AB as much as the black economy and overtime can enhance the apparently lower wage of the C2 and D. From a different standpoint, social class categories are difficult to apply consistently. The variety and complexity of people's jobs make many social classifications inherently subjective rather than objective.

NS-SEC

The weaknesses of the JICNARs approach to social classification and, in particular, its inability to reflect the complexity, differences and subtleties of what we referred to earlier as 'the new consumer', led the government at the beginning of the 1990s to fund the search for an alternative approach. Developed by Professor David Rose of the University of Essex, the new system – known as NS-SEC (National Statistics Socio-Economic Classification) – was designed to provide a far stronger base for the classification and tracking of today's consumers, who have many more facets to their lives than was the case when JICNARs was first developed. At the heart of the system is an essentially classless view of the consumer that reflects three profound shifts in society: the growth of the middle class, the emergence of a new petit bourgeoisie, and the very different role within the workforce played by women. Although it is similar to JICNARs in that it is occupation-based, NS-SEC gives far greater emphasis to people's purchasing power in the labour market. In doing this, it is designed to be a far more accurate tool with which to draw distinctions between purchasing habits.

The initial reaction from the market research industry to the new classification, which is shown in Figure 9.4 alongside the JICNARs approach, was somewhat sceptical. Despite this, there was a widespread recognition

NS-SEC		The old JICNARS	and the new
Class 1a	Large employers, higher level managers: company directors, senior police/fire/prison/military officers, newspaper editors, football managers (with squad of 25 plus), restaurateurs	A Professional	Class 1
Class 1b	Professionals: doctors, solicitors, engineers, teachers, airline pilots	B Managerial/technical	Class 2
Class 2	Associate professionals: journalists, nurses/midwives, actors/musicians, military NCO/junior police/fire/prison officers, lower managers (fewer than 25 staff)	C1 Skilled (non-manual)	Class 3
Class 3	Intermediate occupations: secretaries, air stewardesses, driving instructors, footballers (employee sportsmen), telephone operators	C1 Skilled (non-manual)	Class 3
Class 4	Small employers/managers, non-professional self-employed: publicans, plumbers, golfers/tennis players (self-employed sportsmen), farm owners/managers (fewer than 25 employees)	C2 Skilled (manual)	Class 3
Class 5	Lower level supervisors, craft and related workers: electricians, mechanics, train drivers, building site/factory foremen, bus inspectors	D Partly skilled	Class 4
Class 6	Semi-routine occupations: traffic wardens, caretakers, gardeners, supermarket shelf-stackers, assembly-line workers	D Partly skilled	Class 4
Class 7	Routine occupations: cleaners, waiters/waitresses/bar staff, messengers/couriers, road workers, dockers	E Unskilled	Class 5
Class 8	Excluded: long-term unemployed, never worked, long-term sick	Other	Class 6

FIGURE 9.4   *The JICNARS and NS-SEC approaches to social classification*

that JICNARs, which is essentially a definition of wealth rather than attitude, although adequate for broad consumer definitions, fails to reflect the ways in which consumers have become better educated, move jobs more frequently, and have higher levels of disposable income. It is these sorts of changes that have led to the recognition that class, income and gender are no longer accurate predictors of consumer behaviour.

In Rose's system, consumers are divided into 17 narrow classifications by occupation that take account of employment relationships between managers and the managed. These 17 classifications are then grouped into the eight broad categories that appear in Figure 9.4.

The need for an alternative to classification has also been highlighted by the Future Foundation, which has developed a method designed to capture changing values and systems. Based on the ideas of fuzzy logic, the technique – called 'fuzzy clustering' – allows consumers to be recognized and defined in different ways according to the time of day. Recognition of the complexity of modern society has also led the Henley Centre (2000) to a form of fuzzy clustering. In *Planning for Consumer Change*, the Centre reflected the dimensions of the complex consumer in a classification referred to as *polyglotting*. The thinking behind polyglotting is based not so much on consumer identity as upon modes of acting and behaviour at different times.

Sex

The third demographic category is that of sex. While this variable has obvious applications to such products as clothes, cosmetics, magazines and so on, ever greater attention has been paid in recent years to the ways in which it can be used as a key element in the strategies to market a far wider range of products. In part, this has been brought about by a series of fundamental changes that are taking place within society, including a greater number of working women and the generally higher levels of female independence. One result of this has been an increase in the number of marketing campaigns targeted specifically at women: examples include cigarettes, cars and hotels.

9.10   BEHAVIOURAL SEGMENTATION

The third major approach to segmentation is based on a series of behavioural measures, including attitudes, knowledge, benefits sought by the buyer, a willingness to innovate, loyalty status, usage rates, and response to a product. Of these, *benefit segmentation* (in other words, reasons to believe) is probably the best known and most widely used, and is based on the assumption that it is the benefits that people are seeking from a product that provide the most appropriate bases for dividing up a market.

In applying this approach, the marketing planner begins by attempting to measure consumers' value systems and their perceptions of various brands within a given product class. The information generated is then used as the basis for the marketing strategy. One of the earliest and best-known examples of this is the work conducted on the watch market by Yankelovich (1964). His findings that 'approximately 23 per cent of the buyers bought for lowest price, another 46 per cent bought for durability and general product quality, and 31 per cent bought watches as symbols of some important occasion' were subsequently used by the US Time Company, which created its Timex brand to capitalize on the first two of these segments. The majority of other companies at this stage focused either largely or exclusively on the third segment and Timex therefore faced little direct competition in the early years.

Benefit segmentation begins therefore by determining the principal benefits customers are seeking in the product class, the kinds of people who look for each benefit, and the benefits delivered by each brand. Apple, for example, based its initial strategy, at least in part, on appealing to those looking for a more user-friendly system.

One of the first major pieces of benefit research was the work conducted by Russell Haley (1963), to which we made brief reference earlier. On the basis of his work in the toothpaste market, Haley identified four distinct segments, which, he argued, were sufficiently different to provide a platform for selecting advertising copy, media, commercial length, packaging and new product design. The four segments he identified were: seeking economy, decay prevention, cosmetic and taste benefits respectively.

Haley demonstrated that each group exhibited specific demographic, behavioural and psychographic characteristics. Those concerned primarily with decay prevention, for example, typically had large families, were heavy toothpaste users and were generally conservative in their outlook. By contrast, the group that was more concerned with bright teeth (the cosmetic segment) tended to be younger, were more socially active and in many cases were smokers. Each of these groups, he then demonstrated, exhibited preferences for particular brands: Crest in the case of those concerned with decay prevention, and Macleans and Ultra-Brite for those preoccupied with bright teeth.

The information generated by studies such as these can, as we observed earlier, be used in a variety of ways. Most obviously they prove useful in classifying the specific benefits being sought by particular customer groups, the segment's behavioural, demographic and psychographic characteristics, and the major competitive brands. An additional by-product of this sort of research can also be that it highlights a benefit that customers are seeking, but which currently is not being satisfied. As examples of this:

- In the 1990s, Lucozade developed Lucozade Sport to cater for the fast-growing sports market, while Red Bull developed its product as a functional energy drink targeted at 16–34 sports enthusiasts, students, clubbers and people who need a pick-me-up during the day.

- In the car market, Renault developed one of the first people-carriers, the Espace, in the 1980s in response to the increasingly different ways in which people were using their cars and what they wanted from them.

- In the cereals market, Kellogg's developed Special K as a product to help a predominantly female market with what is referred to as weight and shape management. More recently, the company developed cereal bars such as Nutri-Grain to meet the demand from people who skipped more traditional forms of breakfast, and Optovita designed to help a predominantly male market manage cholesterol levels.

- In the glass market, Pilkington developed Pilkington Activ, a glass that has a coating that, through the action of sunlight and rainwater, leads to it being self-cleaning.

In many markets, benefit segmentation results in the company focusing upon satisfying just one benefit group, with the benefit offered being the unique selling proposition (USP). This is, however, just one of four choices that exist:

1. Single benefit positioning

2. Primary and secondary benefit positioning

3. Double benefit positioning

4. Triple benefit positioning.

These will be discussed in greater detail at a later stage in the chapter.

User status

As an alternative to benefit segmentation, markets can be subdivided on the basis of what is referred to as *user status*. Thus, a number of segments can typically be identified, including non-users, ex-users, potential users, first-time users and regular users. These final two categories can then be subdivided further on the basis of *usage rate* (this is sometimes referred to as *volume segmentation*).

For many firms the marketing task is seen in terms of moving buyers and potential buyers along the buying continuum; thus, non-users and potential users all need to be persuaded to try the product, while first-time users need to be persuaded to become medium users, and medium users to become heavy users. The essence of this approach is reflected in the strategies of a variety of organizations, including those of a number of cigarette companies, which, having been affected by changing smoking habits over the past two decades, have targeted particular user status groups. Across Europe, for example, young females in particular have been identified as a potentially valuable – and vulnerable – segment and a variety of brands developed to appeal specifically to this part of the market.

The attraction of different user status groups tends to vary from one type of organization to another. High market share companies, for example, typically focus on converting potential users into actual users, while smaller and lower share firms will often concentrate upon users of competitive brands with a view to persuading them to switch brands.

Loyalty status and brand enthusiasm

The third technique encompassed by behavioural segmentation is that of *loyalty status*, in which buyers are categorized on the basis of the extent and depth of their loyalty to particular brands or stores. Most typically this leads to the emergence of four categories: hard-core loyals, soft-core loyals, shifting loyals and switchers. In the case of the airlines, for example, the past few years have seen an enormous investment in frequent flyer schemes that are designed to build loyalty. However, as we suggest in Section 6.8, loyalty and the relationships upon which they are supposedly built are not necessarily as straightforward or as deep as they might appear at first sight. It is for this reason that customer promiscuity has become a far more significant and costly issue for many organizations (see pages 242–3).

The implications of loyalty are, of course, significant since, in the case of those markets in which high patterns of loyalty exist, the ability to persuade buyers to shift from one brand to another is likely to be limited, even in the face of high levels of marketing expenditure. Thus, in these circumstances, a share-gaining or market-entry strategy may well prove to be at best only marginally cost-effective. However, the process of categorization referred to above is not by itself sufficient for the strategist. Rather it is the starting point from which the specific characteristics of each category then need to be examined. It may be the case, for example, that those buyers with the highest degrees of loyalty exhibit certain common characteristics in terms of age, socio-economic profile and so on, while those with lower degrees of loyalty exhibit a very different but common set of characteristics. Research designed to identify these differences may well then provide the planner with a far greater understanding and insight into the ways in which patterns of loyalty may prove vulnerable to attack. Equally, analysis of this sort can provide an insight into the ways in which a competitor's products are vulnerable to attack. In the case of soft-core loyals, for example, the strategist needs to identify the brands that compete either directly or indirectly with its own. By doing this, it can then strengthen its position, possibly by means of knocking copy or direct comparison advertising.

Analysis of the final group – the switchers – is also of potential strategic value, since this can provide the basis for understanding in greater detail the brand's weaknesses and the basis for attack.

As an alternative or addition to loyalty status, consumers can often be categorized on the basis of their *enthusiasm* for the product, the five categories that are used most frequently being *enthusiastic, positive, indifferent, negative* and *hostile*. Its major value as a technique is principally as a screening step in that, having identified the category within which the consumer falls, the organization can then focus its energies on the most likely prospects. This process can then be taken a step further by focusing on the *occasions* on which consumers develop a need, purchase or use a product.

Greeting cards companies, for example, have concentrated on increasing the number of occasions on which cards are given in relation to what was the case, say, 30 years ago. A glance at the shelves of any newsagent will reveal the enormous variety of cards that now exist, ranging from Father's Day and Mother's Day through to Get Well and Congratulations on Your Examination Success/New Baby/Moving House/New Job/Passing Your Driving Test, and so on. Ice-cream manufacturers have pursued a broadly similar strategy in order to move away from a pattern of sales that was overly dependent on hot, sunny weather. The result in this case has been the development of a whole series of ice-cream-based desserts and cakes that can be used throughout the year.

Critical events

As a further development of occasion-related segmentation, the past few years have been the emergence of what is usually referred to as *critical event segmentation* (CES). This is based on the idea that major or critical events in an individual's life generate needs that can then be satisfied by the provision of a collection of products and/or services. Typical examples of these critical events are marriage, the death of someone in the family, unemployment, illness, retirement and moving house. Among those who have recognized the potential of CES are estate agents who, during the past decade, have moved away from simply selling houses to providing the whole range of legal and financial services surrounding house sale and purchase. The idea of critical events has also underpinned the marketing approach used by some of the chocolate companies, such as Thorntons, who have focused upon dates such as Valentine's Day, Mother's Day, Christmas, and so on.

9.11   PSYCHOGRAPHIC AND LIFESTYLE SEGMENTATION

The fourth and increasingly popular basis of consumer segmentation stems from work by Riesman *et al.* (1950), which led to the identification of three distinct types of social characterization and behaviour:

1. *Tradition-directed behaviour*, which changes little over time and, as a result, is easy to predict and use as a basis for segmentation

2. *Other directedness*, in which the individual attempts to fit in and adapt to the behaviour of his or her peer group

3. *Inner directedness*, where the individual is seemingly indifferent to the behaviour of others.

Although this relatively simplistic approach to categorization has subsequently been subjected to a degree of criticism, it has provided the basis for a considerable amount of further work, all of which has been designed to provide the strategist with a far more detailed understanding of personality and lifestyle.

The attempts to use personality to segment markets began in earnest in the USA in the late 1950s, when both Ford and Chevrolet gave emphasis to the brand personalities of their products in order to appeal to distinct consumer personalities. Buyers of Fords, for example, were identified as 'independent, impulsive, masculine, alert to change, and self-confident, while Chevrolet owners were conservative, thrifty, prestige-conscious, less masculine, and seeking to avoid extremes'. The validity of these descriptions was subsequently questioned by Evans (1959), who, by using a series of psychometric tests, argued that Ford and Chevrolet owners did not in fact differ to nearly the extent that had been suggested. More recent research has, with just one or two possible exceptions, been equally inconclusive. Among these exceptions is the work of Westfall (1962) and Young (1972). Westfall, for example, has reported finding evidence of personality differences between the buyers of convertible and non-convertible cars, with the former seemingly being 'more active, impulsive and sociable', while Young has pointed to the successful development of personality trait-based segmentation strategies in the cosmetics, drinks and cigarettes markets.

Largely because of the difficulties encountered in using personality as an easy, consistent and reliable basis for segmentation, attention in recent years has switched to *lifestyle* and to the ways in which it influences patterns of consumer demand. Lifestyle has been defined in a variety of ways, but is in essence *how* a person lives and interacts with their environment. As such, it is potentially a long way removed from social class and personality, and instead is a reflection of a person's way of being and acting in the world. An example of how psychographics and lifestyle can be used is that of Gap Inc., which owns the Gap, Banana Republic and Old Navy store chains. Gap customers are categorized as either 'style-conscious' or 'updated classics'. The style-conscious customers are 20- to 30-year-olds, while updated classics are older and more conservative customers (this is the group that felt disenfranchised by Gap's move into younger and edgier designs in 2001). Banana Republic targets sophisticated fashion leaders who want quality clothes and accessories and are not price-sensitive. The 811-strong Old Navy chain consists of large (14 000 square feet) stores with value-priced clothing that attracts young families.

Because of the *apparent* insights offered by lifestyle analysis, a variety of models for categorizing consumers has emerged over the past few years. Prominent among these are the VALS framework, Young & Rubicam's 4Cs, and Taylor Nelson's Monitor.

The VALS framework

Developed in the USA by Arnold Mitchell of the Stanford Research Institute, the VALS framework used the answers of 2713 respondents to 800 questions to classify the American public into nine value lifestyle groups:

1. *Survivors*, who are generally disadvantaged and who tend to be depressed, withdrawn and despairing

2. *Sustainers*, who are again disadvantaged but who are fighting hard to escape poverty

3. *Belongers*, who tend to be conventional, nostalgic, conservative and generally reluctant to experiment with new products or ideas

4. *Emulators*, who are status conscious, ambitious and upwardly mobile

5. *Achievers*, who make things happen and enjoy life

6. *'I-am-me' people*, who are self-engrossed, respond to whims and are generally young

7. *Experientials*, who want to experience a wide variety of what life can offer

8. *Societally conscious people*, who have a marked sense of social responsibility and want to improve the conditions of society

9. *Integrated people*, who are psychologically fully mature and who combine the best elements of inner and outer directedness.

The thinking that underpins the VALS framework is that individuals pass through a series of developmental stages, each of which influences attitudes, behaviour and psychological needs. Thus, people typically move from a stage that is largely need-driven (survivors and sustainers) towards either an outer-directed hierarchy of stages (belongers, emulators and achievers) or an inner-directed hierarchy (I-am-me, experientials, societally conscious); relatively few reach the nirvana of the integrated stage.

From the marketing point of view, the need-driven segments have little apparent appeal, since it is this part of society that lacks any real purchasing power. Outer-directed consumers, by contrast, represent a far more attractive part of the market and in general buy products with what has been described as 'an awareness of what other people will attribute to their consumption of that product'. Typically, therefore, brand names such as Rolex, Gucci, Benetton, Chanel and Cartier will prove to be important. Inner-directed consumers, by contrast, are those people who in their lives place far greater emphasis on their individual needs as opposed to external values. Although in terms of overall numbers this group represents only a small part of the total market, it is often seen to be an important sector in terms of its ability to set trends. It is this group also that is currently showing the fastest growth rate within society, while the number of need-driven consumers declines and outer-directed remains about the same.

Young & Rubicam's 4Cs and Taylor Nelson's Monitor

Developed by the advertising agency Young & Rubicam, 4Cs (a Cross-Cultural Consumer Characterization) divides people into three main groups, each of which is further subdivided along the following lines:

1. The constrained
   (i)   the resigned poor
   (ii) the struggling poor.

2. The middle majority
   (i) mainstreamers
   (ii) aspirers
   (iii) succeeders.

3. The innovators
   (i) transitionals
   (ii) reformers.

The largest single subgroup in the UK is the mainstreamers, said to account for between 30 and 35 per cent of the population.

The principal benefit of 4Cs is that it defines in a fairly precise manner individual or group motivational needs. It does this by acknowledging the multidimensional nature of people and groups by taking the key motivational factors (e.g. success in the case of a succeeder) and overlaying this with other important motivational values to develop a motivational matrix. This can then be used to construct strategic frameworks for marketing and advertising campaigns both domestically and internationally.

A similar framework, labelled Monitor, has been developed by the UK-based market research agency, Taylor Nelson. The Monitor typology divides people into three main groups, which are again subdivided:

1. *Sustenance-driven*. Motivated by material security, they are subdivided into:
   (i) the aimless, who include young unemployed and elderly drifters (5 per cent of the UK population)
   (ii) survivors, traditionally minded working-class people (16 per cent of the population)
   (iii) belongers, who are conservative family-oriented people (18 per cent of the population, but only half of them are sustenance-driven).

2. *Outer-directed*. Those who are mainly motivated by the desire for status. They are subdivided into:
   (i) belongers
   (ii) conspicuous consumers (19 per cent of the population).

3. *Inner-directed*. This group is subdivided into:
   (i) social resisters, who are caring and often doctrinaire (11 per cent of the population)
   (ii) experimentalists, who are hedonistic and individualistic (14 per cent of the population)
   (iii) self-explorers, who are less doctrinaire than social resisters and less materialistic than experimentalists.

The development of approaches such as these has also led to the emergence of a wide variety of acronyms and labels. Prominent among these are Yuppies (Young Upwardly Mobile Professionals), Bumps (Borrowed-to-the-hilt, Upwardly Mobile Professional Show-offs), Jollies (Jet-setting Oldies with Lots of Loot), Woopies (Well-Off Older Persons), Glams (Greying Leisured Affluent Middle-Aged) and Kippers (Kids in Parent's Pockets Eroding Retirement Savings). Although a number of these labels are now rather passé – Yuppies, for example, proved to be a phenomenon of the 1980s and the Big Bang – they have proved to be useful in that they characterize in an easily understood fashion a particular style of life.

9.12 APPROACHES TO SEGMENTING INDUSTRIAL MARKETS

Although much of the work that has been done on segmentation analysis over the past 40 years has focused on consumer markets, many of the variables, such as benefits sought, geography and usage rates, can be applied with equal validity to industrial markets. Recognizing this, a number of writers, including Cardozo (1980) and Bonoma and Shapiro (1983), have concentrated on demonstrating, developing and refining their applicability. Cardozo, for example, has identified four dimensions that can be used either separately or collectively to classify organizational buying situations:

1. Familiarity with the buying task and in particular whether it is a new task, modified rebuy or straight rebuy

2. The type of product and the degree of standardization

3. The significance of the purchase to the buying organization

4. The level of uncertainty in the purchase situation.

Of these, it is arguably the last two factors that are of particular significance, as they reflect the fact that buyers also try to segment potential suppliers by developing assessment criteria and establishing formal vendor rating systems. This general line of thinking has been developed by Johnson and Flodhammer (1980), who, in arguing that the need to understand buyers' needs is as important in industrial markets as in consumer markets, have suggested that: 'Unless there is knowledge of the industrial users' needs the manufactured product usually has the lowest common denominator – price. Quality and service are unknown qualities.'

A slightly different line of argument has been pursued by Bonoma and Shapiro (1984), who have concentrated on developing a classification of industrial segmentation variables and listing the questions that industrial marketers should pose in deciding which customers they want to serve. A summary of these questions, in declining order of importance, appears in Figure 9.5.

Demographic

Industry: on which industries that use this product should we concentrate?

Company: on what size of company should we concentrate?

Location: in which geographical areas should we concentrate our efforts?

Operating variables

Technology: which customers' technologies are of the greatest interest to us?

User status: on which types of user (heavy, medium, light, non-user) should we concentrate?

Customer capabilities: should we concentrate on customers with a broad or a narrow range of needs?

Purchasing approaches

Buying criteria: should we concentrate on customers seeking quality, service, or price?

Buying policies: should we concentrate on companies that prefer leasing, systems purchases, or sealed bids?

Current relationships: should we concentrate on existing or new customers?

Situational factors

Urgency: should we concentrate on customers with sudden delivery needs?

Size of order: should we concentrate on large or small orders?

Applications: should we concentrate on general or specific applications of our product?

Personal characteristics

Loyalty: should we concentrate on customers who exhibit high or low levels of loyalty?

Attitudes to risk: should we concentrate on risk-taking or risk-avoiding customers?

FIGURE 9.5 *The major industrial market segmentation variables (adapted from Bonoma and Shapiro, 1984)*

From this it can be seen that the starting point is the question of which industry to serve, followed by a series of decisions on customer size and purchase criteria.

This method has been employed to great effect by, among others, IBM. IBM's starting point for segmentation has always been the idea that the company sells solutions rather than products. They therefore segment the market by commercial type: banking, transportation, insurance, processing industry and so on, in order to be able to tailor solutions to specific problem areas. Each segment is then divided into a series of sub-segments. Transportation, for example, can be divided into road, air, sea and rail.

Market segmentation and the dialogue of the deaf

The need for the planner to understand markets in detail and to avoid falling into the trap of blindly accepting the market and organizational preconceptions was highlighted by the American futurologist Faith Popcorn. In her book *Eve-olution* (2001), she argues that many (male) marketing planners fail to understand the real differences between men and women and, as a consequence, have been unable to capitalize upon them. To illustrate this, she points to the buying power of women (in the USA it is estimated that women are responsible for or influence 80 per cent of all consumer, healthcare and vehicle purchases, 60 per cent of all electronic purchases, and represent 48 per cent of stock market investors) and to the biological differences that lead to women processing information differently.

Although Popcorn's critics have argued that these differences are not as significant or as far-reaching as she suggests, this can be seen to be part of a more fundamental issue about the relationship between companies and their customers. Almost irrespective of the sector, marketers are finding the gaps between what they think they know and actual buying behaviour are getting bigger. In an attempt to overcome this, marketing planners are spending ever more on technologies that, it is claimed, overcome the problems and imprecision of current segmentation models.

However, in many cases this is likely to have little effect, since there is often a fundamental misunderstanding at the heart of the customer/company dialogue. One example of this was the way in which Monsanto misread the issues surrounding genetically modified (GM) foodstuffs. The company was mesmerized by what it saw as a great scientific revolution and viewed the world through this one framework. How, its planners wondered, could there be objections to developments that had the potential to make food production so much more efficient? What it seemingly could not understand was that consumers viewed the situation very differently, were concerned for their safety and wanted information to make informed choices. The result was a dialogue of the deaf between manufacturer and consumer. It was, instead, the supermarkets that responded to these concerns by launching organically produced and GM-free ranges of foodstuffs.

9.13 MARKET TARGETING

Having decided how best to segment the market, the strategist is then faced with a series of decisions on how many and which segments to approach. Three factors need to be considered:

1. The size and growth potential of each segment

2. Their structural attractiveness

3. The organization's objectives and resources.

The starting point for this involves examining each segment's size and potential for growth. Obviously, the question of what is the 'right size' of a segment will vary greatly from one organization to another. The specialist car manufacturer Morgan has, for example, chosen to concentrate on a very small and specialized segment of the car market. Its customers are seeking the nostalgia of a pre-war sports car and the company has tailored its marketing mix accordingly. In commenting on this, *What Car?* said:

> *The ride's as hard as a rock, comfort and space minimal, noise*
> *levels deafeningly high, and overall the sports car has about as much*
> *refinement as a tractor. Wonderful!*

This is neither a specification nor a segment that has any appeal for, say, Volkswagen or Jaguar, but Morgan operates within it with a high degree of success.

In so far as it is possible to develop broad guidelines, we can say that large companies concentrate on segments with large existing or potential sales volumes and quite deliberately overlook or ignore small segments, simply because they are rarely worth bothering with. Small firms, by contrast, often avoid large segments, partly because of the level of resource needed to operate in them effectively and partly because of the problems of having to cope with a far larger competitor.

With regard to the question of each segment's *structural attractiveness*, the strategist's primary concern is profitability. It may be the case that a segment is both large and growing but that, because of the intensity of competition, the scope for profit is low. Several models for measuring segment attractiveness exist, although arguably the most useful is Michael Porter's five-force model. This model, which is discussed at the beginning of Chapter 11, suggests that segment profitability is affected by five principal factors:

1. Industry competitors and the threat of segment rivalry

2. Potential entrants to the market and the threat of mobility

3. The threat of substitute products

4. Buyers and their relative power

5. Suppliers and their relative power.

Having measured the size, growth rate and structural attractiveness of each segment, the strategist needs then to examine each one in turn against the background of the organization's objectives and resources. In doing this, the strategist is looking for the degree of compatibility between the segment and the organization's long-term goals. It is often the case, for example, that a seemingly attractive segment can be dismissed either because it would not move the organization significantly forward towards its goals, or because it would divert organizational energy. Even where there does appear to be a match, consideration needs to be given to whether the organization has the necessary skills competences, resources and commitment needed to operate effectively. Without these, entry is likely to be of little strategic value.

There are therefore two questions that need to be posed:

1. *Is the segment growing or declining?* Here we are interested in two broad aspects of growth and decline. What is the projected future of the segment in terms of volume sales and profit? Despite much argument to the contrary, there need not be a link between volume sales and profit. Declining volumes in certain market segments can still be extremely profitable for the organizations that service them. It is therefore often more a question of how the segment is managed rather than what the segment is doing.

2. *Is the segment changing?* There are three aspects to this question of change. First, we need to understand how the structure and make-up of the segment are likely to change over time. Is the segment starting to attract new and slightly different members to its centre? What effect will this have on the segment's needs? The second aspect of change relates to the nature of the products and services that we would expect this segment to be demanding in the future. In other words, do we see any significant change in the way in which the members of the segment are likely to translate their needs into buying behaviour? Will they want different products or services in three years' time? The third area of segment change must consider the movements of the segments over time. Do we, for example, see the overall array of segments changing? There are two ways in which this structural change can occur. Segments may merge and combine to create larger, more 'shallow' segments. Alternatively, larger segments may fragment over time into smaller, more precise market targets for the organization to approach.

9.14 DECIDING ON THE BREADTH OF MARKET COVERAGE

The final segmentation decision faced by the strategist is concerned with which and how many segments to enter. In essence, five patterns of market coverage exist:

1. *Single segment concentration.* Here, the organization focuses on just one segment. Although a potentially high-risk strategy in that the firm is vulnerable to sudden changes in taste or the entry of a larger competitor, concentrated marketing along these lines has often proved to be attractive to small companies with limited funds. Left to itself, an organization that opts to concentrate upon a single segment can develop a strong market position, a specialist reputation, and above-average returns for the industry as a whole.

2. *Selective specialization*. As an alternative to concentrating upon just one segment, the strategist may decide to spread the risk by covering several. These segments need not necessarily be related, although each should be compatible with the organization's objectives and resources. One organization that has done this with a high degree of success is Land Rover. Launched at the end of the 1940s as a rugged, utilitarian and easily maintained off-road vehicle, the Land Rover was targeted at a wide variety of geographically dispersed agricultural and military markets. Having dominated these markets for a considerable time, the company subsequently developed the far more luxurious (and expensive) Range Rover, which proved to have an immediate appeal to a very different type of market altogether. Their strategy was then developed further in 1990 by the launch of the Land Rover Discovery and then, a few years later, the Freelander.

3. *Product specialization*. Here, the organization concentrates on marketing a particular product type to a variety of target markets. Examples of this include the Burton Group (now renamed Arcadia) and Next, both of which have concentrated upon selling fashion clothing to a predominantly young market.

4. *Market specialization*. Here, the organization concentrates on satisfying the range of needs of a particular target group. An example of this would be an agrochemicals manufacturer, whose principal target market is farmers.

5. *Full market coverage*. By far the most costly of the five patterns of market coverage, a strategy of full market coverage involves serving all (or most) customer groups with the full range of products needed. Two companies that have increasingly moved towards this position over the past few years are Volkswagen (the small VW Lupo through to the premium-priced VW Phaeton) and Mercedes-Benz (the A-Class through to premium-priced saloons and sports cars).

In deciding which of these five approaches to adopt, the marketing planner needs to take account of two interrelated issues:

1. *The nature of the current strategy*. In discussing this, Fifield and Gilligan (1996, p. 98) suggest that 'market segments ought to be selected according to the broader strategic decisions taken by the company'. For example, the organization aiming for a 'differentiated' position in the marketplace will need to retain a certain degree of flexibility, which will allow it to operate in a number of related market segments while still retaining its differentiated market position. The 'focused' organization, on the other hand, will

necessarily have to get much, much closer to its fewer market segments, and will have to predict fragmentation and merging long before this phenomenon arises. It must be prepared and be able to continue to service changing segment needs as they arise. Failure to do this by the focused organization will leave it very vulnerable to competitive attack in its core markets.

2. *Organization resources and capability.* These need to be harnessed so that the customers' needs within the segments that are chosen are capable of being properly served.

Against the background of the answers to these two issues, the planner can then begin the process of ordering the segments so that a measure of their relative attractiveness across a series of dimensions can be developed.

Market niching and focusing

For small companies in particular, market niching offers a degree of security that is often denied to them if they try to compete in segments which, by virtue of their size, appeal to larger and better-funded organizations (market niching and the characteristics of the supernichers are also discussed in Section 8 of Chapter 12).

An undoubted attraction of many niche markets is the scope they offer for premium pricing and above-average profit margins. In addition, an effective niche strategy has for many firms provided a convenient jumping-off point for entry into a larger market. Both Volkswagen and Toyota, for example, niched when they first entered the North American car market. Their strategies, together with the subsequent growth of the small car market, combined to change what had previously been a niche into a sizeable segment, which the American big three (Ford, General Motors and Chrysler) found difficult to attack because of the entrenched positions of VW and Toyota. Elsewhere, the Japanese have often used a niche as the entry point to a larger market. In the case of motorcycles, for example, 50 cc 'toys' proved to be the niche that gave Honda, in particular, the basis for expansion. Similarly, Volvo developed what was previously a niche that wanted a safe, functional and long-lasting car into a relatively large market. Amongst the others to have started with a strong niching strategy within a specialized, and initially small, market but who have subsequently developed the niche into a sizeable market segment are Body Shop, Harley Davidson, and Häagen-Dazs and Ben & Jerry's ice-creams.

There is, however, a hidden danger in looking at what appear to be niche markets. Many strategists with small brands often deceive themselves by believing they have a niche product. The reality may in fact be very different, with the product being a vulnerable number four or number five brand in a mass market. To clarify whether a brand is a true market nicher, three questions can be posed:

1. Do consumers and distributors recognize the niche or is it simply a figment of the overactive imagination of a marketing planner?

2. Is the niche product or service *really* distinctive and does it have a strong appeal to a specific customer group?

3. Is the product capable of being priced at a premium and does it offer the scope for above-average profit margins?

Unless the answer to all three of the questions is 'yes', it is unlikely that the brand is a true nicher, but is instead simply a poor performer in a far larger market segment, something that leads to the idea that, although it is relatively easy to find a niche, the real secret is to ensure that it is of the right size – large enough to be profitable, but not sufficiently large to attract the far larger players, at least in the early days when the organization is trying to establish a market position.

Although there is a temptation to see niche marketers as small companies, the reality is that many niches are occupied by far larger organizations that have developed the skills of operating with small-volume products.

Given this, the characteristics of the ideal niche are:

1. It should be of sufficient size to be potentially profitable

2. It should offer scope for the organization to exercise its distinctive competences

3. It should/must have the potential for growth.

Other characteristics that favour niching would be patents, a degree of channel control, and the existence of customer goodwill.

9.15 PRODUCT POSITIONING: THE BATTLE FOR THE MIND

The third strand of what we referred to at the beginning of this chapter as STP marketing (segmentation, targeting and positioning) involves deciding on the position within the market that the product is to occupy. In doing this, the strategist is stating to customers what the product means and how it differs from current and potential competing products. Porsche, for example, is positioned in the prestige segment of the car market, with a differential advantage based on performance; Patek Phillipe is positioned as one of the highest quality watches available and for which the 'owner' is simply the product's custodian for the next generation; Mothercare is positioned to appeal to mothers of young children, with its differential advantage being based on the breadth of merchandise for that target group; Duracell is positioned as the longer-life and hence better value battery; brands such as Quiksilver are positioned to appeal to the urban street warrior; while Ryanair and easyJet are positioned as low-cost airlines.

The way in which an organization or a brand is perceived by its target markets (this is not just the existing customers, but also includes those who do not buy currently, might never buy, and so on) is determined by a series of factors including:

1. The nature of the produce and the product range

2. Product quality and performance

3. Pricing levels

4. The nature of the distribution network used

5. The types of advertising appeal, the media used and the nature of anyone used to endorse the product

6. Customer profiles

7. Customer experiences and word of mouth.

Positioning is therefore the process of designing an image and value so that customers within the target segment understand what the company or brand stands for in relation to its competitors. This can perhaps best be understood by considering an example such as grocery retailing, where the major UK retailers have set out to establish distinct market positions. Waitrose, for example, occupies a service and quality position. Aldi and Netto, by contrast, have pursued the low-price/no-frills position, while Sainsbury's and Tesco occupy the quality, breadth of range and convenience position, while Morrison's pursues a position based on freshness and good value. In doing this, the organization is sending a message to consumers and trying to establish a competitive advantage that it hopes will appeal to customers within a sub-segment of the target segment. In the case of Waitrose, therefore, the company hopes that its quality/service position will appeal to the customer to whom these two dimensions are far more important than low prices. In the drinks market, Castlemaine XXXX is positioned as the genuine Australian lager, while in the banking sector the Co-operative Bank is positioned on the basis of an ethical proposition. Given this, the reader needs to recognize that positioning is a battle for the customer's mind, since it is how the customer perceives the company or brand that determines success or failure. As an example of this, in the breakfast cereals market we can see the very different positions occupied by Kellogg's Corn Flakes, Kellogg's All-Bran and Kellogg's Special K.

It should be apparent from this that positioning is a fundamental element of the marketing planning process, since any decision on positioning has direct and immediate implications for the whole of the marketing mix. In essence, therefore, the marketing mix can be seen as the tactical details of the organization's positioning strategy. Where, for example, the organization is pursuing a high-quality position, this needs to be reflected not just in the quality of the product that is to be sold, but in every element of the mix, including price, the pattern of distribution, the style of advertising and the after-sales service. Without this consistency, the believability of the positioning strategy reduces dramatically.

For some organizations the choice of a positioning strategy proves to be straightforward. Where, for example, a particular positioning strategy and image has already been established in a related market, there are likely to be synergistic benefits by adopting the same approach in a new market or with a new product. For other organizations, however, the choice of position proves to be more difficult or less clear and the firm ends up by pursuing the same position as several others in the market. Where this happens, the degree and costs of competition increase dramatically. There is a strong case, therefore, for the strategist to decide in detail on the basis of differentiation: in other words, the organization must identify and build a collection of competitive advantages that will appeal to the target market and then communicate these effectively.

In the light of these comments, it should be apparent that the process of positioning involves three steps:

1. Identifying the organization or brand's possible competitive advantages

2. Deciding on those that are to be emphasized

3. Implementing the positioning concept.

Points 1 and 2 are discussed in detail in Chapter 11; therefore, only point 3 will be considered here.

Capitalizing on the competitive advantage

Having identified the competitive advantage (see Chapter 11) that appears to offer the greatest potential for development, the final step in the process involves communicating this to the market. Ries and Trout (1982), who in the eyes of many are the founding fathers of positioning theory, argue that positioning is first and foremost a communication strategy (this is the issue of the battle of the mind referred to earlier) and that any failure to recognize this will undermine the whole of the marketing mix. All too often, however, and despite having identified potentially valuable competitive advantages, organizations fail to signal these advantages sufficiently strongly. This then leads to one of three errors:

1. *Confused positioning*, where buyers are unsure of what the organization stands for (refer to the comments on the opposite page about Gap's misjudgement of the market in 2001)

2. *Over-positioning*, where consumers perceive the organization's products as being expensive and fail to recognize the full breadth and value of the range (this can be summed up in terms of over-promise and under-delivery)

3. *Under-positioning*, where the message is simply too vague and consumers have little real idea of what the organization stands for or how it differs from the competition.

In order to select the most effective market position, the strategist needs to begin by identifying the structure of the market and the positions currently held by competitors. This can be done in a variety of ways, including by means of the sort of brand map to which we referred earlier. With maps such as these the planner sets out first to plot where the product lies in relation to competitive products and, secondly, to identify those areas in which marketing opportunities might exist either for a new brand or for the existing brand if it was to be repositioned. In taking this second step, the strategist is setting out to position the product in such a way that its marketing potential is fully realized.

As an example of how the greater potential of a different market sector might be realized, the German car manufacturer Audi set out in the 1980s and 1990s to reposition its range of products in order to move further up-market. In doing this, the company recognized that the organizations against which it would be competing would change and that, in this particular case, it would bring itself into more direct competition with both BMW and Mercedes-Benz. At the same time, numerous other car manufacturers have pursued repositioning strategies, with Jaguar targeting a younger market than in the past and Porsche, with part of its product range, pursuing a (relatively) less affluent sector.

In electing for a positioning or repositioning strategy, strategists therefore need to feel confident that, first, they will be able to reach the new market position for which they are aiming, and secondly, that they will be able to operate and compete effectively and profitably in this new position.

For many organizations, however, repositioning proves to be a less than successful exercise. In 2001, for example, Gap reported an $8 million loss against net earnings of $877 million in 2000 and $1.1 billion in 1999, a problem that seemingly had emerged as the result of the way in which they had moved from their previously very clear market position to one that was far more edgy, fashion-forward and less appealing to its traditional markets.

The San Francisco-based company, which had grown dramatically for a decade, was accused by analysts of having alienated its Generation X market by trying to appeal to younger shoppers. However, in doing this, not only did Gap lose some of its traditional and highly loyal customer base, but failed to achieve the penetration of its new target market for which it was hoping. Subsequently, of course, the company has successfully moved back to its core markets. (Refer also to our discussion about Gap and its Banana Republic and Old Navy brands on page 362.)

Against the background of these comments, it should be recognized that very different positioning strategies need to be followed depending upon whether the firm is a market leader, follower or challenger and that, as a general rule, market followers should try to avoid positioning themselves too closely or directly against the market leader. The reasoning behind this is straightforward, since a smaller firm is most likely to succeed if it can establish its own position within the market and develop its own customer base. To compete head-on against an aggressive market leader such as Wal-Mart with a very clear position is to invite retaliation and a costly marketing war (see Illustration 9.2).

The potential pitfalls of weak positioning

The dangers of poor product positioning have been illustrated in the US car market by General Motors. Under Alfred Sloan in the 1920s and 1930s, the company had a clear positioning strategy that was reflected in a product ladder ranging from Chevrolet (low price) to Cadillac (high price) and a slogan 'a car for every purse and purpose'. The clarity of strategic thinking was lost in the 1980s when the company began a move towards 'badge engineering', under which essentially the same car was re-badged for different brands. The net effect of this is that the customer could buy a similar minivan under the Buick, Pontiac, Chevrolet and Saturn names.

Illustration 9.2   Wal-Mart and its positioning by price

With more than 3000 stores serving 60 million people a week and annual revenues in excess of $140 billion, Wal-Mart is the world's largest retailer. The company's positioning statement is simple and unambiguous: 'We sell for less.' In order to achieve this, the founder, Sam Walton, rationalized and controlled costs to such an extent that he was able to undercut every one of his competitors. In commenting on this, Ritson (2002) suggests that:

Walton achieved this control through a revolutionary approach to distribution and inventory management. Taking the company public in 1970 enabled him to use the subsequent funds to build his own distribution network of giant warehouses that each had its own transportation system, linked up with 175 Wal-Mart stores. This network ensured that Wal-Mart handled its own distribution, saving millions of dollars on freight costs. The distribution network also had tremendous bargaining power because of the number of stores served. Walton underlined this power by ensuring that no supplier provided more than 3 per cent of the total Wal-Mart inventory. The message: if you don't price it as low as possible, we'll switch our business elsewhere.

Source: Ritson (2002).

A similar approach emerged in both Procter & Gamble and Unilever with a multitude of overlapping products and brands. The eventual response in both companies was a significant culling of the portfolio. In the case of Unilever, for example, the company's 'Path to Growth' strategy involved 1200 of its 1600 brands being sold or dropped so that marketing resources could be concentrated behind the too 400 high-growth brands. There was then a further culling of the brands in 2007 so that the company could concentrate upon those brands that were the top-two sellers in each segment.

Repositioning strategies

Having developed a position for a brand, there is frequently the need to reposition as the market develops, competitors enter or exit, and customers' expectations and needs change. In thinking about repositioning, the marketing planner has four strategic options:

1. *Gradual repositioning*, which involves a planned and continuous adaptation to the changing market environment. An example of this would be Skoda's move from an essentially utilitarian offer to one that is far more firmly mid-market.

2. *Radical repositioning*, where an increasing gap between what the brand offers and what the market wants leads the management team to think about a major strategic change. As an example of this, Lucozade moved from a position where its primary appeal was to the sick and the old to one where its major appeal is as a lifestyle and health drink.

3. *Innovative repositioning*, where the planner finds a new strategic position that offers market opportunities that have not so far been identified by competitors. Häagen-Dazs recognized the potential of the premium-quality, premium-priced adult ice-cream market, and throughout the 1990s successfully developed this.

4. *Zero positioning*, where the organization maintains an unchanged face to the market over a long period of time and/or it communicates very poorly with the target market, with the result that potential customers have little idea of what the organization stands for.

9.16 SUMMARY

Within this chapter we have focused upon the ways in which a well-developed strategy of market segmentation, targeting and positioning contributes to effective marketing planning.

The rationale for segmentation is straightforward, and is based on the idea that only rarely can a single product or marketing approach appeal to the needs and wants of a disparate group of potential customers. Because of this there is a need for the marketing strategist to categorize buyers on the basis both of their characteristics and their specific product needs, with a view then to adapting either the product and the marketing programme, or both, to satisfy more specifically these different tastes and demands. An effective policy of segmentation is therefore a key contributory factor to the development of a competitive advantage.

A wide variety of approaches to segmentation have been developed, and these were discussed in some detail in the text. Many of the early approaches to segmentation are unidimensional and are incapable of providing the marketing planner with a sufficiently detailed picture of buyers' motives to be of real value. A considerable amount of work has therefore been conducted over the past 30 years to improve segmentation techniques, with the greatest emphasis being placed upon geodemographics and psychographics.

Work within the industrial products sector has, for the most part, tended to lag behind that in the consumer goods field, although the work of Cardozo, and Bonoma and Shapiro, has gone some way towards rectifying this.

Having segmented the market, the strategist should then be in a position to identify those segments which, from the organization's point of view, represent the most attractive targets. In deciding where to focus the marketing effort, the strategist needs to give consideration to three elements:

1. The size and growth potential of each segment

2. The structural attractiveness of different segments

3. The organization's objectives and resources.

Once a decision has been made on the breadth of market coverage, the strategist needs then to consider how best to position the organization, the product range and the brand within each target segment. A number of guidelines for market positioning have been discussed, and emphasis was placed upon the need to avoid making any one of the three most common positioning errors:

1. Confused positioning

2. Over-positioning

3. Under-positioning.

We concluded by returning to the significance of competitive advantage and to the ways in which a well-conceived and properly implemented strategy of segmentation, targeting and positioning can contribute to a highly effective marketing programme.

CHAPTER 10

The Formulation of Strategy 1: Analysing the Product Portfolio

10.2 INTRODUCTION

Against the background of the material covered so far we are now in a position to turn our attention to the ways in which organizations approach the development of a marketing strategy. In this, the first of three chapters on strategy, we begin by examining how strategic perspectives have developed over the past 30 or more years. We then turn our attention to a variety of models of portfolio analysis. In Chapter 11 we concentrate upon the issues surrounding growth, the approaches that are most typically used to achieve it, methods of developing a sustainable competitive advantage, and the ways in which market position influences strategy.

10.3 THE DEVELOPMENT OF STRATEGIC PERSPECTIVES

Although a considerable amount has been written about strategic planning, it should be recognized that, as a discipline, strategic planning and the associated concepts and techniques did not emerge fully until the early 1970s. There are several reasons for this, perhaps the most significant of which stems from the way in which many companies throughout the 1950s and 1960s prospered largely as the result of the growing and continuously buoyant markets that characterized Western economies at the time. In these circumstances, short-term operational planning was often seemingly all that was required. The turbulence of the early 1970s, which followed a series of crises – including oil supply restrictions, energy and material shortages, high inflation, economic stagnation, labour unrest, increased unemployment and then recession – caused many managers to search for a radically different approach to the running of their businesses. At the same time, an influx of low-price but relatively high-quality products from countries such as Japan began to flood Western markets, changing drastically the economics of manufacturing. The revised approach to management planning that emerged was designed to provide organizations with a far stronger and more resilient framework that would enable managers to both recognize opportunities more readily and overcome threats more easily. This new planning process was based on three central premises:

1. The company's business should be viewed and managed in a similar way to an investment portfolio, with each aspect of the business being closely monitored and decisions subsequently made on which products or specific parts of the business should be developed, maintained, phased out, or deleted.

2. Emphasis should be placed upon identifying in detail the future profit potential of each aspect of the business.

3. A strategic perspective to the management of each major element of the business should be adopted. This notion of what has sometimes been referred to as a 'game plan' for achieving long-term objectives required the strategist to plan on the basis of industry position, objectives, opportunities and resources.

It needs to be recognized, however, that for the strategist to be able to adopt this approach to management, there is a need to understand in detail the complexities of the interrelationships that exist between different parts of the organizational structure. In the majority of businesses, three different organizational levels can be identified: the corporate level, the business unit level and the product level.

At the corporate level, the decisions made are concerned principally with the corporate strategic plan and how best to develop the long-term profile of the business. This in turn involves a series of decisions on the levels of resource allocation to individual business units, be it a division, subsidiary or brand, and on which new potential business should be supported. Following this, each business unit should, within the resources allocated by

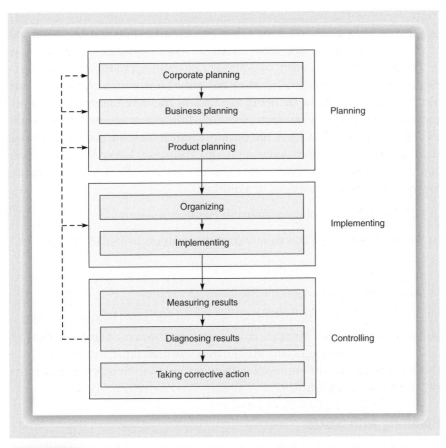

FIGURE 10.1   *The strategic planning, implementation and control cycle*

corporate headquarters, then develop its own strategic plan. Finally, marketing plans need to be developed at the product level. Plans at all three levels need then to be implemented, the results monitored and evaluated, and, where necessary, corrective action taken; this cycle of planning, implementation and control, which underpins the structure of this book, is illustrated in Figure 10.1.

Strategic planning and issues of responsibility

It should be apparent from what has been said so far that the ultimate responsibility for the planning process rests firmly with corporate management. This process, which involves statements of vision, mission, policy and strategy, establishes the broad framework within which plans at the business unit level are then developed. In practice, of course, organizations differ greatly both in how they go about this and in the degree of freedom given to the managers of individual business units. Some organizations, for example, allow the managers of business units considerable scope in developing their own objectives and strategies, requiring only that the promised levels of performance are then obtained: this is typically referred to as *bottom-up planning*. Others, by contrast, adopt an approach that is diametrically opposed to this in that they not only establish the objectives, but also subsequently insist on being involved in the development and implementation of strategy (*top-down planning*). Still others are content to establish the goals and then leave the business unit to develop the strategies for their achievement (*goals down/plans up*). However, irrespective of which approach is adopted, corporate management has the ultimate responsibility for the four major dimensions of planning:

1. The definition of the vision and business mission

2. Establishing the company's strategic business units (SBUs)

3. Evaluating the existing business portfolio

4. Identifying new areas for the business to enter.

The first of these – the definition of the vision and business mission – provided the focus for Chapter 8, and, as we emphasized at that stage, is designed to provide the organization with an overall sense of purpose. Once this has been done, the strategist is then in a position to move on and identify the organization's SBUs.

Planning with SBUs

The idea of SBUs as the basis for planning first emerged in the 1960s, and gave recognition to the fact that the majority of companies operate a number of businesses, not all of which will necessarily be immediately apparent or identifiable. It does not follow, for example, that a company with four operating divisions will have four businesses and hence four SBUs, since one division may in practice contain several quite separate businesses. This typically comes about when the division produces different products for very different customer groups. Equally, two or three divisions may overlap or be interrelated in such a way that in effect they form a single business. It is therefore important that the planner understands in detail the nature and extent of these interrelationships so that the organization's strategy can be developed in the most logical way.

In commenting on this, Levitt (1960, pp. 45–56), along with a number of other writers, has warned against the dangers of simply defining businesses in terms of the products being made. Doing this, he argues, is myopic, since the demand for a particular product is likely to be transient. By contrast, basic needs and customer groups are far more likely to endure. In arguing this, Levitt is reminding us that a business needs to be seen as a *customer-satisfying process* rather than as a *goods-producing process*.

Numerous examples exist of industries that have failed to recognize this, including the American railway companies in the 1950s, the British motorcycle industry in the 1960s, the European cutlery industry in the 1980s and 1990s, and the Swiss watch industry in the 1970s (for a more detailed discussion of the problems experienced by the Swiss watch industry, refer to Illustration 8.1). The net effect of this has been either that opportunities have been missed, or that the business – and on some occasions the entire industry – has gone into decline. It was in an attempt to force managers to recognize the transient nature of demand that Drucker (1973) recommended that periodically they should pose the questions 'What business are we in?' and 'What business should we be in?'

This general theme has also been pursued by Abell (1980), who suggests that businesses should be defined in terms of three elements:

1. The customer groups that will be served

2. The customer needs that will be satisfied

3. The technology that will be used to meet these needs.

Having done this, the planner can then move on to consider how best to manage each business strategically. A variety of frameworks to help with this have emerged over the past 25 years, although at the heart of virtually all of them is the concept of the *strategic business unit* or *strategy centre*. The term 'strategy centre' was first used by the American management consultants Arthur D. Little (1974), who defined it as:

> *A business area with an external market place for goods or services, for which management can determine objectives and execute strategies independently of other business areas. It is a business that could probably stand alone if divested. Strategic Business Units are the 'natural' or homogeneous business of a corporation.*

It follows from this definition that SBUs exhibit a number of characteristics, the three most important of which are that an SBU:

1. Is a single business or collection of related businesses that offers scope for independent planning and that might feasibly stand alone from the rest of the organization

2. Has its own set of competitors

3. Has a manager who has responsibility for strategic planning and profit performance, and control of profit-influencing factors.

The idea of planning based on SBUs developed throughout the 1970s, and has subsequently proved to be useful – not least because for many managers it has to a very large extent clarified what is meant by strategic marketing planning. The identification of SBUs is therefore a convenient starting point for planning, since, once the company's strategic business units have been identified, the *responsibilities* for strategic planning can be more clearly assigned. In practice, the majority of companies work on the basis that strategic planning at SBU level has to be agreed by corporate management. Thus plans are typically submitted on an annual basis, with corporate management then either agreeing them or sending them back for revision.

In going through this process of review, corporate management attempts to identify future potential and hence where investment can most profitably be made. This has in turn led to the development of a variety of frameworks in which products are categorized on the basis of their potential. One of the best known of these was put forward by Drucker (1963), who labelled products as:

1. Tomorrow's breadwinners

2. Today's breadwinners

3. Products that are capable of making a contribution, assuming drastic remedial action is taken

4. Yesterday's breadwinners

5. The also-rans

6. The failures.

By categorizing products or SBUs in this way, corporate management is moving towards a position where decisions regarding patterns of investment in the overall portfolio can be made with a far higher degree of objectivity than is typically the case when each SBU is viewed in partial or total isolation. To help with this, and in order to ensure that the process is analytical rather than impressionistic, a number of models of portfolio evaluation have been developed. Among the best known of these are the Boston Consulting Group's growth–share and growth–gain matrices.

10.4 MODELS OF PORTFOLIO ANALYSIS

The Boston Consulting Group's growth–share and growth–gain matrices

Undoubtedly the best-known approach to portfolio analysis, the Boston Consulting Group's (BCG) growth–share model, involves SBUs being plotted on a matrix according to the *rate of market growth* and their *market share relative to that of the largest competitor*. This is illustrated in Figure 10.2.

In using these dimensions as the basis for evaluating the product portfolio, the Boston Consulting Group forces management to give explicit consideration

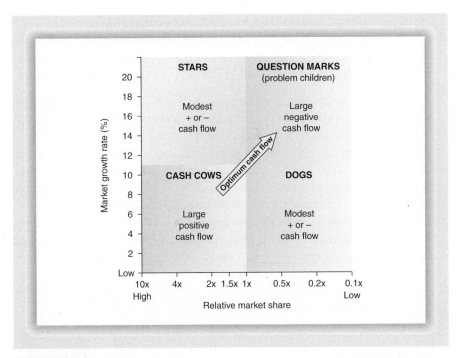

FIGURE 10.2   *The Boston Consulting Group's growth–share matrix (adapted from Hedley, 1977)*

both to the *future potential of the market* (i.e. the annual growth rate) and to the *SBU's competitive position*. Within the model, competitive position is measured on a logarithmic scale against the share of the firm's largest competitor; thus a relative market share of 0.3 in Figure 10.2 signifies that the SBU's sales volume is 30 per cent of the leader's sales volume, while 4.0 would mean that the company's SBU is the market leader and has four times the market share of the next largest company in the market. A ratio of 1.0 signifies joint leadership. The vertical axis is then used to illustrate the largely uncontrollable annual rate of market growth in which the business operates. In Figure 10.2 this ranges from 0 to 20 per cent, with a growth rate in excess of 10 per cent being seen as high.

The 2 × 2 matrix that emerges from this is based on four assumptions:

1. Margins and the funds generated increase with market share largely as the result of experience and scale effects

2. Sales growth demands cash to finance working capital and increases in capacity

3. Increases in market share generally need cash to support share-gaining tactics

4. Growth slows as the product reaches life cycle maturity, and at this stage a surplus of cash can often be generated without the organization experiencing any loss of market share; this can then be used to support products still in the growth stages of their life cycles.

The matrix itself is divided into four cells, each of which indicates a different type of business with different cash-using and cash-generating characteristics; the characteristics of each of these cells are discussed in Figure 10.3.

Having plotted the position of the organization's SBUs, the balance and health of the portfolio can be seen fairly readily. A balanced portfolio typically exhibits certain characteristics, including a mixture of cash cows and stars. By contrast, an unbalanced and potentially dangerous portfolio would have too many dogs or question marks, and too few stars and cash cows. The likely consequence of this is that insufficient cash will be generated on a day-to-day basis to fund or support the development of other SBUs.

Dogs (low share, low growth)
Dogs are those businesses that have a weak market share in a low-growth market. Typically they generate either a low profit or return a loss. The decision faced by the company is whether to hold on to the dog for strategic reasons (e.g. in the expectation that the market will grow, or because the product provides an obstacle, albeit a minor one, to a competitor). Dog businesses frequently take up more management time than they justify and there is often a case for phasing out (shooting) the product.

Question marks (low share, high growth)
Question marks are businesses operating in high-growth markets but with a low relative market share. They generally require considerable sums of cash since the firm needs to invest in plant, equipment and manpower to keep up with market developments. These cash requirements are, in turn, increased significantly if the company wants to improve its competitive position. The title of **question mark** comes about because management has to decide whether to continue investing in the SBU or withdrawing from the market.

Stars (high share, high growth)
Stars are those products which have moved to the position of leadership in a high growth market. Their cash needs are often high with the cash being spent in order to maintain market growth and keep competitors at bay. As stars also generate large amounts of cash, on balance there is unlikely to be any positive or negative cash flow until such time as the state of market growth declines. At this stage, provided the share has been maintained, the product should become a cash cow.

Cash cows (high share, low growth)
When the rate of market growth begins to fall, stars typically become the company's cash cows. The term cash cow is derived from the fact that it is these products which generate considerable sums of cash for the organization but which, because of the lower rate of growth, use relatively little. Because of the SBU's position in the market, economies of scale are often considerable and profit margins high.

Two further groups of SBU's have been identified by Barksdale and Harris (1982). These are **war horses** (high market share and negative growth) and **dodos** (low share, negative growth).

FIGURE 10.3   *The Boston Consulting Group's SBU classification*

Having identified the shape of the portfolio, the planner needs then to consider the objectives, strategy and budget for each SBU. In essence, four major strategies can be pursued:

1. *Build*. In following a building strategy, the primary objective is to increase the SBU's market share in order to strengthen its position. In doing this, short-term earnings and profits are quite deliberately forsaken in the expectation that long-term returns will be far greater. It is a strategy that is best suited to question marks, so that they become stars.

2. *Hold*. The primary objective in this case is to maintain the current share. It is the strategy that typically is used for cash cows to ensure they continue to generate the maximum amounts of cash.

3. *Harvest*. By following a harvesting strategy management tries to increase short-term cash flows as far as possible, even at the expense of the SBUs's longer-term future. It is a strategy best suited to cash cows that are weak or are in a market with seemingly only a limited future life. It is also used on occasions when the organization is in need of cash and is willing to mortgage the future of the product in the interests of short-term needs. Harvesting is also used for question marks when there appear to be few real opportunities to turn them into stars, and for dogs.

4. *Divest or terminate*. The essential objective here is to rid the organization of SBUs that act as a drain on profits, or to realize resources that can be used to greater effect elsewhere in the business. It is a strategy that again is often used for question marks and dogs.

Having decided which of these four broad approaches to follow, the strategist needs to consider the way in which each SBU is likely to change its position within the matrix over time. SBUs typically have a life cycle that begins with their appearance as question marks and then progresses through the stages of star, cash cow and, finally, dog. It is essential therefore that the BCG matrix is used not simply to obtain a snapshot of the portfolio as it stands currently, but rather to see how SBUs have developed so far and how they are likely to develop in the future. In doing this it is possible to gain an impression of the probable shape and health of the portfolio in several years' time, any gaps that are likely to exist, and hence the sort of strategic action that is needed in the form of decisions on new products, marketing support, and indeed product deletion. This process can then be taken a step further if similar charts are developed for each major competitor, since by doing this the strategist gains an insight to each competitor's portfolio strengths, weaknesses and potential gaps. The implications can then be fed back into the organization's own strategy.

The pitfalls of portfolio analysis

Although portfolio analysis is capable of providing a picture of the organization's current position, strategists need to adopt a degree of care in their interpretation and when developing future policy. A common mistake in portfolio analysis is to require each SBU to achieve an unrealistic growth rate or level of return: the essence of portfolio analysis involves recognizing that each SBU offers a different potential, and as such requires individual management. Other typical mistakes include:

- Investing too heavily in dogs, hoping that their position will improve, but failing

- Maintaining too many question marks and investing too little in each one, with the result that their position either fails to change or deteriorates. Question marks should either be dropped or receive the level of support needed to improve their segment position dramatically

- Draining the cash cows of funds and weakening them prematurely and unnecessarily. Alternatively, investing too much in cash cows, with the result that the funding available for question marks, stars and dogs is insufficient

- Seeing models of portfolio analysis as anything more than a *contributor* to decision-making. When the planner begins to use models such as the BCG growth–share matrix to replace evaluation and judgement by relying upon the essentially prescriptive ideas associated with each cell (e.g. *always* milk cash cows, *always* shoot dogs, and so on) as the basis for action, there is the potential for disaster. Given this, a summary of the pros and cons of the Boston matrix – and, by extension, a number of the other models of portfolio analysis examined later in this chapter – appears in Figure 10.4.

It should be apparent from the discussion so far that cash cows are essential to the health and long-term profitability of the organization, since they provide the funds needed if it is to develop and realize its full potential. The reality in many companies, however, is that cash cows are often in short supply and may already have been too vigorously milked. In 1988, for example, Booz Allen Hamilton estimated that, in traditional portfolio analysis terms, 72 per cent of business units in the USA were dogs, 15 per cent were cash cows, 10 per cent were question marks and only 3 per cent were stars. There is little evidence to suggest that the proportions in the UK at the time were radically different – or indeed that they have changed a great deal since then. Recognizing this, the strategist needs to focus upon the long term and consider how best to manage the portfolio and ensure that the organization benefits from a *succession* of cash cows. Any failure to do this is likely to lead to suboptimal management and the sorts of disaster sequences illustrated in Figure 10.5.

Pros	Cons
• It is an easy-to-use guide that helps managers to think about the investment needs of a portfolio of businesses	• It is a guide to investment rather than strategy
• It provides a useful basis for thinking about priorities across a spread of activities	• It rests on the implicit assumption that business planning is driven by just two factors, growth rate and market share, and in doing this ignores the spectrum of factors that influence profitability, such as competitive intensity, competitive advantage and customer needs
	• Cash flow is seen to be dependent upon market growth and market share. In practice, this is not necessarily the case
	• Market share is rarely as easily defined as the model suggests. With the erosion of geographic boundaries and the emergence of a radically different competitive environment, share is often far more fluid and difficult to measure
	• The model fails to come to terms with the nature of the strategy and form of competitive advantage that will lead to success

FIGURE 10.4   *The pros and cons of the Boston matrix*

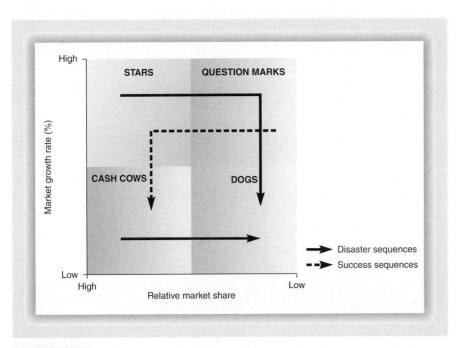

FIGURE 10.5   *Success and disaster sequences in the product portfolio (adapted from The Boston Consulting Group, 1970)*

A second model developed by the Boston Consulting Group – the growth–gain matrix – can go some way towards helping the strategist avoid problems such as those shown in Figure 10.5. The alternative matrix, which is often used in conjunction with growth–share analysis, illustrates the extent to which the growth of each product or SBU is keeping pace with market growth. The matrix, which is illustrated in Figure 10.6(a), features

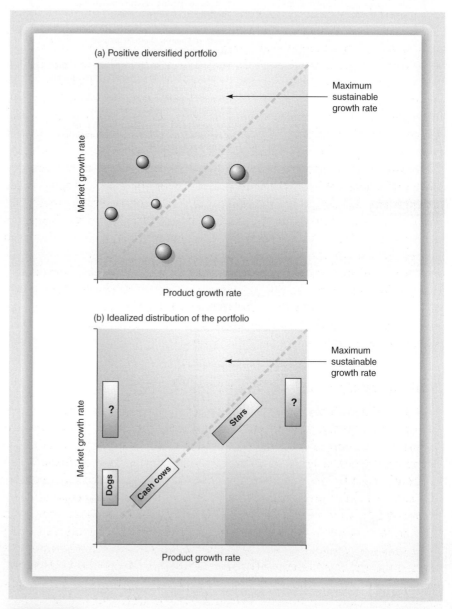

(a) Positive diversified portfolio

Market growth rate

Maximum sustainable growth rate

Product growth rate

(b) Idealized distribution of the portfolio

Market growth rate

Maximum sustainable growth rate

?

Stars

?

Dogs

Cash cows

Product growth rate

FIGURE 10.6 *The product portfolio and maximum sustainable growth (adapted from The Boston Consulting Group, 1970)*

the growth rate of the product (or of its capacity) on the horizontal axis, and the growth rate of the market on the vertical axis. Products with a growth rate just equal to the market growth rate are located on the diagonal. Share losers therefore appear above the diagonal, while share gainers are below.

Figure10.6(b) shows the ideal location of products within a portfolio. Here the dogs are clustered along or near the market growth axis, a position that reflects zero capacity growth. Cash cows are concentrated along the diagonal, showing that market share is being maintained. Stars should appear in the high-growth sector since they should be gaining (or at the very least holding) market share. Question marks then appear in two clusters, with one group receiving little support while the other is receiving the considerable support needed to maximize its chances of producing stars.

In discussing how best to use and interpret the growth–gain matrix, Alan Zakon (1971) of the Boston Consulting Group highlights the significance of the firm's *maximum sustainable growth*; this is plotted as a solid vertical line on the matrix. 'The weighted average growth rate of the products within the portfolio cannot', he emphasizes, 'exceed this maximum sustainable rate.' Where, however, the 'centre of gravity' (i.e. the weighted average growth rate) is to the left of this line, scope exists for further growth. This would typically be achieved by a series of strategy changes to reposition products. As an example of this, extra funds might be shifted to one of the stars in order to achieve even higher rates of growth.

Used in this way, the growth–gain matrix provides a basis for moving the portfolio closer to the 'ideal' position of maximum sustainable growth. Equally, by plotting growth–gain matrices for each major competitor, the strategist can, as with growth–share analysis, gain an insight into the areas of competitive emphasis and react accordingly.

Portfolio analysis: an initial assessment

Although the BCG matrices have a number of obvious attractions a word of caution is necessary, since they do not represent the ultimate management panacea that many of their advocates in the early days argued. It should be recognized that the practical value of portfolio analysis is influenced significantly both by the quality of the basic data inputs, many of which are difficult to define and measure, and the broader political and social environments within which decisions are made. It was therefore in an attempt to give greater specific recognition to a broader spectrum of factors that other approaches to portfolio analysis, including the General Electric multifactor matrix, the Shell directional policy matrix, the Arthur D. Little strategic condition matrix and Abell and Hammond's 3×3 relative investment opportunity chart, have been developed. It is to these models, which are concerned with market attractiveness and business position, that we now turn our attention.

10.5 MARKET ATTRACTIVENESS AND BUSINESS POSITION ASSESSMENT

The two BCG matrices discussed so far are capable of providing the strategist with an understanding of several important strategic relationships, including internal cash flows, and market share and growth trajectories. However, it is generally acknowledged that while the insights provided by these models are undoubtedly of significant value, they are in the majority of cases insufficient if worthwhile investment decisions affecting the future of the business are to be made. More specifically, critics such as Abell and Hammond (1979, pp. 211–12) have highlighted the three major shortcomings of relying simply on growth–share analysis:

1. Often, factors other than relative market share and industry growth play a significant role in influencing cash flow

2. Cash flow may well be viewed as being of less significance than rate of return on investment (ROI) as a means of comparing the attractiveness of investing in one business rather than another

3. Portfolio charts provide little real insight into how one business unit compares with another in terms of investment opportunity. Is it the case, for example, that a star is always a better target for investment than a cash cow? Equally, problems are often encountered in comparing question marks when trying to decide which should receive funds to make it a star, and which should be allowed to decline.

Recognition of these sorts of problems has led to the development of an approach that is labelled '*market attractiveness–business position assessment*', the best known of which is the General Electric model.

The General Electric multifactor portfolio model

The thinking behind General Electric's multifactor model is straightforward and is based on the argument that it is not always possible or appropriate to develop objectives or to make investment decisions for an SBU solely on the basis of its position in the growth–share matrix. The General Electric model therefore takes the general approach a step further by introducing a greater number of variables against which the position of SBUs might be plotted. This model, which appears in Figure 10.7, involves SBUs being rated against two principal dimensions:

1. Industry attractiveness

2. Business strengths.

The circles then represent not the size of the SBU but rather the size of the market in question, with the shaded part of the circle representing the

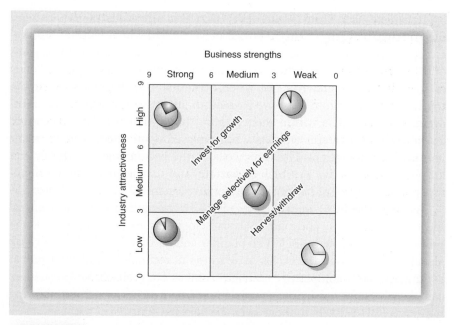

FIGURE 10.7 *The General Electric multifactor portfolio model*

SBU's market share. The thinking behind the choice of the two axes is based on the notion that the success of a company is determined, first, by the extent to which it operates in attractive markets, and secondly, by the extent to which it possesses the sorts of competitive business strengths needed to succeed in each of these markets. The failure on the part of the planning team to acknowledge this is likely to lead to long-term problems, since strong companies that operate in an unattractive market and weak companies operating in an attractive market will almost invariably underperform.

Recognizing this requires the planner to measure each of the two dimensions. In order to do this, the factors underlying each dimension must be identified, measured, and then combined to form an index. Although within each dimension the list of factors that combine to form a measure of attractiveness will be specific to each company, it is possible to identify the sorts of factor that will in nearly every instance be of relevance. *Industry attractiveness*, for example, is determined to a very large extent by the market's size, its rate of growth, the nature, degree and bases of competition, the pace of technological change, the extent to which it is constrained by government or legislative regulations, the opportunities for profit that exist, and so on. Equally, *business strengths* is influenced by such factors as market share, product quality, brand image and reputation, levels of management and operational capability, production capabilities, cost factors, the organization's distribution reach and strength, and the nature of the customer base and levels of loyalty.

It can be seen from Figure 10.7 that the nine cells of the General Electric matrix fall into three distinct areas, each of which requires a different approach to management and investment. The three cells at the top left of the matrix are the most attractive in which to operate, and require a policy of investment for growth. The three cells that run diagonally from the top right to the bottom left have a medium attractiveness rating: the management of the SBUs within this category should therefore be rather more cautious, with a greater emphasis being placed upon selective investment and earnings retention. The three cells at the bottom right of the matrix are the least attractive in which to operate, and management should therefore pursue a policy of harvesting and/or divestment.

As with the BCG matrix, it needs to be recognized that the General Electric approach to portfolio analysis also needs to take account of the probable future of each SBU. The planner should therefore attempt to look ahead by considering life cycles, new forms of technology and their probable impact, likely competitive strategies, and so on. Probable future changes can then be reflected in the matrix by adding a series of arrows showing how each SBU is likely to move over the next few years.

Other portfolio models

Although the BCG and GE models are undoubtedly the best-known approaches to portfolio analysis, a variety of other models have appeared over the years, including the Shell directional policy matrix (Shell Chemical Co., 1975), Abell and Hammond's 3 × 3 matrix (1979), and the Arthur D. Little strategic condition model (1974).

Shell's directional policy matrix (DPM), which is illustrated in Figure 10.8, again has two key dimensions: the company's *competitive capabilities* and the *prospects for sector profitability*. As with the General Electric matrix, each dimension is then subdivided into three categories. SBUs are located within the matrix, and the strategic options open to the company are then identified.

The directional policy matrix has in turn provided the basis for Abell and Hammond's 3 × 3 chart (see Figure 10.9), which is designed to depict relative investment opportunities. Although the terminology used by Abell and Hammond differs slightly from that of Shell's DPM – company competitive capability, for example, is referred to as business position, while prospects for sector profitability is termed market attractiveness – the thinking behind the model is similar, and indeed can be seen to link back to the General Electric approach.

The Arthur D. Little (ADL) model, which is illustrated in Figure 10.10, is again similar in concept, although here the two dimensions used are the firm's *competitive position* and the *stage of industry maturity*.

Competitive position, it is suggested, is influenced by the geographical scope of the industry and the specific product–market sectors in which the

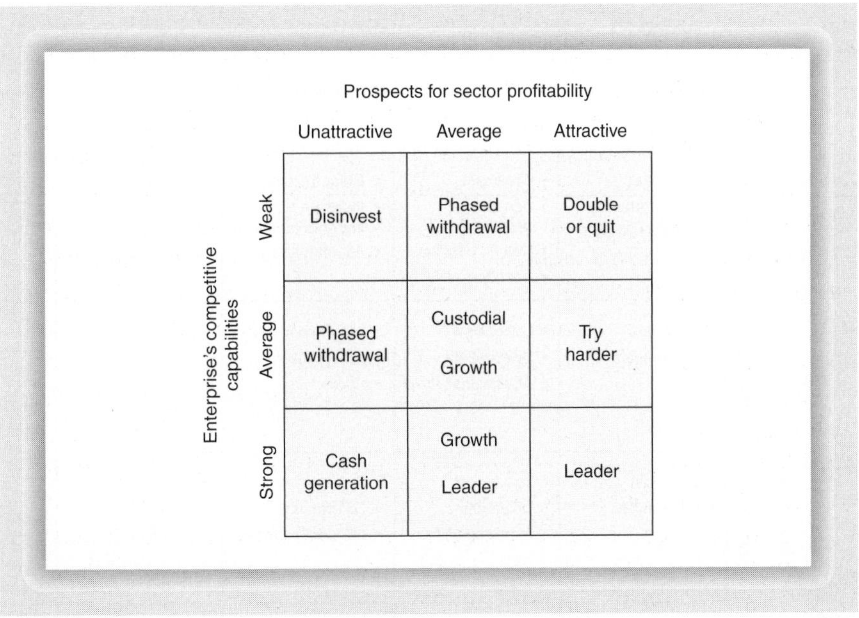

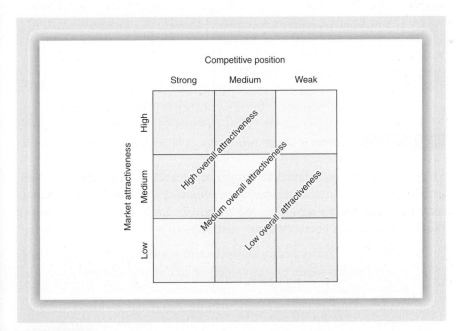

FIGURE 10.8   The Shell directional policy matrix (adapted from Shell Chemical Co., 1975)

FIGURE 10.9   Abell and Hammond's 3 × 3 investment opportunity matrix (adapted from Abell and Hammond, 1979)

		Stage of industry maturity			
		Embryonic	Growth	Mature	Ageing
Competitive position	Dominant	• Grow fast • Build barriers • Act offensively	• Grow fast • Aim for cost leadership • Defend position • Act offensively	• Defend position • Increase the importance of cost • Act offensively	• Defend position • Focus • Consider withdrawal
	Strong	• Grow fast • Differentiate	• Lower cost • Differentiate • Attack small firms	• Lower cost • Differentiate • Focus	• Harvest
	Favourable	• Grow fast • Differentiate	• Lower cost • Differentiate • Attack small firms	• Focus • Differentiate • Hit smaller firms	• Harvest
	Tenable	• Grow the industry • Focus	• Hold-on or withdraw • Niche • Aim for growth	• Hold-on or withdraw • Niche	• Withdraw
	Weak	• Search for a niche • Attempt to catch others	• Niche or withdraw	• Withdraw	• Withdraw

FIGURE 10.10　*The Arthur D. Little strategic condition matrix (adapted from Arthur D. Little, 1974)*

SBU operates. It is not therefore simply market share that influences competitive position, but also competitive economics and a series of other factors, including technology. This led Arthur D. Little to the recognition of five main categories of competitive position:

1. *Dominant.* This is a comparatively rare position, and in many cases is attributable either to a monopoly or to a strong and protected technological leadership. The implications are that the firm is able to exert considerable influence over the behaviour of others in the industry, and has a wide variety of strategic options open to it.

2. *Strong.* By virtue of this position the firm has a considerable degree of freedom over its choice of strategy, and is often able to act without its market position being unduly threatened by competitors.

3. *Favourable*. This position, which generally comes about when the industry is fragmented and no one competitor stands out clearly, results in the market leaders having a reasonable degree of freedom. Companies with a favourable market position often have strengths that can be exploited by particular strategies, and hence a greater than average opportunity to increase market share.

4. *Tenable*. Although firms within this category are able to perform satisfactorily and can justify staying in the industry, they are generally vulnerable in the face of increased competition from stronger and more proactive companies in the market. The opportunities for an organization to strengthen its position tend to be lower than average. The profitability of the tenable firm is best achieved and sustained through a degree of specialization.

5. *Weak*. The performance of firms in this category is generally unsatisfactory, although opportunities for improvement do exist. Often, however, the firm is either too big and inefficient to compete with any real degree of effectiveness, or too small to cope with competitive pressures. Unless the firm changes, it is ultimately likely to be forced out of the market or to exit of its own accord.

A sixth position, that of *non-viability*, can be added to this list, and applies when the firm's performance is unsatisfactory and there are few (if any) opportunities for improvement. In these circumstances it is essentially a case of the strategist recognizing the reality of the situation and withdrawing from the market in the least costly way.

The second dimension of the model – the *stage of industry maturity*, ranging from embryonic to ageing – has, Arthur D. Little argues, significant implications for the strategies open to the organization. Thus once a basic strategy has been identified, there are certain things the strategist must do, might do, and should not do if consistency is to be maintained.

This combination of competitive position and industry maturity provides the basis for determining the SBU's strategic condition and, subsequently, the identification and evaluation of the strategic options open to the company. This typically is a choice between investing in order to strengthen or maintain position, spending in order to maintain the *status quo*, harvesting, or exiting from the industry. In commenting on this, Arthur D. Little states that 'there is a finite set of available strategies for each Business Unit' and that these can be seen in terms of six generic strategic groups:

1. Market strategies (domestic and international)

2. Product strategies

3. Technology strategies

4. Operations strategies

5. Management and systems strategies

6. Retrenchment strategies.

In choosing among these, Arthur D. Little identifies several guiding principles, the most important of which is that 'strategy selection [should] be driven by the condition of the business, not the condition of its managers'. In making this comment, Arthur D. Little is arguing for realism in strategic planning and that it is this that should prevail if the organization is not to overreach itself.

10.6 CRITICISMS OF PORTFOLIO ANALYSIS

Despite the rapid growth, adoption and indeed the apparent attractions of the underlying logic of portfolio analysis, it has been subject to a considerable and growing volume of criticism over the past 15 years. Although it is acknowledged by its critics that the sort of models referred to here have encouraged managers to think strategically, consider the economics of their businesses in greater detail, examine the nature of interrelationships and adopt a more proactive approach to management, many writers have argued that the models are generally too simplistic in their structure. In commenting on this, Kotler (1987, p. 77) suggests that:

> Portfolio analysis models must be used cautiously. They may lead the company to place too much emphasis on market-share growth and entry into high growth businesses, or to neglect its current businesses. The model's results are sensitive to the ratings and weights and can be manipulated to produce a desired location in the matrix. Furthermore, since these models use an averaging process, two or more businesses may end up in the same cell position but differ greatly in the underlying ratings and weights. Many businesses will end up in the middle of the matrix as the result of compromises in ratings, and this makes it hard to know what the appropriate strategy should be. Finally, the models fail to delineate the synergies between two or more businesses, which means that making decisions for one business at a time may be risky.

These sorts of criticisms have been echoed by others, including Baker (1985, p. 75), who has pointed to the way in which many firms managed to cope with the recession of the 1970s and early 1980s not because of a portfolio of products or even a high market share, but rather as the result of a strategy of concentrating upon a single product and market. Equally, many other firms, and especially those in mature markets, he suggests, have not only survived but have also prospered despite having products that, in portfolio analysis terms, would be universally classified as dogs. Brownlie (1983) also discusses these criticisms in some detail, and is worth quoting at length. He suggests that:

> *Additional criticism of the BP [business portfolio] approach tends to focus on its over-simplified, and somewhat misleading, representation of possible strategy positions; and its use of the dimensions growth rate and market share, which are themselves considered to be inadequate measures of, respectively, industry attractiveness and competitive position. As Wensley concludes, this approach to strategy development 'encourages the use of general rather than specific criteria as well as implying assumptions about mechanisms of corporate financing and market behaviour which are rather unnecessary or false'. Indeed, it has been observed that market leadership does not always offer the benefits of lower costs, more positive cash flow and higher profits. On the contrary: the number of highly viable companies occupying market 'niches' is legion, and growing by the day. Recent trends that have favoured the development of greater specialization in some markets include the growth of private label consumer products and the emergence of differential preferences in some industrial markets, for example computers, as customers become familiar with product, or develop relevant in-house expertise.*

The BP approach also tends to overlook other important and strategic factors that are more a function of the external competitive environment – for example, technological change; barriers to entry; social, legal, political and environmental pressures; union and related human factors; elasticity of demand; and cyclicality of sales. The application of the BP to strategic decision-taking is in the manner of a diagnostic rather than a prescriptive aid in instances where observed cash flow patterns do not conform with those on which the four product–market categories are based. This commonly occurs where changes in product–market strategies have short-term transient effects on cash flow.

The limitations and problems of portfolio analysis have also been highlighted by McDonald (1990), albeit from a rather different viewpoint to that of most writers. McDonald suggests that the gap between theory and practice is greater in the case of marketing than in any other discipline. One consequence of this, according to McDonald, is that little evidence exists to show that some of the more substantive techniques such as the Ansoff Matrix, the Boston Matrix, and the Directional Policy Matrix are used in practice. This is supported by research findings not just in the UK but also in Australia and Hong Kong. Reid and Hinckley (1989, p. 9), for example, concluded:

> *Respondents were asked which techniques they were familiar with. The results were skewed towards ignorance of all the techniques to which they were exposed. The majority were not familiar with any by name.*

Similarly, from a study of Australian management practice, McColl-Kennedy *et al.* (1990, p. 28) stated that 'The awareness and usage of planning tools is low'.

McDonald suggests that there are three possible explanations for this:

1. Companies have never heard of them

2. Companies have heard of them but do not understand them

3. Companies have heard of them and tried them, and have found that they are largely irrelevant.

More fundamentally, however, he argues that the gap between theory and practice is due to the failure of most writers' attempts to explain the strategic thinking underpinning such techniques. He illustrates this by discussing the directional policy matrix, which, he suggests, is a well-known but under-utilized and misunderstood planning tool. This misunderstanding is, in one form or another, common to virtually all approaches to portfolio analysis. However, in the case of the DPM, the problems stem from the complexity of the analytical process that is needed if the model is to be used effectively. Thus:

> *The criteria for the vertical axis (market attractiveness) can only be determined once the population of 'markets' has been specified. Once determined, those criteria cannot be changed during the exercise. Another common mistake is to misunderstand that unless the exercise is carried out twice – once for t0 and once for t + 3 – the circles cannot move vertically. Also, the criteria have to change for every 'market' assessed on the horizontal axis each time a company's strength in that market is assessed. Some way has also to be found of quantifying the horizontal axis to prevent every market appearing in the left-hand box of the matrix. If we add to this just some of the further complexities involved – such as the need to take the square root of the volume or value to determine circle diameter, the need to understand that the term 'attractiveness' has more to do with future potential than with any externally-derived criteria and so on – we begin to understand why practising managers rarely use the device.*

Despite criticisms such as these, portfolio analysis has many defenders, including Day (1983), who suggests that:

> *Current criticisms (of portfolio analysis) are unwarranted because they reflect a serious misunderstanding of the proper role of these analytical methods ... what must be realized is that these methods can facilitate the strategic planning process and serve as a rich source of ideas about possible strategic options. But on their own, these methods cannot present the appropriate strategy or predict the consequences of a specific change in strategy.*

In many ways, Day's comments help to put the true role and value of portfolio analysis into perspective. It is not (as some managers appeared to believe in the early days) a set of techniques that guarantees greater success. Rather it is an approach to the formulation of strategy that, if used in the way intended, should force a deeper analysis and give far greater recognition to the interrelationships and implications of these interrelationships to the portfolio of brands or businesses being managed by the company. This in turn should lead to a far firmer base for effective decision-making.

This final point in particular was highlighted in 1979 by the results of a *Harvard Business Review*-sponsored study of strategic portfolio planning practices in *Fortune*'s 1000 companies. The study, by Haspelagh (1982), found that portfolio planning helped managers to strengthen their planning processes, particularly in divisionalized and diversified organizations. The secret to success, however, was found to lie not just in the techniques themselves, but also in the challenge of incorporating the theory of the techniques into managerial practice. The findings of the study did highlight several problems of portfolio planning, including the following:

- If done properly the process is time-consuming, and firms often experience difficulties of implementation

- If the techniques are seen simply as analytical tools, the company sees only limited benefits

- All too often the strategist focuses upon factors that are in a sense inappropriate, e.g. levels of cost efficiency rather than organizational responsiveness

- The techniques are of only limited value in addressing the issue of new business generation.

Despite problems such as these, the techniques were found to be popular for a number of reasons:

1. They were felt to lead to improvements in strategies

2. The allocation of resources was improved

3. They provided an improved base for adapting planning to the needs of individual businesses

4. Levels of control improved.

10.7 SUMMARY

In this, the first of three chapters on strategy, we have taken as our primary focus the nature and development of portfolio analysis. As a prelude to this we examined the development of strategic perspectives since the 1970s,

highlighting the way in which the environmental turbulence that characterized the early 1970s led to many managers rethinking their approaches to
running their businesses. The new planning perspective that emerged was,
we suggested, based on three central premises:

1. A need to view and manage the company's businesses in a similar
   way to an investment portfolio

2. An emphasis upon each business's future profit potential

3. The adoption of a *strategic* perspective to the management of each
   business.

The starting point for portfolio analysis involves identifying the organization's *strategic business units*, an SBU being an element of the business
as a whole that:

- Offers scope for independent planning

- Has its own set of competitors

- Has a manager with direct profit responsibility who also has control
  over the profit-influencing factors.

A variety of approaches to portfolio analysis and planning have been
developed, the best-known of which are:

- The Boston Consulting Group's growth–share matrix

- The General Electric multifactor matrix

- The Shell directional policy matrix

- The Arthur D. Little strategic condition matrix

- Abell and Hammond's 3 × 3 investment opportunity chart.

The conceptual underpinnings in each case are broadly similar, with consideration being given in one form or another to the SBU's *competitive
position* and *market attractiveness/potential.* Each of the portfolio models
also encompasses a series of strategic guidelines, and these were examined.
 Against this background, we focused upon the limitations of portfolio
analysis. Although it is acknowledged that these models have encouraged
managers to think strategically, to consider the economics of their businesses in greater detail and to adopt a generally more proactive approach
to management, critics have argued that the models are overly simplistic in
their structure and often require data inputs that are complex and difficult
to obtain. Because of this, it is suggested, usage levels are generally low.

The Formulation of Strategy 2: Generic Strategies and the Significance of Competitive Advantage

11.1 LEARNING OBJECTIVES

When you have read this chapter you should be able to understand:

(a) the need for a clear statement of marketing strategy;

(b) the types of marketing strategy open to an organization;

(c) the forces that govern competition within an industry and how they interact;

(d) the sources of competitive advantage and how competitive advantage might be leveraged.

11.2 INTRODUCTION

Having used the techniques discussed in Chapter 10 to identify the strengths and weaknesses of the product portfolio, the strategist should be in a far stronger position to focus upon the ways in which the organization is most capable of developing. Against this background, we now turn our attention to an examination of some of the principal factors that influence marketing strategy. We begin by examining Michael Porter's work, in which emphasis is given to the need for a clear statement of a generic strategy and for this to be based upon a detailed understanding of corporate capability and competitive advantage. The remainder of the chapter then focuses upon the nature, significance and sources of competitive advantage, the ways in which, in many markets, competitive advantage is being eroded, and how competitive advantage might possibly be leveraged. We then build upon this in Chapter 12, with an examination of the ways in which market leaders, followers, challengers and nichers might make use of this thinking.

However, before doing this it needs to be emphasized that, although a great deal of thinking on strategy revolves around the idea of a (high) degree of competitive antagonism, the reality in many markets is that a competitive complacency emerges, and indeed is encouraged, so that the status quo remains unchanged. In those markets where major changes in competitive position do occur, this may be the result of fat, lazy, complacent and arrogant managerial thinking that leads to the firm losing its position. Amongst those to have fallen victim of this are Marks & Spencer in the mid to late 1990s, and the major flag carriers in the airlines market. More often though, it is because the management team of a competitor desperately wants to improve its position. It is this mindset of a quiet desperation and a commitment either to exploiting competitors' vulnerabilities or to redefining the market that is an important characteristic of firms that typically manage to strengthen their position.

11.3 TYPES OF STRATEGY

Throughout this book we have tried to give full emphasis to the need for objectives and strategy to be realistic, obtainable and based firmly on corporate capability. In practice, of course, this translates into an almost infinite number of strategies that are open to an organization. Porter (1980) has, however, pulled them together and identified three generic types of strategy – *overall cost leadership*, *differentiation* and *focus* – that provide a meaningful basis for strategic thinking (see Figure 11.1). In doing this, he gives emphasis to the need for the strategist to identify a clear and meaningful selling proposition for the organization. In other words, what is our competitive stance, and what do we stand for in the eyes of our customers? Any failure on the part of the strategist to identify and communicate the selling proposition and strategy is, he suggests, likely to lead to a dilution of the offer and to the company ending up as stuck in the middle or, as it appears in Figure 11.1, a middle-of-the-roader heading into the marketing wilderness.

Porter's thesis is therefore straightforward: to compete successfully the strategist needs to select a generic strategy and pursue it consistently. The ways in which this might be done and the benefits and the problems that might possibly be encountered are referred to in Figure 11.2. Obviously, there is no single 'best' strategy, even within a given industry, and the task faced by the strategist involves selecting the strategic approach that will

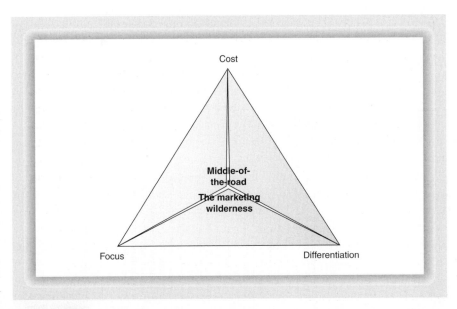

FIGURE 11.1   *Porter's three generic strategies (adapted from Porter, 1980)*

best allow it to maximize its strengths *vis-à-vis* its competitors. This needs to be done, Porter (1979) suggests, by taking into account a variety of factors, the five most significant of which are:

1. The bargaining power of suppliers

2. The bargaining power of customers

3. The threat of new entrants to the industry

4. The threat of substitute products or services

5. The rivalry among current competitors.

Taken together, these factors represent the forces governing the nature and intensity of competition within an industry, and they are the background against which the choice of a generic strategy should be made.

In identifying the three specified generic strategies, Porter suggests that the firms that pursue a particular strategy aimed at the same market or market segment make up a *strategic group*. It is the firm that then manages to pursue the strategy most effectively that will generate the greatest profits. Thus, in the case of firms pursuing a low-cost strategy, it is the firm that ultimately achieves the lowest cost that will do best.

Type of strategy	Ways to achieve the strategy	Benefits	Possible problems	When to use it
Cost leadership	Size and economies of scale Globalization Relocating to low-cost parts of the world Modification/simplification of designs Greater labour effectiveness Greater operating effectiveness Strategic alliances New sources of supply Learning Cost linkages Integration Timing Superior labour and management Advanced technology Smart buying	The ability to: • Outperform rivals • Erect barriers to entry • Resist the five forces	Vulnerability to even lower cost operators Possible price wars The difficulty of sustaining it in the long term	In a price-driven market or in order to gain leadership from a complacent and a high-cost competitor
Focus	Concentration upon one or a small number of segments The creation of a strong and specialist reputation	A more detailed understanding of particular segments The creation of barriers to entry A reputation for specialization The ability to concentrate efforts	Limited opportunities for sector growth The possibility of outgrowing the market The decline of the sector A reputation for specialization which ultimately inhibits growth and development into other sectors	When you are new to a market or have a small market share
Differentiation	The creation of strong brand identities The consistent pursuit of those factors which customers perceive to be important High performance in one or more of a spectrum of attributes The creation of strategic breakpoints The achievement of cost parity or cost proximity relative to its competitor in all areas that do **not** affect differentiation Additional features Packaging innovation Distribution innovation Speed of distribution Distribution breadth and/or depth Higher service levels Better after sales service Superior financing deals Greater flexibility Focused relationship building	A distancing from others in the market The creation of a major competitive advantage Flexibility	The difficulties of sustaining the bases for differentiation Possibly higher costs The difficulty of achieving true and meaningful differentiation Creating differences that customers do not value Focusing too much on the core product in developing bases for differentiation Differentiating on dimensions that become less important to customers over time Losing competitive cost proximity Failing to develop barriers to deter imitation and customer switching	In crowded markets where points of difference are often small, differentiation must be based on factors that competitors see to be important. The points of differentiation must be significant and offer demonstrably more value, making it difficult for the competitor to follow or to copy

FIGURE 11.2 Selecting and pursuing a generic strategy

11.4   PORTER'S THREE GENERIC COMPETITIVE STRATEGIES

Overall cost leadership

By pursuing a strategy of cost leadership, the organization concentrates upon achieving the lowest costs of production and distribution so that it has the *capability* of setting its prices at a lower level than its competitors. Whether it then chooses to do this depends on its objectives and its perception of the market. Saunders (1987, p. 12), for example, has pointed to IBM and Boeing, both of which were for many years cost leaders who chose to use their lower costs not to reduce prices but rather to generate higher returns, which were then invested in marketing, R&D and manufacturing as a means of maintaining or strengthening their position. More commonly, however, firms that set out to be cost leaders then use this lower cost base to reduce prices and in this way build market share. Amongst those to have done this are Amstrad (now trading as Viglen) in the 1980s and, more recently, supermarkets such as Netto, Lidl, Asda and Aldi, the low-cost airlines such as easyJet (see Illustration 11.3) and Ryanair and, of course, Wal-Mart. With sales in 2008 of more than $374 billion, Wal-Mart is now not just the world's largest retailer, but the world's largest company. In reaching this position, the company has pursued a focused and aggressive low price policy that involves working with organizations throughout the supply chain to drive out costs and drive down price.

Although cost reduction has always been an important element of competitive strategy, Porter (1980, p. 35) has commented that it became increasingly popular in the 1970s, largely because of a greater awareness of the experience curve concept. For it to succeed, he suggests that:

> *Cost leadership requires aggressive construction of efficient-scale facilities, vigorous pursuit of cost reductions from experience, tight cost and overhead control, avoidance of marginal customer accounts, and cost minimization in areas like R&D, service, sales force, advertising, and so on.*

In tackling costs the marketing planner therefore needs to recognize in advance the potential complexity of the task, since the evidence suggests that true cost leaders generally achieve this by very tight and consistent control across all areas of the business, including engineering, purchasing, manufacturing, distribution and marketing. An important additional element, of course, is the scale of operations and the scope that exists for economies of scale. However, scale alone does not necessarily lead to lower costs; rather it provides management with an opportunity to learn how the triad of technology, management and labour can be used more effectively. Whether these opportunities are then seized depends on the management stance and determination to take advantage of the potential that exists for cost cutting. Research has shown, for example, that the Japanese are most adept at gaining experience, doing so at a faster rate than the Americans, who in turn are faster than the Europeans.

While the experience curve can provide the basis for cost reductions, manufacturers can also turn to a variety of other areas, including:

- *The globalization of operations*, including brands, in order to benefit from the economies that are not possible by operating purely on a regional basis

- *Concentrating the manufacturing effort* in one or two very large plants in countries such as South Korea, India, China, Taiwan and the Philippines, which (currently at least) offer a low-cost base

- *Modifying designs* to simplify the manufacturing process and make use of new materials

- Achieving greater labour effectiveness by investing in new plant and processes.

A strategy of cost and price leadership has also been at the heart of Ikea's success. With almost 8 per cent of the UK furniture market, the company's aggressive approach to the management of cost is reflected not just in the design and manufacturing processes and the economies of scale from its retail outlets, but also in the way in which the company use its own employees as models for the Ikea catalogue.

The potential benefits of being a low-cost producer are quite obviously significant, since the organization is then in a far stronger position to resist all five competitive forces, outperform its rivals and erect barriers to entry that will help protect the organization's long-term position. In practice, however, many organizations find the long-term pursuit and maintenance of a cost-leadership strategy to be difficult. The Japanese, for example, based much of their success in the 1960s on aggressive cost management but then found that, because of a combination of rising domestic costs and the emergence of new and even lower-cost competitors such as Taiwan, Korea and Philippines, the position was not necessarily tenable in the long term. Although this realization coincided in many cases with a desire on the part of firms to move further up-market, where the scope for premium pricing is greater, the Japanese experience helps to illustrate the potential danger of an over-reliance upon cost leadership. It is largely because of this that many organizations opt sooner or later for an alternative policy, such as that of differentiation.

The difficulties of maintaining a cost-leadership position were also illustrated in the late 1980s and early 1990s in the UK grocery retailing sector, where the low-cost position had been occupied with some considerable success for a number of years by Kwik Save. The organization came under attack from an aggressive new German entrant to the market, Aldi, and then from the Danish company, Netto. Faced with this, Kwik Save was forced into deciding whether to place greater emphasis on differentiation.

The effect of Aldi's entrance was not felt only by Kwik Save. Others, such as Sainsbury's and Tesco, both of which had for a number of years pursued with considerable success a strategy of differentiation, were also forced to respond, albeit in a less direct way. In part, this need to respond can be seen as virtually inevitable in any mature market where the opportunities for substantial growth are limited and a new entrant is therefore able to gain sales only at the expense of firms already in the market. (This is sometimes referred to as a zero-sum game, in that one organization's gain is necessarily another organization's loss.)

It is largely because of the difficulties of maintaining the lowest cost position over time and the vulnerability to a price-led attack that many organizations view cost leadership with a degree of caution and opt instead for one or other of Porter's generic strategies. Most frequently this proves to be differentiation.

Differentiation

By pursuing a strategy of differentiation, the organization gives emphasis to a particular element of the marketing mix that is seen by customers to be important and, as a result, provides a meaningful basis for competitive advantage. The firm might therefore attempt to be the quality leader (Mercedes-Benz with cars, Bang & Olufsen with hi-fi, and Marks & Spencer with food), service leader (Ritz–Carlton), marketing leader (the Japanese with cars), or the technological leader (Makita with rechargeable power tools in the early 1980s and Dolby with noise suppression circuits for tape decks). Other potential bases for differentiation include:

- Speed, by being the first into new market segments
- Levels of reliability that are higher than those of the competition
- Design
- Levels of service and delight
- Unique product features
- The brand image and personality
- New technologies
- A greater number and/or more relevant product features
- Stronger and more meaningful relationships.

Differentiation can also be achieved by means of the brand image and packaging, a ploy that is particularly suited to mature markets in which

> ### Illustration 11.1 Differentiate or die
>
> Over the past 10 years the word 'unique' has become one of the most frequently used – and abused – words in the marketing lexicon. At the same time, 'unique selling proposition' has become an ever more tired phrase that is deployed more in hope than expectation. It is because of this that Jack Trout, seen by many to be the father of positioning, argues that, in a world in which everything can be copied, it is the company's intangible assets that provide the basis for real differentiation. In his book *Differentiate or Die* he suggests that marketing planners should not bother extolling the traditional virtues of quality, customer orientation or even creativity, since these are too easily copied. Instead, he suggests that what really matters are the points of difference rooted in areas such as ownership, leadership, heritage and topicality. Being different on the surface is simply not enough any more. Instead, it needs to be based on issues that are far more fundamental. This focus upon differentiation is of course not new. But the sheer proliferation of products and services is making it imperative to determine just what, if anything, really does make a company different. Trout argues that difference is only real if its essence can be expressed in just one word. In the case of Microsoft, the company could, throughout the 1990s, claim that its describing word was 'innovative'; with its problems with American anti-trust legislation, this is no longer the case. Equally, Marks & Spencer used to be synonymous with 'value' whilst BA was 'British' and Gap was 'cool'. All three have, however, lost sight of their core differentiation. By contrast, easyJet is value, Virgin is 'flair', Nike is 'heroism', Sony is 'miniaturized perfection' and Disney is 'fun'.
>
> *Source*: 'Can You Sum Up Your Brand With A Single Word?', *Marketing*, 20 April 2000, p. 20.

the products are for the most part physically indistinguishable. This might arguably include cigarettes and beer, where blind tests have shown that even highly brand-loyal customers experience difficulties in identifying their favourite brand. The significance of labels and brand images, and hence their potential for differentiation, is also shown in the fashion clothing industry, where brand names and logos such as Benetton, Nike and Lacoste are often prominently displayed and, by virtue of the images associated with them, used as the basis for premium pricing. The fundamental importance of differentiation has been highlighted by Trout and Rifkin (2000), who argue that far too often planners misunderstand what exactly the term means; this is discussed in Illustration 11.1.

As an example of how a strategy of differentiation can be developed and used as the basis of competitive advantage, some of the major airlines, such as Emirates, Singapore Airlines and Cathay Pacific, have all used service to distance themselves from many of the other major flag carriers. In the case of first-class and, increasingly, business-class travellers, the fight for long-haul travellers at the beginning of the twenty-first century revolved around the introduction of beds that folded flat so that passengers could sleep more easily.

Differentiation can, however, prove costly if the basis for differentiation that is chosen subsequently proves to be inappropriate. Sony, for example, developed the Betamax format for its video recorders, but ultimately found that the market preferred JVC's VHS system. Despite this, differentiation is potentially a very powerful basis for strategic development, as companies such as Bang & Olufsen, Bose and Tesco have all demonstrated. Its potential is also illustrated by a McGraw-Hill study of industrial buying, which estimated that most buyers would require incentives that equated to a price reduction of between 8 and 10 per cent before considering a switch to a new supplier. In commenting on this, Baker (1985, p. 110) suggests that:

> *Assuming this applies to the average product with a minimum of objective differentiation, it is clear that sellers of highly differentiated products can require an even larger premium. Given higher margins the firm following a differentiated strategy is able to plough back more into maintaining the perception of differentiation through a policy of new product development, promotional activity, customer service, etc., and thereby strengthen the barriers to entry for would-be competitors.*

It should be apparent from this that, if a strategy of differentiation is to succeed, there is a need for a very different set of skills and attitudes than is suited to cost leadership. Instead of a highly developed set of cost control skills, the strategist needs to be far more innovative and flexible so that me-too companies are kept at a distance.

The strategic significance of differentiation has also been highlighted by Godin (2004), who in his book *Purple Cow* argues that far too many products, services and strategies are, like a large herd of black and white cows, essentially the same and therefore boring and largely invisible. What is needed, he suggests, is something distinctive as remarkable – like a purple cow – that will stand out and be immediately recognizable. Amongst those to have done this are companies such as the budget airline JetBlue, the water retailer Portland Spring, Ikea, the phone service 1-800-COLLECT, and the television show *South Park*.

Focus

The third of the generic strategies identified by Porter involves the organization in concentrating its efforts upon one or more narrow market segments, rather than pursuing a broader-based strategy. By doing this the firm is able to build a greater in-depth knowledge of each of the segments, as well as creating barriers to entry by virtue of its specialist reputation. Having established itself, the firm will typically then, depending upon the specific demands of the market, develop either a cost-based or differentiated strategy. Among those that have used this approach successfully, at least in the short term, at various stages are Laura Ashley, Thorntons (the chocolate manufacturers) and Land Rover. Other firms that have used a focused strategy are Morgan with cars, Steinway with pianos and, perhaps to a lesser degree, Apple with an emphasis upon the design world.

One of the biggest problems faced by companies adopting this approach stems paradoxically from its potential for success since, as the organization increases in size, there is a tendency both to outgrow the market and to lose the immediacy of contact that is often needed. As a general rule, therefore, a focused strategy is often best suited to smaller firms, since it is typically these that have the flexibility to respond quickly to the specialized needs of small segments. (At this stage, it may be useful to refer to the discussion of the supernichers in section 8 of Chapter 12.)

Specializing in this way also enables the organization to achieve at least some of the benefits of the other two strategies since, although in absolute terms the scale of operations may be limited, the organization may well have the largest economies of scale *within* the chosen segment. Equally, the greater the degree of concentration upon a target market, the more specialized is the firm's reputation and hence the greater the degree of perceived product differentiation.

Although Porter presents competitive strategies in this way, many companies succeed not by a blind adherence to any one approach, but rather by a combination of ideas. For many years, for example, the buying power and expertise of Marks & Spencer made it a (relatively) low-cost operator, whilst at the same time it differentiated itself on the basis of service and quality. Equally, Porsche pursues a strategy that combines both focus and differentiation.

It follows from this that the identification, development and maintenance of a long term competitive advantage, and hence a strong selling proposition, is at the very heart of an effective marketing strategy. In practice though, many organizations find this to be a difficult exercise, something that Levi's learned in the 1990s (see Illustration 11.2).

Without an advantage, however, the stark reality is that the organization runs the risk of drifting into the strategic twilight zone of being a middle-of-the-roader or, in Porter's terms, 'stuck in the middle'.

Porter's generic strategies: a brief comment

Although Porter believes strategy needs to be thought about in terms of these three generic approaches, this thinking has been the subject of a considerable amount of criticism in recent years. Given this, Figure 11.3 summarizes the pros and cons of the approach.

Illustration 11.2   The fall and rise of Levi's: the long-term problems of market fragmentation

For eleven consecutive years between 1985 and 1996, Levi's saw its global sales rise, culminating in a peak that year of $7.1 billion. Two years later, with sales in the UK having dropped by 23 per cent, Levi's was forced to rethink its strategy. Having relied for too long upon 501s and a mass-market strategy that allowed a number of fashion brands such as Diesel and YSL to erode its share in a declining or fragmenting market, the company 'fought back with a radically different approach.

In commenting on this, Ellsworth (2000) highlights the way in which:

> The company decided that innovation was the key and in October 1998 shifted its focus from individual product lines to a portfolio of brand bases – aligned with consumer segments – with particular emphasis on the 15- to 24-year-old youth sector. This enabled Levi's to take on smaller brands such as Diesel, own labels such as Gap and some designer ranges. But, like others, Levi's also faced competition from retail areas such as mobiles, CDs and DVDs.
>
> Levi's further rationalized its lines by pulling out of the European children's jeans market to concentrate on 15- to 24-year-olds.

At the same time, the company also launched three premium sub-brands (Levi's Vintage, based on the original Levi's jeans from the 1850s; Red, a 'luxury' sub-brand; and ICD (a joint initiative with Philips that incorporates 'wearable electronics' such as mobile phones into its design) and its Advanced Retail Concept (ARC), which replaced the traditional American theme with a lighter store design that included specific youth-oriented areas. The company also attacked the youth market through the sponsorship of live music events.

But although the strategy and the fight-back has been successful, the question of whether it is capable of achieving its high point of a 21.5 per cent share of the UK market is debatable. At the heart of Levi's problems is that the jeans market, in common with many brand-driven markets, has fragmented. Faced with fifteen rather than five other players, the fight for share becomes ever more desperate.

Source: Ellsworth (2000).

11.5   COMPETITIVE ADVANTAGE AND ITS PIVOTAL ROLE IN STRATEGIC MARKETING PLANNING

Making use of the value chain

The most successful species are those which adapt best to the changing environment. The most successful individuals are those with the greatest competitive advantage over the others.

Charles Darwin, *The Origin of Species by Means of Natural Selection*, 1859

Pros	Cons
• The model highlights the significance of competitive advantage as the basis for competitive success • The idea of three generic strategies gives recognition to the way in which, regardless of the wide variety of variables and industry situations faced by managers, there are in practice only a limited number of meaningful strategic options	• The idea of lowest cost as a meaningful strategic option has, as Porter has acknowledged, largely been invalidated by the pace of change. The notion that economies of scale represent the basis for a sustainable position for organizations faced on the one hand by ultra low-cost and maverick companies from the less-developed world, and on the other hand by fast-moving small companies in the developed world, is now no longer seen to be realistic • The thinking that underpins the model is essentially manufacturer asset-driven rather than being based on an understanding of markets and customers. Since then, a considerable amount of power has shifted from the manufacturer to the consumer • The basis for market success was assumed to rest on the idea that the principal strategic challenge was that of out-manoeuvring competitors. Today, far more recognition needs to be given to the power and role of the distributor and to the way in which retailers and end-users are able to leverage their position • The model is essentially superficial and provides little real insight to the forms of competitive advantage that determine organizational performance.

FIGURE 11.3 *The pros and cons of Porter's three generic strategies*

In discussing competitive advantage, Porter (1985a, Chapter 2) suggests that it:

> grows out of the value a firm is able to create for its buyers that exceeds the firm's cost of creating it. Value is what the buyer is willing to pay, and superior stems from offering lower prices than competitors for equivalent benefits or providing unique benefits that more than offset a higher price. There are two basic types of competitive advantage: cost leadership and differentiation.

He goes on to suggest that a convenient tool for identifying and understanding the potential competitive advantages possessed by a firm is by means of value chain analysis. In making this comment, Porter gives recognition to the way in which a firm is a collection of activities that are performed to design, produce, market, deliver and support its product.

The value chain (introduced in Chapter 3) disaggregates a firm into nine strategically significant activities so that the strategist is more easily able to understand the source and behaviour of costs in the specific business and industry, and the existing and potential sources of differentiation.

These nine value activities consist of five primary activities and four support activities.

The five *primary* activities to which Porter refers are concerned with the process of bringing raw materials into the organization and then modifying them in some way as a prelude to distribution, marketing and servicing them. The *support* activities, which take place at the same time, are concerned with procurement, technology development, human resource management and the firm's infrastructure (e.g. its management, planning, finance, accounting and legal affairs). The strategist's job therefore involves focusing upon the levels of cost and performance in each of the nine value areas in order to identify any opportunities for improvement. The extent to which this is achieved, relative to competitors, is a measure of competitive advantage. However, in making this comment it needs to be emphasized that different firms operating in the same industry are often capable of creating value in very different ways.

In searching for competitive advantage through the value chain, Porter also gives emphasis to the need to look outside the organization and to consider the value chains of suppliers, distributors and customers, since improvements to each of these will also help in the search for an advantage. As an example of this, a supplier or distributor might be helped to reduce costs, with all or part of the savings then being passed back to the company and used as another means of gaining cost leadership. Equally, an organization might work closely with its suppliers to ensure that particular levels of quality or service are achieved. Marks & Spencer, for example, has traditionally worked very closely with its suppliers to ensure that quality levels are maintained. Similarly, the major food retailers work with their suppliers in areas such as product development and cost control. In each case, the rationale is the same – that of achieving a competitive advantage.

Developing a sustainable advantage

The only truly sustainable competitive advantage comes from out-innovating the competition.

(Anon)

This need to understand that the bases of competition and the way in which competitive advantage is achieved should not be seen in any absolute way can perhaps best be illustrated by recognizing that markets can be viewed in a variety of ways and that a product can also be used in many different ways. It follows from this that every time the product–market combination changes, so too does the relative competitive strength or competitive advantage. The implications of this are significant and are reflected by the way in which a key element in any strategy revolves around choosing the competitor whom you wish to challenge, as well as choosing the market segment and product characteristics with which you will compete.

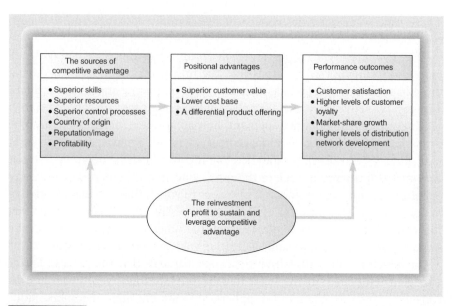

FIGURE 11.4 *Competitive advantage and business performance (adapted from Cravens, 1996, p. 36)*

The problem faced by many companies, therefore, is not how to *gain* a competitive advantage, but how to *sustain* it for any length of time. Most marketers are, for example, fully aware of the profit potential associated with a strategy based on, say, premium quality or technological leadership. The difficulty that is all too often faced in practice, however, is how to guard against predators and capitalize on these benefits *over the long term*. Business history is full of examples of companies that, having invested in a particular strategy, then fall victim to a larger or more agile organization. The question faced by many marketing strategists at one time or another is therefore how best to sustain a competitive advantage.

A framework for thinking about competitive advantage and how it links to the organization's subsequent performance has been proposed by Cravens (1996). This is shown in Figure 11.4.

A fundamental understanding of competitive advantage and how it is capable of undermining the competition was at the heart of the easyJet strategy. This is discussed in Illustration 11.3, and shows how the low-cost airline developed, leveraged and exploited competitive advantage to become a significant player in the European airlines market.

The low-cost business model used by companies such as Southwest Airlines, easyJet and Ryanair is one which, if managed properly, can prove to be enormously attractive. It is also one that is fraught with danger. If an organization is to pursue a low-cost strategy successfully, it is essential that costs are continually and ruthlessly driven out of the business, something that the

Illustration 11.3   EasyJet – competitive advantage through low costs and low prices

In December 1992, the European Union deregulated the airline industry. The implications of this were significant and meant that any European carrier could fly to any European destination and demand landing slots. Recognizing the opportunities that this created, large numbers of new airlines emerged, all of which focused upon offering low prices. However, the majority of these companies quickly encountered problems and, by 1996, 60 of the 80 carriers that had started up after deregulation had gone bankrupt. Given these odds, the success of easyJet is therefore particularly impressive.

The development of the company

Stelios Haji-Ioannou, easyJet's founder, modelled much of his early thinking for the company on the low-cost US carrier Southwest Airlines. Recognizing that the key to success in this sector of the market was the tight control of costs, when he launched the company in 1995 he concentrated upon rethinking and reinventing airline operating practice. An important first step in this was to base the airline at Luton, just north of London, rather than at Heathrow or Gatwick, since it offered lower labour costs and lower airport fees. Whenever possible, he also flew in to the less busy secondary airports in Europe rather than each city's more expensive main airport, which, he calculated, saved £10 per passenger. This approach to the very tight management of costs was also reflected by the way in which the company focused upon:

- One type of aircraft.
- Point-to-point short-haul travel.
- No in-flight meals (this saved £14 per passenger).
- Rapid turnaround times; these averaged 25 minutes.
- Very high aircraft utilization – aircraft flew an average of 11.5 hours per day rather than the industry average of six hours. The net effect of this was that two planes could do the work of three.
- Direct sales rather than via travel agents, since travel agents and computer reservation systems, it was calculated, added 25 per cent to operating costs.
- Booking over the Internet wherever possible. In March 1999, Internet sales accounted for 15 per cent of revenues. By October of that year, it was more than 60 per cent of revenues. By mid-2000, it was more than 70 per cent, a figure that the company aimed to increase yet further by replacing the telephone number livery on its planes with the Internet address.
- Ticketless travel. Customers paid by credit card and were given a six-character reference number. This number was the only information needed for passengers to board the plane.
- Selling drinks and refreshments.
- One class of seating in order to avoid the extra space demanded by business-class passengers.
- The outsourcing of as many services as possible, including check-in and the on-site information desk.

- Yield management in order to sell as large a number of seats as possible. Seats are sold in what could be considered a lottery system – the more people who demand a particular flight, the higher the fare. Put differently, if the load factor (percentage of seats sold) was higher than normal, prices automatically increased. This system worked well for easyJet because it helped to avoid selling out popular flights months in advance. Yield management also served another purpose – it drew potential customers who were in search of cheap fares. Once they found there were no more cheap seats, they usually bought a ticket anyway, since the next highest fare was still cheaper than easyJet's competitors. Stelios defended his policy vigorously: 'We decided that people who are willing to give us their money early should get a better price, and those who want the flexibility of booking late should pay a bit more.' The net effect of this was that load factors were consistently in excess of 80 per cent.

This idea of no-frills travel was based on Stelios's belief that 'When someone is on a bus, he doesn't expect any free lunch. I couldn't see why we cannot educate our customers to expect no frills on board.'

But whilst the company aggressively managed costs, it emphasized that it would never compromise on safety, flew new Boeing 737s and only hired experienced pilots who were paid market rates. Stelios commented: 'If you advertise a very cheap price, people expect an old airplane. But when they come on board and see a brand new plane, they are impressed. Likewise, many customers expect an unhappy staff because they believe they are not paid well, but they come on board and see the staff are smiling.'

The significance of service

In the same way that the company was not prepared to compromise on safety, Stelios believed that low cost and high levels of service and customer satisfaction were not incompatible.

The company saw its principal target market to be people who paid for their own travel. Although they did not target the business market, on some routes, such as London–Amsterdam, London–Glasgow and London–Edinburgh, business travellers typically accounted for 50 per cent of the passengers. However, regardless of whether the passenger was a business or private traveller, punctuality was seen to be important and linked closely to satisfaction. If, therefore, a flight arrived more than four hours late, passengers would receive a signed letter of apology and a full refund.

Taking on the competition

As with many new entrants to a long-established and mature market, the threat posed by easyJet was initially underestimated by some of the major players. When they did begin to recognize that the low-price airlines might possibly be serious competitors, they were initially unsure of how to respond. This was reflected by the way in which, according to easyJet (Rogers, 2000, p. 9):

> … in 1996, Bob Ayling, British Airways chief, approached Stelios in what appeared to be an offer to buy easyJet. Instead, after a three-month

courtship, British Airways abandoned the deal, and one year later, launched Go!, its own budget airline. Still angry over the incident, Stelios got his revenge by buying several rows of seats on Go!'s first flight. He commanded his staff to don orange boiler jackets, and they all boarded the flight like a group of merry pranksters, offering free flights on easyJet to Go!'s passengers. Barbara Cassani, chief executive of Go! Airlines, was on the inaugural flight to welcome new passengers. When she saw what was occurring, she lapsed into stunned silence. The publicity stunt paid off for easyJet. Go! Airlines announced losses of £22 million in 1999.

The low-price airlines market grew quickly as the result of the sorts of activities pursued by easyJet and its major competitor Ryanair, with a host of other companies such as Buzz, BMI Baby and Virgin Express entering the market, albeit with varying degrees of success.

In 2002, the company took its next major step by buying its rival Go!, which, through a management buyout, BA had sold to Cassani and her team.

Source: easyJet and media comments.

low-price grocery retailers such as Aldi and Netto have long realized. As soon as the management team loses sight of this imperative, the organization is likely to suffer in a dramatic fashion as it falls into the marketing wilderness (see Figure 11.1). This was a lesson learned by the retailer Kwik Save.

In the case of the low-cost airlines, although their business model proved to be enormously successful throughout the 1990s and then for much of the early part of the twenty-first century, the intense price-based competition led both to a shake-out across the sector and to the survivors searching for new sources of revenue. Amongst the ways in which they did this was by offering priority boarding (for a fee), charging for baggage that went into the aircraft hold, dispensing with seat pockets, and so on.

However, in 2008 the whole of the low-cost business model began to be questioned as oil prices began to rise dramatically. From an average of $17 a barrel in 2000, prices reached $148 a barrel in 2008 (they rose by more than 35% in just one three-month period). Although oil prices then dropped back, the effect upon the industry was significant, with some players being forced into bankruptcy, whilst others began reporting heavy losses.

The issue of how to develop and sustain a competitive advantage has also been discussed in detail by Davidson (1987a, p. 153). He suggests:

Competitive advantage is achieved whenever you do something better than competitors. If that something is important to consumers, or if a number of small advantages can be combined, you have an exploitable *competitive advantage. One or more competitive advantages are usually necessary in order to develop a winning strategy, and this in turn should enable a company to achieve above-average growth and profits.*

For Davidson, the ten most significant potential competitive advantages are:

1. *A superior product or service benefit*, as shown by First Direct with its combination of service and value; Pilkington with its self-cleaning glass, Toyota and Lexus with their very high levels of reliability; Disneyland with its overall quality of service; and Samsung initially with its price–performance combination and then more recently with its emphasis upon design, quality and value.

2. *A perceived advantage or superiority.* Marlboro, with its aggressively masculine image featuring cowboys, holds a 22 per cent share of the US cigarette market. The brand is well marketed but there is no reason to believe the cigarettes are objectively superior. Other examples of a perceived superiority advantage include designer label clothing and bottled waters.

3. *Low-cost operations* as the result of a combination of high productivity, low overheads, low labour costs, better purchasing skills, a limited product range, or low-cost distribution. Amongst those to have achieved this are the low-cost supermarket chains such as Aldi, Netto and Wal-Mart.

4. *Global experience, global skills and global coverage.* Amongst the most effective global operators are Coca-Cola and McDonald's. In the case of Coca-Cola, the brand's coverage has moved from around 2.26 billion people in 1984 to almost 6 billion today, with the result that there are few places in the world where Coca-Cola is not readily available. For McDonald's, its 35 000 outlets worldwide allow it to serve 50 million plus customers each day.

5. *Legal advantages* in the form of patents, copyright, sole distributorships, or a protected position.

6. *Superior contacts and relationships* with suppliers, distributors, customers, the media and government, and the management of customer databases.

7. *Scale advantages* that enable costs to be driven down and competitors pushed into a position of competitive disadvantage.

8. *Offensive attitudes* or, as Procter & Gamble label it, an attitude of competitive toughness and a determination to win.

9. *Superior competencies.* Ikea's focus upon developing competencies in product design, warehousing, purchasing and packaging, for

example, has allowed it to offer consumers high quality and low prices.

10. *Superior assets*, which may include property or distribution outlets.

Although Davidson's list of the 10 bases of competitive advantage is generally comprehensive, there are several other elements that can be added. These include:

- The notion of intellectual capital, which embraces the knowledge base of staff across the organization (this is typically the basis for the competitive advantage of management consulting firms and advertising agencies)

- Attitudinal issues that give recognition to the idea that creativity and innovation, be it product or process, is ultimately the only really sustainable form of competitive advantage

- Sophisticated service support systems

- Superior knowledge as a result of more effective market research, a better understanding of costs, superior information systems and a particularly highly skilled workforce

- Superior technologies

- Complex selling systems

- Speed to market (time-based competition)

- The brand image and reputation

- A focus upon the customer experience (this is developed at a later stage in the chapter)

- The management of the supply chain.

In so far as there is a single factor that underpins all 20 factors listed here, it is that of adding value to the ways in which the organization interacts with the customer, something that is clearly understood within Tesco (see Illustration 11.4). In the absence of this, there is no real competitive advantage.

An alternative way of thinking about competitive advantage involves categorizing the bases of advantage under four headings: management, behaviour, staff and the marketing mix.

Management advantages include:

- The overall level of management ability

- The willingness and ability of the marketing team to redefine the market in order to create market breakpoints

> **Illustration 11.4   Tesco and its leveraging of competitive advantage**
> A fundamental understanding of the significance of competitive advantage was at the heart of Tesco's strategy throughout the 1990s and early part of the twenty-first century. Their performance outstripped that of the vast majority of retailers and has led not just to the company taking over as the market leader from Sainsbury's in the UK food retailing market, but also to its increasingly successful development of clothes retailing. In doing this, the company has concentrated on developing a series of competitive advantages that, taken together, represent an enormously strong selling proposition, provide consumers with a powerful reason to buy, and put competitors at a disadvantage.

- The ability to identify and manage risk

- Managerial mindsets

- Experience

- A focus upon implementation.

Behavioural and attitudinal advantages include:

- Offensive attitudes (refer also to our earlier discussion on FUD marketing)

- Flexibility and speed of response

- A willingness to take risks.

Staff resource advantages include:

- Levels of creativity

- Networks

- Staff mindsets.

Marketing mix advantages include:

- The nature of each of the elements of the expanded marketing mix

- The speed of innovation

- The management of the distribution network.

However, irrespective of the type of market in which the organization is operating, competitive advantage must always be looked at from the standpoint of the customer since, unless the customer sees something to be significant, it is not a competitive advantage. Recognition of this leads to a three-part test that the marketing planner needs to apply on a regular basis to any proposed form of advantage:

1. To what extent is the advantage *meaningful* to the customer?

2. To what extent can the advantage be *sustained*? The reality, of course, is that in a fast-moving and competitive market few advantages can be sustained for any length of time. Given this, the planner needs to innovate continuously (refer to the comment above that innovation is ultimately the only sustainable form of advantage) by changing the rules of the game, the boundaries of the market, the value proposition, and so on.

3. How clearly and consistently is the advantage *communicated* clearly and consistently to the market?

In the absence of this, the organization runs the risk over time of simply being a 'me-too' player.

Competitive advantage, the growth of the experience economy and the rise of experience marketing

Faced with increasingly competitive markets in which points of differentiation between one product and another have become ever smaller, many marketing planners have responded by focusing upon the broader marketing context and the experience that surrounds the product, the purchase and the brand. Amongst those to have done this are Absolut Vodka with their Absolut Ice bars, Disney with DisneyWorld, Lego with LegoWorld, the Rainforest Café, Virgin with Upper Class, Nike with its Nike Town retail outlets, Apple with the Apple stores, Borders with its book stores, Yo Sushi!, and, in their early days, Starbucks.

The notion of the 'experience economy' was first discussed by Pine and Gilmore (1998) in a *Harvard Business Review* article and then developed in their book (2006) *The Experience Economy: Work Is Theatre and Every Business a Stage*. They argued that we are in the middle of a fundamental economic shift that has emerged out of a culture of mass affluence. With basic needs having been satisfied (the disposable income of most people across Western Europe is double that of 1980), the ways in which people view products and spend money has changed significantly. Because of this, one of the ways in which a company stands out in the market place is not just by offering products and services, but also experiences.

In the case of retailers, for example, shopping malls have reflected the idea of the experience economy by positioning themselves as destinations for a family day out, with scope for browsing, going to the cinema, eating – and shopping. In the case of Toys 'R' Us, for example, there has in its flagship stores been a move away from its traditional approach of 'pile it high, sell it cheap' to an experience which, in the Times Square store in New York, includes an 18m Ferris Wheel, two floors designed as a Barbie house, and an animatronic dinosaur.

As with other companies that have opted for experience marketing, the principal focus is upon developing an emotional attachment between the company and the consumer.

Insofar as it is possible to identify the characteristics of effective experience marketing, they are that the offer is typically characterized by a number of the following features:

- There is a strong sense of engagement both with the brand and the experience (Lego World and the Rainforest café)

- It is different, memorable and consistent (Disney)

- The experience often leads to the customer having a high level of involvement in the delivery of the experience (Lego World)

- The staff involved in delivering the experience are typically well-trained and committed to the organization and its values

- The process by which the customer is managed is often tightly controlled and there is a significant attention to detail (Disney World)

- There is often a sense of fun, excitement and customer delight (Disney World)

- The offer is typically unique or significantly different from much of what is already on the market (Virgin Upper Class)

- There is a high degree of perceived value (Virgin Upper Class)

- The product or service is typically offered at a premium price

- There are frequently add-ons which, in the eyes of the customer, add value to the experience (Disney World, Lego World)

- Everything is underpinned by a strong sense of organizational culture and a high level of staff and customer-buy-in.

In many ways, experience marketing can be seen to be a reflection of the coming together of a variety of trends, including multiculturalism, globalism and a series of demographic shifts. With much larger numbers of leisure activities available than was typically the case 20 years ago, a far greater proportion of the population now has the money to experience them. In the case of women, for example, they participate, on average, in ten different leisure pursuits a year, compared to around six 20 years ago. This desire to experiment and experience a greater variety of activities can, in turn, be seen to be linked to Maslow's hierarchy of needs and the search for self-actualization: recognizing that physical products are not necessarily the key to happiness has led to the search elsewhere for fulfilment.

Customer service and competitive advantage: new paradigms in service management

Two themes to which we keep returning throughout this book are that over the past few years customers have become far more demanding and markets have generally become far more competitive. One of the most significant of the consequences of these changes is that many of the traditional bases of competitive advantage have been eroded. The typical response to this sort of problem in the past is seen by the way in which the marketing planner would concentrate upon the development of a series of product improvements in order to regain the advantages that had been lost. However, the effectiveness of this in a fast-moving market is questionable, since not only are the costs high but it is also almost inevitable that competitors will copy almost immediately. What was therefore – temporarily – an augmented benefit quickly becomes something that is seen by the customer to be a TFG (taken-for-granted).

It is the recognition of this that has led many marketing planners to focus instead upon the development of benefits that are less tangible and therefore harder to copy. Amongst the most obvious of these are customer service, competitive positioning and brand values. It therefore becomes an issue not of what the organization can do, but of the way in which it does it. Amongst those to have done this successfully in the UK is the Co-operative Bank, which has managed to achieve a degree of competitive differentiation by positioning itself as the ethical bank. For those customers who see ethical behaviour to be important, the Co-op has become the preferred supplier – a position that others can attempt to copy but find difficult to beat. Elsewhere, Singapore International Airlines, Emirates and Quatar Airways have for a long time all used service excellence as the basis for their strategies. However, Zeithaml (1990, p. 135) suggest that far too many organizations have still failed to appreciate the strategic significance of service excellence:

> Service with a smile? Not by a mile. The message of commercials is 'We want you!'. The message of the service is 'We want you unless we have to be creative or courteous or better than barely adequate. In that case, get lost.'

Although it might be argued that Zeithaml is being unduly cynical in order to make a point, the reality in numerous cases is that service delivery levels fail to match – or exceed – customers' expectations. The consequences of this are seen in a number of ways, but most obviously in terms of the organization's failure to exploit the customer base to the extent that might be possible by developing higher levels of loyalty. Because of this, far too many purchases prove to be single transactions with customers who, having been attracted to the product or service, often at considerable cost, are then allowed to walk away without a further commitment. While customer loyalty schemes are designed to overcome this, it needs to be recognized that consistently high levels of service quality stem from a far more fundamental reorientation of the business.

It is the acknowledgement of this, together with an appreciation of the way in which the products and prices of competitors are becoming increasingly similar and difficult to differentiate, that has led to a far greater emphasis upon the 'soft' elements of the marketing mix – particularly *people* (staff) and *process management* (how customers are managed from the point of very first contact with the organization through to the point of very last contact.

The pressures to achieve high(er) levels of service have, in turn, been reinforced by the way in which customers – faced with a far greater range of choices – have become more demanding and much less tolerant of service failings. Taken together, these pressures have led to a new service paradigm characterized by a shift in emphasis from *service quality*, with its focus upon meeting customers' expectations, to *service excellence* which gives emphasis to exceeding customer expectations.

The economic rationale for service excellence is typically seen to stem from a variety of studies that have been conducted over the years that have led to the conventional and possibly conventional marketing wisdom which suggests that:

■ The price of acquiring new customers can be five times greater than the cost of keeping current ones

■ Reducing customer defections is said to boost profits by anywhere from 25 to 150 per cent

■ The return on investment to marketing for existing customers can be up to seven times more than for prospective customers

■ The probability is near 100 per cent that very satisfied customers become the best sales promoters of the company.

The importance of service and its contribution to competitive advantage was also highlighted by the results of the PIMS research, which suggested that those organizations that achieved high levels of service charged about 9 per cent more for their goods and grew twice as fast, picking up market share at around 6 per cent per annum; the 'also-rans' lost share at 2 per cent per annum. The PIMS research also revealed that the cost of superior service is often little more than for inferior offerings, with Gale (1994, p. 307) arguing that organizations with inferior quality typically have higher relative direct costs than businesses in any other position.

In discussing the attributes of service, Stone and Young (1992, p. 75) suggest that suppliers often see these in terms of technical features. By contrast, the customer's view will typically include factors such as the time taken to deliver the service; the extent to which the customer wants to or perceives the need to be in control; the effort required to receive the service; the relative importance of the service; the efficiency of the supplier; and the level of skill or professional expertise expected of the service staff.

Parasuraman *et al.* (1985) developed a similar view, based on the results of a series of focus group interviews among representatives from four service sectors – retail banking, credit cards, securities brokerage, and product repair and maintenance – from different parts of the USA. From the responses, an underlying pattern emerged that was consistent across all sectors and regions. These findings were categorized under ten headings or dimensions: tangibles, reliability, responsiveness, competence, courtesy, credibility, security, access, communication, and understanding the customer. These ten dimensions were then further grouped into what Zeithaml (1990) calls their SERVQUAL dimensions:

- Tangibles – the appearance of the physical facilities, equipment, personnel and communication materials

- Reliability – the ability to perform the promised service dependably and accurately

- Responsiveness – the willingness to help customers and provide prompt service

- Assurance – the knowledge and courtesy of employees and their ability to convey trust and confidence

- Empathy – the caring, individualized attention that the firm provides to its customers.

The SERVQUAL model that emerged from this analysis is in many ways one of the best known to audit service within an organization and is based around the identification of a series of gaps. These include:

1. The gap that typically exists between the customer's expectations of service and how management perceives these needs

2. The gap that then emerges between management perceptions and their translation into a policy of service quality

3. The gaps that exist between the often loosely stated service policy and levels of service delivery

4. The gaps between how the organization perceives service delivery and how the customer perceives this.

The problems of these gaps are then often exacerbated by the ways in which organizations often communicate with customers (over-promise and under-delivery) and by the ways in which staff may then put their own interpretation on customers' needs and the delivery of the organization's service.

Service and the rise of the stupid company

Although marketing planners typically argue that their organizations are customer focused and that service and satisfaction are pivotal parts of the marketing strategy, the reality in many cases is that levels of service delivery are often poor and/or inconsistent. In discussing this, Cullum (2006), who, in a report published by the National Consumer Council (NCC), coined the phrase 'The Stupid Company', highlighted the problems of 'businesses over-promising and under-delivering, treating customers in a clinical and patronizing way, and being incapable of getting the most basic things right'. As evidence of this, he points to the 800 000 people each year who make complaints to trading standards departments and to the UK Customer Care Survey of 2005 conducted by Manchester Business School which found that 77 per cent of those surveyed experienced problems with products and services bought in the preceding 12 months.

Amongst the most common complaints were robotic call centres, complex systems, missed appointments and poor after-sales service, with the sectors that received the greatest number of complaints being financial services, telecoms, utilities, electrical retailers and garages. The problems identified by the NCC have, in turn, been discussed by Accenture who find that when telephoning to complain, customers spent an average of six minutes on hold, and spoke to more than two service representatives, and by researchers at Aston University who have argued that the majority of chief executives regard complaining customers as a nuisance and too demanding.

There are several factors that can been seen to contribute to service problems such as these, including a high turnover of staff, staff who are poorly trained, faulty software, and the attempts by companies to 'manage' the customer relationship in an attempt to reduce costs. Most commonly, this has been done by outsourcing service support and by automated call-handling systems that provide options based on the company's organization rather than its customers' problems. These sorts of problems are then compounded by the ways in which many call centres have high levels of staff turnover, relatively low levels of expertise and a focus upon the numbers of calls handled and the time taken to deal with a caller.

In order to overcome problems like this, there is a clear case for marketing planners to view complaints strategically and to see them as a way of gaining market information and building loyalty. Recognition of this led BT to use root cost analysis to identify the five most common complaints each quarter and to focus upon resolving these. At the same time, they have introduced a sensing system designed to anticipate potential problems in any new initiative. Staff are then given ownership of the problem and trained both to restore and create customer value.

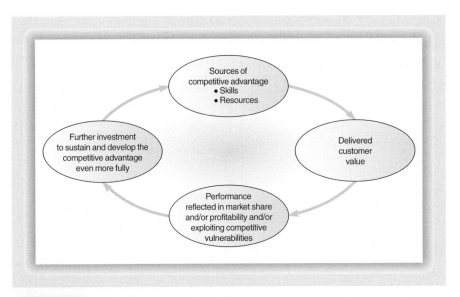

The virtuous circle of competitive advantage

Gaining, sustaining and exploiting competitive advantage: the problems of self-delusion

One of the themes that has been pursued not just within this chapter, but throughout this book is that of the pivotal importance of competitive advantage. In thinking about how to develop competitive advantage, the marketing planner needs to understand in detail the organization's skills and resources, and then manage these in such a way that the business delivers superior customer value to target segments at a cost that leads to a profit. This can be seen diagrammatically in Figure 11.5.

However, in many cases when thinking about competitive advantage, marketing planners appear to suffer from a degree of self-delusion in that they see something that the organization has or does as being far more important or significant than customers see this to be. In order to overcome this, McDonald (1995) argues for the application of the deceptively simple 'So what?' test (see Figure 11.6). Here, the planner begins by identifying the features offered by the product and then – very importantly – translates these into the benefits to the customer. Having done this, the deliberately cynical 'So what?' question is posed. If the benefits that have been identified are essentially the same as those offered by a competitor, then they are of little value. It is only if the benefits pass the test that the advantage can be seen to be at all meaningful.

The problems of sustaining advantage

In developing and, perhaps more importantly, sustaining advantage, the planner needs to recognize that any advantage that an organization or

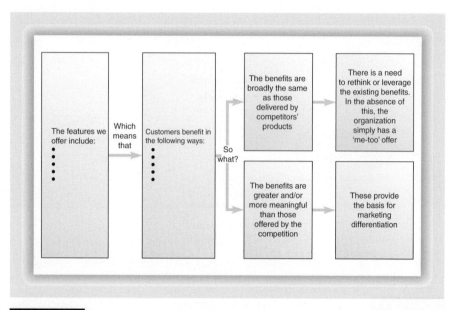

FIGURE 11.6   *The 'So what?' test (adapted from McDonald, 1995)*

brand possesses that is at all meaningful will be copied or improved upon by competitors sooner rather than later. Recognizing this, the planner needs to sustain the advantage in one of several ways. These include product and/or process innovation, clever positioning or repositioning (the Co-operative Bank, for example, developed a position as the ethical bank, something that the other banks then found hard to copy), adding value, new forms of delivery (e.g. Amazon.com), and through higher or different levels of service.

The idea of service as a (sustainable) competitive advantage has proved to be particularly attractive for organizations in highly competitive and fast-moving markets, where there is a recognition that any product innovation is likely to be copied almost immediately. However, there is a problem in that customers' expectations typically rise over time, with the result that something that is different and an order winner today is seen simply to be an order qualifier tomorrow. Because of this, the planner needs to think about the ways in which the customer can be made to be enthused, excited and delighted by the product and/or service offer.

The ways in which order winners are eroded over time and how the delivery of ever higher levels of customer delight become progressively more important are illustrated in Figure 11.7.

Amongst the implications of this are that the planner needs to understand in detail the nature of order qualifiers (those elements that lead to the customer taking the organization or brand sufficiently seriously to consider buying), order winners (those elements that are significant points of

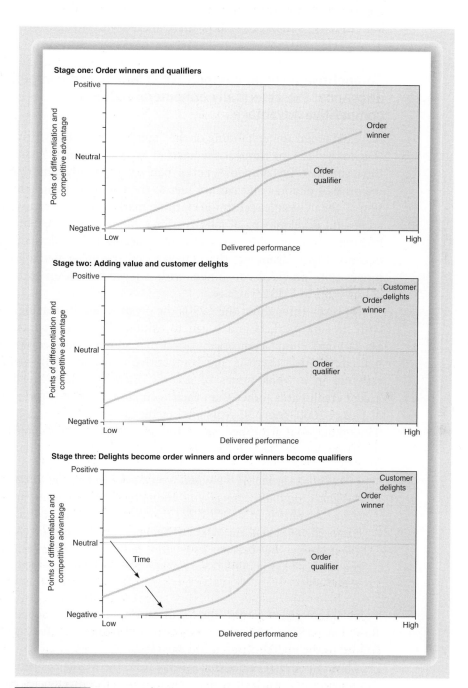

FIGURE 11.7   *Order winners becoming order qualifiers*

differentiation) and areas of customer delight (those elements that provide the basis for extra value and ever more meaningful bases of differentiation), both in today's market and how these are likely to change in the future.

Competitive myopia, competitive sclerosis and competitive arrogance: the essentially ephemeral nature of competitive advantage

A fundamental understanding of the significance of competitive advantage was, for a very long time, at the heart of Marks & Spencer's strategies, with the result that the company's performance consistently outstripped the vast majority of retailers and led not just to the company maintaining its position as the market leader in the clothing market, but also to its enormously successful development of food retailing, financial services and household furniture. In doing this, the company concentrated on developing a series of competitive advantages that, taken together, represented a strong selling proposition, provided consumers with a powerful reason to buy, and put competitors at a disadvantage.

However, throughout the 1990s the organization increasingly lost touch with its core markets and began to exhibit all of the characteristics of a fat, lazy and complacent organization that suffered from competitive myopia, competitive sclerosis and competitive arrogance. This arrogance was reflected in a whole series of actions, including their unwillingness to accept credit cards (other than their own store card) as a form of payment as late as 2000, some 30 years after credit cards were introduced to the UK. This managerial arrogance was summarized by a business journalist who, in writing for the *Daily Telegraph* (21 January 2001, p. 133), said:

> *What other retailer in the world would ask some of the finest designers to produce ranges and then prevent them from putting their own names in them? What the top brass at M&S cannot comprehend is that the Marks & Spencer name, once the group's greatest asset, has become its greatest liability, a Belisha beacon to the clothes buying public that flashes 'Do not shop here! Do not shop here!'*

Subsequently, of course, the organization, under the leadership of Stuart Rose, has pursued a far more aggressive and market-focused strategy which has led to the revitalization of the business.

There are several issues that emerge from the Marks & Spencer story, the most significant of which is that it is managerial competencies and attitudes that are the only *real* sustainable competitive advantage. In the absence of these, the organization's position within the marketplace will inevitably suffer.

Sustainability of competitive advantage can therefore be seen to depend upon:

- A clear understanding by management of a *strategy* for gaining and sustaining competitive advantage

- The single-minded pursuit of the strategy

- A recognition that some sources of advantage are easier for competitors to copy than others

- The continual investment in improving and upgrading sources of advantage.

The speed with which a competitive advantage and strong market position can be eroded was also illustrated in 2003 by the way in which Viagra's dominance of the erectile dysfunction market was attacked by two new drugs, Cialis from Eli Lilly and Levitra from GSK/Bayer. The importance of Viagra to Pfizer was reflected by its sales in 2002 of $1.7 billion and its position as one of Pfizer's three most profitable products. The new entrants to the market based their strategies on a combination of different competitive advantages, including a faster response time to the drug and longer-lasting effects that, together, eroded Viagra's market position.

The nature and significance of competitive disadvantage

Although we have focused so far upon the idea of competitive advantage and the sorts of factors that contribute to this, the reader should not lose sight of the significance of competitive *disadvantage*. This can come about as the result of a series of factors, including a poor brand reputation, the failure to achieve certain service norms within the market, a cost base that is too high, the failure to learn from past experience, the slavish adherence to a previously successful formula, the failure to monitor market conditions, and what might loosely be termed 'country of origin effect'. As an example of the latter effect working against the brand, it is worth thinking back to the way in which many Central and Eastern European products for a very long time – and indeed still today – developed a poor reputation for quality, something that has prevented many of these brands penetrating western markets despite low-price strategies.

Given this, the marketing planner needs to recognize the nature and the very real significance of competitive disadvantage and how any disadvantages are capable of acting as potentially significant inhibitors to their ability to compete effectively. In some ways, the nature of competitive disadvantage, which include issues such as low quality, limited distribution and a poorly managed brand, can be seen to be the opposite of the factors that are identified on pages 420–1. Disadvantage can, however, be far more fundamental. In the case of the car industry, for example, Ford, General Motors and Chrysler have all been struggling with a high cost base that has made the investments in new products, processes and manufacturing capacity that are needed in order to compete effectively very difficult.

In 2007, for example, it was estimated that General Motor's legacy costs of healthcare for staff and pensioners meant that its labour costs in the USA were $25 an hour *more* than those of Toyota (*The Sunday Times*, 2 September, 2007, pp. 13.1 and 3.8). It was this that led Bob Lutz, the company's head of product development, to comment that GM is now the biggest healthcare company in America. The net effect of these legacy costs upon the price of a car in the showroom are significant and, in 2005, were estimated at $1600 per vehicle. These problems are then compounded by customers' perceptions of the different brands and their lack of willingness to pay the price premium that many of the European and Japanese car brands command (*The Sunday Times*, 8 May 2005, p. 3.7).

The situation for both Ford and Chrysler is broadly the same and over the past few years has been reflected both in their share prices and in the lower ratings given to the companies by credit-rating agencies such as Standard & Poor (S&P). The implications of this are in turn reflected in the interest rates that have to be paid on their borrowings.

Creating barriers to entry

Although the development and exploitation of competitive advantage is at the heart of any worthwhile marketing strategy, relatively few organizations prove to be successful at doing this over the long term. Innovators are almost invariably followed by imitators and, because of this, few manage to maintain a truly dominant market position (see the comments above about Marks & Spencer). Tagamet, for example, one of the best-selling and most revolutionary drugs of all time, was quickly eclipsed by an imitator, Zantac. Similarly, Thorn–EMI (with its body scanner) and Xerox (with a series of innovations that helped develop and define the personal computer) are just two companies that, having innovated, came under attack and failed to maintain a dominant position.

The issue that emerges from these and a host of other examples is straightforward: all too often, the resources devoted to *creating* a significant competitive advantage are of little value unless that advantage is subsequently aggressively exploited and sustained. In order to do this and benefit fully from the innovation, Geroski (1996, p. 11) argues that planners need to focus upon understanding two areas:

1. The market's *barriers to entry*, which are the structural features of a market that protect the established companies within a market and allow them to raise prices above costs without attracting new entrants

2. *Mobility barriers*, which protect companies in one part of a market from other companies that are operating in different parts of the same market.

New organizational paradigms and the thirteen commandments for gaining competitive advantage

In 1994, Hamel and Prahalad published their highly influential book *Competing for the Future*. In this, they highlighted the ways in which management paradigms are changing and the nature of the implications of the new paradigm for competitive advantage. Some of the factors that they suggested would characterize the paradigm of the twenty-first century, and how these represent a shift from the 1990s, are shown in Figure 11.8.

The implications of this for competitive advantage and competitive behaviour are obviously significant, and were summarized by Hamel and Prahalad (1994) in terms of the need for marketing planners to:

- Stop playing by the industry rules and, instead, create their own, develop a new competitive space and make others follow (e.g. Swatch, Dell and, in the 1960s to1980s, The Body Shop)

- Get innovative or get dead – in doing this, the planner needs to avoid believing in the idea of sustainable advantage and to focus instead

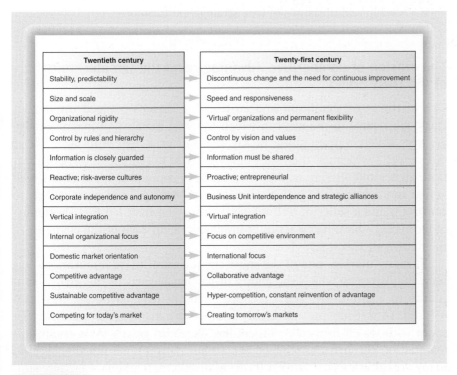

Twentieth century	Twenty-first century
Stability, predictability	Discontinuous change and the need for continuous improvement
Size and scale	Speed and responsiveness
Organizational rigidity	'Virtual' organizations and permanent flexibility
Control by rules and hierarchy	Control by vision and values
Information is closely guarded	Information must be shared
Reactive; risk-averse cultures	Proactive; entrepreneurial
Corporate independence and autonomy	Business Unit interdependence and strategic alliances
Vertical integration	'Virtual' integration
Internal organizational focus	Focus on competitive environment
Domestic market orientation	International focus
Competitive advantage	Collaborative advantage
Sustainable competitive advantage	Hyper-competition, constant reinvention of advantage
Competing for today's market	Creating tomorrow's markets

FIGURE 11.8   *Changing managerial paradigms*

upon creating a culture of constructive destruction (e.g. Direct Line, 3M, Canon and Sony)

■ Scrutinize the company for hidden assets, which then need to be leveraged (e.g. Disney and Harley Davidson)

■ Create a fast action company (e.g. Toyota and CNN)

■ Create an entrepreneurial and experimental business (e.g. Virgin and easyJet)

■ Eliminate boundaries within the organization (e.g. Toshiba and Mitsubishi)

■ Harness the collective genius of staff (e.g. management consultancies such as McKinsey and Bain & Co.)

■ Globalize or perish (e.g. Ikea and Nokia)

■ Emphasize the eco-revolution and use environmental efficiency to set standards for the market (e.g. the Co-operative Bank)

■ Recognize that organizational learning and the ability to learn faster and then apply these ideas more quickly than the competition may be the only real sustainable advantage

■ Develop real measures of true strategic performance.

The erosion of competitive advantage and the (greater) role of the trust brand

One of the most significant and far-reaching themes pursued throughout this book relates to the ways in which the vast majority of markets today are very different from those of say ten and even five years ago. These differences – which are the result of a variety of forces, including globalization; higher and often more desperate levels of competition; customers who are far more demanding and discriminating, less loyal and more willing to complain; and a series of technological shifts that have led to a shortening of life cycles – have had a series of implications for each of the elements of the marketing mix.

In many markets one of the most significant of these implications has been the extent to which the ability of particular parts of the mix to contribute to significant – and sustained – competitive advantage has been reduced. In fast-moving and highly competitive markets, for example, the speed with which firms copy others has increased greatly. As a result, differentiation through the product has all but disappeared. Equally, because many organizations use similar forms of distribution and have broadly similar levels of costs, the ability to differentiate through distribution and price

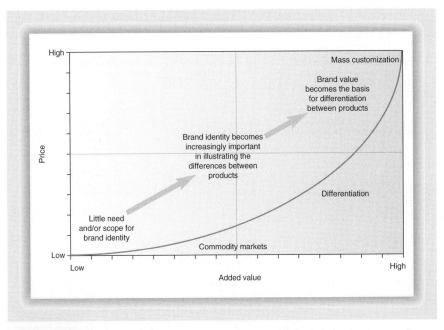

The increasing significance of brands and branding

has also been reduced. Faced with this, many marketing planners have shifted their attention to the brand and to the role that it is capable of playing in creating and maintaining differentiation and advantage.

Brands, which are in essence a form of shorthand that creates expectations about purpose, performance, quality and price, are therefore potentially enormously powerful and provide the basis not just for a high(er) profile in the market, but also for higher levels of customer loyalty and the freedom to charge a price premium. Given this, the effective and proactive management of the brand is, for many organizations, essential.

The increasingly important role played by brands is illustrated in Figure 11.9, which shows the three key stages of a market, ranging from commoditization (in which there is little scope or perhaps need for brand identity) through differentiation (in which brand identity becomes increasingly significant) to mass customization (in which the brand values become the basis for differentiation).

However, these ideas can be taken a step further with the development of thinking about 'trust brands'. These trust brands are the brands in which customers have a fundamental long-lasting and deep-seated faith that emerges both from a rational assessment of the product's capabilities ('I know that this product or service will deliver what I want'), and an emotional assessment of the relationship between the organization and the customer ('I know that I will get a fair deal').

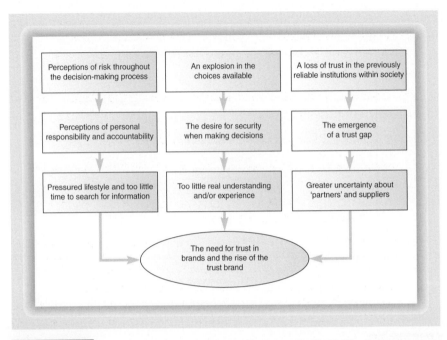

The pressure for trust brands (adapted from Edwards, 1998)

The need for trust brands has grown significantly over the past few years, largely as the result of the privatization of risk within society, something that Edwards (1998) suggests is due to:

> the transfer of risk from the state and from the employer to the
> individual ... (and) accompanied by a long and steady decline in
> popular trust for the institutions in society that individuals used to
> rely on for help in making choices ... In summary, the privatization
> of risk in society means that consumers are seeking new partners to
> help them confront, share and manage that risk. Brands are ideally
> placed to fill this trust vacuum.

These pressures are illustrated in Figure 11.10.

Amongst those brands that have demonstrated high trust credentials are some of the major retailers such as Tesco, and individual brands such as Kellogg's and Nestlé. For Edwards:

> the archetypal trust brand is probably still Virgin. Transferring
> trust apparently effortlessly into new areas, this highly individual
> conglomerate now takes part in diverse activities ranging from
> airlines to finance, and soft drinks to cinemas and weddings. The
> proposition is clear: when you, the consumer, enter an unfamiliar
> market where you do not trust the current providers then Virgin
> will be on your side. Virgin's credentials to enter new markets are

often unclear in the traditional sense (in fact it often operates in partnership with specialist suppliers) – what it actually brings with it from market to market is the brand name and the consumer trust that resides in it.

The work of Edwards and his colleagues at the Henley Centre suggests that six factors contribute to trust:

1. *Packaging* and the product information that it contains

2. *Provenance* and the country or company of origin (included within this is the country of origin effect, which includes the heritage of the country – e.g. Germany for engineering, Japan for high technology – and the reputation of the company)

3. *Performance* over time that leads to perceptions of dependability

4. *Persistence* – once a brand has gained real consumer trust, it demonstrates long-term resilience even though there may be occasions when things go wrong (Persil, for example, has maintained trust despite problems of enzymes and dermatitis at certain stages in its life)

5. *Portability* – having developed trust, the brand can be moved into new and possibly unrelated areas, something that both Virgin and Tesco have demonstrated with their move into a variety of new market sectors

6. *Praise* – when trust is high, the use and power of word of mouth tends to increase dramatically.

Given that markets are now so much more competitive than even a few years ago, it should be apparent that trust brands can play a pivotal role in achieving differentiation and long-term loyalty. The implications for how brands are managed are therefore significant. Edwards (1998) states:

It has long been axiomatic that competitors can quickly copy product or service innovations in most cases. It is therefore crucial that trust and the infrastructure of trust are reinforced through all consumer contacts and relationships. In the field of trust management, marketing becomes everyone's job. All stages of the process are relevant in maintaining trust – R&D, product testing, manufacturing, staff training and policies, distribution, pricing and customer service/complaint handling. All consumer interactions are a marketing opportunity. As the banks have discovered – expensive marketing campaigns are quickly negated by poor customer handling at the branch.

Marketing by trust therefore becomes more of a philosophy than simply the responsibility of a single department. The trust brand places the consumer at the centre of its world; it relies more on understanding real consumer needs and fulfilling them than the particular service or product manifestation at any one time. This means it is not merely responsive but also responsible to the consumer knowing the right thing to do or be even when the customer does not.

In recent years, however, a number of organizations have been faced with the problem of their brands having been undermined by counterfeit products. In a report published in 2000, the Global Anti-Counterfeiting Group estimated that brand counterfeiting costs European business £250 billion a year. Worldwide, the report suggests that the annual cost is at least £600 billion (*Marketing*, 27 April 2000).

The implications of this for the brand marketer are significant and are reflected not just in a loss of revenue and profits, but also in lower levels of customer loyalty, an erosion in customer confidence and a weakening of relationships throughout the distribution chain.

Although virtually all sectors of the economy have been hit to at least some extent by fakes (one argument is that wherever there is a strong brand name there is scope for counterfeiting), the music, software, videos, toys, watches, cosmetics and perfumes industries have proved to be amongst the most vulnerable.

Competitive advantage and the rise of generous brands

As consumers have become more demanding and discriminating (refer to Illustration 6.1 and our discussion of the new consumer in Chapter 6), so their expectations of and relationships with brands have changed. In discussing this, Pearse McCabe (2006) of the design consultants Fitch suggests that 'where once brands were accepted as voices of authority, now consumers want more of a say. Expectations of service, quality and value are growing daily, but above all consumers are seeking more mature, grown-up relationships with brands, based on honesty, openness and the human characteristic of generosity.'

The implications of this are likely to be seen in the way in which if brands are to be trusted, they will increasingly need to be far more open and transparent and, in essence, more human. McCabe refers to the brands that have already moved in that direction as 'the generous brands', not in the sense that they offer special deals, but that they exhibit a more human generosity of spirit. Amongst those to do this, he claims, are Orange, which offers mobile phone chargers in London's black cabs that can be used by anyone; Innocent with its free music festival, 'fruitstock'; The Apple Store with free training and software demonstrations and its 'genius bar' offering free advice; Amazon.com with its development of the referral economy; B&Q with its staff who will give unbiased DIY advice; and Oddbins and Waterstones, both of which have staff who handwrite reviews of wine and books respectively.

The third knowledge revolution and the erosion of competitive advantage

With the arrival of the Internet and the third knowledge revolution (the first and second knowledge revolutions were the printing press in 1455 and broadcasting some 500 years later), the competitive advantage that many firms have traditionally enjoyed has either been eroded or has disappeared completely. In discussing this in their book *Funky Business*, Ridderstråle and Nordström's (2000) core argument is that the world is changing ever faster and that the survivors will be those who embrace the changes and modify their corporate behaviour.

Although this is a view that numerous others have expressed over the past few years, Ridderstråle and Nordström focus upon the way in which managers who are accustomed to controlling their environment by the domination of their staff, customers and markets are likely to be faced with major problems as the new world order demands more than technology, production and distribution. Progressive – or 'funky' – companies will attract custom, they suggest, by understanding in much greater detail what customers want and communicating to them the intangible elements (in essence, the brand values) of their product or service. They then take this philosophy to new heights by predicting a scarily harsh business environment where unforgiving consumers and demanding employees will exert a pincer-movement stranglehold on companies that refuse to 'feel the funk'.

The power of knowledge and the growth of commercial freedom make for a better-informed marketplace than the world has ever seen before. But with that freedom, say Ridderstråle and Nordström, comes the death of corporate loyalty: 'Companies should no longer expect loyalty; they should accept the need to attract and addict people on a continuous basis.' Now that we have moved into a society ruled by over-supply, Ridderstråle and Nordström believe the future no longer belongs to those who control supply but to those who control demand, 'those who help the customer get the best deal'. Prominent amongst the companies that they believe have come to terms with this ('islands of funk') are Virgin and Nokia.

Competitive advantage and the dangers of benchmarking

> In Disney's A Bug's Life, *a moth warns his moth friend not to look at or fly towards the light. 'I can't help it', the doomed insect replies.*

For many organizations, competitive benchmarking – the process by which you identify the best in the sector, determine what it is that has led to such high performance and then copy – has become an integral part of the corporate struggle to stay competitive. But although benchmarking can be of value, it can also lead to problems. Natterman (2000, p. 20), for example, discusses what he terms 'strategic herding'. This happens, he suggests, when managers forget that benchmarking should only be used as an operational tool rather than the determining framework for strategic development. The effects of herding can be seen by the way in which products and services increasingly become commodities and margins shrink as more and more companies crowd into the same market space.

Amongst the examples he cites to illustrate this is that of the German wireless telecommunications providers between 1993 and 1998. The first two carriers entered the business in 1992 and quickly achieved market share of more than 70 per cent with similar strategies in terms of pricing, selling and advertising. When a third company entered the market in 1994, it differentiated itself by targeting segments that the first two were ignoring – similar to the approach adopted in the UK by Orange, when it attacked the two established players, Vodafone and BT Cellnet. Soon there was little to choose between them as they all frantically copied each other's offerings. By 1998, Natterman claims, this led to margins 50 per cent lower than at their peak. The same approach has also eroded margins in computers and consumer electronics.

A broadly similar picture began to emerge in Britain when the American retailer Wal-Mart entered the market in 1999. The established players such as Tesco, Sainsbury's and Safeway, all of which had enjoyed profit margins that were far higher than in many other Western European countries, responded in an almost desperate fashion by cutting prices. One of the few to avoid this strategic herding was Waitrose, which continued with its policy of up-market positioning. It also began targeting its e-shopping at people in their offices rather than at home.

The problems of strategic herding are also increasingly being seen in the high street coffee shop market, with Starbucks and numerous other players all fighting for (an ever larger) share of a market, which, although it has grown rapidly, is ultimately of a finite size. In these circumstances, it is not so much a question of *whether* there will be a shake-out in the market, but simply *when* this will happen.

Returning for a moment to the example of Waitrose given above, Natterman refers to this refusal to follow the pack as a policy of looking for 'white spots' – or those areas that the herd is failing to exploit. Firms such as these, he suggests, may well benchmark, but they then avoid the trap of letting this constrain their strategic thinking.

E-business and competitive advantage

With the development of the Internet and e-commerce, marketing thinking and approaches to marketing planning have undergone a number of radical changes. In part, this has been driven by the way in which e-marketing has the potential for changing not just the rules of the game within a market, but also the market space, and in doing so change the bases for thinking

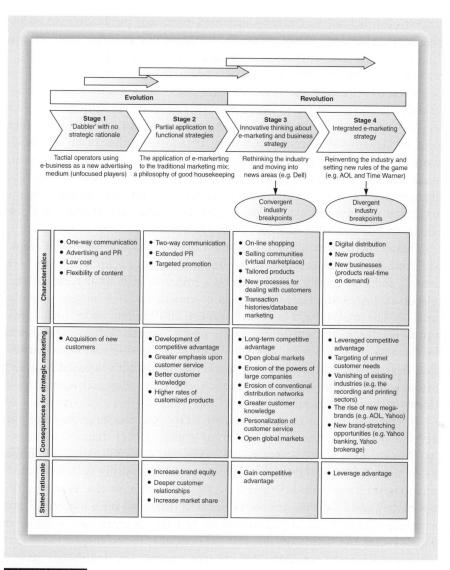

The figure contains the following labelled content:

	Stage 1 'Dabbler' with no strategic rationale	Stage 2 Partial application to functional strategies	Stage 3 Innovative thinking about e-marketing and business strategy	Stage 4 Integrated e-marketing strategy
	Tactial operators using e-business as a new advertising medium (unfocused players)	The application of e-markerting to the traditional marketing mix; a philosophy of good housekeeping	Rethinking the industry and moving into news areas (e.g. Dell)	Reinventing the industry and setting new rules of the game (e.g. AOL and Time Warner)
			Convergent industry breakpoints	Divergent industry breakpoints
Characteristics	• One-way communication • Advertising and PR • Low cost • Flexibility of content	• Two-way communication • Extended PR • Targeted promotion	• On-line shopping • Selling communities (virtual marketplace) • Tailored products • New processes for dealing with customers • Transaction histories/database marketing	• Digital distribution • New products • New businesses (products real-time on demand)
Consequences for strategic marketing	• Acquisition of new customers	• Development of competitive advantage • Greater emphasis upon customer service • Better customer knowledge • Higher rates of customized products	• Long-term competitive advantage • Open global markets • Erosion of the powers of large companies • Erosion of conventional distribution networks • Greater customer knowledge • Personalization of customer service • Open global markets	• Leveraged competitive advantage • Targeting of unmet customer needs • Vanishing of existing industries (e.g. the recording and printing sectors) • The rise of new mega-brands (e.g. AOL, Yahoo) • New brand-stretching opportunities (e.g. Yahoo banking, Yahoo brokerage)
Stated rationale		• Increase brand equity • Deeper customer relationships • Increase market share	• Gain competitive advantage	• Leverage advantage

The top of the figure shows **Evolution** (covering Stage 1 and Stage 2) and **Revolution** (covering Stage 3 and Stage 4).

FIGURE 11.11   *E-marketing and development of strategic thinking and competitive advantage*

about competitive advantage. The ways in which organizations might move from a position in which e-marketing is poorly thought out and reflected largely in the development of web pages that are simply another form of advertising through to the fundamental and strategic integration of e-marketing with the corporate strategy is illustrated in Figure 11.11. Here, organizations move through four stages and, depending upon how proactive they are, are capable of changing the bases of competition in potentially fundamental ways. Those firms that fail to recognize this and continue to focus upon the traditional bases of competition and advantage run the risk of being left behind as the rules of competition and the boundaries of the market develop and change. Amongst the most obvious examples of firms that have done this are Amazon.com, who rewrote the rules of competition within the book-selling market, and easyJet, which took a very different approach to selling airline seats. In both cases, their competitors were put at a disadvantage and forced into a position of copying and catch-up.

The effects of the Internet and the growth of e-marketing have been seen in virtually all markets, but most obviously in the travel, entertainment, books, retailing, telecommunications and music sectors. In many ways, the implications for marketing behaviour have been both obvious and straightforward, in that e-marketing has reduced market entry barriers and increased not just the size of an organization's potential market, but also the speed and flexibility of access to this market.

Driven by the growth by broadband, the effects of this have been graphically illustrated by the growth of on-line marketing (in 2007, the UK e-retail industry grew by 33 per cent, compared with total retail market growth of just 3.5 per cent; forecasts of growth to 2011 suggest that the total on-line market will be worth almost £50 billion, with almost two-thirds of this being within the retail sector [Source: Verdict.co.uk]) and by the way in which there has been a polarization of those organizations that have developed an effective e-marketing model that is based on lower prices, greater convenience, or value (e.g. Amazon, eBay and Ryanair) and those that have struggled.

In the case of the traditional retail sector, the challenge has been to develop an e-marketing model that complements rather than compromises its physical high street operation. In many cases, they have simply failed to do this. Amongst those who have done it successfully is Tesco, which now has the largest on-line grocery operation in the world. However, the difficulties faced by a management team in balancing both a physical and a virtual offer have been highlighted by Natalie Massenet, the founder of Net-A-Porter, the luxury on-line fashion boutique. In the case of the luxury goods industry, she suggests, 'they simply couldn't get their heads around the idea that a three-dimensional retail experience could be reproduced in two dimensions, so instead they stuck their heads "in the sand", something that provided Net-A-Porter with a clear market space' (quoted in *The Financial Times*, 30 May 2006, p. 10).

For many organizations, however, there is increasingly no real option other than to develop a truly effective on-line offer that is run in parallel with the physical offer. With the ever greater technological skills and expectations of the market, but particularly within the youth sector, any polarization between what might loosely be termed digital natives and digital immigrants has significant strategic implications.

The potential implications of the Internet for marketing were outlined in 2000 in a presentation to the Chartered Institute of Marketing by the consultants McKinsey & Co. McKinsey argued that the Internet has the capacity for:

- Creating discontinuity in marketing costs
- Making new and different types of dialogue with the customer possible
- Changing the return on attention equation
- Reinventing the marketing paradigm.

In suggesting this, McKinsey were giving emphasis to the way in which the Internet creates a virtual marketplace in which the buyer is unconstrained by the additional time and geographic boundaries, and has access to an almost infinite number of potential suppliers. In these circumstances, the seller is no longer (so) constrained by the capability of third parties in the distribution channel and can instead approach the customer in a far more direct fashion. At the same time, of course, the buyer is put into a far more powerful position in that there is far greater and far more immediate access to information, and comparisons between alternatives can be made far more easily and conveniently. Given this, the balance of power between the buyer and seller has the potential for changing in a series of radical and far-reaching ways. The implications of this can be seen most readily in terms of the decline of what may be loosely termed 'interruption marketing' and the emergence of a new approach based on permission marketing. (For a detailed discussion of permission marketing, refer to Godin, 1999.) This is illustrated in Figure 11.12.

The implications of the customer's greater access to information are being manifested in three major ways:

1. A downward pressure on the prices of products and services that lack any real competitive advantage or point of differentiation

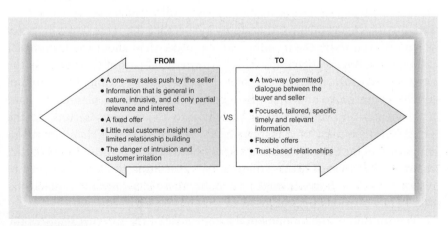

FROM		TO
• A one-way sales push by the seller		• A two-way (permitted) dialogue between the buyer and seller
• Information that is general in nature, intrusive, and of only partial relevance and interest	VS	• Focused, tailored, specific timely and relevant information
• A fixed offer		
• Little real customer insight and limited relationship building		• Flexible offers
• The danger of intrusion and customer irritation		• Trust-based relationships

FIGURE 11.12   *Permission marketing: the new paradigm*

2. A greater potential for demand-led markets

3. Increased customer/consumer expectations of higher product and service quality.

The picture from the standpoint of the manufacturer/producer, however, is not necessarily negative in that the Internet also has the capacity for:

- A reduction in the costs of capturing customer information

- The scope for far deeper customer/consumer relationships

- A greater ability to tailor value propositions

- An ability to price differentially

- A reduction in the cost of targeting customers/consumers.

The implications of this can then be seen in terms of the ways in which there are far greater opportunities for:

- Creating unique value propositions through personalization and customization

- More sophisticated segmentation, marketing and pricing

- New and possibly smaller and far more geographically dispersed competitors to enter the market

- Developing new barriers to switching.

Given the nature of these comments, it should be apparent that the implications of the Internet for marketing have been and are continuing to be potentially enormous, but are often still misunderstood and all too frequently underestimated by many marketing planners (referring back to Figure 11.11, many organizations have still to move beyond Stage 2). Perhaps the greatest danger that many face is that the issue of e-commerce is simply seen to be about selling online rather than about the far broader issue of building relationships with customers. As part of this, there is the need to recognize that the Internet means that, over time, the point of purchase can move and that this requires the marketing planner to have a far greater and more creative insight into the markets served. At the same time, the marketing planner needs to recognize that there are major implications for the organization's speed of response. Because the potential customer has instant access, there is an expectation of a similar speed of response to an enquiry. If this is not done, there is a danger of a deterioration in any relationship that exists or that has begun to emerge.

Recognition of the fundamental significance of the Internet requires the planner to come to terms with the ways in which commercially exploitable relationships might be developed. To do this involves a systematic approach to customer relationship management that has four key characteristics:

1. The need to understand customers in far greater detail

2. The need to meet their needs far more effectively

3. The need to make it easier for customers to do business with the organization than with a competitor

4. The need to add value.

Underpinning all of this, however, is the need to segment the customer base, since not all customers, be they B2B or B2C, view the development of the Internet and e-marketing in the same way. Recognition of this has led the Henley Centre to identify six principal consumer segments:

1. *Habit die-hards*, who are stuck in their ways and who have little knowledge, interest or access to the Internet

2. *Convenience/frenzied copers*, who are responsive to initiatives that save them time

3. *Experimenters*, who are willing to try new things

4. *Ethical shoppers*, who will purchase provided that the product offering is honest and politically correct

5. *Value shoppers/mercenaries*, who will buy on the basis of value

6. *Social shoppers*, who enjoy the social dimensions of shopping.

E-marketing and competitive advantage: a summary

It should be apparent from what has been written so far that the implications of e-marketing for traditional thinking about competitive advantage are potentially significant and can be seen most readily by the way in which some of the traditional bases of advantage can be eroded by a fast-moving and creative e-marketer. It is this that led Fifield (2000) to the suggestion that e-failure emerges from marketing planners seeing the Internet as:

■ Yet another 'push' activity

■ A new paradigm that then becomes the 'set' paradigm

■ Just another form of the same old 'production' mentality.

By contrast, e-success, he believes, will come from:

■ Understanding the needs of e-customers

■ Meeting the needs of e-customers

■ Doing things that can't be done offline

- Doing the boring things – well!

- Taking a strategic approach.

In discussing the contribution of the Internet to marketing, McDonald and Wilson (1999) argue the case for the six 'I's model. The model, which is based on the ways in which IT can add value to the customer and therefore improve the organization's marketing effectiveness, is designed to illustrate how the Internet can be used strategically. The model's six dimensions consist of:

1. *Integration*, and the need to ensure that information on customers from across the organization and across the customer life cycle is brought together, evaluated and then used proactively (e.g. First Direct)

2. *Interactivity*, so that the loop between the messages sent to customers and the messages they send back is closed (e.g. Amazon.com)

3. *Individualization* and the tailoring of products and services to meet the customer's specific needs (e.g. Levi's, Dell and the travel company Trailfinders)

4. *Independence* of location and the death of distance (e.g. Amazon.com, again)

5. *Intelligence* through integrated marketing databases

6. *Industry restructuring* and the redrawing of the market map (e.g. Ryanair, easyJet and, again, First Direct).

Rebuilding competitive advantage: the development of the extra value proposition

Amongst the most obvious consequences of markets becoming more competitive and customers more demanding is that many of the traditional bases of competitive advantage have been eroded. One way in which to combat this is for the marketing planner to differentiate the organization from its competitors by focusing upon the delivery of greater customer value. There are several ways in which this can be done, although before identifying some of these, the idea of the extra value proposition (EVP) needs to be put into context.

The basis for a considerable amount of marketing thinking for many years was the idea of strong selling propositions, in which the customer would be presented with one or more good reasons for buying the product – this is reflected in the notion of 'buy this product, receive this benefit'. From here, thinking moved to the idea of the unique selling proposition (USP), in which the strategy was based upon a feature or benefit that was unique to that organization or brand. However, in highly competitive markets, the scope for retaining uniqueness in anything other than the short term is limited unless the product is protected by a patent. The notion of a USP-based strategy has therefore largely been undermined over the past few years. Where there is still scope for USPs, this stems largely from the brand. Although it is often possible for the product itself to be copied relatively easily, a powerful brand is still capable of acting as a powerful differentiator.

At the same time, many marketing planners have recognized that customers who are generally more demanding are likely to respond positively to an extra value-based strategy, something that has led to a focus upon EVPs. Amongst the ways in which these can be delivered is through providing a greater number of benefits to the customer by:

- Customizing products and services to meet customers' specific needs

- Providing higher levels of customer convenience

- Offering faster service

- Providing more/better service

- Giving customer training

- Offering extraordinary guarantees

- Providing useful hardware/software tools for customers

- Developing membership loyalty programmes

- Winning through lower prices

- Aggressive pricing

- Offering lower price to those customers who are willing to give up some features and services

- Helping customers to reduce their other costs by:
  - showing the customer that the total cost is less despite its initially higher price
  - actively helping the customer to reduce ordering costs and inventory costs, processing costs and administration costs.

- Powerful branding.

Given the nature of these comments, it should be apparent that the marketing planner needs to recognize the pivotal importance of value and, in doing this, come to terms with a variety of issues, including:

- What exactly is meant by value within each segment of the market

- That value is defined by the customer, *not* the organization

- That value can be generated in a variety of ways, including:
  - *the product* (its quality, the levels of consistency, guarantees, and product development;
  - *service* (levels of support, speed, flexibility, convenience, and accessibility);
  - *the price/value equation* (the perceived value for money);
  - the form of *delivery*;
  - *the product/service experience* (refer back to our earlier discussion of experience marketing); and
  - *the brand* and its appeal to the customer
- That the leveraging of value is – or should be – a fundamental element of any marketing strategy
- That value can be damaged or destroyed remarkably quickly and easily.

Recognition of this should lead to the marketing planner auditing the value delivery process on a regular basis with a view to ensuring not only that value in the customer's eyes is leveraged, but also that anything that might damage or destroy customer value and the value of the brand is understood and managed in such a way that, at best, only minimal damage is done.

But although the creation and leveraging of value is at the heart of much of the thinking about marketing strategy, Ramaswamy and Prahalad (2006) have argued that in highly competitive markets, the traditional approach to value creation in which value is typically defined and developed by the organization is increasingly becoming obsolete. Instead, they suggest, if value is to be truly meaningful in the future it will come about as the result of co-creation between company and consumer. The obvious implication of this is that the traditional dividing line between the two sides and the roles they play – those of production and consumption – becomes blurred.

Amongst the examples of the organizations that have already moved in this direction are Amazon.com and eBay. In the case of Amazon, the company sells books, as well as a host of other products, at low prices. However, by building on consumer purchasing data, it can make recommendations to customers on books that are of possible interest. In addition to providing book reviews, customers are invited to provide their own reviews and to rate the books they have read. They are also able to browse a book before they buy by reading sample pages. The net effect of this is that a self-governing system based on an ongoing dialogue between the two sides and reflecting a high degree of trust and loyalty has developed. For Ramaswamy and Prahalad (2006), another good example of co-creation is eBay: 'the initial idea was to change the traditional buying and selling process, offering easy access though online auction to a range of advantageously priced products and services. As the initiative got under way, a community with its own rules evolved, adding further value to buyers and sellers through initiatives such as feedback forums, and ensuring a customer experience.'

Leveraging competitive advantage

Given everything that has been written so far within this chapter, it should be evident that the development, management and leveraging of competitive advantage is at the heart of any truly effective marketing strategy.

However, in a number of ways, one of the biggest constraints on leveraging competitive advantage is a managerial team's adherence to a particular business model. Mitchell (2005) suggests that 'most businesses today still adhere to Ford's core value-adding and innovation agenda: embed useful technologies in products and services; and drive down production costs through standardization; bring them to market as efficiently as possible'. Although the approach was undoubtedly highly effective, it can be argued that over time it also leads to a pattern of (inward focused) silo thinking, with managers becoming fixated on internal efficiency, specialist expertise, and an infrastructure that leads to managers losing sight of how all of this connects with customer value. The net effect of this is the creation of 'an unbridled corporate narcissism, where the corporation's obsessions with its own internal goals, processes, metrics and outputs crowd out virtually all other considerations' (Mitchell, 2005). The gap that this creates between the marketing planner preoccupations and what is seen to be important by the customer is potentially significant and highlights the need for organizations to rethink the underlying business model. Amongst the few to have done this are Toyota's lean production approach which is based on a sense-and-respond model, Dell with its make-to-order system, eBay which pioneered ways of marketing and connecting sellers and buyers, and Primark with its low-cost, speed to market approach.

The argument for taking a radically different approach to thinking about strategy and competitive advantage has also been developed by Kim & Mauborgne (2005), who in their book *Blue Ocean Strategy* argue that companies can be more successful by making 'leapfrogging' strategic moves into new markets rather than competing in an existing marketplace. They suggest that far too many organizations today 'look like mirror images of one another, competing head to head, facing shrinking demand and mounting costs and price pressures'. This, they argue, has come about because although many planners are good at incremental competition-based strategic thinking, too few have any real idea of how to create market dominance, new demand and high profit growth. In these circumstances, products become commodities and the aggressive competition turns the market space – or ocean – bloody.

In order to break away from this, managers need to concentrate not upon a series of incremental changes, but upon a leap in value that has the effect of making the competition irrelevant. In doing this, the company can create a new and, in the short term at least, an uncontested market space (it is these spaces that they refer to as the blue oceans). For Kim and Mauborgne 'value innovation' based strategic thinking is based on the simultaneous pursuit of differentiation and low costs and differs from the more traditional business innovation in that 'when most people think of business innovation they think of new products, new ventures, market pioneering and first-mover advantage. But value innovation is really about challenging assumptions about strategy, redefining market boundaries and making the competition irrelevant rather than competing on established ground. It is geared towards creating new market space and encompasses the entire value chain from product, service and delivery to costs and pricing instead of any one function' (quoted in Bartram, 2005).

Amongst the firms to have done this are Canon, who shifted their strategic focus away from the corporate market and, by using a less advanced technology, created the personal copier market; Starbucks with coffee bars; Nokia with mobile phones; Apple with the i-pod; and in its early days, The Body Shop.

The commercial significance of true value innovation was highlighted by their research findings in which they focused upon 100 companies' new product business launches. Of these, 86 per cent proved to be line extensions or incremental improvements. However, the 14 per cent of the launches that were genuine value innovations accounted for 38 per cent of the companies' revenues and 61 per cent of their profit. Despite this sort of evidence, they found that many organizations, despite significant innovation budgets, are still focusing upon incremental improvements 'such as the 44th variety of spaghetti sauce', but are then surprised by the limited market gains that they make.

The attractions of blue oceans and the need to think differently has also been highlighted by Prahalad (2004), who suggests in his book *The Fortune at the Bottom of the Pyramid* that one of the biggest untapped markets is that of the world's 4 billion poor (people who live on less than $2 a day). The trick, he suggests, lies in turning the poor into consumers. In order to make profits at the bottom of the pyramid (BOP) Prahalad argues that it is not just a case of making small changes to what is offered to the developed world, but to develop a 'forgetting curve' and innovate. For these consumers, cash flow is typically unpredictable and low. Given this, pack size and contents need to be rethought, something that had led to an upsurge in single-serve packaging.

At the same time, however, those in the BOP segment often have very high levels of aspiration towards brands. Recognizing this, the challenge for companies is to change the price-performance relationship of what they produce to take account of different requirements and income levels. As an example of this, Prahalad argues for technology to be used to create 'hybrid' products – those that work with still-evolving infrastructure, such as PCs with in-built back-up power sources.

The potential attractions of the BOP market if a company is able to find the right combination of function, price and distribution are substantial, something that was illustrated by the Monsoon Hungama mobile phone.

GSM mobile phones were first available in India for $1000. As the price fell to $300, the market grew, but only relatively slowly. However, when Reliance, a mobile phone provider, introduced the Monsoon Hungama promotion of 100 free minutes with a multimedia handset for $10 and a monthly payment of $9.25, the company received one million applications in 10 days. The net effect of this was that India became the world's fastest growing wireless market.

11.6 SUMMARY

In this chapter we have examined Porter's work on generic competitive strategies and how the value chain can be used as a platform for thinking about competitive advantage. Competitive advantage is, as discussed in some detail, a fundamental element of the strategic marketing planning process, and the planner must therefore understand the sources of advantage and how advantage might be leveraged.

With markets currently undergoing a series of radical changes, the traditional bases of advantage are being eroded and there is therefore the need for the planner to think creatively how (new) advantages might be developed and leveraged.

CHAPTER 12

The Formulation of Strategy 3: Strategies for Leaders, Followers, Challengers and Nichers

12.1 LEARNING OBJECTIVES

When you have read this chapter you should be able to understand:

  (a) the influence of market position on strategy;

  (b) how organizations might attack others and defend themselves;

  (c) how life cycles influence marketing strategy and planning.

12.2 INTRODUCTION

In Chapter 11 we focused in some detail upon Porter's generic strategies and the nature and sources of competitive advantage. In this chapter we take the analysis a stage further by examining how the organization's position in the market, ranging from market leader through to market nicher, influences strategy and planning. Finally, we turn our attention to the ways in which market and product life cycles need to be managed.

12.3 THE INFLUENCE OF MARKET POSITION ON STRATEGY

In discussing how best to formulate marketing strategy, we have focused so far on the sorts of model and approaches to planning that can help to formalize the analytical process. In making use of models such as these, the strategist needs to pay explicit attention to a series of factors, including the organization's objectives and resources, managerial attitudes to risk, the structure of the market, competitors' strategies and, very importantly, the organization's position within the market. The significance of market position and its often very direct influence upon strategy has been discussed in detail by a wide variety of writers, most of whom suggest classifying competitive position along a spectrum from market leader to market nichers:

- *Market leader*. In the majority of industries there is one firm that is generally recognized to be the leader. It typically has the largest market share and, by virtue of its pricing, advertising intensity, distribution coverage, technological advance and rate of new product introductions, it determines the nature, pace and bases of competition. It is this dominance that typically provides the benchmark for other companies in the industry. However, it needs to be emphasized that market leadership, although often associated with size, is in reality a more complex concept and should instead be seen in terms of an organization's ability to *determine the nature and bases of competition within the market*. A distinction can therefore be made between market leadership that is based primarily upon size, and what might be termed 'thought leadership' that is based not so much upon size, but upon innovation and different patterns of thinking.

- *Market challengers and followers*. Firms with a slightly smaller market share can adopt one of two stances. They may choose to adopt an aggressive stance and attack other firms, including the market leader, in an attempt to gain share and perhaps dominance (market challengers), or they may adopt a less aggressive stance in order to maintain the status quo (market followers).

- *Market nichers*. Virtually every industry has a series of small firms that survive, and indeed often prosper, by choosing to specialize in parts of the market that are too limited in size and potential to be of real interest to larger firms. A case in point would be Morgan specializing in traditional sports cars. By concentrating their efforts in this way, market nichers are able to build up specialist market knowledge and avoid expensive head-on fights with larger companies.

This approach to classification has, in turn, led to a considerable discussion of the strategic alternatives for leaders, challengers and nichers, with numerous analogies being drawn between business strategy and military strategy. The idea has been to show how the ideas of military strategists, and in particular Karl von Clausewitz, Sun Tzu and Basil Liddell-Hart, might be applied to the alternatives open to a company intent on gaining or retaining a competitive advantage. Within this section we will therefore examine some of these ideas and show how market leaders might defend their current position, how challengers might attempt to seize share, and

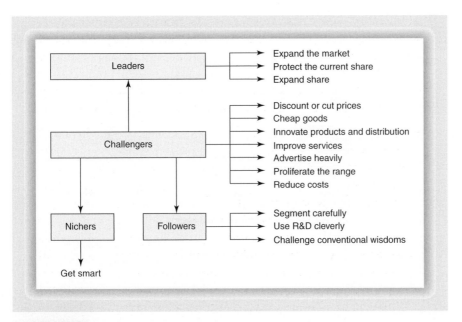

FIGURE 12.1 *Leaders, challengers followers, and market nichers*

how followers and nichers are affected by this. An overview of how this might be done appears in Figure 12.1.

12.4 STRATEGIES FOR MARKET LEADERS

Although a position of market leadership has undoubted attractions, both in terms of the scope that often exists to influence others and a possibly higher return on investment, leaders have all too often in the past proved to be vulnerable in the face of an attack from a challenger or when faced with the need for a major technological change. If, therefore, a market leader is to remain as the dominant company, it needs to defend its position constantly. In doing this, there are three major areas to which the marketing strategist needs to pay attention:

1. How best to expand the total market

2. How to protect the organization's current share of the market

3. How to increase market share.

A summary of the ways in which leaders might do this appears in Figure 12.2. Of these, it is an *expansion of the overall market* from which the market leader typically stands to gain the most. It follows from this that the strategist needs to search for new users, new uses and greater usage levels of his or her firm's products. This can be done in a variety of ways.

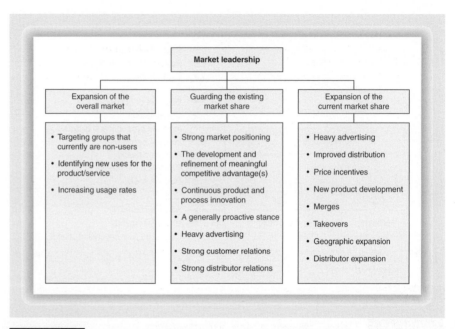

Market leadership

Expansion of the overall market

Guarding the existing market share

Expansion of the current market share

• Targeting groups that currently are non-users

• Identifying new uses for the product/service

• Increasing usage rates

• Strong market positioning

• The development and refinement of meaningful competitive advantage(s)

• Continuous product and process innovation

• A generally proactive stance

• Heavy advertising

• Strong customer relations

• Strong distributor relations

• Heavy advertising

• Improved distribution

• Price incentives

• New product development

• Merges

• Takeovers

• Geographic expansion

• Distributor expansion

FIGURE 12.2 *Strategies for market leaders*

In the 1960s and 1970s, for example, Honda increased its sales by targeting groups that traditionally had not bought motorcycles. These groups, which included commuters and women, were seen to offer enormous untapped potential. The company unlocked this by developing a range of small, economic and lightweight machines, which they then backed with a series of advertising campaigns giving emphasis to their convenience and style. Moving into the 1980s, the strategy began to change yet again as the company recognized the potential for selling motorcycles almost as an adjunct to fashion. Styling therefore became far more important. This repositioning was then taken several steps further in the late 1980s as Honda, along with other manufacturers, began targeting the middle-aged executive market with a series of larger motorcycles that were supported by advertising campaigns giving emphasis to the re-creation of youthful values.

As a second stage the strategist might search for *new uses* for the product. Perhaps the most successful example of this is Du Pont's Nylon, which was first used as a synthetic fibre for parachutes and then subsequently for stockings, shirts, tyres, upholstery, carpets and a spectrum of industrial and engineering uses. This is illustrated in Figure 12.3. A broadly similar approach of market development through a series of new uses has been taken with Teflon. Developed initially as a high-performance lubricant for the American space programme, the product has been reformulated for applications in cooking, motor oils, and as a protection for fabrics, clothing and carpets.

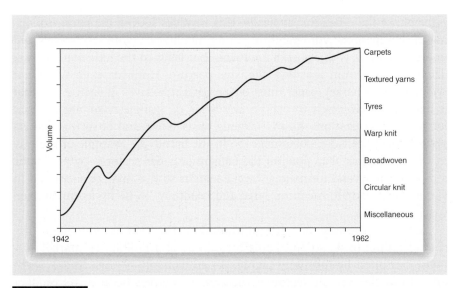

FIGURE 12.3   *Nylon's product cycle (adapted from Yale, 1964)*

The third approach to market expansion involves encouraging *existing users* of the product to *increase their usage rates*, a strategy pursued with considerable success by Procter & Gamble with its Head & Shoulders brand of shampoo, which was promoted on the basis that two applications were more effective than one.

At the same time as trying to expand the total market, the market leader should not lose sight of the need to *defend its market share*. It has long been recognized that leaders represent a convenient target since, because of their size, they are often vulnerable to attack. Whether the attack is successful is often determined largely by the leader's ability to recognize its vulnerability and position itself in such a way that the challenger's chances of success are minimized. The need for this is illustrated by examples from many industries, including photography (Kodak having been attacked in the film market by Fuji and in the camera market by Polaroid, Minolta, Nikon, Canon and Pentax), soft drinks (Pepsi attacking Coca-Cola), car hire (Avis against Hertz), razors (Bic and Wilkinson Sword attacking Gillette), photocopiers (Xerox being attacked by numerous players) and computers (IBM being attacked by Apple, Compaq and Dell among numerous others).

Although there are obvious dangers in generalizing, the most successful strategy for a market leader intent on fighting off attacks such as these lies in the area of continuous product and/or process innovation, something that involves the leader refusing to be content with the way things are, and leading the industry in new-product ideas, customer services, distribution effectiveness and cost cutting. It therefore needs to keep increasing its competitive effectiveness and value to customer by applying the military principle of the offensive. Typically, this involves setting the pace, exploiting the competitors' vulnerabilities, and generally behaving aggressively and unpredictably. It is this sort of approach that leads to the idea that the best defence comes from a strong offensive posture. However, even when not attacking, the market leader must ensure that it behaves in such a way that it does not allow itself to expose any areas of weakness, something that for many organizations means keeping costs down and ensuring that its prices reflect the value customers see in the brand. An example of the way in which this has been done in the consumer goods sector is by producing a product in several forms (e.g. liquid soap as well as bars of soap) and in various sizes (small, medium, large and economy) to tie up as much shelf space as possible.

Although the cost of 'plugging holes' in this way is often high, the cost of failing to do so and being forced out of a product or market segment can often be infinitely higher. As an example of this, Kodak withdrew from the 35 mm sector of the camera market because its product was losing money. The Japanese subsequently found a way of making 35 mm cameras profitably at a low price and in this way took share away from Kodak's cheaper cameras.

Similarly, in the USA, the major car manufacturers paid too little attention in the 1960s and early 1970s to the small car sector because of the difficulties of making them at a profit. Both the Japanese (Toyota, Mazda and Honda) and the Germans (Volkswagen) took advantage of this lack of domestic competition and developed the small car sector very profitably. The long-term consequence of this has been that the domestic manufacturers, having initially conceded this market sector, subsequently entered into a series of joint ventures with the Japanese (e.g. Ford with Mazda, General Motors with Toyota, Isuzo and Suzuki, and Chrysler with Mitsubishi), the long-term results of which have often proved questionable.

The third course of action open to market leaders intent on remaining leaders involves *expanding market share*. This can typically be done in a variety of ways, including by means of heavier advertising, improved distribution, price incentives, new products and, as the brewers have demonstrated, by mergers, takeovers, alliances and distribution deals.

It should be apparent from what has been said so far that leadership involves the development and pursuit of a consistently proactive strategy, something which Pascale (1989) has touched upon; this is discussed in Illustration 12.1.

The PIMS study and the pursuit of market share

The significance of market share, and in particular its influence upon return on investment, has long been recognized, and has been pointed to

Illustration 12.1   Change, transformation and a market focus – reasserting market leadership

Three of the best-known and most successful organizational change programmes in the 1980s and 1990s took place at British Airways ('from Bloody Awful to Bloody Awesome'), Grand Met and SmithKline Beecham. In each case, a slow-moving and increasingly unsuccessful organization was refocused and transformed into a marketing leader. However, the problems of achieving transformation *and maintaining* a successful profile are highlighted by the way in which, only five years after the publication of Peters and Waterman's 1982 bestseller *In Search of Excellence*, all but 14 of its 43 'excellent' companies had either grown weaker or were declining rapidly. Similarly, BA, having been successfully turned around, was then hit very hard by a combination of factors, including the European low-cost airlines such as easyJet and Ryanair (see Illustration 11.3), and was forced into massive restructuring. In commenting on this, Richard Pascale (1989) argues that too few managers really understand what is involved in transforming an organization. To him, transformation involves not only a discontinuous shift in an organization's capability, but also the much more difficult task of sustaining that shift. Faced with the need for change, he suggests, companies come to a fork in the road. About 80 per cent take the easy route, stripping themselves 'back to basics', searching for the latest tools and techniques, and going on to risk stagnation or decline. Only a fifth of companies take the much tougher, alternative route. This involves three big steps: the first he refers to as 'inquiring into their underlying paradigm' (that is, questioning the way they do everything, including how managers think); attacking the problems systematically on all fronts, notably strategy, operations, organization and culture; and 'reinventing' themselves in such a way that the transformation becomes self-sustaining. It is only in this way that truly intellectual learning is matched by the emotional learning that is needed and transformation truly becomes embedded in the organization.

by a variety of studies over the past 35 years, the best known of which is the PIMS (Profit Impact of Market Strategy) research.

The aim of the PIMS programme has been to identify the most significant determinants of profitability. The factors that have shown themselves to be persistently the most influential are:

1. *Competitive position* (including market share and relative product quality)

2. *Production structure* (including investment intensity and the productivity of operations)

3. The *attractiveness of the served market* (as shown by its growth rate and customers' characteristics).

Taken together, these factors explain 65–70 per cent of the variability in profitability among the firms in the PIMS database. By examining the determinants of profitability it is possible to address a series of strategic questions, such as:

- What rate of profit and cash flow is normal for this type of business?

- What profit and cash flow outcomes can be expected if the business continues with its present strategy?

- How will future performance be affected by a change in strategy?

One of the key notions underlying strategic marketing management is, as already emphasized, that of the relative position of a firm among its competitors, particularly with regard to unit costs, quality, price, profitability and market share.

The respective contribution of each of these factors to overall profitability is estimated by means of a multiple regression model. This allows the impact of weak variables to be offset by strong variables – a low market share might, for example, be offset by high product quality. Once the model has been applied to a given company, it can then be used to assess the relative strengths and weaknesses of competitors in order to identify the best source of competitive advantage. From the viewpoint of the marketing strategist, this has most typically been seen in terms of the organization's relative market share, a factor which has been given considerable emphasis by successive PIMS reports: 'The average ROI for businesses with under 10 per cent market share was about 9 per cent ... On the average, a difference of 10 percentage points in market share is accompanied by a difference of about 5 points in pretax ROI.' The study has also shown that businesses with a market share of more than 40 per cent achieve ROIs of 30 per cent, or three times that of firms with shares under 10 per cent.

In the light of these findings, it is not at all surprising that many organizations have pursued a goal of share increases, since it should lead not just to greater profits, but also to greater profitability (that is, return on investment).

Although the findings and conclusions of the PIMS study have an initial and pragmatic appeal, the general approach has been subjected to an increasing amount of critical comment in recent years. In particular, critics have highlighted:

- Measurement errors

- Apparent deficiencies in the model

- The interpretations of the findings.

Perhaps the main concern, however, is over the practice of deriving prescriptions about strategy from unsupported causal inferences. It is therefore important in using PIMS data to understand the limitations of the approach. When used as intended, data from the PIMS programme can, its defenders argue, provide valuable insights into effective marketing and corporate strategy. In particular, they point to some of the broad conclusions from the programme, which can be summarized as:

1. In the long run, the single most important factor affecting performance is the quality of an enterprise's products/services relative to those of its competitors.

2. Market share and profitability are strongly related:
   - ROI increases steadily as market share increases
   - Enterprises having relatively large market shares tend to have above-average rates of investment turnover
   - The ratio of marketing expenses to sales revenue tends to be lower for enterprises having high market shares. The PIMS programme has demonstrated the linkages among superior relative quality, higher relative prices, gains in market share, lower relative costs and higher profitability. These linkages, which are portrayed in Figure 12.4, indicate the causal role that relative quality plays in influencing business performance.

3. High investment intensity acts as a powerful drag on profitability:
   - The higher the ratio of investment to sales, the lower the ROI; enterprises having high investment intensity tend to be unable to achieve profit margins sufficient to sustain growth.

4. Many dog and wildcat activities generate cash, while many cash cows do not.

5. Vertical integration is a profitable strategy for some kinds of enterprise but not for others.

6. Most of the strategic factors that boost ROI also contribute to long-term value.

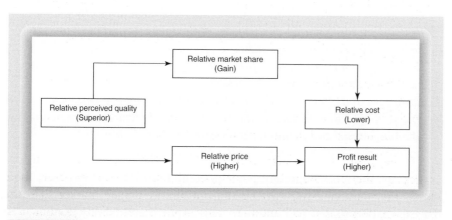

FIGURE 12.4   *Some PIMS linkages (adapted from Buzzell and Gale, 1987)*

Despite these comments, however, the reader should bear in mind the very real reservations that have been expressed about the study, since the relationship between profit and market share that is claimed as the result of the PIMS study may well be due more to flexible definitions of market boundaries than to market realities (see Baker, 1985, p. 110). Similarly, Porter (1980, p. 44) suggests that:

> *There is no single relationship between profitability and market share, unless one conveniently defines the market so that focused or differentiated firms are assigned high market shares in some narrowly-defined industries and the industry definitions of cost leadership firms are allowed to stay broad (which they must because cost leaders often do not have the largest share in every sub-market). Even shifting industry cannot explain the high returns of firms which have achieved differentiation industry-wide and held market shares below that of the industry leader.*

A number of other writers have also argued that the study's findings are generally spurious. Hamermesh *et al.* (1987), for example, have pointed to numerous successful low-share businesses. Similarly, Woo and Cooper (1982) identified 40 low-share businesses with pretax ROIs of 20 per cent or more.

Findings such as these suggest the existence not of a linear relationship between market share and profitability but rather, in some industries at least, of a V-shaped relationship. This is illustrated in Figure 12.5. In such an industry, there will be one or two highly profitable market leaders, several profitable low-share firms, and a number of medium-share, poorly focused and far less profitable organizations. This has been commented on by Roach (1981, p. 21):

> *The large firms on the V-curve tend to address the entire market, achieving cost advantages and high market share by realizing economies of scale. The small competitors reap high profits by focusing on some narrower segments of the business and by developing specialized approaches to production, marketing, and distribution for that segment. Ironically the medium-sized competitors at the trough of the V-curve are unable to realize any competitive advantage and often show the poorest profit performance. Trapped in a strategic 'no man's land', they are too large to reap the benefits of more focused competition, yet too small to benefit from the economies of scale that their larger competitors enjoy.*

Perhaps the most important point to come from this sort of observation is that the marketing strategist should not blindly pursue market share in the expectation that it will automatically improve profitability. Rather it is the case that the return will depend upon the *type* of strategy pursued. In

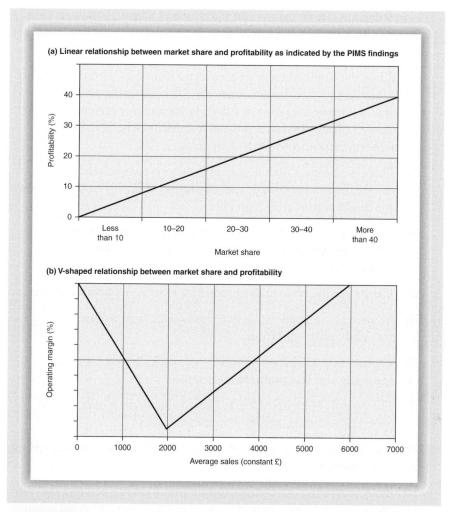

(a) Linear relationship between market share and profitability as indicated by the PIMS findings

(b) V-shaped relationship between market share and profitability

FIGURE 12.5 *The relationship between market share and profitability*

some cases, for example, the cost of achieving a share gain may far exceed the returns that are possible. There are therefore twelve factors that need to be taken into account in deciding whether to pursue a share-gaining strategy:

1. The cost of gaining share and whether this will be higher than the returns that will follow. This is likely to occur in various situations, but most obviously when the market is in or near maturity, since in these circumstances sales (and hence share) can only be gained on the basis of what would typically be a zero-sum game (this would in effect lead to a pyrrhic victory in which the benefits of victory are outweighed by the costs of achieving that victory). In other words, the only way in which a company can gain sales is at the expense

of someone else in the market. By contrast, when the market is in the growth stage, sales can be gained without the need to pursue a confrontational strategy.

2. When the implication of gaining extra share has a knock-on effect to another part of the organization. This might happen when a firm is already operating at full capacity and any increase would involve a heavy investment in new capacity. The likelihood of achieving a positive ROI is then small.

3. There is already a high degree of loyalty to competitors' products among the customer base and this loyalty can only be broken down at a disproportionately high cost.

4. The company intent on gaining share has few obvious or sustainable competitive advantages and hence a weak selling proposition.

5. The future life cycle of the product or market is likely to be short.

6. An increase in share is likely to lead to the firm running foul of anti-monopoly legislation.

7. The increase in share can only be gained by moving into less appealing and less profitable segments.

8. The pursuit of higher share is likely to spark off a major – and potentially unmanageable – competitive fight.

9. It is unlikely that any gain in share can be maintained for anything other than the short term.

10. By increasing share, a larger competitor begins to perceive the organization as an emerging threat and decides to respond when, assuming the organization had not decided to grow, the two firms would have coexisted peacefully.

11. The organization has developed a reputation as a specialist or niche operator and any move away from this would compromise brand values and the brand equity.

12. By growing, the organization would fall into a strategic 'no man's land' in which the firm is too big to be small (in other words, it would no longer be a niche operator), but too small to be big enough to fight off the large players in the market on an equal footing (see Figure 12.5).

In addition, of course, share-gaining strategies can also be argued against when the management team has neither the ability nor the *fundamental* willingness to develop and sustain an appropriate and offensive strategy.

These sorts of points have also been referred to by Jacobson and Aaker (1985), who, in an article entitled 'Is Market Share All That It's Cracked Up To Be?', raised a series of fundamental questions about the value of chasing share gains. It is, however, possible to identify the two conditions under which higher share generally does lead to higher profits. These are: first, when the company offers a superior quality product that is then sold at a premium price, which more than offsets the extra costs of achieving higher quality; and, secondly, when unit costs fall significantly as sales and share increase.

These two points have been developed by Buzzell and Wiersema (1981), who, by using PIMS data, concluded that companies that successfully achieved gains in market share generally outperformed their competitors in three areas: *new product activity*, *relative product quality* and *levels of marketing expenditure*. Thus:

1. The successful share gainers developed and added a greater number of new products to their range than their competitors

2. Companies that increased their relative product quality achieved greater share gains than those whose quality stayed constant or declined

3. Those companies that increased their marketing expenditures more rapidly than the rate of market growth gained share

4. Companies that cut their prices more rapidly than competitors rarely – and perhaps surprisingly – did not achieve significant share gains.

In summary, therefore, it is possible to identify the factors that the PIMS researchers believe act as the triggers to profit. These are illustrated in Figure 12.6.

–	Profitability	+
• Weak	Relative market share	• High
• Inferior	Relative quality	• Superior
• High	Investment intensity	• Low
• Low	Capacity utilization	• High
• Below par	Productivity	• Above par
• Low or in decline	Market growth	• High
• None	New products	• Some
• High	Market spread	• Low
• Low	Market concentration	• High
• Complex	Logistics	• Simple

FIGURE 12.6   *PIMs and the triggers of profit*

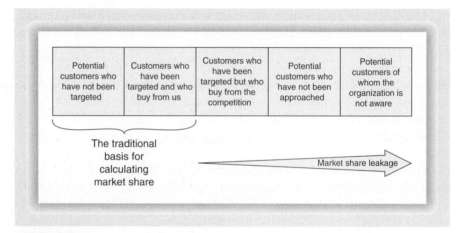

FIGURE 12.7 *Broadening the redefinition of market share*

Market share and the definition of market boundaries

Given the importance placed upon market share by the PIMS researchers, it is essential that the marketing planner understands in detail the boundaries of the market in which the organization or the brand is operating. In analysing an organization's market share and performance, the marketing planner needs to begin by taking as broad an approach as possible. In doing this, a distinction can be made between that part of the market of which the organization has a share and the broader market, which either has not been approached or has 'leaked' away (see Figure 12.7).

12.5 MARKETING STRATEGY AND MILITARY ANALOGIES: LESSONS FOR MARKET LEADERS

It has been suggested in the past that there are, in essence, two sorts of people: those 'who make change and those who talk about making change. It's better to be in the first group; there is often far less competition' (Anon).

The greater intensity of competition that has taken place throughout the world in recent years has led to many managers developing an interest in models of military warfare with a view to identifying any lessons that might be learned and applied to business. From the viewpoint of a market leader intent on defending his position, there are six military defence strategies that can be used: position defence, mobile defence, flanking defence, contraction defence, pre-emptive defence and counter-offensive defence. However, if military history is to teach the marketing or business strategist anything at all, it has to be that some of these strategies are likely to be far less successful than others.

> **Illustration 12.2   Sun Tzu and the art of war**
>
> Sun Tzu was a Chinese general who lived around 290 BC. During his life more than 300 wars were fought between the largely separate Chinese states and it was from these that he learned the principles of warfare that appear in his book *The Art of War*. The essence of the book is that strategy is everything and that preparing the battle is often more important than fighting it. He argues also that you should never wage war on an army that is deeply committed to its cause. According to Sun Tzu, the art of war is identifying where your rivals are weakest and then exploiting this. In applying these sorts of ideas to marketing, one lesson that planners have had to learn is that every brand has committed and brand-loyal customers who will only rarely consider changing their brand. Any advertising messages aimed at them will be ignored and, in some cases, may strengthen their commitment to the existing brand. Instead, it is those who are not brand-loyal and who are the potential defectors who should be the target. Although this sort of comment may seem self-evident, the reality is that many marketing campaigns are poorly focused and, as a result, waste resources.

Amongst the best known of the writers on warfare are Basil Liddell-Hart and Sun Tzu. Of the two, it is Sun Tzu who has been the most influential in marketing, with his book *The Art of War* (1963) having been used extensively by marketing strategists (see Illustration 12.2).

However, in thinking about strategy and what might be learned from looking at other organizations, it is worth remembering a comment made by Sun Tzu:

> *All men can see the tactics whereby I conquer, but what none can see is the strategy out of which great victory is evolved.*

The issue that emerges from this is that the slavish adoption of another organization's winning strategy is not guaranteed to work. Rather, it is the 'softer' elements of marketing and the mindset of the management team that are of far greater significance.

Position defence

Arguably one of the consistently least successful methods of defence, the position defence or fortress, relies on the apparent impregnability of a fixed position. Militarily, parallels are often drawn between this and the wartime French Maginot and German Siegfried lines, neither of which achieved their purpose. To overcome a position defence, an attacker therefore typically adopts an indirect approach rather than the head-on attack that the defender expects. Among the companies that have adopted a position defence only to see it fail is Land Rover, which was attacked initially by Toyota, Suzuki and Subaru, and then, more recently, by others such as BMW and Mercedes-Benz. In the case of Land Rover, the company, which had developed a strong international reputation for well-made and very rugged four-wheel drive vehicles, did relatively little in the 1960s and 1970s either in terms of product or market development, and subsequently fell victim to an attack based on a lower price and 'fun' appeal. Rather than responding in an aggressive way to this, Land Rover continued with only small modifications to its strategy of selling primarily to farmers and the military, and was then faced with a second-wave attack from Mitsubishi.

There are a series of lessons to be learned from examples such as this, as Saunders (1987, p. 15) has suggested:

> *A company attempting a fortress defence will find itself retreating from line after line of fortification into shrinking product markets. The stationary company will end up with outdated products and lost markets, undermined by competitors who find superiority in new products in the marketplace. Even a dominant leader cannot afford to maintain a static defence. It must continually engage in product improvement, line extensions and product proliferations. For instance, giants like Unilever spread their front into related household products; and Coca-Cola, despite having over 50 per cent of the world soft drinks market, has moved aggressively into marketing wines and has diversified into desalination equipment and plastics. These companies defend their territory by breaking it down into units and entrenching in each.*

(Author's note: In 2000, Unilever announced a major review of the company's product portfolio and subsequently axed 1200 of their 1600 consumer brands. The rationale for this was to concentrate investment behind 400 high-growth brands and, in this way, strengthen the organization's position. Seven years later, as part of the 'One Unilever' project, the company sold its US laundry business, a move that ended years of price wars with Procter & Gamble.)

Mobile defence

The second approach, a mobile defence, is based in part on the ideas discussed by Theodore Levitt (1960) in his article 'Marketing myopia'; here, rather than becoming preoccupied with the defence of current products and markets through the proliferation of brands, the strategist concentrates upon market broadening and diversification. The rationale for this is to cover new territories that might in the future serve as focal points both for offence and defence. In doing this, the intention is to achieve a degree of strategic depth, which will enable the firm not just to fight off an attacker, but to retaliate effectively. At the heart of a mobile defence, therefore, is the need for management to define carefully, and perhaps redefine, the business it is in. Several years ago, for example, the bicycle manufacturers redefined their business by recognizing that their future was that of leisure and health rather than that of cheap and generally functional transport.

However, in pursuing a strategy of market broadening, the marketing strategist should never lose sight of two major principles – the *principle of the objective* (pursue a clearly defined and realistic objective) and the *principle of mass* (focus your efforts upon the enemy's point of weakness). The implications of these are perhaps best understood by considering for a moment the oil industry. In the 1970s, faced with the likelihood of oil reserves being exhausted in the twenty-first century, the oil companies were encouraged to redefine their business from that of petrol and oil to that of 'energy'. This led several companies to experiment with, and in some cases invest in, nuclear energy, coal, hydroelectric power, solar energy and wind power. In the majority of cases, however, success has at best been limited and in some instances has diluted the company's mass in the markets it is operating in currently. A strategy of market broadening should therefore be realistic and reflect not just the two principles referred to above but also, and very importantly, company capability.

The second dimension of a mobile defence involves *diversification* into unrelated industries. Among those who have done this, in some cases with considerable success, are the tobacco manufacturers, who, faced with a declining market, have moved into industries such as food and financial services, both of which offer greater long-term stability and profits. The net effect of this has been that their vulnerability to predators has been reduced significantly, although there is an irony in the linking of tobacco products with life assurance, which could produce another related net effect.

Flanking defence

It has long been recognized that the flank of an organization, be it an army or a company, is often less well protected than other parts. This vulnerability has several implications for the marketing strategist, the most significant of which is that secondary markets should not be ignored. This lesson was learned the hard way in the 1960s by Smith's Crisps, which, at the time, dominated the UK's potato crisp market. This market consisted primarily of adults, with distribution being achieved mainly through pubs. The children's market was seen by the company to be of secondary importance, and it was therefore this flank that Imperial Tobacco's Golden Wonder attacked with a strategy aimed at children. Distribution to this market then took place through newsagents, sweet shops and the grocery trade. The net effect of this was that, within just a few years, Golden Wonder had taken over as market leader. Subsequently, market leadership was taken over by yet another player, Walker's.

This need to monitor closely the organization's flanks is shown also by the way in which the low-cost airlines deliberately chose not to attack the major airlines such as BA, KLM and Lufthansa head-on, but to pursue a flanking strategy that involved redefining the market (see Illustration 11.3). A similar approach was taken by Dyson, who flanked Hoover and Electrolux (see Illustration 12.3).

Illustration 12.3 Dyson's reinvention of the vacuum cleaner market

One of the biggest marketing success stories of the 1990s was the launch of the Dyson Dual Cyclone™ vacuum cleaner. Following a five-year development period that started in 1978 and involved more than 5000 prototypes, ten years getting it to the market, and grudging retail acceptance, the product took off in a spectacular fashion. Within just a few years of its launch the company had become the UK's market leader, with more than 52 per cent of the home market in value, and had penetrated some of the most difficult overseas markets in the world, including Japan. By 1999 the company was the fastest growing manufacturer in the UK and had forced companies such as Hoover and Electrolux on to the defensive. Annual sales had grown from £2.4 million in 1993 to £170 million, and profits from £200 000 to £22 million. Worldwide, sales were well in excess of £1 billion.

The origins of the market and product

The vacuum cleaner was invented by Hoover at the beginning of the twentieth century, and, by the final quarter of the century, the market had seemingly reached long-term maturity, with the major players all offering a broadly similar product and fighting desperately for market share, Dyson's approach was very different and involved doing away with the vacuum pump and bag that had been the basis of traditional machines and replacing them with two cyclones, one inside the other, that spun the air at very high speeds and filtered particles as small as cigarette smoke and allergens, which were then collected in a transparent bin.

At the beginning of the 1990s, having developed the product, James Dyson began approaching the leading players of the time, including Bosch, Siemens, Philips, Miele and Electrolux, with a view to their manufacturing and marketing the product in return for a royalty. Having been ignored or rejected by all of them – in part, he felt, because the product would have led to the collapse of the immensely valuable replacement bag market – Dyson decided in 1993 to set up his own manufacturing organization.

Twenty-three months later, and despite selling at twice the price of the conventional vacuum cleaner, the Dyson Dual Cyclone™ had become Britain's best-selling vacuum cleaner.

Niche or mass-market product?

In the early stages of the product's life, many commentators focused upon the product's design and colourful style and suggested that it was 'basically a niche product for technocrats' (Vandermerwe, 1999, p. 6). James Dyson disagreed. The aesthetics were not, he said, 'the defining and differentiating characteristics'. Instead, it was the performance. 'Because everyone has dust, vacuuming is something that everyone has to do.' Despite its technology and its looks it was, in his eyes, a product designed not for a niche but for the masses. Everyone, he felt, would want to take advantage of what he saw to be a major leap in performance, *and they would be willing to pay for it* (our emphasis). The technology, protected by numerous patents, demanded a high(er) price, which the market would, he believed, pay if it was convinced it was better than the competition.

The competitive response

The failure on the part of some or all the competitors to respond quickly and aggressively to Dyson's new technology and entry to the market was seen by some analysts to be surprising. Others saw it to be predictable, and a manifestation of the lazy and complacent attitude that often develops in stable and mature markets. Rebecca Trentham, Dyson's Marketing Director, suggested that, even when Dyson was making steady inroads into the competitors' territories, they stayed 'pretty much asleep' and, if pushed, would comment that the product was 'just a fad', 'a gimmick', 'a funny-looking niche product', and 'the Dyson is nothing but a shooting star'.

For James Dyson, this failure to respond was entirely predictable:

> There was a huge opportunity for someone to come along with different and better technology and something which looked different. The market seemed impenetrable because it was dominated by big multinationals. I thought it presented a great opportunity because they were all sitting back on their fat market shares without really doing anything, it was all too cosy ...

The second stage: building upon success

Having established the company as the UK market leader Dyson reinforced its position with a number of new models, including:

- The Dyson Absolute, targeted at asthmatics and others with respiratory problems. The Absolute was the only vacuum cleaner that not only removed pollens but also, due to its bacteria-killing screen, killed certain viruses and bacteria such as salmonella and listeria.

- The De Stijl, a brightly coloured model that was a homage to the Dutch modernist art movement of the early twentieth century.

- The Dyson Antarctica, produced as part of the company's sponsorship of the attempt by Sir Ranulph Fiennes to be the first person to walk across the entire Antarctic continent and, in doing this, raise £5 m for breast cancer research. Dyson donated almost £2 m to the appeal.

In 1999 the company took the product a step further still by launching a new model featuring a filter that did not have to be thrown away, but could instead be cleaned.

By the end of the decade, the competition had come to terms with the inevitable and responded by developing their own products characterized by bright colours, see-through plastic parts and cyclone-type design.

The retail and service philosophy

Although the product's performance was from the outset far superior to anything offered by the competition, Dyson – in common with many inventors of new and different products – faced difficulties in breaking into the established retail networks. As Vandermerwe (1999, p. 9) commented:

> The first retailers approached by Dyson had been sceptical about stocking a strange-looking product with an unknown brand from an unheard-of company – and costing a premium on top of it all. Moreover, several were uneasy with the idea of having this apparatus which graphically showed, as

it was being used, the amount of dirt and dust in their stores. Perhaps most importantly, Dyson believed that nobody – be it at the trade or consumer level – really knew that there was anything wrong with the bag – this was part of the educational process.

The Dyson sales force overcame this by focusing upon a variety of techniques to overcome the reluctance, including:

- Encouraging the store staff to use the product themselves so that, having been impressed by its performance, this would then sell the product far more enthusiastically and proactively
- Giving retailers' sales staff a free 30-day home trial
- Offering store staff discounts on the product.

Once anyone bought this precious piece of technology, the company had a responsibility to keep that person happy till the very end. This translated into making the entire process of buying, owning, using and maintaining a Dyson as easy as possible – and, once Dyson had defined its service philosophy, it determined that it couldn't be fulfilled by having any independent, third-party service dealers involved; it would all be done in-house.

> One of the first steps in implementing the service philosophy stemmed from a suggestion from one of the people on the Dyson assembly line during the company's early, cottage industry days. 'Why don't we put a helpline number on every machine?' he suggested. The result was that each model in the Dyson range had a prominently displayed label with the Dyson Helpline number on it. The helpline was open seven days a week, from 8.00 am to 8.00 pm, including most bank holidays. By 1999, the company had 100 trained customer service staff manning these helplines.

> (Vandermerwe, 1999, p. 10)

These helplines led to many day-to-day problems being sorted out over the phone. Where this was not possible, Dyson would send a courier to the customer's home to collect the machine that day and return it the next. This was then followed by an experiment in 1999 whereby a service engineer would go directly to the customer's home to deal with any problems.

The next step

Given the strength of the brand and its market position at the beginning of the twenty-first century, the company faced an interesting set of strategic choices. With only 5 million of the 23 million households in the UK owning a Dyson, there was still scope for significant growth. Similarly, overseas markets offered enormous potential. There was also, Dyson felt, a tremendous opportunity to 'Do a Dyson' within other product categories such as washing machines, refrigerators and dishwashers. The company was, however, only too aware that the competition, having been hit so hard, was inevitably going to continue to become far more proactive.

(Source: Vandermerwe, 1999)

Dyson: a postscript

Following on from the enormous success of the Dyson Vacuum cleaner, James Dyson launched his next new product – a washing machine – in November 2000. Named the Dyson Contrarotator, the product was the result of an investment of £25 million and four years of research, which involved going back to the first principles of clothes washing and concluding that hand-washing was more effective than even the best of the existing machines on the market. This led to the invention's unique feature: a split drum that rotates in two directions at the same time in order to pummel and flex clothes. When launching the new product, the company claimed that the machine could reduce the time of a family wash by almost two-thirds.

The Dyson Contrarotator featured 49 patented improvements, including a 'sealless' door, a window to retrieve trapped objects such as coins, and a retractable rollerjack to make the machine easy to move. Priced initially at £999 for the basic model with full automatic programming (this compares with the £400–£580 of the competition), the pricing strategy again reflected Dyson's belief that customers recognize innovation and higher performance, and are willing to pay a premium for them.

Contraction defence

There are occasions when, faced with an actual or potential attack, a company will recognize that it has little hope of defending itself fully. It therefore opts for a withdrawal from those segments and geographical areas in which it is most vulnerable or in which it feels there is the least potential. It then concentrates its resources in those areas in which, perhaps by virtue of its mass, it considers itself to be less vulnerable. Militarily, it is a strategy that was used by Russia to great effect in defending itself against Napoleon and, subsequently, Hitler. It was, however, a strategy that was used far less effectively by the British motorcycle industry in the 1960s and 1970s, which, when faced with an attack upon the moped market in South-East Asia by the Japanese, retreated. The rationale for this was explained by the management teams at the time in terms of the way in which they believed that the Japanese development of the small bikes sector would ultimately stimulate demand for large(r) British bikes. In the event, the British manufacturers were forced successively on to the defensive in the 125 cc bikes sector and then the 250 cc and 350 cc sectors. The effect of this was to force out the majority of the British players until only Norton and Triumph were left. Subsequently, even these two were squeezed to such a degree that they became irrelevant. (Author's note: Subsequently, Triumph has come back into the market, albeit as a small and specialist manufacturer.)

Pre-emptive defence

Recognizing the possible limitations both of a position defence and a contraction defence, many strategists, particularly in recent years, have begun to recognize the potential value of pre-emptive strikes. This involves gathering information on potential attacks and then, capitalizing upon competitive advantages, striking first. Pre-emptive strikes can take one of two broad forms: either the company behaves aggressively by, for example, hitting one competitor after another, or it uses psychological warfare by letting it be known how it will behave if a competitor acts in a particular way, a strategy which has been labelled FUD marketing – that is, spreading 'fear uncertainty and despair'.

Among the companies that have successfully used pre-emptive defences are Procter & Gamble and Seiko. In the case of Procter & Gamble, pre-emptive behaviour has been a fundamental element of their strategy for the past few decades and takes the form of consistent and broad-ranging product development, heavy advertising, aggressive pricing and a general philosophy that is sometimes referred to as 'competitive toughness'. A similar philosophy has been pursued by Seiko, which, with more than 2000 different models of watch worldwide, was designed to make it difficult for competitors to get a foothold. The general lesson to be learned from these two companies, and indeed other market leaders, is that the company should never rest even after it has achieved domination, but should instead offer a broad range of products that are replaced frequently and supported aggressively. Any competitor is then faced with a target that is infinitely more difficult to penetrate.

Equally, Tesco, having taken over as the market leader of the UK groceries market, has reinforced its position with a series of astute strategic moves that have seen the business develop into a number of other markets, including books, CDs, computer games, DVDs, brown goods (televisions and vacuum cleaners), finance, flowers, gas and electricity, insurance, clothes, travel services, and so on, all of which have been underpinned by speed and agility.

Counter-offensive defence

The final form of defence tends to come into play once an attack has taken place. Faced with a competitor's significant price cut, major new product or increase in advertising, a market leader needs to respond in order to minimize the threat. This response can take one of three forms:

1. Meet the attack head-on
2. Attack the attacker's flank
3. Develop a pincer movement in an attempt to cut off the attacker's operational base.

Of these, it is the first that is arguably the most straightforward; this was seen in the way in which airlines responded in the 1970s to Freddie

Laker's attack on prices on the North Atlantic routes. Faced with Laker's price cutting, other airlines flying these routes also cut their prices. Laker's company was eventually forced into liquidation through an inability to service its debts.

As an alternative to this sort of response, market leaders can try searching for a gap in the attacker's armour, a strategy that was used in the USA by Cadillac when faced with a stronger marketing push by Mercedes. Cadillac responded by designing a new model, the Seville, which it claimed had a smoother ride and more features than the Mercedes.

The final counter-offensive move involves fighting back by hitting at the attacker's base. In the USA, for example, Northwest Airlines was faced with a price-cutting attack on one of its biggest and most profitable routes by a far smaller airline. Northwest responded by cutting its fares on the attacker's most important route. Faced with a significant drop in revenue, the attacker withdrew and prices were restored to their original levels.

Defending a position by behaving unconventionally

In defending an organization against its competitors, there is often the need for the marketing planner to behave in a way that at first sight might appear counterproductive, something that was once summed up in terms of 'It's better to shoot yourself in the foot than have your competitors aiming for your head.'

It was this sort of thinking that led Canon, the Japanese camera, copier and printer company, to launch a range of inkjet printers, knowing that it would damage its own dominant position in laser printers. However, in doing this, Canon ensured that it remained the leader in the printer market as a whole rather than dominating just one part of it. But whilst the rationale for this is straightforward, numerous managers have failed to understand this and have responded too late to take advantage of radical shifts within a market or technology.

In discussing this, Loudon (2002, p. 46) has attempted to identify how organizations try to catch what he refers to as 'the next wave of innovations'. The industry's Goliaths, he says, have been awakened from their slumbers by the new-economy Davids, and the two camps are now getting together in three distinct ways. One is internal venturing, whereby companies promote competition between their divisions, an approach that has long been used by Procter & Gamble and Wal-Mart. Another is corporate venture capital, where companies make investments in third-party operations with a view to eventual pay-off in both financial and strategic terms, something that has been done by Intel and Reuters. The third way involves acquisitions, exemplified by Bertelsmann's buyout of Napster, the online operation. This shows how an old-economy giant can acquire new-technology thinking simply by writing a cheque.

In bringing these ideas together, Loudon has developed the concept of networked innovation. Established companies that want to catch the second (profitable) wave of the Internet revolution need to make sure that they link into the relevant web through networked innovation. In arguing the case for this, Loudon recognizes the potential problems that exist, but cites Volvo as an example of a company that has successfully set up a separate subsidiary to handle this type of innovation.

Unconventional or innovative behaviour has also been used by, amongst others, Cadbury's, with its drum-playing gorilla advertisements for Dairy Milk chocolate, Sony with the Bravia coloured balls, and Honda with a succession of advertisements, including the cog and wheel and with what was claimed to be the first live television advert in the UK. In this, a group of skydivers freefall and, as they do this, spell out H O N D A. The event, which was extensively trailed beforehand, represented an attempt to differentiate the company's advertising approach and was a reflection of the campaign line 'Difficult is worth doing'. The press coverage that the advertisement attracted was substantial and during a time in which media audience are fragmenting and dwindling, led to large numbers of people seeing the advertisement.

Unconventional behaviour has also been at the heart of Red Bull's marketing strategy. Launched in 1984, the sales strategy focused in the early years upon small distributors who were required to have a dedicated Red Bull sales force. The sales reps would then identify five key accounts in their area, including clubs and bars, where they provided DJs, bar staff and individuals identified as trendsetters with Red Bull and Red Bull branded merchandise. They then targeted universities, gyms and petrol stations rather than the large retail outlets in which they would face a fight for shelf space from companies such as Coca-Cola and Pepsi. The brand strategy, which was based around the company's cartoon character and the slogan 'Red Bull gives you wings', relied heavily upon word of mouth and buzz marketing rather than the more traditional – and expensive – advertising techniques of television, radio, posters and the print media. The company also focused upon spreading the Red Bull message through a programme of stealth marketing and their association with energy and danger:

> a major part of Red Bull's marketing [has been the] sponsorship of extreme sports events. Many of these had a flying theme, consistent with the brand's slogan. Rather than merely sponsoring events, Red Bull also developed its own extreme sports events such as BMX biking, kite-boarding, extreme snowboarding, freeskiing, paragliding and skydiving. Soon the drink became associated with dangerous, on-the-edge, adrenaline-fuelled activities, such as the Red Bull King of the Air kiteboarding event in Maui, Big Wave Africa Surf Competition on the Cape peninsula and the infamous Red Bull

Flugtag where amateur pilots build their own flying machines and
leap off a parapet into water.

Red Bull also sponsored pop culture events, many of which were
participatory. For example, the Red Bull Music Academy (RBMA)
brought together aspiring musicians and DJs for two weeks to attend
workshops and studio sessions, and listen to guest lecturers. The
academy was held in different cities: Berlin in 1998, Dublin in 1999,
New York in 2001, London in 2002, Capetown in 2003 and Rome in
2004. (Kumar et al., 2005)

It was in this way that Red Bull developed a cult following among
Generation Y consumers, many of whom are sceptical of marketing and
who saw Red Bull as the anti-brand brand.

Market leadership and a customer focus

It should be apparent from what has been written so far that, for an organization to become a market leader and – perhaps more importantly – retain
its leadership position over anything other than the short term, the marketing planner needs to develop a clear view of what the future will or can be.
As part of this, it is typically argued that there needs to be a strong focus
upon the customer and that the organization must, of necessity, be customer-led: indeed, this is a fundamental element of the marketing concept.
However, it needs to be recognized that a strong argument can be developed *against* being wholly customer-led in that customers only rarely have
a detailed or useful vision of what they will want in the future. (It is important to recognize that, in arguing against being customer-led, we are not
arguing against customer satisfaction.) As an example of this, if Sony had
relied upon the results of customer research when developing the Walkman,
they would have dropped the product at an early stage, since few customers
appeared to value the concept. Equally, 3M persevered with its Post-it notes
despite initially negative customer research findings.

The lesson that many market leaders have learned from these, and
indeed numerous other examples of products that have succeeded in the face
of customer myopia, was summed up by Akio Morita, the then chairman
of Sony:

Our plan is to lead the public with new products rather than ask
them what kind of products they want. The public does not know
what is possible, but we do. So instead of doing a lot of market
research, we refine our thinking on a product and its use and try to
create a market for it by educating and communicating with the
public.

This sentiment, which has been echoed by many other consistently innovative companies such as Toshiba, with its Lifestyle Research Institute,

highlights the need for the marketing planner to ask – and answer – two questions:

1. What benefits will customers see to be of value in tomorrow's products?

2. How, through innovation, can we deliver these benefits and, in this way, pre-empt our competitors?

In posing the first of these two questions, the marketing planner must, of course, take a very broad view of who the customer is in that, if tomorrow's customers are defined in the same way as those of today, it is almost inevitable that the firm will be eclipsed by others in the market. Recognition of this leads to us being able to identify three types of organization:

1. Companies that insist on trying to take customers in a direction in which they do not really want to go

2. Companies that listen to their customers and then respond by producing products and services that customers are aware they want, but that others in the market are either producing currently or will produce shortly

3. Companies that take their customers where they want to go, even though they may not yet be aware that this is a direction in which they want to go and that the product will deliver value to them.

It is this third type of organization that can be seen to have moved beyond being customer-led and that, as a result, is creating its own future. In doing

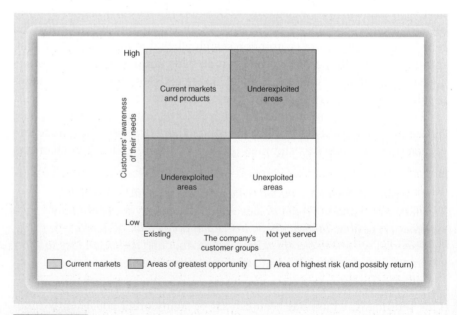

FIGURE 12.8 *The step beyond 'customer-led'*

this, the matrix illustrated in Figure 12.8 is of value in helping managers to focus their thinking (see also Illustration 12.4).

The rise and fall of market leaders

Although market leaders typically have a number of significant advantages, including resources, relationships and market power, there is a considerable body of evidence to suggest that few remain as leaders for more than a relatively short time. In discussing this and the factors that contribute to it, it has been suggested that sustained corporate success is the exception and that few companies managed to achieve real growth once they have lost the momentum that enabled them to reach a leadership position. It is also estimated that only about one in 10 companies manage to outperform the stock market over a decade or more, something that suggests that market leadership is less of a competitive advantage than might appear.

In the case of those organizations that do manage to succeed over the long term, Christensen suggests that they do this by avoiding the temptation simply to repeat the strategies that they have used in the past. Instead, they focus upon developing new technologies, business models and organizational skills, even though these reinventions might radically change the basis on which the organization was built. As an example of this, Toyota built its initial competitive advantage around ideas of lean production and attention to quality. As others in the industry copied these ideas, Toyota's focus shifted to vehicle design and marketing, something that led to the Lexus and Scion brands. As the competition again learned from this, Toyota began developing hybrid power technology, initially for the Prius, but now being applied across the range.

This sort of thinking can be seen to be linked to Hamel and Prahalad's (1994) ideas of stretch goals (to be the most innovative and largest car maker) and to possess the foresight to 'develop competences far in advance of products' (refer back to pages 435–6), a strategy that was reflected in the development of hybrid technology when the conventional wisdom was that this company's technology could never be profitable.

The mistake that many other market leaders seemingly make, and which ultimately leads to their (relative) decline, often stems from a reluctance to invest in the low technology and low margin products that will possibly appeal to new customers. Instead, they move ever further upmarket, leaving space for new competitors to enter the market and change the sector's dynamics. It was the recognition of this that led Pascale (1989) to suggest that 'The ultimate and largely ignored task of management is one of creating and breaking paradigms. The problem is that we devote 99 per cent of energy to squeezing more out of existing paradigms.'

The potential vulnerability of market leaders to an attack can also be seen by the way in which companies such as Eastman Kodak, IBM, Cisco, Dell, General Motors, Xerox, Digital Equipment Corporation and Texas

Illustration 12.4 Moving beyond customer-led

Amongst the organizations that have at various stages taken on board the idea of moving beyond being customer-led in the traditional sense are Renault, with its launch in the 1980s of the Espace people carrier; Swatch, with fashionable high-design/low-cost and ultimately disposable watches; and Ryanair and easyJet, with low-cost, no-frills airline travel. Rather than researching customers and tweaking the existing type of service, Michael O'Leary of Ryanair and Stelios Haji-Ioannou of easyJet both identified a need that consumers were not really aware that they had, set about educating them and, in doing this, provided a quantum leap in value. The move beyond being customer-led and the development instead of a strategy based upon consumer insight and a deeper understanding of changes within society was also at the heart of product and market development within the European car industry in the 1990s. Companies such as Mercedes, BMW and Porsche all identified a series of changes in the profiles of consumers and an often fundamental rethinking of values within this market, and responded by launching sports cars that were lower in price than their traditional products. At the heart of this was the emergence of a sizeable cash-rich ageing baby boomer generation intent on recapturing its youth. The characteristics of this market and the ways in which their values were changing are illustrated in Figure 12.9.

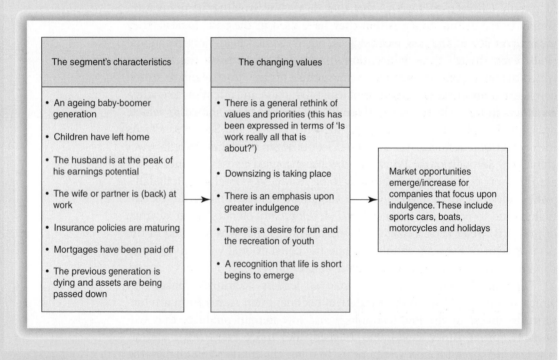

FIGURE 12.9 *Changing markets and marketing opportunities*

Instruments have all been hit hard by competitors with more limited resources, inferior technologies and less market power. Interestingly, most – if not all – of these companies might have appeared impregnable when examined within the context of Porter's five-forces framework.

12.6 STRATEGIES FOR MARKET CHALLENGERS

The Romans didn't build a great empire by organizing meetings.
They did it by killing people.

(Anon.)

Companies that are not market leaders are faced with a straightforward strategic choice: either they attack other firms – including perhaps the market leader – in an attempt to build market share and achieve leadership themselves (*market challengers*), or they pursue a far less aggressive strategy and, in doing so, accept the status quo (*market followers*). In deciding between the two, several factors need to be taken into account, the most significant of which are the costs of attacking other firms, the likelihood of success, the eventual probable returns, and the willingness of management to engage in what in most cases will prove to be a costly fight. In commenting on the issue of returns, Fruhan (1972, p. 100) has highlighted the dangers of spending unwisely, arguing that, particularly in mature markets, management can all too easily fall into the trap of chasing market share that proves not to be cost-effective.

This theme has, in turn, been picked up by Dolan (1981), who has suggested that competitive rivalry is typically most intense in industries faced with stagnant demand, high fixed costs and high inventory costs. The implications for a firm in this situation are potentially significant since, while there may well be a need to gain share in order to benefit from greater economies of scale, not only are the costs of doing this high, but the likelihood of the sort of pyrrhic victory referred to above also increases dramatically. Recognition of this should then lead the strategist to a clearer perception of the course of action that is likely to be the most cost-effective. In practice, this means choosing between:

1. Attacking the market leader

2. Attacking firms of similar size to itself, but which are either underfinanced or reactive

3. Attacking smaller regional firms.

In making this choice a variety of factors needs to be considered, but particularly the competitive consequences. Picking off a series of small regional players is, for example, often far more profitable than attacking the market leader. This point has been highlighted by Porter (1985b), who suggests that:

Trying to take business away from the competition that holds the
largest share of a market, or makes the most money from that
market, may be the most dangerous competitive move a company
can make ... the leader, by virtue of its pre-eminent position, can
afford to cut prices, rain down new products on rivals, or bury their

offerings under an advertising blitz – in short the big guy can make the business miserable for everyone else.

In making this comment, he highlights the way in which a well-established – and clever – market leader can often afford to slash prices, launch a series of new products and boost levels of advertising spend so that the smaller aggressor is unable to gain share. However, he does recognize that, if the challenger behaves cleverly and strategically, many market leaders are vulnerable. In part, he suggests that this is due to the way in which they become complacent and unwittingly allow the competition to make small inroads that then provide the basis for a more serious attack.

More broadly, he identifies a set of principles that provide a framework for challengers who are thinking of attacking. At the heart of these is the idea that they should never attack head-on with a strategy that simply imitates the leader. Instead, he suggests:

> *a successful attack against a strong leader requires that a challenger meet three basic conditions: First, the assailant must have a sustainable competitive advantage, either in cost or in differentiation – the ability to provide the kind of value that commands premium prices. If the challenger's advantage is low cost, the troublemaking upstart can cut prices to lure away the leader's customers or, alternatively, maintain the same price but take the extra money it earns on each product and invest in marketing or R&D. If, on the other hand, the challenger can successfully differentiate itself or its product, then it can invest the proceeds from its premium prices to try to lower its costs or otherwise nullify the leader's cost edge. Whichever advantage the assailant banks on though, must be sustainable – the challenge has to have enough time to close the market share gap before the big guy can come roaring back with his own version of whatever it was that made the challenger successful.*
>
> *Second, the challenger must be able to partly or wholly neutralize the leader's other advantages, typically by doing almost as well as the leader what the leader does best. An upstart relying on differentiation for example, can't have costs that are hopelessly worse than the leader's – the leader will use his higher returns to bring out a similarly superior product, or will cut prices to make the challenger's offering look pricey indeed.*
>
> *Finally, there must be some impediment to the leader's retaliating – don't launch an attack without one. The impediment may derive from the leader's circumstances: it's having trouble with the antitrust enforcers, say, or is strapped for cash because of diversification into other businesses. Or the impediment may arise because of the nature of the upstart's challenge: the leader has hundreds of millions of dollars invested in turning out a*

product based on a particular technology; the challenger attacks with substitute incorporating a new technology which has to be manufactured differently.

At the heart of Porter's ideas is the belief that a challenger must have some kind of strategic insight, something that he or she believes comes from a new or a different way of doing business. The three most common ways of doing this are by:

1. *Reconfiguration*, in which the challenger finds a new and innovative way of performing some of the business's essential activities, such as design, manufacturing, marketing or delivery. An example of this was the way in which Amazon.com used the Internet as the basis of its strategy.

2. *Redefining the market*, either geographically and/or through the product. Federal Express, for example, began by focusing on small packages that required overnight delivery, and operated its own aircraft. easyJet and Ryanair also redefined the market by offering low-cost, no-frills flights, and in this way avoided attacking head-on the established players such as BA, KLM and Lufthansa.

3. *High spending*. Although this is potentially the most costly and risky of the three approaches, it has been used by firms such as Amazon.com to establish both the technological infrastructure and high levels of brand awareness.

Whilst ideally the challenger will meet all three of these conditions, fulfilling just one or two can often offset a degree of weakness in meeting the others. In the USA, for example, the no-frills airline People Express began with the benefits of a lower cost base than its competitors – pilots' salaries were lower than the norm, staffing levels were low, and there was little job demarcation – which meant value was passed on to customers in the form of lower prices. Their product, a cramped seat, was sufficiently similar to the cramped seats of other operations for the market leaders to be unable to persuade customers there was a difference. The condition that People Express was unable to meet was the lasting impediment to retaliation, and eventually others in the industry fought back by matching the People Express prices. Having exhausted the growth potential offered on routes that the majors had largely neglected, People Express was forced to look to the more competitive routes if it was to continue growing, and this sparked off a further round of price-cutting and retaliation.

A successful attack by a challenger is therefore typically based on a degree of reconfiguration of the activities that make up the business, be it in the form of design, manufacture or delivery; it was this approach that

> **Illustration 12.5   The Dolls Wars: Bratz – the anti-Barbie doll**
>
> Launched by Mattel in 1959, Barbie dominated the dolls market for more than four decades. However, in 2001 MGA Entertainment launched its Bratz range and the market began to change dramatically. Positioned as multicultural and streetwise and targeted at the tweens – girls aged between seven and 11 who want to distance themselves from their younger sisters – Bratz sales reached $600 million within just 18 months.
>
> Mattel responded quickly with the launch in 2002 of My Scene, a group of highly fashionable dolls, and then, in 2003, the Flava dolls with names such as P Bo and Happy D. Flavas were a mixed-race range, but faced with a disappointing response from the market, were quickly dropped.
>
> In 2005, Bratz announced a 56.6 per cent share of UK fashion doll sales, a figure that showed that Bratz were selling at twice the level of any other fashion doll in the market and accounted for almost 5 per cent of the total toy market. The strategy pursued since then has been aggressive and designed to keep Barbie at a distance. With additions to the range and cinema releases such as *Bratz : the movie*, the strategic focus was firstly that of developing the Bratz brand as a lifestyle with a series of Bratz-branded consumer electronics, entertainment, music, furnishings and sports products.
>
> Mattel's response was two-pronged, with a combination of Barbie and My Scene, both of which they suggest mothers prefer because they are stylish but safe and arguably less provocative than Bratz. The company also believes that Bratz's tweens market is essentially brand-promiscuous: what they like today, they drop tomorrow.

characterized Dyson's attack on the market leader, Hoover. If the challenger is unable to do this, the safest option is often to ignore the leader and to pursue instead others in the industry who are of equal size or who are smaller and potentially more vulnerable. In this way, any competitive response is likely to be more manageable.

The dimensions of an effective challenge strategy have also been illustrated by Bratz's attack upon the market leader, Barbie, in the dolls market (see Illustration 12.5).

Deciding upon whom to challenge

Given what has been said so far, the choice of *whom* to challenge is fundamental and a major determinant not just of the likelihood of success, but also of the costs and risks involved. However, once this has been done, the strategist is then in a position to consider the detail of the strategy that is to be pursued. Returning to the sorts of military analogies discussed earlier, this translates into a choice between five strategies: a frontal attack, a flanking attack, an encirclement attack, a bypass attack and a guerrilla attack. But before choosing among these we need to return for a moment to the more fundamental issue referred to above of *whom* to attack and *when*. In deciding this, the options, as we have suggested, can be seen in terms of an assault on the market leader (a high-risk but potentially high-return strategy), an attack upon companies of similar size, or an attack upon the generally larger number of smaller and possibly more vulnerable firms in the industry. In choosing among these various targets the strategist is likely to be influenced by a variety of factors, including perception of the leader's likely response, the availability of the resources needed to launch an effective attack, and the possible pay-offs. In addition, however, the strategist should also perhaps be influenced by the findings of the military historian Basil Liddell-Hart. In an analysis of the 30 most important conflicts of the world from the Greek wars up to First World War (this included 280 campaigns), Liddell-Hart (1967) concluded that a direct head-on assault succeeded on only six occasions. By contrast, indirect approaches proved not only to be far more successful, but also more economic. This thinking, when applied to business, has led to a series of guidelines for challengers, which are summarized in Figure 12.10.

It has long been recognized that market challengers only rarely succeed by relying on just one element of strategy. Instead, the challenging strategy needs to be made up of several strands that, together, provide the basis for competitive advantage. The eight most commonly used and successful strategic strands are:

1. Price discounting

2. Product and/or service innovation

3. Distribution innovation

4. Heavy advertising

5. Market development

6. Clearer and more meaningful positioning

7. Product proliferation

8. Higher added value.

Frontal attacks

The conventional military wisdom is that for a frontal or head-on attack to succeed against a well-entrenched opponent, the attacker must have at least a 3:1 advantage in firepower; history suggests that broadly similar lessons apply to business.

In launching a frontal attack, a market challenger can opt for either the *pure frontal attack* (by matching the leader product for product, price for price, and so on) or a rather more *limited frontal attack* (by attracting away selected customers). Although the record of success with a pure frontal attack is, as we commented above, generally limited, examples of companies

It has long been recognized that market challengers only rarely succeed by relying on just one element of strategy. Instead, success depends on designing a strategy made up of several strands that, by virtue of their cumulative effect, give the challenger a competitive advantage. The ten most commonly used and successful strategic strands used by challengers are:

1. *Price discounting*. Fuji attacked Kodak by offering photographic film and paper that they claimed was of the same quality as the market leader, but 10 per cent cheaper. A similar strategy was pursued by Amstrad in the personal computer market.

2. *Cheaper goods*. Aldi's attack in the grocery retailing market was based on providing a different quality–price combination to that of the other players in the market. Similarly, the coach travel company National Express has based its attack upon the rail industry on a strategy of lower prices.

3. *Product innovation*. By offering a constant stream of new and updated products, a challenger gives buyers a powerful reason for changing their purchasing patterns. Among those to have done this successfully are Polaroid with cameras and, in the 1970s, Apple with microcomputers.

4. *Improved services*. Avis challenged Hertz, the market leader in the car hire market, with a strategy that promised a faster and higher level of service. Its advertising slogan, 'Avis, we're number two, we try harder', is now part of advertising mythology.

5. *Distribution innovation*. Timex watches achieved considerable sales success as the result of a strategy that pioneered a new approach to watch distribution. Rather than selling the product through specialist jewellery stores, the company opted for a far broader approach by distributing through chainstores and supermarkets.

6. *Intensive advertising*.

7. *Market development*. Walker's Crisps achieved considerable success in the 1960s by focusing on the previously ignored market sector of children. The market leader, Smith's, had traditionally concentrated on adults and had distributed through pubs. The attack on such a different front took Smith's by surprise.

8. *Prestige image*. Much of the success achieved in the car market by Mercedes and BMW has been based on the development of an image of quality, reliability and consumer aspiration.

9. *Product proliferation*. The success of Seiko's attack on other watch manufacturers owes much to its strategy of developing some 2400 models designed to satisfy fashion, features, user preferences and virtually anything else that might motivate consumers.

10. *Cost reduction*. Many Japanese companies entered the European and North American markets in the 1960s and 1970s on the back of a cost-reduction, price-led strategy designed to put pressure on domestic manufacturers. Subsequently, a large number of these Japanese companies have modified their approach and repositioned by, for example, emphasizing quality, reliability and prestige. Their place has now been taken by a second wave of companies, this time from Korea, Taiwan and the Phillippines, which are emphasizing cost reduction and lower prices.

FIGURE 12.10 *Attack strategies for market challengers*

that have adopted this approach and succeeded do exist. Included among these is Xerox, which in the copying market attacked companies such as Gestetner and 3M and, by virtue of a better product, captured the market. (Subsequently, Xerox has itself been attacked by a large number of companies, including Sharp, Canon, Panasonic and Toshiba.)

A similar frontal attack was used to great effect by the Japanese producers of magnetic recording tape. Having pioneered the market in the 1960s, 3M fell victim to a series of aggressive pricing moves in the 1970s, led by

TDK. The effect on 3M was significant and by 1982 it had been forced into the position of a minor player.

More frequently, however, it is the case that a frontal attack proves to be both expensive and ultimately self-defeating, something that both Safeway and Sainsbury's have found in attacking the market leader, Tesco.

Flank attacks

As an alternative to a costly and generally risky frontal attack, many strategists have learned the lesson from military history that an indirect approach is both more economical and more effective. In business terms, a flanking attack translates into an attack on those areas where the leader is geographically weak and in market segments or areas of technology that have been neglected. It was the geographical approach that was used in the late 1960s and early 1970s by Honeywell in competing in the USA against IBM. Quite deliberately, the company concentrated its efforts on the small and medium-sized cities in which IBM's representation, while still high, was not as intense as in the major cities. A similar geographical approach was adopted by the Japanese motorcycle industry, which concentrated its efforts progressively on Asia, the USA and then Europe.

As an alternative, many companies have opted for *technological flanking* or leap-frogging. Among those to have done this with considerable success are the Japanese in the car industry, who rewrote the rules of how to mass produce cars to such an extent that they not only managed to undercut the traditional market leaders, but also reversed the flow of technology transfer in the industry.

Others to have used technological flanking include Michelin against companies such as Goodyear, Firestone and Uniroyal, and the state-owned French helicopter manufacturer Aerospatiale. Aerospatiale's competitors – Bell Helicopter, Sikorsky and Boeing – worked to full capacity for several years to satisfy the enormous military demand for helicopters in the Vietnam war and had little time for major technological developments. Aerospatiale took advantage of this and in 1980 simultaneously introduced three new-generation fast, twin-turbine models designed to cover all conceivable military and civilian needs. These models all featured Aerospatiale-developed fail-safe rotor blades manufactured not from conventional metal but from composite materials.

Segmental flanking has been used to equal effect by numerous companies, over the years, including Hewlett–Packard with mini-computers, Apple with micro-computers, and Toyota and Volkswagen in the USA with small, economical cars. The lesson in each case is straightforward: identify the areas of market need not being covered by the market leader and then concentrate resources on building both size and share. In doing this it is, however, essential that the attacker moves quickly, since the challenge becomes clearer over time and can lead to a sudden competitive response in which the company being attacked regains the initiative. In the majority of cases, however, the company being attacked either fails to recognize the significance of the challenge or is unsure of how best to retaliate and, as a result, responds only slowly. Bic, for example, flanked Gillette in razors by developing the low-priced sector, while Knorr and Batchelor flanked Heinz with the introduction of low-priced soups shortly after Heinz had fought off a head-on attack by Campbell's. In both cases, the defender was slow to respond, possibly because of a fear that a stronger reaction would speed up the growth of the low-price sector.

Encirclement attacks

Whereas flanking in its purest form involves an attack on just one front, encirclement has parallels with a blitzkrieg in that it involves launching an attack on as many fronts as possible in order to overwhelm the competitor's defences. In this way, the defender's ability to retaliate effectively is reduced dramatically. Whilst this is an expensive strategy to pursue, and one that is almost guaranteed to lead to significant short-term losses, its record of success in the hands of certain types of company is impressive. Seiko, for example, has made use of a strategy of encirclement not just with the sheer number of models that are changed constantly, but also by acquiring distribution in every watch outlet possible and by heavy advertising that gives emphasis to fashion, features, user preferences and everything else that might motivate the consumer. Similarly, the Japanese motorcycle, audio and hi-fi manufacturers, having started with flanking strategies, quickly developed these into encirclement strategies with an emphasis on rapid product life cycles, frequent and radical new product launches, wide product ranges, aggressive pricing, strong dealer support and, in the case of the motorcycle companies, a successful racing programme. Other companies that have made use of encirclement, admittedly with varying degrees of success, include Yamaha against Honda and the Japanese construction machinery manufacturer Komatsu in its attack on the market leader, Caterpillar.

In the case of Komatsu and Caterpillar, Komatsu's attack on the market leader was based on the slogan used internally, 'Encircle Caterpillar'. This translated into a series of attacks on market niches, improvements in product quality, extensions to its product range, and pricing at levels 10–15 per cent lower than those of Caterpillar.

Bypass attacks

The fourth approach, a bypass attack, is (in the short-term at least) the most indirect of assaults in that it avoids any aggressive move against the defender's existing products or markets. Instead, the strategist typically concentrates on developing the organization by focusing on *unrelated products* (the Japanese consumer electronics firms developing video recorders and compact discs rather than traditional audiovisual products), *new geographical markets* for existing products and, in the case of the hi-tech industries, by *technological leap-frogging*. Among those to have used a bypass attack successfully are Sturm Ruger and YKK.

Sturm Ruger, a small US gun manufacturer, recognized in the early 1950s that it did not have the resources to develop a product range that would enable it to compete effectively against Colt, Remington and Browning. It therefore concentrated on a bypass strategy by producing a limited range of high-quality and competitively produced guns that earned a reputation for being the best in their class. In this way, Sturm Ruger managed over a 30-year period to capture almost 20 per cent of the US domestic sporting guns market.

A broadly similar strategy was pursued in the zip fasteners market by YKK. The North American market had long been dominated by Talon. YKK therefore concentrated on avoiding a head-on confrontation with the market leader and, by selling direct to fashion houses, managed both to bypass Talon and turn its zip fasteners into a high-fashion item that commanded a premium price. By doing this, YKK captured 30 per cent of the US market. The same strategy was subsequently used in Europe to achieve broadly similar results.

Guerrilla attacks and ambush marketing

The fifth option open to a challenger is in many ways best suited to smaller companies with a relatively limited resource base. Whereas frontal, flanking, encirclement and even bypass attacks are generally broad-based and costly to pursue, a guerrilla attack is made up of a series of hit-and-run moves designed to demoralize the opponent as a prelude to destabilizing and keeping the competitor off balance. In practice, this typically involves drastic short-term price cuts, sudden and intensive bursts of advertising, product comparisons, damaging public relations activity, poaching a competitor's key staff, legislative moves, and geographically concentrated campaigns. The success of such a strategy has been shown to depend in part upon the competitor's response. In some cases, for example, the competitor chooses to ignore the attack, as has been seen with the way in which the major airlines in the early to mid-1990s chose deliberately not to respond to Virgin's lower prices on the North Atlantic routes. In others, however, the competitor fights back quickly and aggressively in order to minimize any long-term threat. All too often, dealing with guerrilla attacks proves to be difficult.

Guerrilla attacks and No Logo

The attractions and growth of guerrilla marketing have also been highlighted by Naomi Klein (2000), who, in her book *No Logo*, argues that advertisers are extending their tentacles as never before, commercializing

---

Illustration 12.6   Guerrilla marketing

The difficulties faced in responding effectively to guerrilla marketing tactics were illustrated in 1996 by the way in which easyJet managed to gain a considerable amount of press coverage of a stunt on the inaugural flight of BA's budget airline, Go! EasyJet staff bought several rows of seats on the flight and then, wearing bright orange jackets, began offering free easyJet flights to Go!'s passengers.

BA was also the victim of a guerrilla marketing products stunt when their staff on an early-morning flight from Manchester to London, tried to stop a dwarf wearing a T-shirt with the slogan 'Shorter journey times with Virgin Trains' from boarding the plane.

---

public spaces, branding celebrities and finding new ways to appeal to the traditionally hard-to-reach groups such as the gay market and ethnic minorities. The result has been an enormous upsurge in the volume of advertising and a reduction in the impact of individual advertisements. (Estimates in the USA suggest that each American now sees some 1500 commercial messages a day. Jupiter Communications estimates that, by 2012, wired consumers will be exposed to almost 1500 online advertisements a day, three times the figure for 2000.)

The problems that this has created have, in turn, been compounded by the degree of media fragmentation, with an ever greater number of magazine titles, the growth of cable and innumerable Internet pages. In an attempt to overcome this, a number of organizations have turned to guerrilla marketing, in which the firm adopts either a strategic approach to attacking its competitors (see Illustration 12.6) or resorts to a series of what are essentially gimmicks. Amongst those to have done this are Pizza Hut, which put a 10-metre-high advertisement on a Russian space programme rocket; Mattel, the toy firm that makes Barbie, which painted a street pink to promote its doll; and Jim Thompson, a Canadian, who created interest in medical applications for the Palm Pilot through his 'Jim's Pal pages' site.

However, a problem that has emerged is that guerrilla marketing campaigns often have a relatively superficial appeal and the stunts are neither memorable nor big enough to raise brand awareness and boost sales, something that led Anita Roddick, the founder of Body Shop, to call most guerrilla campaigns 'the masturbatory indulgences of ad men'.

How challengers defeat the market leaders: lessons from *Eating the Big Fish*

In his book, *Eating the Big Fish*, Adam Morgan (1999) shows how challengers have succeeded against large and well-entrenched brand leaders, and the lessons that emerge from their experiences. Amongst the best of these, he suggests, are:

- *Dyson*, who recognized the vulnerabilities of the established players in the vacuum cleaner market and, with a combination of new technology and new marketing thinking, quickly eclipsed companies such as Hoover and Electrolux (see Illustration 12.3).

- *Orange*, which overcome people's technological fears by creating a warm and reassuring vision of the future. In doing this, they demonstrated how to build a new technology brand and overtook the established players such as BT.

- *Charles Schwab*, the US discount broker, which launched e-Schwab in 1996. Although they knew that the new division would cannibalize their existing business, they recognized how the market was moving and believed that they had to be the first to create a category killer and redefine the market. The result was that they quickly overtook the market leader, Merrill Lynch.

- *Bertelsmann Napster*. As the number four player in the media world, Bertelsmann was the first to recognize that the firm that was potentially its greatest threat – Napster, the company that allows consumers to swap music online via MP3 technology – could also provide huge opportunities. Given this, Bertelsmann formed an alliance with Napster and, in doing this, not only neutralized the threat but also redefined the industry.

Others who have taken on the big fish within the market include Red Bull who, with the creation of the energy drink market, took Coca-Cola by surprise; Airbus against Boeing; easyJet and Ryanair against the traditional full-service legacy airlines such as BA, KLM and Lufthansa; and Sainsbury within the clothing market.

The single most important lesson to emerge from organizations such as these, Morgan (1999, p. 19) argues, is that of the managerial mindset. The key issue, he suggests, is to think like a challenger rather than to accept the marketing status quo and conventional wisdoms. The ways in which this might best be done include:

1. Forget how the data collectors traditionally define your category. Define it by the way the user thinks of it. Now who is your most dangerous potential competition?

2. Look long and hard at your marketing group's thinking. Be brutal: how much is high interest and how much is low interest? And what are you going to do about the latter?

3. The consumers don't want to know what you think about them. They want to know who you are and what you believe in. Do you know? Honestly? And do they?

4. Everything communicates. How much of your available 'media' – and not just the conventional media you pay for, but the way you act and the way your staff represent you – is projecting your identity?

	Leaders forced to defend their position	Challengers and underdogs intent on strengthening their position
Resources	• Generally substantial	• Often limited
The concept of the future	• A focus on protecting what they have already • Growth from the existing base	• High aspirations • 'Pioneers of a whole new order'
The relationship to the past	• Extrapolation from experience • Fine-tuning of a winning formula	• Expediency • Break the rules where possible

FIGURE 12.11   *Leaders and challengers: the significance of mindset*

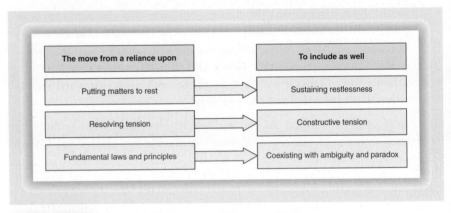

FIGURE 12.12   *The challenger's contextual shift*

5. Take away your primary communications medium. How would you build an emotional relationship with people without any television advertising at all?

6. What is the category killer in your market, and what should you risk to create it yourself?

A similar theme has been pursued by Richard Pascale (1989), who, in explaining the success of market challengers and the often relatively poor performance of leaders forced into a defence of their position, has highlighted three areas that need to be considered: resources, the management's concept of the future, and the relationship to the past (see Figure 12.11).

At the heart of Pascale's ideas of how a challenger can succeed is the development of a particular mindset that requires the sort of contextual shift in management that is shown in Figure 12.12.

12.7   STRATEGIES FOR MARKET FOLLOWERS

As an alternative to challenging for leadership, many companies are content to adopt a far less proactive posture simply by following what others do. The attractions of this have been pointed to by a variety of writers, including Levitt (1966) and Kotler (1997, p. 393). Levitt, for example, suggested that a strategy of product imitation can often be as profitable as a strategy of innovation. Similarly, Kotler has pointed to the way in which:

> An innovator such as Sony bears the huge expense of developing the new product, getting it into distribution, and informing and educating the market. The reward for all this work and risk is normally market leadership. However, other firms can come along, copy or improve on the new products – for example, Panasonic rarely innovates. Rather, it copies Sony's new products, then sells them at lower prices. Panasonic turns a higher profit than Sony because it did not bear the innovation and education expense.

For many firms, therefore, the attractions of being and indeed remaining a market follower can be considerable. This is particularly so when the full costs and risks of challenging an entrenched leader are recognized. If a company is to challenge a market leader successfully, it is essential that the basis for challenging is really worthwhile and meaningful. In practice, this would generally mean a major breakthrough in terms of innovation, price or distribution, something that in relatively long-established and stable industries is often difficult to achieve. Without a major breakthrough such as this, any attack is almost certain to fail, since most market leaders will not only have the benefit of better financing, but will also be more firmly entrenched.

Recognizing this leads the majority of market followers to accept the status quo, and to pursue a course of action that avoids the risk of confrontation and retaliation. In strategic terms, this often translates into copying the market leaders by offering broadly similar products, prices and levels of service: this is sometimes referred to as a *me-too strategy*. The net effect is that direct competition is avoided and market shares tend to remain relatively stable over a considerable period.

These comments should not, however, be taken to mean that market followers do not have their own distinct strategies. Indeed, as Saunders (1987, p. 21) has pointed out, the strategies of successful low-share followers tend to exhibit a number of common characteristics, including:

1. Careful market segmentation, competing only in areas where their particular strengths were highly valued.

2. Efficient use of limited R&D budgets – they seldom won R&D battles but channelled their R&D spending into areas that were most likely to generate the greatest financial pay-off, in terms of return

on R&D expenditure. Where R&D capabilities were available, they concentrated on truly innovative products.

3. They thought small and stayed small. They tended to emphasize profitability rather than sales growth and market share, concentrating on specialization rather than diversification, high value added rather than mass products, quality rather than quantity.

4. The companies were willing to challenge conventional wisdom – their leaders were often strong willed, committed and involved in almost all aspects of their companies' operations.

It follows from this that the need for a follower to develop a clear and well-formulated strategy is just as great as it is for an infinitely more proactive market leader or challenger. In practice, however, many market followers fail to recognize this and pursue a 'strategy' that is largely implicit and derivative. At the very least a follower needs to recognize the importance of positioning itself so that its customer base is not eroded, that sales increase in line with rates of market growth, and that it is not overly vulnerable to more aggressive and predatory market challengers. This is particularly important when it is remembered that challengers can gain share in three ways, including by taking sales from smaller or equal-sized competitors. A market follower in these circumstances can often prove to be an attractive and vulnerable target.

Followers do therefore need to decide how they intend operating and, in particular, how closely they intend following the market leader. In doing this, it is essential that the firm reduces its vulnerability as much as possible by a combination of tight cost control, an early recognition of developing opportunities, and a clear product and service strategy. This final point is particularly significant, since there is a danger of seeing market followers quite simply as imitators of the market leader. Where this does happen the dangers of confusion among customers increases and the reasons for buying from the follower decrease markedly.

It is possible to identify three quite distinct postures for market followers, depending on just how closely they emulate the leader:

1. *Following closely*, with as similar a marketing mix and market segmentation combination as possible

2. *Following at a distance*, so that, although there are obvious similarities, there are also areas of differentiation between the two

3. *Following selectively*, both in product and market terms, so that the likelihood of direct competition is minimized.

12.8   STRATEGIES FOR MARKET NICHERS

The fourth and final strategic position for a firm is that of a market nicher. Although niching is typically associated with small companies, it is in practice a strategy that is also adopted by divisions of larger companies in industries in which competition is intense and the costs of achieving a prominent position are disproportionately high. The advantages of niching can therefore be considerable since, if properly done, it is not only profitable but also avoids confrontation and competition.

The attractiveness of a market niche is typically influenced by several factors, the most significant of which are:

1. It needs to be of sufficient size and purchasing power to be profitable

2. There is scope for market growth

3. The niche is of little immediate interest to the major competitors

4. The firm has the abilities and resources to be able to serve the niche effectively

5. The firm is capable of defending itself against an attack through areas such as customer loyalty.

It is specialization that is at the heart of effective niching, something which has been recognized by retailers such as Aga, Bang & Olufsen and Ann Summers, and by car companies such as Porsche (the world's most profitable car company in 2007) and Ferrari.

Specialization can, however, prove dangerous if the market changes in a fundamental way, either as the result of greater competition or an economic downturn, and the nicher is left exposed. For this reason, there is often a strong argument for multiple niching rather than single-sector niching.

The potential profitability of niching has been pointed to by a variety of consultants and authors over the years, including McKinsey & Co. and Biggadike. For example, two of McKinsey's consultants, Clifford and Cavanagh (1985), found from a study of successful mid-size companies that their success was directly attributable to the way in which they niched within a large market rather than trying to go after the whole market. Equally, Biggadike (1977), in a study of 40 firms that entered established markets, found that the majority chose to concentrate upon narrower product lines and narrower market segments than the rather better established incumbents.

The supernichers

The potential attractions of market niching have also been highlighted by Hermann Simon (1996), who, in his book *Hidden Champions*, identified a group of what he referred to as 'the supernichers'. These firms, he suggests, typically have a particularly detailed understanding of their markets and have achieved the position of being the largest or second largest player within the world market for their products or the largest in the European market. Amongst these organizations are Hohner (85 per cent of the market for harmonicas), Loctite (80 per cent share of the super-glue market), Swarovski (67 per cent of the cut-cross jewellery market), Tetra (80 per cent of the tropical fish food market) and Steiner (80 per cent of the military field glasses market). Although some of these markets might at first sight seem slightly esoteric, the attractions of being a (successful) market nicher are substantial and include a depth of penetration that makes it difficult for others to attack effectively.

Simon identifies 11 lessons that emerge from the supernichers:

1. Set and then aggressively pursue the goal of becoming the market leader in the chosen market

2. Define the target market narrowly

3. Combine a narrow market focus with a global perspective

4. Deal as directly as possible with customers across the globe

5. Be close to customers in both performance and interaction

6. Ensure that all functions have direct customer contacts

7. Strive for continuous innovation in both product and process

8. Create clear-cut advantages in both product and service, and continually strengthen the selling propositions

9. Keep core competencies in the company and outsource non-core activities

10. Select employees rigorously and retain them for the long term

11. Practice leadership that is authoritarian in the fundamentals and participative in the details.

12.9 MILITARY ANALOGIES AND COMPETITIVE STRATEGY: A BRIEF SUMMARY

Given the nature of our comments about the parallels between military strategy and business strategy, these can perhaps best be summarized by referring to von Clausewitz's thoughts, discussed in his book *On War* ([1832] 1984). In this, he argues for planners to adopt eight principles:

1. Select and maintain the aim

2. Use surprise in the form of originality, audacity and speed

3. Maintain morale

The principles of offensive marketing warfare

1. The major consideration is the strength of the leader's position
2. Search for a weakness in the leader's strength, and attack where he is most vulnerable
3. Always launch the attack on as narrow a front as possible

The principles of defensive marketing warfare

1. Only the market leader should consider playing defence; all others should think more offensively
2. The best defensive strategy involves attack
3. Strong competitive moves should always be blocked; never ignore or underestimate the competition

The principles of flanking marketing warfare

1. Flanking moves must be made into uncontested areas
2. Tactical surprise should be a key element of the plan
3. The pursuit is as critical as the attack itself

The principles of guerrilla marketing warfare

1. Find a segment of the market that is small enough to defend (and is worth defending)
2. Regardless of how successful you become, never act like the leader by becoming fat, lazy, complacent and arrogant
3. Be prepared to retreat at short notice when faced with a threat you cannot deal with

FIGURE 12.13 *Military analogies and competitive strategy: a brief summary*

4. Take offensive action

5. Secure your defences and never be taken by surprise

6. Maintain flexibility

7. Use a concentration of force

8. Use an economy of effort.

These ideas are also summarized in Figure 12.13.

Competitive strategy as a game

It has long been recognized that competition between organizations can be seen in much the same way as a game, in that the outcome in terms of an organization's performance is determined not just by its own actions but also by the actions and reactions of the other players, such as competitors, customers, governments and other stakeholders. However, as the pace of environmental change increases and the nature, sources and bases of competition alter, markets become more complex and the competitive game consequently becomes more difficult to win, something that has been illustrated by a spectrum of markets, including colas, films and cameras, airlines, detergents, disposable nappies, tyres, computer hardware and software, and newspapers. In markets such as these, the ever-present danger is of one company taking a step such as a price cut, which then proves to be mutually destructive, as everyone else responds in a desperate attempt to avoid losing customers, volume and share. From the customers' point of view, of course, moves such as these are often attractive, particularly as they can lead to a different set of expectations, which any individual firm then finds difficult to reverse.

It follows from this that the need to manage competition and the competitive process, while often difficult, is essential. Although there are no hard and fast rules, it is possible to identify a number of very broad guidelines that companies might follow. These include:

- *Never ignore new competitors*, particularly those who enter at the bottom end of the market, since almost inevitably once a firm gains a foothold it will start targeting other segments of the market. Examples of this include the early manufacturers of calculators, who ignored Casio; IBM, which ignored a series of initially small players such as Apple, Dell and Compaq; the UK motorcycle manufacturers, who underestimated the Japanese such as Honda, Yamaha, Kawasaki and Suzuki; and Xerox, which was hit hard by Canon.

- *Always exploit competitive advantages* and never allow them to disappear unless they are being replaced by an advantage that, from the customer's point of view, is more powerful and meaningful.

- *Never launch a new product or take a new initiative without working out how the competition will respond* and how you will be affected by this.

Although these three guidelines are in many ways self-evident, the reality is that numerous organizations develop and implement strategies that reflect little real understanding or awareness of the competition. Others, however, do manage to develop competitive strategies in the truest sense. According to Day (1996b, p. 2), there appear to be several factors that set these companies apart, including:

- An intense focus upon competitors *throughout* the organization

- The desire and determination to learn as much as possible about each competitor, its strategies, intentions, capabilities and limitations

- A commitment to using this information and the insights it provides in order to anticipate how they are most likely to behave.

The outcome of this sort of approach is, as Day (1996b, p. 3) comments, that:

They formulate strategies by devising creative alternatives that minimize or preclude or encourage cooperative competitive responses. They adroitly use many weapons other than price, including advertising, litigation, and product innovation. They play the competitive game as though it were chess, by envisioning the long-term consequences of their moves. Their goal is long-term success, rather than settling for short-run gains, or avoiding immediate losses.

However, in developing a competitive strategy, many managers appear to make the mistake of focusing upon what competitors have done in the past rather than what they are most likely to do in the future. Whilst behaviour in the future is often influenced by what has been done previously, even small changes on the part of a competitor can invalidate the assumptions being made.

At the same time, much thinking about competitors and the interpretation of competitive intelligence is based on mental models that reflect a simplification of reality. Although this simplification is understandable – and may well prove to be adequate in relatively static markets – it is unlikely to be suited to markets in which there is any real degree of competitive intensity. Because of this, competitively successful organizations appear to put a great deal of effort into learning, not just about competitors, but also into developing a detailed understanding of distributors' perceptions and expectations, and the extent to which these are being met. They appear also to devote significant resources to learning from their own experiences so that future strategies can then be built upon this understanding.

Marketing strategy and the search for future competitiveness

We suggested earlier that, if an enterprise is managed a little better than customers expect, and if this is done in a slightly better way than competitors can manage, then the enterprise should be successful (see page 3). Although the need for a competitively superior approach has long been at the heart of marketing strategy, the search for greater competitive capability has increased dramatically over the past few years. Several factors have contributed to this, a number of which are referred to in the discussion of the strategic challenges facing organizations (pages 153–5) and the dimensions of the new customer and the new forms of competition (pages 201 and 251–2 respectively). Together, these have put pressures on managers to develop strategies that are not only far more clearly focused upon the market, but also infinitely more proactive, flexible and innovative. However, for many managers, the problem is not necessarily that of identifying or gaining an advantage initially, but of *sustaining* it over any length of time. In highly competitive and largely mature markets, for example, an ever greater number of organizations are having to compete directly against competitors who offer almost identical products across 70–80 per cent of the range. Because of this, the focus of competitive advantage is increasingly shifting away from major product and technological breakthroughs to an emphasis upon a series of process improvements. These are illustrated in Figure 12.14.

However, in order to achieve this, it is essential that the interrelationships that exist both internally (between marketing and other functional areas of the business) and externally (between the organization and its suppliers and distributors) are refined – and perhaps rethought – so that the

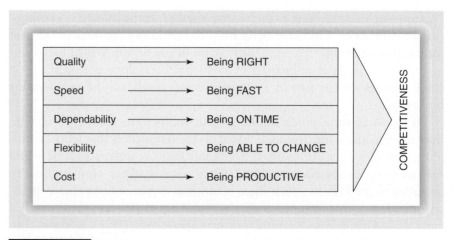

FIGURE 12.14   *The contribution of process improvements to greater competitiveness*

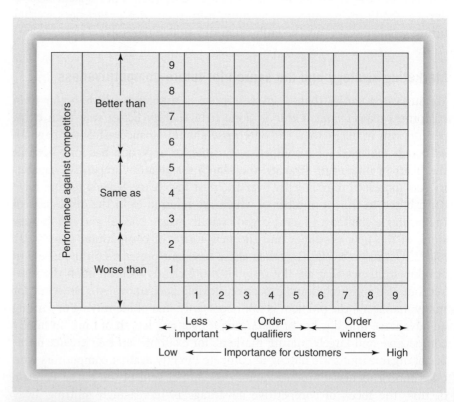

FIGURE 12.15   *Performance against competition*

five dimensions of quality, speed, dependability, flexibility and cost referred to in Figure 12.14 are operating optimally.

As part of this, the marketing planner also needs to develop a far more detailed understanding of what customers see to be of importance and how

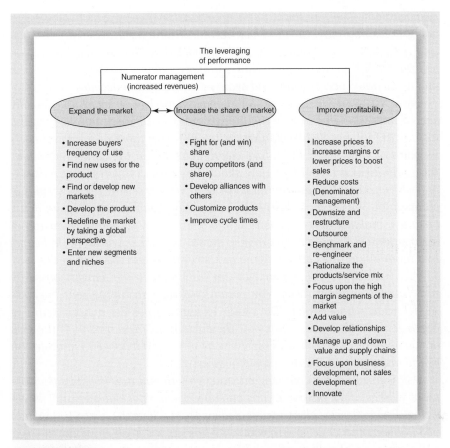

Leveraging performance (adapted from Hooley and Saunders, 1993)

the organization's product range compares with those of its competitors. A framework for this is illustrated in Figure 12.15.

This search for competitiveness has been pursued by numerous writers over the years, including Hooley and Saunders (1993) and Hamel and Prahalad (1994). In discussing how to improve performance, Hooley and Saunders focus upon the detail of marketing activity, arguing that there are three areas to which the marketing planner needs to pay attention (these are illustrated in Figure 12.16).

These ideas are taken further by Hamel and Prahalad (1994), who, in *Competing for the Future* (one of the most influential management books of the 1990s), argue that managers need to rethink their strategies in a series of fundamental ways. However, in many organizations they argue that all or most managers have still failed to come to terms with this and are wedded to old patterns of thinking and old formulae. As a test of this, they suggest posing a series of questions (Hamel and Prahalad, 1994, pp. 1–2).

Look around your company. Look at the high profile initiatives that have been launched recently. Look at the issues that are preoccupying senior management. Look at the criteria and benchmarks by which progress is being measured. Look at the track record of new business creation. Look into the faces of your colleagues and consider their dreams and fears. Look toward the future and ponder your company's ability to shape that future and regenerate success again and again in the years and decades to come.

Now ask yourself: Does senior management have a clear and broadly shared understanding of how the industry may be different ten years in the future? Are its 'headlights' shining further out than those of competitors? Is its point of view about the future clearly reflected in the company's short-term priorities? Is its point of view about the future competitively unique?

Ask yourself: How influential is my company in setting the new rules of competition within its industry? Is it regularly defining new ways of doing business, building new capabilities, and setting new standards of customer satisfaction? Is it more a rule-maker than a rule-taker within its industry? Is it more intent on challenging the industry status quo than protecting it?

Ask yourself: Is senior management fully alert to the dangers posed by new, unconventional rivals? Are potential threats to the current business model widely understood? Do senior executives possess a keen sense of urgency about the need to reinvent the current business model? Is the task of regenerating core strategies receiving as much top management attention as the task of re-engineering core processes?

Ask yourself: Is my company pursuing growth and new business development with as much passion as it is pursuing operational efficiency and down-sizing? Do we have as clear a point of view about where the next $100 million or $1 billion of revenue growth will come from as we do about where the next $10 million, $100 million, or $1 billion of cost savings will come from?

The answer to these and a number of other questions, they suggest, is that far too often, far too little really detailed thinking about how best to compete in the future is going on. As a first step in overcoming this, they suggest that managers focus upon the factors that contribute to greater competitiveness. These are illustrated in Figure 12.17.

They go on to argue that, although many managers have focused upon the first two dimensions in Figure 12.17 (which, it needs to be emphasized, are inward-looking and, in the case of downsizing, if taken to the extreme, can lead to 'anorexia industrialosa', which can best be summarized as the desperate attempt to be ever fitter and ever leaner, leading to emaciation and ultimately death), relatively few have managed to come to terms with the third, even though it is this area that offers the greatest opportunity for an organization to make a major competitive advance. At the same time, of course, it is this area that offers the scope for the greatest competitive dis-advantage if a competitor reinvents the industry or strategy first.

Among the organizations that have successfully reinvented the indus-try and/or regenerated strategy are Xerox, which in the 1970s redefined the

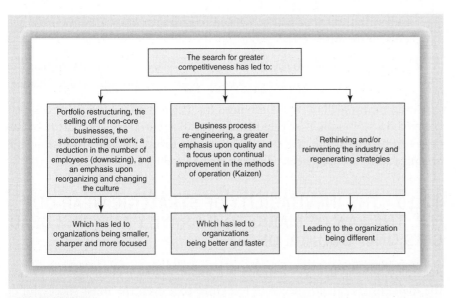

FIGURE 12.17 *The search for greater competitiveness (adapted from Hamel and Prahalad, 1994)*

document-copying market; Pentax and Canon, which developed highly reliable and low-cost 35 mm cameras; Canon, which, in the 1980s, developed small, low-cost photocopiers and, in so doing, opened up vast new markets that, despite its initial innovatory zeal, Xerox had largely ignored; Compaq, which developed the low-cost PC market; Swatch, with fashion watches; The Body Shop, which pioneered the environmentally friendly health and beauty market; Sony with, among other products, the Walkman; Direct Line, which developed the direct selling of insurance; and Häagen-Dazs and Ben & Jerry's which developed the market for premium-quality, premium-priced ice cream.

At the heart of Hamel and Prahalad's thinking on strategy is the idea that, in order to cope with the demands of the future, managers need to make a series of fundamental changes. The starting point in this process, they suggest, involves getting off the treadmill of day-to-day activities and moving away from existing patterns of thought. A fundamental part of this involves managers in 'learning to forget'. In other words, managers need to recognize that, by adhering to the old but possibly successful formulae and to the existing cultural paradigms, failure is almost certain. There needs, therefore, to be an emphasis upon a series of steps, including:

- *Competing for industry foresight* by identifying how the market will or can be encouraged to develop. 'The trick', Hamel and Prahalad (1994, p. 73) suggest, 'is to see the future before it arrives.'

- Having developed a picture of the future, the emphasis then shifts to *crafting the strategic architecture* or blueprint for developing the skills and structures that will be needed in order to compete in the new environment.

- In turn, this leads to the *stretching and leveraging of strategy* so that the organization's resources are focused, developed and exploited to the full.

Underpinning all of this is the need for a clear understanding of the core competences or skills that the organization has currently, the nature of the core competences that will be needed in the future and how therefore the organization's competences will need to be developed.

12.10 THE INEVITABILITY OF STRATEGIC WEAR-OUT (OR, THE LAW OF MARKETING GRAVITY AND WHY DEAD CATS ONLY BOUNCE ONCE)

Regardless of whether the company is a leader, follower, challenger or nicher, the marketing strategist needs to recognize that even the most successful of strategies will, sooner or later, begin to wear out and lose its impact. It is therefore essential that strategies are modified both to anticipate and meet changing competitive challenges and consumer needs. Among the companies that have failed to do this are Polaroid and the large mail order companies. In the case of Polaroid, its winning strategies of the 1960s and 1970s failed to change sufficiently to come to terms with the radically different markets of the 1980s as non-instant competitors improved product performance and the high street witnessed an explosion in the number and reliability of shops offering one-hour and 24-hour photographic development services.

Similarly, the mass-market mail order companies failed in the 1970s to come to terms with the changing role of women, their greater spending power, the smaller numbers staying at home during the day, the greater attractions of the high street, and the greater availability of instant credit. The result was a rapid decline in their share of consumer spending, an increasingly tired-looking sales formula and, perhaps more fundamentally, an apparent absence at the time of any real understanding of how to fight back. Subsequently, organizations such as Littlewoods have moved online, whilst new(er) entrants to the market such as Land's End and Next have based their strategies on clearer targeting and a move up the socio-economic scale and down the age scale.

The problems of strategic wear-out have also been illustrated by Eastman Kodak. As the long-term market leader in the traditional film business, Kodak's key challenge in recent years has been to build a strong digital imaging business. However, in doing this, the organization has been faced not only with a very different technology and set of consumer buying and usage patterns, but also with the need to compete effectively against a large number of Asian rivals in the digital photography market where margins are typically very thin and the need for technological advances high. Despite this, in 2004, the company took the lead in digital camera sales in the USA, with 22 per cent of the market compared with Sony's 19 per cent.

Quite obviously, the vulnerability of a company to a predator in these circumstances increases enormously and highlights the need for regular reviews of strategy. In many cases, however, and particularly when a company has been successful, management often proves reluctant to change what is seen to be a winning strategy. The need for change often becomes apparent only at a later stage, when the gap between what the company is doing and what it should be doing increases to a point at which performance and prospects begin to suffer in an obvious way. It is by this stage that an observant and astute competitor will have taken advantage of the company's increased vulnerability. The argument in favour of regular environmental and strategic reviews is therefore unassailable and reinforces the discussion in the earlier parts of the book. Specifically, the sorts of factors that contribute to strategic wear-out and strategic drift include:

- Changes in market structure as competitors enter or exit

- Changes in competitors' stances

- Competitive innovations

- Changes in consumers' expectations

- Economic changes

- Legislative changes

- Technological changes, including in some instances the emergence of a new technology, which at first sight is unrelated or only indirectly related to the company's existing sphere of operations

- Distribution changes

- Supplier changes

- A lack of internal investment

- Poor control of company costs

- A tired and uncertain managerial philosophy.

Some of these are shown diagrammatically in Figure 12.18.

We commented at an earlier stage in this book that, for many companies, strategic development often proves to be a painful and unnatural process. Recognizing this, it is perhaps understandable that, having developed a seemingly successful strategy, many management teams are content either to stick with the strategy or change it only marginally over time.

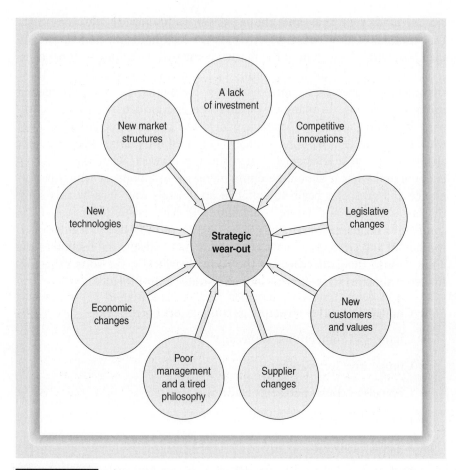

FIGURE 12.18 *The dangers of strategic wear-out*

The law of marketing gravity

The law of marketing gravity states that, regardless of how big or powerful an organization or brand becomes, sooner or later its performance will almost inevitably decline.

Amongst those to have experienced this are Marks & Spencer in the late 1990s, BA and Hoover. According to Mazur (2000), the four principal contributors to marketing gravity are:

1. *Marketing myopia*, or the tendency to apply the letter of marketing while ignoring the spirit. BA's decision to redesign the tailfins of its planes, play down the Britishness of the airline and to focus upon premium-paying first- and business-class passengers had an apparent strategic appeal that was lost in the implementation. The new tailfin designs blurred what had previously been a strongly defined and unique image, whilst the focus upon just a small

number of passengers failed to recognize the imperfections of market segmentation and that not all business executives fly business class.

2. *Marketing arrogance*, or ignoring the impact of your actions on the brand's success. Amongst those to have fallen victim to this was Marks & Spencer's management team, with its belief for a long time that the company did not really need marketing and that they had an unerring feel for customers' needs. The inward-looking culture that emerged led to a series of mistakes and an unprecedented degree of customer disillusionment and defection. The company's revival only came about once new management was brought in from the outside and a new externally focused culture developed.

3. *Marketing hubris*, or believing your own PR to the detriment of the corporate brand. Amongst those guilty of this have been Bill Gates, with his belief that Microsoft should be free of the sorts of constraints that affect other organizations, and Douglas Ivester (the former head of Coca-Cola), who, for some time, ignored the problems faced by the brand when stories began to emerge in Europe of the possible contamination of the product.

4. *The marketing silliness* that affects the organization when it puts common sense to one side in the interest of decisions that are claimed to be 'creative'. A case in point was Abbey's choice of the name Cahoot for its Internet bank.

Dead cats only bounce once

Having come to terms with the law of marketing gravity and the apparent inevitability of strategic wear-out, management teams should never lose sight of the investment analysts' management adage that, at best, dead cats only bounce once. In other words, once the organization's strategy loses its impact (this is the idea of strategic wear-out that is referred to above), the management team typically only has one opportunity to recapture its lost position. If it fails to do this, levels of loyalty and the customer franchise rapidly disappear, and market share begins to slide.

Recognizing this, it should be apparent that many organizations run the risk of competitive oblivion, not least because of the way in which the Internet drives margins downwards. Faced with this, the need for the marketing planner to focus upon strategies that create unique value for customers is self-evident, but all too often ignored. Instead, many organizations rely upon friction as a reliable service of profit (friction is defined as customer ignorance or inertia). The banks, for example, have traditionally derived much of their income from customers' perceptions of the difficulties of transferring their account to another bank and/or a belief that, even if they do transfer, the way in which they will be treated will be little different.

However, with the development of Web-based strategies, a decline in technophobia and generally higher levels of customer promiscuity, the extent to which organizations will be able to rely upon friction is likely to decrease dramatically.

It was the recognition of this that has led companies such as Gateway and First Direct to rethink the ways in which they might interact with customers. In the case of Gateway, having been hit by the economic downturn in the USA in 2001, the company focused upon a two-pronged strategy that involved going 'back to basics' in reducing its product lines and concentrating upon customer satisfaction. As part of the back to basics approach, the company streamlined the number of PC options so that there were fewer chances of things going wrong. The customer strategy concentrated upon satisfaction levels, part of which involved Gateway's employees going to a customer's home or office to guide them through setting up a new PC. The results of this were seen initially in terms of a dramatic reduction in the number of calls to the company's helpline, but then a leap in the number of add-ons that customers bought as the result of a company employee demonstrating their value.

A similar approach, in which the organization rediscovered the business benefits of thinking from their customers' point of view, has been adopted by the telephone and Internet banker First Direct, which has encouraged staff to deal with customers in the same way that they would want to be treated.

There is, however, a more fundamental problem that many organizations face as they grow and that stems from past success. Where an organization has been successful, there is an understandable tendency to continue with what appears to be a winning formula (this is a reflection of the idea that only the very brave or the very stupid change things when they are going well). However, in doing this, the management team may well be sowing the seeds of their own destruction, since the alternative view would be that it is when the organization is doing well that it is in the strongest position to take the next (strategic) step. In practice though, and particularly when faced with a challenging and rapidly changing market, a tension develops within organizations in which the management team finds itself unable to break away from the past and is unable to invent its future.

12.11 THE INFLUENCE OF PRODUCT EVOLUTION AND THE PRODUCT LIFE CYCLE ON STRATEGY

The product life cycle (PLC) is arguably one of the best-known but least understood concepts in marketing. In making this comment, we have in mind the idea that, whilst the concept has an inherent appeal and logic, there is little hard evidence that marketing managers use it in a particularly effective manner when developing strategy. There are several reasons for this, the most obvious being the difficulty in predicting the precise shape of the life cycle curve and the position of the company on the curve at any particular time. Nevertheless, the idea of the PLC has undoubtedly influenced the thinking of many marketing strategists, albeit at a general rather than a specific level.

The rationale of the life cycle is straightforward and reflects the way in which products and services pass through a number of distinct stages from their introduction through to their removal from the market. Recognizing this, the planner needs to develop strategies that are appropriate to each stage of the life cycle.

The strategic implications of the life cycle are thus potentially significant and can be summarized as follows:

1. Products have a finite life

2. During this life, they pass through a series of different stages, each of which poses different challenges to the seller

3. Virtually all elements of the organization's strategy need to change as the product moves from one stage to another

4. The profit potential of products varies considerably from one stage to another

5. The demands upon management and the appropriateness of managerial styles also varies from stage to stage.

In terms of operating practice, the most obvious and immediate implication of a model of product and market evolution such as this can be seen as the need for strategy to change over time and to reflect the particular demands of the different stages. These stages, which are illustrated in Figure 12.19, are typically designated as introduction, growth, maturity and decline, and follow an S-shaped curve.

However, despite the simplicity and apparent logic of the life cycle concept, a series of problems are typically experienced in its use. The most common of these stems from the difficulty of identifying where on the life cycle a product is and where each stage begins and ends. In most cases, the decision is arbitrary, although several commentators have proposed rather more objective criteria. Probably the best-known of these is an approach devised by Polli and Cook (1969), which is based on a normal distribution of percentage changes in real sales from year to year. Others, such as Cox (1967), advocate an historically based approach whereby the strategist examines the sales histories of similar products in the industry. If this reveals that in the past the average length of the introductory, growth and maturity periods has been 5, 14 and 48 months respectively, these time scales are, all other factors being equal, assumed to apply to the product in question. The problem, of course, is that other factors almost invariably do intrude, with the result that historical analysis is at best only a vague guide

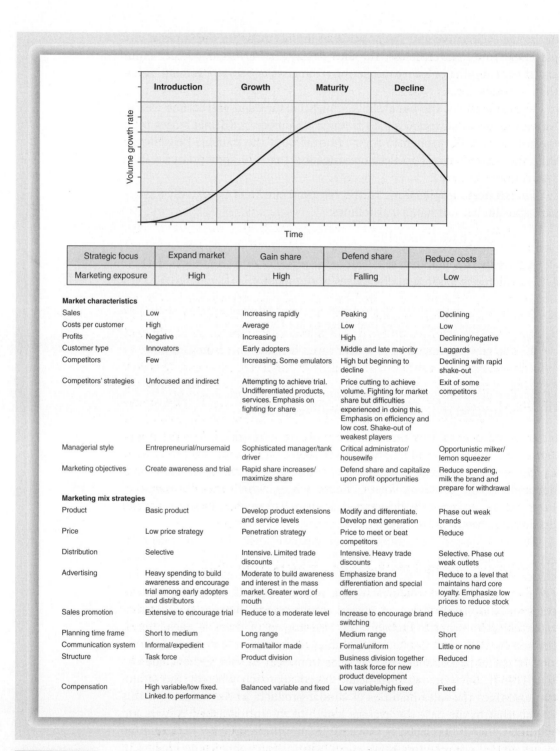

	Introduction	Growth	Maturity	Decline
Strategic focus	Expand market	Gain share	Defend share	Reduce costs
Marketing exposure	High	High	Falling	Low

Market characteristics

Sales	Low	Increasing rapidly	Peaking	Declining
Costs per customer	High	Average	Low	Low
Profits	Negative	Increasing	High	Declining/negative
Customer type	Innovators	Early adopters	Middle and late majority	Laggards
Competitors	Few	Increasing. Some emulators	High but beginning to decline	Declining with rapid shake-out
Competitors' strategies	Unfocused and indirect	Attempting to achieve trial. Undifferentiated products, services. Emphasis on fighting for share	Price cutting to achieve volume. Fighting for market share but difficulties experienced in doing this. Emphasis on efficiency and low cost. Shake-out of weakest players	Exit of some competitors
Managerial style	Entrepreneurial/nursemaid	Sophisticated manager/tank driver	Critical administrator/housewife	Opportunistic milker/lemon squeezer
Marketing objectives	Create awareness and trial	Rapid share increases/maximize share	Defend share and capitalize upon profit opportunities	Reduce spending, milk the brand and prepare for withdrawal

Marketing mix strategies

Product	Basic product	Develop product extensions and service levels	Modify and differentiate. Develop next generation	Phase out weak brands
Price	Low price strategy	Penetration strategy	Price to meet or beat competitors	Reduce
Distribution	Selective	Intensive. Limited trade discounts	Intensive. Heavy trade discounts	Selective. Phase out weak outlets
Advertising	Heavy spending to build awareness and encourage trial among early adopters and distributors	Moderate to build awareness and interest in the mass market. Greater word of mouth	Emphasize brand differentiation and special offers	Reduce to a level that maintains hard core loyalty. Emphasize low prices to reduce stock
Sales promotion	Extensive to encourage trial	Reduce to a moderate level	Increase to encourage brand switching	Reduce
Planning time frame	Short to medium	Long range	Medium range	Short
Communication system	Informal/expedient	Formal/tailor made	Formal/uniform	Little or none
Structure	Task force	Product division	Business division together with task force for new product development	Reduced
Compensation	High variable/low fixed. Linked to performance	Balanced variable and fixed	Low variable/high fixed	Fixed

FIGURE 12.19   *The characteristics of the product life cycle and the implications for strategy*

to strategy and at worst misleading. This is particularly so when levels of competitive intensity increase. Moreover, the planner should not lose sight of the way in which life cycles generally are shortening. Other problems with historical analysis stem from the very different life cycle curves that products exhibit. One particular piece of research, for example, has identified seventeen different life cycle patterns (see Swan and Rink, 1982). The combined effect of these few points raises a significant question mark over historical analysis and argues the case for a rather more cautious and individual approach than is normally suggested.

Nevertheless, despite these criticisms, the PLC does offer some scope as a broad planning, control and forecasting tool. As a planning tool its value should be seen in terms of the way in which it highlights the need for marketing strategy to change over time and, indeed, identifies the types of strategy that are best suited to each of the four stages. As a control tool it can be used as a basis for a comparison of a product's performance against broadly similar products in the past, while as a means of forecasting it provides a broad indication of how a product might develop. These are brought together in Figure 12.19, which summarizes the characteristics of the life cycle, and the objectives and strategies best suited to each of the four major stages.

One final word of caution that needs to be uttered here is that life cycle thinking traditionally revolves around the product. In practice, PLCs are just one element of life cycle management, the others being market, brand and technological life cycles, all of which need to be taken into account in the strategic marketing planning process. As an example of this, the development of digital cameras (a significant step on the camera technological life cycle) has implications both for the film processing industry and for the number and type of players within the market, with organizations that previously did not operate within the market but which had digital expertise recognizing the opportunities that were opening up to them.

The influence of market evolution on marketing strategy

The PLC is, as we commented earlier, a model of both product and market evolution. In practice, emphasis tends to be placed on the product's life cycle rather than that of the market, with the result that many strategists work to a product-oriented picture rather than to a market-oriented picture. There is, however, a strong argument for the strategist to take a step sideways and to focus periodically upon the market overall in an attempt to identify how it is likely to evolve and how it will be affected by changing needs, new technology, developments in the channels of distribution, and so on. This, in turn, points to the need for the strategist to recognize the nature of the interrelationships between the demand life cycle curve and the technology life cycle curve, and how in turn these should be reflected in the management of particular brands.

In doing this, the starting point involves focusing upon the demand life cycle, since it is the demand life cycle that is concerned with the underlying need. The technology life cycle, by contrast, is concerned with the particular ways in which this need is satisfied. One of the most commonly used examples to illustrate this point is that of the need for calculating power. The demand life cycle for this is still growing rapidly and looks as if it will continue to do so for the foreseeable future. The technology life cycle is concerned with the detail of how this need is met. This was done initially with fingers and then subsequently with abacuses, slide rules, adding machines, hand-held calculators and then, most recently, with computers. Each of these has a technology life cycle that exists within the overall framework of the demand life cycle. The strategic implications of this need to be seen in terms of what and who the firm is competing against, something which takes us back to Peter Drucker's questions of 'What business are we in?' and 'What business should we be in?' In practical terms, this can be seen by a manufacturer of slide rules in the 1960s continuing to see its competitors as other manufacturers of slide rules rather than the new and emerging forms of technology such as adding machines and low-priced calculators, which subsequently forced slide rules into decline. For a computer manufacturer today the issues are broadly similar as a series of technologies begin to converge. However, although a great deal of the thinking that underpins the life cycle reflects the idea that the marketing planner can, to a greater or lesser extent, manage the pattern of the cycle, the reality is often very different. In 2001–2, for example, the music industry witnessed a major shift in buying patterns as CD sales slowed and Internet downloads increased. Faced with significant drop in their earnings, the music industry initially pursued a strategy designed to close down the internet sites offering downloads. It quickly became apparent, at least to those outside the industry, that the strategy was doomed to failure.

This sort of example highlights the very real need for a company to identify clearly what type of demand technology to invest in and when to shift emphasis to a new technology, something that has been discussed in some detail by Ansoff (1984), who refers to a demand technology as a strategic business area (SBA), 'a distinctive segment of the environment in which the firm does or may want to do business'. The problem faced by many firms, however, is that, confronted by a variety of different markets and technologies, all of which are changing, there is little scope for mastering them all. The strategist is faced with the need to decide where the firm's emphasis is to be placed. In essence, this involves a choice between investing heavily in one area of technology or less heavily in several. This latter strategy, while offering less risk, has the disadvantage of making it less likely that the firm will either become or retain market leadership. Rather it is the pioneering firm that invests heavily in the new technology that is likely to emerge and remain as the leader.

	Stage of industry development		
	Growth	Maturity	Decline
Strategic position of the firm	Keep ahead of the field Discourage other possible entrants Raise entry barriers	Hit back at challengers Manage costs aggressively Raise entry barriers further Increase differentiation	Redefine scope Divest peripherals Encourage departures Squeeze distributors
Leader	Develop a strong selling proposition and competitive advantage 'Lock in' distributors Build loyalty Advertise extensively	Encourage greater usage Search for new uses Harass competitors Develop new markets Develop new products and product variations Tighten control over distributors	Manage costs aggressively Increase profit margins
Challenger	Enter early Price aggressively Develop a strong alternative selling proposition Search for the leader's weaknesses Constantly challenge the leader Identify possible new segments Advertise aggressively Harass the leader and followers	Exploit the weaknesses of leaders and followers Challenge the leader Leapfrog technologically Maintain high levels of advertising Price aggressively Use short-term promotions Develop alternative distributors Take over smaller companies	If the challenging strategy has not been successful, manage the withdrawal in the least costly way to you but in the most costly way to others
Follower	Imitate at lower cost if possible Search for joint ventures Maintain vigilance and guard against competitive attacks Look for unexploited opportunities	Search for possible competitive advantages in the form of focus or differentiation Manage costs aggressively Look for unexploited opportunities Monitor product and market developments	Search for opportunities created by the withdrawal of others Manage costs aggressively Prepare to withdraw

FIGURE 12.20 *Competitive strategies for leaders, challengers and followers*

This line of thought can be taken a step further by relating the development stage of an industry (growth, maturity or decline) to the organization's strategic position (leader, challenger or follower), since the strategic implications of the interplay between these two dimensions is potentially significant. This is illustrated in Figure 12.20.

Managing in mature markets

Although growth and how it might best be managed has been the focus of a considerable amount of management writing over the past two decades, the reality for the majority of organizations is that most if not all of their products and markets are a long-term maturity. For Larréché and Hamel-Smith (1985), this demands a particular approach to marketing management which, they suggest, is all too often misunderstood. In making this comment, they argue that many managers suffer from strategic astigmatism in which there is a mismatch between the manager's strategic focus and the demands of the market. There are several possible reasons for this, although the most significant is the failure to distinguish between *behavioural* marketing and *structural* maturity.

For Larréché, and Hamel-Smith a market can be seen to be behaviourally mature when there are typically no new competitors and no new products. Marketing investment is often limited, market shares tend to be stable, and there is little or no growth. When a market is structurally mature, there is little or no change – or likelihood of change – in customer preferences, the technologies, or the distribution networks.

Faced with this, Larréché and Hamel-Smith argue that many marketing planners respond by forgetting about the specifics of market segmentation and pursue instead a policy of undifferentiated marketing. They then compound the problems that this creates by adhering too closely to the generalized assumptions that underpin conventional PLC theory about how to behave in each of the stages. The net effect of this in many cases is a move away from any real thinking about marketing strategy to a focus upon short-term promotions and price incentives.

The weakness of this sort of approach is also reflected in the over-simplistic application of portfolio theory which is underpinned by life cycle thinking about how to manage products and which to retain, invest in, delete or milk. Taken together, the poor application of the two concepts is capable of sending clear messages to a competitor about the organization having lost its focus and commitment to a product, thereby making it an attractive target for an attack. This was illustrated in the 1980s and early 1990s in the floor care market which had long been dominated by Hoover. The market, which exhibited all of the classic signs of a sector in long-term maturity with few, if any, opportunities for growth, proved to be vulnerable when Dyson entered the market with a radically different approach and a far more innovative product (refer to Illustration 12.3). Equally, in the canned soups market which had long been dominated by Heinz, new entrants such as the Covent Garden Soup Company illustrated only too easily the scope for innovation and premium pricing.

The lessons that emerge from examples such as these highlight the way in which mature markets and products need to be managed and managed cleverly. If this is done, maturity is potentially profitable. If done badly, the move towards commoditization and the loss of the consumer franchise is speeded up. Recognition of this raises a question about the value of two of the traditional pillars of marketing thinking: PLC theory and brand share.

Although life cycle theory is, as we suggest earlier, one of the oldest and best-known marketing frameworks, the reality is that the generalized thinking about growth, maturity and decline is often difficult to apply in a marketing planning sense to consumer packaged goods and to services. Instead, it is simply a framework for looking back at the life and sales pattern of a product and identifying where it *has* been. Equally, although brand share theory suggests that share and profitability are closely linked (the higher the share, the higher the profit), the reality is far more complex and is often influenced as much by the way in which the market is defined as anything else.

Given this, in thinking about how to manage products in what appear to be mature markets, a more logical starting point involves identifying the factors that damage or destroy the product's position in the market. In essence, these fall into two main areas:

- a lack of marketing activity; and

- activities that are inappropriate and/or are taken at the wrong time.

Included within the first of these is a lack of marketing expenditure to support the product, a failure to innovate, poor positioning, and the too aggressive milking of the product's revenues.

The second set of factors that destroys both the product and the market is inappropriate activity or what might be termed *random walk marketing* in which the marketing team fails to pursue a consistent or meaningful approach to positioning, differentiation and the meaning of the brand. Amongst the most obvious examples of this are Woolworths, which at the end of 2008 announced that it was closing all of its UK stores, and WH Smith (in the case of WH Smith, a far greater clarity of marketing thinking emerged from 2005 onwards). Faced with a weakening of the product or brand's position in the marketplace, management teams often respond with a sense of desperation, including aggressive short-term price cuts, retailer promotions, and badly focused advertising. Although these might have a short-term effect, they are often essentially self-destructive and lead to commoditization. As an example of this, numerous consumer products sold through supermarkets in the UK have been faced with having to cope with the supermarket's own-label products, many of which are similar in concept and packaging to branded products, but sold at much lower prices. The scope for a manufacturer's brand to compete on price in these terms is often limited, but despite this, many have taken this approach. A strategically more logical step would be to focus upon unique benefits such as higher quality and the brand image.

Life cycles and managerial style

Although a considerable amount has been written on product and market life cycles and how strategies need to reflect life cycle stages, relatively little has been said about the appropriateness of managerial style. There is, however, a strong argument for the style of management to be tailored to the particular demands of different stages. In the introductory stage, for example, there is a need for an entrepreneurial style of management in which emphasis is placed upon the rapid identification and seizing of opportunities, flexible structures and a risk-taking culture. In the growth stage this needs to be modified slightly, with greater attention being paid to long-term planning and control. In maturity this needs to change again in order to capitalize on the profit opportunities that exist, something which argues the case for what Arthur D. Little (in Patel and Younger, 1978) refers to as a critical administrator and is particularly important bearing in mind that the majority of products spend most of their lives in the mature stage. In the final stage of the life cycle the managerial needs change yet again, with the focus tending to shorten, costs being reduced and the need for an increased emphasis upon opportunities milking styles. These ideas have been expressed in a slightly different, albeit more colourful, way by Clarke and Pratt (1985), who argue for four styles of management: nursemaid, tank driver, housewife and lemon squeezer.

12.12 SUMMARY

This chapter has focused on the need for a clear statement of marketing strategy and for this strategy to be based on a detailed understanding of corporate capability and competitive advantage. Here, we have examined how the strategic marketing planner, against the background of an understanding of the organization's competitive advantages, needs to begin developing the detail of the strategy. In doing this, explicit consideration needs to be given both to the organization's objectives and to its position within the marketplace.

Bibliography

Abell, D.F. (1980) *Defining the Business: The Starting Point of Strategic Planning*. Englewood Cliffs, NJ: Prentice-Hall.

Abell, D.F. and Hammond, J.S. (1979) *Strategic Market Planning: Problems and Analytical Approaches*. Englewood Cliffs, NJ: Prentice-Hall.

Abrahams, T. (1999) *The Mission Statement Book: 301 Corporate Mission Statements from America's Top Companies*, 2nd edn Berkeley, CA: Ten Speed Press.

Abratt, R. (1986) Industrial buying in high-tech markets, *Industrial Marketing Management*, **15**, 293–8.

Advertising Works 5 (1990) New York: Holt Rinehart Winston.

Albrecht, K. (1979) *Stress and the Manager*. Englewood Cliffs, NJ: Prentice-Hall.

Anandarajan, A. and Christopher, M.G. (1987) A mission approach to customer profitability analysis, *International Journal of Physical Distribution and Materials Management*, **17(7)**, 55–86.

Ansoff, H.I. (1957) Strategies for diversification, *Harvard Business Review*, **25(5)**, 113–24.

Ansoff, H.I. (1968) *Corporate Strategy*. Harmondsworth: Penguin Books.

Ansoff, H.I. (1984) *Implementing Strategic Management*. Englewood Cliffs, NJ: Prentice-Hall.

Ashridge Management College (1993) *Industrial Buying and Issues of Loyalty*.

Assael, H. (1987) *Consumer Behaviour and Marketing Action*. Boston. MA: Kent Publishing.

Baker, K. (1982) quoted in E. Clark (1982) Acorn finds new friends. *Marketing*, **16 Dec**, 13.

Baker, M.J. (1985) *Marketing Strategy and Management*. London: Macmillan.

Baker, M.J. (1987) One more time – what is marketing?, in M.J. Baker (ed.), *The Marketing Book*. London: Heinemann, pp. 3–9.

Barksdale, H.C. and Harris, C.E. (1982) Portfolio analysis and the PLC, *Long Range Planning*, **15(6)**, 74–83.

Barlow, J. and Møller, C. (1996) *A Complaint Is a Gift: Using Customer Feedback as a Strategic Tool*. San Francisco, CA: Berrett-Koehler.

519

Barnard, C.I. (1956) *The Functions of the Executive*. Cambridge, MA: Harvard University Press.

Barrett, R.F. (1980) Modular data base system, *International Journal of Physical Distribution and Materials Management*, **10(4)**, 135–46.

Bartram, P. (2005) Why the competition doesn't matter, *The Marketer*, **Jun**, 20.

Berkowitz, E.N., Kerin, R.A., Hartley, S.W. and Rudelius, W. (1994) *Marketing*, 4th edn Boston, MA: Richard D. Irwin.

Biggadike, R. (1977) *Entering New Markets: Strategies and Performance*. Cambridge, MA: Marketing Science Institute.

Bliss, M. (1980) Market Segmentation and Environmental Analysis. Unpublished MSc thesis, University of Strathclyde.

Bonoma, T.V. (1985) *The Marketing Edge: Making Strategies Work*. London: Collier Macmillan.

Bonoma, T.V. and Shapiro, B.P. (1983) *Segmenting the Industrial Market*. Lexington, MA: Lexington Books.

Bonoma, T.V. and Shapiro, B.P. (1984) Evaluating market segmentation approaches, *Industrial Marketing Management*, **13**, 257–67.

Booz Allen Hamilton (1994) *Marketing in the 1990s*, a presentation at the Institute of Directors, 8 Feb.

Booz Allen Hamilton (1998) *Imbalances in the Product Portfolio: The Implications for Marketing Strategy*. Working paper, New York.

Boston Consulting Group (1970) *The Growth-Share Matrix as a Basis for Planning*. Discussion paper, Boston, MA.

Brady, J. and Davies, I. (1993) The failure of marketing, *McKinsey Quarterly*, **7**, 3.

Brannan, T. (1993) Time for a new definition of marketing, *Marketing Business*, **Nov**, 3.

Brown, S. (1995) *Post-Modern Marketing*. London: Routledge.

Brownlie, D.T. (1983) Analytical frameworks for strategic market planning, in M.J. Baker (ed.), *Marketing: Theory and Practice*. London: Macmillan.

Brownlie, D.T. (1987) Environmental analysis, in M.J. Baker (ed.), *The Marketing Book*. London: Heinemann.

Brownlie, D.T. and Saren, M.A. (1992) The four Ps of the marketing concept: prescriptive, polemical, permanent and problematic, *European Journal of Marketing*, **26(4)**, 34–47.

Bucklin, L.P. (1978) *Productivity in Marketing*. Chicago: American Marketing Association.

Business Week (1977) The market mishandles a blue chip, *Business Week*, **20 Jun**, 17.

Business Week (1996) America, land of the shaken, *Business Week*, **Mar**, 64–5.

Button, K. (1994) Spies like us, *Marketing Business*, **Mar**.

Buzzell, R.D. and Gale, B.T. (1987) *The PIMS Principles: Linking Strategy to Performance*. New York: The Free Press.

Buzzell, R.D. and Wiersema, F.D. (1981) Successful share building strategies, *Harvard Business Review*, **59(1)**, 135–44.

Cannon, J.T. (1968) *Business Strategy and Policy*. New York: Harcourt, Brace & World.

Cardozo, R.N. (1980) Situational segmentation of industrial markets, *European Journal of Marketing*, **14(5/6)**, 264–76.

Carlzon, J. (1987) *Moments of Truth*. New York: Ballinger.

Carson, R. (1963) *Silent Spring*. Boston, MA: Houghton Mifflin.

Chandler, A.D. (1962) *Strategy and Structure*. Cambridge, MA: MIT Press.

Chisnall, P.M. (1989) *Strategic Industrial Marketing*, 2nd edn London: Prentice-Hall.

Christopher, M.G., Majaro, S. and McDonald, M.H.B. (1987) *Strategy Search*. Aldershot: Gower.

Christopher, M.G., Payne, A. and Ballantyne, D. (1991) *Relationship Marketing: Bringing Quality, Customer Service and Marketing Together*. Oxford: Butterworth-Heinemann.

Christopher, W.F. (1977) Marketing achievement reporting: a profitability approach, *Industrial Marketing Management*, **3**, 149–62.

Clarke, C. and Pratt, S. (1985) Leadership's four part progress, *Management Today*, **Mar**, 84–6.

Clausewitz, Karl von ([1832] 1984) *On War*, edited and translated by Michael Howard and Peter Paret. Princeton, NJ: Princeton University Press.

Clifford, D.K. and Cavanagh, R.E. (1985) *The Winning Performance: How America's High and Mid-Size Growth Companies Succeed*. New York: Bantam Books.

Clutterbuck, D. and Dearlove, D. (1993) The basic lessons of change, *Managing Service Quality*, **3(1)**, 97–101.

Collins, J.C. and Porras, J.I. (1998) *Built to Last: Successful Habits of Visionary Companies*. London: Random House.

Coopers & Lybrand (1993) *The Status of Marketing*, p. iv. London: Coopers & Lybrand.

Cox, W.E. (1967) Product life cycles as marketing models, *Journal of Business*, **40(4)**, 375–84.

Cravens, D.W. (1986) Strategic forces affecting marketing strategy, *Business Horizons*, **29(5)**, 77–86.

Cravens, D.W. (1996) *Strategic Marketing*, 94th edn Homewood, IL: Irwin.

Cullum, P. (2006) *The Stupid Company: How British Businesses Throw Away Money by Alienating Consumers*. London: National Consumer Council.

Cunningham, J. and Roberts, P. (2007) *Inside Her Pretty Little Head*. London: Cyan Books.

Cunningham, M.I. and Roberts, D.A. (1974) The role of customer service in industrial marketing, *European Journal of Marketing*, **8(1)**, 15–19.

Cyert, R.M. and March, J.G. (1963) *A Behavioral Theory of the Firm*. Englewood Cliffs, NJ: Prentice-Hall.

D'Aveni, R.A. (1999) Hypercompetition closes in, in *Financial Times, Mastering Global Business*, 57–62 (London: FT Pitman Publishing).

Daft, RL. (1998) *Principles of Management*. Chicago: Dryden Press.

Darwin, C. (1859) *The Origin of Species by Means of Natural Selection*. London: Murray.

Datamonitor Analysis (1996) *The Rise of One-to-one Marketing*. London: Datamonitor.

Davidson, J.H. (1987a) *Offensive Marketing or How to Make Your Competitors Followers*, 2nd edn Harmondsworth: Penguin.

Davidson, J.H. (1987b) Going on the offensive, *Marketing*, **16 Apr**, 24–9.

Davidson, J.H. (2007) Making the most of your assets, *The Marketer*, **May**, 34–5.

Day, G.S. (1983) Gaining insights through strategy analysis, *Journal of Business Strategy*, **4(1)**, 51–8.

Day, G.S. (1990) *Marketing Driven Strategy*. New York: The Free Press.

Day, G.S. (1996a) How to learn about markets, *Financial Times, Mastering Management*, **Part 12**, 12 (London: FT Pitman Publishing).

Day, G.S. (1996b) Keeping ahead in the competitive game, in *Financial Times, Mastering Management*, **Part 18**, 2–4 (London: FT Pitman Publishing).

De Kare-Silver, M. (1997) *Strategy in Crisis: Why Business Urgently Needs a Completely New Approach*. Basingstoke: Macmillan.

Denison, M. (1994), *Marketing*, **8 May**, 4.

Dibb, S., Simkin, L., Pride, W.M. and Ferrell, O.C. (2005) *Marketing: Concepts and Strategies*, 5th edn Boston, MA: Houghton Mifflin.

Diffenbach, J. (1983) Corporate environmental analysis in large US corporations, *Long Range Planning*, **16(3)**, 107–16.

Dolan, R.J. (1981) Models of competition: a review of theory and empirical evidence, in B.M. Enis and K.J. Roering (eds), *Review of Marketing*. Chicago, IL: American Marketing Association.

Doyle, P. (1987) Marketing and the British Chief Executive, *Journal of Marketing Management*, **3(2)**, 121–32.

Doyle, P. (2002) *Marketing Management and Strategy*, 3rd edn London: Prentice-Hall.

Dromgoole, A., Carroll, S.J., Gorman, L. and Flood, P.C. (2000) *Managing Strategy Implementation*. Oxford: Blackwell.

Drucker, P.F. (1955) *The Practice of Management*. London: Heinemann.

Drucker, P.F. (1959) Long range planning: challenge to management science, *Management Science*, **5(3)**, 238–49.

Drucker, P.F. (1963) Managing for business effectiveness, *Harvard Business Review*, **41(3)**, 53–60.

Drucker, P.F. (1969) *The Age of Discontinuity*. New York: Harper & Row.

Drucker, P.F. (1973) *Management Tasks, Responsibilities and Practices*. New York: Harper & Row.

Edwards, P. (1998) The age of the trust brand, *Market Leader*, **Winter**, 15–19.

Ellsworth, J. (2000) Engineering a revival for Levi's, *Marketing*, **19 Oct**, 25.

Engel, J.F., Kollat, D.T. and Blackwell, R.D. (1968) *Consumer Behaviour*. New York: Holt, Rinehart and Winston.

Ernst & Young (2001) *Online Retailing: The Future*. London: Ernst & Young.

Evans, F.B. (1959) Psychological and objective factors in the prediction of brand choice: Ford versus Chevrolet, *Journal of Business*, **32(4)**, 340–69.

Festinger, L. (1957) *A Theory of Cognitive Dissonance*. Stanford, CA: Stanford University Press.

Fifield, P. (1998) *Marketing Strategy*, 2nd edn Oxford: Butterworth-Heinemann.

Fifield, P. (2000). Marketing in the Post-Internet Age, A Presentation to the Sheffield branch of the Chartered Institute of Marketing, Oct.

Fifield, P. and Gilligan, C.T. (1996) *Strategic Marketing Management: Planning and Control, Analysis and Decision*, 2nd edn Oxford: Butterworth-Heinemann.

Fisk, P. (2006) *Marketing Genius*. Mankato, MN: Capstone.

Foxall, G.R. (1984) Marketing's domain, *European Journal of Marketing*, **18(1)**, 25–40.

Foxall, G. (1987) Consumer behaviour, in J.J. Baker (ed.), *The Marketing Book*. London: Heinemann.

Freedman, A. (2004) The age of the hollow company, *The Sunday Times*, **25 April**, 32.

Freedman, M. (2003) The genius is in the implementation, *Journal of Business Strategy*, **24(2)**, 2.

Friedman, T.L. (2006) *The World Is Flat: A Brief History of the 21st Century*. London: Picador.

Fruhan, W.E. (1972) Pyrrhic victories in fights for market share, *Harvard Business Review*, **50(5)**, 100–7.

Galbraith, J.K. (1958) *The Affluent Society*. Harmondsworth: Penguin Books.

Galbraith, J.K. (1977) *The Age of Uncertainty*. London: BBC/André Deutsch.

Gale, B.T. (1994) *Managing Customer Value: Creating Quality and Service that Customers Can See*. New York: The Free Press.

Geroski, P. (1996) Keeping out the competition, *in Financial Times, Mastering Management*, **Part 16**, 11–12 (London: FT Pitman Publishing).

Gerson, R. (1992) Dealing with the customers who complain, *The Straits Times*, **27 Apr**, 18.

Giles, W. (1995) cited in Piercy, N.F. (2002) *Market-led Strategic Change: A Guide to Transforming the Process of Going to Market*, 3rd edn Oxford: Butterworth-Heinemann, pp. 593–4.

Godin, S. (1999) *Permission Marketing, Turning Strangers into Friends, and Friends into Customers*. New York: Simon and Schuster.

Godin, S. (2004) *Purple Cow: Transform Your Business by Being Remarkable*. Harmondsworth: Penguin.

Grashof, J.F. (1975) Conducting and using a marketing audit, in E.J. McCarthy, J.F. Grashof and A. Brogowicz (eds), *Readings in Basic Marketing*. Homewood, IL: Irwin.

Greenley, G.E. (1986) The interface of strategic and marketing plans, *Journal of General Management*, **12(1)**, 54–62.

Greenspan, A. (2007) *The Age of Turbulence*. London: Allen Lane.

Gregory, M. (1994) *Dirty Tricks*. Boston, MA: Little, Brown & Co.

Guiltinan, J.P. and Paul, G.W. (1988) *Marketing Management: Strategies and Programs*, 3rd edn New York: McGraw-Hill.

Gummeson, E. (1987) The new marketing – developing long-term interactive relationships, *Long Range Planning*, **20(4)**, 10–20.

Hakansson, H. (ed.) (1981) *International Marketing and Purchasing of Industrial Goods: An Interaction Approach*. Chichester: Wiley.

Haley, R.J. (1963) Benefit segmentation: a decision orientated research tool, *Journal of Marketing*, **27(3)**.

Hamel, G. (2001) *Leading the Revolution*. Boston, MA: Harvard Business School Press.

Hamel, G. and Prahalad, C.K. (1994) *Competing for the Future: Breakthrough Strategies for Seizing Control of Your Industry and Creating the Markets of Tomorrow*. Boston, MA: Harvard Business School Press.

Hamermesh, R.G., Anderson, M.J. and Harris, J.E. (1987) Strategies for low market share businesses, *Harvard Business Review*, **65(3)**, 95–102.

Handy, C. (1994) *The Empty Raincoat: Making Sense of the Future*. London: Random House.

Harvey-Jones, J. (1988) *Making It Happen*. London: Collins.

Haspelagh, P. (1982) Portfolio planning: its uses and limits, *Harvard Business Review*, **60(1)**, 58–73.

Hedley, B. (1977) Strategy and the business portfolio, *Long Range Planning*, **10(1)**, 9–15.

Henderson, B.D. (1981) Understanding the forces of strategic and natural competition, *Journal of Business Strategy*, **2**, 11–15.

Henderson, B.D. (1982) *Henderson on Corporate Strategy*. New York: Mentor.

Henley Centre (2000) *Planning for Consumer Change*. Henley Centre.

Herzberg, F. (1966) *Work and the Nature of Man*. London: Collins.

Heskett, J.L., Jones, T.O., Loveman, G. *et al.* (1994) Putting the service profit chain to work, *Harvard Business Review*, **Mar–Apr**, 164–74.

Hill, R.W. (1972) The nature of industrial buying decisions, *Industrial Marketing Management*, **2**, 45–55.

Hill, S. and Lederer, C. (2002) *The Infinite Asset: Managing Brands to Build New Value*. Boston, MA: Harvard Business School.

Hofer, C.W. and Schendel, D.E. (1978) *Strategy Formulation: Analytical Concepts*. New York, NY: West.

Hollingworth, C. (2001) *Future Shock 21st Century Marketing*. London: organized by The Marketing Society.

Hooley, G.J. and Lynch, J.E. (1985) Marketing lessons from the UK's high-flying companies, *Journal of Marketing Management*, **1(1)**, 65–74.

Hooley, G.J. and Saunders, J.A. (1993) *Competitive Position: The Key to Market Strategy*. London: Prentice-Hall International.

Hunter, V.L. (1997) *Business to Business Marketing: Creating a Community of Customers*. New York: McGraw-Hill.

Hutton, W. (1995) *The State We're In*. London: Jonathan Cape.

Illich, I. (1973) *Tools for Conviviality*. New York: Harper & Row.

Jackson, K.F. (1975) *The Art of Solving Problems*. London: Heinemann.

Jacobson, R. and Aaker, D.A. (1985) Is market share all that it is cracked up to be?, *Journal of Marketing*, **49(4)**, 11–22.

Jobber, D. (2004) *Principles and Practice of Marketing*, 4th edn Maidenhead: McGraw-Hill.

Johnson, G. and Scholes, K.A. (1988) *Exploring Corporate Strategy*, 2nd edn Hemel Hempstead: Prentice-Hall.

Johnson, G. and Scholes, K.A. (2002) *Exploring Corporate Strategy*, 6th edn Hemel Hempstead: Prentice-Hall.

Johnson, G., Scholes, H.K. and Whittington, R. (2008) *Exploring Corporate Strategy*, 8th edn Hemel Hempstead: FT Prentice-Hall.

Johnson, H.G. and Flodhammer, A. (1980) Industrial customer segmentation, *Industrial Marketing Management*, **9**, 201–5.

Johnson, R. and Pound, E.T. (1992) Hot on the trail of trade secret thieves: Private eyes fight all manner of snakes, *Wall Street Journal*, **12 Aug**, 131, B4.

Kakabadse, A. (1999) Art of visioning, *Management Focus*, **11**, 10–11.

Kanter, R.M. (1989) *When Giants Learned to Dance*. New York, NY: Simon and Schuster.

Kashani, K. (1996) A new future for brands, *in Financial Times, Mastering Management*, **Part 3** (London: FT Pitman Publishing).

Kelly, J.M. (1987) *How to Check Out Your Competition*. New York: Wiley.

Kim, W.C. and Mauborgne, R. (2005) *Blue Ocean Strategy: How to Create Uncontested Market Space and Make the Competition Irrelevant*. Boston, MA: Harvard Business School Press.

Klein, N. (2000) *No Logo: Taking Aim at the Brand Bullies*. London: Flamingo.

Kohli, A.K. and Jaworski, B.J. (1990) Market orientation: the construct, research propositions and managerial implications, *Journal of Marketing*, **54**, 1–18.

Kotler, P. (1987) *Marketing: An Introduction*. Englewood Cliffs, NJ: Prentice-Hall.

Kotler, P. (1988) *Marketing Management: Analysis, Planning, Implementation and Control*, 6th edn Englewood Cliffs, NJ: Prentice-Hall.

Kotler, P. (1991) *Marketing Management: Analysis, Planning, Implementation and Control*, 7th edn Englewood Cliffs, NJ: Prentice-Hall.

Kotler, P. (1997) *Marketing Management: Analysis, Planning, Implementation and Control*, 9th edn Upper Saddle River, NJ: Prentice-Hall.

Kotler, P. and Keller, K.L. (2008) *Marketing Management: Analysis, Planning, Implementation and Control*, 13th edn Upper Saddle River, NJ: Prentice-Hall.

Kumar, N., Linguri, S. and Tavassoli, N. (2005) *Red Bull: The Anti-Brand Brand*, (CS-04-006). London: London Business School.

Larréché, J.C. and Hamel-Smith, N. (1985) New life in old markets, *Issues: The PA Journal of Management*, **3**.

Lehmann, D.R. and O'Shaughnessy, J. (1974) Differences in attribute importance for different industrial products, *Journal of Marketing*, **38(2)**, 36–42.

Levitt, T. (1960) Marketing myopia, *Harvard Business Review*, **38(4)**, 45–56.

Levitt, T. (1966) Innovative imitation, *Harvard Business Review*, **44(5)**, 63.

Lewis, D. and Bridger, D. (2000) *The Soul of the New Consumer: Authenticity, What We Buy and Why in the New Economy*. London: Nicholas Brearley Publishing.

Lewis, K. (1995) *World-changing Megatrends*. London: A presentation to Abbey National.

Liddell-Hart, B.H. (1967) *Strategy*. New York: Praeger.

Little, Arthur D. (1974) see Patel, P. and Younger, M. (1978) A frame of reference for strategy development. *Long Range Planning*, **11(2)**, 6–12.

Littler, D. and Wilson, D. (eds) (1995) *Marketing Strategy*. Oxford: Butterworth-Heinemann.

Loudon, A. (2002) *Waves of Innovation*. Harlow: Pearson Education.

MacLennan, N. (2000), *Financial Times*, **31 Jul**, 13.

MacLuhan, M. (1964) *Understanding Media: The Extension of Man*. London: Routledge.

Madrick, J.G. (1995) *The End of Affluence: The Causes and Consequences of America's Economic Decline*. New York: Random House.

Market Research Society (1990) *Occupational Groups: A Job Dictionary*. London: MRS.

Martilla, J.C. (1971) 'Word of mouth' communication in the industrial adoption process, *Journal of Marketing Research*, **3(2)**, 173–8.

Martin, R. (2007) *The Opposable Mind: How Successful Leaders Win Through Integrative Thinking*. Boston, MA: Harvard Business School Press.

Maslow, A.E. (1954) *Motivation and Personality*. New York: Harper & Row.

Mazur, L. (1999) Loyalty cards are a waste of companies' time, effort and money, *Market Leader*, **Spring**, 15–18.

Mazur, L. (2000) Past experience is no guide to the future, *Marketing*, **15 Jun**, 20.

McCabe, P. (2006) The rise of generous brands, *Market Leader*, **Spring**, 8.

McCarthy, M.J. and Perreault, W.D., Jr. (1990) *Essentials of Marketing: A Global-Managerial Approach*. Homewood, IL: Irwin.

McClelland, D.C. (1961) *The Achieving Society*. New York: The Free Press.

McColl-Kennedy, J.R., Yau, O.H. and Kiel, G.C. (1990) Marketing planning practices in Australia: a comparison across company types, *Marketing Intelligence and Planning*, **8(4)**, 21–9.

McDonald, M.H.B. (1984) *Marketing Plans: How to Prepare Them, How to Use Them*. London: Heinemann.

McDonald, M.H.B. (1989) Ten barriers to marketing planning, *Journal of Marketing Management*, **5(1)**, 1–18.

McDonald, M.H.B. (1990) SMEs – twelve factors for success in the 1990s, *Business Growth and Profitability*, **1(1)**, 11–19.

McDonald, M.H.B. (1995) *Marketing Plans: How to Prepare Them, How to Use Them*, 3rd edn Oxford: Butterworth-Heinemann.

McDonald, M.H.B. (1998) A slice of the action, *Marketing Business*, **Jul–Aug**, 47.

McDonald, M.H.B. (2007) *Marketing Plans: How to Prepare Them, How to Use Them*, 6th edn Oxford: Butterworth-Heinemann.

McDonald, M.H.B. and Wilson, H. (1999) Research for practice: the Internet and marketing strategy, *Marketing Business*, **Jun**, Special feature.

McGonagle, J.J. and Vella, C.M. (1993) *Outsmarting the Competition*. London: McGraw-Hill.

McKay, E.S. (1972) *The Marketing Mystique*. New York: American Management Association.

McKinsey & Co (1993) *The Future of Marketing*. London: McKinsey.

Merriden, A. (1998) The Japanese mind, *Financial Times*, **13 Apr**, 17.

Miles, R.E. (1980) *Macro Organisational Behaviour*. Glenview, IL: Scott, Foresman.

Miles, R.E. and Snow, C.C. (1978) *Organizational Strategy, Structure and Process*. New York: McGraw-Hill.

Milton, F. and Reiss, T. (1985) Developing a competitive strategy, *Accountancy Ireland*, **17(5)**, 19–23, 28.

Mintel (1998) Customer loyalty in retailing, Mar.

Mintzberg, H. (1987) Crafting strategy, *Harvard Business Review*, **65(4)**, 66–75.

Mintzberg, H. (1994) *The Rise and Fall of Strategic Planning*. Hemel Hempstead: Prentice-Hall International.

Mintzberg, H., Ahlstrand, B. and Lampel, J. (1998) *Strategy Safari: A Guided Tour Through the Wilds of Strategic Management*. Hemel Hempstead: Prentice-Hall Europe.

Mintzberg, H., Ahlstrand, B.W. and Lampel, J.B. (2005) *Strategy Bites Back*. Harlow: Pearson Education.

Mitchell, A. (1997) *Marketing Business*, **Feb**, 18.

Mitchell, A. (2005) Driving forward, *The Marketer*, **Jun**, 17.

Morgan, A. (1999) *Eating the Big Fish: How Challenger Brands Can Compete Against Brand Leaders*. Chichester: Wiley.

Morgan, A. (2000) Ten ways to knock down a giant, *Marketing*, **11 Jan**, 19.

Narver, J.C. and Slater, S.F. (1990) The effect of a market orientation on business profitability, *Journal of Marketing*, **54**, 20–35.

Natterman, P. (2000) Best practice does not equal best strategy, *McKinsey Quarterly*, **Summer**.

Naumann, E. (1995) Creating customer value: the path to sustainable competitive advantage, *National Productivity Review*, **14(1)**, 16–17.

Neilson, G.L. and Pasternack, B.A. (2005) *Results: Keep What's Good, Fix What's Wrong and Unlock Great Performance*. Boston, MA: Harvard Business School Press.

Neugarten, B. (1968) *Middle Age and Aging*. Chicago, IL: University of Chicago Press.

Newell, F. (2003) *Why CRM Doesn't Work*. London: Kogan Page.

Nicosia, F.M. (1966) *Consumer Decision Processes*. Englewood Cliffs, NJ: Prentice-Hall.

Nilson, T.H. (1995) *Chaos Marketing: How to Win in a Turbulent World*. Maidenhead: McGraw-Hill.

O'Brien, S. and Ford, R. (1988) Can we at last say goodbye to social class?, *Journal of the Market Research Society*, **30(3)**, 289–332.

Ohmae, K. (1983) *The Mind of the Strategist: The Art of Japanese Business*. Harmondsworth: Penguin.

Ormerod, P. (2006) *Why Most Things Fail: Evolution, Extinction and Economics*. London: Faber & Faber.

Ouchi, W. (1983) *Theory Z*. Reading, MA: Addison-Wesley.

Packard, V. (1957) *The Hidden Persuaders*. Harmondsworth: Penguin Books.

Parasuraman, A., Zeithaml, V.A. and Berry, L.L. (1985) A conceptual model of service quality and its implications for future research, *Journal of Marketing*, **49(Fall)**, 41–50.

Pascale, R.T. (1989) *Managing on the Edge: How Successful Companies Use Conflict to Stay Ahead*. New York: Simon and Schuster.

Peters, T.J. (1988) *Thriving on Chaos*. London: Macmillan.

Peters, T.J. (1992) *Liberation Management*. New York: Knopf.

Peters, T.J. and Waterman, R.H. (1982) *In Search of Excellence: Lessons from America's Best Run Companies*. New York: Harper & Row.

Piercy, N.F. (1991) *Market-led Strategic Change*. London: Thorsons.

Piercy, N.F. (1997) *Market-led Strategic Change: Transforming the Process of Going to Market*, 3rd edn Oxford: Butterworth-Heinemann.

Piercy, N.F. (1999) Relationship marketing myopia, *Marketing Business*, **Oct**.

Piercy, N.F. (2002) *Market-led Strategic Change: A Guide to Transforming the Process of Going to Market*, 3rd edn Oxford: Butterworth-Heinemann.

Piercy, N.F. and Morgan, N. (1990) Making marketing strategies happen in the real world, *Marketing Business*, **9**, 20–1.

Pine, B. and Gilmore, J. (1998) Welcome to the Experience Economy, *Harvard Business Review*, **Jul–Aug**.

Pine, B. and Gilmore, J.H. (2006) *The Experience Economy: Work Is Theatre and Every Business a Stage*. Boston, MA: Harvard Business Press.

Planning Review (1987) Competitive Intelligence Issue, **15(5)**.

Planning Review (1989) Competitive Intelligence Issue, **7(3)**.

Polli, R. and Cook, V. (1969) The validity of the product life cycle, *Journal of Business*, **42(4)**, 385–400.

Popcorn, F. (2001) *Eve-olution: The 8 Truths of Marketing to Women*. London: HarperCollinsBusiness.

Porter, M.E. (1979) How competitive forces shape strategy, *Harvard Business Review*, **57(2)**, 137–45.

Porter, M.E. (1980) *Competitive Strategy*. New York: The Free Press.

Porter, M.E. (1985a) *Competitive Advantage: Creating and Sustaining Superior Performance*. New York: The Free Press.

Porter, M.E. (1985b) How to attack the industry leader, *Fortune*, **111**, 97–104.

Porter, M.E. (1990) *The Competitive Advantage of Nations*. New York: The Free Press.

Porter, M.E., Sala-I-Martin, X. and Schwab, *The Global Competitiveness Report 2007–2008*. World Economic Forum/Palgrave Macmillan.

Prahalad, C.K. (2004) *The Fortune at the Bottom of the Pyramid: Eradicating Poverty through Profits*. Philadelphia, PA: Wharton School Publishing.

Publicis (2002) *The New Assertiveness*. London: Publicis.

Ramaswamy, V. and Prahalad, C.K. (2006) *The Future of Competition: Co-creating Unique Value with Customers*. Boston, MA: Harvard Business School Press.

Rapp, S. and Collins, T.L. (1990) *The Great Marketing Turnaround: The Age of the Individual and How to Profit From It*. Englewood Cliffs, NJ: Prentice-Hall.

Ratnatunga, J.T.D. (1983) *Financial Controls in Marketing: The Accounting–Marketing Interface*. Canberra: Canberra College of Advanced Education.

Reicheld, F. (2006) The ultimate question: the one number you need to grow, *Harvard Business Review*, **Mar**.

Reid, D.M. and Hinckley, L.C. (1989) Strategic planning: the cultural impact, *Marketing Intelligence and Planning*, **7(11/12)**, 4–11.

Reinartz, W. and Kumar, V. (2002) The mismanagement of customer loyalty, *Harvard Business Review*, **Jul**, 4–11.

Resnik, A.J., Turner, P.B.B. and Mason, J.B. (1979) Marketers turn to counterseg-mentation, *Harvard Business Review*, **57(5)**, 100–6.

Richards, M.D. (1978) *Organizational Goal Structures*. St Paul. MN: West Publishing Co.

Richardson, S. (2001) *The Young West: How We are All Growing Older More Slowly*. San Diego, CA: University of California.

Richardson, W. and Richardson, R. (1989) *Business Planning: A Strategic Approach to World Markets*. London: Pitman.

Ridderstråle, J. and Nordström, K. (2000) Funky Business: Talent makes Capital Dance, FT.com

Ridderstråle, J. and Nordström, K. (2004) *Karaoke Capitalism*. Hemel Hempstead: FT Prentice Hall.

Ries, A. and Trout, J. (1982) *Positioning: The Battle for Your Mind*. New York: Warner Books.

Ries, A. and Trout, J. (1986) *Marketing Warfare*. New York, NY: McGraw-Hill.

Riesman, D., Glazer, N. and Dinny, R. (1950) *The Lonely Crowd*. Newhaven, CT: Yale University Press.

Ritson, M. (2002) Wal-Mart: a shopping revolution, *Business Life*, **Mar**, 21.

Rivkin, J. (1995) *The End of Work: The Decline of the Global Labour Force and the Dawn of the Post-Market Era*. New York: G.P. Putnam's Sons.

Roach, J.D.C. (1981) From strategic planning to strategic performance: closing the achievement gap, *Outlook*, **Spring** (New York: Booz Allen & Hamilton).

Robinson, P.J., Faris, C.W. and Wind, Y. (1967) *Industrial Buying and Creative Marketing*. Boston, MA: Allyn & Bacon.

Rogers, B. (2000) *easyJet 2000*. Lausanne: IMD.

Roslender, R. and Wilson, R.M.S. (eds) (2008) The Marketing/Accounting Interface, *Journal of Marketing Management*, **24(7–8)**, 659–876.

Rothschild, W.E. (1984) *How to Gain (and Maintain) the Competitive Advantage*. New York: McGraw-Hill.

Salancik, G.R. and Upah, G.D. (1978) *Directions for Inter-organisational Marketing*, Unpublished paper. University of Illinois.

Saunders, J.A. (1987) Marketing and competitive success, in M.J. Baker (ed.), *The Marketing Book*. London: Macmillan.

Scherer, F.M. (1980) *Industrial Market Structure and Economic Performance*, 2nd edn Chicago, IL: Rand McNally.

Schiffman, L.G. and Kanuk, L.L. (1983) *Consumer Behaviour*, 2nd edn Englewood Cliffs, NJ: Prentice-Hall.

Sevin, C.H. (1965) *Marketing Productivity Analysis*. New York: McGraw-Hill.

Seybold, P. (2001) *The Customer Revolution*. London: Random House Business Books.

Shell Chemical Co. (1975) *The Directional Policy Matrix: A New Aid to Corporate Planning*. London: Shell.

Sheth, J.N. (1969) *The Theory of Buyer Behaviour*. New York: Wiley.

Sheth, J.N. (1973) Industrial buyer behaviour, *Journal of Marketing*, **37(4)**, 50–6.

Shuchman, A. (1950) The marketing audit: its nature, purposes and problems, in A.R. Oxenfeldt and R.D. Crisp (eds), *Analysing and Improving Marketing Performance*. New York: American Management Association Report No. 32.

Simmonds, K. (1980) *Strategic Management Accounting*. Oxford: Paper presented to ICMA Technical Symposium.

Simmons, W.W. (1972) Practical planning, *Long Range Planning*, **5(2)**, 32–9.

Simon, H.A. (1960) *The New Science of Management Decision*. New York: Harper & Row.

Simon, H. (1996) *Hidden Champions: Lessons from 500 of the World's Best Unknown Companies*. Boston, MA: Harvard Business School Press.

Slack, N., Chambers, S., Harland, C. *et al.* (1998) *Operations Management*, 2nd edn London: Pitman Publishing.

Solomon, M.R., Marshall, G.W. and Stuart, E.W. (2006) *Marketing*. Pearson/Prentice-Hall.

Stacey, R. (1991) *The Chaos Frontier: Creative Strategic Control for Business*. Oxford: Butterworth-Heinemann.

Stacey, R.D. (1992) *Managing Chaos: Dynamic Business Strategies in an Unpredictable World*. London: Kogan Page.

Stacey, R.D. (1994) Order from chaos, *Management Today*, **Nov**, 62–5.

Stacey, R.D. (2007) *Strategic Management and Organisational Dynamics*, 5th edn London: FT Prentice Hall.

Stone, M. and Young, L.D. (1992) *Competitive Customer Care: A Guide to Keeping Customers*. London: Croner.

Strebel, P. (1996) Breakpoint: how to stay in the game, *in Financial Times, Mastering Management*, **Part17**, 13–14 (London: FT Pitman Publishing).

Sun Tzu (1963) *The Art of War*. London: Oxford University Press.

Swan, J.E. and Rink, D.R. (1982) Variations on the product life cycle, *Business Horizons*, **25(1)**, 72–6.

Taylor, J. and Watts, W. (1998) *The 500-Year Delta: What Happens after What Comes Next*. New York: HarperBusiness.

Thaler, R. and Sunstein, C.R. (2008) *Nudge: Improving Decisions about Health, Wealth & Happiness*. New Haven, CT: Yale University Press.

Thomas, M.J. (1984) The meaning of marketing productivity analysis, *Marketing Intelligence and Planning*, **2(2)**, 13–28.

Thomas, M.J. (1986) Marketing productivity analysis: a research report, *Marketing Intelligence and Planning*, **4(2)**.

Thomas, M.J. (1993) Marketing – in chaos or transition?, in D. Brownlie (ed.), *Rethinking Marketing*. Coventry: Warwick Business School Research Bureau, pp. 114–23.

Thomas, M.J. (1994) Marketing's Future as a Profession, Keynote Presentation to the Annual Conference of the Chartered Institute of Marketing, Harrogate.

Toffler, A. (1970) *Future Shock*. New York: Bantam Books.

Toffler, A. (1980) *The Third Wave*. New York: Bantam Books.

Transparency International (1997) The corruption index, cited in *The Economist*, **7–13 Mar**, 12.

Trout, J. and Rifkin, S. (2000) *Differentiate or Die: Survival in Our Era of Killer Competition*. New York: Wiley.

Vandermerwe, S. (1999) *Doing a Dyson (A)*. London: Imperial College, London.

Vargo, S.L. and Lusch, R.F. (2004) Evolving to a dominant new logic in marketing, *Journal of Marketing*, **68(Jan)**, 1–17.

Veblen, T. (1998) *The Theory of the Leisure Class*. London: Macmillan.

Vroon, V.H. (1964) *Work and Motivation*. New York: Wiley.

Walker, O.C. and Ruekert, R.W. (1987) Marketing's role in the implementation of business strategies: a critical review and conceptual framework, *Journal of Marketing*, **51(3)**, 15–33.

Walton, P. (1999) Marketing rivalry in an age of hypercompetition, *Market Leader*, **Spring**, 33–7.

Webster, F.E. (1970) Informal communications in industrial markets, *Journal of Marketing Research*, **7(2)**, 186–9.

Webster, F.E. (1988) The rediscovery of the marketing concept, *Business Horizons*, **31(3)**, 29–39.

Webster, F.E. (1999) Is your company really market driven?, *Financial Times, Mastering Global Business*. London: Pitman Publishing.

Webster, F.E. and Wind, Y. (1972) *Organisational Buying Behaviour*. Englewood Cliffs, NJ: Prentice-Hall.

Weihrich, H. (1982) The TOWS matrix: a tool for situational analysis, *Long Range Planning*, **15(2)**, 60.

Weihrich, H. (1993) Daimler–Benz's move towards the next century, *European Business Review*, **93(1)**.

Weinberg, R. (1969) Paper presented at a seminar on Developing Marketing Strategies for Short-Term Profits and Long-Term Growth, sponsored by Advanced Management Research Inc., Regency Hotel, New York, 29 Sep.

Wells, W.D. and Gubar, G. (1966) Life cycle concepts in marketing research, *Journal of Marketing Research*, **3(4)**, 355–63.

Wensley, J.R.C. (1987) Marketing strategy, in M.J. Baker (ed.), *The Marketing Book*. London: Heinemann.

Westfall, R. (1962) Psychological factors in predicting product choice, *Journal of Marketing*, **36**, 34–40.

Whittington, R. (1993) *What Is Strategy and Does It Matter?* London: Routledge.

Wills, G.S.C., Wilson, R.M.S., Hildebrandt, R. and Manning, N. (1972) *Technological Forecasting*. London: Penguin Books.

Wilson, R.M.S. (1988) Marketing and the management accountant, in R. Cowe (ed.), *Handbook of Management Accounting*, 2nd edn Aldershot: Gower, pp. 255–95.

Wilson, R.M.S. (ed.) (1997) *Strategic Cost Management*. Aldershot: Dartmouth/Ashgate.

Wilson, R.M.S. (1999) *Accounting for Marketing*. London: ITBP.

Wilson, R.M.S. (2001) *Marketing Controllership*. Aldershot: Dartmouth/Ashgate.

Wilson, R.M.S. and Chua, W.F. (1993) *Managerial Accounting: Method and Meaning*, 2nd edn London: Chapman & Hall.

Wilson, R.M.S. and Fook, N.Y.M. (1990) Improving marketing orientation, *Marketing Business*, **11**, 22–3.

Wilson, R.M.S. and Gilligan, C.T. (2005) *Strategic Marketing Management: Planning, Implementation and Control*, 3rd edn Oxford: Butterworth-Heinemann.

Wind, J. (1996) Big questions for the 21st century, in *Financial Times, Mastering Management*, **Part 15**, 6–7 (London: Pitman Publishing).

Wind, Y. (1978) Issues and advances in segmentation research, *Journal of Marketing Research*, **15**(**3**), 317–37.

Wong, V. and Saunders, J.A. (1993) Business orientations and corporate success, *Journal of Strategic Marketing*, **1**(**1**), 20–40.

Woo, C.Y. and Cooper, A.C. (1982) The surprising case for low market share, *Harvard Business Review*, **60**(**6**), 106–33.

Yale, J.P. (1964) *Modern Textiles Magazine*, **Feb**, 33.

Yankelovich, D. (1964) New criteria for market segmentation, *Harvard Business Review*, **42**(**2**), 83–90.

Young, S. (1972) The dynamics of measuring unchange, in R.I. Haley (ed.), *Attitudes Research in Transition*. Chicago: American Marketing Association.

Zakon, A. (1971) *Growth and Financial Strategies*. Boston, MA: Boston Consulting Group.

Zeithaml, V.A. (1990) SERVQUAL: the strategic significance of service quality, *Marketing Productivity*, **1**(**2**), 135–8.

Index